THE GIFTS OF AFRICA

How a Continent and Its People Changed the World

Jeff Pearce

Prometheus Books

Guilford, Connecticut

Prometheus Books

An imprint of Globe Pequot, the trade division of The Rowman & Littlefield
Publishing Group, Inc.
4501 Forbes Blvd., Ste. 200
Lanham, MD 20706
www.rowman.com

Distributed by NATIONAL BOOK NETWORK

British Library Cataloguing in Publication Information Available

Library of Congress Cataloging-in-Publication Data

Names: Pearce, Jeff, 1963– author.
Title: The Gifts of Africa : how a continent and its people changed the world /
  Jeff Pearce.
Description: Lanham, MD : Prometheus, an imprint of Globe Pequot, [2022] |
  Includes bibliographical references and index. | Summary: "Past works
  have reinforced misconceptions about Africa, from its oral traditions
  and languages to its resistance to colonial powers. Other books have
  treated African achievements as a parade of honorable mentions and
  novelties. This book is different-refreshingly different. It tells the
  stories behind the milestones and provides insights into how great
  Africans thought, and how they passed along what they learned"—
  Provided by publisher.
Identifiers: LCCN 2021029574 (print) | LCCN 2021029575 (ebook) | ISBN
  9781633887701 (cloth) | ISBN 9781633887718 (epub)
Subjects: LCSH: Civilization, Western—African influences. |
  Africa—Civilization. | Africa—History. | Africa—Intellectual life.
Classification: LCC DT14 .P39 2022 (print) | LCC DT14 (ebook) | DDC
  960—dc23
LC record available at https://lccn.loc.gov/2021029574
LC ebook record available at https://lccn.loc.gov/2021029575

To the greatest African I know

IMRU ZELLEKE
Witness, Survivor, Ambassador

And this book is offered respectfully to the
peoples of Africa, in the sincere hope that I have
properly depicted their history and cultures.

Contents

Introduction

Leo Frobenius had exciting news to share as 1911 got started. On his expedition into the "hinterland of Togo," he had visited a shrine outside Ife in what is now modern Nigeria and had found a sculpted head. But it was of such extraordinary beauty that he decided it couldn't have originated from an African mind or have been crafted by black hands. No, this fine specimen, so beautiful and lifelike in its naturalism, was "indisputable" evidence of another civilization at work. And that's exactly how the *New York Times* heralded it on its front page: "German Discovers Atlantis in Africa."

"The head of the bronze is hollow," reported the *Times*, "and this construction helps to establish the period of the work. It is entirely devoid of Negro characteristics, and there is no doubt that it cannot have been of local casting." Frobenius estimated that it dated back to "ages before the day of Solon." It took several paragraphs before the paper quoted a voice of caution, a professor of Greek archaeology and art at Columbia University, James Wheeler, who suggested tepidly that "it would seem difficult to prove anything one way or the other about his find."[1]

In fact, the head probably wasn't bronze at all but was made of brass and copper alloys. So taken with his theory of Atlantis living on in Africa that Leo Frobenius wrote a two-volume book on his expedition to promote it. And like Schliemann with Troy or Howard Carter digging away in the Valley of the Kings, he vividly recalled the moment of discovery. He stood for many minutes in front of the sculpture. "Then I looked around and saw the blacks, the circle of the sons of the 'venerable priest'. . . and his intelligent officials. I was moved to silent melancholy at the thought that this assembly of degenerate and feeble-minded posterity should be the guardians of so much classic loveliness."[2]

At the time, Frobenius was celebrated as one of the most respected ethnographers in the world. And, believe it or not, he was even considered a champion of African cultures, suggesting they deserved greater study and respect—if you can call his views respectful. He railed publicly at how the British looted the palace of Benin but went home from the Belgian Congo in 1906 with 8,000 artifacts. He extolled the moral virtue of Africans, romanticizing them in "noble savage" terms, and wrote about the destructive impact of colonialism, such as the rubber trade. Yet he complained to American missionaries about keeping blacks in their place: "I want to underscore, explicitly, that I see the Negro as a primitive form of mankind, and it is demonstrable, based on the history of all colonizing nations and on the lives of almost every individual, that if the Negro is deprived of the sentiments of his primitive kind, and if he falls prey to the obscurity of equalization in matters of cultural production, he puts not only the cultural work of the white race, but also himself in great danger."[3]

Such was the racism of the man that he literally failed to recognize that the head he found at Ife displayed black features—one can recognize them clearly in the plate included in his book. Indeed, they *had* to have them because the head was sculpted by the Yoruba people in an age before any contact with Europeans.

His dating estimate was also way off the mark. But just because the head isn't ancient doesn't mean we can't delight in its brilliance. The walled city-state of Ife thrived between the twelfth and the fifteenth centuries, which means, as art critic Michael Glover once put it, "at the same historical moment that Andrea del Verrocchio was doing his wonderfully painstaking, high-Renaissance drawing of a female head, anonymous artisans in Ife were working with brass, bronze, copper and terracotta to

A terra-cotta bust sculpted between the twelfth and fifteenth centuries by one of the great Ife artists of what is now southwestern Nigeria. Part of the Leo Frobenius collection in 1913.

produce a series of exquisite heads that are not only the equal of Donatello in technical brilliance, but also just as naturalistic in their refinement."[4]

Frobenius wouldn't entertain this possibility. Like many experts of his time, he subscribed to the grand idea of "cultural diffusion"—that anything good in civilization originated from the mighty empires of the past in Europe and the Middle East. They were sure that a "white residue" could be traced in the finest expressions of African culture. But his take on it was unique, creating an elaborate backstory for an African Atlantis. He spent years in the field, acquiring valuable relics and prehistoric stone paintings, studying, gaining knowledge of the indigenous peoples of Nigeria, Sudan, and the Congo, and yet despite some brilliant insights, you often see in his works the rationale of a quack who could have been easily and simply challenged over his assertions.

In one paper, for example, he argued, "The Ethiopian Negro culture is not directed as it develops toward some goal or purpose determined intellectually, but on the contrary is guided under the aegis of emotional life." Of course, Frobenius had his own way of defining Ethiopian culture, but even allowing for that, when these words appeared in print in 1928, men from independent Ethiopia journeyed as government-sponsored students to attend the Sorbonne, Oxford, and universities across Europe and in the United States. For Africans abroad, however, he had three questions over "whether they have remained true to their 'nature' while in exile . . . 1) Is the Negro in a strange culture still capable of emotional exaltation and ecstasy (e.g., in church)? 2) Is the Negro still musical? 3) Has he kept his sense of humor, i.e., has he still a sovereign superiority of soul able to smile without cynicism or mockery at any fate?"[5] His paper, by the way, was titled, "Early African Culture as an Indication of Present Negro Potentialities."

By now, you might ask, why should we care about Leo Frobenius at all? Especially in a book about *African* ideas? Today, he has his apologists, though he's rarely cited, nor have his theories survived the test of modern research. But when it comes to the thread of African ideas, everything is not always as it seems. He had black American and African admirers in his own time. Legendary activist and writer W. E. B. Du Bois admitted that Frobenius "indulged his imagination" but still thought, "He looked upon Africa with unprejudiced eyes and has been more valuable for his interpretation of the Negro than any other man I know."[6] Léopold Sédar Senghor and Aimé Césaire—whom we'll meet as the founders of *Négritude* in 1930s Paris—were highly enamored of him and learned whole sections of his first book by heart. Of course, later generations have been more critical. When Wole Soyinka was awarded the Nobel Prize for Literature in 1986, he quoted in his acceptance speech Frobenius's lines about discovering the head sculpture and offered a scathing rebuke, calling them "a direct invitation to a free-for-all race for dispossession, justified on the grounds of the keeper's unworthiness."[7]

Frobenius and his Atlantis theory is only an extreme example of how white academics denied Africans their own accomplishments. But to borrow another phrase of Soyinka's lecture, "the purpose is not really to indict the past, but to summon it to the attention of a suicidal, anachronistic present." We need to remember that mainstream respect for African culture is very much a *recent* development, and if this point isn't clear, a few examples should bring the lesson home.

Consider this dedication in 1920 by Francis Fuller for his book *A Vanished Dynasty* on the Asante (Ashanti) people; it's to his colleagues who "so loyally and ably assisted me to convert a sullen and suspicious people, still smarting from defeat, into a contented and prosperous people." In that same decade, Oxford professor H. E. Egerton wrote that colonialism "was the introduction of order into blank, uninteresting, brutal barbarism." You may reply, "Well, that was a century ago." Let's keep advancing through the decades then.

Historians and anthropologists were challenging old presumptions in the 1940s, but you could walk into a theater in the United States in 1943 and see *Jungle Drums*, the Fleischer cartoon in which Superman confronts dancing, drum-beating Africans with stereotype thick lips and wild eyes under the thrall of a Nazi officer in a white mask and cloak. Live-action films were rarely better in their depictions. In 1948, a collection of sculptures from Ife were put on display at the British Museum (others had been found in 1938, the year Frobenius died), and on the positive side, the *Illustrated London News* declared this was "African art worthy to rank with the finest works of Italy and Greece" with "Donatellos of medieval Africa." The land of these Donatellos, however, stayed within the British Empire until 1960.

Still too far back? But we're already within generations still with us. And when fossils of hominins were discovered at Olduvai Gorge in Tanzania in the early 1960s, huge portions of the continent remained under European colonial rule, including what became the independent nations of Mozambique, Angola, Djibouti, Zimbabwe, and Namibia.

"When I was growing up," James Baldwin said in 1965 during his famously excoriating address at Cambridge, which put conservative William F. Buckley in his place, "I was taught by American history books that Africa had no history, and neither did I; that I was a savage about whom the less said the better, who had been saved by Europe and brought to America. And of course, I believed it. I didn't have much choice. Those were the only books there were." Little seemed to have changed when Baldwin was an adult. Hugh Trevor-Roper informed the BBC in 1962, "Perhaps in the future, there will be some African history to teach. But, at present there is none: there is only the history of the Europeans in Africa. The rest is darkness" and what he considered "the unedifying gyrations of barbarous tribes in picturesque but irrelevant corners of the globe."

Even with this recent past—comfortably distant in black-and-white film—we can feel intellectually and morally superior. But we shouldn't. It was only in 1980 that Rhodesia finally had elections that overturned white rule, and, lest we forget, South Africa had its first elections that allowed all races to vote only in 1994. In 1999, when the Smithsonian Museum opened its exhibition hall called "African Voices," its curator of African Ethnography and Art, Mary Jo Arnoldi, told the *Washington Post* that U.S. knowledge of Africa was measured in a survey to help develop the project. Most Americans, the staff discovered, didn't know that Africans lived in cities and assumed they were only in villages; the Americans, in fact, refused to believe that Africans used paper money.[8]

As editor of *The Spectator*, Boris Johnson wrote a column that referred to Africans in general as "piccaninnies" and Congolese in particular as "tribal warriors" with "watermelon smiles."[9] For a column on his visit to Uganda, he called the small children in a choir "little AIDS-ridden choristors" and quoted an unnamed British official who compared Africans to the boys who turned feral in *The Lord of the Flies*. "The best fate for Africa," wrote Johnson, "would be if the old colonial powers, or their citizens, scrambled once again in her direction; on the understanding that this time they will not be asked to feel guilty."[10] This was how the future prime minister of Great Britain perceived the history and cultural dynamics of an entire continent in 2002.

Each time, it seems, as we progress a little further to understand more of African history, we must cope with Soyinka's "suicidal, anachronistic present."

While for the most part sensible, intelligent people will acknowledge that great civilizations once existed in Africa, each example is too often a kingdom without a face. We know Genghis Khan and Kublai from the Mongols. We in the West can rattle off at least half a dozen names of painters, princes, and thinkers in the Italian Renaissance, from Borgias to Machiavelli. But aside from Shaka Zulu, most people in North America and Europe would be hard pressed to name another historical African ruler from before the twentieth century, let alone a writer or philosopher.

What we normally get in books and documentaries—when we get it at all—is a presentation of impressive ruins in Africa, sometimes the beautiful vistas, and what amounts to a kind of eulogy and postmortem. The inhabitants of these ancient places may be talked about, but we rarely meet their citizens, either high and low, and so they cannot come alive in our imaginations. In some cases, it's forgivable. We know, for instance, that there was the ancient kingdom of Meroe. We know their lion god, Apedemek; we know they made pyramids, and we know they had a flourishing empire that clashed on occasion with the Romans. Unfortunately, scholars are still at work deciphering

Meroitic script, so most of their secrets remain kept from us—for now.

But in other cases, even when there's overwhelming evidence that the ancient African kingdoms had flourishing trade with Europeans, we tend to think of their achievements and empires as a "closed system." They weren't closed at all—in many cases, far from it. We often think of geography, too, in a lazy way, more so thanks to the ability now to summon Google Maps on our smartphones. An app can tell you where Dar es Salaam is, but it can't tell you how to think. The writer Jacques Barzun (whom we'll come back to much later) reminds us, "Europe is the peninsula that juts out from the mass of Asia without a break and is ridiculously called a continent."[11]

So why don't we ever discuss the debt that Western, indeed world, civilization owes to *African* thinkers and innovators? It only stands to reason that there must be a legacy, just as we can trace the thread of Confucius and Buddhism influencing Western thought and acknowledge how Islamic scholars rescued Greek classics from oblivion.

There are other assumptions in general knowledge of history that have proved remarkably persistent. In elementary and middle school, I was taught—with little attention to the finer details—that civilization sprang out of Mesopotamia. I don't think I was a particularly clever little boy, but I found this difficult to reconcile with the other premise I was taught, such as that hominins evolved in East Africa. The brilliant discoveries by the Leakeys made it undeniable that humans originated in the region. Then in 1974, the famous "Lucy" skeleton was found in Ethiopia (known as *Dinknesh* to Ethiopians, which is Amharic for "you marvel"). And hieroglyphics came from Egypt, which is in Africa. So, I reasoned, why would ancient people leave an environment with a wealth of natural resources and migrate thousands of miles up to the Near East before they got around to becoming "civilized"?

It never occurred to my teachers, I suppose, that several African civilizations logically had to come first. We never heard about Kerma or Kush, let alone the empires of Mali or Zimbabwe. But teachers can pass on only what they have the initiative themselves to learn and share. James Loewen wrote a bestseller on how the American history curriculum gets it wrong; is it any wonder then that there is such ignorance over Africa?

This book was written because I simply couldn't find one like it available. Yes, there are very good and comprehensive histories of Africa, but they tend to stick to the themes of genocidal colonial expansion, failed development, famine, or war. The facts can't be denied, but such books reflect an air of general defeatism. The authors despair over Africa's lack of stability, its despots, its corruption, its poverty. (One notable and welcome exception is Dayo Olopade's recent work on the new generation of African reformers and entrepreneurs, which she understandably titled *The Bright Continent*.) Well, let's consider for the moment the history of Europe.

Within the span of my own lifetime, we've had the last autocratic years of Franco in Spain, the bloody reign of Ceaușescu in Romania, terrorist bombings by left-wing, right-wing, and Basque separatist groups across Europe in the 1970s and 1980s long before the specter of Islamic fundamentalism, the Irish Republican Army, the kidnapping and assassination of Aldo Moro in Italy, the breakup of the Soviet Union, the Bosnian genocide, war in Kosovo, and all the rest of the tragedies of the crumbling of Yugoslavia. Today, we have Brexit. We have Russia's seizure of the Crimea. And we have a Russia that's under the thumb of a ruthless oligarch, one who doesn't hesitate to have a political opponent shot dead on a bridge in front of the Kremlin. *That's* our supposedly stable and civilized Europe.

My point is not to deny Africa's problems but to argue that we manage just fine to have perfectly accessible histories of Europe that can trace the patterns of intellectual progress and the development of technology while keeping perspective on its troubles. So why don't we do that with Africa?

This book is my answer to that question, and I believe we should start with a new approach. This book is *not* intended to be a traditional, complete, and linear history of the continent. Rather than dwell on the famines, bloody civil wars, and colonialism, it attempts to trace ideas by Africans, ones that started in Africa, and even a few ideas *about* Africa that had impacts on the West. This book has other ambitions, too. It will explore some ideas that gained traction in Africa thanks to thinkers from elsewhere. And it will try to demolish a couple of destructive misconceptions about African history that stubbornly endure and affect how we see it.

This book expects the reader to have at least some passing familiarity with the eras of the Atlantic slave trade and European colonialism. In 2020, as the police murder of George Floyd sparked a tidal wave of Black Lives Matter protests around the world and the statue of merchant and slave trader Edward Colston was pulled down in Bristol and dumped in the harbor, a few pundits reminded everyone that European colonialism was barely taught in British schools. The conclusion is inescapable. How can you have an intelligent conversation on African history if you don't even know, let alone acknowledge, this legacy? To write at length on this background, however, would mean practically doubling the length of this work, and there are good books already available for that. Colonialism is part of Africa's story, yes, but far too often, it becomes a narrative about Europeans in Africa (Trevor-Roper's smug vision) rather than about the Africans themselves. And so I touch on colonialism when it's necessary to give the discussion context or to shed light on our misguided perceptions.

We start with northern Africa because this was the first and most natural point for its cultures to have contact with the outside ancient world. But as we'll see, it wasn't only the north that developed mutually beneficial cultural and trade exchanges with Europe, the Middle East, and Asia. It's then unavoidable to follow the chronological early path of European invasion and African resistance (but there are surprises here, too, that defy our assumptions). As the African diaspora grows, our narrative quickly becomes less about "what Africa first gave the world" and more about the multiple traffic lanes of ideas back and forth between the continent and Britain, the United States and continental Europe, and the rest of the globe.

Take the example of Edward Wilmot Blyden. He was born in the Caribbean, but as we'll see, he made his mark in Liberia, worked in Liberia, and represented Liberia as its diplomat in

Europe. His ideas had a great impact not only on Africans but also on another son of the West Indies, Marcus Garvey, who further inspired Caribbean and African thinkers and activists, and on it goes.

If we look for them, we can find certain themes echoing down through the centuries, from a Roman African penning a rollicking adventure tale of magical metamorphosis to an activist of Nigerian Igbo descent, trying to assert his humanity and identity in Georgian England. In the 1700s, the British vexed and complained about the "Black Poor"—free and recently manumitted Africans in the slum districts of London. Close to three centuries later, Europeans wonder what should be done about waves of African refugees desperate for asylum within their territory. Both then and now, prominent African expatriates took strong positions on the crisis and have influenced our thinking. Today, as we'll see, Africans have changed our minds about economics, environmentalism, science, and even our comfortable notions of how justice should be dispensed. We'll meet a few of them.

Since the 1990s, we've had several popular history books that did cheerleading for authors' chosen peoples, the most successful examples being *How the Irish Saved Civilization* and *The Basque History of the World*. I always found it interesting that there were so few books that advanced similar cases for Africa.

Unfortunately, the few ones available tend to be older works—still popular in cheap reprint editions—that are often shallow polemics, so poorly researched as to be worthless. In *From Babylon to Timbuktu*, a book that came out first in 1969 and still ranks high on Amazon's online bestseller list, Rudolph R. Windsor treats the Bible's genealogy as historical fact. In a book that passes itself off as reliable history, this claim appears in an early citation of its endnotes: "There were two Ethiopian nations; one in eastern Africa as we know of it today, and the other Ethiopia was situated near the Persian Gulf in the Garden of Eden."[12] Another work from the late 1980s finding new popularity in e-book form indulges in blatant slurs of Arabs, makes sweeping generalizations about African monotheism, and is riddled with factual errors.

One of the best, indeed brilliant, introductions to African history and with due attention to precolonial cultures is Kevin Shillington's *History of Africa*, which through the years has been regularly updated and revised. But it's a textbook, a highly readable one at that, but not meant for the general reader and with a textbook's expected price.

All this means that there's little out there for those who want to learn about Africa's intellectual legacy. You can find efforts online to redress the balance, but internet articles are invariably short, made for quick reads, and can't offer much depth—nor do you usually get sources you can check and verify. And we keep getting served African intellectual achievements as a parade of honorable mentions and novelties. They're not provided with any context in terms of their own cultures and countries and tell us nothing in the end about Africa. In sharp contrast, when we read, say, Tamim Ansary's *Destiny Disrupted*, with its brilliant sweep and fresh eyes on the spread of Islam, or Jenny Uglow's *The Lunar Men*, about Enlightenment thinkers in the English Midlands, we get the sense of *acquired knowledge having a cultural momentum*. Portraits add up to a tableau.

The use of the word "Enlightenment" is in vogue lately for the titles of cultural histories. Frederick Starr has given us *The Lost Enlightenment*. Christopher de Bellaigue gave us *The Islamic Enlightenment*. But it would be highly misleading to use the word on my cover. For one thing, across a vast continent in which the United States could fit three times, there was never a single oppressive force like Christianity that held back *all* of Africa's numerous and diverse peoples in the *same* exact era for an extended period the way Europe was kept in check. How could there be?

And while it might be tempting to focus on a single era rich in advancement and/or a renaissance in culture, we would soon return to the familiar counterfeit image projected onto the continent: the implication is that if there was glory, it was "the glory that was," allowing readers to shake their heads over the modern upheavals and crises routinely reported on Western television of disease, civil war, and political instability.

And which region, people, and era do we single out anyway for our crowning label of Enlightenment? Do we stick with the Maghreb, which gave us classical writers and a Roman emperor? Do we concentrate on the boom in scholarship during the Middle Ages in Morocco and Mali, especially Timbuktu? Or do we limit coverage simply to the postwar explosion of pan-African writers, activists, and scientists who are more readily familiar? Why restrict the conversation to one era at all?

Jacob Bronowski, famous for his documentary series *The Ascent of Man* and its companion volume, teamed up with Bruce Mazlish to work on a wonderful book published in 1960, *The Western Intellectual Tradition*. Sadly, it's almost completely forgotten today. "Ideas are not dead thoughts, even when they are no longer contemporary," wrote Bronowski and Mazlish, "for they remain steps in the evolution of contemporary ideas." They considered their work "a history of the life of ideas: active, mobile, and changing." In this same spirit, I've tried to cover the whole expanse of Africa's life story up until now, concentrating on its intellectual development and how it contributed to the world, to try to offer a tapestry of gradually acquired knowledge that built a cultural momentum—hence the title *The Gifts of Africa* and why my subtitle is *How a Continent and Its People Changed the World*.

Here is what this book is *not*. Anyone expecting a compilation of dust-dry, esoteric philosophy won't find it here. Nor is this book a mere compilation of biographical portraits; sometimes there is no single architect for a key idea or issue that needs examination (for instance, discussion of the Benin Bronzes in chapter 6). And such a parade would leave the reader without any context for how these great minds arrived at their conclusions. It is also not intended to be a mere hagiographical exercise. It's important to consider these thinkers critically and evaluate what worked for them and what didn't and to examine ideas that had an impact in the same way.

This book isn't intended as a mere cheerleading exercise either because Africa doesn't need one. Go online, and you can find an article in which a highly impressionable writer rattles off how the Dogon people of Mali knew about Jupiter's moons and Saturn's rings and more. Impressive—except it's ridiculous. Simple common sense reminds us that none of these astronomical phenomena can be seen anywhere on Earth with the naked eye, and unless the Dogon were secret masters of grinding telescope lenses, they gained these tidbits of knowledge from outside contact with travelers.

As we'll see, there are many African accomplishments in science, democracy, and wondrous architecture that can be celebrated—and verified. For example, when Michael Palin ventured to remote Chinguetti in Mauritania for his miniseries *Sahara*, he visited a library of 1,400 invaluable manuscripts. As Palin puts it in his companion volume to the show, "They have a book on astronomy dating from the fourteenth century, clearly showing the planets of our solar system circling the sun, proving that Arab scholars knew something that the authorities in Europe refused to acknowledge for a further 200 years."[13]

Chinua Achebe once argued, "I do not see that it is necessary for any people to prove to another that they build cathedrals or pyramids before they can be entitled to peace and safety. Flowing from that, I do not believe that black people should invent a great fictitious past in order to justify their human existence and dignity today."[14] These lines, however, should be seen in context. Achebe was fully aware that Africans *had* built cathedrals and pyramids; on the same page, in fact, he cites the example of the spectacular Benin City. His argument was that the accomplishments were already there.

I have needed to be arbitrarily selective in what's covered and in weighing emphasis. There's no agenda in this, certainly not a conscious one, only a sincere desire not to publish an unwieldy tome. For instance, we *could* spend far more time on the debt the world owes to the ancient Egyptians or pause to consider the impact of Gamal Nasser. But there are literally thousands of books available to readers on Egypt, both ancient and modern. Not so for the rest of the continent. Readers would be hard pressed to walk into a bookshop in New York or London and find more than two books—if you can find one stocked at all—about ancient Somalia or modern Ghana. Yes, there are whole cultures and peoples that are left out. And a fair criticism might be that say, Kenyans, Nigerians, or Ethiopians are over-represented, but the impact made by individuals was a more vital factor for their inclusion than their nationality.

Of course, this book can't possibly be exhaustive over its subject and will obviously be forever incomplete. There will be some great minds overlooked or not given as much space as they deserve. I have deliberately avoided and left out many famous political leaders, so the reader may well ask, Where's the discussion of the ideas of Julius Nyerere? Where are your profiles of Kofi Annan and Thabo Mbeki? But they would lure us too far off our path. To examine them all means that we need an evaluation of each of their political careers, which can't be separated from the development of their nations, and then we'd wind up with yet another conventional history of the continent.

Yes, figures such as Jomo Kenyatta and Léopold Sédar Senghor later entered the political ring, but I cover them in depth only in terms of their intellectual contributions, such as Senghor's role in the *Négritude* movement. I've also chosen to steer clear of literary giants such as Chinua Achebe or Wole Soyinka, mentioning them only in passing in certain contexts, because there is so much already written about them that can be found elsewhere, and the reader can—and should—turn to their great contributions to world literature.

You'll find discussion in these pages of African art and its impact on modern painting. But you'll find little about music. No one can deny that African music is the mother of jazz and blues and continues to spread its influence throughout the world today. But our focus here is on ideas, and I wouldn't even know how to start to trace a lineage of ideas through music; let's just leave it at the fact that I'm hopelessly unqualified. With a couple of notable exceptions, I've also ignored the world of film, another specialized realm of mood and feeling, as again it would lead us into an avenue of artistic criticism that takes us far away from our main exploration.

You might ask, But why have the visual arts but not cinema or music? The answer is that African sculpture and painting stood for certain concepts in specific eras and, as we saw with Frobenius, sometimes prejudices. These works of art have been interpreted and reinterpreted down through the ages for a variety of arguments. They are inextricably linked to the evolution of the continent's intellectual legacy.

The Gifts of Africa are still being developed, and more great thinkers and champions of human rights, technology, and literature are still to come. This book can (hopefully) be a door but never the whole mansion.

I firmly believe, as I've written elsewhere, that no work of history should be read without considering the context of the times in which it was written.

Today, we live in an intellectual climate of perverse fear. There has been a chilling wave of far-right racist nationalism around the world. Besides the spectacle of open and unashamed bigotry, it sometimes expresses itself in toxic efforts to nullify the genuine historical record. A handy and current example is the increasing circulation of the idea that "Irish slaves" preceded Africans taken by ship to America, and it's implied that they merit the same sympathy, that the destruction of culture and historical impacts on society were on the same scale. Its exponents are pushing it on—where else—various social media. The truth is that during the time of Oliver Cromwell, some Irish were cruelly sent into forced labor and indentured servitude in the Caribbean and America, but their lot was a far cry from the horrors perpetrated on captured Africans, and to try to equate the two is grotesque propaganda.

The Gifts of Africa was written to counter such backsliding to a dangerous mind-set from the previous century. Those who want to deny the holocaust of slavery don't have to step far to revive the equally outrageous claims that colonialism was a noble endeavor or that Africans owed everything to Western civilization.

Not everyone, of course, has a racist agenda, and we shouldn't always believe that there are sinister motives behind what amounts to a defensive posture for frustrated centrist liberalism. The defenders will concede, when pushed, that brutality occurred, horrible crimes of theft and massacre; at the same time, you get this kind of logic: "Do you genuinely believe the legacy of colonialism was *only* negative?" replied the premier of South Africa's Western Cape, Helen Zille, in a Twitter debate in 2018. "Then let's scrap the constitution including concepts such as the separation of powers. Let's scrap formal education institutions, the English language etc, etc." To be fair, Zille later apologized if her remarks offended anyone. But her rationale was similar to the one that Africans should forgive the British, Italians, French, and others because they made good roads—as if Africans wouldn't have chosen to build their own (which they often did).

In his illuminating biography of Henry Stanley (of "Dr. Livingstone, I presume?" fame), Tim Jeal proves the man was more complex than the imperialist image we have of him, but he grumbles in his introduction, "It appears to be widely imagined today that Africa was a paradise before Stanley and other explorers entered it," and then blames Arabs for their slave trading on the continent before Europeans arrived. But a wrong conception of an African "paradise" is beside the point. As a rule, we don't find historians nostalgically wishing the Mongols succeeded in invading Europe because of the widespread scientific ignorance, plague, and political infighting of the thirteenth century. Jeal goes on to write, "Would Stanley number among the genuine idealists, or the exploitative money makers who urged on the earliest Empire builders in Africa?"[15]

In terms of a biography, this is a perfectly valid question. But within the wider context of Africa's colonial history, it's irrelevant. As we discuss later in this book, one of the arguments made by pan-African thinkers in the 1930s was that imperialists shouldn't be given credit for their supposed benign intentions; colonialism doesn't ever have a benevolent face. The "colonialism wasn't all bad" argument is also a disingenuous one because its goal is not to weigh the merits of historical legacy but to gain a tacit acceptance that genocide and oppression are the cost of civilization. If you want schools, sorry, you must have the massacre first. Those nicely paved roads can come only from a subjugation of a people rather than foreign investment and cooperative development.

To fight this kind of propaganda (for that is what it is), we don't require a litany of African "firsts" or an autopsy of ideas that may have been stolen or borrowed without due credit to African thinkers. What a narrow vision that would be! Instead, this book tries to piece together a rich mosaic that deserves to be celebrated. It should be obvious then that I did not write this book only for Africans, though it's my hope that they will enjoy it as well and that Ethiopians, South Africans, those from Cameroon, Niger, Sudan, or Botswana can enjoy the anecdotes and thrill at the private battles of the individuals portrayed in these chapters. This book was written for anyone who is curious about Africa. It treats African ideas as world heritage that needs to be preserved.

About 140 years ago, Edward Wilmot Blyden, wrote, "Africa is no vast island, separated by an immense ocean from other portions of the globe and cut off through the ages from the men who have made and influenced the destinies of mankind. She has been closely connected, both as source and nourisher, with some of the most potent influences which have affected for good the history of the world."[16]

This fact should be obvious, yet it seems the lesson needs to be learned by each new generation. My hope is that as we navigate through an era of bitter and violent political extremes, the reader gains a new appreciation of the truth of Blyden's words in these pages and realizes that the African intellectual tradition is a rich legacy not just for Africans and the black diaspora but for every human being. The West will begin to understand Africa when it realizes it's not talking to a child—it's talking to its mother.

Comparative Chronology

BCE: Before Common Era; CE: Common Era

Note: To avoid punishing the reader, I have left out a tedious list of colonial benchmarks as well as the parade of dates for when countries in Africa became independent. Certain events are part of the book's narrative, but other events have been included here that are not covered but may still help give the reader a fix on the flow of history.

The chronology emphasizes accomplishments, and yes, some were obviously made in the United States and Europe, but it often makes more sense on a case-by-case basis for our purposes here to put them under the "In Africa" side of the ledger.

In Africa	Europe, Near East, Asia, U.S.
4.4 million years ago	
First hominins in Ethiopia	
2 million to 200,000 years ago	
Humans migrate and spread from Africa to rest of the world	
	4100–2000 BCE
	Sumerian civilization
4000 BCE	
Rise of ancient Egypt	
3500 BCE	
Egypt: philosophy, writing, invention of paper, the nilometer, early surgery	
2500–1500 BCE	
Kingdom of Kerma	
	2000 BCE
	Old Assyrian Empire
1000 BCE–350 CE	
Kingdom of Kush	
	1500 BCE
	Iron Age in eastern Europe, Asia
800 BCE	
Iron Age in parts of Nigeria	
	753 BCE
	Foundation of Rome
590 BCE	
Kingdom of Meroe	
	550 BCE
	Persian Empire, Cyrus the Great
	circa 400 BCE
	Plato active in Greece
	330s BCE
	Alexander the Great defeats Persian Empire

In Africa	Europe, Near East, Asia, U.S.

In Africa

30 BCE

Egypt becomes Roman province

27 BCE

Roman Republic falls

circa 100 CE–circa 960 CE

Rise and fall of Kingdom of Aksum

160 CE

Apuleius writes *The Golden Ass* in Numidia

circa 160 CE

Buddhism spreads to China

circa 320 CE

King Ezana of Aksum adopts Christianity

397–400 CE

Augustine of Hippo writes *Confessions*

476 CE

Roman Empire falls

610 CE

Birth of Islam

615 CE

King Armah of Aksum shelters Othman and other Muslim refugees

circa 600s CE

Byzantine Empire

Tang dynasty in China

700s–early 1200s CE

Rise and fall of Kingdom of Ghana

711–788 CE

Al-Andalus, "Islamic Spain," begins with Umayyad Caliphate conquest of Hispania

800 CE

Reign of Charlemagne

Vikings sack Europe

859 CE

Founding of Qarawiyyin in Tunisia, oldest university in the world

circa 860 CE

Somalia trades with China

871 CE

Alfred the Great reigns in England

In Africa	Europe, Near East, Asia, U.S.
	1160
	Work begins on Notre Dame Cathedral, Paris
1187	
Work begins on construction of great churches in Lalibela, Ethiopia	
1200–1450	*1202–1204*
Great Zimbabwe	Fourth Crusade
1300s–1600s	*1300s*
Ajuran Sultanate in Somalia region	Avignon papacy
1306	
Ethiopia reportedly sends first diplomats to Europe	
1324	
Mali's Mansa Musa makes pilgrimage to Mecca, promotes Timbuktu as center of scholarship	
	circa 1350
	Black Death in Europe
1378	
Ibn Khaldun writes *Muqqadima*	
	1389
	Battle of Kosovo
circa 1400	
Golden age of the Kingdom of Benin	Renaissance in Western Europe
1415	*1415*
Portuguese capture Ceuta, northern Africa	Battle of Agincourt, France
1463	
Sonni Ali Ber of Gao ruler of Songhay	
1468	
He captures Timbuktu	
	1455–1487
	War of the Roses in England

In Africa	Europe, Near East, Asia, U.S.
1493–1529	*circa 1500*
Reign of Askia Muhammad I	Leonardo da Vinci, Michelangelo
University of Sankoré, Timbuktu	
	1526
	Leo Africanus finishes *Description of Africa* in Rome
circa 1600–1650	*1558–1603*
Inoculation against smallpox in use across East Africa and possibly sub-Saharan Africa	Elizabethan Age in England
	William Shakespeare
Use of public streetlamps reported in Benin City	
	1619
	First African slaves transported to American colony of Virginia
	1620
	Mayflower sails for New England colony
1620s	
Ethiopia's Walatta Petros active, preaching rebellion against Emperor Susenyos after he adopts Catholicism	
1628	
Queen Njinga of Ndongo in Angola starts her long fight against the slave-trading Portuguese	
1632	*1630s*
After Battle of Lasta against his son, Fasilides, Emperor Susenyos reverses policy on Catholicism, allows religious tolerance	Thirty Years' War over religion convulses Europe (ends 1648)
	1633
	Galileo faces Inquisition
	1641
	Irish Rebellion
1656	
Queen Njinga negotiates peace with Portugal on her terms	

In Africa	Europe, Near East, Asia, U.S.
	1666
	Great Fire of London
1667	
Ethiopia's Zera Yacob finishes his *Hatata*, his "Inquiry"	
1670	
Osei Tutu founds the Asante Empire	
	1706
	Jenner tests his smallpox vaccine
1783	
Olaudah Equiano reads about the *Zong*, encourages antislavery legal action	
1789	*1789*
Olaudah Equiano writes his *Interesting Narrative*	George Washington inaugurated as first U.S. president
	French Revolution
	1791
	Haitian Revolution
1792	
Founding of Freetown, Sierra Leone	
	1807
	Slave Trade Act becomes British law
	1815
	Napoleon defeated at Waterloo
circa 1832	
Vai written script of Liberia developed	
1840s–1870s	*1840s*
African "Spartacus" Bilali runs sanctuary for escaped slaves and leads rebellions against native kings in Sierra Leone	Opium Wars in China "Great Game" in Afghanistan
1861	
Edward Wilmot Blyden tries to draw African American immigrants to Liberia	
	1861–1865
	American Civil War

In Africa	Europe, Near East, Asia, U.S.
	1865
	Reconstruction begins in U.S.
1868	
Sierra Leone's James Africanus Horton, *West African Countries and Peoples*	
	1883
	France colonizes Indochina
1887	
Ethiopians defeat invading Italians at the Battle of Dogali near Massawa, Eritrea	
Edward Wilmot Blyden brings out *Christianity, Islam and the Negro Race*	
1896	*1896*
Ethiopia hands Italy's invasion force a crushing defeat at the Battle of Adwa	U.S. Supreme Court upholds racial segregation in *Plessy v. Ferguson*
1897	*1897*
British invade the Kingdom of Benin; looting of the Benin Bronzes	William McKinley U.S. president
	Klondike gold rush
	Diamond Jubilee of Queen Victoria
1900	*1900*
Yaa Asantewaa sparks Asante "War of the Golden Stool" against the British	Boxer Rebellion in China
	First Pan-African Conference in London
1912	*1912*
Forerunner of African National Congress founded	*Titanic* hits iceberg and sinks
	U.S. Marines invade Nicaragua
circa 1912	*1912–1913*
Gebrehiwot Baykedagn, *State and Economy of Early 20th Century Ethiopia*	First Balkan War
1914	*1914*
Somalis from Aysha sail to New York via France to appear in human zoos	Senegal's Blaise Diagne elected to France's Chamber of Deputies

1914–1918

World War I

In Africa	Europe, Near East, Asia, U.S.
1915	*1914—1918*
John Chilembwe's antiwar uprising Nyasaland (Malawi)	Antiwar activism in U.K., Italy, U.S.
	1916
	Picasso's *Les Demoiselles d'Avignon* first exhibited in Paris

1918–1920

Global Spanish flu pandemic

1920s	*1920s*
African art popular in Europe	Jazz grows in popularity
	Marcus Garvey, Back to Africa movement in U.S.
	1922
	Mussolini's March on Rome
1923	
Ethiopia becomes member of League of Nations	
	1925
	The New Negro, edited by Alain Locke
	La Revue Nègre and Josephine Baker in Paris
1926	
Liberia signs extortionist deal with Firestone Tire and Rubber	
1929	*1929*
Igbo "Women's War" protests in Nigeria	Wall Street crash in New York
1930s	*1930s*
Pan-African activists studying and developing ideas at U.S. colleges and in London and Paris	*Négritude* movement in Paris
	Depression across North America and Europe
	1933
	Hitler becomes chancellor of Germany
1934	
Mussolini orchestrates the Walwal Incident that sparks the "Ethiopia Crisis"	

In Africa	Europe, Near East, Asia, U.S.
1935	*1935*
Fascist Italy invades Ethiopia	Hitler rearms Germany, Nuremberg Laws go into effect
1936	*1936*
Documentary on South Africa, *My Song Goes Forth*, features Paul Robeson	Spanish Civil War begins
1937	*1937*
Graziani massacre: Italian Fascists murder 20,000 Ethiopians; 6,500 sent to concentration camps	Bombing of Guernica
1938	*1938*
Jomo Kenyatta, *Facing Mount Kenya*	Kristallnacht in Germany

1939–1945

World War II

African and Caribbean colonial soldiers fight for the Allies	War in Europe, Africa, Asia
1940	*1940*
Gerard Sekoto's *Yellow Houses— Sophiatown* exhibited in Johannesburg Art Gallery	Nazis sweep across Western Europe
	Churchill becomes British prime minister
	British escape from Dunkirk
May 5, 1941	*December 7, 1941*
With a coalition of British, colonial African, and Indian forces, Ethiopia becomes the first occupied nation to be liberated in World War II	Attack on Pearl Harbor
1943	*1943*
End of World War II in Africa	Soviets win Battle of Stalingrad
Somali Youth League founded	Warsaw Ghetto Uprising
1944	*1944*
Dini ya Msambwa revolt in Kenya	Liberation of Paris
Eric Williams, *Capitalism and Slavery*	Battle of the Bulge
1945	*1945*
Placide Tempels, *Bantu Philosophy*	World War II ends in Europe and the Pacific
Fatima Massaquoi wins her lawsuit against Fisk University	

In Africa	Europe, Near East, Asia, U.S.
	1948
	Windrush brings 800 West Indian migrants to Britain
	Marshall Plan in Europe
1950	
UN Four Power Commission gives Italy trusteeship of Somaliland	
1950s	*1950s*
Artist Ben Enwonwu becomes international star	Korean War, Cuban Revolution, McCarthyism in America
1952	*1952*
Mau Mau Uprising	Elizabeth II becomes Queen of U.K.
Frantz Fanon, *Black Skin, White Masks*	Anne Frank's *Diary of a Young Girl*
1954–1962	
Algerian War for Independence	
1956	*1956*
Suez Crisis in Egypt	Revolt in Hungary
Conference of "Negro-African Writers and Artists" in Paris	
1957	
Ben Enwonwu's sculpture of Queen Elizabeth II unveiled at exhibition in London	
1958	*1958*
Chinua Achebe, *Things Fall Apart*	Kenneth Galbraith's *The Affluent Society*
1959	*1959*
Tom Mboya organizes airlift to U.S. for 81 Kenyan students	Hawaii becomes 50th state of U.S.
	U.K. grants independence to Cyprus
1961	*1961*
Frantz Fanon, *The Wretched of the Earth*	*Catch-22*
Patrice Lumumba assassinated	Freedom Riders in U.S.
	Bay of Pigs in Cuba
1963	*1963*
Haile Selassie makes "Until the philosophy" speech to United Nations	Kennedy assassination
Organization of African Unity formed	U.S. involvement in Vietnam War

In Africa	Europe, Near East, Asia, U.S.
1964	*1964*
Nelson Mandela sentenced to life in prison and sent to South Africa's Robben Island	Civil Rights Act becomes U.S. law
1967–1970	*1967–1970*
Student protests in various African capitals	Student protests across U.S., Europe
Nigerian Civil War	
Somalia's Aden Osman becomes first African president to voluntarily give up power after election	
1968	*1968*
Steve Biko leads "Black Consciousness" movement in South Africa	Martin Luther King Jr. assassinated
	Prague Spring
	My Lai massacre in Vietnam
1969	*1969*
John Mbiti, *African Religions and Philosophy*	Maya Angelou's *I Know Why the Caged Bird Sings*
1970	*1970*
Aswan High Dam begins operation	Kent State shootings in U.S.
	October Crisis in Canada; the equivalent of martial law briefly imposed
1974	*1974*
English translation published of Cheikh Anta Diop's *The African Origin of Civilization*	Watergate scandal ends, Richard Nixon resigns as U.S. president
Dinknesh ("Lucy") skeleton found in Ethiopia	
1975	*1975*
Angolan Civil War begins	Vietnam War ends
Haile Selassie assassinated	
1976	*1976*
Soweto uprising	Alex Haley's *Roots* best seller
1977	*1977*
Steve Biko murdered in police custody in South Africa	Jimmy Carter becomes U.S. president
	New York blackout

In Africa	Europe, Near East, Asia, U.S.
1979	*1979*
Ali Mazrui outlines his Pax Africana in BBC Reith Lecture	*Roots* airs on U.S. television
	Margaret Thatcher becomes British prime minister
1980s	*1980s*
Wangari Maathai leads Green Belt movement in Kenya	Reagan era in U.S., Thatcher era in U.K.
1984	*1984*
Desmond Tutu wins Nobel Peace Prize	CIA mines Nicaragua's harbors
Famine in Ethiopia	
1985	*1985*
Marxist Derg regime squanders relief funds	Live Aid concerts for famine relief
George Ayittey's "A Double Standard in Black and White," runs in the *Wall Street Journal*	
Ken Saro-Wiwa's *Sozaboy*	
1986	*1986*
Ali Mazrui's *The Africans: A Triple Heritage* airs on PBS in the U.S.	*Challenger* space shuttle explodes
Wole Soyinka wins Nobel Prize for Literature	Chernobyl nuclear disaster
	1989
	Berlin Wall falls, Tiananmen Square massacre in Beijing
1990	*1990*
Nelson Mandela freed after 27 years of imprisonment; ban lifted on African National Congress	Poland withdraws from Warsaw Pact
	Poll tax riots in Britain
1990s	*1990s*
Ken Saro-Wiwa lobbies for human rights causes, for the Ogoni people, and against Royal Dutch Shell in Nigeria	O.J. Simpson case
	Monica Lewinsky scandal
1992	*1992*
George Ayittey's *Africa Betrayed*	Margaret Busby's *Daughters of Africa*

In Africa	Europe, Near East, Asia, U.S.
1993	
South Africa's Nelson Mandela and Frederik Willem de Klerk jointly win Nobel Peace Prize on ending apartheid	
1994	*1992–1995*
Nelson Mandela elected first black president of South Africa	Bosnian War
Rwandan genocide	
1995	*1995*
Ken Saro-Wiwa hanged at army base in Port Harcourt, Nigeria	Bosnian genocide
1996	*1996*
Televised Truth and Reconciliation Commission hearings in South Africa	First Chechen War (ends 1996)
2001	*2001*
South Africa's Kofi Annan wins Nobel Peace Prize	World Trade Center attacks in U.S.
	Invasion of Afghanistan
2002	
Angolan Civil War ends	
2004	*2004*
Kenya's Wangari Maathai wins Nobel Peace Prize	Mark Zuckerberg creates Facebook
	2005
	7/7 London Bombings in U.K.
	Hurricane Katrina
2006	*2006*
Ellen Johnson Sirleaf of Liberia elected first female head of state in Africa	Saddam Hussein executed by hanging
December 2010–2011	
Protests in Tunisia start Arab Spring	
2011	*2011*
South Sudan becomes independent after referendum	U.S. military raid kills Osama bin Laden

In Africa

Europe, Near East, Asia, U.S.

2012

Librarians in Timbuktu rescue more
than 377,000 precious manuscripts as
al-Qaida militants capture and terrorize
most of Mali

2014–2015

ISIS destroys priceless works of cultural
heritage in Iraq and Syria, including
ancient Assyrian artifacts in Mosul and
structures and sculptures at the World
Heritage site of Palmyra

2018

African migration crisis worsens

Asfa-Wossen Asserate's *African Exodus*

44 members of African Union sign
African Continental Free Trade Area
agreement

2018

Trump administration scandal over
migrant children in cages

2019

Debate over return of African artifacts

Ethiopia's Abiy Ahmed wins Nobel
Peace Prize

2019

U.K. Brexit woes continue

Donald Trump's first impeachment

2020

George Floyd police murder

Black Lives Matter protests

Slave-trader and Confederate statues
pulled down in U.K. and U.S.

2020–2022

Global COVID-19 pandemic

2021

African Continental Free Trade Area
Agreement comes into effect

Former Nigerian finance minister
Ngozi Okonjo-Iweala becomes
the first woman and first African
director general of the World Trade
Organization

2021

Joe Biden elected U.S. president

Donald Trump incites insurrection
and attack on U.S. Capitol building;
impeached a second time

Part I

CONTOURS

A map of Africa made in 1635 from the printing operation of Dutch cartographer Willem Blaeu. This map is clearly intended to be more decorative than functional. For all its exquisite attention to detail, we can see that much of its "information" is fanciful and inaccurate.

1

Building Blocks

Humanity started in Africa. We have the bones to prove it, the skeletal remains of our early ancestors in Ethiopia from millennia ago. Everything that followed came from these ancestors on *this* continent who learned how to walk upright, who first learned how to hunt and live in communal groups. Whoever you are reading this book—whether your roots are Croat or Brazilian, Scottish or Chinese, whether you're brown, white, Asian, one of the aboriginal peoples of the Americas or Australia or New Zealand—you carry this heritage of ancient Africans within you. Africans were the first wanderers, the first explorers, the first human beings who looked up at the night sky and shuddered in terror at its vast dark canvas—and then held the original, orphaned, brave speculations of curiosity.

They wandered, spreading the family of mankind, but by 8000 BCE, when the Sahara experienced a very different climate, Africans were already fishing, farming, and making pottery across a long swath of the continent above what is now The Gambia all the way east across to the Ethiopian Highlands. From at least 4000 BCE, cattle herders were tending their animals in the central Sahara, but climate change likely drove them west toward the Nile Valley of Upper Egypt. When we say, "Upper" or "Lower Egypt," by the way, we mean upstream and downstream on the Nile, and these terms are carryovers from early

3

translations. For instance, one of the titles of the pharaohs was translated into English as "King of Upper and Lower Egypt," but the original form of these terms were emblems: the sedge for "Upper" and the bee for "Lower."

While those cattle herders were moving into the valley, at the same time, what the experts call the Afroasiatic people who roamed over northeast Africa, the Badarians (named after the town of el-Badari, where their culture was first discovered), put down roots in a countryside of rich, arable soil. And to the south, the people who would come to be known as the Nubians also grew cereal crops and tended herds, but they had less arable land and so became highly skilled at hunting and fishing.

With its advantages of geography, Egypt rose to become the first superpower. As has been pointed out many times before, it lasted for 3,000 years mostly because of a system of monarchical despotism; we usually don't dwell on this when we're slack-jawed tourists on holiday staring up at the grandeur of the pyramids and the Sphinx. And because there's so much focus on interactions with the Middle East and Greece, we lose track of the reality that this was a formidable nation-state *within Africa*. It made its presence felt on its neighbors, who in turn had some influence on its culture and power structures.

Down through the centuries, Egypt kept its eye on the south, where the Nubians developed their own powerful kingdom of Kush while selling the Egyptians gold, ivory, and other products. The Nubians' first capital was Kerma, south of the Nile's Third Cataract, a fortified city of mud-brick temples, houses of stone, and impressive palaces. Friction grew between the two powers, and during the First Dynasty of about 3000 BCE, the Egyptians built a fortress and customs post on the island of Abu—it amounted to a billboard that said, "This is as far as you go."[1] But as the centuries rolled on, Egypt was hungry for more territory, not to mention the gold and other goods available, and they pushed the Nubians farther south and then took them over completely as a client state some time close to 1500 BCE. The Nubians earned fame as brilliant archers, and the Egyptians often referred to Nubian territory as "Ta-Sety," which meant "The Land of the Bow."

Meanwhile, in the thirteenth and twelfth centuries BCE, the tribes in what we now call Libya made steady incursions on Egyptian territory. The Egyptians fought back, stealing cattle and forcing their prisoners to be army conscripts. Our very word for Libya, in fact, comes from the name of a specific tribe, the *Libu*, which is recorded in ancient Egyptian inscriptions. The Libyans were known for being skilled charioteers and for wearing headdresses with feathers.[2] The Egyptians first fortified their borders against the Libyans, then integrated them into their warrior ranks and eventually high offices, and after the death of the pharaoh Ramesses XI around 1078 BCE, it was the Libyans who ran Egypt for four centuries.

While experts today debate to what extent these new leaders were "Egyptianized," their own culture had an impact. Those in charge wore their feathers with pride; they governed in a style that reflected their nomadic, tribal roots, and they scorned the more grandiose tombs and burial practices of their predecessors.[3] These Libyan overlords felt "an indifference to elaborate long-term preparations for death," an attitude that reflected "the customs of a (semi-) nomadic people who habitually buried their dead where they fell, without ostentation or prior concern."[4]

Four hundred years later, however, Egypt didn't have the clout it used to, and the Nubians established a new capital, Napata, on the west bank of the Nile not far from the Fourth Cataract. Today, it's the town in northern Sudan called Karima, about 400 kilometers from Khartoum. Their kings managed to rule in Egypt for sixty years, but in 670 BCE, they had to contend with another player—Assyria, the fabulous empire that was once based near Mosul in the Kurdistan region of Iraq. Creators of their own magnificent palaces. Builders of iconic winged bulls and lions and writers of a cuneiform language all their own.

The Assyrians managed to drive the Egyptians out of Palestine and what is today Jordan, and they forced the Kushites to abandon Egypt itself. While the Kushites put up a bitter fight to take Egypt back, their efforts failed, and they were left with only their original domain. Only a few decades passed before the Kushites felt the need to retreat farther south and move their capital from Napata to Meroe (near the modern Sudanese town of Shendi). The reason this time wasn't the Assyrians—it was the Persians who were now moving into Egypt. In 525 BCE, Cambyses, son of Cyrus the Great, launched his invasion, soon prompting the Libyans and Greeks of the towns of Cyrene and Barca to surrender and send gifts in tribute.[5] But the Nubians were defiant.

Cambyses sent spies as ambassadors to the royal court in Meroe, where, given the dates, the ruler must have been Amaninatakilebte at the time. He immediately figured out what these "ambassadors" were up to and handed one of them a large Nubian bow. He then told them words to the effect, "When you Persians can bend a bow as easily as I can, come march against us."[6]

Cambyses accepted that challenge—and failed. It's unclear how because many historians don't trust a leading source for events. This was Herodotus, the Greek "Father of History," who held a clear bias against the Persians. In his account, the Persians never ended up fighting the warriors of Kush at all. Cambyses was apparently so enraged over how the Nubian king bested his envoys that he sent his advance force "without ordering any provision for food, nor giving any rational consideration to the fact that he was about to lead his army to the edges of the earth."[7] His men soon ran out of supplies. First, they ate their pack animals. Then they tried to forage off the land. But when they hit the desert, they allegedly wound up resorting to cannibalism. When the story got back to Cambyses in Thebes, he chose to break off his invasion of Kush. Or so the story goes.

The point of this whirlwind summary of events, the almost dizzying list of empires and kingdoms, is that we have to start with the question the Egyptologists and historians will patiently ask you: *which* ancient Egypt do you want to talk about? And we'd still have a lot of ground to cover before Alexander the Great and the Romans show up. Then there's the matter of the geography. We should consider Egypt—and Kush—in the context of a wider world. Just think of Assyrian cavalry and warriors hurling javelins and slinging rocks against Nubian archers. Imagine Persians marching proudly within sight of the Nile toward Sudan and ending up humiliated by the geography.

All of it happened long before Sparta's King Leonidas defended the Hot Gates of Thermopylae. It was before Plato started his academy and before Alexander the Great rode out of Macedon.

Africa was *the* power of the ancient world, and even when Egypt was no longer on top, Egypt and Nubia were arenas where great empires tested their limits.

That great old sage of the twentieth century, Bertrand Russell, started his magisterial *History of Western Philosophy* with the Greeks. While he acknowledged the Greeks owed a few things to the ancient Egyptians, he didn't have much use for the civilization on the Nile. "The Egyptians were preoccupied with death," he wrote, insisting that religious conservatism after the third millennium BCE "made progress impossible." He soon moved on in his book to early Babylonian influences on civilization, transfers of culture between Egypt and Crete, and then we're off to discussing the rise of Greece. But he offered this extraordinary footnote on his very first page. "Arithmetic and some geometry existed among the Egyptians and Babylonians, but mainly in the forms of rule of thumb. Deductive reasoning from general premises was a Greek innovation."[8]

Well, no, it wasn't, and this is a rather bizarre and sweeping statement to come from one of the world's greatest modern philosophers. No single culture holds the patent on logic, and the notion is absurd on its face. We know, for instance, that the Egyptians were considered leaders in medicine in the ancient world, and they couldn't have practiced surgery without some level of deductive reasoning to go with their empirical discoveries. But Russell wrote his book in 1945. It was a best seller (and is still in print and widely read today), and it won him the Nobel Prize for Literature. To be fair, he could work only with the sources he had available, and scholarship in Egyptology has made huge leaps and bounds since then, and, being one of the most liberally progressive and open-minded thinkers of our modern age, he probably would have changed his mind, given the new information. But . . . he could have looked further.

The way ancient Egypt used to be taught in schools—perhaps it still is in some places—would have you believe it was a dreary place. "What survives of Cretan art gives an impression of cheerfulness and almost decadent luxury," wrote Russell, "very different from the terrifying gloom of Egyptian temples." And there in one line is the problem. Ancient Egypt to most of us has meant tombs, death, mummies. A static, sterile culture that couldn't get past a morbid fascination with the afterlife, so it was up to others to borrow its few accomplishments and build on them.

We are long overdue to toss out the narrow-minded notion that ancient Egypt—well, really, ancient northeast Africa—has little relevance to us. A dead culture. That certainly isn't true for modern Egyptians. Complex innovations of music and harmony were first developed for war marches, harvests, and religious celebrations and naturally to give joy to the ancient Egyptians the way music does for us today. Cairo-born scholar Sherif Abouelhadid notes that "Sufi chanters still adopt the same posture as 'Iti, a singer depicted more than 4,000 years ago on a tomb wall at Saqqara. Clapping to adjust rhythm and tempo is inherited in a form of singing in Upper Egypt known as 'Al Kaf,' which means 'palm' (it stands for clapping). Singing while feeding a child can be seen in every street in modern Egypt. Last but not least, one word used to describe the act of singing (hst) in the ancient Egyptian language is still used in modern Egypt to ask someone 'to describe sounds, Hs.'"[9]

The Western view of Africa has long ignored examples of Egypt's innovative technology. Yes, the exception to the rule has always been the pyramids, these great feats of engineering. But let's consider a marvel that resonates into our modern era. The Nile River was life to these ancient Africans. Every year, the river flooded the Nile Valley, dumping its stores of rich, black, fertile silt and carrying a promise of agricultural production. If you could figure out how much the farmlands would flood, you could predict crop yields. You could rearrange public events and religious festivals, and while you were at it, you could figure out how severe or light you wanted to tax the subjects of your realm.

Some clever soul came up with the nilometer—which is exactly what we call it in English. In its most basic form, it was a vertical column structure sunk into the waters of the Nile, with markings calibrated in Egyptian cubits to indicate the depth of the water. If that doesn't impress you, consider that this technology, with only a few improvements in design, was in use for centuries all the way through the Roman era and the Middle Ages to well into the twentieth century. The most celebrated example of a nilometer is one that was built during the eighth century CE on the southern tip of Egypt's Roda Island. Beautifully decorated, it boasted both a circular well and a marble column and was able to measure floods up to about nine and a half meters, or a little over thirty-one feet. Such ingenious structures didn't become obsolete until work was finished on the Aswan High Dam in 1970.[10]

This very book in your hands, whether in physical pages or on a digital screen, is testimony to the greatest African achievement of all time. Because the Egyptians helped to give us writing. Hieroglyphics. True, the consensus has been for many years that writing first developed in Mesopotamia, with the supportive evidence of cuneiform found in ancient cities such as Uruk. But in 1989, a team led by German archaeologist Gunther Dreyer worked in a spot called Abydos close to the Nile and about six miles from the modern town of El Araba El Madfuna. Here, they discovered small labels of hieroglyphs carved in ivory and bone, likely used as tags "attached to bolts of linen and containers" in royal tombs and dating perhaps as far back as at least 3300 BCE.

"A rougher set of similar inscriptions was found on nearby vessels," noted *Science* magazine. "About fifty signs seem to represent humans, animals, and a palace facade. Later findings nearby included pot marks dating to about 3500 BCE."[11] Even if we confirm one day that Mesopotamia was first for giving the world written script, we know that Africa should get a lot of credit for helping the process develop.

According to Professor Konrad Tuchscherer, various forms of "proto-writing," such as knotted cords, rock art, and pottery designs, likely helped spur the development of hieroglyphics. "The Egyptian system drew from many highly codified African graphic systems, which, even if not phonetic, were highly systematized and recorded as well as communicated information. Such systems—which included rock art, geometric pottery motifs, cattle brands, weaving designs, scarification, etc.—existed not only in Upper Egypt . . . but far to the south, which by the fourth millennium [BCE] was engaging in robust exchanges with Egypt."[12]

Now if you're a regular person, you can't name an ancient Egyptian writer off the top of your head. We're not familiar with their great philosophers or literary geniuses the way we know Aristotle and Sophocles, and Egyptologist Toby Wilkinson explained why in the introduction to his translation of ancient Egyptian writings: "First is the strangeness and apparent impenetrability of the script," and, second, with the exceptions of a few revered thinkers and administrators, "pharaonic culture valued perfection within an established tradition over individual creativity."[13]

But another innovation the Egyptians gave us would unlock the creative potential of individuals.

First, think of all those inscriptions bragging about the acts and conquests of the mighty pharaohs on their stone monuments. Most common people would have been illiterate, and even for those who could read, if I as a pharaoh have my name and life story carved in stone, *you* must come to *me*. The king and his officials controlled the block, and they dictated the message, and even then, the amount of space they had to convey their message—no matter how huge the surface and grandiose the setting—was always finite. The effort to create that message was also labor intensive. Just try some time engraving stones by hand.

But the Egyptians came up with an alternative for stone and brick. They already relied on an all-purpose reed to construct boats and to make baskets, mats, and wicks for oil lamps; they were so good at using it that they turned it into a product for a brisk international trade. Much, much later, the army of Persia's Xerxes used these reed fibers for tethering a pontoon bridge so that it could cross the Hellespont (what we now call the Dardanelles in Turkey).[14] And they used these reed fibers for something else . . .

Yes, we're talking about *papyrus*, which is where we get our word "paper." And the minute an Egyptian began writing on it, the world witnessed the birth of a technological and intellectual revolution. The Greeks adopted papyrus. The Romans used it. It was relied on for centuries until better, more durable materials for scrolls and ordinary paper were invented. So much attention is naturally given to the invention of writing itself that we can easily forget the medium. Even if the Mesopotamians invented writing, the Africans were the ones who *freed* it. They made knowledge *portable*, and in doing so, their innovation held the genesis of the democratization of learning. True, the high priests and scribes of ancient Egypt—just as their medieval counterparts later in the churches of Europe—would be a privileged class, keeping tight control on what was written down and who could read it. But the ancient Egyptians themselves recognized this invention changed everything.

One specific text offers an extraordinary perspective. "Be a writer," an instructor encourages his students in a papyrus kept in the British Museum, and he argues, "Man perishes; his corpse turns to dust; all his relatives pass away. But writings make him remembered in the mouth of the reader. A book is more effective than a well-built house or a tomb-chapel in the West [meaning the land of the dead], better than an established villa or a stela in the temple!" The text was intended to be read out loud, and it suggests "that the schooling of scribes was not, perhaps, as traditional or stultifying as it might appear."[15]

The invention of writing was obviously crucial to human development. As neurologists will tell you, the very act of reading changes the way we think. It stimulates connectivity in our brains and helps us with abstract thinking, even with our empathy toward others according to some psychologists. The power of the written word on a portable medium must have made an impression first with its practical value. Then it sunk in how much it molds us on comprehensive and personal levels. Before its wide use, you accepted new details most of the time in either a verbal consultation—or even a possible confrontation. I know who's telling me this, but I may not know who told *them*. Have they garbled the message? Do I trust the messenger? Ah, but now I have this paper, so I can interpret the message for myself.

Moreover, writing on papyrus opened the door to reading as an act that could be done *in privacy*. The stones that hold the boasts of pharaohs were declarations to be read in public surroundings. By the time that anonymous teacher was urging his students to "be a writer," at least a privileged few in Egyptian society had the luxury to *enjoy* text for its own pleasure, not for the king's purpose. They could savor words and consider their value to themselves personally.

This innovation was to the ancient world what the internet was for us in the past twenty-five years. Its usage no doubt started off slowly, and then, just as with our digital revolution, it took off and spread. True, the hard reality would still be that most ordinary Egyptians knew only what they needed to know in terms of their work—after all, no one required a manual for how to plow a field or sell wares in a market stall. But like our internet, papyrus could be your gateway to learning about astronomy, zoology, history, geology, and other subjects . . . exactly the ones the ancient Egyptians began to write about.

One of the virtues of a powerful technology is that it spurs and quickens other innovations and their dissemination. A text known as the Rhind Mathematical Papyrus offers a collection of mathematical problems and their solutions, such as how to calculate the volume in a grain silo or a rectangular storage unit and how to figure out the slopes on pyramids.[16] The great Egyptologist Rosalie David has called Egyptian arithmetic "clumsy yet effective," but it's certainly impressive (at least to us slower pupils in math class) that the Egyptians could figure out the surface area of a trapezoid or that they relied on a base-10 decimal system for counting.[17] The science historian Marshall Clagett devoted three painstaking volumes to considering ancient Egyptian science and wrote that "some early historians of mathematics would find in the Egyptian expression of equations and in their solutions of problems involving unknowns the nascent procedures that carry over into later algebra."[18]

We know, of course, how Egyptian innovations, including math, impacted the world because of the testimonials of a recipient culture: the Greeks. Herodotus and the geographer Strabo claim Egypt gave the world geometry. In *Phaedrus*,

Plato attributes the Egyptian god Thoth as the creator of letters, astronomy, math, and dice. The Greeks also recognized the Egyptians as leaders in medicine. While one scholar has argued that yes, okay, there's a huge chronological stretch between the medical texts written in papyrus in ancient Egypt (around 1800 BCE) and those scribbled down in Greek after Hippocrates lived (around 460 BCE), "the pharmacopeia of Hippocratic medicine expressly mentions products from Egypt, such as nitrate, alum and oil."[19]

One Egyptian text recommends a bizarre—to us—medical test for whether a woman will experience a normal birth: a clove of garlic is inserted into a woman's vagina and left overnight; the next day, the physician checks her breath. Garlic breath means standard delivery, no garlic breath is a problem. The Hippocratic treatise of "On Infertile Women" suggests the same test, only its purpose is to check if a woman can't conceive.[20]

As the experts will remind us, these examples are anecdotal and by no means conclusive, but the complimentary references to Egypt in Greek classical texts do add up. In Homer's *Odyssey*, we're told, "Every man is a healer there, more skilled than any other men on earth—Egyptians born of the healing god himself."[21] According to Diogenes Laertius, who wrote in the third century CE, Plato visited Egypt with Euripides, and the playwright fell ill but "was cured by the priests, who treated him with seawater." Diogenes thought this experience might have inspired Euripides' line, "The sea washes away all human ills" and referenced the lines above from Homer.[22]

Herodotus could be notoriously wrong sometimes, but he did visit Egypt himself, and he tells us the medical men on the Nile were keen on specialization. "The art of medicine is divided so that each physician treats just one illness and no more. Doctors are everywhere, as there are specific physicians for the eyes, the head, the teeth, the abdomen, and still others for illnesses that are invisible."[23] Herodotus, in fact, mentions several times how "Egyptian doctors were sought-after throughout the rest of the world." Rulers in the Near East "surrounded themselves with doctors from Egypt." Persia's Cyrus the Great had problems with his eyes, and he insisted the pharaoh Amasis send him the best ophthalmologist available. After Darius hurt his ankle from jumping off his horse, he turned to Egyptian doctors first for relief.[24]

There has been a lot of quibbling over whether the great minds of ancient Greece—mathematicians and philosophers such as Thales and Pythagoras—ever visited and received additional education in Egypt. But it's telling that the Greeks were keen to include Egypt on the résumés of their important thinkers. Here was the first wellspring of African Ideas.

For about sixty years, the pot has been simmering over how much ancient Greece owes to Egyptian civilization, and we'll touch on this controversy in a much later chapter. Then there's the impact that Egypt had on the Middle East. Well, what about ancient Egypt in the context of the rest of Africa? Historian Basil Davidson once humorously skewered the attitude of those who treated its location as "merely a geographical irrelevance." For years, Egypt "has been explained to us as evolving more or less in total isolation from Africa or as a product of West Asian stimulus. On this deeply held view, the land of Ancient Egypt appears to have detached itself from the delta of the Nile . . . and sailed off into the Mediterranean on a course veering broadly towards the coasts of Syria."[25]

Add to this a certain reflexive thinking. Who are the great explorers? Why, the Europeans, of course, such as Columbus and Vasco da Gama, even though these luminaries often raided, pillaged, and devastated the populations they famously visited. We *do* think of the ancient Egyptians as conquerors, but they, too, set out on journeys of discovery.

One famous episode gives us the tantalizing case of a run-in with another culture impressively distant from Egypt. During the Sixth Dynasty, the pharaoh's chief of scouts, Harkhuf, made four expeditions through Nubia, the first one made with his father, with later ones to the land of Yam (its location is still something of a mystery). On his fourth and final mission, Harkhuf sent word home that in addition to his usual bounty of exotic goods from foreign lands, he was sailing back with an unusual captive: likely one of the Forest Peoples of Central Africa.* At the time, a six-year-old boy, Pepi II, was ostensibly ruling Egypt while a regency council handled the actual affairs of state. Pharaohs and nobles enjoyed having Little People and various "misshapen human beings" at court, and Pepi II—thrilled as a spoiled child would be at the prospect of having his own human mascot—sent off a letter to Harkhuf. "If he goes down into a boat with you, choose trusty men to be beside him in his tent. Inspect him ten times during the night. My Majesty longs to see this [person] more than the spoils of the mining country and of Punt!"[26]

We don't know what Harkhuf originally wrote to Pepi II, but one Egyptologist suggested with reasonable logic, "The original letter seems to have spoken of the captive as a wild and fierce creature continually seeking to escape."[27] Well, of course. Like any kidnap victim, this terrified individual—ripped from his home and probably not speaking his captor's language—wanted to escape. But who was he? Forest Peoples make up more than one single ethnic group, such as the Mbuti of the Congo or the Batwa of the Great Lakes region, and they're scattered across a wide swath of the continent all the way from Botswana up to Guinea and Gabon to Rwanda and Uganda.

Harkhuf didn't have to travel deep into central Africa either to obtain his captive but likely purchased him through an intermediary. These would have usually been warriors taken prisoner. And while ancient powers could force their new slaves across vast distances, given the arduous geography involved, it makes more sense that Harkhuf's victim might have been taken from a locale closer to Sudan, such as in Uganda or the Congo region; after all, a lot of ground needed to be covered, and any newly acquired captive still needs to be fed and provided for until dispensed with. So, perhaps Harkhuf's gift to his pharaoh was either a Batwa or a Mbuti man. Perhaps the person wasn't from one of these ethnic groups at all but someone who had a

---

* In translations and in past academic descriptions, the word "pygmy" has been used, but given its pejorative connotations today, this text opts for the modern term "Little People"—or, better still, seeks to refer to him as what he was, a captive—and a person.

genetic condition, such as dwarfism. But this is only speculation, and we have no real evidence.

Then there's the mystery of the land of Punt, which we know the ancient Egyptians visited since at least around 2500 BCE and during the reigns of different leaders. From Punt, the Egyptians could obtain ebony, incense, gold, ivory, and other goods. But where was Punt? The experts still can't be sure, though they've long suspected it was in the Horn of Africa. The modern autonomous region of Somalia, Puntland, takes its name from the fabled Land of Punt.

But some fascinating research was done at the British Museum that indicates Punt might have been elsewhere. Scientists studied the hairs of baboons, which they know the ancient Egyptians obtained from Punt and mummified, and they were able to make an educated guess on where the animals likely came from (although there's room for error). By using oxygen isotope analysis, the researchers developed a working theory that Punt covered all of what's now Eritrea and a portion of eastern Ethiopia. In fact, their work led to the possible location of an ancient harbor, near the modern Eritrean city of Massawa, where the Egyptians would have loaded up their goods and riches to send back home.[28]

So it's quite possible then that the Egyptians ventured down the Red Sea to reach what was sometimes called "Land of the god"—quite an ambitious undertaking.

The Egyptians also might have explored a direction that few have considered before: southwest. In the ancient Egyptian literature of the sixteenth century BCE, the *Amduat* is a funerary text, one that chronicles the journey of the sun god Ra through the underworld, dividing up his voyage across vast distances into separate hours. In his second hour, for instance, Ra gets to a fertile landscape and then, in the third hour, a "sweet-water ocean." The *Amduat* has been examined as literature, even with speculations that it's a forerunner of modern psychotherapy, but suppose—just suppose—its detailed descriptions refer to actual physical geography of a distant land? This is the argument of Thomas Schneider of the University of British Columbia, who thinks the Egyptians might have traveled as far as the Chad Basin of Central Africa.[29]

Schneider's case is built on scrutinizing the specific geographical references in the text and linking them to evidence of the ecological changes in the region of central Africa over the millennia. For instance, the "intermediate realm between the sunset and the second hour is designated, in the first hour of the *Amduat*, as a 'gateway' or 'portico,'" and Schneider notes that this is "an architectural term for the approaches to palaces or temples." Perhaps that portico then was one of the stunning rock formations in the Tibesti mountain range in the north of Chad or the Ennedi Plateau in the northeast of the country, such as the Ennedi's Aloba Arch or the Bammena Massif.[30]

Schneider's theory generated a fair amount of buzz among scholars, with one citing that there are, after all, "comparable linguistic features" between the Egyptian and Chadic languages.[31] As usual, the experts advise caution in jumping to any conclusions; more study, more exploration required. But it's an intriguing theory, and it reminds us—just as with the example of Punt—that these ancient Africans didn't focus all their attention on the Middle East but on their own continent's wonders and riches as well.

Much of the Egyptians' interest—as well as their greed, scorn, and weaponry—was spent on Nubia.

It's been speculated that perhaps Nubia got its name from the ancient Egyptian word for gold, *nub*, given that Nubia had the richest supply.[32] But if we're going to talk about its people, we have to watch out for a pitfall with terminology. The label "Nubians" is a convenient term, but we need to keep track of who we're referring to because at certain times, the Egyptians had their Nubian colonies while not always occupying Kush, and then we might also refer to the Nubians who were subjects of the later kingdom of Meroe. Adding to the confusion, ancient writers often referred to the lands beyond Egyptian territory in a vague way as "Ethiopia" when a region may not have been Ethiopian at all. In fact, our whole view of Nubian lands is skewed because scholars unfortunately have needed to rely heavily on Egyptian texts—the Meroitic language developed by the Nubians still hasn't given up most of its secrets.

In fact, it's only in the past forty years or so that the Nubians have finally gotten a spotlight. We can put some of the blame on the ancient Egyptians, "who made Nubia the target of relentless negative propaganda."[33] In various inscriptions, they referred to "vile Kush" and "wretched Kush," which prompted one archaeologist to ask, was Kush *really* wretched? Probably not. Near the ancient fortress colony of Askut, about 350 kilometers from Aswan, artifacts such as cookpots have been found, and the evidence from tombs and pyramids suggests that during Egypt's Middle Kingdom, its Second Intermediate Period and its New Kingdom, Egyptians and Nubians may well have lived next to each other and even shared households. Rather than passive acceptance of occupation, Nubian women in the community of Tombos stuck to their own cultural ways, using burial practices that asserted their "ethnic identities within [an] otherwise strongly marked Egyptian cemetery."[34]

The latest archaeological evidence and scholarship strongly suggests that while the Egyptians had a huge influence on Nubian culture, the Nubians made a substantial impact in turn on the Egyptian one. Scholar Peter Lacovara suggests that the Kushite kings who ruled in the Twenty-Fifth Dynasty didn't merely usher in a "renaissance" of Egyptian art and architecture but presided over a "complex and studied reinvention of past styles and a reinterpretation of pharaonic motifs and themes" that lasted almost 1,000 years.[35] Susan Doll believes that during the same dynasty, the Nubians reinvigorated a classic form of the Egyptian language, "replete with erudite literary allusions and echoes of earlier writers and themes . . . Kushite Egyptian is sometimes so direct that the reader wonders if it was not indeed composed, at least in part, by the kings themselves."[36]

We also know the Kushites got around. Though the Assyrians failed to capture Kush, Nubians before the invasion by Cambyses in the sixth century BCE and afterward had a presence in Assyria. In 732 BCE, official rations of wine were dispensed to different groups of foreigners in the capital of Assur—among them, Nubians from Kush. Nubian women worked as musicians, scribes, smiths, stoneworkers, even as barbers and bakers. They can be found immortalized in ancient

Assyrian art objects and on wall reliefs. Kushites were perhaps valued most by the Assyrians for their expert breeding and training of fine horses, and "several documents mention Kushite horse-experts living in Assyria."[37] In the West today, we don't regularly associate African cultures with equestrianism, yet the Greeks and Romans often depicted Africans as grooms, charioteers, or cavalry men in their art, and later in the Middle Ages, Sudan's Funj kingdom of Sennar would provide horses for the empire of Ethiopia.[38]

We may never know the true extent of Nubian influence because the evidence has been literally flushed out of our reach. There are archaeological finds under Lake Nasser, flooded after the Aswan High Dam was built, while other valuable sites were ruined with the construction of the Merowe Dam at the Nile's Fourth Cataract.[39] Even if you visit Abu Simbel, the stunning temples cut out of rock for Ramses II and his wife, Nefertari, you're not seeing them in their original location, which was 250 kilometers south of Aswan in Lower Nubia. They were moved in the late 1960s for the sake of the Aswan High Dam. Preserved, thankfully, yes, but still they were chopped up, dismantled,

The spectacular Great Temple of Abu Simbel built by the ancient Nubians.

carted off, and reassembled at an exorbitant cost at an artificial hill above their original location.[40]

And yet researchers can still tell us a lot. Though the Meroitic script is mostly impenetrable (for now), we know the Nubians did something with their language that was simple yet groundbreaking. The Egyptians didn't do it. Neither did the Greeks in their earliest texts. The Romans often didn't do it either. Hint: You're looking at it right now as you read this line. It's the dividing up of words. For Egyptian hieroglyphics, just as in Chinese ideograms, this is unnecessary, but in syllabic systems, it helps comprehension immeasurably, only we take it for granted. Suppose we mash the words together for a line by the Roman poet Horace: DULCEETDECORUMEST. Difficult to follow, isn't it? (And annoying.) *Dulce et decorum est*, or "It is sweet and fitting to die for one's country," is now much easier to read with spaces than in what's called *scriptio continua*. Instead of gaps, the Nubians used two or three dots after a word.

It's been suggested that Nubians could have spoken Meroitic for perhaps a millennium before they got around to devising their alphabetic and syllabic system, but after they did, their professional classes—not just the clerks working for officials—were quite literate.[41]

One of the most fascinating aspects of Nubian culture is how their queens and royal figures enjoyed a respect and higher regard during the Napatan and Meroitic periods, in some ways more than their Egyptian counterparts. During the Napatan era, "the king had to be born to a woman who had the title Sister of a King," while the king's mother was a key figure at coronations and gave an important speech to the god Amun.[42] According to scholars Joyce Haynes and Mimi Santini-Ritt, "Queens could also share in rites normally reserved for kings in Egypt," and they and the king's mother are featured prominently on reliefs and stelae.[43] At the ancient city of Naqa during the Meroitic period, one queen, Amanitore, is shown as defender of the nation.[44]

The Kingdom of Meroe is thought to have extended its reach far south of Khartoum, and though at one point Rome tried to seize Lower Nubia, a peace treaty was signed in 24 BCE that lasted more than 300 years.[45] When Meroe fell, it gave way to the rising new power of the Kingdom of Aksum, which we'll examine in the next chapter.

More than a century ago, the massive rerouting of the Nile didn't merely exile much of Nubia's past to underwater depths but also many of Nubia's twentieth-century descendants.

In 1902, they were first pushed out of their ancestral lands by work on the Aswan Low Dam intended to regulate the great river's annual flooding. Then more were pushed out in 1912 and 1933. But the biggest displacement happened from 1961 to 1964 when the Aswan High Dam was built, submerging numerous villages. About 135,000 residents were forcefully evicted from their homes and dumped in desert communities, while what remained of their historic territory, as one journalist put it in 2014, "hugs a thin, sparsely populated strip of land along the Nile that's now bisected by the Egypt-Sudan border and is crossable only by boat."[46] Officials in Cairo promised the Nubians that one day they could return, and if they couldn't go back to their original homes, they could live and work in newer pastures along Lake Nasser.[47] The Nubians are still waiting.

In Egypt's tumultuous year of 2014, there was a brief interlude of hope when the new constitution was overwhelmingly passed in a referendum; it promised in one of its articles to "bring back the residents of Nubia to their original areas and develop them within ten years."[48] A committee was formed, and it met with Nubian and nongovernmental organization representatives. A draft bill was written up. Rules were created over land use. Things started to look promising. Here was hope and progress. The bill was ready to go to parliament—but never did. Since then, well-known Nubian activist Fatma Sakory has suggested the Egyptian authorities never intended to make good on the constitutional promise and only considered it as "a way in order to silence the Nubian community" for the short-term future.[49]

In late November 2014, President Abdel Fattah el-Sisi issued an executive order that created a new military zone, one that was carved out of the coastal towns of Ras Hadraba and Arfeen and a region that had sixteen former Nubian villages. Then, four years later, the government swooped in to develop the "southernmost parts of Upper Egypt, including most of the Nubians' ancestral territory not already flooded, sold off, or declared a military zone."[50] The Nubians can be forgiven for not putting any more faith in government promises. And they still wait to go home. "The government is not sensitized to any human rights of all the population," Sakory told a reporter in 2017. "They are violating Nubian rights in the same way they are violating Coptic rights, in the same way they are violating Bedouin rights."[51]

Displacement, however, hasn't meant the complete extinction of Nubian culture—not yet anyway. Amazingly, even as archaeologists and other experts try to decipher the script of the ancient Nubians, some of their descendants are trying to revive their ancestral tongue. It hasn't been an easy task. While the script died out, the spoken form morphed into two dialects, Kenzi and Fadiji. As with dialects anywhere, speakers of one don't necessarily know the other, and non-Nubian Egyptians can't speak them either. But language classes in the dialects are being held for Nubians living in Alexandria and Cairo. Nubian businesswoman Hafsa Amberkab and several volunteer researchers launched what they called the *Koma Waidi* ("Tales from the Past") initiative, traveling to different villages and filming Nubian elders, collecting folk stories and expressions. The first fruit of their labors was a booklet published in 2020, a dictionary of rare Nubian words. There are versions in English, Arabic, and Spanish.[52]

Even before the dictionary made headlines, software developer Momen Taloosh brought out "Nubi," a mobile application. Though he lives in Alexandria, he's of Nubian descent and wanted the language to live on. The app offers Nubian proverbs and traditional songs in both Kenzi and Fadiji translated into Arabic. The lyrics of one tune include, "My son, as you leave for the old village, remember me when you get there . . . and do not forget to greet it for me."[53]

What should this remind us of? Only pages ago, I quoted scholar Sherif Abouelhadid on the ancient Egyptian singing forms and clapping in the country's modern streets. Nubians have a similar miracle of continuity from ancient times, only theirs has been eroded by the steady progress of the dominant Arabized culture. But it's still there. And there are lessons for us if we look for them. The West, after all, has repeatedly congratulated itself for cracking the code of hieroglyphics and for Howard Carter's discovery of Tutankhamun. It seems only fitting that when experts pay more attention to ancient Nubia, Nubians themselves are taking the initiative to rescue the most practical and vital component of their ancient heritage.

We'll see this phenomenon again and again through the ages: while some African figures made huge impacts on culture and civilization through their thinking and written work, there were also ethnic peoples on the continent quietly innovating, developing, progressing . . . and who were ignored by the rest of the world for considerable stretches of time. We'll explore later what I call "African Antecedents" as well as other unique approaches to language and to conveying information. But for now, our road leads to Rome, where the later empire turned out to be more African in spirit than you might think.

2

Tall Tales and Confessions

Our collective imagination has an image of Rome that's as misleading as the one we have of ancient Egypt. It's colored by movie portrayals and classic paintings of men in togas or in legionnaire breastplates and with plumed helmets—oh, and these figures are invariably depicted as white. But we forget that the Roman Empire, vast in its conquests and stretching from what is now southern Spain and Algeria all the way to Jordan, Egypt, and Iraq, was also a multicultural one.

This wasn't merely because of trade. From early on, the Romans got smart and realized they were better off recruiting men for their army legions from the locals in their occupied territories. If you fought for Rome, you had certain privileges and earned yourself land and citizenship. And some of the empire's greatest figures were from north Africa. The very word *Africa* is a Roman one, derived from the Latin term *Afri*, which referred to occupants in a region of ancient Libya. As the empire gobbled up more territory along the coast, they thought nothing of mixing the word in to refer to their new possessions, and over time, "Africa" became more generic. When westerners rather sloppily refer in conversation to "taking a trip to Africa" or "African politics," it shows some things have never changed.

But Romans had their finer distinctions, too, and ones we should remember. When we talk of Hannibal and his elephants from Carthage crossing the Alps to fight Rome, we're referring to a culture that was once based geographically in Tunisia and that had its own language (known as Punic). *But* it was started by the Phoenicians of ancient Lebanon. And in the east were the Libyans—the Romans called them Libyans to distinguish them from the non-Punic Africans.

It's important to keep in mind the Romans didn't think in terms of race the way we do, and their attitudes were more ambiguous. Of course, they were as subject to biases and xenophobia as anyone now, and there's considerable academic debate over how much color prejudice existed in the ancient world. But class and money certainly played major and decisive roles in their society. We can't be completely sure of his ethnic background, but we know Suetonius, who wrote the history of the *Twelve Caesars* during the reign of Hadrian, was from the province of Numidia. The playwright Terence came from Carthage, while Marcus Fronto—the tutor of Marcus Aurelius—was another Numidian. The later emperor, Septimius Severus, came from Libya.

Septimius was perfectly fluent in Punic, but he always spoke Latin with a slight accent, which prompted sneers from his critics and enemies. Looking at a classical white bust of Suetonius or Septimius will tell you little because they were portrayed in the typical heroic style with European features. This is highly misleading because according to research going all the way back to at least the 1980s, such busts weren't "finished" as white at all but would have been decorated with colored pigments. How faithful to their portrayed subjects we don't know, but with either Suetonius or Septimius, they might have looked as different from their white marble sculptures as Jesus—a Jew of the Middle East—would differ from his image in a pie plate in the tourist gift shops near the Vatican.

What we do know is that the Libyans at this time, as well as Numidians like Suetonius and Septimius, were all from the various communities of *Imazighen*, the people known in the West as Berbers. Some cultural descendants don't like to be called that, as the word *Berber* is derived from the Greek term for "barbarian," while others don't mind so much. There's scholarly debate over where their own name for themselves came from and which specific tribe should get the credit, but one common explanation for Imazighen is "free people," and it's the plural of *Amazigh*—a single individual—in the language of Tamazight. Because "Amazighs" is becoming increasingly common as the plural, we'll use that from now on.

The various Amazigh tribes put up a long fight for decades before they were gradually absorbed by the Romans. And even as Latin was spoken in the larger towns of, say, Numidia, and togas were worn along their crowded market streets, Amazigh culture continued along a parallel course, especially in the rural areas. Out in the country, they spoke their own languages and lived as they pleased.

Ancient Amazighs were tough and tribal, and their brilliant horsemen proved especially valuable to Hannibal on his punishing marches, relying on an ingenious neck rein all their own instead of a bridle.[1] We tend to think of them reflexively as pastoral, and they were, herding their sheep and goats and sometimes farming. But they were builders, too. You can see a beautiful example of their ancient architecture if you visit the Mausoleum of Dougga in Tunisia, believed to have been constructed on the order of a Numidian prince. Where we want to concentrate, however, are two Numidians, separated by hundreds of years, who gave us classics that are each still having an impact on our thinking.

This is how one classic book starts: "Business once took me to Thessaly, where my mother's family originated; I have, by the way, the distinction of being descended through her from the famous Plutarch. One morning after I had ridden over a high range of hills, down a slippery track into the valley beyond, across dewy pastures and soggy ploughlands, my horse, a white Thessalian thoroughbred, began to puff and slacken his pace."[2]

With these opening words, we're off on a rollicking adventure, one in which a man is accidentally turned into a donkey. This is *The Golden Ass*, the only ancient Roman novel you can read complete from beginning to end. And it's been influencing world literature ever since it was "hot off the scrolls."

Now if we're exploring African ideas, why should we care about an ancient novel in Latin? Because it's only deceptively Latin. The author's language is vivid, dynamic, and, with the right translator, such as Robert Graves (the man who turned the lives of the Caesars into a potboiler soap opera, *I, Claudius*), quite compelling. Graves thought the writer was "parodying the extravagant language which the 'Milesian' storytellers used [ones from Ionian town of Miletus], like barkers at county fairs today as a means of impressing simple-minded audiences."[3]

Perhaps, but maybe he was up to something else.

The author was Apuleius, a rhetorician, priest, and mystic who lived during the reigns of Hadrian, Marcus Aurelius, and Commodus, from about 125 to 180 CE. He was from a town called M'daourouch or Madauros in Numidia. We know his roots because he comments on them in one of his other works, telling us how he was "half-Numidian, half-Gaetulian." Gaetulia was another Romanized region in the desert south of the Atlas Mountains and bordering the Sahara. The Gaetulians were a nomadic people who deeply resented anyone telling them what to do but who were happy to trade goods and intermarry other cultures, such as the Persians.

So it's possible Apuleius wasn't always thinking of parody and that he was really calling on the oral traditions of Amazigh folktales, the kind that goatherds enjoyed around their fires late at night and which amused the merchants as they passed the time at their stalls on a dusty corner. It's been suggested that there are traceable narrative motifs from the Amazigh tradition in his novel, and a couple of scholars believe that even his retelling of the Cupid and Psyche story could have relied on different Amazigh versions. In one of them, instead of the male hero of the story being a Hellenic god, he's a supernatural being, *Asfer n Ilhwa*, "Whistling of the Rain."[4]

It's important as well that *The Golden Ass* is a novel about ordinary people. Yes, it has gods and magic in it, but its characters include a baker, a magistrate, a cook, and a trio of bandits. We get a window on the world of ordinary lower-class citizens of Roman society, a colonial society at that, and it's bawdy in spots. Who else could tell such a tale but a person who has one foot outside the highborn life? Apuleius traveled widely, but he lived and worked in Roman Africa, against the backdrop of his own culture. While he set his novel in Thessaly in Greece, he ended it—rather tellingly—by revealing that his protagonist was from his own hometown, M'daourouch.

Now consider that tales from *The Golden Ass* have been filched by Boccaccio for his *Decameron*, and this rambling adventure yarn with its many digressions has clearly left its stamp on writers through the ages. You can spot its influence in Voltaire's *Candide* and *Don Quixote* by Cervantes, certainly in *Pinocchio* by Carlo Collodi and Franz Kafka's helpless salesman turning into a giant insect in Henry Fielding and C. S. Lewis and countless others. It's inspired an opera and comic books.

And at heart, it's an African novel with an *African* hero.

Our second Numidian made two major contributions to literature, which were definitely *not* meant as entertainments and stirred very different reactions in his readers. His name was Aurelius Augustinus, and we know him as St. Augustine of Hippo.

Augustine was born in 354 CE in a town called Thagaste in the wooded highlands of northeastern Numidia, not that far, in fact, from M'daourouch. There's still a town there today, now called Souk Ahras. His family must have been what we would call lower middle class, as they habitually spoke Latin at home, but his father still had to save up enough money to send Augustine off to Carthage to study law. As a youth, he was distant from his father and closer to his mother, who was a devout Christian, but the boy didn't pay that much attention, as can be typical with teenagers with strongly devout parents. She also got on his nerves with what today we'd call a lot of passive-aggressive guilt-tripping and lecturing.

In writing about himself, Augustine paints a portrait of an adolescent suffering growing pains and questioning life. He steals from a pear tree not because he's hungry but because he can, and he's thrilled at getting away with it. He hears his pals "bragging about their depravity," the equivalent of locker room sex talk, and he joins in, regretting it later.[5] He goes to Carthage, and, like young people today leaving home for the first time to attend university, he overindulges in sex, wine, and fun, loving the theater, and enjoying all the cool things a big city has to offer. At the same time, his hedonistic pleasures often make him feel hollow. Augustine coined a phrase in a brief prayer to God that even a wit like Oscar Wilde would appreciate. The best colloquial translation for the joke is "Oh, God, please make me pure—but not yet."

To cut to the chase in his story, Augustine abandoned law to become interested in philosophy and teach rhetoric, and between the influence of Mom, who kept nagging, and his various travels and the mentorship of such figures as Ambrose of Milan, he finally heard the call (literally, with a voice in his head). At the age of thirty-one, he read the Bible and became a Christian. In 391 CE, he was ordained as a priest in the town of Hippo Regius—now Algeria's Annaba—and a handful of years later, he was made its bishop, which is why he's known as "Augustine of Hippo."

In joining the church, he was following in the footsteps of many other Africans who helped give the religion its distinctive character and rituals. Scholar D. A. Masolo considers it "reasonable to think that many elements of the indigenous customs and everyday or seasonal activities and practices of the peoples of North Africa may have found their way, by way of adaptation, into the conceptions of Christianity as African thinkers endeavored to systematize Christian beliefs into an organized and coherent thought system."[6] Origen, who lived more than a hundred years before Augustine and whom scholars believe was either Punic or Amazigh, is credited by experts with influencing how Christians thought about the Holy Trinity. Tertullian of Carthage, whose life span overlaps part of Origen's era, was a prolific writer of Christian theology. Tertullian was so hostile to philosophical musings, in fact, that he's often been thought of as a materialist. "What has Athens to do with Jerusalem?" he demanded. His blunt, commonsense approach did have its limits. For instance, Tertullian pondered a while about God and decided his divine creator had both a spirit and a physical body.[7]

But as a thinker and a guiding light for his faith, Augustine would eclipse all his African predecessors because he left behind two profoundly influential works of literature and philosophy, the *Confessions* and *The City of God*.

We'll get to their significance in a moment, but first, it's worth pausing to consider a question posed by a scholar named Maurice Frost in a theological journal back in 1942. "One would welcome," Frost wrote, "some attempt to assess Augustine's importance as an African in the history of North Africa, and to consider his thought in the light of his Berber background. How far do Augustine's ideas show traces of the Berber surroundings in which he grew up?"[8] It's clear that few if any scholars in the West in the mid-twentieth century thought of Augustine this way any more than they gave a passing thought to Apuleius's background or to that of Origen. Fortunately, more recent historians have looked into the matter.

And Augustine left several references that he thought of himself as African and used that word for himself. He called Apuleius "the most notorious of us Africans" and referred to someone else as "an African man writing of Africa . . . or at any rate, with that flat nose that you see in Africans." When he got into a heated theological argument with someone, his opponent lost his temper and referred to him as Punic, a person from Carthage such as Hannibal. It was meant as a slur, and according to one of his modern biographers, Augustine "effectively played the race card" and reminded the man that one of his own favorite bishops was from Carthage.[9] Many a young black intellectual today can relate to Augustine's situation how, having "graduated" to a position of prestige, they suddenly find themselves yanked back to a status set by their color or heritage.

But we can answer Frost's question about Amazigh surroundings and African influence another way: by what Augustine *didn't* do. For this, we need to look at a schism in early Christianity that most of us have never heard of or remember. In schools in Europe and North America, we learn about Martin Luther and the Protestants breaking away from the Catholic faith, but it wasn't the first split in the church, and this one would last from the fourth to the sixth century. It essentially came down to a rivalry between Catholicism and what came to be known as Donatism, named after a bishop in Numidia named Donatus.

The background is this: When the emperor Diocletian infamously persecuted Christians in 303 CE, having their churches burned down and rounding up their numbers to be executed, a good portion of the faithful understandably wanted to stay alive. In fact, during the first decades of the fledgling cult, persecution or not, many people worshipped Christ right alongside the old pagan gods (which annoyed and vexed Christian priests no end). A Roman governor in north Africa happened to be more tolerant, simply asking Christians to make a gesture of rejecting their faith by handing over their scriptures. This became a class issue as well because the wealthier Christians could more easily do this and get themselves out of trouble.

After Diocletian died in 311 and the persecutions ended, the poorer classes in Numidia held a lot of resentment toward the folks they called *traditores*, essentially "traitors." And Bishop Donatus didn't want the clergy who had temporarily renounced their faith to go back on the job. The Donatists even believed "that sacraments administered by unworthy priests were invalid."[10] Augustine, of course, was a walking, talking example of a man who had been brought up with the church, who had rejected it for his own personal reasons, and who then came back to it. From his perspective, it made no sense to treat the church as a private club where if you left the membership, you were out forever. He was also, lest we forget, a very Romanized African who had spent years among the sophisticated thinkers in Rome and Milan. When it came time to choose sides, he went with Catholicism.

Now why should any of this matter in terms of Africa, even though the dispute broke out there?

Well, by Augustine's era, the state apparatus of Rome was in steady decline across the empire. The era was counting down to the ultimate disaster when barbarians invaded Italy and the Visigoths sacked the imperial capital. Of course, the fall of the empire didn't happen overnight, and the rot had already set in. Sure, for a long time, the Romans could hold on to their colonial backwater of Numidia with a single legion of 5,000 men.[11] But the world was different now, and the locals were getting sick and tired of their colonial overseers.

Coinciding with the dismal state of affairs in Rome and the rise of Christianity was a revival of local cultures, particularly among the lower classes across Roman Africa, Egypt, and Syria. We've seen the same thing in our own modern era after political upheavals, showcased in the worst way with the ethnic fighting of the Balkans after the breakup of Yugoslavia and the bitter chaos that has plagued Iraq since the fall of Saddam Hussein. So it was with the Donatists, who began to widen their interests. They got involved with peasant rebellions and championed certain Amazigh chiefs.[12] Their uncompromising view of Christianity perhaps fit the rugged individualism of Amazigh tribesmen, but in the grand scheme of things, they *were on the losing side.*

As Donatism diluted and mixed with the local beliefs, it lost its cohesive power, and so Christianity never really took hold in this part of Africa, leaving it fertile ground for another religious import down the line: Islam.[13]

For Augustine, his choices had repercussions, which is how we ended up with one of his classics. After he came home to Numidia and was recognized as a rising talent, it was natural that some wanted to put him on the fast track in Hippo before another church snapped him up, but apparently the right references hadn't been obtained. "Augustine was clever and therefore distrusted," noted the British theologian Henry Chadwick. "Many recalled how combative he had once been against the Catholic Church before his conversion. . . . His lurid youth had not been forgotten." The presiding bishop in Numidia wrote an angry letter to Augustine's sponsor, and it was leaked. "In Numidia, the Donatists were in the majority in both town and countryside and notably in Hippo itself," Chadwick reminds us. "The Donatists got hold of the presiding bishop's letter and used it as a rod to beat Augustine."[14]

So, many see Augustine's *Confessions* as partly an answer to his critics. It's also fair to say that even though written in Latin, the book is an *African* thinker writing *to and for other Africans,* making his case. After all, he didn't need to argue the sincerity of his conversion or plead his case to his allies in Rome or Milan. It was many of his fellow Africans who were the Donatists and the ones who needed persuading. To point this out isn't a case of afterthought tokenism either—a careless "oh, and they were Africans." At the time, no one could be sure, Augustine included, that the Donatists would lose the great debate. It was quite possible that Roman Africa might change the course of Christian theology.

Instead, it was changed by a single African, Augustine.

His *Confessions* are just that. While he does sometimes refer to God in the regular third person, his book is studded with instances where he addresses God as "you," in a very personal monologue. It's the work of a philosopher, pondering important issues and questioning scripture, but we're not eavesdropping on a pretentious coffee shop debate over terminology either. This is a quest of the heart as much as one for the mind. "I realized that I was now thirty years old and was still floundering in the same quagmire because I was greedy to enjoy what the world had to offer, though it only eluded me and wasted my strength. And all the time I had been telling myself one tale after another. 'Tomorrow I shall discover the truth. I shall see it quite plainly, and it will be mine to keep.'"[15] One of his first breakthroughs was to decide that the Bible shouldn't always be taken literally, and he settles on the idea that evil is a perversion of the will.

Stephen Greenblatt in an article for *The New Yorker* in 2017 phrased Augustine's dilemma over Adam and Eve rather pithily: "The archaic story of the naked man and woman, the talking snake, and the magical trees was something of an embarrassment. It was Augustine who rescued it from the decorous oblivion to which it seemed to be heading."[16] What he came up with was a rationale over the concept of Original Sin, passed down from the Bible's original man, Adam.

We don't need to debate the validity of his ideas here; suffice to say they found enough support to ensure his place in history. It's the candor of his life story that gives the book its real power. His *Confessions* may go on the Religion shelf, but it's considered a milestone in autobiography. It's unrelenting in its examination of character, and it sometimes delves into the most peculiar minutiae. Early on, he recalls a time when he and his father, Patricius, were at the bathhouse and his father spotted a sign that his teenage son had sprouted pubic hair or he caught a glimpse of an involuntary partial erection (the language isn't terribly clear). When the two returned home, Patricius eagerly told his wife how the boy was ready now to provide them with grandchildren. "It is easy, even across a vast distance in time," remarks Greenblatt, "to conjure up a teenager's exquisite embarrassment."[17]

We don't always sympathize with Augustine either. He enjoyed a convenient sexual relationship with a lowborn woman that began when they were both teenagers, one that lasted fifteen years and produced a son. But Augustine packed her off to Carthage as his career improved and when he needed to marry someone more suitable to his position. He feels terrible about it later—but not so terrible that he didn't get himself another mistress.

Unlike regular autobiography, Augustine's narrative arc is a mental one. Its climax isn't obtaining a great career post or other achievements, it's his spiritual enlightenment. And for Christians well into the Middle Ages, it was a long yet effective recruiting pamphlet. With its almost excruciating intimacy of disclosure, it told them, "Consider me, I was miserable, I had these questions, too! But now I've resolved them." They could arrive at faith not merely through prayer (because quite possibly, that wouldn't be enough) but by thinking their way to it.

In only a few years, Augustine set his scope wider. After the sack of Rome, there were those who believed the disaster happened because Romans had abandoned the old pagan gods and taken up Christianity. *The City of God* was Augustine's response. He devotes a lot of space to critiquing the pagan religions and why he considers them invalid. Interestingly, he chooses to pick on Apuleius several times, perhaps because his fellow Numidian had stayed popular and was a clever advocate in some of his writings for the old pagan beliefs. The rest of Augustine's book outlines his view of Christian theology, and its ideas—from his analysis of scriptures and sexuality to how he viewed the battle between good and evil—left an indelible stamp on the Roman Catholic Church for centuries. Augustine basically believed in free will, and we're still debating that one. He influenced not only Catholics, such as Thomas Aquinas, but Protestants, such as John Calvin.

Nor did his impact stop there. The philosophers Martin Heidegger and Ludwig Wittgenstein reference him. At the University of Heidelberg in 1929, a young Hannah Arendt wrote a dissertation on Augustine's concept of love. Our old friend Bertrand Russell, who had little use for Christianity, gave Augustine a fair hearing when evaluating his philosophy and declared that he didn't agree with the saint's subjective concept of the nature of time, "in so far as it makes time something mental. But it is clearly a very able theory, deserving to be seriously considered."[18] Russell went further, saying it was a great advance over the Greeks and Emmanuel Kant.

An African philosopher, sending ripples down through civilization and into modern thought today.

3

A Historian Meets a Khan

Between the lifetimes of Numidia's favorite sons, Apuleius and Augustus, another region of the continent—what is now northern Ethiopia—became important to the rest of the world. The Empire of Aksum was a mighty realm that exported glass crystal, copper, brass, frankincense, and myrrh to the Romans and Egyptians. (Because no one ever remembers, frankincense and myrrh are resins used in perfumes and sometimes in traditional medicine.) The Aksumites were the only Africans aside from those in client states for Rome to issue their own national coinage, which they used from about the late third to the seventh century.[1] Today, Aksum is most remembered for its remarkable stelae—stone pillars that weigh tons and rise like skyscrapers. They even have carved fake windows and doors, and they're thought to be funerary monuments. But why the Aksumites matter to us here is that they once mattered to everyone else around them.

Look at a map of the southern Red Sea. By the time that Apuleius was chuckling over the jokes in the rough draft of his novel, Rome had expanded so much—stretching from Spain to deep into Armenia and Mesopotamia—that Emperor Hadrian finally said enough is enough. The legions had taken all they could handle. But the Romans naturally still wanted to hold on to their conquests, and they had problems on multiple fronts.

The nomadic Beja of Sudan made incursions in Egypt. The famed legions were running into trouble with the Persians. Roman ships in the Red Sea region were attacked—not in the waters themselves but when they put into shore to trade and pick up supplies.

For all these struggles, Aksum stepped in as a valuable ally. In the typical monarch boasting for the inscriptions of ancient times, one king tells us, "I subjugated the Solate people and ordered them to protect the seacoast. Having dispatched a war fleet, I subjugated the rulers who lived along that side of the sea . . . having commanded them to pay tribute and conduct affairs peacefully on land and sea."[2]

We also know that early Christian bishops and scholars from Aksum visited India and Sri Lanka and that Indians, in turn, traveled to Aksum. Cosmas of Alexandria, an early traveler to India himself, refers to Aksumite ships conducting a brisk trade in the north of the subcontinent, particularly in emeralds, while the Greek scholar Procopius talks about ships from Aksum making trips to southern Arabia. When Justinian ruled the Byzantine Empire, he suggested the Ethiopians act as the middlemen in the silk trade, buying the cloth from the Indians to sell to Romans. The deal fell through, however, because "the Persians, who inhabited the land adjoining with the Indians, used to come to the ports where the Indian ships pulled in, usually taking [all] the cargo from them [the Indians]."[3]

Even before this, Byzantium was keen to enlist the Aksumites as allies against its main foe at the time, the Persians. But the Aksumites had their own priorities, eager to put down the Jewish Himyarite kingdom in the southern Arabian Peninsula (in what today is Yemen). Christians had long appealed to Aksum, complaining of persecution under the Jewish monarch, Yusuf, who ruled around 520 CE. Yusuf, known as Dhu-Nuwas, had a ruthless streak and managed to antagonize the various ethnic groups under his reign.

The Aksumites sailed across the Red Sea, using a military public relations trick familiar to us today: they were on a "rescue mission." And they quite neatly captured the Himyarite capital, Zafar, and other strategic centers. Then the bulk of their forces headed home and left a detachment behind. Dhu-Nuwas—in a move worthy of a Borgia—sent a message to Zafar, promising the Aksumites could have safe passage home if they abandoned his capital. Unfortunately, the Aksumites fell for the ruse, and he promptly had them slaughtered, trapping more than 280 of those who had stayed behind in a church, which was then set on fire.

Feeling confident after this reversal, Dhu Nuwas went on the warpath up and down the Himyarite lands and, if Christian sources are to be believed, committed massacres in the port town of Muhvan and the northern city of Najaran. The seasonal winds didn't allow the Aksumites to save Najaran, and they strangely dithered for a few years over getting payback (perhaps because of internal politics).[4] In the meantime, Dhu Nuwas looked around for allies, hoping he could win over the Persians. He didn't. But his autocratic, unpredictable reign hurt trade and alienated all his neighbors enough that the Romans now considered him a threat, especially if he was going to throw in with the Persians. Emperor Justin I suggested to Aksum, Hey, why don't we *both* invade the Himyar? Under Justin's strategy, the Byzantines would come down via Egypt to link up with the Aksumites in Ethiopian territory.

Aksum, however, was cool to the idea, which is understandable from its point of view. Yes, there was the short-term gain of superior numbers and a united force for the invasion, but in the long term, you now had the Eastern Roman Empire on your turf, and even if it kept its word about only passing through, should the invasion succeed, the Romans would be camped in your backyard.. Aksum's emperor at the time was Kaleb—or, to use his imperial name, Ella Asbeha—a ruler who would become both a legend and a saint in Ethiopian culture. Sticking to the maxim of "if you want something done," he chose to invade Himyar himself.

Kaleb executed a clever plan. All this time, a population of disaffected Christians had become refugees in the Aksum kingdom, along with other exiles, such as members of a Jewish clan persecuted by Dhu Nuwas. They would sail over first as an advance strike force, sowing rebellion. In the summer of 525 CE, the invasion got under way, relying in part on Byzantine ships because the Aksumites didn't have enough of their own. The chronicles for events then get sketchy and sometimes contradict each other. In one account, at least part of the invasion fleet was lost at sea.

Despite this setback, we can be sure most of the Aksumites and their exile rebels made landfall, and Dhu Nuwas reportedly couldn't persuade the nobles along the Arabian coast to gather for his defense. In a climactic battle on the shore, the Himyarites suffered great casualties, and their men lost their nerve and fled. Dhu Nuwas was confronted by an ordinary Ethiopian warrior and. . . . He lost the fight, his body dragged out of the foam washing along the beach, his head chopped off.

The Aksumites made quick work of taking Zafar and then finishing off the rest of the Himyarites, and one of Dhu Nuwas's own relatives escorted Kaleb on his victory parade. While some Aksumites went on a vengeful spree of killing Himyarite Jews, this didn't happen on Kaleb's orders, and it speaks to his reputation for tolerance that some Himyarite nobles made direct complaints and appeals to him over the slaughter. Nevertheless, when the killing stopped, Christians were in top positions of power while pagan temples and Jewish synagogues were reduced to rubble and smoldering ashes. After seven months, Kaleb sailed home, and Himyar was now a vassal state of Aksum.

In time, Aksum's hold waned, and the Himyarites took back full control over their land. But the era of influence from across the Red Sea should make us adjust our view of the region. History is replete with examples of the Arabization of Africa and the impact of the Middle East on African countries. We forget that there was a time when power flowed the other way, with a major empire affecting the destiny of a part of southern Arabia. As well, our casual understanding of Rome relies on our impression of how much it dominated the known world, forgetting that it both occasionally needed and feared other powers.

One of those was Aksum: a civilization that impressed the Romans, traded with the Indians, and for a short while ruled some of the Arabians.

As Aksum started to decline and Augustine's works were widely discussed in Christian Europe, followers of Allah rode away from their homes near the Red Sea to spread their faith across the Middle East and then along the coast of northern Africa, which they referred to as the *Maghreb* (the "West" from their perspective, because they meant west of Egypt).

It's important to recognize, however, that conversion to Islam in Africa didn't always result from conquest. Take the case of the Empire of Ghana (which was quite some distance from the postcolonial modern country that adopted its name). Tales of Ghana's fabulous wealth in gold and its opulent court in its capital of Kumbi saleh in the 700s reached all the way to Baghdad. And the traditional thinking right into the late twentieth century was that the Amazighs pushed their way down across the Sahara and subdued Ghana in 1076 CE, getting the locals to become Muslims.

But it's been persuasively argued that "there is no direct evidence for any conquest, still less a violent and destructive conquest, of Ghana by the Almoravids."[5] The original sources for pushing this alleged "fact" are all Arabic, and each writer had a political ax to grind. You won't find the conquest of Ghana, as you'd surely expect to, in the *Tarikh-al-Sudan*—the "History of the Sudan," which is the famous chronicle of the Songhay Empire in the western Sahel—and even the great Amazigh scholar of the sixteenth century, Ahmad Baba, denied it ever happened.[6] European writers and historians, however, picked up the wrong idea and ran with it. Adding to the confusion is that the Amazighs had long held a spot on the edge of the Sahara, Awdaghust, and though it was written that this used to be the capital of the Empire of Ghana, it certainly wasn't by 1076.[7]

Similarly, we don't see Islam grow in places like Nigeria and coastal Kenya from invading armies. Instead, it flourished through trade. The badly misunderstood idea of *jihad* is such a political trope now for the modern West, along with vague recollections from school about the Crusades, that it barely registers that Islam could have had something to offer to African cultures, just as Christianity would prove attractive as well to Africans at various points in history. In fact, Islam in Africa provided something you couldn't get in the rainy, cold patches of medieval Europe: a really thorough further education.

For example, one of the great generals of the Umayyad Caliphate founded a small city, Qarawiyyin, in the middle of a dense forest of what is now Tunisia. He also founded its Great Mosque, and Qarawiyyin is home to beautiful examples of Islamic architecture and a picturesque *souk*, or market. But in the late 700s, the place to be was nearby Fez because Morocco was enjoying its first independent Islamic regime, and this minor town—known until then for its tannery work—had adopted it as its capital. The trouble was that a recent population boom meant there were not enough mosques or *madrasas* (colleges) in Fez to accommodate the citizens. Luckily, two daughters of a wealthy businessman in Qarawiyyin, Mariam and Fatima, inherited their father's fortune after he died, and Fatima al-Fihri put her share to good use. In the *Dictionary of African Biography*, Osire Glacier concedes that we know hardly anything about Fatima but given her legacy, speculates that "one can sense some of her personal qualities, among which were probably generosity, intelligence and clairvoyance."[8]

She first bankrolled the construction of a mosque with a comparatively humble minaret and then decided there should be a madrasa as well; and it's the madrasa that put Qarawiyyin on the map of intellectual development. It became one of the oldest and most prestigious universities of the ancient world.

To attend Qarawiyyin must have been equivalent in its day to getting into Cambridge, Harvard, and MIT all rolled into one. With a library full of precious manuscripts, students could learn law, astronomy, medicine, and mathematics. UNESCO calls it the oldest university in the world, founded in 859 CE. By comparison, Oxford—often touted as Europe's model that started the university experience—got rolling only by the eleventh century. The Sorbonne was founded later in 1150. Fez's casbahs would have bustled with traders and eager students arguing passionately over the Koran, their homes and shops guarded by thick stone walls with watchtowers.

Over the next few centuries, some of the greatest minds of the Middle Ages went to Qarawiyyin. Ibn Rushd, better known as the philosopher Averroes, studied there and would later write commentaries on Aristotle. He also tried to figure out the motions of the planets and dash off a general treatise on the principles of medicine. Another alumnus was Moses ben Maimon, the Jewish scholar known as Maimonides, who was revered for his inspired interpretations of the Torah and who wrote several influential books in Arabic on medicine, covering everything from aphrodisiacs to how to treat poisons and hemorrhoids.

But this African university drew other curious minds from across the Mediterranean. In the tenth century, a French cleric and scientist named Gerbert d'Aurillac was a student; he would eventually become Pope Sylvester II, but he's more important to us because he introduced the concepts of Arabic numerals and the decimal system to Europe. Later in the 1600s, the Dutch mathematician Jacobus Golius, an enthusiastic collector and translator of Arabic manuscripts, visited Qarawiyyin. Thanks to Golius, Europeans working on physics and math would come to know an important treatise on optics. For several centuries, this university in Africa served as a nourishing lifeline of ideas and research between Christian Europe and the Islamic East.

Of course, different historians have made persuasive cases to champion individual cultures they think deserve credit for gathering knowledge during the Middle Ages. The traditional view is that Arabs rescued Greek classics from oblivion during Europe's so-called Dark Ages. And Frederick Starr has argued recently that many great figures wrote their seminal works in Arabic, but they were ethnically from Central Asia. Well, then, what about Africa? A long quarrel has persisted on whether certain innovators should be thought of as Arabs, given all the contributions by those who came out of north Africa and Islamic Spain, or if their achievements should be ticked on the "Africa" side of the ledger. But with no insult intended to the respective cultures, I would suggest this is an ultimately irrelevant argument.

First, take the case of the Ottoman Empire. It took in Muslims, Jews, Christians, and a patchwork quilt of ethnicities, such as Armenians, Kurds, Yezidis, Egyptians, Assyrians, and so on. But you'll search in vain through the records for anyone who referred to themselves in a village of Mesopotamia or in the Balkans *at the time* as an "Ottoman." Identity and race in the Middle Ages were more fluid, and if we take, as an example, the great explorer Ibn Battuta (whom we'll meet later), we can think of him as a Moroccan, or we can think of him as an African or a Muslim. But he may well have thought of himself as an Amazigh in one sense, as a Muslim in another, and as an African in a wider context. As he flitted across the world, he would have been constantly in positions to define and redefine himself.

Second, let's remember a point made in the introduction: the *dissemination* of ideas was crucial. At the University of Qarawiyyin, regular students and visitors translated and passed along important medical texts by Ibn Zuhr from Seville, a physician who did pioneering work on the tracheotomy, and texts on astronomy and botany by the Adalusian Ibn Bajja. Yes, it was wonderful when a Muslim polymath in Cairo or Córdoba had a breakthrough in physics or dreamed up a new way to treat a debilitating disease, but consider how slowly information traveled in this dark era of plague, suspicion, periodic droughts, and famine . . . along with the occasional Crusade. Africans helped spread the word of their discoveries. Africans incorporated them and taught them, keeping them alive. As the centuries rolled on and Europeans made the long trip to the madrasa, their pilgrimage to know more says a lot about how a distant university in Morocco—in Africa—was well respected.

Today's bookshops have been full of best-selling tomes that try to interpret the world around us: Thomas L. Friedman's *The World Is Flat*, Francis Fukuyama's *The End of History and the Last Man*, Paul Kennedy's *The Rise and Fall of the Great Powers*, *The Clash of Civilizations and the Remaking of World Order* by Samuel Huntingdon. And on the roll call goes. Plus, we're still debating how much Karl Marx got right and wrong.

But it was an African who first developed an intellectual framework for looking at the rise and fall of great civilizations and the dynamics of a society. It's not overselling it to call this scholar from Tunis the father of modern sociology. After all, he claimed himself to have invented it. His name was Ibn Khaldun.

He was born in 1332 into a prominent family from Andalusian Spain and claimed his roots went back to Arabs from Yemen. But his biographer Mohammad Enan poured cold water on this, suggesting, "To be of Arab origin was considered, in Andalusia, to be a coveted honor on account of their dominance and influence. But doubt entered into the genealogies of many chiefs and racial leaders." Moreover, Ibn Khaldun showed in his writing "strong antagonism and prejudice towards the Arabs, while in another part of his history, he praises the Berbers and extols their character and qualities."[9]

Nevertheless, he came from a privileged class, and he also studied at the University of Qarawiyyin; he would later donate his most famous book to its library, which still has it. After his education and while still in his early twenties, he earned himself a high position at the court of the sultan in Fez. He was on the fast track. Now this was a time of almost constant political upheaval and shifting alliances in the Maghreb, and a cunning man would learn to keep his head down. The problem is that Ibn Khaldun was often his own worst enemy. He had opinions, and he was ambitious, and the two can be a dangerous mix.

His career, which has been compared to that of Machiavelli, is a winding one, but the short version is that he got involved in a political conspiracy against his boss, got caught, and wound up in prison. After his sentence, he moved to Granada and managed to land another high position. But once again, he became embroiled in political rivalries, which pushed him to return to north Africa. At one point, he was sent on a mission to go collect taxes and raise armies from the various nomadic Amazigh tribes, even lead them sometimes into battle. As modern biographer Allen Fromhertz puts it, "Not many philosophers have been obliged to eat their own horse."[10]

After his sponsoring sultan died, he switched allegiances yet again, wound up on the wrong side of a feud between factions, and was taken captive. After his release, he'd had enough of intrigues and slashing and parrying his way up and down the status ladder, and he eventually managed to win passage back to his hometown of Tunis in 1378 to focus on writing. But after a couple of years, he went to Cairo, where he became a legal professor, then a *qadi* or Islamic judge, then lost that job, then won a new appointment, and you can see the pattern of his tumultuous life.

In 1400, he was lured away from his desk to join a defensive effort against the invading Tatars led by Timur—Tamerlane, as he's often known. Armies clashed at Damascus, but when the two sides finally started negotiating peace, there was dissension in the camp of the latest emir, who was Ibn Khaldun's boss. Fearing a coup, the emir fled to Cairo. That left his military officials bickering over terms for the surrender of Damascus. As this went on and on, Ibn Khaldun suddenly decided he should be the man of the hour. He marched right out and convinced the soldiers to lower him down the side of the city's wall. He then talked his way into an audience with Timur, finding the Tatar leader in a tent, stretched out and sampling wares from platters of food.

Timur fancied himself a descendant of Genghis Khan (he wasn't), and he dreamed of bringing the glory of the Mongol Empire back. He could appreciate scholars, liked them, sponsored them, but he was also sadistically cruel to people he didn't like. As an example, after invading Turkey, he kept its sultan in a cage and forced him to watch as he raped the man's wives and daughters.[11] But he and Ibn Khaldun hit it off, and the two had an amicable chat . . . and then kept meeting for more than a month.

Ibn Khaldun flattered Timur a little, expounded on his new theories, and did his best to try to win better terms for Damascus. Among other things, Timur was interested in Ibn Khaldun's mule, which Ibn Khaldun wisely decided to give up. He impressed his host well enough that Timur asked him to write a treatise on North Africa, of which he was very curious. This alone is remarkable. Here were the Tatars of the East—a mix of Turkic-Mongol peoples—learning maybe for the very first time about Africans. Ibn Khaldun must have thought his "lone gun" diplomacy was a success. He wrote up his treatise, and Timur's response was a thanks very much, calling for it to be translated into Mongolian, and—

Then Timur promptly sacked Damascus. We can perhaps forgive Ibn Khaldun for not knowing who he was dealing with, though the Tatars had already sacked Aleppo, and there were reports from there of horrific scenes of carnage. It was no different in Damascus, where people were crushed in presses, burned alive, and subjected to other tortures.

But Ibn Khaldun managed to stay on Timur's good side, mainly through nauseating flattery, and at the right moment, he secured permission to leave for Cairo. There, he got to be a judge again, and his career went through its familiar pattern of doing well until he stepped on the wrong toes. He annoyed the powerful by not taking bribes and for refusing to wear the Egyptian *qadi* dress instead of his regular wardrobe. He was deposed, was made a judge again, and was still writing away just before his death.

His magnum opus is a set of books called the *Kitab al-Ibar*, the "Book of Lessons," but most of the attention on him in the West has gone toward the introductory first book, the *Muqaddimah*. He originally set out just to write a history of the Amazighs, but then he grew ambitious. Why not a history of the world? Of course, the world to Ibn Khaldun was a smaller one than our own, but his real accomplishment was developing principles for how to examine his subject. "The inner meaning of history . . . involves speculation and an attempt to get at the truth," he tells us from the beginning, "subtle explanation of the causes and origins of existing things, and deep knowledge of the how and why of events. History, therefore, is firmly rooted in philosophy. It deserves to be accounted a branch of it."[12]

Though he never worked as a professional historian, he had scornful remarks about certain revered scholars in the field, pretty much dismissing them as gullible hacks (though as a man of his time, he bought into certain superstitions himself). Partisan biases can creep in, he warns us, and sometimes those providing information may not fully understand the significance of an event. Allen Fromhertz considers that Ibn Khaldun's "inspired method involved the simple application of the logic of cause and effect" and that he believed the true spark for events could be found in natural social forces and organizations.[13] The *Muqaddimah* ambitiously discusses what effect climate has on people and society (and, given the limits of scientific knowledge at the time, blames a lot on the air). He also considers the scarcity and abundance of their resources.

In looking at the Bedouin, the Amazighs, and the various dynasties, Ibn Khaldun came up with a cyclical view of history. He theorized that great civilizations rise, but they inevitably succumb to decadence after three or four generations and fall. His biographer Robert Irwin points out an interesting contrast between him and Edward Gibbon, who wrote *The Decline and Fall of the Roman Empire*. Gibbon chalked up Rome's collapse to barbarism and religion, while Ibn Khaldun believed barbarism and faith served as engines of empire.[14]

We can see now that back when Ibn Khaldun was roaming around Amazigh territories and collecting taxes, he wasn't merely doing his job—he was also performing what anthropologists might consider amateur fieldwork. It was research, though not in today's conventional sense. Still, he put his insights to use. And Ibn Khaldun did have his own natural biases. He considered the Amazighs "a powerful, formidable, brave and numerous people; a true people like so many others this world has seen—like the Arabs, the Persians, the Greeks, and the Romans."[15]

He also anticipated many of the core concepts of economics: "Profit is the value realized from labor." He understood the principle of excess capital, shrugged off inflation as a natural problem with urban living, and tied much of his analysis of economics to the productivity in cities and towns (the bigger the town, the greater the wealth), which is a little surprising for someone who extolled the virtues of nomads.[16] Interestingly, as his biographers point out, he mulled over the question of just who had it better, those in the cities or the people who lived in rural settings or relied on the nomadic life.[17]

It took a couple of centuries for Ibn Khaldun's work to receive wide recognition, but it eventually gathered momentum, first by Ottoman and Arabic scholars and then in Europe. For much of the twentieth century, the field of popular history was dominated by the British professor Arnold Toynbee, who arguably did more to popularize Ibn Khaldun than anyone else in the West. Toynbee gushed that the *Muqaddimah* was "undoubtedly the greatest work of its kind that has ever been created by any mind in any time or place" and that Ibn Khaldun "gave me a vision of a study of history bursting the bounds of this world."[18] Ronald Reagan once notoriously tried in 1981 to paraphrase Ibn Khaldun's ideas to justify his trickle-down economics—and got everything wrong, including even what century the scholar lived in. Reagan should have known better, given that he was an economics and sociology major in college.

Today, there are statues to Ibn Khaldun in Tunis and Cairo. There are awards and an essay contest. His portrait is on a Tunisian currency note, and in 2011, Google even commemorated his birthday with one of its doodles, which appeared on millions of screens in the Middle East and northern Africa. But the most lasting tribute is always the longevity and reinterpretation of ideas. When history is taught well, it isn't a mere recital of calendar dates. We may no longer accept his notions about the rise and decline of great powers, but we think about their causes and evolution in a different way thanks to Ibn Khaldun. We think about the levers of society and what pulls on them—all thanks to an ambitious philosopher from the Maghreb who once sat in a tent with the self-appointed "heir" of Genghis Khan.

4

An African Midas

Imagine you're a traveler in an antique land. It's the early fourteenth century. Exhausted by the beating sun and slapping the dust of the road off your clothes, eager to rest, you're about to enter Cairo. And this is what you see: a fabulous procession for a king winding its way to the city, with 60,000 warriors proudly marching in front as he rides on horseback, red banners of silk streaming with the breeze. There's a personal retinue of 14,000 female slaves for the ruler and 500 more slaves in the caravan, every one of them gripping a staff made of 500 *mithqals* of gold, roughly four pounds, or 1.8 kilograms, *each*. Stories soon circulate of this king's fabulous wealth; one unlikely tale even suggests that he built a swimming pool in the desert so that his wife and her female servants could bathe. His visit will be talked about in the city for years after he's gone.

And we are still talking about him, for this king was Musa I of the Mali Empire, sometimes called different names but most popularly known as Mansa Musa. The *mansa* refers to his title, which translates as "Sultan" or "Emperor." We have no idea if the numbers given for his procession were accurate, as they vary according to sources and might well be exaggerated. But Musa has captured the imagination for centuries right into our modern era, and the most compelling part of his legend is rooted in this anecdote by an Arab scholar, Shihab al-Umari. While on his pilgrimage to Mecca, Musa "spread upon Cairo the flood of his generosity; there was no person, officer of the court or holder of any office of the sultanate who did not receive a sum in gold from him. . . . So much gold was current in Cairo that it ruined the value of money."[1]

Time, Money, and *Business Insider* still gush over him in articles. Far too often, a portrait of Mansa Musa is a gilded one because it stops with his gold and very few specifics on what else he did or may have thought. But as with so many things, the reality is more interesting than the image. A case can be made that as the Black Death racked up its gruesome body count and Britain and France became ensnared in what turned out to be the Hundred Years' War, Musa inspired Europe and the Middle East. He did it—albeit unconsciously—with a relatively new and radically different concept that was a change of pace from religion and nation: big, flashy, *loud* capitalism.

Before we get to Musa, however, we need to look at his empire and wade into another legend, one that has to do with his predecessor. The Mali Empire of the Malinke people was built up during the thirteenth century by its ruler, Sundiata Keita. He inspired his own come-from-behind heroic epic in the oral tradition: he was the second son born to a king and an allegedly ugly, hunchbacked woman; at first lame, he developed into a powerful hunter and conqueror, and it's still a cornerstone of traditional Mali literature today. The truth is almost as impressive because he was a rebel with the odds against him.

The Malinke had faced trouble because their region not only relied on rich croplands of sorghum, millet, and rice, it also had gold—lots of it—in the area around Bure in the south near the Niger River. This attracted the interest of the Sosso, who had taken over the empire of ancient Ghana. Their leader, Sumaguru Kante, lives on in the *Epic of Sundiata* as a larger-than-life sorcerer villain. We don't know what he was really like, but Sundiata must have sold an equally damaging image of Sumaguru because he managed to organize several chiefs to follow his lead, and the Malinke won their battle against the Sosso near a spot on what today is the modern metropolis of Bamako.

Sundiata Keita consolidated power, and so the mansa subsequently made all the major decisions and was both the supreme governor and religious authority. He was the first to rule an empire that would eventually stretch from the Atlantic coast below the Senegal River to what is now Nigeria, from the southern tropical zone to outposts in the southern Sahara. With the empire in the perfect spot along the route of major trading caravans, the mansas wisely taxed all the goods coming and going through their realm. But it was gold that made the real difference. The gold was mined in the areas around Bambouk and Bure on the upper Niger River and then loaded up for caravans that meandered their way through the major trade outposts of Walata, Timbuktu, and Gao.

Mali was the ultimate case of "he who has the gold makes the rules." Even with a standing army at court, a mansa's power only went so far. While the rulers and their people were Muslims, the workers of the goldfields were animists, and they preferred to worship as they pleased and to handle the mines their own way. The mansas learned that if they tried to push an agenda, the miners wouldn't hesitate to strike or reduce their production to a trickle. In fact, a *qadi* in Egypt later asked Mansa Musa, "Why don't you take this land by conquest?" Musa replied that it had been tried before, with the gold promptly drying up. Left to its own devices, Bure produced, and the most effective way to keep the gold coming was through a long understanding with the locals that the gold be provided through tribute.[2]

Still, the arrangement being what it was, the mansa was the main person who got wealthy. Money isn't everything, and one of Sundiata Keita's successors was interested in something else. This was a leader named Muhammad. In many accounts, he's misidentified as Abu Bakr, but it's a mistake we've inherited thanks to, funnily enough, Ibn Khaldun misreading a source text and getting the Mali kings genealogy wrong.[3] Mansa Muhammad longed to see what was across the Atlantic Ocean, and he sent out a reconnaissance fleet of 400 ships. These would have been large pirogues—dug-out canoes with small sails—and while perhaps it's not completely impossible for them to have made the trek (consider the feats of adventurer Thor Heyerdahl), only one ship came back. It returned with a tantalizing and bizarre report of a "river in the middle of the ocean." Mansa Muhammad was hooked on the mystery. He decided to lead a new and larger expedition himself, sailing with a thousand pirogues for his men and another thousand ships stocked with supplies. In 1311, just before his vessels disappeared beyond the waves, he left his kingdom in the hands of Musa.

What became of Mansa Muhammad? We don't know. The information that he made the trip at all relies on one source, Musa himself, and nobody ever recorded Muhammad's return. The arguments start when it comes to discussing whether he was successful. Traditional academics have never bought the premise that Mansa Muhammad or any other medieval African made it across the Atlantic. Historian Gaoussou Diawara suggested in 2000 that traditional scholars and historians of Mali "found his abdication a shameful act, not worthy of praise. For that reason, they have refused to sing praise or talk of this great African man."[4]

But let's return to Mansa Musa because he made a much bigger difference. He also understood how fate had smiled on him. "If I have become the master of Mali," he once told the son of the sultan of Cairo, "it is only because my predecessor refused to believe that the ocean was infinite."[5] Reading between the lines, one gets the impression that Musa was appalled at the risk his leader was taking, but nevertheless, he was now in charge. It's been suggested he was only twenty-three when he ascended the throne in 1312.

What earned him lasting, international fame was his pilgrimage to Mecca. The ancient accounts seem to agree on the year—in fact, they can even claim the date Musa arrived at his stop in Cairo, July 18, 1324 (it was a Wednesday).[6] Nothing gets tongues wagging like a huge entourage, and there's the old folktale that he bankrupted Cairo's economy. But if you check the chronicles, the reality is that Cairo probably bankrupted Musa. Most sources report that he stayed about a year, but this doesn't seem credible because of the conditions and time lines, so it was probably a shorter period, and at some point, he ran out of funds and was forced to borrow from the city's wealthy merchants.

They didn't hesitate to gouge him in terms of steep interest rates on their loans, others bragging about how they took advantage of these naive Mali pilgrims.[7]

Despite his hefty loans, Musa had enough money and prestige that he could use the return leg of his trip for recruiting, and he hired Abu Ishaq Ibrahim Al-Sahili, a renowned poet and architect from Granada. For the assignment of building a mosque in Timbuktu, Al Sahili didn't come cheap; he wanted about 200 kilograms of gold, slaves, fancy clothes, real estate along the Niger River, and the list went on.[8] It's thought that he designed Timbuktu's Djinguereber mosque, a remarkable achievement in construction given that it's built out of earth, straw, and wood, though it's doubtful he supervised the work himself. Historical accounts agree that Musa did have him design a *madugu*, a royal palace for the emperor's stays in the city that was suitably impressive (Musa kept his capital elsewhere, in Niani).

Aside from these landmarks, what Mansa Musa really accomplished was to create an atmosphere in Mali that attracted the best and the brightest. The city's University of Sankoré (by the way, another madrasa founded by a woman) had already been around for more than 200 years, but doctors, teachers, imams, and scholars were now flocking to Timbuktu. Your reputation was not always enough to earn you a place. Writers Marq de Villiers and Sheila Hirtle note how in one chronicle, an Egyptian scholar "accompanied Mansa Musa to Timbuktu when he returned from Mecca, expecting to take a teaching role there. Instead, he found the standards so rigorous he was obliged to depart for Fez and Marrakesh to further his studies before he was allowed to teach at any of the city's schools."[9]

We know some fascinating details about the Mali court because Africa's own version of Marco Polo, an Amazigh named Ibn Battuta, visited only fifteen years after Musa's death in June of 1352, during the reign of Musa's successor, Suleyman. It's from Ibn Battuta that we learn the ceremonial customs of the mansa court, how the emperor would hold audiences out in the palace yard from a platform carpeted in silk and with cushions laid out, shaded by an umbrella that was decorated with a golden bird. On reaching his seat, "he stops and looks round

Mansa Musa as depicted in the Catalan Atlas.

the assembly, then ascends it in the sedate manner of a preacher ascending a mosque-pulpit. As he takes his seat, the drums, trumpets and bugles are sounded. Three slaves go out at a run to summon the sovereign's deputy and the military commanders, who enter and sit down."[10] It would have been no different in Musa's time.

Ibn Battuta also serves as a keen if not always objective observer of Mali culture. He listed what he deemed to be the citizens' admirable qualities. "They are seldom unjust and have a greater abhorrence of injustice than any other people. . . . There is complete security in their country. Neither traveler nor inhabitant in it has anything to fear from robbers or men of violence. They do not confiscate the property of any white man who dies in their country, even if it be of uncounted wealth."[11] But while noting how they diligently learned the Koran, Ibn Battuta was scandalized by women commonly walking around naked.

He took an ethnographic interest in the people and their customs, but for most Africans, the attraction to Mali would have been trade and education. For Europeans, it was the lure of what glitters. As for Mansa Musa, his fame reached such a height that his portrait was included in what's called the Catalan Atlas. This exquisite document, thought to have been made by cartographers in 1375 for France's Charles V, provides us with a wealth of information on what Europeans back then understood about their world. Its accompanying text informed sailors how to navigate tides and marked out major cities in the Christian and Islamic realms; it even offers us clues as to certain locales in India and China.

And right in the lower corner of the first of four leaves is Mansa Musa sitting on a throne, crowned in gold, holding in his left hand a gold scepter topped with a *fleur-de-lis* and in his right hand an orb. An inscription offers his name and tells us, "This king is the richest and most noble lord of the whole region because of the abundance of gold that is collected in his land."[12] Mansa Musa is shown as a king equal to the other illustrated sovereigns, a black man depicted as an emperor.

By 1518, the Renaissance was in full bloom in Europe. Michelangelo had finished the Sistine Chapel in Rome and had moved on to Florence, while Copernicus was working on the early drafts of his earth-shaking hypothesis of heliocentrism. And still to come in the century was Tycho Brahe for astronomy, while Paracelsus and William Harvey would make their contributions to medicine. And as all this was going on, Spanish corsairs roamed the Mediterranean, plundering coastlines and attacking passing vessels. During the summer of 1518, one of their raids scooped up a young captive named Hasan ibn Muhammad al-Wazzan al-Fasi. We know him today as Leo Africanus.

He was born to an important and well-off family around 1494 in Granada, not long after Spaniards took back this last holdout of the Andalusian Moors. Under a treaty, the Muslims who found themselves with new Christian rulers were supposed to be allowed to keep their own language, schools, and customs, but the writing was on the wall, given how Jews had already faced expulsion. It would only be a handful of years before Muslims were persecuted, their books burned, and facing threats of mass conversion. As for Hasan ibn Muhammad al-Wazzan al-Fasi, it's possible that his parents simply didn't want to live in territory newly dominated by the infidels, but whether it was for personal taste or shrewd caution, his family decided at some point to move to Fez. The "al-Fasi" in his name means "of Fez."

He was clever enough to later attend the University of Qarawiyyin, and between studies, he worked in a hospital that catered to foreign patients and the poor and which had a mental asylum.[13] He must have done well because he ended up as a diplomatic aide to the second Wattasid sultan of Morocco. His writings mention trips to Istanbul, Beirut, and Baghdad. We know roughly when he was taken by the Spanish because it's recorded that pirates captured a cargo vessel with sixty Turks off the eastern coast of Crete; Hasan had been on his way to Tunis.[14] Any other hostage would have been condemned to life as a galley slave, and he spent a few miserable months imprisoned in Rhodes. What saved him was his obvious intelligence—this man, reasoned his captors, was clearly no peasant. So by October 1518, he was taken to Rome and kept in the Castel Sant'Angelo.

The pope at the time was Leo X, the second son of Lorenzo de'Medici, who had the cunning or the brazenness, depending on your point of view, to get his boy named a cardinal while still a teenager. Legend goes that the pope reacted to his new job the way you'd expect from a rich merchant's son: "Since God has given us the papacy, let us enjoy it." He was, according to many sources, a bundle of decent values and quite a few hedonistic vices, loving music, charities, art, boys, and vulgar comedy, not necessarily in that order. He was the pope who angered Martin Luther by selling indulgences, the money going to renovations on St. Peter's Basilica and for general redecorating of the Vatican. But he also knew a good thing when it came along, and one of them happened to be an African diplomat.

Exit Hasan ibn Muhammad al-Wazzan al-Fasi and enter Johannes Leo or Giovanni Leone, the names of his powerful patron—but he would be better known one day as "Leo Africanus." Far from home and converting to Christianity, the new Leo understood how to adapt to survive; he even wrote that when he heard people talk about Africans, he would say he was from Granada, and if present company held a grudge against Granada, he would claim to be African.

The pope was thinking of launching a new Crusade, focusing on north Africa because Turkish pirates had made a good portion of the Mediterranean into an Ottoman lake. It made perfect sense then to accept every scrap of new information that Leo could provide. We know Leo Africanus probably wrote or at least dictated his manuscript in Italian, for which he would have already had some degree of fluency—and he didn't disappoint.[15] Over nine volumes, his *Description of Africa*—finally finished in 1526—examined northern parts of the continent and dazzled his readers with more detailed reports of the fabulous gold in Timbuktu. The African Crusade never got off the ground, but the book was a best seller across Europe.

Its publisher was Giovanni Ramusio, one of the top officials in Venice and something of an encyclopedist over geography, and he made significant edits to the book so it could be, in his opinion, more palatable to his European readers; he adjusted Leo's style, made a few disparaging statements about Africans even stronger, and added some insults about Islam.[16] Not surprisingly, Ramusio had his own agenda and sounded the call in 1563 for merchants to make their fortunes in Africa. "Let them go and do business with the king of Timbuktu and Mali," he wrote, "and there is no doubt they will be well received there with their ships and their goods and treated well and granted the favors that they ask."[17]

Yet by the time Ramusio put quill to paper, his own information was out of date. The great mansas were gone, and so was the Mali Empire.

Musa's immediate heirs were incompetent. The reign of one of them was quite brief thanks to assassination, and, inevitably, other cultures moved in to gobble up their territory. First Tuaregs, an Amazigh people, and then a ruthless animist chieftain named Sonni Ali from Gao started the Songhay Empire by capturing Timbuktu in 1468. Unlike previous conquerors who left the scholars alone, Sonni Ali slaughtered and humiliated many of them and sacked the town.[18] It would not be the first or last time that the keepers of Timbuktu's knowledge needed to fade into shadows or flee into the Sahara and hide their treasures, reappearing only when conditions were safe again.

Sonni Ali reigned until 1492, but after his death, his son was ousted within a year by Muhammad Ture, originally from the Soninke people of Senegal. Muhammad Ture expanded the Songhay Empire into a vast realm, first conquering parts of the Sahara and Mali and then gobbling up Hausa city-states. But why we care about him is that he turned things around in recreating an atmosphere where the scholars were welcome again.

Known to historians as Askia Muhammad I, he was a devout Muslim but wasn't interested in making all his subjects into converts, and thanks in part to his less restrictive rule, traditional ways of animist religion and life—clothing, sacred drums, even hairstyles—managed to survive down to our own time. He standardized taxes, weights, and measures, and he was intensely curious about the intricacies of Islamic law. The Songhay Empire enjoyed an age of unparalleled prosperity that allowed the realm's intellectuals to keep reading and scribbling away, with many top astronomers, doctors, mathematicians, and other specialists at the University of Sankoré enjoying the financial sponsorship of Askia Muhammad himself.[19]

Mahmud Kati, the author of the *Tarik-al-fattash*, the great chronicle of the Songhay Empire, wrote of how Timbuktu had no equal under Askia Muhammad. It was known for its "political liberties, the purity of its morals . . . its courtesy towards students and men of learning and the financial assistance which it provided for the latter; the scholars of this period were the most respected among the believers for their generosity, force of character, and their discretion."[20] As scholar Toby Green writes, with the gold trade, "West African rulers . . . developed a style of government that welcomed strangers, and a worldview that was plural and could accommodate different faiths."[21]

And with the trans-Sahara trade route under Songhay's control, gold and slaves kept flowing to Morocco and other parts of northern Africa; the slaves were usually captives of the Mossi people, ones taken in battle from what is now Burkina Faso. At this time, Europeans knew nothing of the Mossi, Malinke, Soninke, Hausa, or other peoples of the interior. For them, north

Africa contained a seemingly impenetrable wall of Islam and Sahara sand. But the gold! The gold of folktales and then Leo Africanus's *Description of Africa* haunted them.

The Portuguese, who had driven the Arab invaders from their land even before the Spanish, were eager to get their hands on it, and if they could push the Moors out of their sphere of influence as well, all the better. All in the name of Christendom, of course. They struck first across the Sea of Gibraltar in 1415 to take the Islamic port of Ceuta, and then after years of figuring out how to navigate around the treacherous Cape Bojador off the Western Sahara, they began trading with kingdoms along the west coast of Africa. In exchange for gold, they offered the Africans copper, brass, and European cloth. It was the legend of Mansa Musa and the brisk trade in West African gold that helped fuel the Renaissance, helped pay for stunning masterpieces and cathedral domes, and no doubt bankrolled the *condottiere*, the mercenary soldiers who fought for the Italian city-states.

Throughout the fourteenth century, however, a powerful empire on the east coast of Africa had been busy with trading partners even farther away than Portugal—the Chinese.

Think for a moment about the legendary sea vessels and traditions that live in our imagination. You have Spanish galleons, Lord Nelson's three-mast *Victory*, German U-boats of World War II. The British are steeped in the lore and detail of Portsmouth Harbour; the French have Marseilles. We know the scallop-like sails of junks in Hong Kong, and Europe and Asia symbolically meet as you stand on a bridge, watching the waves crest on the Bosporus. Africa has a coastline that runs more than 30,000 kilometers, and yet aside from possibly Cape Town, we don't easily summon an image of a majestic naval history for Africa. It's one of the cruel ironies of history that Somalia—infamous today for piracy—once had a sultanate that was a significant coastal empire.

Its unique geography made it a natural center for international trade and the development of a sophisticated culture. Islam penetrated early into Somalia, and one of the oldest mosques on the continent, Fakr ad-Din, was built in Mogadishu in 869 CE. We also know that the people accomplished great feats of engineering with limestone wells and cisterns. What came to be known as the Ajuran Sultanate tried to push west, but it was ultimately kept in check by a powerful rival, which we'll get to later.

The beginnings of the Ajuran are rooted in traditional folklore, and we need to take the oral tradition seriously because until our current era, much of the written history of the Somali people was made by a succession of tweedy colonial officials—British, French, Italian—who were less concerned with accuracy and more with using history to keep the wandering Somalis and their cattle herds in check. Still, it is true that for centuries, the Somalis had little political cohesion as the West would define it; fluid clans and kinship groups held power in a "nation of nomads with a long pastoral tradition."[22]

The Ajuran have been traced to the Hawiyya clan, and when they swept to power in the thirteenth century, it was with a powerful army and imams who led by stern decree. For centuries, they flexed their political muscles over the pastoral territories, and they also embraced the sea, building lighthouses and castles to defend the southern coastline. They sent out fleets of *beden* ships, one- or two-mast sailing vessels about forty-nine feet long, for trading missions. Ibn Battuta, the consummate tourist of the fourteenth century, visited the Ajuran Empire and considered Zeila "the dirtiest, most abominable and most stinking town in the world. The reason for the stench is the quantity of its fish and the blood of the camels that they slaughter in the streets."[23] Rather than stay overnight in town, he spent the night aboard ship despite rough seas.

Yet he didn't seem offended by Mogadishu, which he called "an enormous town. Its inhabitants are merchants and have many camels, of which they slaughter hundreds every day [for food]."[24] And Portugal's Vasco da Gama, whose ship came within sight of the capital later, reported the city had "houses of several stories, big palaces in its center and four towers around it."[25]

By the time Ibn Battuta was holding his nose over the bad fish in the Zeila marketplace, the locals in the region had been trading with Romans, Greeks, Nabateans, Arabs, Persians, Indians, and Egyptians. There are reports that make clear they traded from as early as the eleventh century with China, which referred to their home as *Zeng-dan*, "Land of Blacks." Han dynasty porcelain has been discovered along the east coast of Africa, while a Chinese coin helped spark fresh archaeological curiosity when it was found a few years ago in a village on Kenya's north coast.[26] About a dozen pieces of Chinese pottery from the thirteenth and fourteenth centuries were found in Aydhab, Sudan, a busy market town on the pilgrim route to Mecca.[27]

The traffic in the region wasn't one way either. We know the name of at least one Somali lawyer and diplomat who visited China, Sa'id of Mogadishu. Ibn Battuta claims to have met him in India and considered him a pious Muslim "of fine figure and character."[28] Some scholars believe that instead of making the trip to China himself for his *Travels*, Ibn Battuta may have appropriated details he learned from Sa'id.

Then for a while, travel literature was all that Africans could get. Under the Mongols, China put a tight leash on its private traders, and things didn't open up again until Zhu Di, the progressive leader of the Ming dynasty, came to power. He was known as the *Yong Le* emperor. (Yong Le means "Eternal Happiness.") In 1414, the Chinese sailed again across the ocean blue, and anthropologist Samuel Wilson paints a compelling scene of the trade armada that crossed the Indian Ocean under a skilled explorer, Zheng He: "The undertaking far surpassed anything Columbus, Isabella, and Ferdinand could have envisioned. The fleet included at least sixty-two massive trading galleons, any of which could have held Columbus's three small ships on its decks. . . . More than one hundred smaller vessels accompanied the galleons. All told, 30,000 people went on the voyage, compared with Columbus's crew of ninety-some."[29]

Zheng He and his expedition reportedly made contact with the people of Malindi on the Kenyan coast, who made a gift of a pair of giraffes. Today, there's an excellent example of a Chinese painting with a giraffe and its handler in the collection of the Philadelphia Museum of Art. The Yong Le emperor was so delighted with his new treasures that he invited envoys of other

African kingdoms to visit, including the Ajuran Sultanate.[30] The African diplomats came with ivory, unique medicines, tortoise shell, zebras, and ostrich. In return, they took home silk, spices, and other goods. A flourishing trade and a clear relationship of mutual respect began.

This is remarkable on many levels. Here are *African* nations granted diplomatic courtesies by a power so foreign and distant for that time that it might as well have been on Mars. We can reasonably assume they must have treated each other more or less as equals, without any signs of hostility or competition, eager to learn about each other's lands. Consider how things might have progressed had this unique relationship been allowed to continue.

Unfortunately, it didn't, and the reason was simple: regime change. After the Yong Le emperor died, those running the Ming dynasty decided to end the great and costly experiment of trade across the Indian Ocean. Call it isolationism, call it "growth begins at home," but Africa became a continent too far.

Why should we care? Because the idea of the Africa–China relationship flips the long narrative we're familiar with of only Arabs and white men supposedly "opening up" the continent. While the Chinese had superiority in naval power over the Somalis (and the Europeans, for that matter), the two sides would have been technologically equal in other respects. For quite a while, the Ajuran Sultanate and other kingdoms could hold their own impressively well against white invaders. And after the Chinese bowed out of the trade sphere of the Indian Ocean, the Somalis were required to prove it.

In 1507, for instance, the Portuguese came to take the key port city of Barawa, and by then, they had formidable muskets and artillery. Still, the residents of Barawa put up a ferocious resistance with 4,000 soldiers and impressive fortifications. Two thousand of the Ajuran rushed out of their garrison to keep the invaders at bay but were pushed back inside their walls. The Portuguese were made to pay in blood for their spoils, and "several were dangerously wounded." A hail of blazing torches rained down on the invader, but the Europeans eventually broke through, plundering the town and indulging in such an orgy of greed that "they cut off the arms of several women to come at their rings and bracelets the more readily."[31] Some of the looters packed a longboat so much with silver and gold that eighteen men were lost at sea. Then the Portuguese burned down the town, and the Ajuran fled inland from the ruins. Their enemy, having satisfied its bloodlust, moved on to Mogadishu.

Such raids went on for decades. The Ajuran, with the help of their Ottoman allies, sometimes won, sometimes lost engagements, anxious to secure their own waterways and protect their coastal towns. By the 1580s, an Ottoman pirate named Mir Ali Bey gave the Portuguese a lot of trouble, and we know his forces had help on key occasions from Somali galley ships.

By now, however, the Ajuran Sultanate was imploding. A common thread in Somali clan narratives is that ordinary people, sick of its tyrannical rule, finally booted the Ajuran out. According to scholar Lee Cassanelli's research, the first group to revolt was the Darandoole, who were furious at being told they could water their herds only at night. "The leaders decided to make war on the Ajuran," goes the traditional narrative, and they first ambushed the governor of Mogadishu. This apparently happened in the early 1600s. Then after a few years, some rebels "found the imam of the Ajuran seated on a rock near a well called Ceel Crawl." As they struck him with a sword, "they split his body together with the rock on which he was seated. He died immediately, and the Ajuran migrated out of the country."[32]

The Portuguese were quick to move in and take over the spice trade routes and the slave trade, but there's a big difference between looting a town and dominating it. Business suffered. Towns lost residents in a culture already bifurcated between urban dwellers and the cattle herders on the harsh terrain. The Portuguese found their East African realm slipping away as the century wore on, and the Somalis would confound other colonial powers with their proud, roaming nomads who wandered as they pleased. And so the greatness of the Ajuran Sultanate faded from historical memory.

Instead, another image of Africans captured the European imagination and inspired further efforts to explore the interior. But this idea sent ripples that turned into waves, rolling down the centuries and carrying the promise of a resurgent continent.

5

Church and State . . . of Mind

If you visit Ethiopia, you can take a trip to the Zege Peninsula on Lake Tana, which is the source of the Blue Nile, where a puttering, creaky motorboat can whisk you off to a charmingly peaceful and wooded island that hides a few national treasures. These are building complexes, and several more dot the surrounding coastal region of the lake. They look for all intents and purposes like the conical huts of thatch, mud, and wood found in the rural areas of the country. But surprise—walk into one of them, and you see stunningly beautiful paintings of religious figures in the Ethiopian style. You've walked into a Christian monastery.

For a Western visitor, the juxtaposition is a fascinating and exotic one. In a land where warriors with toga-like garments, *shammas*, fought with spears and shields right into the twentieth century, a place where hyenas can still lope through the old, cracked streets of a town at night and baboons munch grass in a national park, this country is home to some of the most devout followers of Jesus.

Only a handful of years before Augustine was born, a group of Christian pilgrims made the journey from Alexandria in Egypt to the Aksumite Empire, and the first Aksumite ruler to convert to Christianity was King Ezana. "Reluctant though some authorities have been to accept it," wrote scholar Stuart Munro-Hay, "it seems as if Ezana has very strong claims to be the first ruler anywhere to use the Christian cross on his coins, since some of his gold coins with the cross are of the weight used before [Rome's] Constantine the Great's reform of the currency in 324."[1] In fact, Ethiopia was Christian in the early fourth century well before many places in Europe.

And because of another turn of events of diplomacy, Ethiopia's fate went in a very different direction than the rest of Africa. As a result, its political and cultural status would again influence the rest of the world.

In 2018, I sat in the audience of a lecture hall at Toronto's Art Gallery of Ontario, where a rising young star from Princeton University gave an excellent lecture to the general public on beautiful illuminated manuscripts of the Ethiopian Orthodox Church. When the lights came up and it was time for questions, a local teenager took the borrowed microphone and asked with touching sincerity why it was that Ethiopia—surrounded by Muslim countries—managed to stay Christian and not be turned to Islam?

There was an awkward, uncomfortable silence. It was a good question, but it seemed to come out of the blue, and it had nothing to do with ancient illuminated manuscripts. Perhaps folks didn't like the idea of having to think of one religion against the other. Then there's the current climate of self-censorship and political correctness where virtually anything casually said might result in a backlash. No one really gave the young woman an answer that evening—but of course, there is one.

Let's start with a name. Arabs called the land *al-Habesha*, which got corrupted in Latin to "Abyssinia." But the Ethiopians never called their land "Abyssinia," though you still find the occasional historian and journalist thinking this was the old name of the country. Confusing the issue more, some Ethiopians commonly refer to themselves today as "Habesha." It's also commonly thought that the ancient Greeks loaned the country its name, as their word, *Aithiops*, that is, an Ethiopian, was a person with a "burnt face"—and so for Europeans, "Ethiopian" became synonymous for a long time with all Africans. But it's also worth remembering that with Christianity came translations of the Bible into the Ethiopians' ancient language of Ge'ez.

"At village churches today," wrote a historian in the 1960s, "the priests still teach young children that the father of the nation, Ethiops, one of the twelve descendants of Cush, the son of Ham, is buried at Aksum."[2]

A fiercely independent people, Ethiopians borrowed both these terms and made them their own.

Ethiopia also has Judaism, animist believers, and there are strong links to Islam. As an infant, Muhammad's nurse was an Ethiopian woman named Baraka, and his maternal grandfather made frequent trips to Aksum. When the Quraysh tribe in Mecca began persecuting the new faith, it was only natural that the Prophet consider Ethiopia a good choice as a temporary haven for his followers. In 615 CE, Muhammad's son-in-law and eventual successor, Othman, was among a group that sought refuge in the Ethiopian highlands. A delegation of Arabs soon followed to try to persuade the Aksumite king, Armah, to hand the Muslims over.

Armah listened to the ambassadors patiently, then listened to the Muslims, and then finally told the Arabs, "If you were to offer me a mountain of gold, I would not give up these people who have taken refuge with me." In time, the Muslims returned home, but Muhammad never forgot Armah's integrity and compassion, and after Armah died, he prayed for this foreign king's soul. More importantly, Muhammad told his adherents, "Leave the Ethiopians in peace." Other lands might be fit targets for conversion and *jihad*, but these people were off limits.[3]

It should come as no surprise that even with a warning from the Prophet, this still didn't settle the matter, and Islam did gain footholds in Ethiopia. It was carried along on trade routes, and it penetrated through what's now Eritrea. By the 1300s, the Islamic state of Ifat swept west from Zeila and gave the Christian Ethiopians a hard time. After Ifat had its day, the Adal Sultanate kept pressing hard from the West, and one of the legacies of Christian Africans versus Muslim ones in the region is Harar, a picturesque town that is home to more than eighty mosques, small and large, some humble, others ornate and stunning, all within its old, traditional quarter. Muslim sultanates, such as Hadiyya and Ifat, were integrated as vassals into the Christian kingdom, and Muslim-born princesses even intermarried with the Christian dynastic line.

The first report of Ethiopian diplomats—a group of about thirty—to reach Europe was apparently in 1306, visiting Spain and Pope Clement V in Avignon and later Rome and Genoa.[4] While details are scant, they must have proved an astonishing sight to their Catholic brothers in the lands of the early Renaissance. These dark-skinned individuals might have resembled "Moors," but they wore crosses and were fluent in the Gospels. Spain paid attention. So did Rome. Within a few years, the king of France got a briefing on how important these Ethiopians were. Then in July 1402, ambassadors sent by Ethiopia's Emperor Dawit II—led not by an Ethiopian but an Italian representative—arrived in the Republic of Venice, bringing impressive gifts for the city's ruling elites, including exotic animals, such as four live leopards (and the logistics of transporting such animals in that era—like the pair of giraffes sent to China—boggles the mind).

What did Dawit want from the Venetians? What did Ethiopians ever want from the Europeans with their envoys traveling so far? The standard line among scholars used to be that they were primarily after technical know-how, appreciating that they lagged behind European nations, and that a military alliance wouldn't hurt either against steady encroachment by Muslims. But historian Verena Krebs of Germany's Ruhr University has pored over the source texts and suggests these weren't the main reasons at all. And when you think about it, the old assumptions play into another comfortable Western bias: Africans, supposedly knowing they're backward, seek out white help. But how would they know of any technological disparity at all?

Instead, Krebs makes a compelling case that the Ethiopians had other interests. There was something of a monumental building boom in Ethiopia during the fifteenth and sixteenth centuries, when scores of Orthodox churches and monasteries went up by royal order. Well, it would be nice to have those decorated with rare and exotic items, wouldn't it? Exotic to Ethiopians, in coming from far-off Europe. In the case of Dawit, he sent off multiple delegations from 1402 to 1404—to Venice and

Rome—because he was after ecclesiastical relics and treasures as well as skilled artisans who could make more.

One Ethiopian source describes a European traveler as his emissary, ordered to bring him back a piece of the True Cross. Not only was this diplomat reportedly successful in collecting such a fantastic item, but in returning from Venice via Alexandria, he brought back exquisitely made chalices and priest garments, bowls, and other religious objects. Dawit was ecstatic. Clapping his hands and stamping his feet, he went around a church, "praising God and singing together with his priests, and the chiefs of his army, and all his troops were with him."[5] The focus in this account is all on the wonderful treasures bought, not on any forged alliance or successful recruitment of foreign experts.

It was the same with Dawit's son and successor, Yeshaq, who was eager as well to acquire sacred objects and skilled tradesmen. Off went his ambassadors, who turned up at the court of Alfonso V of Aragon likely in late 1427. But they also passed along the emperor's novel plan of allying his kingdom with Aragon, not through just one marriage but *two*. Yeshaq would take as his bride King Alfonso's second cousin, while Alfonso's younger brother would marry an unnamed princess of the Ethiopian court.[6] But nothing came of this intriguing proposal.

As far as the military matters go, it looks a lot as if the Europeans were the ones eager to get the Ethiopians to throw in with them because they feared the encroachment of Mamluk and Ottoman forces. The Ethiopians, for their part, didn't need their arms or technicians—they did their shopping for horses, well-crafted swords, and smiths in Egypt and other parts of the Middle East, and Arabic was a useful lingua franca for trade even within the Ethiopian kingdom.[7] Nevertheless, Alfonso sent his ambassadors to Africa in May 1428, charging his top man, Petrus, with finding out all he could about Ethiopia and conveying a message to Yeshaq too confidential to trust to paper; he was also supposed to talk Alfonso up in front of the emperor. "In particular," writes Verena Krebs, "he was to stress the Aragonese strength in naval warfare."[8] But Petrus and the rest of his delegation never made it to Yeshaq's realm; instead, they suffered "great ruin on the dangerous way and perished."[9]

Throughout the 1400s, clusters of Ethiopians could be found in spots such as Rhodes, Jerusalem, Bethlehem, Cairo, and even as far away as what is today Lebanon and Syria.[10] The likenesses of Ethiopian diplomats and pilgrims can be found in a few of the most prized works of Renaissance art in the Vatican. In 1441, delegates from the Ethiopian monastery in Jerusalem attended the Council of Florence, and they were later depicted on the central door of St. Peter's Basilica. Go to the Sistine Chapel, and you'll see on a wall *Temptation of Moses*, in which Sandro Botticelli painted blue-turbaned black men—and used the likenesses of Ethiopian ambassadors who had met with Pope Sixtus IV in 1481.[11]

What did Ethiopians think of their European hosts whenever they came to visit? Well, some were probably mystified by the responses they got from Europeans, who usually asked what news did they have of Prester John? In 1400, for instance, England's King Henry IV sent off a letter addressed to "the King of Abyssinia, Prester John." The Ethiopians had never had an emperor called that, and the name meant nothing to them.[12] In 1404, nobles and scholars in Rome mistook three of Dawit's envoys for subjects of Prester John, and the Ethiopians, apparently wanting to be good guests, didn't bother to correct them.[13] As the decades rolled on, the confusion still wasn't cleared up. Why did the Europeans keep asking after this Prester John? Who were they talking about?

The legend of a Christian king in a distant land—safely beyond the reach of invading Muslim armies—had gathered shape in the twelfth century, first placing this mythical figure in India and then within the Mongol Empire. It was the kind of tale designed to reassure French and Italians who trembled at the thought of Muslims putting their villages to the torch, forcing them to convert. But after the first Ethiopian diplomats visited, the myth was transplanted to the *ambas*—the flat-topped, green mountains—below Egypt and Sudan.

For the Portuguese, as historian Roger Crowley put it, the myth "is what lured them even farther south down the African [western] coast, hunting for the River of Gold or the river that would take them to Prester John."[14] It was an incredibly resilient story. In 1520, the Portuguese missionary and explorer Francesco Alvarez reached Ethiopia, and when he was led past the woven, checkerboard curtains that enveloped the royal camp and ushered into the tent of the current emperor, Lebna Dengel, he still referred to him in his writings as "the Prester."[15] There was quite a culture clash between the Portuguese and the Ethiopians in terms of devotional behavior, one that didn't bode well for the future. For instance, it was customary for Ethiopians to remove their footwear before entering church (no different than Buddhists in Asian temples), but Alvarez reported they were scandalized "at our coming into church with our shoes on, and still more at our spitting in it."[16]

As the age of gunpowder began, the Adal Muslims from the west threatened to completely overrun the highland Christians until Ethiopia took the unusual step of seeking help from Portugal. To the rescue came Vasco da Gama's son Christovao and 400 seasoned musketeers, arriving in Massawa in 1541. The charismatic imam leading the Adal invaders soon found himself literally staring down the barrels of cannon, and he sent word to bring in help for *his* side. Now the Ottomans got involved. The heart of ancient Ethiopia was reduced to a battlefield occupied by foreign armies, its monasteries razed, its priceless manuscripts burned, and its populations scattered. Christovao da Gama ended up giving his life for his African allies in 1542. He was captured during the fighting and then beheaded. As we hinted at in the previous chapter, the Islamic invaders, from both the Adal Sultanate and the Ajuran, were eventually driven back. But when the musket smoke cleared, a fascinating thing happened that was almost wholly unique.

Emperor Galawdewos got on with rebuilding his kingdom, but his Portuguese allies now grew presumptuous. They wanted the Ethiopians to become Catholics. They wanted them to replace their Orthodox spiritual head or *abuna*—who traditionally came from Egypt—with the pope of Rome. The emperor chose a masterstroke of strategic diplomacy. His response amounted to a polite thank you for your service, but we're fine here, thank you *so* much, really . . . and then he sent the Portuguese officials out to the hinterlands of the realm with the excuse that way out beyond, they would be in a better position to defend the empire from any further Islamic invasion. Bye, bye, good luck, off you go.

The lesson would never be entirely forgotten. In the centuries to come, as we'll see, shrewd rulers of Ethiopia would figure out how to outwit European visitors who were often shamelessly brazen in their colonial ambitions. These emperors would keep the foreigner at bay, sometimes pit them against each other, and they recognized that while Europeans occasionally brought exciting innovations, they should be allowed to visit but never to put down roots.

Only a few decades later in the early 1600s, the role of the Catholic Church caused trouble once more in Ethiopia. The emperor at the time was Susenyos, who faced all kinds of challenges: the usual rebellions, raids from the Oromo people in the region, plus a feud with the Funj Sultanate of Sudan. Perhaps thinking he could get military help from Portugal and Spain or perhaps feeling genuinely persuaded—or, who knows, both— Susenyos converted to Catholicism in 1622. This did *not* go down well with most of the population, especially when on at least one occasion, he sported Portuguese clothes; still, as many as 100,000 Ethiopians followed the example of their emperor and switched faiths.[17]

A Jesuit priest named Afonso Mendes adopted the title of patriarch and started throwing his weight around, condemning certain practices, such as the Saturday sabbath and fasting. At a ceremony with the emperor in attendance, Mendes insisted that priests needed to be reordained, that altars had to be reconfigured in the Portuguese style, and that ordinary Ethiopians were outside the faith unless they were rebaptized. There is the ugly anecdote of a poor woman who was mentally ill. The attitude at the time in Ethiopia was that such individuals were special to God, but Mendez had her thrown into prison as a witch. Many Ethiopians were outraged, and what's also interesting here is that they deeply resented what Mendez's accusation of witchcraft implied; to them, it suggested two Gods at work, which was an intolerable contradiction.[18] It wasn't long before Susen-yos had an open and bitter revolt on his hands. High-ranking nobles, some from the Ethiopian Orthodox Church, and his own son, Fasilides, or Fasil for short, fought against him.

There are few conflicts more bitter and bloody than a civil war. The Portuguese missionary and ambassador Manuel del Almeida tells us that the Ethiopians of this era were "good troops" who were "inured to toil, enduring hunger and thirst as much as can be imagined."[19] Launching themselves into battle with their half-lances and buffalo shields, they wielded clubs and short swords at close quarters. Muskets had appeared around this time, but they weren't used very effectively. This was war close-up, screaming in your face, the enemy hurtling himself at you with blade and spear and fist, only your foe was your neighbor. There was a climactic battle at a spot called Lasta in 1631, and given the forces of emperor and son, it didn't look good for Susenyos. Some of his men mutinied, and there were reports he faced overwhelming numbers. Yet when the dust cleared, he was victorious.

Some 8,000 peasant warriors lay dead on the battlefield, prompting Fasil to make an impassioned speech to his father. "Look at these men slaughtered on the ground—they're not pagans or Muslims—we could have celebrated killing *their* kind. But these are Christians. They were your subjects, your country-men—some of them your own relatives. This isn't victory. In killing them, you drive a sword into your own guts! And how many more will you kill? We're a cautionary tale now, even to the pagans and Muslims, just for having this war and for turning our backs on God."[20]

Susenyos was shaken by this. He didn't hold a feast, he didn't celebrate. He went back to his capital of Danquaz and consulted with Mendes, who tried to pump up his leader's ego over defending the true faith. But the emperor decided enough was enough. He reversed his policy, and about a year later, he issued a final decree: if you were Catholic, you could go on being Catholic. No forced conversions anymore. As for the Orthodox, "we restore to you the faith of your forefathers. Let the former clergy return to their churches, let them put in their altars, let them say their own liturgy."[21] There were enthusiastic celebrations in the streets.

It's an astonishing episode not only for Ethiopia but also for African history. If it superficially resembles the religious schisms we learned about in Western schools, well, consider what was happening in 1631 in Europe. It was convulsed in the incredibly bloody Thirty Years' War, which began along religious fault lines and turned into a clash of nation-states, taking millions of lives. Henry VIII had already made his land grabs and turned the English aristocracy upside down by leaving the Catholic Church, and his daughter Mary chose to switch her allegiance to Rome and turn the calendar back, sending close to 300 people to be burned at the stake for heresy.

Yet in the most well known part of Africa, an emperor had changed his mind after a mere decade and opted for religious tolerance.

Only the court policy was short lived. Susenyos died a mere three months after his decree, and when Fasil took over as emperor, he promptly showed the Jesuits the door. He seemed to care less about the faith itself than the advance and influence of a foreign power, the Portuguese, and he negotiated treaties with pashas in Massawa and Suakin (in modern-day Sudan) just to keep them out; and for good measure, he had envoys on the South Arabian coast, watching for Portuguese ships.[22] Once again, an African emperor outwitted a European power that had logistical and technological advantages. Fasil made a new capital for himself at Gondar, where today you can roam the grounds of what was once his palace and royal enclosure. Here is where many of his successors would base themselves, some adding to the complex. It's something to see, these architectural marvels combining elements of Nubian, Arab, Baroque, and even Hindu styles, set in the Horn of Africa. As for Fasil, according to one source, while he started off well, in time he turned cruel, and his reign was marked by famine and plague.

But there are two remarkable legacies from that failed experiment with the Roman Catholic Church. And one of them could be considered a role model for African feminism.

The castle of Ethiopia's Emperor Fasilides at Gondar.

After his conversion, Susenyos ordered one of his counselors and a convert like himself, a man named Malkiya Kristos, to help suppress the rebellion against the newly imposed faith. The man's wife, however, wanted to stay with the Orthodox Church, and she walked out on her husband. She would become known as Walatta Petros, meaning "Daughter of Saint Peter."

Now is as good a place as any to clear up a misconception. Ethiopian names, particularly for those of saints and sovereigns, don't follow Western conventions. Without getting too bogged down in the details, to call Walatta Petros just "Walatta" would be to convert her name into gibberish. In a similar vein, we can look to the example of the country's last and most well known emperor, Tafari Makonnen, better known by his imperial name, Haile Selassie. When American or European writers refer to him as just "Selassie," it's equivalent to calling Winston Churchill "Church" or Barack Obama "Obam."

But let's get back to Walatta Petros. Different folks in the Orthodox Church and at court tried to get her to return to her husband, hoping she could be a moderating influence on his cruelty, and in a case of stunning emotional blackmail, Malkiya Kristos promised to slaughter a whole town if she didn't come back. But she learned that her husband supported the killing of the Orthodox patriarch, even accepting the patriarch's clothes as a reward from the king for his loyalty and service.[23] That did it; she left him once and for all, shaved her head, and became a nun in 1617. She was twenty-four years old.

And she apparently had no intention of being a meek and mild, "passive" nun. Walatta Petros organized nonviolent resistance, persuading priests not to offer any of the usual praises to Susenyos during Mass, becoming such a thorn in the emperor's side that he had her arrested and considered executing her. Her family talked him out of it. Sent north, she still preached rebellion. Again, she was almost put to death. Susenyos exiled her farther away—Sudan. That didn't stop her either. Walatta Petros started a religious community in Sudan, then six others over the years, also founding her own monastery.

Considered a saint within the Ethiopian Orthodox Church, there are moving stories about her as you find with saints in the Western Christian tradition. For instance, she was supposedly set on cutting herself off from the world in accordance with the strict monastic tradition, but God charged her with the mission of saving souls—and she turned God down. She wasn't up to the job, she protested, being "made of mud and soil. . . . How is it possible for me? How can I save others when I am unable to save myself?" According to the legend, God "brought her doves and precious glasses, saying, 'These are the pure souls of your children, keep them for me.'" She still didn't feel worthy. "What if they fly away from me and return to the world? What if they get broken?" God then made a special promise, a covenant with rigorously tested saints known as the *Kalkidan*, which would bestow on her the "divine power to perform miracles or other acts."[24]

Devotional historiography aside, we should still be impressed by this formidable figure. Here is an example of an African individual—no doubt having made serious sacrifices in her social and financial status—rejecting the idea of monarch and church as an inseparable authority. Like the notion put forward by European thinkers, Walatta Petros insisted on a loyalty to God that supersedes that of the earthly monarch, and she left a lasting impact on her nation.

In stark contrast to Walatta Petros, a young priest in his twenties, born into a poor family near Aksum, had been minding his own business when Susenyos wrenched his kingdom over to the Catholic faith. His name was Zera Yacob.

By his own account, as a teacher he presented the arguments and ideas of *ferenji* (foreigners, such as Europeans) and of Coptic (Egyptian) believers without too much editorial comment: "This and that is good for us, if we are ourselves good. Therefore, I was hated by all, for the Roman Catholics thought I was with the Egyptians, and the Egyptians that I was with the Europeans."[25] A fellow priest in Aksum named Walda Yohannes thought this was the perfect time for career advancement and denounced him directly to Susenyos, claiming he wanted to kick out the Portuguese and assassinate the emperor. Zera Yacob had to flee for his life. With thirty ounces of gold, he headed south to Shoa, but along the way, he discovered a "beautiful uninhabited place." It was a cave in a valley not far from the Takazze River where he could hole up for a couple of years and develop an intricate philosophy.[26]

After Susenyos died, Zera Yacob left his cave, but he would be no fan of the emperor's son and successor. In fact, he is our source that Fasilides "did not persevere in goodness, he became a wicked king . . . " One who "came to hate and persecute" the Europeans, who sent out his soldiers to plunder the land and raid the houses of the poor and had people executed without trial.[27] Despite these dark times, Zera Yacob didn't return to hiding and spent much of the rest of his life in a town called Emfraz.

Today, it's eclipsed by the nearby historic city of Gondar. But Emfraz was where the imperial courts of Ethiopia sometimes made their camps during the rainy season, making it a natural nexus for commerce and society, so it was a smart choice. So, he settled down and taught in the area, married, and had a family. Oddly enough, like one of Hollywood's convenient moments in medieval epics, he had another run-in with his old nemesis, Walda Yohannes, who had managed to keep his head down during the civil war, switching sides and casting off his Roman Catholicism. Having returned to the Orthodox Church, Walda Yohannes also worked his way into the good graces of Fasilides. And after peddling the lie that Zera Yacob was against the Europeans, now he was back and pushing the libel that the philosopher was *pro*-foreigner, teaching their doctrines in secret!

But in a strange irony, Walda Yohannes got what he wanted. He was put in charge of several parts of the region of Dembiya, where his autocratic rule infuriated the locals so much that an unknown resident assassinated him. Meanwhile, Zera Yacob found a wealthy patron who hired him to teach the man's sons and write a book of Psalms for him, and he lived to the ripe old age of ninety-three. It was Walda Heywat, his top student and a son of his patron, who asked him to write down his autobiography and his philosophy. And in 1667, when Zera Yacob was sixty-eight years old, he finished his treatise, which came to be known as *Hatata*, or "Inquiry." Walda Heywat would expand on his teacher's work with his own *Hatata*.

But let's stick with Zera Yacob, for he's a true original, and his "Inquiry" is an amazing document. Ethiopians knew of the Greek philosophers and were already familiar with their works, but Zera Yacob came up with specific arguments and concepts on his own, without reference to any predecessors. According to his *Hatata*, he asked himself if there really was a God. And if so, did God bother to listen to him? He wondered, "Is the inventor of the ear unable to hear?" What about his own origins as a rational human being? Working backward, thinking how each generation was created before, he decided God "must be an uncreated essence who is and will be for all centuries [to come], the lord and master of all things." Endowing human beings with the gifts of intelligence and reason implies that God is a rational being as well.

Being rational himself, Zera Yacob mulled over the validity of the scriptures. Were they correct? But here was another problem because the adherents of each religion held their faith to be true. "If I had asked the Mohammedans and the Jews, they also would have interpreted according to their own faith. . . . As my own faith appears true to me, so does another one find his own faith true; but truth is one." The way out of this cul-de-sac was to rely on your own wits. He decided that human beings make the choice in whether to be good or evil but that many don't put in the proper critical examination of situations.[28]

Much of what we're discussing here resembles the kind of approach and the thinking of René Descartes. Even if most of us have never cracked open a Penguin edition of his *Discourse on the Method*, we (hopefully) remember from school his famous phrase, "I think therefore I am." In philosophy studies, Descartes is Rational Man, and it appears that, at least in spirit, he had a long-lost African brother. The Canadian scholar Claude Sumner noted that in reading both, "we find an occasion for a critical investigation, the need for such an inquiry, a criterion which leads to the establishment of a basic principle that is applied in both authors to theodicy, ethics, and psychology (and in Descartes to cosmology). Although the method of enquiring is revolutionary in both cases, its roots are deeply theological in both philosophers."[29]

Zera Yacob is rightly celebrated as a rationalist, but he was also a skeptic with a delightful contrarian streak, well ahead of his time over social values. He believed in men and women being equals in marriage and practiced what he preached with his own wife. He had no patience with the sexist notion that women were somehow "impure" because they menstruated. As for diet, "God does not order absurdities, nor does he say: 'Eat this, do not eat this; today eat, tomorrow do not eat; do not eat meat today, eat it tomorrow,' unlike the Christians who follow the laws of fasting. Neither did God say to the Mohammedans:

'Eat during the night, but do not eat during the day,' nor similar and like things. Our reason teaches us that we should eat of all things which do no harm to our health and our nature, and that we should eat each day as much as is required for our sustenance."[30]

He also rejected entirely the notion that slavery had justification on any moral grounds or even had sanction in the Bible and the Koran. When the Gospels talked about slavery, its directives "cannot come from God." In the same vein, "with our intelligence we understand that this Mohammedan law cannot come from the creator of man who made us equal, like brothers, so that we call our creator our father, But Mohammed made the weaker man the possession of the stronger and equated a rational creature with irrational animals; can this depravity be attributed to God?"[31]

For such a progressive thinker, you'd think he would be better known. Yet he remains obscure as far as the rest of the world is concerned. Granted, he has his fans. One Norwegian writer gushed over his ideas in an online article and asked, "What if the Enlightenment can be found in places and thinkers that we often overlook?"[32] Except this question forgets a basic principle: for there to be an Enlightenment, you need a substantial number of folks to be enlightened.

Unfortunately, it would take centuries for Zera Yacob to leave a major impact on Ethiopian spiritual thought and philosophy. *How* he became known again is something that scholars still debate. An Italian Capuchin missionary, Giusto d'Urbino, lived in Ethiopia for close to a decade in the mid-1800s, learning its languages, and he made copies of manuscripts written by both Zera Yacob and Walda Heywat. Depending on which academic you want to believe, the missionary either copied them in good faith in 1852 or committed heinous forgeries.

But the person who brought Zera Yacob to the forefront of African ideas in our own time was Claude Sumner, who came to teach at Addis Ababa University and used to say he was "Canadian by birth, Ethiopian by choice." As someone who loved his adopted country but still carefully evaluated its intricacies, the *Hatatas* were genuine—of course, they were. Neither

Giusto d'Urbino nor his scribe knew enough Ge'ez to pull off such a fraud. The trouble is that the issue remains unresolved for the academics, and there was a whole conference devoted to the subject, "In Search of Zera Yacob," held in 2021 at Oxford University's Worcester College. Unfortunately, this won't be the last time in this book that the authenticity of an African thinker is called into question.

To Sumner, the matter was settled, and "modern philosophy, in the sense of a personal rationalistic critical investigation, began in Ethiopia with Zera Yacob at the same time as in England and France."[33] This is huge, and in the end, it doesn't matter whether Zera Yacob's ideas spread beyond Ethiopia. After all, we have examples of Greek thinkers seemingly banished by the ages, only for scholars in Islamic Spain to reintroduce them to the world. Zera Yacob only needed a little longer. So no, we can't credit him with sparking an Enlightenment, but what's important is that he *did* develop his specific method and ideas, proving through his work that Europe has never held the monopoly on critical thinking.

Meanwhile, the myth of Prester John that first drove European curiosity had to die, and in 1684, a German scholar named Hiob Ludolf closed the casket. It was the right time for it; this was the same year when Isaac Newton—grumpy, antisocial, but nevertheless a genius—wrote from a drafty room in Cambridge to Edmond Hillary about planetary orbits. Facts were needed for a dawning Age of Reason, not legends, and after befriending an Ethiopian priest named Gorgoryos who was visiting Rome, Ludolf learned Amharic and wrote a long and meticulous study, *A New History of Ethiopia*. His book had the long-winded subtitle that it was "a full and accurate description of the kingdom of Abyssinia, vulgarly, though erroneously called the empire of Prester John."

A new legend replaced the old. The term "Ethiopian" remained a frequent generic term for Africans, one used by white Europeans and sometimes free Africans living abroad. A romanticism developed over the country. Samuel Johnson— yes, *that* Johnson, followed around by his young, sycophantic biographer, James Boswell—wrote a popular novella that came out in 1759, *The History of Rasselas, Prince of Abyssinia.* It was a fable about a prince and his sister trying to escape their sheltered life at a palace in a "happy valley." What's interesting for us is that Johnson depicted Ethiopia as a dominion where oppression is "neither frequent nor tolerated."

Generations of African slaves—cut off from their cultural homelands, forced to adopt the native tongue of their oppressors—relied on the shorthand reference that they were from Ethiopia. It was, after all, a land properly vetted with mentions in the Bible. It also gave transplanted slaves and free black individuals a separate touchstone of faith and culture. Slaves might think of the Christianity of Portugal, England, France, and other parts of Europe as a foreign c   onstruct. Their white masters' faith insisted that their souls would be saved . . . eventually . . . while their physical bodies and minds were subjected to the vilest of humiliations and sadistic bondage.

But then there was Ethiopia: Christian and stubbornly independent, ruled by black people like themselves.

In the early United States, there was a Barbados immigrant named Prince Hall who fought in the Revolutionary War and who founded the African Masonic Lodge. One of the country's first, fiery black activists, he attacked slavery and racism as he spoke to a group of black Masons in 1797, invoking mentions of Ethiopia in the Bible. By 1829, a black abolitionist in New York named Robert Young, who was something of a messianic character as well, put out a pamphlet of African rights, the *Ethiopian Manifesto.* By 1854, at the Western Reserve College in Cleveland, Frederick Douglass was ready to debunk the notion that the best in Western culture had always had a pale complexion; instead, "the arts, appliances and blessings of civilization flourished in the very heart of Ethiopia, at a time when all Europe floundered in the depths of ignorance and barbarism."[34]

Ethiopia lived and breathed as an idyll; blacks in the great diaspora responded to its power as much as white Europeans culturally romanticized ancient Greece and Rome.

Throughout the late 1800s, in fact, articles in mainstream American newspapers referenced the lineage of the Ethiopian emperor going back to the Queen of Sheba and King Solomon.[35]

And the Ethiopian tradition would continue to impact history and the African sense of identity, right through the Scramble for Africa on to the Roaring Twenties and still further to the postwar independent African states.

6

African Antecedents

In a late October issue of *The Economist* for 1992, a job ad appeared for a "Democracy/Governance Advisor" for the USAID Mission to Zambia. The successful applicant would "coordinate and implement a program of initiatives to promote accountable government in Zambia. The advisor will coordinate initiatives in four areas: (i) constitutional reform and civic education, (ii) the development of an independent press, (iii) strengthening the Zambian National Assembly, (iv) policy analysis and management in the Cabinet Office." Besides operating with the American embassy, the adviser would also "work extensively with relevant ministries and agencies of the Government of the Republic of Zambia and with relevant groups in the private sector."

The ad appeared a *full year after* Zambia, having already adopted a new constitution, held multiparty elections. Ugandan intellectual Yash Tandon was prompted to write, "The patronizing audacity of a U.S. offer of 'technical' assistance to develop the instruments of 'democracy' and 'governance' in Zambia is simply breathtaking."[1]

Which brings us to our theme here. One of the most pernicious and lasting misassumptions about Africa is that it "had to be modernized." Technology *must* be an import. Africa *had* to be taught democracy. Breaking away from the divine right of kings to representational government was yet another gift from more enlightened Western powers. Wrong on all counts. From antiquity right throughout the Middle Ages, much of Africa was often on a level playing field with Europe in terms of government, law, medicine, infrastructure, and technology—in several cases, the Africans were superior.

We can also find astonishing parallels. For instance, there were African kingdoms that had their own codes of chivalry that resembled those of the feudal Europeans. "Be welcome here, bold herald," says Seku Amadu of the Niger Delta during a pause in a battle, and he warned the messenger to tell his king, "Let me know that my submission is already to God and will be made to no man." As Basil Davidson pointed out, the words are strikingly similar to a speech given in Shakespeare's *Henry V*.[2] The Ngoni people of southern Africa in the seventeenth century created a system of army regiments which placed men by age rather than local or familial loyalties, and with their martial skill came principles of a chivalric code and dueling rules that are familiar to westerners. In a magnanimous gesture, a noble "might reveal to another what his magical protections were and how he might be killed. Sometimes a young hero declined to fight an older man who resembled his father."[3] It was common practice to offer your opponent the chance to strike first with his cutlass or shoot first with his gun. The rules even extended to fighting battles or launching an attack on a city, with greetings first traded between the warring sides. Your enemy wasn't ready yet? No problem, the attacker would wait.[4]

In the kingdom of Benin at its height in the Middle Ages, the succession of the ruler, or Oba, followed through the eldest son, and while his mandate depended heavily on a religious and spiritual aura, his powers were far from absolute. He couldn't declare war or pass laws without consulting an executive council of nobles, and he also worked with town chiefs and a group of palace bureaucrats who were "freeborn commoners from any part of the kingdom." The Oba could invent new titles and dispense them as he saw fit, but at the same time, town chiefs held enough power and performed multiple functions so that the whole system worked efficiently with its own checks and balances.[5]

In fact, Ghana's politician and historian Albert Adu Boahen considered Benin's unwritten constitution one of the top reasons why the kingdom lasted for centuries, right up to 1897 when the British invaded. "Because of the very fact that most of the offices and titles of the state were non-hereditary but appointed by the Oba, no powerful lineages and family groups with large followings could develop. . . . On the other hand, since the Oba had to rely on [the chiefs] for soldiers, labor, tribute, as well as for the administrative services both in the kingdom and in the conquered states, and for the rituals needed to prop up his position, the Oba could not ignore the views of those people."[6]

Then there was the king of the Asante, who enjoyed a spectacular court with elaborate rituals and splendid decoration, but his rule was checked by the powers of a national assembly of 200 regional senior chiefs who kept their hands firmly on the administration of the state. Every day, the king consulted the *Asante Kotoko*, the "Asante porcupine," an elite council of nobles, officials, and technocrats.[7] We also know that at least as far back as the early nineteenth century, the ruler had access to sophisticated intelligence on foreign affairs far beyond his kingdom. When a British visitor in 1817 tried to persuade King Osei Bonsu that his country's intentions were to share the benefits of knowledge and civilization, the king consulted with an adviser and replied shrewdly, "If such are today the purposes of your nation, why then have you behaved so differently in India?"[8]

The Xhosa, too, put checks and balances on their chiefs and kept him in line with a group of advisers called the *amapakati*, the "middle ones." To fail to consult it or to ignore its rulings would be almost unthinkable. If the poorest citizen had a grievance, he was entitled to his day in court in front of the chief and his advisers, some of whom served as the walking libraries of oral legal history, carrying an "enormous background of precedents, customs and rulings."[9]

A missionary named William Holden wrote in 1866 about the prowess in logic of the Xhosa: "Some would-be wise Englishman has endeavored to parody the black man by representing him as shaking hands with a baboon or a monkey," but Holden wrote he would like to bring such a racist to three days of Xhosa discussion. "They have deceived and outwitted our ablest governors, our most astute diplomatists, and our very acute officers and magistrates. They are equal to any English lawyers in discussing questions which relate to their own laws and customs; and the man who attempts to speak contemptuously of them only betrays his own ignorance, weakness or folly."[10]

The Mende people of what is now Sierra Leone didn't bother with a hereditary system at all; their elders reflected on the merits of potential chiefs and kings and then elected them on their records as warriors or traders. A Mende king had a "speaker" who conveyed instructions to administrators, served as the ruler's spokesman, and acted as his deputy if he was sick or away; he was more a premier than what we today would call a parliamentary speaker. Similarly, the Temne people also relied on their elders to elect a king who was sequestered for months with officials who educated him on his responsibilities to his subjects.[11]

For the Loango people of what is now the Republic of the Congo, a king had to prove his merit through a challenging seven-year probation period. This was followed by a year "on the road," visiting every corner of the realm. There were tests of his physical prowess and even his self-restraint, with a beautiful virgin for temptation. And yet after he passed all these trials, he earned himself a life of relative seclusion. He was the go-between for the Loango supreme god of Nzambi and treated practically as a god himself, which meant he needed to stay within the grounds of the royal court.[12] The Oyo Empire of the Yoruba people (in what's now western Nigeria and modern Benin) also preferred to keep their ruler in relative seclusion, "appearing in public only on ritual occasions, three times a year and always heavily veiled—it would not do for the ordinary populace to look on the Son of Heaven."[13]

Now all this secrecy and mystique shouldn't seem strange to us. In Russia in the mid-1800s, common serfs and uneducated peasants were taught to think of Tsar Alexander II as an emissary of God. In Japan, the role of the emperor withered away until he was mostly a figurehead, never seen by the public, and yet he was considered an actual god by generations from the Middle Ages right into the twentieth century. After Japan's defeat in World War II, ordinary Japanese were shocked at a photograph revealing Hirohito's short, somewhat frail body compared to the relative bulk and height of American general Douglas MacArthur.

A king of the Oyo had arguably more power than Hirohito ever enjoyed, and he used his slave eunuchs like chess pawns to exert their administrative will.[14] But this could get him into serious trouble. As in other cultures, the king relied on a cabinet of nobles who not only had chosen him but held his very life in their hands. If they turned on him, he was duty-bound to go kill himself. What kept this check on his power from getting abused was that a key member of the nobles was required to commit suicide as well.

For the Mossi people of Burkina Faso, their ruler or *Moro Naba* (also *Mogho Naba*) relied on five ministers who represented the five provinces. When "the fire had gone out" and the king died, the chief minister, or *Ouidi Naba*, gathered his colleagues to start the process to appoint a new monarch, and an elaborate set piece of political theater played out—but its cues very much had a purpose. The Ouidi Naba urged the other ministers to weigh the qualifications of the eldest son of the late king, along with others vying for the job. The lesser ministers would reply, "You are our superior, and the right to make the choice rests on you alone." The ritual satisfied, they got down to deciding but by convention usually elected the eldest son of the last Moro Naba.[15]

The Ouidi Naba then informed the minister of war, "My mind is not at ease because I fear that those whose hopes have not been fulfilled will resort to violence." The war minister's stock reply was, "That will be against tradition and justice to the dead ruler. Do not fear; I am here with my arms to see that your decision is respected." Then the choice was announced to the other ministers, who declared, "You have expressed our will and the will of all the people." The ministers would then present their new ruler before the public, with the chief minister shouting, "Here is he who has the power of life and death over you."[16]

Yet while the Moro Naba was invested with huge autocratic powers and couldn't be deposed, he ruled through his ministers. A minister "couldn't interfere in the internal affairs of a district, nor could the district chief complain to the Moro Naba about a minister. Everyone was required to observe the strict hierarchy; the only sanction that the district chief exercised over his minister was to appeal to another minister in the hope that the Moro Naba would come to his aid."[17] The system wasn't perfect. There were cases of defiance over payment of tribute and at least a couple of civil wars, plus petty corruption by district chiefs. But locals had their own way of dealing with a bullying chief in their district—they simply left his territory.[18]

When the French set up their colonial administration in the late 1890s, they severely limited the powers of the Moro Naba and his district chiefs. And yet there is still a Moro Naba today, even if his realm has shrunk to Burkina Faso's capital of Ouagadougou, and he is still considered an important cultural and spiritual leader. We can see the influence in two peculiar episodes in Burkina Faso's history. In 1958, the ruler at the time, Naba Kougri, orchestrated a coup to try to impose a constitutional monarchy. He failed, and yet he stayed in his position until his death in 1982, and his son, Naba Baongo II, took over. In 2015, during the spectacularly incompetent coup by the Regiment of Presidential Security, the coup's leader, General Gilbert Diendéré, felt it necessary to visit the palace of Naba Baongo, supposedly to "update him on the situation." Diendéré claimed he cut the audience short when a crowd massed outside in the courtyard because "that could upset him." *SlateAfrique.com* suspected the truth might have been quite different, and it was the Moro Naba who chased off the general "to prevent an angry crowd from lynching him."[19]

What are we to think then of all these examples of government, the Asante and the Oyo, the Xhosa, Benin, the Mossi, and others?

Well, consider for a moment our intellectual inheritance of Western feudal government. Generations of schoolchildren have been taught about the Magna Carta, and their more informed teachers let them know it was really about power sharing between King John and his barons and how there was very little thought given to Joe Peasant. For its 800th anniversary in 2015, *The Atlantic* grumbled that this long document in spidery script signed in a pleasant little town in Surrey (Runnymede) is "often invoked in the U.K., the U.S. and around the world as a font of freedom, the touchstone for today's constitutional democracy. But its specifics are largely forgotten."[20]

And there's the rub. By now it should be clear that the kingdoms of West Africa were at least, if not more, enlightened than their Western feudal counterparts. And in cultures that didn't rely on the written word, they could be remarkably, astonishingly vigilant through the centuries over preserving the rights and privileges of ruler and adviser, chief, and common man. True, the Xhosa had walking, talking libraries of pedantic legal scholars. And you might think, Well, of course, these societies would have written their rules and policies down if they could. But that's the point: unlike our societies in Europe, *they didn't need to.*

For many of these West African kingdoms, civic understanding functioned like good manners, passed down from generation to generation. The rulers knew their limits, even when it was proclaimed that they had the power of life and death and were considered mystical figures. Compliance with "the rules" didn't evolve from blind following of ritual or because the technology of the written word was lacking; the strength of conviction in institutions arose from something more profound, from the ties that bind in a community. We'll return to this point later in discussing a remarkable success story in African democracy, and we'll examine it further when one of the giants and the martyrs of the antiapartheid struggle summed up a core concept of African philosophy.

For now, it's worth considering that in our modern era, we've fetishized the documents that represent our democratic genius, but we also mourn how both the spirit and the letter of the law have been ignored with rising corruption and populism. We're shaking our heads over not merely the gleeful, callous abandon of laws by the villains but our fears of the breakdown of civilization. If we look harder, we'll notice the pattern: the good manners always die *first*, then the laws. And we can see now that one of the great lessons of traditional African culture is that social cohesion is possibly the true fulcrum underneath a government and a society that lasts.

In Western schools, children learn about the blessings and blights of the industrial revolution in the early 1800s, the rise of steam locomotives thundering across the American landscape, and the dark, brooding mills of the English Midlands—and so there is another void of ignorance over what was happening at the same time in Africa. These young pupils don't learn what is common knowledge to generations of African Studies majors: that the continent wasn't sitting around and waiting to "graduate" from the dissolution of the slave trade to the harnessing of its resource wealth by Europeans. Their indigenous peoples were, in fact, doing this job quite nicely, thank you, all on their own.

Take one region. In the 1830s, the palm oil traded from the coastlines of what is now modern Benin and Ghana satisfied an insatiable British appetite. It was a product with versatile uses, such as an ingredient in margarine and soap. At the same time, West Africans were importing millions of meters of British cotton. (In the northeast, in Sudan, cotton products had already been produced for centuries with local workers carrying out all the steps of production, such as spinning and dyeing.) In the 1840s, Senegalese traders reserved tons of their peanut crops for sale to the French, while in Angola, clever entrepreneurs recognized the market for rubber trees.[21] Instead of us thinking of an industrial backwardness in comparison to Europe, we should remember that West Africa "had a range of manufacturing industries which closely resembled those of pre-industrial societies in other parts of the world."[22]

But let's return for a moment to our Western classroom and the industrial revolution. We're taught that Europe and North America experienced a technological boom, and we're left with the impression that soldiers and architects of empire merely arrived with an industrial and commercial prowess the Africans didn't have. In truth, Europe already relied—and was in some cases, *vitally dependent*—on goods from and established trading relationships with Africa. As Basil Davidson reminds us, these African economies were self-sustaining and quite adaptive to changing markets. "Save in very barren regions, existing populations probably fed better than they ever would later, if only because the pre-colonial export booms had not yet cut seriously into land and labor resources available for growing food."[23] In the Ivory Coast, the cocoa farmers in the 1900s practiced their own version of profit sharing—*abusa*.[24]

Yet one of the most pernicious barnacles of the colonial era that clings to historical discussion is that empires "created wealth." In truth, as Davidson observed, they usually took over the *existing means* of creating wealth. When the term "Third World" fell out of favor in the 1990s, the neologism that replaced it was the "developing world"—ignoring the fact that Africa was already at a stage of sophisticated economic development. And as we continue along the road of African intellectual thought, we should remember that several of the thinkers and activists who emerged in the 1800s and the turn of the twentieth century worked in a context that often recognized—because the evidence was already there or within collective memory—the continent's potential for self-determined prosperity.

African medicine also defies Western expectations of its lack of advancement. And no, we're not about to wander down a path romanticizing traditional prescriptions of herbal remedies, rediscovered by those of perhaps a New Age bent who prefer alternative therapies. We're talking about accomplishments that can stand up to scientific scrutiny. The South African writer E. A. Ritter recalled a practice by Zulu healers of boiling jimsonweed and the urine deposits of rock rabbits to create a natural antiseptic; the healer would then pressure squirt the mixture through a reed tube into serious gashes and wounds and bandage the injuries with the leaves. We know this treatment worked because one of Ritter's own friends was cured with it in 1910 after being attacked by a leopard.[25]

As scholar Ioan Lewis reports, "Traditional medical lore also included smallpox vaccination and the isolation of patients with diseases which were known to be infectious . . . Somalis knew from observation of their haunts that mosquitoes carried malaria before this was known to Western science."[26] Inoculating against smallpox was known to other parts of the continent as well. In the early 1700s in Boston, American minister Cotton Mather asked one of his African slaves, renamed Onesimus, if he had ever had smallpox. Onesimus told him yes—and no. As Mather put, while a young boy, Onesimus had "undergone an operation, which had given him something of ye smallpox, and would forever preserve him from it."[27] Britain has several statues and paintings in tribute to its patron saint of immunology, Edward Jenner, yet we have none to that anonymous pioneer in Africa who lived generations before Jenner ever started his important work.

Then there's surgery. It would be easy to assume that as a scientific discipline, it was the monopoly of the early Romans and medieval Europeans. But it's clear that it also developed in parts of Africa. The traditional practice of bone setting in Nigeria, often handed down from father to son, survived among the Yoruba into the modern age, and a study published in 1980 noted how the contemporary bonesetters "were conversant with the classical signs of fracture which are swelling, pain, loss of function." Their use of a specific splint "parallels the use of plaster of Paris in modern orthopaedic practice."[28]

The disadvantages of the traditional methods are obvious, as the study pointed out: no X-rays for confirmation of diagnosis, unhygienic conditions that could lead to infection, plus joint manipulation that could be excruciatingly painful without anesthetics.[29] But from a historical point of view, these conditions were no grislier than those endured by countless patients in surgeries in London, Paris, or Philadelphia right until the closing decades of the nineteenth century.

Ugandans had a surgical treatment for pleuritis, the inflammation of the lung membranes that can cause shortness of breath and chest pain. "For inflammation of the lungs or pleurisy," wrote the British colonial official Harry Johnston in 1902, "they pierce a hole in the chest until air escapes through it. In a few days [the patient] appears to be quite well, and simply dress the wound with butter." Johnston also noticed "they have no professional medicine men but are content with women doctors."[30]

British observers routinely poured scorn on traditional healers but paid grudging respect to surgeons. "Surgical skill had reached a high standard," wrote John Roscoe about the Baganda people in Uganda in 1921, impressed that "even a bone pressing upon the brain [caused by head trauma from a blow of a club or from a flung stone] could be removed, and the patient saved." According to Roscoe, many wounds and mutilations resulted from battle or due to punishment imposed by a chief, and "men whose stomachs had been ripped open with the bowels protruding had a piece of gourd shell placed inside to keep the stomach in position, and the flesh was then stitched over it."[31] The Ekoi people of Nigeria used the same procedure. A British official saw the patient for himself. "The shape of the calabash can be clearly seen, but he has quite recovered and is able to take his share of any hard labor, such as road work."[32]

Even a highly dangerous operation for centuries, the caesarean section, wasn't unknown to sub-Saharan Africa. In the West, we know it was always a last-ditch measure in antiquity and the Middle Ages because the mother usually died. But before we get to how Africans operated, it's worth pausing to consider the supposed "first case" of the procedure in which both the mother and the child survived.

A few years ago, Czech researchers thought they might have discovered it in the court documents of the king of Bohemia. His second wife, Beatrice of Bourbon, gave birth in late February 1337. According to one of the researchers, Dr. Antonin Parizek, "Beatrice most likely passed out during delivery, and was believed dead. The surgeons opened her only to save and baptize the child. The pain from the operation then likely led to her awakening." Shock "may have saved her life by keeping her from bleeding excessively." The *New York Times* headlined its feature, "A Breakthrough in C-Section History: Beatrice of Bourbon's Survival in 1337."[33]

Now we can't possibly know exactly when sub-Saharan Africans first used the procedure, but we do have a fascinating example of the operation. The English explorer and later mystic Robert Felkin visited Uganda while a medical student, and in 1879, he was allowed to observe a C-section performed on a twenty-year-old woman of the Ganda people. Just as in Europe, the easiest anesthetic available was always alcohol, and the young woman—bound tightly with restraints—was half drunk on banana wine. But notice this incredible aspect of the surgery, which took place "only two years after [Joseph] Lister had moved to London to spread his gospel of antisepsis." After muttering an incantation, the surgeon *"washed his hands and the patient's abdomen first with banana wine and then water* [emphasis added]."[34]

The banana wine would have contained 7 percent alcohol, far more if distilled, and as one modern commentator observed, "The whole conduct of the operation as Felkin has described it suggests a skilled, long-practiced surgical team at work conducting a well-tried and familiar operation with smooth efficiency and unhurried skill. . . . Lister's team in London could hardly have performed with greater smoothness. The leader of the team was helped all through by assistants who seemed familiar with their roles. The after treatment followed a clear routine."

We can only wonder how long such efficient practices were standard, but it's reasonable to assume they had some extensive duration comparable to other traditional methods. Were they around at least a century before Felkin bore witness? Two centuries? More? We'll never know. Poor Beatrice of Bourbon survived with her child in Prague only by sheer accident, and this is still considered a possible medical milestone. Isn't the possibility worth considering that the Ugandans might have got there first? And that they were well ahead of the Europeans in enlightened surgical care?

West Africans also showed a sophistication in city planning and infrastructure that could rival and even exceed European development.

The Asante, for instance, tamed the thick, wild rain forest into submission for their elaborate network of roads, allowing them better movement of trade and easier travel. Each one was policed by its own deployment of soldiers and depots.[35] In the Kingdom of Benin at the height of its medieval glory in the seventeenth century, the capital boasted walls that "extended 16,000 kilometers in all, in a mosaic of more than 500 interconnected settlement boundaries." They were "four times longer than the Great Wall of China and consumed a hundred times more material than the Great Pyramid of Cheops. They took an estimated 150 million hours of digging to construct and are perhaps the largest single archaeological phenomenon on the planet."[36]

Sadly, very few remnants of these foundations are still around. But we do know at night, residents in Benin City walked under one of the first systems of urban street lighting, with metal lamps running on palm oil and used in particular near the capital's palace.[37] "The Towne seemeth to be very great when you enter it," reads a Dutch report from about 1602. "You go into a great broad street, not paved, which seemeth to be seven or eight times broader than the Warmoes Street in Amsterdam." Its houses "stand in good order, one close and even with the other, as the houses in Holland stand."[38] It was natural for the arts to flourish in a place like this, and the royal palace took up almost half of its capital. One European described how the Oba's court was "divided into many magnificent palaces, houses and apartments of the courtiers, and comprises beautiful and long square galleries, about as large as the exchange in Amsterdam, but one larger than another, resting on wooden pillars, from top to bottom covered with cast copper, on which are engraved the pictures of their war exploits and battles, and are kept very clean."[39]

This ingenuity in African city planning goes even deeper. American mathematician Ron Eglash captured the public imagination with his innovative and fascinating study of African cities, arguing that fractal patterns can be found in many examples of their architecture. Fractals, for those of us who were terrible at math or just asleep in class, are complex, recursive patterns; you see them in nature, such as the nautilus, and they're now a staple of computer graphics. "Although there is great diversity among the many cultures of Africa," wrote Eglash, "examples of fractal architecture can be found in every corner of the African continent."[40] To Eglash, the designs testify to an indigenous understanding of fractal geometry, something that didn't sink in for Europeans until centuries later.

And the legacy of African fractals still goes on. Spanish architect Xavier Vilalta was commissioned in 2009 to build a vocational school in the Ethiopian town of Mekelle. Eager to design a building that connected with the nation's culture, he dove into researching Ethiopia and other countries and came across Eglash's book. "This opened new possibilities in terms of architectural design. Thinking with fractals and geometry in designs was like a complete new world."[41] Vilalta went on to use fractals in the award-winning Lideta Mercato in Addis Ababa, which is also "inspired by the beautiful, bold patterns found on Ethiopian women's dresses" and his proposed design for a university in Angola.[42]

Wired magazine gushed in 2017 how "from Kenya to Morocco, a string of world-class buildings" represented "the very best of modern architecture." It described how Diébédo Francis Kéré of Burkina Faso relied on a "smart blend of traditional and vernacular construction techniques and materials— mud bricks and corrugated steel sheets—with contemporary design."[43] The materials were chosen deliberately with local workers in mind. And British Ghanaian architect David Adjaye suggests "the most enduring and inspirational architecture on the continent generally demonstrates an extraordinary apposite response to the climate. It offers many examples of age-old innovations that have endured and from which we can learn."[44]

One of Adjaye's protégés is the award-winning architect Mariam Kamara of Niger, whose elegant design of the Niamey Cultural Center will include curved towers that will rely on natural ventilation and will be constructed with "compressed earth bricks—a breathable material responsive to Niger's desert climate and a reflection of local vernacular architecture."[45]

What are we to make of all these antecedents and innovations? An appreciation for law and decent governance, the rise of mathematics and medicine, meticulous artisans and artists—the point is staring us right in the face: these are not merely signs of sophisticated cultures, which have their own self-evident rights, but markers of civilization. The essayist and great journalistic provocateur Christopher Hitchens liked to declare that civilization didn't need *Western* in front of it—if the term "means the sum of human intellectual accomplishment, it needn't be qualified by an adjective."[46] And what follows in this book will make sense only if we appreciate that Europe didn't barge into Africa and paint its values across a blank canvas or traumatize a mass collection of happy, simple-minded pastoralists (i.e., "noble savages"). They interrupted the give-and-take of societies, the flow of cultural transmission itself that helped build both Africa *and* Europe.

This is a very different point from hammering home again the devastation of the Atlantic slave trade and colonialism. And the tragedy of what happened to the Kingdom of Benin can help illustrate. The details are worth a closer look because the ugly episode touches on so many themes for our discussion.

The Kingdom of Benin had achieved the miracle of enduring for centuries with only the occasional incursion by Europeans and their limited interference. When the Portuguese, for example, made themselves a continual nuisance around the early 1500s, the Beni restricted them to trading from São Tomé.[47] The centuries rolled on, and the British supplanted the Portuguese in colonizing the region, carving out a healthy portion of Nigeria. Yet the Kingdom of Benin somehow had eluded the covetous eyes gazing all the way from Whitehall.

The Beni were not fools, and the Oba insisted on payment of custom duties—what both sides called "presents"—as well as the rich trade in goods that was run as it always had been through royal monopoly, using the appointed middlemen and the trading associations of court nobles. This frustrated the British to no end; they knew the country was full of wonderful commodities, such as palm oil, rubber, gum, and minerals, and they wanted to get their hands on them, but those troublesome custom duties. . . . They resented anything that clogged up business. In other words, whatever impacted their greed. And they considered the "fetish practices" of Benin, its religious worship of ancestors and reliance on human sacrifice (often of criminals), to be another obstacle. But this was just an excuse. The only thing that had ever changed was the British attitude, and the king of Benin and his advisers kept a tight grip on administration just like their predecessors. By 1892, however, London's point man on the scene managed to nudge the Oba, Ovonramwen Nogbaisi, into signing a treaty—or, rather, Ovonramwen's aide to sign it because the king wouldn't even touch the pen.[48]

As far as Ovonramwen was concerned, these pushy whites could go away now and leave his kingdom alone. Business would go on as usual, and if he wanted to place an occasional embargo on something—oh, like maybe the kernels for palm oil—he was well within his rights. But the British thought their piece of paper made all the difference in the world, and they grew impatient with the trade obstacles. The consul general of what eventually was called the Niger Coast Protectorate wrote bluntly in 1895 to Britain's Foreign Office, "At the first opportunity, steps should be taken for opening up the country if necessary by force."[49]

Less than two years later while the consul general was on leave in London, his second in command, James Phillips, spoke to chiefs in the region and to trading firms. He decided "there is only one remedy, to depose the king of Benin from his stool." Then he asked the Foreign Office for permission to kick out the Oba and replace him with a native council, supremely confident that ordinary natives would support the British removing a "tyrant." As for the cost of such an expedition, well, confiscating a large supply of ivory from the king would underwrite that. The Foreign Office had concerns that there weren't enough soldiers for the job yet in the end worked with the War Office and Colonial Office to put arrangements in place.[50]

Phillips dispatched a message to the Oba, declaring that he was on his way and bringing a customs duty "present." This was a cynical ruse, but Ovonramwen Nogbaisi wouldn't take the bait. According to Alan Boisragon, a minor official with Phillips, the Oba sent a reply that thanked Phillips for the present but explained he "could not see any white men just then as he was celebrating the 'custom' [ceremony] of his father's death." The British knew this involved the ritual sacrifice of hundreds of slaves. Offering an olive branch of sorts, Ovonramwen was willing to see Phillips in a couple of months, but with "no other white men."[51]

Phillips was determined to barge into Benin, so he took a force of eight white officers that led a column of more than 200 African soldiers disguised as porters, their revolvers hidden in the baggage. Phillips even brought along a drum-and-fife band, which he later sent back. He had somehow got it into his head that the people of Benin had no standing army or fighting tradition despite being aware that they had already obtained some guns from traders.[52] Custer had more men and showed more sense at the Battle of Little Big Horn.

The Beni might have kept many traditional cultural practices, but they had not stood still. They had some outdated rifles and knew how to use them and on learning about the column coming their way treated it correctly as an invasion. With guns and machetes, they wiped out the column, including Phillips, and only two white officers managed to frantically escape. London now had martyrs and an excuse to move in, and in less than a month, in February 1897, a "punitive expedition" with 1,400 British troops under the command of Admiral Harry Rawson from Cape Town sailed to the Nigerian coast and linked up with a force of hundreds of local black troops and thousands of porters from a military base in Sierra Leone. Then they pushed on to the Kingdom of Benin.

The naval surgeon who was with the expedition, Felix Roth, marked in his diary how "our black troops with the scouts in front and a few Maxims do all the fighting." Rawson's units were ruthless. Knowing that the enemy liked to ambush the head of a column advancing through the forest, soldiers would fire volleys "every few minutes low down into the bush on each side," and if the Beni returned fire, the soldiers would strafe the area with a machine gun. For all their superior firepower, though, Rawson's army encountered fierce resistance, and his three columns were hounded by guerrilla fighters in the bush and with open attacks. The British response was to shell villages, put them to the torch, and fire their machine guns into the trees to catch fleeing defenders. "For Benin 1897," writes scholar Dan Hicks, "perhaps most telling is the sustained silence in both official and informal documentation of any prisoners of war, or any injured African casualties," or, for that matter, any hospital care for wounded African civilians or caring for ordinary people displaced by the British attacks.[53]

When Rawson's troops closed in on Benin City, firing rockets and shelling different positions, they found it mostly deserted, with many of its residents fleeing into the countryside. Both Felix Roth and a Reginald Bacon described grotesque scenes of human sacrifice and bloody crucifixions: "live women-slaves gagged and pegged on their backs to the ground, the abdominal wall being cut in the form of a cross. . . . The altar was deluged in blood, the smell of which was too overpowering for many of us," while others were "roused to fury."[54]

Roth and Bacon published books in the same year as the expedition, their memories fresh, and since they were so unwittingly forthcoming about the army's conduct—perpetrating acts that today we'd consider war crimes—we should consider they weren't exaggerating over what they saw. But already by 1926, the question was, Did they really *understand* what they saw? Ethnographer Percy Talbot argued that the bodies might have been really those of "executed criminals and those who had died of some infectious disease, etc. to whom decent burial was denied." Criminals might have preferred being a sacrifice for the gods to other forms of execution, while those who were tied to trees were accused wizards and witches "and so guilty in native eyes of the worst possible crime. The idea of Benin rule, therefore, as one of bloodstained despotism, appears at variance with the truth."[55]

Nevertheless, in 1897, Felix Roth, Reginald Bacon, and others rushed to get their versions of what happened into print, and Bacon opened his lurid account with these lines: "Truly has Benin been called the City of Blood. Its history is one long record of savagery of the most debased kind."[56] Purporting to know something of native funereal rites, he suggested, "the killing of wives and slaves to accompany the dead man into the next world is not without its redeeming side."[57] What seemed to offend him more than the gore itself was the scale of it. The gruesome tales from the expedition are thought to have helped inspire Joseph Conrad's *Heart of Darkness*. Six months after the British forces took Benin City, Ovonramwen Nogbaisi was finally captured, given a show trial (with the consul general as judge), and sent into exile to Calabar.

Rawson's soldiers spent about three days in the city and soon began burning and destroying the royal houses and compounds. On their last day of occupation, a careless fire—later conveniently blamed on a servant—spread quickly from a thatch roof of an ordinary home and engulfed the rest of the city, burning up a good portion of the army's supplies. The only reason why it didn't obliterate the legacy of Benin art altogether is because soldiers had already emptied the complexes, taking away thousands of examples of precious sculptures and plaques, carved ivory tusks, and coral beads. One officer, Captain Herbert Walker, casually mentioned how he was due to leave the site soon and wrote in his diary, "Busy packing loot!"[58]

There is no doubt the men recognized their value. In Bacon's account, after casual references to the laziness of Africans (using the *n*-word) and listing a veritable catalog of army slaughter along with self-righteous descriptions of the Beni's atrocities, he mentions how he explored the storehouses of one compound where "buried in the dirt of ages in one house were several hundred unique bronze plaques, suggestive of almost Egyptian design, but of really superb casting. Castings of wonderful delicacy of detail, and some magnificently carved tusks were collected."[59]

But in ransacking the brass heads and bronze plaques, Rawson's expedition destroyed the chain of Benin history. His men carted off "the Benin equivalent of chronological records. Since each head represented an Oba, this recorded a dynasty back to the twelfth century. When an Oba died, a formal head was cast in bronze as a furnishing for an altar erected to his memory."[60] In the royal palace, the plaques that were once fixed to the wooden columns for the roof had offered "a detailed picture of the Benin court at the height of its glory and power," and many of them "show European traders in the costume of the day."[61] Rawson's

Plaque from the Benin Bronzes on display at the British Museum in London in 2018.

soldiers succeeded in vandalizing and carelessly scattering valuable clues to European history as well.

In an anniversary feature on the expedition in 1997, *The Independent* noted that for the display of Benin Bronzes at the

The inside of the royal palace when it was looted in 1897.

main staircase of the British Museum, the theft and destruction by Rawson's army went "unmentioned in the museum's accompanying wall notice."[62] Aside from these pieces—plus a small collection of works found later and kept in Africa—most of Benin's magnificent art is sitting in foreign museums or in private collections. And in most history books, the looting of the bronzes is summed up in a few quick paragraphs. The trip by an arrogant Phillips is listed as the spark, then we're told about Rawson putting the city to the torch, and . . . We cut to the looting and disbursement of the treasures. It makes for an easy tale of colonial hooliganism.

But when Western writers pack the story into a single page, they're doing us a disservice because no one can really understand the tragedy without examining more of the details. The British weren't undermining a tyrant; they were trying to extinguish a whole system of governance. In the many years leading up to the invasion, the Beni had followed protocols of diplomatic relations. They could understand them like any official in France's Quai d'Orsay or in the U.S. State Department.

And the story doesn't make sense at all unless you appreciate that Benin's Oba and his advisers—for he wouldn't have made decisions without them—were acting on traditional but highly developed administrative practices to protect their economy, which was completely reliant on their natural resources and their control of their own trade.

Now consider what was happening in the rest of the world in February 1897 when the British expedition was launched. Greece and Turkey were fighting each other but would negotiate a peace treaty later that year. Boston would open the first subway in North America, while Edison and his team of hired geniuses worked away on developing a movie projector. If you were in Paris, you could take in the very first performances of *Cyrano de Bergerac*, and if you were in London, you could buy the first edition of Bram Stoker's *Dracula*. Before the new century had even arrived, the modern world was intruding with icons and technology that are still with us.

Against this background, the Kingdom of Benin never stood a chance. Superior firepower was important, yes, but that's *not* what almost caused the extinction of a culture. Looking back with our progressive sensibilities, we fully expect Phillips and Bacon to be racists, but the matter is not that simple either. Reginald Bacon held the plaques and sculptures in his hands, and he acknowledged the craftsmanship, but he saw it as a separate thing, detached from the rest of the Beni's reality. Admiring the plaques as he did, he still couldn't make the leap to thinking these works of art reflected a sophisticated culture.

That should bother us because many people, with no malice in their hearts, will still unconsciously hold the attitude that the Beni must have been primitives.

Today, the liberal mind-set will acknowledge the crime but, like the imperial apologist, grant it a statute of limitations. Surely, the Kingdom of Benin must have been frozen in time. Its intellectual and technological advancement must have stopped, and that's why British soldiers with machine guns could cruelly take away their land, their goods, their way of life. Such a shame, but oh, well. And then we go on looking at the sculptures, removed from their context.

Yet the Beni had rifles and other weapons, they had the technology to fight back for their form of government, for their economy and way of life, all of which coalesced to form the environment that made that sculpture flourish. *This* is why we need to look at African antecedents because we can then shed this sense of defeatist inevitability.

It's high time we recognized that the Africans didn't modernize or "grow up" with exposure to European ways—no, the Europeans and American regressed in their appreciation of African culture. And though the story of the slave trade has been told many times, it still holds a few revelations.

7

Immortal Queens

When it comes to the European slave trade and its impacts on Africa, there is an interesting aspect that so far still earns minimal attention: resistance.

The focus has always been—because of the sheer numbers involved—on the slave trade to *America*, with minor attention paid to the occasional and swiftly quelled rebellions in the United States and the Caribbean. But the Europeans began the trade by first taking slaves back to their home countries and even selling them to the Middle East, and so the hard, early battles in Africa have been relegated to quick references in history books. This is comparable to retelling the narrative of the Holocaust and perfunctorily skipping over the Warsaw Ghetto Uprising. Like the slowly moving tide of prisoners forced onto trains for the concentration camps, we have an image, too, of Africans led to their fate, accepting it with a stoic docility that would become a crude stereotype.

First, let's dissect another cliché, that "Africans sold themselves into slavery first." True, it is an irrefutable fact that African cultures had a tradition of slavery, but it's forgotten that Europeans also kept and sold slaves from *their own* populations as well, all the way to the era of Joan of Arc and Gutenberg. There were objections from the papacy in the 1300s, but these didn't last long after the profits became clear, and much of the trade was conducted by merchants from Venice and Genoa, with slaves sold to the Sultanate of Egypt.[1]

So much for the Europeans. What was slavery then to Africans? In many African kingdoms, it was far closer to feudal serfdom than what we associate with the chained-beast-of-burden horrors that came to epitomize the Atlantic trade. In the culture of the Asante of southern Ghana, for instance, it's true that masters had the right to dispense with a slave as a human sacrifice, and slaves could end up as military conscripts or performing backbreaking labor.[2] At the same time, however, slaves were allowed to marry and own property.

It's important to realize this is not a modern interpretation. Martin Delany—educated at Harvard, a trained physician, and the first black man to be given a field commission by Abraham Lincoln—traveled to Liberia and wrote later, "It is simply preposterous to talk about slavery, as that term is understood, either being legalized or existing in this part of Africa. It is nonsense. The system is a patriarchal one, there being no actual difference socially between the slave (called by their protector son or daughter) and the children of the person with whom they live."[3] Delany exaggerated, but his essential point is correct. In form and approach, slavery in much of Africa usually bore little resemblance to the practices of Europe.

The attitudes of early Europeans to their African slaves were also strikingly different at the infancy of the trade as opposed to later. It was the Portuguese who first started it, and the chronicler Gomes de Azurara wrote that his people didn't find their new slaves "hardened in the belief of the other Moors [those from North Africa]. . . . They made no difference between them and their free servants born in our own country; but those whom they took while still young, they caused to be instructed in the mechanical arts, and those whom they saw fitted for managing property, they set free and married to women who were natives of [their] land."[4]

That prompts a natural question: why take slaves later from the west coast and the center of the continent at all? Why didn't the trade evolve from military strikes in the north? Simple: religion at the time was far more important than color. The

Europeans feared that slaves from northern Africa might spread Islam and undermine Christianity. For their part, the Africans preferred to sell slaves who were not natives of their own kingdoms; they were often captives from the losing side of a battle. That worked out well for the Portuguese—and later the Dutch and British—who made their incursions along the southwest and southeast coasts. They could repeatedly take advantage of the regional politics in Africa to loot, pillage, and capture ground. In one battle in Angola, the Portuguese took the noses of slain warriors as trophies—and not just one or two but *hundreds*—while after another battle, the bodies covered the ground so widely that Portuguese soldiers were forced to step on top of them to cross.[5]

The "Africans sold themselves" trope has become so widely accepted as a mitigating factor that it's almost forgotten in the public imagination how relentless the European incursions into African territory were, how these invasions offered staggering riches to those who could supply the demand for slaves and who ruthlessly beat down any native opposition. But there *were* formal protests.

King Afonso of Kongo (in what is now Angola and parts of the two modern Congo states) wrote to Portugal's Jao III in 1526, and in doing so, he wasn't naive. Making such an appeal made perfect sense, because from the sixteenth to the nineteenth century, Kongo enjoyed an impressive network of diplomatic correspondence, ambassadors, and merchant relations across Europe.[6] "Each day," Afonso wrote, "the traders are kidnapping our people—children of this country, sons of our nobles and vassals, even people of our own family. . . . The corruption and depravity are so widespread that our land is entirely depopulated." He described how his people were branded with hot irons and taken away to the slave ships. Portugal's monarch replied haughtily that he was told Kongo was vast, with plenty of slaves still available.[7]

Nor was Afonso's letter an isolated case. A king of Dahomey, Agaja, conquered nearby city-states of Ardrah in what's now Benin, and he took advantage of a visit by an Englishman in 1724 to relay a message back to London: enough is enough. He wanted the slave trade of his people to stop. In 1789, the imam who essentially ruled Futa Toro in northern Senegal at the time took on the French slave traders, telling them, hands off his people; he returned several presents the slave-trading company had given him, warning that "all the riches of that company would not make him change his mind." The French found a new route down the coast and a more accommodating market where they could buy and drag away human beings.[8] As with the other examples, the ruler's noble effort failed, but it's significant that an *imam* took this stand.

In the 1580s right into the 1600s, the Portuguese also ravaged the kingdom of Ndongo—located in the northwest of Angola—while forcing its neighboring territories to become vassal states and extorting tributes of slaves. Then, in 1622, a remarkable meeting took place in Luanda, the main town occupied by these pale invaders from across the sea. A procession of men and women entered the coastal town, with male slaves proudly carrying their leader on their shoulders while more slaves brought gifts. There was to be a meeting between Portugal's colonial governor, João Correira de Sousa, and the envoy of Ndongo's ineffectual, erratic king, Ngola Mbande, of the Mbundu people. The envoy was Ngola's sister, Njinga, who was dressed to impress in beautiful robes, her arms and legs covered in jewels, her hair decorated with feathers; even her female entourage sported impressive outfits.

Njinga was a larger-than-life figure who was determined to get her way. She knew how to swing a war ax, and by the time she met the governor, she was close to forty years old and quite likely a veteran of the battlefield. She would later lead her own armies into combat, and when she was well past eighty years old, she still impressed one Portuguese observer with her arms skill during a military parade.[9] She also liked sex and had many lovers. One court official was foolish enough to complain about her promiscuity; she had the man's son put to death in front of him before she had him killed as well. A legend goes that when she came face-to-face with de Sousa, he sat on a fancy chair and offered her a carpet on the floor. Njinga wasn't about to put up with that, so she gestured to a female attendant, who promptly dropped to all fours and became a human chair for the negotiation session.[10]

That story of her response has been retold many times, but what is more impressive is how Njinga held her own. The governor and his officials demanded that her brother pay a yearly tribute in slaves to Portugal's monarch. The implication was clear—such a move would make Ndongo's ruler subservient. But Njinga told them, "He who is born free should maintain himself in freedom and not submit to others."[11]

She soon became queen after her brother died from poisoning (whether it was an accident, self-inflicted, or murder is still unknown), and she employed a political cunning worthy of Machiavelli. But our interest here is how she recognized the Portuguese as a threat and dealt with them. They predictably hoped to replace her with a handpicked stooge who would do as he was told, and they did their best to muddle into Mbundu politics. They didn't have this woman's measure. Within a couple of years, whole villages rushed to support her. Slaves in the hundreds were fleeing their Portuguese masters, and vassal lords were switching allegiances. Njinga may have been defiant on her visit to Luanda, but she strung her enemy along with a series of clever and polite denials. Slaves? No runaway slaves here, sorry. The governor was in a panic, writing home to Lisbon how Njinga threatened the whole colonial system.

When open hostilities broke out in 1628, the Portuguese used musketeers and cavalry as well as Angolan warriors to hunt down the impertinent monarch. Njinga, however, was a seasoned fighter who understood guerrilla warfare. Her exploits even rise in some cases to action film set pieces. For instance, the Portuguese managed to track down her camp in May 1629, prompting her to escape with her followers to a narrow cliff. Now imagine the Mbundu fighters for the Portuguese spotting her position and then trying to rush her. But instead of taking her in, they slipped and plummeted over the side to their deaths. Her loyal warriors didn't wait for another try—they formed a human barrier around their queen. And then in an astonishing scene, Njinga climbed down what was either a rope or a vine into a ravine! More of her people stood ready below to take her to safety.[12]

A hand-colored lithograph portrait of Njinga made in the 1830s and now in the collection of the National Portrait Gallery in London.

Even on the run, she was able to draw other Mbundu lords and kingdoms to her cause. The Portuguese tortured their members, hoping they would give her up—they didn't.

Njinga's resistance went on for years. There were times when she sincerely seemed to look for a diplomatic, dignified way out of trouble, which is understandable given the odds. Other times, her overtures may have been delays or distractions. But let's consider things from her point of view: the Portuguese had demonstrated time and again they would break their word, treat Africans with horrific cruelty, and were hypocrites to the Christian faith they continued to push on the indigenous peoples.

She allied herself with the Imbangala, who inspired pure dread in other peoples of the region. The Imbangala didn't believe in sticking to one territory. They were marauders who practiced cannibalism and rituals of child sacrifice and drinking of blood (if such practices offend the tender Western sensibility, keep in mind the ancient Greeks and Romans practiced child abandonment and infanticide on a regular basis). After finding refuge with them, Njinga rose to become one of their most powerful leaders. And when the Dutch came on the scene as key rivals for the Portuguese, she learned how to manipulate them, too, to advance her own ends.

There is a fascinating aspect of gender politics to Njinga's political and spiritual evolution. Having made herself into a force to be reckoned with, striking fear into both the Portuguese and the Angolans who dared oppose her, she declared herself a man, and her male concubines were required to wear women's clothing and sleep in the same quarters as her female retainers. And if the men made sexual advances on the women, they would be promptly executed. Her ladies-in-waiting were also formed into a battalion and served as her personal guard.[13]

By 1645, she had built up an impressive court for herself and her retainers, one that dazzled with its finery of silks and tapestries, and she amassed an army of 80,000 soldiers, which put the fear into the Portuguese. Yet even with her brilliant tactical thinking and Dutch support, she had military setbacks. The war and the diplomatic overtures dragged on until 1656, when she negotiated a peace with Portugal and agreed to accept Christianity again. Lest anyone think she was trapped and finally succumbed to pressure, she carefully checked and challenged the wording of the peace treaty, and in the years that followed, she kept up a steady letter-writing campaign to Rome, doing her best to steer through the intricate Catholic rivalries, all to protect her realm and her people from more foreign incursions. She died in 1663.

Early on, Europeans seized on the legend of Njinga, played up what they knew or thought they knew, and recast her as a sexually voracious monster. In his *Philosophy in the Boudoir*, published in 1795, the Marquis de Sade wrote that Njinga, "queen of Angola, the cruelest of women, slaughtered her lovers after they enjoyed her. She often had warriors clash before her, and she became the winner's prize. To gratify her bloodthirsty soul, she entertained herself by condemning all pregnant women under thirty to be stacked up in a lime pit."[14] In his *Lectures on the Philosophy of History* given in Berlin, Georg Hegel infamously declared that Africa was "no historical part of the world" and went on a rant about African barbarism, indirectly referring to her when he described "a state composed of women, at whose head was a woman," where she supposedly "had the blood of pounded children constantly at hand."[15]

Of course, anyone who digs into the backgrounds of the great figures of the Enlightenment will find they could be as bigoted as a Virginia plantation owner. In 1742, David Hume wrote, "I am apt to suspect the Negroes, and in general all other species of men, to be naturally inferior to the whites." Voltaire, who wrote so eloquently about tolerance, had none for black people and didn't think they were even human. "Their round eyes, their flattened nose, their lips which are always large, their differently shaped ears, the wool of their head, that very measure of their intelligence, place prodigious differences between them and the other species of men."

Both tried to bolster their revulsion with a pseudoscientific rationale. They needed to because racism is that most absurd of bigotries. If Hume and Voltaire rejected African cultures, even the humanity of black people, is it any wonder then that black scholars went in search of African heroes they could claim as their own? And naturally, Njinga was a perfect icon for the anticolonial fight. In 1959, a talented poet named Agostinho Neto, who had been in and out of prison over his political activism, wrote "The Hoisting of the Flag," his poem "dedicated to the heroes of the Angolan people"—one of the heroes referenced was Njinga.[16] Sixteen years later, Neto became the first president of an independent Angola. And the tributes continue. Today, a larger-than-life statue of Njinga stands in Luanda. In 2013, a film with impressive production values and beautiful cinematography was made, *Njinga: Queen of Angola*, starring Lesliana Pereira. With Njinga inspiring modern women in the greater black diaspora, it truly is a case of long live the queen.

But she is not the only female monarch to live on as a reinterpreted embodiment of feminism and black resistance.

Here are lines from a song of the Asante:

Yaa Asantewaa
The mere woman
Who faces a cannon[17]

Yaa Asantewaa was born in 1840, and she was the queen mother of Edweso, a small Asante kingdom near the larger and more powerful one of Kumase, which dominated the confederacy of states in southern Ghana. But for our purposes, Yaa Asantewaa's story really begins more than halfway through her life.

The Asante had a sophisticated culture, one that the British, whether invading or studying, failed to fully appreciate for a long time. Its aristocrats valued cleanliness and decorum, its slaves were treated with relative decency, and Asante women could divorce their partners if they chose. While the Zulus are famous as warriors, the Asante also had a disciplined military machine that built them an empire. An Asante army on the move traveled with an entire satellite infrastructure: carpenters, blacksmiths, stall owners for providing food and drink, even moneylenders. The army's drums, along with tunes played on elephant tusk horns, made a clever forest internet to send recon details about the enemy, and the Asante recognized the tactical value of muskets. In fact, they used the same European tactic of a suppressing musket fire, with the next line advancing and firing while the other reloaded.

Their fearsome reputation was well earned, but the Asante were also skilled diplomats. A top envoy carried a golden ax, which confused the British, who presumed it was a grand weapon—it was actually a symbol for cutting obstacles in the way of their mission.

In 1896, the conquering British arrested the Asante king Prempeh and the rulers of individual Asante states and then, after exiling them to various points, such as the Seychelles, declared Asante a protectorate. By 1900, in a move stunning in its callous heavy-handedness, the governor of the Gold Coast, Frederick Hodgson, visited the key state of Kumase and had the remaining Asante rulers meet him in the new British fort. There, he announced that the old powers of the king were now invested in Queen Victoria and her administration. As well, British officials could yank ordinary Asante as they pleased for forced labor on construction projects, such as road works. And while they were at it, they wanted the Golden Stool, the embodiment of the Asante nation and its royal lineage. They assumed that confiscating the stool would take away a symbol that was useful for any lingering cultural revolt.

"Where is the Golden Stool?" Hodgson demanded of the rulers. "Why am I not sitting on the Golden Stool at this moment?" He assured them that the British government would rule over them "with the same firmness as if you had produced it."[18]

The Asante rulers swallowed this insulting treatment with stoic reserve and left quietly, but at a secret meeting later that night, they got a scathing lecture from the sixty-year-old Yaa Asantewaa, whose son had been an ally of Prempeh and had been exiled by the British. She wanted to know how these men could just sit there meekly and listen. "If you, the chiefs of Asante, are going to behave like cowards and not fight, you should exchange your loincloths for my undergarments." And to further make her point, she yanked a rifle out of the hands of a nearby chief and fired it into the ground.[19]

The men decided that evening to resist, and three days later, the "War of the Golden Stool" began. At first, the honor of being in charge and leading the war was given to the ruler of Kokofu, Asibe, but he was captured, bravely escaped, was captured again and then sent into exile. The rulers eventually chose Yaa Asantewaa as their new military leader, the first time a woman ever held the post.

The war has been characterized as the last gasp to fend off the British, but there were Asante who were loyal to the colonizers and fought on their side, along with Hausa soldiers. As glorious final showdowns go, however, the engagements speak to Asante ingenuity and valor. The conflict started with a boy leading British officers and their Hausa on a merry chase for the coveted stool (at one point, the officers ordered the Hausa to whip children to betray its whereabouts, with nothing useful learned). The climax of this episode, as you can probably guess, was an ambush. The Asante took potshots from their cover and wounded many enemy soldiers.

The British tried small sorties and attacks. The Asante proved they were a skillful match at guerrilla fighting. They cleverly cut the telegraph wires and sometimes used booby traps with trip wires rigged to guns. They punished the Hausa for aiding the British, torching one of their villages near the Kumasi fort. In fact, they soon had their enemy's fort surrounded, and the British were horrified to discover they had a siege on their hands, one that would last for months. Those within had to put up a listless defense while they slowly starved to death. Asante rulers who were hostages inside suggested a truce and peace negotiations, but the British rejected their terms and took advantage of the lull to sneak in a reinforcement column arriving with food and arms. Once they found out, the Asante beyond their walls naturally resumed the siege.

So, too, did ferocious battles beyond. In early June, the Asante fought British reinforcements from Nigeria, and the fighting was so intense, it literally destroyed the nearby tropical vegetation. The British were stunned to see their enemy shooting at them through holes in a thick fortification that extended for almost a quarter of a mile. With appalling casualties, the British still decided—incredibly—to launch a bayonet charge against the Asante position (with 100 Yoruba troops sacrificed to this suicidal maneuver). They were saved only because the Asante chose at that moment, like true guerrillas, to pack up and melt into the jungle.

Despite small victories like this, the Asante couldn't turn them into lasting gains, and it's been argued that their seemingly impregnable fortifications, as robust as they were, might have contributed to their undoing. When one fell, it demoralized those based at the others. Nor did the various district armies ever come together in a truly unified force. But we need to remember they faced an enemy with cannon and Maxim guns, one that kept replenishing its ranks with warriors from rival kingdoms, as well as Sikhs in the imperial army and men from distant England. The Asante fought with incredible valor.

As time passed, both sides must have felt desperate. We know for a fact the British did. One officer thought of the awful casualty toll and then hatched a daring change in tactics: a night raid on a stockade. His soldiers climbed over the top with an ease that astonished even them, and the British later heard a report that the setback so alarmed Yaa Asantewaa that she gathered her commanders in a hurry to figure out countermeasures.[20]

Independence for the Asante, however, was doomed. The "rebellion" was put down, its leaders deported into exile and their kingdom made an official colony in 1901. Yaa Asantewaa lived on for decades in exile in the Seychelles, finally dying at close to ninety years old in 1921. The British never did find the Golden Stool, but it says something about the spite of colonial officials that they kept looking for it until 1920.[21] Prempeh was allowed to come back to Kumase a few years later, and he managed to negotiate the return of the remains of those who died so far from home, among them Yaa Asantewaa. About two decades after her death, a thick, authorized *History of Ashanti* was developed but never published. It relied on oral traditions that naturally had their own political and possible gender biases, and it barely mentioned her.[22]

It's an unfortunate paradox that even though she's closer to our own time, we know less about her than we do of Njinga. We have no idea, for instance, how much she planned the war effort or if she was ever in the thick of the fighting. For that matter, we don't know if her role was mainly a symbolic one. And yet as our picture of the real woman has receded, her status as an icon has only grown. By 1960, there was a girls' school named after her in Ghana. By 1986, a community center in Maida Vale, London, renamed itself the Yaa Asantewaa Arts and Community Centre (today, it's known casually as the Yaa Centre). By 2000, the late Ghana historian Kwame Arhin eulogized her this way: "She shall for long be remembered as a personal symbol of Asante's final stand against British imperialism, and as proof that, for the Asante, gender was irrelevant to leadership."[23]

In that same year, however, opponents in Ghana's elections tried to capitalize on her memory, and politics even overshadowed a fire that gutted the small museum dedicated to her. Yet a steady tide of interest in her continues, especially from the United States. There have been websites, print portraits, pop music references, a documentary, and even a stage show. Professor Tom McCaskie of London's School of Oriental and African Studies has written on how those who adopt her as a heroine sometimes have little regard for the nuances of her culture, and he noted, "In private many Asante chiefs angrily mock Africans from the diaspora who think they have somehow returned home and been reintegrated because they wear cloth, speak greetings in Twi and buy Nkosuo stools." At the same time, "Young, urban and all too often unemployed inhabitants of Kumase take pride in Yaa Asantewaa and those like her, but only when more pressing matters allow them time to think about history or culture."[24]

Where does this leave us then? In the end, with the same potential for durability as any other cultural hero. Eyebrows might rise over how African Americans take to an Asante queen, but is this any more cultural appropriation than hip-hop finding new expression in The Gambia or Côte d'Ivoire? As for the arguable flaws in our warrior queens, well, both Jefferson and Churchill have had their halos dimmed by relentless scholarship. In time, the images of Njinga and Yaa Asantewaa may evolve into more realistic impressions, and given that Njinga's portrayal has been such a lurid caricature for centuries, it's hardly an outrage that the scales are tipped the other way in the popular imagination for a while.

There is one truth from our warrior queens that cannot be denied, and it's that African resistance often had a female face . . . and a female fist.

When the Spanish Armada loomed, Elizabeth I put on a silver breastplate and inspected the troops in Essex, giving a rousing speech, but this was a public relations exercise. She never wielded a sword in a crush of soldiers. Neither did Catherine the Great, who presided over wars with the Turks and the Persians and who carved up Poland. Compare that to African queens who were willing to lead by example, to raise the sword and fire the rifle. And while movies and novels might retrofit Elizabeth and Catherine as feminist heroines, when it comes down to it, we sympathize more with a leader who joins the battle and takes the personal risks rather than shouting orders while safely behind the barricades—or back home in the palace.

Of course, you didn't always have to be the queen to fight colonial invaders. There's the example of the so-called Dahomey Amazons, who have inspired writers like Zora Neale Hurston and the makers of *Black Panther*. These female warriors formed an elite unit for the kingdom of Dahomey (in what is now modern Benin). Skilled in archery, rifles, and blades, they were reportedly ferocious in combat, and we can't help but be fascinated by them.

Historians remind us, however, that in their society, men and women weren't considered "equals in any meaningful sense," and the women "were thought to become 'men' usually at the moment they disemboweled their first enemy."[25] In fact, they may have been conscripted in the first place because one of their original enemies, the Yoruba, outnumbered them ten to one.[26] But go online, and you'll find suggestions that the unit was started by Hangbe, a queen who lived around the turn of the seventeenth century and who was deposed as regent after perhaps as little as three months; one reporter who visited Benin insisted that "her legacy lived on through her mighty female soldiers."[27]

Only it may not have been her legacy at all. This isn't a case of male historians wanting to deprive a female accomplishment (there is evidence Hangbe did exist). It's just that there are practical dilemmas with attributing the Amazons to her. For one thing, the chronology doesn't fit, and the evidence seems to favor another scenario: that a king in the 1700s, Agaja, conquered the kingdom of Whydah and borrowed its concept of "royal wives as police." It's one of the reasons why their fighting unit were known among the people early on as the *Ahosi* (king's wives). Out of this practice evolved a palace guard of women, which became in time an elite fighting force.[28]

Things aren't even conclusive over Agaja, but the issue doesn't come down to king versus queen so much as *which* king. Nevertheless, by 1772, a British visitor to the palace in Dahomey's capital, Abomey, could notice, "In the guard house, were about forty women, armed with a musket and cutlass each; and twenty eunuchs, with bright iron rods in their hands."[29] Today, because the label "Amazons" carries the unnecessary freight of European connotations, the term *Mino*, meaning "our mothers" in the language of the Fon people of the region, is gaining more circulation.

It shouldn't have to be said, but in case it does, it takes little away from the rich legacy of the Ahosi or Mino to assign another origin for them. Far more interesting than whether it was a king or queen who founded their corps is the fact that women were also *generals* who often *commanded other women*. And the tales of their skills and conduct are certainly impressive.

One story—which can't be authenticated but bolsters their reputation—goes that in 1889, as tensions increased with the encroaching French, Dahomeans raided a colonial trading post run by a Senegalese worker. As historian Stanley Alpern tells it, a French official assured his appointee from Senegal he would be protected by the famous tricolor. "But the Dahomeans killed or wounded his whole staff and wounded and captured the Senegalese. 'So you like this French flag?' said the Dahomean war chief. '*Eh bien*, it will serve you.' He gave a signal to the Amazon, who then beheaded the Senegalese with one blow of her cutlass." The head was then wrapped in the flag and the victim's wife forced to carry it to another outpost.[30] In another anecdote, as the second and final war went badly for Dahomey, their female warriors seduced French officers, waited in bed for them to drift off, and then slit their throats.

However much or little basis in fact these stories have—and there's good reason to believe there is a lot—these women, to use the modern colloquialism, were badasses. The Amazons of Greece were mythical. The female warriors in Africa were real, and, better still for our modern sensibilities, they were patriots, defending their ancestral homeland.

Part II

COLORS

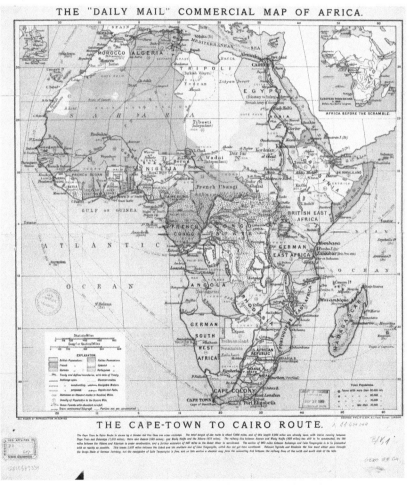

Africa as seen in 1898 by the *Daily Mail* newspaper, reflecting a greater precision in geographical details and knowledge of the interior. But it's a continent divided up and labeled according to European possession, and many of its highlights are the industrial innovations of the occupiers: steamer routes, telegraph lines, and railways.

8

The Activist

London in the 1700s: a metropolis teeming with bookshops and printers on Paternoster Row, anatomy schools in Covent Garden, and Smithfield butchers dumping their castoffs and rubbish on the piers by the Thames. There were theaters and coffeehouses. There were raucous shouts that called for gin and more genteel debate that could be heard in the quiet houses of Marylebone. London was where the French Huguenots built new lives in exile and where other Europeans would flee for refuge. Africans were here, too, with their Caribbean brothers and sisters, some slaves and some free, and of those free, many worked as servants for the well to do. In 1764, a letter to a prominent magazine estimated there were 20,000 Africans in London, but the number could be a severe exaggeration, as newspapers later put the figure much lower.[1]

Many of them lived as best as they could on their low wages, some forming small networks to socialize together when they had the chance, and they were expected—according to the unwritten codes of behavior of the day—to know their place and keep quiet. But in 1788, in an ordinary newspaper called *The Public Advertiser*, there was a scathing review of a pro-slavery book that included this mild threat, that "were I to enumerate even my own sufferings in the West Indies, which perhaps I may one day offer to the public, the disgusting catalogue would be almost too great for belief."

The next year, the writer did exactly that, with his book given the typically overlong Georgian title, *The Interesting Narrative of the Life of Olaudah Equiano, or Gustavus Vassa, the African, Written by Himself.*

The flip side to the ignorant refrain that "Africans sold themselves into slavery" is the important fact that Africans played a key role in abolition. This has been largely overlooked because the spotlight on the crusade usually goes to William Wilberforce, Granville Sharp, and Thomas Clarkson, British gentlemen one and all, of firm resolve and good conscience. And what they accomplished was truly remarkable. We can hardly conceive today just how monolithic and institutionalized the business of slavery was in their time. It was simply a fact of life, and to question it at all in the beginning was to be dismissed as a crank.

Unlike in the United States, the issue was never decided in the crucible of a bloody civil war, with a Lincoln using an executive order (the Emancipation Proclamation). In Britain, it was a tide washing against a rock. The activists hammered away for years, slowly changing minds and strategically working for the goal of ending the *trade* first, not slavery itself. The trade stopped with an act passed in Parliament in 1807. It would take another twenty-six years for a Slavery Abolition Act to stamp it out in the British Empire.

And what helped change minds were Africans speaking for themselves, using their own voices, asserting themselves *as* Africans.

Equiano's *Narrative* is one of the earliest memoirs in what became a genre that would eventually include Solomon Northup's *Twelve Years a Slave* and *Up from Slavery* by Frederick Douglass. But his book is unique in many respects. Millions of slaves would be robbed of their names and their history, but in this account, we're given a brief summary of life in Africa before bondage. Our hero tells us he was the son of an Igbo chief in what is now southern Nigeria, and he was given the name of Olaudah Equiano. While life in his village had its idyllic side, he doesn't hesitate to mention his people had their own slaves. Then, at around the time he was about eleven years old, before the ritual scarification that would have marked his forehead, he

Olaudah Equiano in a painting by the artist Daniel Orme used as the frontispiece for *The Interesting Narrative*.

was kidnapped along with his sister and ripped from the only home he'd ever known.

His book is often quoted because of the vivid portrait he drew of the slave's nightmarish ordeal: the "loathsomeness of the stench" below deck on the ship taking him away and how, when he refused to eat, one of the sailors tied his hands and feet "while the other flogged me severely." Through his eyes, we understand what it must have been like to be shocked at the sight of the ocean for the first time. Equiano was taken first to Barbados and then Virginia, which was then still under British rule. And he was forced to adopt a new name, Gustavus Vassa, which he used throughout his life. Equiano eventually had the chance to buy his own freedom and settled in England.

But his book is more than just a catalog of injustices he suffered. It's a rich chronicle of adventure. While still a slave during the Seven Years' War, he served the Royal Navy, and General James Wolfe—soon to be a national martyr in the Battle of the Plains of Abraham in Quebec—"saved me once a flogging for fighting with a young gentleman." At the siege of Louisburg, he "saw some of the ships set on fire by the shells from the batteries, and I believe two or three of them were quite burnt." At one point, he was shipwrecked in the Bahamas, and on other voyages, he traveled to Turkey, Greece, and Portugal. He also went with a former employer onboard the *Racehorse* for a unique expedition in 1773. It tried to find a passage to India via an approach to the North Pole. The thrills of the voyage were spotting whales and sampling the meat of polar bears; the lows were the teeth-chattering cold and the brink of death. "Our deplorable condition, which kept up the constant apprehension of our perishing in the ice, brought me gradually to think of eternity in such a manner as I never had done before."

He had a profound religious experience, converting to Christianity, and like the abolition crusaders he would later meet, his faith drove his social conscience. In 1774 and by now a free man in London, he tried to save a black cook from being kidnapped from a ship in harbor and taken away to the man's former master, a William Kirkpatrick, who usually lived in St. Kitts. "I proved the only friend he had, who attempted to regain him his liberty if possible, having known the want of liberty myself." Now consider these extraordinary lines: "My intention was then to apprehend Mr. Kirkpatrick, who was about setting off for Scotland . . . he, suspecting something of this kind, set a watch to look out." Here was an African in Georgian London— an ex-slave who by color and class could be subjected to regular, casual abuse—and he went to the trouble of obtaining a writ of habeas corpus and a bailiff to track down Kirkpatrick at his home near St. Paul's churchyard. He even whitened his face as a disguise to "stake out" the man's home.

Unfortunately, the story does not have a happy ending. Equiano spent a considerable sum on a lawyer to try to rescue his friend, but the man was still taken to St. Kitts, where he was "according to custom, staked to the ground with four pins through a cord, two on his wrists and two on his ankles, was cut and flogged most unmercifully, and afterwards loaded cruelly with irons about his neck." Equiano received two letters from him before the man died, still enslaved. The brave effort to save the cook remains significant for two reasons: one, it shows how Equiano acted on his own initiative, and, two, it brought him to the door of Granville Sharp.

This was a smart tactical move. Only two years before, Sharp had financially and publicly backed the defense of an escaped slave named James Stewart who had been snatched by thugs out of Covent Garden and kept in chains on a ship that was due to sail to the West Indies. Unlike the doomed cook, Stewart's acquaintances obtained a writ and got his case heard. In what was a groundbreaking precedent, the judge, Lord Mansfield, avoided the thornier issue of slavery's legal status and decreed in painfully opaque language that slaves couldn't be taken out of the country against their will. Historians think there's a good reason Mansfield was so cautious in his decisions—he had a family secret. Right in his home lived a mixed-race young woman named Dido, the product of his nephew in the Royal Navy and an African slave named Maria. Equiano couldn't save his friend, but he made a powerful ally in Granville Sharp.

Then in 1783, Equiano was reading a newspaper when he came upon a story about a court case involving a slave ship called the *Zong*. The *Zong* had sailed for Jamaica with more than 400 sick and terrified Africans packed into its hold. But the ship got lost and becalmed. Its novice captain, who was thoroughly incompetent, used to be a ship's doctor. Water supplies became dire. Each slave was insured as "cargo," and the captain knew if his cargo died while on board, the loss was the ship owners', but if "they were thrown alive into the sea, it would be the loss of the underwriters." Over the first mate's objection, 133 Africans were tossed to their deaths or forced to jump.[2]

The story Equiano read had to do with the insurance claim filed. Because the insurers refused to pay, the matter was being heard in court. He realized the lawyers and underwriters were haggling over a massacre.

Equiano was determined to act, and Granville Sharp recorded in his diary on March 19, 1783, "Gustavus Vassa Negro called on me with an account of 130 Negroes being thrown live into the sea, from on board an English Slave Ship."[3] Sharp came up with a clever stratagem, no doubt calculated to gain public sympathy rather than perhaps succeed in law. He would lobby for a charge of murder against the crew members and told the Admiralty he "had been earnestly solicited and called upon by a poor Negro for my assistance to avenge the blood of his murdered countrymen."[4]

The campaign failed, but we remember the Zong today as one of the ghastliest episodes demonstrating the evil of the trade, and Equiano was the first to be outraged, the first to recognize its power to shock those with a soul. He was coming up in the world, becoming a minor name in London as he wrote protest letters to newspapers and reviews of abolition books.

By then, many black Loyalists from the losing side of the American Revolution had turned up in London and had become the so-called "Black Poor." Their race made them stand out, and their wretchedness—freezing and starving to death on the cobbles around Covent Garden or in slum neighborhoods—made them a public embarrassment. What to do about them? Why not, some asked, resettle them on the very continent where they had been taken? One scheme backed by the government would take willing black individuals to Sierra Leone, which was smack in the middle of the slave trade routes.

Equiano tells us he was at first "very agreeably surprised" over the plan, but the organizers, which included Sharp, wanted him to go with the passengers to Africa. Equiano was willing to help but not this far, and he expressed his objections, which included "difficulties on the account of the slave dealers, as I would certainly oppose their traffic . . . by every means in my power." We don't know exactly how they convinced him in the end to go, though one compensatory plum had to be that he was made the government's commissary of provisions and stores for the mission, an office no black resident of Britain had ever held before.

But the Sierra Leone plan was a disaster from start to finish. It was hatched by a con man named Smeathman who promised to whisk the "troublesome blacks back to Africa," taking them to a warm paradise of gentle climate and easy farming. Smeathman had already been to Sierra Leone and knew better. He had been infected himself with various tropical diseases and was familiar with how the region experienced regular monsoons (he died before the transport ships ever sailed). Unfortunately, the Committee for the Black Poor fell for his pitch, and its members in turn won over the government. Hundreds of African and Caribbean men and women, trying to eke out an existence under the steel-gray clouds of England, were attracted to the idea of having their own farms and their own homes in what they considered an ancestral homeland. Sharp even kicked in a donation to buy gifts to help smooth relations with the local African rulers.[5]

Delays meant applicants were forced to wait while more than 200 passengers were stuck on ships in the Deptford harbor, enduring the cold winter of 1786. Equiano, in performance of his new duties, learned how many didn't have blankets and beds, decent clothing, wood for fires, and water. It was clear to him that money for supplies was being embezzled, but when he raised a fuss, he was kicked off both the mission and his ship at Plymouth, along with other passengers who were considered troublemakers. The story of the appalling conditions and appropriated funds hit the papers, and Equiano took the case of his dismissal to the government, winning £50 in compensation. He wrote of this triumph in his *Narrative*, "Certainly the sum is more than a free negro would have had in the western colonies!!!"

If he could have known all that befell the passengers in Sierra Leone, he might have thanked his stars again for how things turned out. The settlers faced punishing heat, brutal storms, near impene-trable jungles, and swarms of malarial mosquitoes. Their numbers were decimated by the conditions, and after a visiting navy marine fired a shot that set a hut on fire, they faced the wrath of the indig-enous Temne people, who wanted them gone in a hurry. After the few remaining survivors fled, some ended up working for nearby slave traders, while others tried to resettle elsewhere.[6]

The whole episode didn't seem to dampen Equiano's relent-less drive to do something meaningful, something powerful that could fight slavery and the injustices against his people. He was among a group of black abolitionists writing letters to newspapers and calling themselves the "Sons of Africa." In 1788, he drafted a petition that appealed to Queen Charlotte. It was a waste of time and energy to appeal to George III, given that he was known to be unsympathetic (and sometimes out of his mind with porphyry). Equiano may have also helped his friend and ally Ottobah Cugoano write a book titled *Thoughts and Sen-timents on the Evil and Wicked Traffic of the Slavery and Commerce of the Human Species*, which came out in 1787. Scholars have always been amazed and mildly befuddled that Cugoano, born a Fanti in what is today Ghana, devoted only a few pages to his personal experiences, so it's possible that Equiano weighed the reception of Cugoano's work and chose a different approach.

Today, we understand that we ought to let victims speak for themselves. We have initiatives like the Memory Project of the Holocaust Memorial Museum in Washington, D.C., for just such a purpose. Journalists track down persecuted Rohingya and Yezidi. And yet, as Adam Hochschild reminds us in *Bury the Chains*, the abolitionists had "strikingly little interest in the testimony of any of the thousands of former slaves in Britain, some with whip scars on their backs." These valuable witnesses didn't join the crusaders when they gave their speeches, nor did Sharp or Wilberforce bother to take down their accounts, even though the Africans were readily available.[7]

There were slavery advocates who even taunted abolitionists like Thomas Clarkson to offer a black witness to back up their argu-ments: "I defy him to produce a negro of character who would not *turn pale* in fabricating such assertions [emphasis in the original]."[8]

Equiano could have proved a devastating opponent in debate, and maybe he wondered himself why he wasn't given the opportunity; if so, this could have been further motivation for his *Narrative*.

His book was a best seller, and public hearings over the latest effort at an abolition bill helped sales. He traveled across England, making stops in Cambridge, Leeds, Manchester, Nottingham, and other towns, venturing over to Glasgow and getting a warm reception in Belfast. An author doing readings and promotion is part sage-on-cue and part performer, and Equiano knew how to write advertisements to bring in the curious, and he knew how to charm. As he toured, he became interested in the situation and aspirations of the working white poor. He also made connections with Irish radicals. His book, after all, had come out not only against the backdrop of the slave trade but as the French Revolution ignited new lines of thinking and terrified the rich and wealthy across Europe.

His interest almost landed him in serious trouble. The French thought their revolution exportable, and they promised military aid to any people willing to overthrow their government. At the time, William Pitt the Younger was prime minister, a port-guzzling, passionless man who barely knew other parts of England beyond his native Kent. Pitt had habeas corpus suspended and used a network of secret police to keep tabs on radicals and Irish activists. As mass arrests spread fear and sent the outspoken into hiding, Equiano was moved to write friends over "false reports" that he was a target.

He had checked with "gentlemen in power—my friends—and they went to the Privy Council and were told that there was not any messengers after me [*sic*]." He later contributed to a defense fund for radicals languishing in prison, at least one of whom was a friend.[9]

Equiano died three years later. His autobiography had come out in multiple editions, with one in New York, another in Dublin and a translation in Dutch. In one way, we can see him as the heir to both Apuleius and Augustine. In the *Narrative*, we see how slavery transformed him, set him on a path of both tragedy and adventure until he rescued himself and fixed his own destiny. At the same time, he was on a journey toward profound convictions in his adopted faith. But what he accomplished with the *Narrative* was also unique, a pioneering literary work.

With his natural eloquence and by sharing scenes of his life in Nigeria and his later adventures, he created a face above the chains. He demonstrated truths that we take as self-evident today but which had to be stubbornly and painfully earned in the Georgian era, including the revolutionary notion that his people had as much potential for the richness of life and for accomplishment as any European. When we truly appreciate that an African played a vital role in the rescue of a race and in changing the conscience of the world, we can dispense with the paltry label often assigned to his book of "slave narrative" and call it what it is: a milestone in world literature.

At this point, we need to confront an issue that involves how everyone chooses to see Equiano—because incredibly, there's a theory he may not have been African at all. The *Narrative* had faded into obscurity until it was rediscovered by scholars in the 1960s and became popular all over again. Then in the early 2000s, Professor Vincent Carretta of the University of Maryland argued that Equiano didn't come from a village in Nigeria but was, in fact, born in South Carolina. And he claimed that he found two persuasive documents to make his case.

As you might expect, this revision of heritage did not go down well with some academics. When Carretta defended his argument at a conference in Britain in 2003, discussions apparently got heated, and the well-known Nigerian American writer and professor Obioma Iwuanyanwu was one of those who voiced strong objections. By 2005, Carretta put his arguments into a new book, *Equiano the African: Biography of a Self-Made Man*, and the controversy made great feature bait for newspapers and possibly helped his book's sales. When the Associated Press contacted Iwuanyanwu, he replied in an e-mail, "His kind of scholarship, which invests excessive energy in pseudo-detective work, devotes too little time to critical analysis, disavows scholarly fellowship, and indulges in vast publicity gamesmanship."[10]

Carretta suggested in interviews that he never intended to disprove Equiano's origins. He was, he claimed, shocked by his own discoveries and understood the anger of his critics. After all, Equiano "is a Nigerian national hero. It would be the equivalent of saying George Washington was actually born in France."[11] But let's consider his evidence.

There are multiple issues, but Carretta's theory rests mainly on two documents. The first is a record of baptism from St. Margaret's Church, London, on February 9, 1759. Now Carretta doesn't only dispute where Equiano was born but *when*, arguing that he was born not in 1745 but in 1747 and brought to England younger than he claimed. While there are problems with chronology and sometimes accuracy in Equiano's book (as you might expect in an autobiography), Paul Lovejoy of York University in Toronto points out "it is another matter to assume that he consciously misled virtually everyone he knew about his place of birth. Why not assume that the age he remembered at the time of his enslavement is approximately correct, as are his recollections of key events during the Seven Years' War in 1756–1763, and by extension backward, to his purchase . . . in 1754?"

When it comes down to it, the baptism record works as evidence only if you rearrange the facts to your liking.

What about the second document? "No one had ever looked at his naval records," Carretta told the *Washington Post* in 2005. "He tells us the month and year and place he was baptized."[12] Then again, maybe he doesn't. In his book, Carretta insists that on the ship heading to the Arctic, the *Racehorse*, Equiano "was entered on the first muster list as 'Gustavus Weston' and on the second as 'Gustavus Feston.' . . . Even more familiar names were apt to be misspelled."[13] In an academic journal in 2003, his language was less sure, suggesting that "Weston and Feston are both plausible approximate phonetic spellings of Vassa." Which unfortunately doesn't settle things at all. Fordham professor John Bugg offered at least three other candidates these entries could have referred to.[14]

And as he and others point out, even if you want to accept that "Weston" was Vassa, there's a compellingly valid reason for a different date and a place of birth—South Carolina—to be entered on the record. "Those of African birth," counters Bugg, "were more likely to be suspected as slaves seeking escape through maritime service than those of American birth, who could more plausibly claim manumitted status. In fact, the fluidity of sailors' identities led the United States government in 1798 to demand that mariners hold 'Seaman's Protection Certificates,' which verified their nationalities. On ship board, Equiano may have listed an American birthplace to deflect those pursuing runaway slaves."[15] Carretta's reply to this is that two other black sailors aboard the *Racehorse* listed Africa as their places of birth. Bugg's rejoinder is that "Equiano was more adept at identity politics than the average sailor."[16]

Carretta's theory, despite remaining controversial among scholars, has managed to gain traction. The Oxford World's Classic 2018 edition for Equiano's *Narrative* presents his birthplace as an either/or proposition, West Africa or South Carolina. And Carretta has his defenders. In a review of his book in *The Guardian*, the accomplished Guyanese novelist and diplomat David Dabydeen wrote that Carretta "deserves applause, not resentment, for his indefatigable research." And he argued, "That the early chapters may have invented a life in Africa only adds to our appreciation of Equiano's imaginative depth and literary talent."[17]

Well, no, they wouldn't—they would make Equiano a liar. There are reasons why we have the separate categories of *fiction* and *nonfiction*, and authenticity was valued in Equiano's time just as it is today. When a William Langworthy recommended the book to a correspondent in Bath in 1793, he wrote that "the simplicity that runs through his narrative is singularly beautiful, and that beauty is heightened by the idea that it is *true*; this is all that I shall say about this book [emphasis in the original]."[18] If black lives are to matter, if African lives are to matter, then truth must matter.

Here are the modern stakes: In 2013, a British government document was leaked, and it was reported that Equiano and other social reformers were to be dropped from the National Curriculum in schools. There was widespread protest. Operation Black Vote in the U.K. sent a petition of more than 36,000 signatures, while American civil rights activist Jesse Jackson wrote a critical letter to the *Times* of London. It was only after these steps that Education Secretary Michael Gove did a reverse course, and Equiano stayed put. But what if the plan had gone through? It would be far easier for the politically callous to substitute a work of literature in the classroom, insisting one pseudo-novel is as good as the other, than an authoritative auto-biographical (and factual) account.

In the U.S., if one is to believe the Southern Poverty Law Center, the main problems for history teaching seem to be cultural amnesia, bad instruction, and outright distortion. The center came out with a study in early 2018 that indicted the American education system: "High school seniors struggle on even the most basic questions about American enslavement of Africans. Only eight percent of high school seniors surveyed can identify slavery as the central cause of the Civil War."[19]

Three months later, a news story reported that at a charter school in San Antonio, Texas, students were asked on a work-sheet titled "The Life of Slaves: A Balanced View [sic]" to list the positive and negative aspects of slavery. According to the textbook used by eighth graders for about decade at the school, *Prentice Hall Classics: A History of the United States*, "While there were cruel masters who maimed or even killed their slaves (although killing and maiming were against the law in every state), there were also kind and generous owners" and that many slaves "may not have even been terribly unhappy with their lot, for they knew no other."[20]

It's with these prevailing conditions that high school students and general readers on both sides of the Atlantic may reach for a paperback of *The Interesting Narrative*. Now Carretta concedes that Equiano's account is "remarkably" accurate over most details when these can be independently verified. So, as others have asked, why presume the man lied about his own birth?

If there is one constant to literary fantasists, it's that they lie as a pattern of behavior and that "lies and inventions pervade the entire book."[21] In the 1930s, the *Toronto Star* correspondent Pierre van Paassen claimed he spent time in Dachau—at a time when Dachau didn't exist. Dig deeper, and you discover his reportage on Africa is riddled with holes. Laurens van der Post, a guru figure of the 1970s, achieved fame by popularizing the Kalahari Bushmen, with whom he claimed he spent years of his life; a biographer figured out that he spent only a couple of weeks with them. He also lied extensively about his war record and other matters.

The Polish writer Ryszard Kapuściński has had a hugely destructive influence; in his books, he encouraged the myth that he was friends with Patrice Lumumba when he visited the Congo only after Lumumba was dead, and he invented absurd rituals and ridiculous titles that never existed at the court of Ethiopia's emperor Haile Selassie. His books are still popular. Worse, they're still cited and quoted by leading authors and academics.[22] Kapuściński is often defended as a talented storyteller whose work is meant to be taken as allegorical, but as writer Peter Englund—a self-confessed fan of his works—argued in the *Financial Times*, "the 'literary'" in 'literary reportage' doesn't absolve you of your duty to the facts."[23]

In the case of Equiano, there is doubt about the most essential element of his identity, despite his being vindicated on other details. And it gets worse because if the theory is true, it would mean a string of lies related to his account of being transported across the sea—one of the core aspects of what is rightly considered an African Holocaust. So it's understandable that some, especially in Nigeria, might find it repugnant to recast Olaudah Equiano as a brilliant rogue with good intentions but incomplete bona fides for all his suffering and that instead of relying on him as a witness, we should celebrate his creative mendacity. One might also ask why all the creative spinners of tall tales should be indulged for Africa when we set a higher bar for everywhere else.

As it happens, Equiano dealt with a "birther" controversy within his own lifetime. For a 1792 edition of *The Interesting Narrative*, he wrote a note to the reader on how "an invidious falsehood" had "appeared in the *Oracle* of the 25th and the *Star* of the 27th of April of 1792 with a view to hurt my character, and to discredit and to prevent the sale of my *Narrative*, asserting that I was born in the Danish island of Santa Cruz [St. Croix] in the West Indies." He appealed to friends "who knew me when I first arrived in England and could speak no language but that of Africa." He then offered several letters from associates who backed up his claim. One of them was from abolitionist James Ramsay, who in his reply put a rhetorical question: "Can any man that reads your Narrative believe that you are not a native of Africa?"

Long after Olaudah Equiano's death, a partially deaf history student explored the green commons of Oxford and the streets near Russell Square in London in the 1930s. And he planned to kick a myth about the end of slavery off its pedestal.

Eric Williams was from Trinidad and Tobago, islands which had been wrestled back and forth among the Spanish, French, British, and Dutch for centuries. Then the British showed up with an invasion fleet in 1797 that prompted the Spanish governor to clear his throat and wisely surrender. With immigrants from other parts of the Caribbean and white colonial settlers from different corners of Europe—as well as a small population of Africans brought over in the tail end of the slave trade—Trinidad's history is reflected in the rainbow tones of its people. Williams's own mother had French Creole roots. And when the British put their stamp on the islands, it meant Whitehall treated them no better than their African colonies. Only a single university scholarship was offered each year for the *entire population.*

Williams beat racism and poverty to get to Britain thanks to a £50 grant, and his friends in the capital were a mix of the best and the brightest thinkers from Africa and the Caribbean. We'll meet them in a later chapter, but right now we want to focus on him, toiling away on his doctoral thesis. Because he zeroed in on what he considered a glaring conceit. "The view was that a band of humanitarians—the Saints, they had been nicknamed—had got together to abolish slavery," recalled Williams, "and had after many years succeeded in arousing the conscience of the British people against man's greatest inhumanity to man." But despite all the popular academic backing, "that view could claim no support from the historical records."[24] The issue was not whether these men had tried but whether they really won their fight. His thesis would evolve into the landmark book *Capitalism and Slavery*, published in 1944.

Williams tunneled through the dusty files of the Public Record Office in London, papers at the British Museum, even custom receipts and stock ledgers. Free of any romantic illusions, he pointed out how the abolitionists were not radicals but reactionaries at heart, especially when it came to labor and the economy: "Wilberforce was familiar with all that went on in the hold of a slave ship but ignored what went on in the bottom of a mine shaft."[25] And, as he reminded his reader, the Saints cared at the beginning of their movement solely about ending the slave *trade*, content to leave emancipation for a distant day.

To be clear, Williams gave the abolitionists proper credit for their lofty aims, but he also cited their occasional narrow vision and hypocrisies. For instance, it never seemed to occur to them that freed slaves might want or feel entitled to the land they worked on in Antigua or Barbados. His most crucial argument was that economics played a far bigger role in ending slavery than altruism. Forget the sentimentality of a noble social movement. As early manufacturing evolved in Britain, those with vested interests were more inclined to be receptive to abolitionist appeals. Moreover, the very capital built from slavery and the resulting division of markets—sugar, tobacco, ginger from the Caribbean, iron works and textiles from England—sealed the doom of this evil institution.

"The commercial capitalism of the 18th century," wrote Williams, "developed the wealth of Europe by means of slavery and monopoly. But in so doing, it helped to create the industrial capitalism of the 19th century, which turned round and destroyed the power of commercial capitalism, slavery and all its works."[26]

Here was a scholar from the Caribbean—a descendant of people transported against their will in ships from Africa—offering a bold new interpretation of how African slavery ended. And this was in 1944, a time when Africa was *still* carved up by the colonial powers of Britain, France, Belgium, and Portugal.

When his book came out, it was controversial. With surgical analysis, Williams dismissed the cozy, warm narrative that white Western culture relied on to let itself off the hook: good men had stepped forward to act. Well, yes, they did, argued Williams, but market forces accomplished far more. And he was downright caustic over how other historians romanticized the abolition movement, even calling out Reginald Coupland (an Oxford don known as a cheerleader for the British Empire and its civilizing mission) for "this deplorable tendency."[27]

Williams went on to become the first prime minister of an independent Trinidad and Tobago, but his ideas went out of fashion for a while. Some modern scholars have been quick to dismiss his work, yet in 2020, Sally-Anne Huxtable, the head curator of Britain's National Trust, rendered a different verdict: "Although historians have interrogated almost every aspect of Williams's thesis, it remains the foundational text on the economic history of Caribbean slavery and its abolition."[28] And it's telling that new books on economics and slavery keep rolling off the presses each year. Greg Grandin, author of *The Empire of Necessity: Slavery, Freedom and Deception in the New World*, notes, "Each generation . . . seems condemned to have to prove the obvious anew: Slavery created the modern world, and the modern world's divisions (both abstract and concrete) are the product of slavery."[29]

Williams proved it first. Durham University's Richard Huzzey has summarized his legacy well, noting "his work has defined all later examinations, and focused attention on the way economic ideas and morality co-exist in society. As much as people have disagreed with his conclusions, he asked new questions that historians are still trying to answer."[30] That is about the best posterity a historian can ask for.

Olaudah Equiano lost his native home and his culture years before he began his activism. But what of African slaves who never left the continent?

One of the standard legends around the world is the tale of the fallen prince. Somehow, he loses his status and must regain it through heroic deeds. If he doesn't get back all that he lost, there's at least a symbolic or psychological accomplishment. Africa had such a prince, a real one. Now consider the other familiar tale of the noble "common man" hero who fights against impossible odds. And who's the most famous underdog of ancient Rome, the hero who still inspires us today? The answer, of course, is Spartacus. Books, political organizations, movies, even television series still bear his name. Spartacus, we know, was a real human being, and though the sources are sketchy on his origins in Thrace, we know he really did lead a slave rebellion.

Well, Africa had its own Spartacus who was a fallen prince. While his influence wouldn't be as great as the gladiator of legend, his example alters the way we think of African resistance to slavery. It should also adjust our view on Britain's changing role in Africa *and*, interestingly, African attitudes to Islam.

In 1807, slavery was extinguished for good, at least as far as British law was concerned, but the British themselves still often treated ex-slaves as a problem for disposal instead of victims of human rights abuse. And Sierra Leone, made a British colony a year later, proved the perfect dumping ground to settle Yoruba and Igbo people captured from what is modern Nigeria. They could also resettle free black Nova Scotians, who had already been betrayed by the lack of land and representation promised to them when they served in the Revolutionary War. The British cared little for the fact that there were indigenous peoples already in Sierra Leone, such as the Temne, who didn't like their territory being encroached on—they simply used their military might to push the Temne back and extort a deal for the real estate. The British were often background players to our story here, but they would play a crucial role in its final act. For the most part, this is a narrative of *African* resistance to *African* slavery.

Its leader was a man named Bilali, and he was born to the king of the Soso people in Kukuna at some date after the turn of the nineteenth century. What affected his destiny was his mother's status because she was a slave. It could be no accident that he was named after Bilal, one of the Prophet Muhammad's most trusted followers, his first *muezzin*, caller to prayer, and a former slave himself (incidentally, this Bilal also had African roots, as his mother was Ethiopian). Bilali's father made sure he received a proper education, that he learned the Koran, and that he was trained in how to be a warrior. And yet the old man never formally acknowledged him as his son, only declaring that Bilali gain his freedom after the king's death. No surprise, Bilali's troubles began the moment his father passed. One after another, the king's successors refused outright to accept he was free.

This stance made the Soso kings into obvious hypocrites. Islam tolerated slavery just as Christianity did, but Islam had an arguably more enlightened view. Muhammad had repeated the prohibition in his final sermon that masters could not mistreat slaves, and, unlike Christianity, a Muslim could not buy slaves on his own and rip them away from their family—it was either take all the family members or none. But most pertinent of all to Bilali's case, Muslims, by definition, could *not* be slaves, and a child born of a Muslim and a slave was supposed to be free.

Bilali chose to be a *murtah*, a runaway in the Soso language, and he didn't do it alone, taking a group of family members and supporters with him to a nearby village.[31] But he was still in relative danger, and by 1838, he found a new home in the Tonko region among the Limba people, who were sympathetic given their ongoing battles with slave raiders. He was free. He was among allies. His story might have ended there, but here's where it becomes extraordinary. Still practicing Islam and recalling his military training, he founded a sanctuary for escaped slaves called Laminyah. Satellite colonies for more escapees sprung up around it. As far as the neighboring chiefs and slaveholders were concerned, this, of course, would not do. As with the Spartacus of old, it's one thing to lose a single runner, it's another thing to tolerate an escapee who challenges the entire system.

But woe to those who took Bilali on, and there were many. The Soso, Malinke, and Temne tried to stamp out his movement. They were beaten back. Other ethnicities became embroiled: the Bena, Sumbuya, Samu, Magbema, Kawlah, and others.[32] For more than thirty years, Bilali and his followers held their own against different armies uniting to put him down. Bilali, wrote Edward Wilmot Blyden in 1872, "has succeeded in forming a powerful party, and in rousing amongst a large portion of the servile population, not only a devotion to the idea of liberty at any price, but a strong attachment to himself and a hatred for all who hold slaves; and he is by no means scrupulous as to the price he pays for their support."[33] At one point, the king of Moriah recruited and armed slaves to attack Laminyah—a risky gambit no matter how you look at it.

And still Bilali kept winning engagements. Blyden, acting as an intermediary on behalf of the British colonial government in Freetown, noted the strength of the rebellion and described how it took more of a toll on the Soso than it seemed to have on the resistance; "men thirty years of age . . . had not known one day of peace" and were haunted by the "constant fear of invasion." Bilali had outlasted one of his father's successors, and the next king, Almany Mumini, "is now reduced to extreme poverty. His resources have all been exhausted in the war, and he is the unfortunate victim of his warriors. Whenever these robbers return from an unsuccessful marauding excursion, they seize upon everything in the shape of food and clothing that they can lay their hands upon and appropriate it."[34]

The king told Blyden he was now old and tired of the war, and he hoped the British colonial government might intervene on the behalf of the Soso and their allies. For the British, this conflict was a headache. It didn't *want* to be involved in this struggle, not when the public conscience had shifted back home. Backing slaveholders? It was now unthinkable. But nothing focuses self-interest like a balance sheet, and war was bad for commerce, especially in the normally prosperous market town of Kambia. Traders had petitioned the Freetown government.

"It occurs to me that this matter can be settled only by a concession on both sides," wrote Blyden. "The Soso and Temne chiefs must abate their impetuous contempt of Bilali on account of his servile origin, and agree to make no demands upon him in the future for the surrender of their fugitive slaves; and he should agree to encourage no more surrender of their fugitive slaves; and he should agree to encourage no more slaves to resort to his asylum."[35] This was exactly what was done. The British, fortunately, listened to Blyden and negotiated a deal. The exhausted chiefs finally learned to leave Bilali and his supporters alone in return for an important concession: Bilali's influence would now be limited.

But there can be no doubt who the real winner was because over three decades, the various powers were worn down through attrition, failing to grasp why this Spartacus was so resilient and his cause so effective. Bilali could always afford to be patient, and in the end, he was rewarded for it. Unlike the original rebel against Rome, he did not have to die on the battlefield for his dream of freedom.

9

Two Economists and a Diplomat

In the 1830s when Bilali was seeking refuge with the Limba people, another native of Sierra Leone was growing up who would later champion a different way to emancipate Africans. And in doing so, he came up with new perspectives on Africa that no one had bothered to consider before.

James Beale Horton was born in the village of Gloucester near Freetown in 1835, the son of a Nigerian Igbo man liberated from a slave ship. Thanks to missionary philanthropy, he was able to get an education. Around that time, the British War Ministry decided to train Africans to replace British medical officers in West Africa, mainly because the white English, Scots, and Welsh couldn't handle the harsh conditions (not to mention the malaria), nor were they likely to be fluent in the native languages. With his sharp mind, young James was one of only three students from his college to be selected to go to the University of London's King's College. So off went the impressionable twenty-year-old, trading the dirt paths and stunning ocean views of his hometown in 1855 for the hard pavement of the Strand.

Horton was lucky in his education. He had the chance to roam the wards of King's College Hospital, which was considered state of the art for the era. Then he learned that even after four years of hard work, a medical student wouldn't be entitled to an MD (the common practice in England then was to study for six). But in Edinburgh, he could get one, so he finished his fourth year there. The city had developed an impressive reputation as one of the best places in the world to study medicine. At some point as he rushed to classes or wandered near Surgeon's Hall or the city's Grassmarket, he decided to give himself a new name, "Africanus." And on his books and pamphlets, he would style himself as "James Africanus Horton."

Unfortunately, there's little information outside his writings that can bring him to life in terms of his personality. We know what he looked like from a photo of him as a proud young officer, his hand posed gallantly on the hilt of his sword for the camera. We know he married twice, his first bride dying tragically young and his second wife the descendant of a black settler family from Nova Scotia. We know that after leaving the British army, he moved successfully into commercial banking and even the gold mining business. We can infer he was good at his job, as he returned to Sierra Leone after university and was made assistant surgeon to the British forces in the Gold Coast, what today is Ghana, and he eventually reached the rank of surgeon major. And we know he served during the Asante rebellions when the legendary Yaa Asantewaa was still a young woman. His work took him all over West Africa, where treating and dealing with the local populations must have made a deep impression on him.

As early as 1861, he lobbied the War Office to set up a small school in Sierra Leone where Africans could get their first medical training before taking further studies, just as he had done over in Britain. And while the government was at it, it should put an African instead of a European in charge of the college because, after all, a native individual would feel more personally invested and relate to the students better. In fact, he nominated himself for the job. What's refreshing is that the governor of the Gold Coast endorsed the idea of giving Africans a chance; what doesn't surprise is that the harrumphing clerks and overseers in London stuck his proposal in a file cabinet and didn't give it a second thought.[1]

Their reasons went beyond simple racism, although there was that, too. The British had built the greatest empire in history, but there had never been a grand vision or consistent policy behind its steady acquisitions. As a result, there was always a lot of schizophrenic second-guessing back in Whitehall, and by the time Horton wrote to the secretary of war, the government was poring over dire reports of fierce Asante warriors. It considered quitting West Africa altogether. In the end, it didn't, which meant white British doctors would still have jobs. And soldiers and doctors alike got to stay in Africa as the revolutionary usage of quinine proved its worth. It made little sense then from the colonizers' point of view to sink time, money, and effort into the education of Africans, people whom the British thought of mostly as a convenient labor force for the empire.[2]

Horton, however, wasn't about to let the matter go, and education became a major theme for him. Having written several dry medical texts, he now put pen to paper to fight European racist attitudes toward the African. But *how* he did it is what's so special. Horton looked at Africa in terms of economics.

No one up to that point had given the continent much serious thought along those lines. Of course, the explorers and military adventurers who sailed over had dreamed of gold and profits and wonderful markets, but they didn't apply economic *theory* to the continent, and neither had those who followed. As Craufurd Goodwin of Duke University put it, "The white men who came to British West Africa did little to stimulate local economic enquiry. A few newspapers, dominated by emigrant Britons, applied classical market theory to local situations and described home country practices and institutions, but there was little strength to sustain this beginning. . . . Economic enquiry was viewed mainly as the application of a few moral principles or laws to domestic conditions."[3]

In prose that's sometimes casual, other times bitterly scolding, Horton took his reader on a journey through the West African region to debunk white supremacist myths and to explore the potential. He noted how there was untapped wealth in Africa's agricultural resources while at the same time "the trading propensity is most extensively developed among every tribe." He quoted a report from the colonial administration in The Gambia that complimented Africans for being frugal. "If Adam

Smith's theory is pronounced orthodox, that it is to the principle of parsimony we owe our capital, and again to capital we owe our comforts and enjoyment, we certainly have this desideratum in the African, who is for the most part a parsimonious citizen, ambitious to rise in the world, and consequently to save and amass."[4]

This was solid, proper observation that any racially enlightened white economist could have made—if only one were available. But Horton took it further by suggesting the colonial administration should thoroughly educate itself on each colony's "revenues and expenses, its commerce and agriculture," as well as the national character of the locals, so that it could step in when necessary. What sounds like common sense to us was a highly innovative attitude for the time.[5] In 1868, Horton's best-known and most important work came out, *West African Countries and Peoples, British and Native: A Vindication of the African Race.*

In the book, he envisioned Africans taking part in their governments and African states trying different political forms to eventually find what worked. He also developed a novel argument against domestic slavery. Rather than raise the familiar moral objections, he underlined the waste of lost potential and how the enslaved couldn't contribute to an economy: in the Gold Coast, "a few of the slaves work for three or four hours of the day and sleep away the rest of it. They are fed by their masters, who give them a piece of . . . fish in the morning and evening. They possess no energy; there is no life in anything they do; no intellectual vigor; no effort such as springs from the rights, duties, responsibilities, and cares of property."[6]

This is also a devastating argument against racism. Perpetual bigotry simply makes no economic sense and is downright destructive. In western Africa, he wrote, "there are no prizes held out to ambition; in all well-constituted societies for the progressive development of a community there must be a wholesome stimulus to the aspirants." Given the arrogance and the spirit of oppression on the part of the privileged class, Horton warned British governors that they should remember there has to be "motive to industry; and that when a people is kept under mental depression and dejection, indolence, poverty, and stupidity are the inseparable concomitants."[7]

Yet he was harshly critical of the indigenous African institution of leadership by a council of elders, which to his mind "produces a most depressing and decrepit effect on the rising generation of that race. They possess a secret, freemason-like influence which checks any exuberance of spirit and of enterprise in their young, and thus produces an injurious result on the race." He thought their influence stifled investment and entrepreneurship. "This influence is certainly dying away, but much still remains which tells against the body politic of the nation."[8] Whether elders were a reactionary force or not, he was dead wrong on its dying influence. Such traditional councils would prove remarkably resilient across Africa despite the upheavals of colonialism.

Horton, of course, didn't think in terms of the broader diaspora of African peoples. He focused on the western region alone, and given the patriotism of a colonial, he can easily be charged with gross naïveté over the motivations behind British imperial expansion. He was trained as a doctor, a profession the English long treated as *middle class*, and working as a surgeon and tropical disease specialist in the field—sometimes in the middle of battlefields—it was natural for him to turn to London as the beacon of culture and opportunity.

He never doubted that his fellow West Africans needed to be "civilized" and that the British were the ones who should do the job. Colonial subjects, therefore, shouldn't demand independence before they gained all the practical advantages and the benefits Mother Empire had to offer. In fact, he believed that when it came to the more defiant or "barbarous" tribes, "to bring up the governed rapidly to advancement in industrial pursuits, education, and general social condition, *a little despotism is absolutely necessary* [emphasis in the original]."[9]

After close to two centuries, a modern reader may find it hard to forgive such a paternalistic attitude, especially when it's advocated by one who must have known intimately how a little despotism can turn into a lot. But Horton never forgot who he was or where he came from. To rename himself "Africanus" was a public statement, and it declared that he was perfectly comfortable with his origins. If he couldn't make the intellectual leap of treating disparate cultures as equals, we can laud his imagination for treating Europe and Africa as equal models worthy of economic discussion. He gave careful thought to the reforms he suggested, which carried the natural implication that colonial Africans deserved to be treated as loyal, contributing subjects of empire as any citizen in Canada or Australia.

Horton gained considerable respect and attention within his own lifetime for his work, earning several stories in the *African Times*, the newspaper of the African Aid Society published in London. Its editor once gushed in 1869 that "every educated African ought to consider it a matter of duty to possess" one of Horton's books. The *Freetown Express* was naturally proud of its hometown son and later "greeted his death [in 1883] as a national disaster." He was still having an impact on other writers and thinkers well into the twentieth century.[10]

Modern scholars consider him ahead of his time, and he certainly was when certain passages in his work anticipate the soaring eloquence of civil rights leaders almost a hundred years later. "It must be remembered," he wrote near the end of *West African Countries*, when he called on Africans to take up the challenge of development, "that there is no royal road to greatness—that it cannot be said that this or that man possesses a heaven-born reputation, greatness or talent. It must be bought by severe perseverance, by an undaunted courage and industry, by real hard work and application, with a love for the undertaking we have in hand, by an uncompromising, disinterested adhesion to the truth."[11]

The first years of the twentieth century: horse traffic is giving way to trams, trains, and bicycles. The internet of the Victorian age, the telegraph, still dominates, linking Britain to the jewel in its crown, India, and even spanning oceans, putting California in touch with Washington, D.C. The overwhelming majority of black people in the U.S. still live in southern states of the union. In Africa, the Zulu Wars are over, the Boers are defeated, Egypt is a pawn for Britain, and after horrific massacres, France has its boot firmly on Algeria. What we think of today as former British colonies, what became Tanzania and Botswana, "belong" around this time to Germany before they'll be confiscated by the Great Powers after the debacle of World War I. But Germans have already gotten away with genocide, that of the Herrero people in the land that's now called Namibia.

And yet for a while, a citizen of an African nation, Liberia, is one of the most respected authors and thinkers in the world. He is awarded a Coronation Medal by Britain's Edward VII. The British government grants him a modest pension "in recognition of his literary services," and he can stroll into one of the most hallowed reserves of male privilege of the time, the London gentlemen's club, in this case the Athenaeum Club. The sultan of the Ottoman Empire, the bey of Tunis, and the French government all give him prestigious honors.

This man was Edward Wilmot Blyden, and he practically invented pan-Africanism. If his name is obscure to you today, it's probably because those who followed absorbed his ideas, incorporating them into their own, and they eclipsed him as they grew in stature in the troubled times to come.

Blyden was born in 1832 in St. Thomas in the Danish West Indies in what would eventually become the U.S. Virgin Islands. Looking for a career, he tried Venezuela and found only menial jobs, then tried America but got turned down from entering various religious colleges. After seven months, he decided to emigrate to Liberia. Unfortunately, at eighteen years old, he was trained only to be a tailor, and there was no market for him—the wealthy elite of Monrovia preferred to get their clothes from Paris and New York. Nevertheless, it was here where he would put down roots and build a distinguished career, one well beyond his youthful expectations. To understand Blyden, we need to know a little about the early and misunderstood history of Liberia.

Liberia takes its name from the Latin word *liber*, for "free man," while Monrovia was named after James Monroe, serving as U.S. president at the time and a backer of the colonization scheme (he helped raise the modest $100,000 that fueled the initial efforts). As with the Black Poor headed from London to

Sierra Leone, the idea of black people going back to Africa from the U.S. didn't start from any altruistic motive. Men who are venerated today as great heroic figures in American history— Daniel Webster, Francis Scott Key (who wrote the lyrics to "The Star Spangled Banner"), Henry Clay—all got together in 1816 in Washington because they wanted to get rid of a "useless and pernicious" population. Oh, and perhaps, as an afterthought, save Africa from "barbarism." These were the roots of the American Colonization Society. And when they first floated their scheme in a Philadelphia church of shipping free individuals off to Africa, most of the 3,000 African Americans at the meeting practically shook the walls with a loud "no" for the vote.[12]

But there was a handful—eighty-two individuals—who *did* want to go. They must have bitterly regretted it later. First, they were betrayed by the white organizers of the expedition, who decided they would take charge of both the trip and the settlement, only they didn't feel like sharing that conclusion with the passengers until they were on board. After enduring storms, the settlers discovered there was no drinkable local water, and supplies needed to be brought in. The indigenous people were justifiably suspicious and resentful of these strangers who turned up without an invitation. And on top of all that, a large portion of the settlers collapsed in the delirium and agony of malaria, many dying, as their new home was surrounded by swamps. The British stationed in nearby Sierra Leone were no help, abandoning the settlers to their fate. And if that wasn't enough, then came the rainy season.

And yet some survived. More colonists kept arriving, pushing into a land that already had indigenous peoples. After the Songhay Empire had fallen and the glory of Timbuktu faded, its citizens had headed south. It's believed that many of those who spoke the Mel and Kwa languages also migrated from the lands of the Niger Delta stretching all the way into what's now Sierra Leone. Far from being "uncivilized," they were brilliant at agriculture, taming the jungle to sow the stubborn earth for rice and cassava, the starchy tuber. The Kru people claimed the sea and its fishing stocks, and in time, they would be recruited by Europeans as reliable sailors.[13]

The saga of Liberia makes for fascinating if often grim reading. Contrary to the myth of a nation founded by African Americans, whites kept a tight, jealous grip on power for years over the early settlements under the auspices of the American Colonization Society. Disease and shortened life spans for settlers were the norm for a long time. There were clashes with the native peoples, who were no match for muskets. Inevitably, as word circulated back to the U.S. of how terrible conditions were, the ACS didn't hesitate to brazenly lie or blame the problems on the settlers.

The populace of Monrovia in the 1830s, writes historian James Ciment, gave it "an exoticism few American settlements could match, as half-naked Dey tribesmen, robed Mandingo traders, suited mulatto merchants, leather-aproned black American workers, and the occasional uniformed white U.S. Navy man mingled on the grid of broad grassy streets."[14] As they built their new society into a commonwealth, the settlers often adopted children from the native peoples and reportedly treated them as little better than slaves. This went on despite the efforts by emigrant evangelicals to stamp out slavery among the Africans. So, by the time that Edward Blyden sailed over, mixed-race residents—"mulattoes" was the term still often used—had risen to the top of the social and economic hierarchy, dominating the merchant class, the local administration, and the educational facilities of the tiny settlement (the population was still well under 10,000 around that time). Some darker-skinned black individuals, however, were able to advance.

"Society in Liberia is as good as can be reasonably expected," wrote one condescending white observer, "indeed, we found a degree of refinement and taste for which we were not prepared. The people desire to live in comfortable and pretty houses, the ladies and beaux dress in the fashion, and an aristocracy of means and education is already set up. The people generally dress above their means, extravagantly so, and the quantity of kid gloves and umbrellas displayed on all occasions does not promise well for a nation whose hope rests on hard and well developed muscles."[15]

As time went on, those at the top chafed at white men from across the Atlantic calling the shots on their government, even as the American Colonization Society took in less revenues to support Liberia and Congress lost interest in the great experiment. Likening themselves to America's founding fathers taxed without representation and kept from holding high office, Liberia's elite leaders issued a "Declaration of Rights" in late July 1847. They wanted to be independent. Interestingly, less affluent Liberians opposed the idea of the country going it alone but were outvoted.

A Liberian, as the Declaration of Rights defined it, was "originally an inhabitant of the United States of America." When the leaders of the new country drafted their constitution, they included an article that piously discussed "the improvement of the native tribes" while at the same time excluding thousands of Africans from the same rights of citizenship. Into this muddled landscape of color, class, and heritage and only three years after Liberia's independence wandered Edward Wilmot Blyden.

With his remarkable intellect and a gift for languages, he soon developed a career as a teacher and a respected professor. He was also in demand as a journalist and a useful diplomatic operative for the British in their colonies, which is how he got involved over the revolt by the African "Spartacus," Bilali, in Sierra Leone. Early in Blyden's new life in Liberia, he saw his adopted country as a black haven and wrote passionately for it in pamphlets and articles for religious quarterly magazines. Africa, he felt, was where black people could earn the esteem of the world by creating new, modern nations on the continent that showcased Western civilization and values, and as a young man, he literally thought God was on their side.

But if God was, young Blyden was convinced mixed-race people weren't. They frequently showed open contempt toward their darker-skinned brothers and sisters, and Blyden, in turn, developed a seething bigotry toward them. The irony was that they awarded him many of his greatest career opportunities.[16]

He had a vision of "civilized" African states, but this alone shouldn't earn our attention—after all, he was backing a colonizing power, tiny as it was, and early in his career, he applauded a military attack on the Kru. In 1853, he got his own chance to fight native Africans; he was conscripted into the militia to battle the

Vai people. The Vai had earned the respect of the settlers, with even Liberia's president at the time, Stephen Benson, suggesting they were intellectually superior to many of the Americans who came over. Blyden recognized for himself how advanced they were, amazed at the sophisticated fortifications in the Vai capital and their impressive literary heritage.

He made trips deep into the countryside, learning more about another people, the Boporu, and came away with a generous reappraisal, unique for its time: "Interior people have the advantage over us in never having been under foreign masters, in never having imbibed a sense of inferiority or a feeling of self-depreciation," he wrote in 1871. "They had never had to look up to white men for anything, so as to form in their minds comparisons between themselves and others disparaging to themselves. They are entirely free from the mental and moral trammels which the touch of the Caucasian has imposed upon us."[17]

Away from settlers, white colonial powers, and foreign influence, Blyden saw practical communal living. He saw attentive, responsible governorship. He walked clean pathways that served as streets. And he found these long before white European ethnographers came along and sang their praises. Impose American and European civilization on *these* people? Instead of fighting them or making incursions on their territory, he thought, the settlers should be collaborating with them. When he took over as president of Liberia College in 1881, he wrote, "We must not suppose that the Anglo-Saxon methods are final. . . . We must study our brethren in the interior who knows more than we do the laws of growth for the race."[18]

His passion through the decades was the campaign to bring more immigrants from the United States to Liberia, but it's a controversial legacy. Never graduating from his ingrained contempt toward mixed-race people, he was relentless in trying to bar them from coming over. Meanwhile, the ebb and flow of new arrivals always depended on the changing politics and the attitudes of black Americans, over which he had no control. And with a spite that must have been unattractive to his contemporaries, he enjoyed when discrimination made black lives more miserable, such as the Supreme Court throwing out the Civil

Rights Act of 1875, which he presumed only helped his cause and would drive more settlers across the sea to Liberia. It didn't work out that way.

He moved into politics and diplomacy, traveling widely in the 1860s and 1870s, making trips to London, where he rubbed shoulders with and got to know the likes of Gladstone, Herbert Spencer, and scholars in Islamic and Arabic Studies. Writing often for magazines about Christianity and Islam as they related to black people, he became a popular speaker on the lecture circuit and racked up a collection of honorary degrees. He learned Hebrew and took a trip to the Middle East, advocating strongly for the creation of Israel as a secular state. It was in the final two decades of the nineteenth century that he was at the height of his intellectual powers and literary influence.

He also held views that modern readers will surely find troubling. Consider this jarring passage from one of his books, which argues that, with the slave trade, "Africa has never lost the better classes of her people. As a rule, those who were exported—nearly all the forty millions who have been brought away—belonged to the servile and criminal classes. Only here and there, by the accidents of war or the misfortunes of politics was a leading African brought away."[19]

His masterwork was his book called *Christianity, Islam and the Negro Race*, a collection of essays that rely heavily on the articles he published in British and American periodicals. The heart of the book—and what gained it the most attention around the world—was its comparative analysis between Christianity and Islam in Africa. African Muslims, he argued, "quietly disseminate" their faith, often on trading expeditions, far less obtrusively than Christians, and in terms of politics, Africans had been left to their own devices. "Christianity, on the other hand, came to the Negro as a slave, or at least as a subject race in a foreign land. Along with the Christian teaching, he and his children received lessons of their utter and permanent inferiority and subordination to their instructors, to whom they stood in the relation of chattels."[20]

He pointed out how "the painting and sculpture of Europe, as instruments of education, have been worse than failures"—their depictions of Jesus, apostles, prophets, saints, and God himself as white serving only to alienate blacks. Islam, for the most part, didn't have this problem. It's important to note that it's a myth that Muhammad can't be visually depicted, and in fact, there's nothing in the Koran to ban the practice; you can easily find Ottoman, Persian, and Mongol paintings of scenes from his life, including his birth and his fighting at the Battle of Badr. But it's true that visual depiction of Islamic prophets has often been avoided, particularly in Africa. Blyden suggested that in this absence, the Muslim "sees God in the great men of his country." He also argued—as we discussed earlier—"The slave who becomes a Muhammadan is free" and noted the "distinguished" Africans in Islamic history.[21]

In his analysis of Christianity, Blyden virtually ignored the unique case of Ethiopia, which certainly didn't acquire its dominant faith through racist European missionaries. This is peculiar because Blyden extolled Ethiopia as a "cradle of civilization" only pages later, and he had to have possessed some knowledge of its early history. As well, his historical analysis of Islam is a flattering one that ignores certain realities: yes, it's true that in many cases, Muslim proselytizers and Islamists didn't exert political pressure on Africans, but then, how could they? This fact had less to do with ambition than with distance, geographic barriers, and the balances of military technology for the age.

There was much in Blyden's work that was exciting and fresh for readers. Why was Jesus, a Jew in the Middle East, supposed to be accepted as *white* by blacks in America and Africa? Why should they accept a faith at all that denigrated them when there was a compelling alternative that ignored color? What was the relationship that Africans had with Islam? Because Europeans and Americans reflexively saw Muslims—as many still do—as only Arabs, Persians, and Turks, ignoring the obvious fact that millions of Africans, as well as Malaysians, Indonesians, Pakistanis, Bosnians, Kurds, and others, also turn toward Mecca. They had never given much consideration to the African context of the faith.

What also leaps out for the modern reader is how Blyden debated in his pages some issues we still grapple with today. For instance, quoting a writer's charge in Britain's *Quarterly Review* that Islam stifled reforms and that it "consecrated polygamy," he suggested this kind of rhetorical flourish could be used against Christianity as well: "Christianity has consecrated drunkenness . . . it has consecrated war."[22] The social ills identified by critics in Muslim lands, he argued, were due more to human passions than to Islamic teaching.

Gifted as he was and having met with indigenous peoples in the hinterland of his country, he might have gone further. Ultimately, he still viewed the Middle East faiths through the prism of race and the individual. He forgot the virtues of African ways that he learned about miles away from Monrovia. In *Destiny Disrupted*, Tamrin Ansary makes the crucial point that a core element of Islam is what he calls the "social project," the righteous community. In Christianity, too, are doctrines of communalism, of forgiveness and redemption that appeal to Africans, but they are present as well in the indigenous religious and social practices. Blyden, however, was a man of his time who was repelled by and bigoted toward the "pagan" religions of Africa, seeing them mainly in opposition to Christianity and Islam.

Despite his book's deficiencies—both those of his era and ones we see with hindsight—it was a brilliant success when it came out. In England, it was a shock to reviewers that such an erudite volume could be authored by a black man, and they harped on the fact. One critic even cast aspersions on whether he was a "full-blooded" black man at all. In the second edition, Blyden made sure to include a photo of himself as the frontispiece. The reviewer for the *Times* of London gushed that the book "may yet prove the greatest contribution of the age on the gigantic subject of Christian missions." Off in New York, *The Nation* was impressed with the essays in the book that demonstrated the author's "minute investigation [and] surprising mental alertness." Newspapers and journals in Istanbul, Damascus, and Beirut also gave the book high praise, and they enjoyed how Blyden's advocacy for Islam outraged certain British critics.[23]

Blyden relished the attention. He could be a difficult man to deal with, and even his most thorough and insightful biographer, Hollis Lynch, conceded he could sometimes show great charm yet was "a brilliant but self-righteous, intolerant, dilettantish, suspicious and paranoid individual."[24] Naturally bookish and introspective, he couldn't connect intellectually with his mixed-race wife from an upscale family or with his children (one daughter was mentally retarded). "I live among an unsympathetic people—and an unsympathetic family," he once complained in a letter back in 1875. "My wife seems entirely unimprovable. . . . I am persecuted *outside*, but more inside. Uncongenial, incompatible, unsympathetic, my wife makes the burden of my life sore and heavy."

His solution was to have an affair with an African American woman he deemed in private to be of "first-class intellect."[25] Perpetually ill, he endured Liberia's sweltering humidity and dodged or survived its diseases like malaria. Yet he had a stubborn physical constitution that helped him live into his seventies.

In 1884, an extraordinary meeting of thirteen European countries and the Ottoman Empire took place in Berlin. The delegates were there to figure out how to carve up the spoils of an entire continent. It didn't matter at all what Africa's inhabitants wanted. In fact, the diplomats at the German chancellor's palace on the Wilhelmstrasse drew up borders and demarcations for a lot of territory no European had ever seen. Out of the Congo Conference, which lasted more than three months until late February 1885, was born the Scramble for Africa and its associated miseries of rape, genocide, plunder, and even environmental devastation. The Europeans did nothing to hide their plan for the greatest landgrab in history, and the progress of their negotiations was widely reported in the newspapers.

Largely forgotten is how the United States reacted. The administration of President Chester Arthur didn't like being left out of these talks, especially when lucrative trade was to be had in the Congo, but more interesting was how a concern was worded in a report by Arthur's secretary of state, Frederick Frelinghuysen, and submitted to Congress. Arthur's government, invoking the example of Liberia and trotting out the Monroe Doctrine, "hopes to see an agreement reached by the conference which shall fix the formalities necessary to show that foreign occupation is established with the consent of the natives and to remove questions of title from dispute."[26]

This was a lot of smoke, and the European powers would get their imperial shares whether America disapproved or not. What matters is that an educated man like Blyden who followed current events had to know what was going on. He was perfectly aware of the Belgian atrocities in the Congo but chose to ignore them. In fact, he had developed a close friendship with a shipping magnate getting rich from investments in the Belgian Congo, and he had even sat down to lunch with King Leopold. Taking Europeans at their word over their good intentions, he never did revise his volume to reflect the horrific information coming out of central Africa, the accounts of forced labor for the rubber trade, the rapes and mutilations on a terrifying scale. And by 1900, he even suggested it was necessary for great masses of Africans to be "taken into exile for discipline and training under a more advanced race" and that it naturally followed that after a period of separation, certain chosen descendants should return so they could guide Africans "into the path of civilization."[27]

This amounts to a warped rationale justifying slavery. Looking back on his progression of thought, it shouldn't be such a surprise given how he once presumed that "criminals" had been loaded onto the slave ships crossing the Atlantic. But it's also a complete reversal of his views on Christianity's influence, and it undermines his unique evaluation of the good of African cultures. What happened to the prospect of collaborating with Africans who knew more about "the laws of growth for the race"?

Instead, an African American journalist, lawyer, and historian named George Washington Williams would be one of the first to expose the truth about the Congo Free State. Leopold worked his charm on Williams for an interview in 1899, but unlike Blyden, the black reporter went to see conditions for himself the next year. For his "Open Letter" to Leopold in 1890, which was widely circulated to newspapers, Williams wrote, "Against the deceit, fraud, robberies, arson, murder, slave-raiding, and general policy of cruelty of your Majesty's Government to the natives, stands their record of unexampled patience, long-suffering and forgiving spirit, which put the boasted civilization and professed religion of your Majesty's Government to the blush."[28]

Williams tore away the veil. But one of the lesser-known stories about the nightmare of King Leopold's Congo is that once again, as they did with fighting slavery, Africans played an important role in efforts to reveal their plight. A Western-educated Congolese evangelist named Frank Teva Clark was a key source for Roger Casement, the British consul who had shown up on a fact-finding mission. He supplied crucial evidence about sexual assaults and mutilations, which made for grisly reading in the consul's *Congo Report*. Scholar Derrick M. Nault considers the report "a landmark in human rights history," in part because it included victim testimonies, allowing the Congolese to speak for themselves and tell what was happening to them.[29]

"We had to go further and further into the forest to find the rubber vines," a Congolese man named Moyo explained to Casement, "to go without food, and our women had to give up cultivating the fields and gardens. Then we starved. Wild beasts—leopards—killed some of us when we were working away in the forest, and others got lost or died from exposure and starvation, and we begged the white man to leave us alone, saying that we could get no more rubber, but the white men and their soldiers said: 'Go! You are only beasts yourselves.' . . . When we failed and our rubber was short, the soldiers came to our towns and killed us. Many were shot, some had their ears cut off; others were tied up with ropes around their necks and bodies and taken away."[30]

At his advanced age by then, Blyden could hardly be expected to go investigate conditions for himself, but he had the voice and the fame to at least highlight the work of Williams, Casement, and others and champion the cause. This was a unique missed opportunity, and it's tragic that he of all people didn't help bring the situation to light.

Despite this major failing, when we assess Blyden's life and his ideas, it's clear he left behind a strong foundation of Pan-African thought for others. We can also think of Blyden as an important bridge in the development of African ideas. Olaudah Equiano and James Horton presumed just as whites did that the African needed the import of civilization. Blyden frequently did as well, but he was one of the first to publicly assert that Africans had civilizations of their own and contributions to make.

He had a profound influence on others, among them Casely Hayford, a journalist and writer from the Gold Coast, who wrote an introduction for a short book of Blyden's speeches, believing them worthy of "the earnest attention and study of all Africans."[31] Hayford expanded on Blyden's themes of African identity, lobbying hard for land rights and political reforms. Blyden also influenced one of Nigeria's publishers, John Payne Jackson. There were enough rising African intellectuals and activists by 1885 that the exasperated Portuguese governor of Angola dismissed them as "useless visionaries and detestable clerks."[32]

Just as Blyden inspired Casely Hayford, so Hayford would pass the torch and lend support and funds for the start-up of a newspaper in London, the *African Times and the Orient Review.* Its founder was a remarkably successful Egyptian Sudanese actor, Dusé Mohamed Ali, who gave up the footlights for Pan-Africanism. Moved to dispel all the White Man's Burden talk about Egypt, Ali wrote a history, *In the Land of the Pharaohs,* that became the toast of Pan-Africanists and sympathetic liberals. Just one problem: he blatantly plagiarized work by other scholars. The stain on his reputation was remarkably short lived, and he blithely carried on and founded his newspaper.

His first edition included a recruiting ad for contributors, the "young and budding Wilmot Blydens, Frederick Douglasses and Paul Laurence Dunbars."[33] Among those who answered the call was a stocky, impoverished young Jamaican student. Ali didn't put him in front of a typewriter but instead gave him a job first as a messenger and handyman. This was Marcus Garvey. In the paper's office in Fleet Street, Garvey would take volumes of Edward Blyden down from the shelves to give them a thorough read. Deeply inspired, he memorized some of the most rousing inspirational sections. Colin Grant, Garvey's best biographer, observed that in reading Blyden, Garvey "felt himself let into an amazing secret; given a privileged glimpse back to the dawn of Ethiopia, through amber dusk and pastoral twilight, when Africa was the 'gateway of all the loftiest and noblest traditions of the human race.'"[34]

When Marcus Garvey was a nine-year-old boy in Jamaica's St. Ann's Bay, Ethiopia gave the world a vivid reminder of its cultural power. There's talk and there's action, and nothing speaks to the notion that black people can do whatever whites can like a massive African army defeating a European one with ruthless efficiency. It had never happened before. Yes, the Zulus beat the British at Islandwana, but in the end, the Union Jack still flew over South Africa. When the Ethiopians purged the Italian forces from their mountains and valleys of the Tigray region, one single battle decided an entire war and sent a shock wave through Europe. Because of Adwa, Ethiopia had a direct impact on the course of European politics and finance and made a lasting impression on African American and Caribbean self-esteem for more than a century.

It happened like this. Britain was spending a small fortune on maintaining the port of Massawa and, just to keep it out of the hands of the French, decided to sell it behind Ethiopia's back to Italy. Italian settlers soon moved into the new colony of Eritrea and pushed ever southward, running into Ethiopians and creating tensions, much the same way as when white settlers (and often incompetent would-be farmers) imposed themselves on the land of the Choctaw and Creek Indians in the American West. The Italians also tried a little divide and conquer with the various political factions of Ethiopia. They even sold rifles and ammunition to the future emperor Menelik II. The Italians presumed this bought his allegiance—they were disastrously wrong.

Then they tried a charm offensive to lure Ethiopia into becoming a protectorate, drafting a treaty which turned out to have different phrasing in the Italian draft than the one written in Amharic. This cheap trick failed as well. At each stage, despite repeated setbacks and all signs to the contrary, the Italians clung to their perception that they were dealing with a bunch of unsophisticated savages. But Emperor Menelik, though never formally educated, was a shrewd leader who appreciated technological innovations (he was delighted by the lightbulb) and understood the drives and vanities of powerful men. There is a wonderful anecdote that he once laid out a feast for nobles in his home region of Shewa, and knowing how they looked down on blacksmiths, he deliberately left out knives from the meal settings just to teach them a lesson.[35] Menelik knew how to marshal his forces. As well, his right-hand man, Makonnen Walda-Mikael, could have taught a master class in realpolitik.

When Italy declared war, its general in charge of the invasion, Oreste Baratieri, promised to bring Menelik back to Rome in a cage. Only Baratieri and his Italians didn't have a clue what they were in for. First, in daring to invade the northern highlands of Ethiopia, they were stepping into the natural fortress of the defender. Second, Menelik showed up with an army of an estimated 100,000 men, outnumbering the Italians likely five to one. At the decisive Battle of Adwa on March 1, 1896, the Italian tactic of firing in volleys couldn't overwhelm the sheer scale of warriors rushing toward them with buffalo-hide shields and spears. Some officers saw the thundering charge of the Ethiopian cavalry and promptly pointed their revolvers at their own heads.[36] Tales of legendary heroism in battle would be passed down among the Ethiopians, especially about Makonnen Walda-Mikael and Empress Taitu, who each rallied troops in the thick of the fighting.

When it was over, thousands lay dead, but there was a hideous reckoning for the captured. Many wounded Italians were stripped naked and castrated. Every native soldier fighting for Italy, the *askaris*, had his right hand and left foot chopped off. Menelik strongly disapproved of these mutilations, but his orders against them were ignored. Italy's humiliation was front-page news around the world, and only two weeks later, the government of Francesco Crispi fell. Rome's elite had never imagined its army could lose, and having emptied its treasury, it had to pay 10 million lire for the maintenance of prisoners of war, who sailed home about a year later.

How could this happen, an army of African warriors defeating an army of "civilized" Europeans? For some whites, the best answer was to rewrite the facts and pretend it didn't. They preferred to blame Italy's general, Baratieri, as a bumbling incompetent rather than give credit to Menelik, Makonnen, and the Ethiopians' brilliant general, Ras Alula, for strategic and tactical brilliance. Anyone on the battlefield would have seen that the Ethiopians had wisely invested in guns and weapons manufactured in Europe, which put the opposing armies on a relatively equal footing. Race, however, was the issue that haunted these critics. So there circulated the idea—dwelling on the Semitic roots of the Tigrayan and Amhara people, whose nobles had dominated the historical narrative thus far—that the Ethiopians *weren't really black.*

They must be something else, a kind of Caucasian. In the aftermath of the battle, for instance, American newspapers such as the *Atlanta Constitution* and the *New York World* printed stories with this claim. The *World* informed its readers that "the majority of the inhabitants of Abyssinia are of the Caucasian race," and they were "well formed and handsome."[37]

It hardly mattered that the idea had no legitimacy among Ethiopians themselves. While it was true that ethnic rivalries could be fierce, Menelik himself, when trying to enlist the help of Muslim Dervishes for the battle, had told them, "I am black, and you are black. Let us unite to hunt our common enemy."[38] The theory persisted well into the twentieth century and was even adopted by a few well-intentioned liberals who were on Ethiopia's side when Mussolini threatened invasion. "The Ethiopians are a superior race of men," declared Nikola Tesla in an article in July of 1936. "I am almost tempted to say a race of supermen, chiefly Caucasian whites like ourselves."[39]

Black residents of North America and the Caribbean, of course, naturally never bought into this fiction and celebrated the battle as a triumph for the extended family. For African Americans, as scholar Sylvia Jacobs suggested, Adwa may have become "a kind of folk story that was well known to all blacks and passed among individuals within the black community in beauty shops and barber shops, at church congregations,

Le Petit Journal

Le Petit Journal
CHAQUE JOUR 5 CENTIMES
Le Supplément illustré
CHAQUE SEMAINE 5 CENTIMES

SUPPLÉMENT ILLUSTRÉ
Huit pages : CINQ centimes

ABONNEMENTS

SEINE ET SEINE-ET-OISE   3 fr.   3 fr. 50
DÉPARTEMENTS   2 fr.   4 fr.
ÉTRANGER   2 50   5 fr.

Neuvième année

DIMANCHE 28 AOUT 1898

Numéro 406

Le Négus Ménélik à la bataille d'Adoua

TABLEAU DE M. Paul BUFFET (SALON DE 1898)

Menelik at the Battle of Adwa, as depicted in a popular magazine of the era.

at various meetings and gatherings, and in family circles."[40] For Ethiopians, the battle remains a source of national pride, its name a touchstone for them as much as "Bunker Hill" is for Americans or "Agincourt" is to the English. It's celebrated each year in the country and by Ethiopians in Minneapolis and Washington, Toronto and London. And yet the Battle of Adwa did more than keep Ethiopia independent; once again, Africa changed the world.

The Adwa defeat was a crushing blow to Rome's prestige, and it can be argued that Italy's military reputation never really recovered. The coup de grâce was Italy's dithering neutrality at the beginning of World War I and then its poor performance for the rest of the conflict, which alienated the Great Powers. Italy, saddled afterward with debt, lobbied for African colonies as spoils of war at Versailles in 1919, and when European and American representatives refused to meet its demands, Prime Minister Vittorio Orlando broke down and wept before walking out on the talks. Adwa, therefore, started the decline of a nation and reshuffled the power hierarchy in Europe.

It has other significance. After Adwa, Great Britain, France, and Italy set up proper diplomatic legations in Ethiopia, and while they engaged in yet more skullduggery to try to carve up the nation, Menelik—slowly dying of syphilis—still managed to foil their efforts. With Menelik's passing, the country went through political upheavals, but its more seasoned court officials kept European intriguers at bay. And what no doubt began as a cynical charade at diplomacy turned within a few short years into genuine and formal deference. Russia had a presence in Addis Ababa. The Americans established their own legation. The Swedes took an interest in the country and in time formed close ties with Ethiopia's people. The Japanese studied Ethiopia's trade markets and crops.

We're taught that the Non-Aligned Movement began in the 1950s, and it did, with Yugoslavia's Tito, Egypt's Gamal Nasser, and India's Jawaharlal Nehru each fending off the bullying and coaxing of the United States and the Soviet Union. But if we are open minded, we can trace the roots of the nonalignment strategy further back to Menelik.

Consider that after Adwa, for the very first time, a sovereign African nation was pursued by multiple powers for the sake of investment, alliance, and trade. It had to be taken seriously. British and French diplomats would pay their calls on Menelik, who listened politely and then asked them quite pointed questions. Menelik's later successor, Tafari Makonnen—the son of his old ally Makonnen Walda-Mikael and who became the emperor, Haile Selassie—proved even more skillful at steering an independent course, keeping Ethiopia out of the fray of international rivalries in the 1920s.

It may be difficult at first to buy this notion because we're used to the Cold War narrative that viewed the world in binary terms, Americans and the Soviets. But more than 100 years ago, there were more than two superpowers: Great Britain, France, tsarist Russia, and Germany; the United States didn't really emerge as a force to be reckoned with by European standards until the Great War. Ethiopia, then as now, was in a strategic spot (especially important for the British and French). It sat below Egypt and Sudan and close to the Red Sea and Gulf of Aden. At the time when the cannon smoke of Adwa finally dissipated, the Suez Canal was little more than a couple of decades old. Not even the ailing and slowly shrinking Ottoman Empire had avoided seeking out firm alliances, forever needing to guard itself against Russian incursion and looking for help from the British and French through the second half of the nineteenth century. In sharp contrast, an "uncivilized" African nation defied the arm-twisting of superpowers.

In the post–World War II landscape, Britain and France still spoke to newly independent nations as if they were children in desperate need of Western civics lessons. But here was Ethiopia, which could boast a long tradition of dealing with the West as diplomatic equals. It had set up embassies and consulates abroad. Its delegates attended the Paris peace talks after World War I, turning heads as they wore their traditional toga-like *shammas*. Ethiopia sent bright young men (alas, no women) to the best universities across Europe and the U.S. in the 1920s on the understanding that they would become educated technocrats, helping to guide their country into the modern age.

None of this could have happened without the Battle of Adwa. As a result, other nations had to think of Africa in different ways and adjust their strategic views.

As Ethiopia took its first tentative steps into the modern world, one of its people was coming up with new ways to do it—and became a bold innovator in what's now called development economics. His name was Gebrehiwot Baykedagn, and his brief life had episodes of incredible adventure.

Born in the district of Adwa ten years before the famous battle, he lost his father to the Battle of Gallabat, where Emperor Yohannes IV died as well fighting the forces of the Sudanese in 1889. When Menelik took over and secured his reign, young Gebrehiwot was among the refugees who streamed into the Italian colony of Eritrea and wound up at a Swedish missionary school near Massawa. He was a bright child and an astonishingly daring one. At the age of seven, he talked his way onto a German ship to look around the vessel with friends. After it cast off, the captain was surprised to find little Gebrehiwot still aboard. Even more amazing, after the ship made port, the captain didn't just abandon his stowaway but placed him with a rich Austrian family. Gebrehiwot thrived in his new, strange surroundings, learning German and eventually studying medicine in Berlin.[41]

He later returned to his native land and learned Amharic, and with a little networking help, he managed to get employment as a private secretary and interpreter for the emperor. But these were the years when Menelik's health was deteriorating, and Gebrehiwot found himself caught up in court intrigue over the old lion's condition and on the wrong side of Empress Taitu. He wisely took himself out of the game, relocating to British Sudan in 1909. Coming home to Massawa after a couple of years, he fell seriously ill, but he was strong enough during his recovery in the hospital to write *Emperor Menelik and Ethiopia*. In his book, he sounded a warning note on the stark differences between the development of his own country and its neighbors, where "a desert can be transformed into a Garden of Eden when ruled by such intelligent people like the British. All around us colonies are marching ahead undeterred by any obstacles."[42]

Scholar Bahru Zewde suggests he was writing mainly for an audience of one, the incoming new emperor, Iyasu.[43] But Iyasu would prove to be a political disaster. An impulsive, arrogant young man who reveled in cruelty (he once slaughtered 300 people in camps in the Danakil region apparently for his own amusement), he alienated the regional princes and Ethiopian Orthodox clergy, neglecting his duties as ruler for long periods, and he alarmed French, British, and Italian diplomats by giving supplies to Somali colonial rebels. It was only a matter of time before powerful Ethiopian aristocrats kicked him out, and he was replaced by someone who could truly appreciate Gebrehiwot's ideas, Tafari Makonnen, better known in the West as Haile Selassie.

He recognized Gebrehiwot's administrative talent and gave him various posts, including the job of inspector of the Addis Ababa–Djibouti Railway and chief of commerce in the town of Diredawa. He's been celebrated in part for his wit, and there's a great story about a time when he thought he was dying. Go get the priests, he asked someone. But word came back that the Ethiopian Orthodox priests wouldn't come (maybe because Gebrehiwot was known as a Protestant or, worse, an atheist), although the Catholic priests were willing to make the trip. Gebrehiwot shot back, "If the butchers disagree, does that I mean I am not to get my meat? Bring the Catholics!"[44]

Unfortunately, Gebrehiwot was another victim of the worldwide flu pandemic and died in 1919, but Haile Selassie backed the effort to have his writings collected for one of the first offerings of the Berhanena Selam Press in 1924.[45] As a result, Gebrehiwot's work has lived on in new reprintings and translations. Years before his most important book found a translator in English, Gebrehiwot was considered one of the most learned Africans of the early twentieth century in Japan.[46]

For our purposes, it's this second book that's worth a closer look, which was published in English in the 1990s as *The State and Economy of Early 20th Century Ethiopia*. He brought his magnificently agile mind to a part of Africa that, on the one hand, was an agrarian society that still had feudal lords and *rases*, the equivalent of dukes, as well as its own insular system of slavery.

On the other hand, the country had a railway line built largely by the French that connected it to Djibouti. Gebrehiwot studied the nation's crops and its markets, its social structure, and its history, and he came up with what one modern reviewer once suggested could have been written for contemporary Ethiopia.

We can see from the very first chapter why Gebrehiwot speaks to current generations. "When the property and knowledge of people increases, the government's policy and wealth parameters also increase. As people's knowledge and wealth develop, the government's instrument of policy implementation acquires additional strength."[47] In this slim volume, which hopscotches from tariff discussions to labor theory and even includes an explanation of banking systems, Gebrehiwot brought a refreshingly original perspective to his country's economics—and one that could be used to analyze other African regions.

For instance, he recognized a glaring problem with the country's trade. Even if ordinary people made a profit from the sale of raw exports, that would give them only a temporary benefit. Crops would exhaust their fertility, and in time, people had to abandon the land. In the same vein, foreign traders with access to modern banking infrastructure profited on interest while local merchants—demoralized by poor returns—migrated to other locales where they could do better. The poor "will not care whether their government is strong or perishes."[48] Today, we recognize this argument as *unequal exchange*, one of the key rationales behind not only fair trade but what's come to be known as ethical trade. He stated bluntly that in his age, the leaders in technology and knowledge were Europeans and Americans, and he made a crucial point that leaps off the page to shake anyone contemplating Africa's current dilemmas: "It is said that we Ethiopians have independence. The true meaning of independence is not only a people with their own government. It means people who are self-sufficient."[49] A warning for independent Africa written before 1919 . . . !

Instead of wearing and using products that were the result of native craftsmanship handed down through the generations, argued Gebrehiwot, Ethiopians wore imported cloth and ate with utensils manufactured abroad; they bought foreign-made furniture and even tilled their fields with plowshares that were imported. And we can easily recognize today's examples of his warning over the import of Western consumer culture leading to African ruin. "Although roads are constructed in all directions and railways are built, people will continue to borrow more, if through time, knowledge does not expand simultaneously. And in order to pay the principal and the interest on this borrowed money, [the peasants] will have to labor more for the benefit of the foreigners. Since they do not have the capacity to pay off the loan, it will have to be repaid from the resources of the land."[50]

As his English translator Tenkir Bonger has noted, he was even prescient over what we now call "green issues." The land, Gebrehiwot reminds us, doesn't give but *loans* us its benefits, and if the debt isn't repaid, "she pesters the borrowers like the banks." Listing off Ethiopia's exports such as coffee, ivory, and livestock, he warns, "Even if we do not feel the consequences now, the Ethiopian people will do when there is scarcity of land due to population pressure."[51]

He detailed in his book the crushing tax burden faced by ordinary peasants, and he pointed a finger at the *shiftas*, the bandits, who were a plague across the land. "More than the impediment to progress posed by soil and the climate, there is another one which is an even greater obstacle, and that is banditry and war."[52] He wanted taxes on speculators, the breakup of monopolies, schools that employed not only European teachers but Ethiopian ones as well to instill the national culture—reforms that would create, as one scholar put it, "what we would call today a productive middle class."[53]

The book has its flaws. As Tenkir Bonger points out, Gebrehiwot was probably familiar with the theories and writings of European economists and thinkers, but he scrimps on references. While acknowledging the destructive effects of ethnic rivalry, he wasn't above making a few ignorant comments on ethnicities, and his vision of history is a markedly biased one that is irrelevant to his economic arguments. And yet tucked in with the observations of this autodidact is some astonishingly visionary thinking. Gebrehiwot Baykedagn speaks to our concerns over the development of Africa more than a century after he wrote his manuscript.

He has been bashed as Eurocentric, but this is unfair. He had the experiences of life and an education in Europe, which he turned into penetrating insights into how foreign capital took advantage of Africa. Such criticism of him amounts to "blaming the messenger," and being a *modernist* does not equal being Eurocentric. Marxists have also wanted to claim Gebrehiwot Baykedagn as one of their own, but he was no Marxist—far from it. He sought reform, not revolution, and while he understood class struggles, he appreciated market forces even more.

If anything, he was a pioneer of that most elusive concept that's still being hotly debated and has yet to find persuasive expression—ethical capitalism.

10

Words, Bards, and "Tribes"

In chapter 1, we explored the heritage of Egyptian writing and efforts to revive the Nubian language. A common assumption in the West is that African cultures south of the Maghreb were mostly oral ones, without a written tradition. Not true, and you'll recall we already touched on certain forms of early "proto-writing." You can add to those a couple more examples. In Mali, the Bamana women make a mud-dyed cloth called *bogolanfini*, and their "geometric designs and patterns have specific names and convey different levels of meanings," while chiefs and warriors of the Limba people of Sierra Leone stamp intricate symbols on a traditional red gown.[1]

The Sabaeans of southern Arabia bequeathed their written language to the Ethiopians, who transformed it over time into ancient Ge'ez, and Ge'ez gradually gave way to written Amharic. The Christian Nubians of medieval Sudan used their own written script from the 700s to the thirteenth century CE before Islamic influence and the use of Arabic took over. In fact, the first use of written Arabic in Africa can be traced as early as the first millennium in Mali. For centuries, Arabic writing proved its great versatility and usefulness for those who spoke Fula, Hausa, and Swahili.

Some written languages in western and southern Africa developed later, such as the Vai script of Liberia in 1832 or 1833, while a couple of written scripts, such as those of the Kpelle and Loma peoples, were developed in the 1930s. Because Vai men wound up working as laborers and bearers for European colonizers, their written language spread to such spots as Cameroon and the Congo. And experts have found several examples where African monarchs and important leaders were inspired by European languages and chose to invent new ones for their own people. But as it turns out, even our presumption that "Africans had no writing" sometimes received a little help from those with an ax to grind.

In 1917, a British artillery officer in Cameroon, L. W. G. Malcolm, learned about the unique written script used by the Bagam people, which had characters that represented not only syllables but sometimes whole words. The script was based on the systems of signs developed by Sultan Ibrahim Njoya, the king of the nearby Bamum people. The Bagam occasionally used the Bamum script when they needed to, even though the characters originated from a clearly different system. And here is where the story gets interesting. Malcolm wrote about all this in an article for the *Journal of the African Society*, and he bothered to include reproductions of the script characters. His article made it into print in 1920—the script characters did not.

The editor, Sir Harry Johnston, claimed it was too expensive to put them in. But it turns out Johnston held a deep contempt for African invented languages. He had written off the Vai script as "clumsy adaptations" of Roman letters or of European signs. And for Malcom's article, he undermined it by slapping in a prefatory note that blamed his budget for not publishing the characters, adding, "It is quite sufficient to say that they are, most of them, imitations or perversions of Roman capitals or else of the trade marks stenciled on the goods of European traders. . . . [They are] copied from the white man's symbols."

The trouble is that after that, no one else saw the Bagam characters or had a copy of the script to judge for themselves. Johnston died in 1927, Malcolm in 1946. Scholars knew the script existed but had nothing to work with. Through the 1950s and right into the 1980s, the historians and academics commented and made guesses on the "lost script of the Bagam." It was only when an American doctoral student played detective in the 1990s that there was a breakthrough. The student—and later professor—Konrad Tuchscherer chose to follow Malcolm instead of the script. And sure enough, after digging through the archives of Bristol Museum and then turning to Cambridge, his clever method paid off. Tuchscherer found a copy of the characters appended to an unpublished thesis by Malcolm written in 1922.[2]

What does it say, if anything, about West African peoples for developing written languages so "late" if we measure them by our Western timetable? But are they late at all? Maybe instead of dismissing these cultures for being "behind," we should congratulate them for their ingenuity and sidestepping the complete adoption of colonial imports. Some of these languages are still used in limited form today. Africanus Horton argued in 1865 that "the African, in common with the most enlightened people, may be animated with feelings of philosophical speculations; and this is proved in the existence of a written language amongst them, designed entirely by themselves."[3]

African innovation in language certainly didn't stop in the 1930s. One day in 1944, a businessman from Guinea named Souleymane Kanté—working at the time in the Côte d'Ivoire—was reading a French magazine when he came across this passage: "African voices are like those of birds—impossible to translate."[4] Annoyed, Kanté wanted to fire a response back in his own Maninka language, a member of the largest Mandé family of languages in West Africa, but translating it into Arabic or French wasn't getting the job done.

So in 1949, he created his own script: N'ko. The name itself means "I say." With a businessman's savvy, Kanté knew to start first with religious texts, ones written in Arabic; then he moved on to science and technology books and developed his own N'ko dictionary and teaching aids.[5] His new written language did well in his native Guinea—but what makes it remarkable is how it gained popularity in Mali, Nigeria, Senegal, Sierra Leone, The Gambia, and Côte d'Ivoire. More texts have been published in N'ko than "in all the other West African scripts combined."[6]

Kanté also appreciated how language could protect indigenous institutions. He gave himself the additional task of locating traditional healers and cataloging their methods and the medicinal plants they used. As scholar Dianne Oyler noted, "He had to convince each individual, aging healer of his own altruistic intentions in the preservation of their knowledge." By using N'ko, many healers were comforted by their techniques being safeguarded in a "secret code."[7]

In giving people a new written script that granted access to knowledge on their own terms, as well as a tool to preserve pieces of their own culture, Kanté changed the intellectual landscape and accelerated the spread of African Ideas.

For the renowned Kenyan writer Ngũgĩ wa Thiong'o, language is a war zone. "African languages were weaponized against Africans," he reminded Rohit Inani in *The Nation* in 2018, conceding that "It is okay to make English our own or French our own. Any individual writer can make a language his own, but you can't tell me that by writing in English, [Joseph] Conrad was somehow helping the Polish language."[8] Only a year before, Thiong'o captured headlines with a powerful lecture on language at South Africa's University of the Witswaters and (known as Wits University). For the sake of preserving heritage, he argued, Africans should lobby their governments to incorporate native languages into educational institutions. Knowing English without knowing your mother tongue was "akin to enslavement." Instead, he urged his audience to "Use English, but don't let English use you."[9]

The author of such acclaimed novels as *Weep Not, Child* and *A Grain of Wheat*, Thiong'o has practiced what he preaches. Though educated in English at Kenyan schools, at Makerere University in Uganda and the University of Leeds, he chose in the 1970s to write in Kikuyu and Swahili. Imprisoned over the controversial play he cowrote with Ngugi wa Mirii, he even famously wrote another novel in Kikuyu on prison-issue toilet paper.

Any language is a constantly evolving thing, and government intervention doesn't always solve the problem. The U.S., for instance, has never made English its official language as much as right-wing pundits and politicians wish it had given the steady rise of Spanish. In Nigeria, English reigns, while Igbo, Hausa, and Yoruba are "the languages of national culture and integration."[10] In fact, as journalist Socrates Mbamalu reported in 2017, "In most East African countries Kiswahili has been made an official language. However, the elevation of Kiswahili leaves other indigenous languages out of the picture, which raises questions. What is the possibility of the survival of African languages surviving without language policies to support their existence?" He pointed out that in the southern region of Kaduna State in northern Nigeria, "within eight local governments, thirty languages exist. In different parts of Nigeria there are similar examples. The government's plan for the protection and preservation of many of the indigenous languages is not clear."[11]

Preserving Africa's more than 2,000 languages is an urgent matter because as Orwell warned us, when you take away the words, you lose the power to express an idea. Think of how many common philosophical concepts have been our inheritance through the cross-pollination of language. We associate democracy with ancient Greece, and the word itself still carries the freight of its roots: *demos*, which evolved in Greek to mean "common people," and *kratos*, "rule." Anyone who studies martial arts or traditional Asian healing—or has even watched action movies in the past forty years—learns the idea of *ch'i* (Chinese) or *ki* (Japanese), the vital life energy in all living things. From Montevideo to Bucharest, you'll find folks who know what *democracy* and *ki* mean. But how many Romanians, Greeks, or Japanese for that matter know what *ubuntu* is?

Ubuntu is a word that can be traced back to the Xhosa, Zulu, and other languages of southern Africa, and it can be defined as "humanity." But like *democracy*, a rough translation hardly sums it up. *Ubuntu* is a whole philosophy related to community spirit. One of the easiest ways to think about it is how it was explained to me: an American or European says, "I am because I am." But an African says, "I am because *we* are." The Ugandan human rights activist and lawyer Nicholas Opiyo casually summed up the essence another way in a tweet to me in 2019: *Umuntu, ngamuntu, ngabantu,* that is, "A person is a person because of people." After attacks on foreign nationals of African descent in Johannesburg in September 2019, *Daily Show* host Trevor Noah criticized the wave of xenophobia and finished with the line, "Share for spirit of *Ubuntu.*"[12]

There have been many suggestions that *ubuntu* is a reasonable equivalent to humanism, but even this doesn't quite satisfy because *ubuntu* has wider aspects of community hospitality, of wealth sharing, and even social standards of mutual respect. Like so many other African concepts, it doesn't need to be redefined in terms of the European experience; it stands on its own moral authority. But for the sake of our understanding here, we should consult an expert on the subject, Christian Grade, who traced Western written references to the concept all the way back to 1846. *Ubuntu* has been defined as everything from "human nature" to "manhood, virtue, politeness, liberality," and more.[13] And this is a concept that isn't vital only to a single culture's expression—it spans nations. It's articulated in the cultures, for instance, of South Africa, Tanzania, Nigeria, Zimbabwe, and Malawi. Imagine then the multiplicity and subtlety of meanings we lose with words when a language dies.

Another expert on *ubuntu,* academic Michael Onyebuchi Eze, has explored the subject eloquently. He found that it encompasses an idealism that suggests "humanity is not embedded in my person solely as an individual; my humanity is co-substantively bestowed upon the other and me. Humanity is a quality we owe to each other. We create each other and need to sustain this otherness creation. And if we belong to each other, we participate in our creations: we are because you are, and since you are, definitely I am. The 'I am' is not a rigid subject, but a dynamic self-constitution dependent on this otherness creation of relation and distance."[14]

This, of course, is as intricate and sophisticated as anything one might find in a book by the European philosophers of the eighteenth century onward. And as with any compelling idea, it's asserted itself on major political events in history. The word and the concept of *ubuntu* may remain known mostly to

Africans—for now—but one of its aspects has already taught the world a powerful lesson about justice, which we'll take up in a future chapter.

In his novel *Fahrenheit 451*, Ray Bradbury reminds us that books are "only one type of receptacle where we stored a lot of things we were afraid we might forget." There's nothing magical in them, a character tells the protagonist Montag. "The magic is only in what books say." One of the most moving scenes in the novel is the revelation that a group of exiles, fleeing their dystopian society where books are routinely, spitefully burned, has memorized classic texts and can recite them on demand. Montag is casually introduced to a man who "is" Plato, another who "is" Jonathan Swift, and still another who can bring back Darwin.

But in the real world, West Africans have practiced something close to this, at least to its spirit, for centuries.

On a day in 2020 when a winter storm was punishing the eastern seaboard, Ali Al Haji Papa Bunka Susso—better known to his friends and admirers as Papa Susso—was settling in again at his apartment in the Bronx after a flight back from Africa and calling around to friends and contacts to book some gigs. He likes to stay busy. And his reputation is so great that in his seventies, he is still in demand. For Papa Susso is a *griot*, that unique mix of historian and musician from West Africa.

He comes from The Gambia, a thin wedge of a nation almost completely sandwiched by Senegal, with its capital, Banjul, sitting on its modest coast. Though born in the village of Sotuma Sere into a family that already boasted prestigious griots, his life could have been very different. After getting a scholarship to enrol at Cuttington University in Liberia and earning his degree in business administration, he was all set for a career as an accountant. He worked at The Gambia's Ministry of Works and Communications and later as a financial attaché and liaison officer for his country's embassy in Sierra Leone.[15]

"That was a civil service job," he explained in a phone interview, "and at the time, people may think if you're working in the government, you'll be making big money. But later it was proven to me that that was wrong." Luckily, he decided to fall back on the "family business" of being a griot. Later, he would become the chief *kora* player for the Gambia National Ballet.[16] Over a career spanning generations, he's performed for several heads of state and political figures, such as Nelson Mandela, and with an impressive number of orchestras, including the London Philharmonic and with the Kazumi Watanabe Opera in Tokyo. He's played Carnegie Hall twice. "So this has made me a well known fellow all over the world, and it has generated a lot of money for me to support my family, send my children to school, and to do whatever I wanted to do. I think I am comfortable to work as a griot now."[17]

Griots—and *griottes* for women in the profession—hold a job that can be hard to define, and it's one that's unique to Africa. If westerners hear of them at all, they often vaguely assume a griot is a kind of poet-musician, skilled in playing the lute, the kora, or the balafon. Yes, griots can be musicians like Papa Susso, but they don't have to be. Genealogist, singer of praises, historian, political adviser, spy, mediator, translator, teacher—griots have been all these things and more.

It is griots who passed down the *Epic of Sundiata*, which tells us about the founder of the Mali Empire, Sundiata Keita (mentioned in chapter 4). A griot accompanied Askia Muhammad on his pilgrimage to Mecca. In western Niger and eastern Mali, a griot is a *jeseré*. For the Mandinka of parts of the Mande region of Senegal and The Gambia, he is a *jali*. In Mauritania, he can be an *iggio*.[18] As a genealogist, the griot can be valuable for providing a window on the history of a nation. In 1935, a French governor-general in Dakar recognized their value and sent a memo out to colonial officials, requesting they collect oral history accounts and written records so the French could educate themselves on the "wars between tribes, migrations, and . . . the social and economic situations in these African countries."[19]

Ibn Battuta wrote about the esteemed griot, Dugha, when he visited the court of Mansa Suleyman. After a couple of months of trying to talk to the sultan and getting nowhere, he appealed to Dugha, who replied, "Speak in his presence, and I shall express on your behalf what is necessary." But as Ibn Battuta discovered, the griot performed more functions than being

The celebrated griot Tinguizi of Naimey, memorialized on a postage stamp for Niger. *Courtesy Thomas A. Hale.*

simply an interpreter. On certain days, Dugha came to the audience chamber with the sultan's four wives and close to 100 slave women, all in "beautiful robes." On these occasions, "a chair is placed for Dugha to sit on. He plays on an instrument made of reeds with some small calabashes at its lower end, and chants a poem in praise of the sultan, recalling his battles and deeds of valor. The women and girls sing along with him and play with bows."[20]

In this context, the women appear to be relegated as Dugha's backup band, but it's worth remembering that women have also been accomplished griottes in West Africa. Western scholars overlooked them in the past thanks to another universal tradition, gender bias, and the women also faced their own professional glass ceilings. Until recently, men tended to monopolize the history field through recitals of grand epics, while women did praise singing.

Respect in North America and Europe for griots and griottes seems to have been hard won. Around the time that I had my short interview with Papa Susso in 2020, social media buzzed with the story that inspectors for the Transportation Security Administration callously destroyed the kora of another renowned griot, Ballaké Sissoko, when he took a night flight to Paris after a successful American tour. Ballaké opened the hard case for his custom-made instrument, only to find it in pieces along with a note from the TSA in Spanish with the motto: "Intelligent security saves time."

With photos on Ballaké Sissoko's Facebook page showing the note and the damage, British music producer Lucy Durán wrote a scathing account of the incident. Durán also happens to be a professor at London's School of Oriental and African Studies, and she pointed out the bitter irony of how jihadists in Mali have tried to ban music and cut out the tongues of singers, yet it was U.S. Customs who managed to destroy Ballaké's unique instrument. Would they have "dared do such a thing to a white musician playing a classical instrument?"[21]

Papa Susso told me how he experienced this kind of wanton destruction himself to his kora in the past—twice. Once while flying from Austin, Texas, to New York and once on a flight from Los Angeles to Seattle. Neither time was he compensated. Does he attribute it to racism? Stupidity? "I think they just don't care."[22]

For the episode involving Ballaké Sissoko, others have asked if more might have been going on. It happened in the context of the Trump administration adding another four African countries to its travel ban, and while Mali wasn't on the travel ban list at the time, its citizens were occasionally "subject to 'extreme vetting' measures," reinforcing the idea that Homeland Security "has stepped up aggressively discriminatory tactics to isolate Muslims and Africans."[23] But whether through casual negligence or deliberate malice, the effect is the same: denial of freedom of speech. A griot musician needs his kora or other instrument the way a broadcast journalist needs a microphone. The instrument can be integral, even vital to the process.

Still, the profession is a resilient one. It's survived the onslaught of movies, video games, other musical genres, and the internet, and Papa Susso fully expects it to live on. In 1995, he won $20,000 in the New York State Lottery and put a chunk of his windfall into the institution he founded in The Gambia, the Koriya Center for Research on Oral Tradition.[24] Here, the younger generation, particularly westerners, can train in playing the kora. Meanwhile, he works regularly with universities in the Northeast—departments of history, African Studies, anthropology, and others—whose academics want to know more about the playing of the traditional instruments, the songs played, and how they developed. He points out that "young griots change the music. They change it into a different style, but still, there are a few among them whose interest is to continue with the historical songs."

"In a way, you're keeping some of that history alive," I said. "Exactly."[25]

One of the world's experts on griots and griottes is Thomas Hale, a professor (now retired) who researched them across four countries and interviewed more than 100 of them; he and Papa Susso are friends. Hale recorded and translated the recital of *The Epic of Askia Mohammed*, the legendary ruler of the Songhay Empire, by griot Nouhou Malio, who lived in Niamey, the

Griots Harouna Beidari and Idrissa Souley performing *The Epic of Askia Mohammed* at Karma, Niger, in 1981. *Courtesy Thomas A. Hale.*

capital of Niger. He considers them "time binders"—those who link the past to the present and who can be a valuable witness to current events. "In this sense, the griot's role as historian is somewhat more dynamic and interactive than what we have in the Western tradition—the scholar who spends years in libraries going through archival sources."[26]

He offers a dynamic example of how the griot's role can span the ages. "An event happens in the past, griots witness it, they mentally record it, they recount it over and over and over after several generations. Then a new leader comes in . . . and his griots say, 'Okay, you're going to go off to battle tomorrow. What am I going to tell people in the future about you . . . ? Your father did this, that and the other, are you going to measure up or not?' So the battle takes place, and the soldiers are really great because they don't want to be left out. If they don't do anything, they will disappear from the narrative." In the development and recital of the final product, the griot "influences the future with what he tells about the present which is rooted somewhere in the past."[27]

The westerner reflexively sees such epics and recitals as mere stories. But Thomas Hale cautions, "This is their history. They believe in it."[28] At the same time, Hale notes that according to two important African source texts, the griots also faced stiff competition over a ruler's attention from scribes who "hint at the need to corroborate information from their competitors by speaking with other people."[29]

Which brings us to the bitter and remarkable debate that erupted when the griot legacy fused with best-selling fiction.

In 1972, at a historic conference in the School of Oriental and African Studies in London, more than twenty griots from Senegal, Mali, and The Gambia took part in workshops and discussions while some of them charmed the British media with their musical performances. The first of its kind, the conference was exceptional in another respect. Alex Haley was in attendance. Having helped shape Malcolm X's autobiography into a page-turner that's inspired millions, he was there to give a talk about his exploration of his own genealogy. The British filmmaker Geoffrey Haydon, who was working on a documentary about blues and jazz antecedents in West Africa, was also at the event, commonly known as the Manding Conference.

He recalled that Haley's lecture "was an emotional affair; a triumph of rhetoric in the face of some discreet academic head-shaking. When he reached the climax of his impassioned tale, Professor Haley brought forward musicians from The Gambia who repeated in song his story of capture by slavers of his great-great-grandfather, Kunta Kinteh [sic]."[30]

Here is a fascinating moment that may be unfamiliar even to those who know the story of Roots. Alex Haley was offering a kind of dress rehearsal for his ancestor's story. And he gave it in a bilingual and cross-cultural format, his English version, and then its West African griot counterpart. It must have been something to see. If those watching and listening could have known what a phenomenon Roots would become, they might have marked it as Haydon did. But a good portion of the scholarly audience was extremely skeptical. And unfortunately, they had good reason to be. The tradition of griots proved to be essential to Haley's work and, in the end, crucial to parsing the truth.

There are two essential problems with *Roots*. The first—to put it bluntly—is that Alex Haley plagiarized a substantial portion of his monumental classic. Long before his book rolled off the presses, a novel came out in 1967 from an anthropologist and novelist named Harold Courlander. Courlander couldn't fail to notice how *Roots* became a publishing sensation, and he sued Haley in 1979 in Manhattan's federal district court for more than half the profits of the best-selling juggernaut.

In Courlander's novel, *The African*, the hero, Hwesuhunu, is captured by French slave traders, and he eventually is brought to a Georgia plantation. Haley didn't steal the entire plot outright; there are significant differences between the two novels. But it was clear to the presiding judge (there was no jury) that Haley had copied more than *eighty* passages from Courlander's work. When confronted in court with specific instances, he insisted that he'd never heard of *The African* and blamed it all on "someone," possibly student volunteers helping with his manuscript who may have passed along material from Courlander's book.[31] This is weak tea indeed, so much so that the judge informed Haley's defense lawyer that he thought the author had perjured himself.[32]

And as it turned out, Haley did. When he lectured at Skidmore College in upstate New York, Native American writer Joseph Bruchac was an instructor there, and he gave Haley his own copy of *The African*, suggesting it might provide insights. Haley thanked him and said, "I'll read it on the plane." Bruchac didn't realize the significance of what had happened until after the trial.[33] It would have been the fatal blow in the lawsuit, but the two sides ended up settling. Courlander was paid $650,000—three times what Haley originally offered to make the case go away—plus an important admission: "Alex Haley acknowledges and regrets that various materials from *The African* by Harold Courlander found their way into his book, *Roots*."[34] The word *found* is overly generous, but the point was made.

Haley also admitted during the trial that he plundered from other works, including *Slave Narratives* collected by the Federal

Writers Project back in the 1930s and Carl Sandburg's once-popular biography of Lincoln.[35] For our discussion, the plagiarism is not the key issue, but it does go to credibility, which is important for consideration of the second problem.

Roots was called a novel when it was first released in 1976, and Haley never claimed the dialogue between characters reflected actual conversations—how could he? But Doubleday promoted it as *nonfiction*, and it's been stacked as such on library and store shelves to this day. Haley himself blurred the lines between categories as it suited him, sometimes conceding in interviews that he got details wrong or consciously changed them, other times insisting combatively that he was being persecuted. In his final chapter, he stated, "To the best of my knowledge and of my effort, every lineage statement within *Roots* is from either my African or American families' carefully preserved oral history, much of which I have been able conventionally to corroborate with documents."[36]

He wrote of traveling to Juffure in The Gambia and meeting a supposed griot, Kebbi Kanji Fofana, a man who gave him vital information about his alleged ancestor Kunta Kinte. "I sat as if carved in stone. My blood seemed to have congealed. This man whose life time had been in this back-country African village had no way in the world to know that he had just echoed what I had heard all through my boyhood years on my grandma's front porch in Henning, Tenn." Haley wrote movingly of how he began to sob. Only a recording from his collected papers and tapes shows he didn't. Moreover, Fofana did have a way of knowing. More about that later.

By April 1977, a reporter for the London *Sunday Times*, Mark Ottaway, challenged many of Haley's claims after retracing his steps in Juffure and digging into the background of Fofana, who died in 1976. Ottaway argued that Juffure simply wasn't as Haley depicted it in his novel—instead of an unspoiled patch of Africa, it had been a white trading post for almost a century, and it was first set up with the permission of the king of Barra, who demanded from whites that none of his subjects ever be enslaved. The reporter also suggested the date for Kunta Kinte's capture in 1767 was way off (assuming it happened at all). On top of all that, he discovered that after *Roots* had been published, Kebbi Fofana gave a deposition to The Gambia Archives, "which said that Kunta Kinte was a member of a generation that would have been living in Juffure in the 1820s." Ottaway concluded that the probabilities that Kunta Kinte "disappeared much later than 1767, that he was never shipped as a slave to America and that he was not an ancestor of Haley at all far outweigh any possibility that he did or was."[37]

Readers didn't seem to care. The accolades still poured in, and Haley won the Pulitzer Prize only eight days after the *New York Times* ran a story on Ottaway's exposé. It seemed nothing could kill the book's astonishing popularity, especially after it was adapted for television. It's hard to convey the impact of the original miniseries in the 1970s. Keep in mind, this was an era of only *three* U.S. networks and before videotape recorders became common in American living rooms. Viewers were glued each night to their sets for the eight episodes. Scored by Quincy Jones and with a cast including top stars, *Roots* was an *event*. The nightly news ran stories on how people named their newborn babies after the characters. The miniseries had two sequels plus a remake of the original in 2016.

But in 1993, a year after Haley died, the *Village Voice* carried an incendiary investigative article by journalist Philip Nobile titled "Alex Haley's Hoax." Burrowing through the collection of Haley's private papers and tapes at the University of Tennessee in Knoxville, Nobile found even more damning evidence against the validity of the *Roots* narrative. "All of Haley's ripping yarns about his search for Kunta Kinte and his ten year struggle to write *Roots* were part of an elegant and complex make-it-up-as-you-go-along scam."[38] And key to Nobile's stinging indictment was Haley's dealings with his griot, Fofana, who was coached and fed prearranged questions; Haley "registered no surprise"—let alone a cathartic emotional response—to Fofana's answers because he already knew what was coming.[39]

It was difficult for supporters of Haley to criticize Nobile's muckraking—so they took issue with his tone and his perceived motivations. For Donna Britt writing in the *Washington Post*, Nobile "gleefully" challenged the author's reputation. Clarence

Page's language in the *Chicago Tribune* was almost as harsh as Nobile's, referring to arguments in general from critics of *Roots* as the "trashing" of Haley's memory and as a "lynching."

Supporters of Haley preferred to overlook the author's abuse of facts for a greater good. "If Nobile is correct, it means Haley lied about things too important to be falsified," wrote Britt. "It means that part of what made me weep for fifteen minutes after watching *Roots II* was a lie. Whatever the truth of Nobile's conclusions, I'm grateful to Haley for having given all African Americans a family tree whose branches stretched clear to Africa."[40] Page suggested that Nobile "missed the larger, more important truth. If *Roots* was a hoax, it was a hoax Americans wanted desperately to believe, which says something more important about Americans than anything Nobile says about Haley."[41]

Nobile's scorn has not diminished with time. In 2018, he looked back at the controversy and his reportage, knocking the Pulitzer Board for not rescinding Haley's award. Nobile still considers Alex Haley "an irredeemable literary scoundrel who polluted black history and genealogy with an avalanche of lies."[42]

If the reader recalls, the "larger truth" argument was employed to justify any fabrications that Olaudah Equiano might have had in his memoir. By now it should be clear that time and again, whether justified or not, the theme of authenticity intrudes on African Ideas. Outside of whether Shakespeare wrote his own plays, it's hard to imagine Western authors and thinkers being doubted as much as their African counterparts, but we can see the gleam of the sword's double edge. Why should Haley get a pass? Are the criticisms fair?

Let's return as best we can to Haley's crucial source, the griot, for this tells us something important about how information from Africa is disseminated and how its treatment differs substantially from Western tradition.

First, Ottaway uncovered the fact that Haley's griot wasn't a real griot at all. The prestigious job in Juffure was a hereditary one, but the elders there were unimpressed by Kebbi Fofana's lack of Koranic training and his living the high life. Haley was already writing about his search for his ancestor and his meeting with Fofana by 1972 for an article in the *New York Times Magazine*. "Now the whispering hushed—the musicians had softly begun playing kora and balafon, and a canvas sling lawn seat was taken by the griot, Kebba Kanga Fofana [*sic*], aged seventy-three 'rains' (one rainy season each year). He seemed to gather himself into a physical rigidity, and he began speaking the Kinte clan's ancestral oral history; it came rolling from his mouth across the next hours . . . 17th- and 18th-century Kinte lineage details, predominantly what men took wives; the children they 'begot,' in the order of their births; those children's mates and children."[43]

But when historian Donald Wright visited Juffure in 1974 and went looking for elders who could give him details on the history of the village, Fofana wasn't even mentioned. Wright did finally interview Fofana, and just as Ottaway had learned, the man was apparently an entertainer who made at best a marginal living. His information on Kunte Kinte seemed so sketchy that the historian spent time talking about Kinte to "a man who appeared to be better informed than Fofana." In analyzing Haley's amateur fieldwork, Wright zeroed in on the fact that the author had tipped his hand in relating "his history to at least eight people, who undoubtedly told it to others, and who went out looking for someone to provide Haley what he wanted."[44] Nobile, with the advantage of access to Haley's papers, saw deliberate fabrication. Wright, penning a journal article in 1981, saw shoddy research.

Our griot expert from earlier, Thomas Hale, did his own detective work on *Roots* in the 1990s, but he arrived at a unique perspective, one more charitable than the usual criticisms in magazines and newspapers. Having his own doubts over the book, he found it "highly unlikely that a Songhay griot could have recalled specific incidents associated with the name of an ordinary citizen two centuries earlier unless that person was of royal origin and had accomplished something significant in life."[45] As it turns out, Hale interviewed Haley three months before the author died, and Haley soon proved he had limited knowledge of griots (it didn't occur to him, for instance, that there could be griottes).

But knowing the practices and cultural history well, Hale recognized that griot narratives "contain a degree of symbolism." He concluded that Haley had taken his partial facts and data and had "created *Roots* in a way that echoed the griot tradition"—it was one that "simply had to be interpreted at a symbolic level." When author met professor in late 1991, Haley accepted Hale's description, and he explained how after criticisms of the book began, he felt no need to parse fact from fiction "because he was operating as a modern-day griot, telling a story of great social and cultural significance to audiences that until then had little opportunity to learn anything positive about their African past."[46]

Hale concedes that to reporters—who get the commandment of "stick to the facts" hammered into them from day one in journalism school, and to historical scholars, who certainly can't indulge their imaginations—the notion of the author as America's griot might appear "revisionist at best and downright naïve at worst."[47] But it's an intriguing premise.

I put it to Hale that if this was the author's intention, it's a noble one, but Haley could have achieved the same literary effect while adhering more closely to the facts or simply making the book definitively historical fiction. Hale countered there simply were no hard facts three centuries ago that Haley would have been able to access. No griot would have been able to provide such specific details. Nevertheless, whether it's stories or hard data, "all of this information is on the same spectrum of learning about Africa, whether it's how many slaves came over or what their names are or what life was like back in those days. . . . It's all bringing, let's say, new perspectives on Africa."[48]

If we put Alex Haley aside for a moment, we should think about what the controversy says about how we treat African source material and whether we impose standards that don't reflect the traditions of the culture. Does anyone take *The Iliad* as literal history? Of course not. Yet Heinrich Schliemann found what he claimed was Troy, and archaeologists look to grand epics to help them unearth secrets. In several Asian cultures, if a temple burns down, its monks and patrons often don't distinguish between the one that was built centuries ago and lost and the one more recently constructed; to them, it's the same temple.

It's worth pausing here to consider another work of history. The South African writer E. A. Ritter, born in 1890, was the son of a British officer and magistrate in Natal. Zulu was his first language, learned from his nurses, and as a child, he eagerly listened to the tales of Shaka from his father's court orderly, the son of a warrior who fought in Shaka's ranks. Ritter himself served as a trumpeter for a Natal cavalry regiment that fought a rebellious Zulu contingent in 1906. His 1955 biography, *Shaka Zulu*, was an attempt "to portray Shaka, the founder of the Zulu nation, as the Zulus saw him, particularly at the turn of the last century."[49] Though a westerner, Ritter clearly retained the respect and empathy he developed in his formative years for Zulu culture, and he spoke to multiple witnesses and elders tied with the Zulu royal family.

And yet his book has been criticized by later historians for its supposed romanticism and alleged embellishment. Go online, and you'll find spots where *Shaka Zulu* is referred to as a novel; the Wikipedia page for Shaka sneers that it's "a potboiling [*sic*] romance that was re-edited into something more closely resembling a history."[50] The only way to explain this elitist and inaccurate characterization is to attribute it to a strange, indirect racism and reflexive dismissal of African sources. The reality is you couldn't ask for better bona fides for a historian. A witness who knew your subject personally? Ritter had one. Others who were living vaults of Zulu culture and its history? Ritter had access to them as well. He spoke the language fluently, not to mention he had personal experience with Zulu fighting methods. Where then is the problem with his book?

The answer is that his critics don't like his *style*. Here is a brief scene from Ritter's narrative, taken from his chapter on the Tembu War: "And while they thus conversed, there came to Shaka, in breathless haste and excitement, a messenger saying, 'O King, our army has been beaten from the field, and it is even now in full retreat.' Shaka arose in a towering rage—'as angry as a lion in a net'—and roared to his attendants to 'kill the babbling fool'—the ill-starred messenger who had at once betrayed his deceit and his disgrace. The unfortunate man stood rooted to the ground and with horror-stricken eyes looked mutely at Shaka as the executioner approached and crushed his skull with a heavy club."[51]

It's interesting that Ritter divulged in his introduction the push-back he received from his own publisher and editor over certain passages. They were considered "too imaginative-seeming for biography, and that it was extremely important to avoid any question of a fictitious element in a work of serious purpose." Ritter explained to his editors that "his first sources were oral, and when Zulus give an account of an historical event their method is not dry reportage, it is more akin to drama, and the *feelings and words of all protagonists are recounted as in epic poetry* [emphasis added]." Ritter "wanted to tell his story as nearly as possible as it was told to him," and he also "had his Zulu readers much in mind." In fact, Ritter originally intended to copiously endnote his book for his scholarly references, but his editors scotched this, thus undermining their own case for the book's need to impress with its validity.

So, on the one hand, we have Alex Haley, whose novel has transmogrified over time into "nonfiction," and, on the other hand, we have Ritter's meticulous work of biography—a work that sincerely keeps to the spirit and a fairly accurate rendition of Zulu history telling—marginalized and dismissed as a hack novel fare. But the truth is we can learn to appreciate both.

When we consider the storytelling of Zulu elders and the griots, their traditions force us to consider history in a different way. The conceit of the written word in Europe and America has always been that it's inherently superior; it's definitive as a tangible, permanent thing, checked and measured. But this is illusory. Socrates wrote nothing down. Much of what we know of him comes from the account of his student Plato. And what is so permanent? From the burning of the Great Library of Alexandria to the burning pyre of classics in Nazi-era Berlin to our ever-shrinking attention spans, the printed word remains vulnerable. But then what about perspective? The physicist raconteur Richard Feynman once said, "The first principle is that you must not fool yourself—and you are the easiest person to fool." A bias is a bias, whether printed, spoken, or sung.

Now here is the griot, who doesn't hold the conceit of a Western historian that he's objective or even rigorous over factual details but that his recitation still has value.

In another case of taking us full circle, *Roots* popularized the word *griot* in the Western vocabulary. There is no denying the profound influence that the book had on connecting black Americans to their African heritage, inspiring many to try as best they could to trace their own backgrounds to another continent. As Thomas Hale notes, when the story of Haley's research was dramatized in *Roots II: The Next Generation*, the role of Fofana was played by "one of the most talented *jalolu* of The Gambia, Al Haji Bai Konte," meaning that "large audiences saw for the first time an actual griot recounting a genealogy."[52] We know that Haley didn't rely in the end on a "legitimate" griot for his book, but it is no small thing that Americans turned on their TVs and saw the genuine article. African truth still found its way across an ocean and across time.

Like the myths over African language, the concept of *tribe* remains stubbornly persistent. "We can see the absurdity of the current usages," Ngũgĩ wa Thiong'o wrote in 2009, "where thirty million Yorubas are referred to as a *tribe*, but four million Danes as a *nation*. A group of 250,000 Icelanders constitutes a nation, while ten million Igbos make up a tribe [emphasis in the original]."[53] As he points out, most African languages don't have an equivalent word for this often lazy, inexact, and pejorative term, one that colonial powers brought into wide circulation. Martin Meredith quotes a chief in Zambia observing that his people "were not Soli until 1937 when the Bwana D.C. [district commissioner] told us we were."[54] Kenya's Kikuyu people never had chiefs prior to the colonial period. The British apartheid regime appointed chiefs for them, creating a whole social layer of hated collaborators, who were rewarded with choice parcels of land for their submissiveness.

Moreover, as writers Marq de Villiers and Sheila Hirtle have pointed out, tribes weren't static. White scholars and colonial bureaucrats, having assigned a culture a label, thought, okay, that was that—ignoring that change is inevitable. "Most of the tribes David Livingstone encountered along the Zambezi no longer exist," while Zulus "were merely an obscure Nguni subclan until the military genius of Shaka took hold of them; but after his death, and the death of his murdering brother Dingaan, the Zulu name would, in the African way, have gone into decline or shifted to something else, except that by that time the missionaries and the settlers had arrived with their busy recording pencils. The Zulus remained the Zulus because the language they spoke was called Zulu by the missionaries and written down, codified for history."[55]

The way Europeans categorized Africans, in fact, set parts of the continent on the path to self-destruction. When the Belgians ran Ruana-Urundi (modern Rwanda), they forced Hutus and Tutsis to carry identity cards and stacked education and work opportunities in favor of the Tutsis. Ethnic tensions between the two peoples naturally predate the Belgians showing up (and the Germans who held the country before them), but colonial administrators were only too happy to exacerbate rivalries. An influential Catholic bishop urged the Belgian regime in the 1920s to favor the Tutsis: "The government must work mainly with them." Some Hutu chiefs were summarily kicked out of their positions, with Tutsi ones installed.[56]

Then in the years counting down to Rwanda's independence in 1962, amid increasing frictions with the Tutsi elite, the Belgians "felt betrayed by their erstwhile protégés," and switched sides; with cynical ruthlessness, they began working with Hutus to take their vengeance in government and spheres of influence against the Tutsis.[57] In the civil war and genocide of Rwanda about thirty years later, the outside world—particularly the Western media—glossed over nuances of how Hutus and Tutsis had much in common culturally and portrayed it as a "tribal conflict."

When Sudan's Darfur region captured headlines, the Western media defaulted to its usual habits and portrayed the conflict as northern Arabs slaughtering black African southerners. The trouble is that while racially all Sudanese are African, nothing is cut and dried in terms of their complex ethnic diversity or even their migrations. Down through the centuries, you had Arabized groups, as well as peoples that we might consider more "classically African" to Western perceptions, such as the Dinka or the Nuba, and then there's the intermingling and nomadic dispersion to consider. In his fascinating book about Khartoum, *A Line in the River*, Jamal Mahjoub reminds us, "If all the focus is on explaining the violence as racially and ethnically motivated we risk missing other essential factors, such as climate change, which played a key role; with delayed and insufficient rains forcing herders to move onto farming land earlier than normal, breaking the interdependence between the two groups. Without addressing this issue, we run the risk of perpetuating the conditions for other similar conflicts to arise in the future."[58]

Yes, lingering on white perceptions of Africans takes us away from our main theme. But it's worth pausing here to consider one standout episode in the early twentieth century. In 1914, about two months prior to World War I scorching across Europe, a special group of sixty passengers disembarked from the *SS Chicago* at Ellis Island, having sailed from Le Havre, France. The arrivals were later mistakenly identified in historical reports as "Abyssinians," and to this day, there are posts on social media reinforcing the claim that these people were Ethiopians. Only the information available suggests they weren't that at all—they were, in fact, Somalis from the Issa clan either from near Aysha or from Djibouti.

Louis Takács, an independent researcher in the Netherlands, notes that the Chicago's manifest only adds to the confusion. A shipping agent in Le Havre wrote that they were "Abyssinians," while an inspector at Ellis Island treated them as colonials from France. The discrepancies start to make sense when we remember that Aysha was in a region of Ethiopia highly populated with Somalis, and given the porous borders at the time, it would be easy for westerners to presume it fell within the realm of nearby French Djibouti. Other documents and facts back up Takács's argument. Among the arrivals, "five were musicians, three shepherds, and one a shoemaker—the rest of the men were most likely pastoralists while the women were listed as homemakers. None spoke English or had any money." The family names included Abdalla, Aïcha, Aiga, Aigale, Akmad, Mera,

Mohamed, Oigale, Oufune, and Saïd. A few of them had the misfortune to be deported soon after they were processed.[59]

"Ellis Island had quite a flutter when the Somali outfit arrived," chirped the *Washington Post* ten days later. "Brass buttoned folk looked up books to see if they were Arabians, Egyptians, Mohammedans, fire worshipers, Hottentots, philosophers, or just plain 'cullud folks' [sic]. The immigration officials couldn't for the life of them tell whether the Somalis were 'undesirable aliens' or the very latest fashion models from Paris."[60]

But why had they made the long journey? As Takács puts it, "The Somalis had come to the U.S. to literally *perform* their ethnicity, their culture . . . as white Westerners wanted it" (emphasis in original). From the 1850s, circuses, music halls, and sideshow operations in America and Europe liked to put Africans on display. Some of the Issa Somalis had, in fact, performed for several months at the "Magic City" amusement park in Paris, two blocks away from the Eiffel Tower.[61] When the U.S. immigration officials inquired what kind of show the Somalis would perform, one of their sponsors and subsequent managers replied, "They will have a native village where they will do a war dance."[62] Mere days after their ship crossed the temperamental Atlantic Ocean, the ones who were let into the country appeared in the "Dreamland" sideshow at Coney Island and with the Barnum & Bailey Circus at Madison Square Garden.

Ticket buyers could visit "Somaliland" and had the chance twice daily to see "Earth's most curious people shown in their native haunts and in their weird pursuits."[63] Their weird pursuits included simple tasks, such as making handicrafts, or the more interesting spectacles of dancing and mock warfare. "Every day and night the men divide into rival camps and fight a Somali battle with shields and arrows for weapons and wild cries as the chief means of inspiring terror," observed one reporter. "They worship in an open, roofless house in kneeling posture, their faces turned toward Mecca."[64] We can only wonder what the Somalis thought of being stuck in one spot for an extended period and displayed for a few cents.

After Madison Square Garden, the Somalis were taken to Coney Island to perform. As the circus season ended, many of

A typical postcard depicting Somali performers at "Magic City" in Paris. Some of them would come to New York, and this image was reused and captioned falsely that it was taken at Coney Island. *Courtesy Louis Takács.*

them longed to return to Africa, while others wanted to stay on and keep working. While some presumably took the dangerous journey home—happening as it did when the Great War got under way—those willing to work were packed off to miserable conditions in a tenement on the outskirts of Jersey City. It was now December 1914, and a New Jersey winter is no place for tribesmen used to the warmer temperatures of East Africa. Their manager abandoned them, only to return and talk them into going west to perform at the World's Fair in San Francisco in 1915.

But the Somalis proved they weren't one thing: pushovers. They held their own strike, insisting the show would not go on because they were owed back wages. Officials at the fair eventually took over the concession yet still refused to pay them and then arranged to have them packed off to infamous Angel Island, where thousands of immigrants—most of them Chinese—were kept in squalid and sometimes nightmarish conditions.

The story only becomes more tragic from there. With one last gig booked in Chicago by their frequently disappearing manager (whom they ultimately fired), the Somalis decided to take their fate into their own hands and manage themselves. But they were ripped off yet again and in trying to confront their latest client were rounded up and hauled off to jail. Even those of the troupe who left the engagement early and tried to make a living as buskers in New York soon ended up as pitiful, starving vagrants. A tragic reunion of the remaining twenty-three Somalis happened at Ellis Island, where they were all deported that October.[65]

Throughout their time in the U.S., they were referred to as either "Abyssinians" or "Somalis," sometimes called "savage," occasionally billed as "cannibals." They were recruited to confirm a prejudice rather than dispel it. They were hired for their exoticism and little else, to embody an *idea* of Africans for strangers without any threat of contradiction from reality. And this is the most important takeaway: not that these circus shows, consciously or not, reinforced the public relations of colonial empire—that's obvious. What is harder for westerners to concede, even today, is that this was done to people from cultures that may not have been technologically on par with the West at the time but *were as philosophically and spiritually sophisticated.*

In a way, the case of the Somalis deported from Ellis Island can be viewed as a bridge from one era to another. The human zoos of exotic Africans, Burmese, and Aboriginal peoples would unfortunately stay popular right into the 1930s, but World War I—with its poison gas, its rat-infested trenches, and its machine gun bloodbaths—mocked almost every old "civilized" value in Europe and America. It's easier to understand then why westerners created a new myth of the Africans, camouflaging them in "primitive chic." Only this time, the Africans wouldn't stay wrapped. They would bust free and change Western art forever.

11

Masks

Africa was far from quiet at the turn of the twentieth century. There is so much focus on the "Scramble" and alternatively on independence after World War II that we're often left with the impression that the European countries, recognizing the day of empire was over, suddenly came to their senses and in good conscience "let" their former colonies go. But Africans were not passive recipients of any "gift." While, yes, the war depleted the resolve of the European nations, the relinquishment of their empires didn't happen overnight, and it certainly didn't spring out of initiative in London or Paris. There was already sporadic momentum in many African countries for freedom, human rights, and better working conditions during the 1900s right through to the 1930s.

Resistance in this era often took an evangelical form, with several colorful, charismatic figures who attracted their own followings. Onyango Dundo of the Luo people of Kenya invented his own religion, Mumbo, which worshipped a great serpent and rejected European clothing and culture. Acolytes were promised a day of deliverance; what they got instead was "deportation, prison or dispersal by an indignant colonial power."[1] Elliot Kamwana of Nyasaland (Malawi) fared mildly better. Mentored by the English radical missionary Joseph Booth, Kamwana managed to convert thousands to his own brand of the Jehovah

Witnesses in Nyasaland, South Africa, northern Rhodesia, and the Congo. Colonial powers kept deporting him around the continent, but they never managed to silence him.

These messianic leaders didn't have a structured platform or philosophy. They didn't think in terms of building nation-states. But there was a man who bridged the gap between faith and politics: John Chilembwe, the leader of Nyasaland's 1915 uprising.

As a young man, Chilembwe had been a house servant for Joseph Booth and had accompanied him on a trip to the United States, an experience that had a profound effect on his thinking.[2] As a Baptist minister, he promoted sobriety among men and education among women, once declaring in a letter that "the ordinary African woman in her heathen state is ignorant, uninteresting and unlovable. . . . It is sad to see a young mother, little more than a girl, with an infant on her back and know that she is thrust into responsibility for which she is quite unfit, and that at a time when she should be taken care of."[3] Chilembwe soon turned activist over the shameful treatment of plantation workers but then took on a new cause.

Adding to the injury from a terrible famine in 1913 was the insult the following year of the British conscripting Africans to serve, mostly as laborers, in World War I. They would help the British capture the German colonies, and, in fact, Malawian soldiers distinguished themselves in battle, defeating the Germans at Karonga in September 1914 in what's been called "the only significant military engagement of the war on Nyasaland soil."[4] Chilembwe sent a letter to the *Nyasaland Times* in November that amounted to a manifesto: "We understand that we have been invited to shed our innocent blood in this world's war which is now in progress throughout the wide world." But while police were marching into villages and rounding up fresh men, he wondered, "will there be any good prospects for the natives after the end of the war? Shall we be recognized as anybody in the best interests of civilization and Christianity after the great struggle is ended? . . . Let the rich men, bankers, titled men, storekeepers, farmers, and landlords go to war and get shot. Instead, the poor Africans who have nothing to own in this present world, who in death, leave only a long line of widows and orphans in utter want and dire distress are invited to die for a cause which is not theirs."[5]

This is as passionately eloquent as anything written by anti-war activists in Europe and later in the United States. Compare his line about Africans with "nothing to own" and "orphans in utter want and dire distress" with what American Socialist Eugene Debs told a court after he was found guilty of sedition in 1918 for opposing America joining the war. "I am thinking this morning of the men in the mills and factories; I am thinking of the women who, for a paltry wage, are compelled to work out their lives; of the little children who, in this system, are robbed of their childhood . . . and forced into the industrial dungeons, there to feed the monster machines while they themselves are being starved and stunted, body and soul."[6] Debs was known for weaving evangelical language into his radical speeches—in fact, he invoked the "Southern Cross" in his court statement. Though separated by culture and thousands of miles, the sentiment is the same. American radicals like John Reed and Emma Goldman are remembered for their antiwar stands, while Britain can count Sylvia Pankhurst and Bertrand Russell. Chilembwe is in good company.

His letter, however, wouldn't be widely read at the time. Wartime censors suppressed it from the paper's November 26 edition, and the sympathetic white editor tipped Chilembwe off that he should hide the original copy—the heat was on. Only the warning would do him no good. The authorities had been watching him, and the governor wrote to his counterpart in Mauritius in January about deporting Chilembwe there. We can't be sure, but it's quite possible that Chilembwe knew he was about to be arrested.[7] By now, there were members of his congregation willing to be a small army, and it was the time to act. Chilembwe was moved by the story of the American abolitionist John Brown, and, like Brown, he saw himself as a martyr. He and his followers decided, "Let us strike a blow and die."[8]

The plan was to raid white settlements and hopefully pick up popular native support along the way. On the night of January 23, his followers attacked a couple of Europeans, including a temperamental and often cruel estates manager. They cut off that man's head and later put it on a pole outside Chilembwe's church mission for all to see. While this is horrific, it wasn't without precedent, as both Malawi warriors and European soldiers indulged in this practice from the 1890s.[9] The manager's wife, a couple of other European women and their children were taken away from the area but weren't hurt. Another group of followers raided the African Lakes Company in Mandala.[10] But the rebellion failed to catch on and was soon put down by the authorities, with Chilembwe himself killed by a military patrol as he tried to escape to Mozambique. The colonial regime obliterated his church and put each of his remaining followers in a noose or against a wall to be shot.

But Chilembwe would be proved right. Africans would suffer substantial casualties in World War I, losing limbs and lives with hardly anything to show for their sacrifices. Most couldn't even face the risks armed with a weapon. South Africa was adamantly against putting rifles in black hands, even to carry them for whites. The French had no such qualms, sending about half a million African troops into the conflict.[11] Moroccan soldiers took part in the battles of Verdun and Aisne, and they suffered more casualties than their French counterparts.[12]

It would take almost a century for African soldiers in the Great War to get proper recognition for their service. But after Nyasaland gained its independence in 1964, becoming Malawi, John Chilembwe would be celebrated as a national hero, honored with his own public holiday on January 15 and his likeness on currency notes.

Then there were the educated African elites who were certainly not interested in leading night raids on farms or stealing ammunition supplies. They didn't want to throw out the machinery of Western colonial government—reforms and representation would be enough. And there were ample venues for their opinions to be heard. At the turn of the twentieth century, Sierra Leone had thirty-four newspapers. The Gold Coast had nineteen papers, while Nigeria could boast seven.[13]

Nigeria's press was especially dynamic. There was Liberian John Payne Jackson—as mentioned before, strongly influenced by Edward Wilmot Blyden's ideas—who started the *Lagos Weekly Record* in 1891. The paper often flirted dangerously with the limits that the regime extended to the native press: "There can be no question," thundered Jackson in one editorial in 1919, "that if the Nigerian system is not scrapped within the next five years, the unfortunate experiences of the Indian agitation will be witnessed in West Africa."[14]

But not all the elites were firebrand reformers. Kitoyi Ajasa was a lawyer who spent more than a decade from his teens into adulthood living in England, which turned him into a staunch conservative and believer in assimilation. Good friends with the colony's governor, Frederick Lugard, Ajasa founded the *Nigerian Pioneer* in 1914 and unashamedly backed the regime most of the time. His competitors—the *Record*, the *Standard*, the *Times of Nigeria*—didn't hesitate to lambaste the *Pioneer* when it predictably defended the British administration during uprisings by native peoples such as the Egba.[15] When Ajasa's paper offered criticism of the government at all, it was anemic. For instance, it conceded in an editorial in 1917 that "it might be suicidal for any empire to let the subject races into its secrets by having them employed in positions of trust," but the administration "should look upon the educated natives as an asset of the empire to be utilized in imperial interests."[16]

It's been suggested that the experience of World War I removed any illusions about white invincibility, but this is a poor argument—and a rather patronizing one at that. To borrow Maya Angelou's phrasing, the colonizers had long ago shown Africans who they were, and the Africans believed them the first time. What mattered was having the means and opportunities to fight back. If anything, the postwar economic slump in the colonies, combined with the ravages of the Spanish flu epidemic, brought an urgency to thoughts of rebellion. As the 1920s began, more people than ever before chose or were forced to live in the cities of colonial Africa instead of rural settings, which made organization easier.

Yet the methods for rebellion, the thinking, did not advance much. In 1912, a wide selection of teachers, lawyers, church ministers, journalists, and office managers all got together to form the South African Native National Congress. The main goal was to champion the rights of black citizens—but it would do this with petitions and protests that minded the law. How did this go over? With a yawn. The group was painfully ineffectual, and it would be for some time. The only thing that changed soon after the war was their name, a new one adopted in 1923: the African National Congress. It took another seven years for women to be granted affiliate member status in the ANC, and women wouldn't be granted full membership until 1943.

Had these early ANC leaders with their professional credentials and their smart suits paid attention, they might have admitted women earlier. There was a lesson for them in Nigeria's struggle. In late 1929, it was the scene for what came to be known as the "Women's War," an extraordinary set of protests and riots.

In the traditional Igbo society of Nigeria, women were never the equal of men, but they still held important roles in farming and trading, and they enjoyed significant political rights as well as rights to property and inheritance.[17] They also developed a fascinating set of protest tactics involving boycotts and strikes and a practice that was called "sitting on a man" (though sometimes the target could be a woman).

Say a man was abusive to his wife or flouted the market rules or allowed his cattle to munch away on valuable crops of a neighbor. Women might then gather at his compound late at night, sing songs that rattled off their complaints (and sometimes insult his sexual prowess), and make a general racket by hammering on his hut with pestles used for pounding yams. "Although this could hardly have been a pleasant experience for the offending man," observed scholar Judith Van Allen, "it was considered legitimate and no man would consider intervening."[18]

The British colonial system did much to upheaval native traditions, and they relied on proxies to do a lot of the dirty work of colonial administration. Top Igbo leaders, so-called warrant chiefs, were given power, and as these stand-ins became more corrupt and abusive, it only helped to undermine a culture's foundations. When the warrant chiefs were charged with tallying herds and checking who owned what, everyone expected a new round of tax grabs. The incident that's considered the spark for the rebellion was when a particularly officious warrant chief named Okugu visited a compound and told a woman named Nwanyeruwa to count her goats and sheep; Nwanyeruwa understood what was going on and wasn't having it: "Was your mother counted?" Okugu didn't appreciate her wit and became violent, and Nwanyeruwa fought back. In the wake of the incident, thousands of women protested in the town of Oloko. The warrant chief later spent two years in prison for assault and for spreading news that caused a panic.

Meanwhile, the movement spread, with thousands more women taking to the streets of Aba and other communities in late November and December. They stormed into native courts, occupied European warehouses stocked with the essential commodity of palm oil, released inmates from a prison, and even raided Barclay's Bank. Domestic servants "refused to cook for their white masters and mistresses, and some of them made the attempt to bring the European women by force into the markets to give them some experience of what work was like."[19]

In mid-December, police turned their rifles and a machine gun on women marching in one community in Calabar province, killing eighteen. At a protest in another town soon after, the police opened fire, mowing down thirty-nine women and one man; eight other women were pushed by a panicking, fleeing crowd into a river, where they drowned while bullets wounded another thirty-one. The British authorities justified their actions with the all-purpose slur that they had to quell "savage" behavior on the part of a "frenzied mob."

Not surprisingly for the era, the Colonial Office in London was happy to rubber-stamp an initial report that claimed officials in Nigeria had handled the situation perfectly fine. This was met with howls of protest, and another commission was formed—but this time pressure worked to get two Africans on the board. Despite this progressive step, the Aba Commission interviewed only about 100 women as witnesses out of a rebellion of thousands.

And when it came to investigating the Women's War, the Britons in charge—whether in Aba or Oloko or Lagos—failed to see the women at all. Nigeria's colonial secretary blamed Soviet agent provocateurs. District officers in the field blamed a secret society, even though they couldn't find it. All, of course, presumed men had been the leaders of the protests. It didn't occur to the authorities that the men gave their tacit support. At the hearings, women stepped forward to give evidence, assuming the actual point was to put on trial certain warrant chiefs, and though they might have misunderstood the real motivations, they were wise enough to keep their organizational secrets to themselves.

Some commissioners, in turn, were smart enough to suggest, "In view of the women's movements in the past, the independent character . . . and leadership which some of the women displayed, we consider that more attention be paid to the political influence of women . . . as a factor to be reckoned with more directly by the administration."[20] But this was the minority view. The British enacted changes in the early 1930s, doing away with the warrant chiefs for a system of judges, yet the erosion of the cultural traditions and the role of Igbo women rolled on. Still, the Women's War was significant. Some historians believe that it helped inspire similar tax protests and rebellions over the next three decades. It's also a landmark in the feminist struggle for women of color.

In 1910, the lanky, owlish author and art critic, Gelett Burgess—who looked like Buster Keaton playing an accountant—was living in France and went to see an exhibition of revolutionary new artists. Burgess gave us the word *blurb* and is sometimes remembered, if at all, for his comedic rhymes. He decided that many of the paintings at the exhibition were ugly. "If you can imagine what a particularly sanguinary little girl of eight, half-crazed with gin, would do to a whitewashed wall if left alone with a box of crayons then you will come near to fancying what most of this work was like."[21] But trying to keep an open mind (and sell a feature article), he visited the top Fauvists and Cubists at their studios. He paid a call on Picasso, "whom here and there, one has heard so much," and thought the Spaniard was more interesting than his art—"the only one of the crowd with a sense of humor."

Burgess put all his observations and opinions, studded with exclamation marks, into a piece lavishly illustrated with photographs. And on the pages discussing Picasso, in a left-hand corner, is the first published shot of Les Demoiselles d'Avignon. Here for the first time, albeit in black and white, was one of the greatest works of modern art in the world, the five famous women of the brothel, with the two on the right having faces that resemble African masks.

The composition was given no title, only labeled "Study by Picasso." Perhaps the magazine's editor took his cue from Burgess, who wrote, "I doubt if Picasso ever finishes his paintings. The nightmares are too barbarous to last; to carry out such profanities would be impossible. So we gaze at his pyramidical women, his sub-African caricatures, figures with eyes askew, with contorted legs, and—things unmentionably worse, and patch together whatever idea we may."[22]

Burgess was wrong. Picasso had finished Les Demoiselles, painting it in 1907, and he knew exactly what he was doing. He had collected African masks and sculptures ever since Henri Matisse strolled into Gertrude Stein's Paris apartment in 1906 and showed him his latest purchase from a curio shop, a Vili wooden sculpture from the Congo. While Les Demoiselles is the most celebrated of his works with African influence, there are many others, but the Great Master could be appallingly uncharitable. Asked once about it, he infamously replied, "L'art nègre? Connais pas." [African art? Never heard of it.]

The art historian and first director of the Museum of Modern Art, Alfred Barr, curated a retrospective of Picasso's work in 1939, and in the companion book for the exhibition, he called Les Demoiselles "the masterpiece of Picasso's Negro period." Barr highlighted how "the masks of the figures at the right are more directly derived from the Negro art of the Ivory Coast or the French Congo," and he went further, pinning down the influence of a masked dancer figure to "the metal-covered grave figures of the Gabon."[23] Whether Barr had his ethnography right

Picasso's *Les Demoiselles d'Avignon.*

(and scholars quibble over this), an incensed Picasso arranged for a disclaimer to be put in his catalog of works that *no*, African art did *not* play any part in his compositions.

Yet it did and is still plain for all to see. Crowds poured into Johannesburg's Standard Bank Gallery in 2006 to see eighty-four of his works with twenty-nine similar African pieces. *The Guardian* newspaper picked up on the huge debt that Picasso clearly owed the African artists in terms of not only inspiration but *technique*—something most casual art fans may not discern right away. These included "reversing concave and convex lines in a face or figure," while one of his sculptures clearly borrowed from "guardian figures from Gabon . . . in which abstract head figures perch on leg-like pedestals."[24]

These modern shows still, by implication, make Picasso out to be a visionary. Well, he was indeed a genius, but he wasn't alone in raiding African art to replenish his own creativity. So did Matisse, so did Modigliani. Picasso already had a high profile by the time he painted his controversial masterpiece in 1907, but Les Demoiselles d'Avignon wasn't exhibited until 1916. We forget in our Instagram-Twitter world that art in the early twentieth century circulated at a far slower, sometimes even glacial pace, and his brothel ladies in Avignon didn't really make an impact until the early 1920s. By then, the world, recovering from the horrors of Ypres and the Somme, was ripe for new ideas and aesthetic shocks. And something else was going on, which meant that the Master also had great timing.

African art was getting discussed, debated, analyzed. Exhibitions of it were held in London, Paris, and the U.S. André Salmon, the French critic and friend of Picasso who championed Cubism, wrote a defense of "Negro Art" in 1920, even if today we can find in it some truly cringe-worthy lines: "The black sculptor was . . . scrupulous and believed that he ought not to neglect any detail. It is because of this virtuous application, devoid of any mischievous intent or any violent sensuality, that the wooden sculpture of savages—especially those of Western Africa, is occasionally indecent."[25]

Salmon unintentionally tripped over an interesting point, writing that "it often happens that masks of feast and mourning, weddings and funerals, only reach us deprived of their beards and fleeces of wool, tow, hair or raffia. . . . But our aesthetic joy in the genius of barbarism does not suffer in consequence. The value of these ornaments is sometimes purely symbolic, more religious than aesthetic . . . which warn us of the time when over-refinement and false civilization will ruin the whole. Negro sculpture is admirable through its balance, its nobility of form, its sum of naked beauty."[26]

Buried in all that salon blather is the familiar issue of context, one that a curator in Montreal would parse more clearly almost 100 years later and for a unique Picasso exhibition that also showcased the work of contemporary African artists. Erell Hubert used the example of a mask of the Dan people of Ivory Coast. Yes, Picasso might borrow its striking features, but the item wasn't created to be hung on a wall—it was meant to be worn with pride by the winner of a ritual competition. "The mask is never meant to be seen on a neutral background like this," explained Hubert. "It's meant to accompany a headdress, a costume, music, dancing, performance, and the body with it. In [any museum] context, this mask is incomplete."[27]

Which begs the question . . . Just what did *Africans* think when they saw Picasso's masterpiece or other paintings inspired by African art? Few if anyone in the bastions of mainstream newspapers and magazines—at least the English ones—apparently thought to ask them, even though Paris had a substantial population of African expatriates in the 1920s.

Nevertheless, African art was a hot topic for discussion on both sides of the Atlantic. For the *American Magazine of Art*, Adeline Adams, critic and professional boor, wrote in 1926, "At a little dinner table of the rich, chance placed me between a modernist art editor and a modernisticated [*sic*] manufacturer of rayon-mixture lingerie, if you get what I mean. Wealth, thought I, knows strange table-fellows!" The businessman wanted to buy modern art, of which she disapproved. "Surely no person of sense has any especial slant against African sculpture, per se; it is interesting enough in its own ethnological niche, and indeed as art expression. . . . But is it not true that those who linger too long in the caverns of the goblins become in the end fatally unmindful of the beauty, the harmony, the radiance of life in the higher, non-goblin world?"[28]

African art did have its defenders. A couple of months later, there was a blistering review of a book called *Primitive Negro Sculpture* by art historian Thomas Munro and the dealer Paul Guillaume, who sold works by Matisse and Picasso and who organized one of the first African art exhibitions in Paris. The reviewer was offended by the book's condescending tone and its sweeping generalizations. "Such statements about Negroes as 'One fact does emerge, unquestionably; they developed no durable intellectual culture, no technique of applied science or logic of abstract reasoning,' are put forth. Perhaps ironworking is not applied science; nor the proverbs, conundrums, and other literary forms of the natives do not involve abstract reasoning. But it seems to me that they do."[29]

The reviewer was a young anthropologist named Melville Herskovits, who later founded and directed the first African Studies program at an American college. The unfortunate irony is that for all the good Herskovits did as a pioneer, he brought his own attitudes of condescension to the field, convinced that African American scholars couldn't be objective. He went out of his way to undermine W. E. B. Du Bois's initiative to create an African encyclopedia, claiming it would be "loaded with propaganda," and his conduct has tarnished his reputation with academics even to this day.[30]

In 1925, the year that art deco was born and *The Great Gatsby* was published, there was another case of adapted Africana that took Paris by storm, and this one didn't stay fixed on canvas but came to bold, beautiful life, cartwheeling and gyrating on the stage of the Théâtre des Champs-Elysées. It was *La Revue Nègre*, a dance show of all-black performers from the U.S., which happened to feature a kooky, high-spirited nineteen-year-old named Josephine Baker. What made the French audience gasp was a specific number called "The Dance of the Savages." Baker, according to Janet Flanner of *The New Yorker*, "made her entry entirely nude except for a pink flamingo feather between her limbs; she was being carried upside down and doing the split on the shoulder of a black giant. . . . The two specific elements had been established and were unforgettable—her magnificent dark body, a new model that to the French proved for the first time that black was beautiful, and the acute response of the white masculine public in the capital of hedonism of all Europe—Paris."[31]

The black giant who was her talented dance partner had a name, Joe Alex, but he was practically forgotten as Baker emerged as the breakout star. And to be fair, she earned her acclaim. The choreographer's idea of jungle mating was the stuff of crude caricature, but Josephine was such a luminous talent that she lifted the material above its stereotype. That she was no flash in the pan was confirmed when she performed in her iconic banana skirt the next year for the Folies-Bergère. Luckily, there's footage of her early performances (many in which she sports a bikini-style top to satisfy the mores of the day), and they can be viewed on YouTube, where modern viewers can't help but notice what the comments correctly identify as "the original twerking." Beyoncé, in fact, considers Baker a personal hero and wore an outfit styled after Josephine's for a performance in 2006.

She was born into crushing poverty in St. Louis, where she had to go to school barefoot in the same filthy dress day after day. Having faced the corrosive racism of America, Josephine was as ambitious as any black performer. Her persona up to then and even for a few numbers in *La Revue Nègre* was as a comic buffoon, pulling elastic, cartoonish faces like a female Jim Carrey. The producers saw in her something else for "The Dance of the Savages," and Josephine was so overwhelmed by her success on the opening night—some people rushed the stage—that she ran into the theater wings.[32] But the spotlight could have easily fizzled out. Another dancer might have lasted just for the show's run, reduced only to a prop for an idea of African culture. To Josephine's credit, she embraced her new celeb status and realized she could stand for something else, an expression of female sexuality, and black sexuality at that. It was not always a consciously crafted persona, but in time, it would be.

The artist Jean-Paul Domergue painted her in the nude, with white flowers in her hair, leaning forward expectantly. There is an equally well known picture of her taken by the celebrated photographer George Hoyningen-Huene, again nude but holding a dress in front her body as a faint tease of a drape, her features calm, the pose almost that of an award statuette. But the lighting and affectations are so elegant that the composition gives us the "Black Venus" as she was sometimes called. This is no lurid stereotype of a female African "savage" but a Josephine who is an individual, with her own dignity and personality and very much in control of her own sensuality.

Josephine Baker became the most famous woman in the world, white or black. There were Kewpie dolls on sale with her image, records, movies, postcards, concert engagements. She

Josephine Baker, as photographed in 1929 by George Hoyningen-Huene. *Used with permission from © George Hoyningen-Huene Estate Archives.*

had hot and cold running lovers, with a voracious sexual appetite and a constant ache of loneliness and self-doubt. She owned her own chateau and walked a pet cheetah down the Champs-Elysées. Like our era's Lady Gaga, her image had to evolve out of professional necessity away from scandal over wardrobe and her publicity stunts to the real work: her dancing and, later, singing and acting. But there was no Gaga before her, no Madonna or Aretha Franklin, certainly no triple threat of a female dancer, singer, and actor who rocketed to so much fame and wealth so quickly. Whether she liked it or not, she had to be a pioneer.

And if an idea about Africa sparked her fame, as we'll see later, her comments on Africa would nearly be her undoing. The controversy took her in a surprising direction that helped change the world.

12

Attitudes

In the 1920s and the 1930s, black intellectuals from the French Empire often thought of themselves at home *as* French—until they stepped off a ship in Marseilles or another port and discovered all too soon that the French saw them in a completely different way. Black people in the British Empire, of course, often went through the same bitter rite of passage, discovering in London how they were outsiders. But France was a different environment with its own unique paradoxes. Despite the regular racism toward Africans, Senegal's Blaise Diagne was elected to the Chamber of Deputies in 1914, and he was reelected for several terms; Britain didn't see a black member of parliament until 1987.

The scene in Paris also offered consolations that you couldn't get in the British capital, with multiple sources of inspiration for new ways of thinking. In a word, Paris was jumping. Jazz bands made nightclubs swing, imported books from America were changing minds, and the cafés were lively with talk of dealing with colonialism and reinventing black identity. Countless movies have recycled the myths of Hemingway, Fitzgerald, and the rest of the Lost (and white) Generation that hung around the Shakespeare & Company bookshop, so it's a shame that Hollywood hasn't mined the exciting parallel scene—tiny as it was in comparison but still vibrant—of African American, African, and

West Indian painters, writers, poets, and musicians in the City of Light. Among them were the artists who came up with a new approach they called *Négritude*.

Just what was *Négritude*? It depended on who you asked. Too malleable to be called a philosophy, too diffuse to be a discipline, it was nevertheless a movement. Each exponent had his or her own ideas of what it was about, but, as scholar Tyler Stovall eloquently puts it, "above all, it stood for an affirmation of blackness. Rejecting the assimilationism frequently espoused by upper-class mulattoes and blacks from the French Caribbean in particular, its young partisans emphasized the integrity and beauty of a culture whose roots lay in Africa."[1] It had many inspirations, all synthesized into a new way of looking at race and culture.

One of those inspirations was poetry. While most Europeans thought black people had no history or redeeming values, there were a couple of poets who spun veils of romantic exoticism. Charles Baudelaire, for example, famous for writing *The Flowers of Evil*, rhapsodized about the hair of his Haitian lover and muse, Jeanne Duval. Rejecting civilization, a young Arthur Rimbaud penned the lines, "I am a beast, a Negro." And when his absinthe-drenched, opium-smoked, abusive relationship with fellow poet Paul Verlaine blew up, he quit writing poetry altogether, quit France altogether, and wound up in Ethiopia, where he sold coffee and antiquated guns in Harar. In fact, Rimbaud's house became a well-kept if little-visited tourist spot in the old casbah of the city.

As the twenties stopped roaring and a new decade took over, a young student from Senegal was in Paris, Léopold Sédar Senghor, hoping to become a teacher. "I hear him still, reciting to me *The Flowers of Evil* in a grave voice, a bit muffled, monotonous," recalled his friend Georges Pompidou. "It was the tone of an incantation, the very tone of the bards of Senegal."[2] In 1931, Senghor made another lifelong friend in Aimé Césaire, a student from Martinique who later remembered how they would share books and delight in the work of the same poets.

Senghor and Césaire accomplished something interesting with their friendship. Many of the French-speaking black residents of the West Indies were apt to dismiss Africans as savages as easily as whites. *They* had culture, *they* weren't black—Africans were black. *They* were different. Caribbean women in France often sneered at Senghor behind his back. Africans returned this snobbery, writing off the West Indians as the petty clerks of their colonizers. Césaire, however, appreciated his African heritage and traveled to the Casamance region in southern Senegal decades later. According to Césaire, both he and Senghor were tormented by the same question: "Who am I? For us, it was not a question of metaphysics, but of a life to live, an ethic to create, and communities to save. We tried to answer that question. In the end, our answer was *Négritude*."[3]

"The average French Negro has no idea that there are important men and important work in Negro art in America," wrote Eslanda Goode Robeson, wife of Paul Robeson. "In Martinique, the Negroes think all American Negroes are prize fighters, because a prize fighter once visited the Antilles. . . . The Negroes from the French West Indies (Antillean) dislike African negroes because they have an older civilization; cultured Antilleans are often sent to Africa as civil servants by the French government."[4] Eslanda Robeson accepted as a given that the West Indians had an older civilization.

But if blackness and being African were to have any value beyond the aesthetics and the pretty lines of Baudelaire, it needed more history. History was a weapon that could fight the argument of colonialism that Africa had been a blank page except for barbarism. Both Senghor and Césaire tunneled their way through the works of Leo Frobenius, learning whole sections the way they learned favorite poems. They found comfort, too, in the liberal conclusions of French ethnographer Maurice Delafosse, who wrote a flawed but significant history of early African civilizations, *The Negroes of Africa*. "I am aware of the fact that many Negro princes have distinguished themselves by massacres and capital punishment rather than by acts of clemency and pity," wrote Delafosse in the 1920s, "but we know of kings of France and other countries, who nevertheless were great kings . . . who had nothing to learn in this respect from such and such a Negro king or chief."[5]

It's been pointed out before that it's a little peculiar for Senghor and others to enjoy the constructed images and romanticism of African cultures by white experts and authors, but to be fair, they must have felt they were working mostly in a vacuum. Knowledge wasn't available then at the touch of a keyboard. It was built through long hours in libraries, in the lightning serendipity of a magazine reference or the casual mention by a colleague of an interesting new study. A Senegalese student in 1931 didn't need a Frenchman to tell him his people were capable of morality; what was needed in those tentative beginnings was validation of core inklings, the notions before any formal declaration of one's own ideas . . . and in time, the castoff of white validation altogether.

As it was, white civilization didn't seem to be doing too well lately, or so thought many of Europe's leading lights. It's important to keep in mind the mood of an era, and customers who walked into French bookshops in the 1920s and thirties could flip through tomes of doom: *The Decline of Europe* or *Decadence of the French Nation*. Oswald Spengler's *The Decline of the West* was popular.

Spengler—seeming to channel some fragments of Ibn Khaldun—observed historical maturing and collapse, but instead of thinking in cycles, he treated cultures like delicate plants in a garden, the Chinese, Egyptian, Classical Greco-Roman each having their day. Spengler wrote about their roots and had his own odd ideas on race as well. "A race has roots," he declared confidently and argued that a "landscape exercises a secret force upon the plant-nature in them, and eventually the race-expression is completely transformed by the extinction of the old and the appearance of a new one."[6] If this strikes a modern reader as disturbingly close to the "blood and soil" claptrap of white supremacists, it's worth remembering that he despised the Nazis and wrote critically about them. He had little if anything useful to say about Africa, but Senghor and Césaire still grappled with defining an African and black identity against the competition of ideas like his.

Strangely, neither of them had heard of Edward Wilmot Blyden, who once wrote, "Every race . . . has a soul."[7] According to Senghor, he and Césaire weren't familiar at all with his writings, though years later, he acknowledged that all the themes that he and his circle were developing in Paris had been covered by Blyden. Senghor and Césaire merely visited another branch on the family tree of ideas, those who *had* read Blyden. And *Négritude* owed a lot to the literary swagger of the Harlem Renaissance, its belated influence working its magic on the City of Light.

It happened like this. Paulette Nardal, a young West Indian, ran a literary salon out of her apartment on Sundays. Black expats met there to dance to the latest jazz records and talk ideas, and her circle began publishing a magazine, *La Revue du Monde Noir* ("The Review of the Black World"). In its first issue in the autumn of 1931, it stated its aim was to give to the intelligentsia of the black race "and its partisans an official organ in which to publish their artistic, literary and scientific works. To study and to popularize, by means of the press, books, lectures, courses, all which concerns NEGRO CIVILIZATION and the natural riches of Africa, thrice sacred to the black race."[8] It was in the *Revue*'s pages that Senghor and Césaire each read for the first time poetry by Claude McKay and Langston Hughes.

Senghor helped out a little with the magazine and hung out more with its other contributors and editors. In its pages, he found essays on black art and on Liberian politics, more poems, and the odd short story. *La Revue* also noted an incident which shows the spirit of the times: an infamously tactless white professor at a girls' school in Martinique gave the pupils this essay subject: "Why does the sight of an African Negro dressed in European clothes provoke the laugh of the white man?" The pupils, observed the magazine, "declared, among other things, that they would never forget their African origins."

La Revue didn't last long, extinct before the end of 1932, but it was influential, and it's still cited today by historians. One of the magazine's most important pieces was a long essay by Paulette Nardal about race consciousness, which focused on the evolving viewpoints of West Indian and African American writers. Nardal didn't bother to include Africans, but she could have been writing as well about their feelings of alienation in European and American culture and trying to find their voice. She did, however, have the prescience to note that long before black men in Paris, "colored women . . . felt the need of a racial solidarity which would not be merely material."

What's particularly interesting is how Nardal still speaks to us today; she marked how as black students developed their ideas, "their intellectual curiosity applied itself to the history of their race and of their respective countries. They thus came to regret the absence of such interesting matters in the educational programs of the Antillean schools. Instead of despising their unheeding brothers or laying aside all hope about the possibility of the black race being on a par with the Aryans, they began to study."[9]

Senghor, of course, would have read this with interest, just as he pounced on the work of another writer referenced in *La Revue*, Alain Locke. In 1925, Locke, a philosophy professor at Howard University, expanded one of his most impactful articles, "The New Negro," and put it into an anthology under the same title with stories, poems, and essays by others. The book was also handsomely illustrated by African American artist Aaron Douglas and contained several photos of sculptures and masks, including a Benin bronze and Congo portrait statue. There were, wrote Locke, "constructive channels opening out into which the balked social feelings of the American Negro can flow freely. . . . One is the consciousness of acting as the advance-guard of the African peoples in their contact with 20th century civilization; the other, the sense of a mission of rehabilitating the race in world esteem from that loss of prestige for which the fate and conditions of slavery have so largely been responsible."[10]

The New Negro is considered a landmark work of the Harlem Renaissance, but it had an impact as well on colonial Africans. Nnamdi Azikiwe—who would one day be a publisher, then Nigeria's first president, and later its governor-general—came to study in the U.S. in the 1920s. Azikiwe had the stimulating opportunities to meet and know some of the great minds emerging in African American and Pan-African thought. He worked as a private assistant for Alain Locke. He was later a classmate of Thurgood Marshall. He corresponded with Marxist radical

George Padmore of Trinidad and his fellow Nigerian, activist Ladipo Solanke. For Azikiwe, "the idea of a new Negro evolved into the crusade for a new Africa," while the exchanges among young students like himself and activists "started a chain reaction in the fermentation of ideas which ultimately crystallized into the struggle for the complete emancipation of the African colonial territories from European imperialism."[11]

The influence naturally weaved its way into the francophone African diaspora as well. Léopold Sédar Senghor promptly took the term "New Negro" and adapted it into French, *le nègre nouveau*, as a kind of abstract idyll of his early conclusions. In March 1935, Césaire changed the name of the *Journal de l'Association des étudiants Martiniquais en France* to *L'Etudiant noir* and invited Senghor as well as poet Léon Damas, originally from French Guiana, to help edit it.[12] It was in the pages of the magazine's May–June issue of that year where Césaire used the term *Négritude* for the first time.

Through the rest of the decade and into the forties, he and Senghor wrote provocative essays on assimilation and black culture, developing divergent interpretations of *Négritude*. Césaire's examinations leaned toward a historical view. Senghor sought to capture the concept's defining attributes. Though allies, the two disagreed over their core idea. For Césaire, the black person taken out of his African cultural environment could lose what provided him with *Négritude*. Culture carried the day, not biology. For Senghor, to be black or mixed race was enough—it automatically conferred *Négritude*—and he focused more on a genetic view of how culture could be transmitted, as exemplified in his phrase, "Emotion is Negro, as reason is Hellenic."[13]

To understand Senghor's perspective, consider these lines from "What the Black Man Contributes," a 1939 essay: "You have brought to us Africans logical reasoning: we bring to you Europeans, you Latins, intuitive reasoning by which *Négritude* is defined, *Négritude* being total comprehension of the world. . . . To atheistic materialism, we oppose spiritualistic materialism, which is incarnated in History and whose precursor was the Arab-Berber, the African—Ibn Khaldun. *Credo quia absurdum.* [I believe because it is absurd.] Tertullian's sentence, taken up by Saint Augustine. . . . What these two Berbers, these two Africans, mean is that logic by itself is incapable of comprehending reality. That there is a superior reason: this vital **élan**, this intuition of faith in which subject and object are mingled in an amorous embrace."

It's clear how black American writers left their stamp on his thinking from lines he wrote that same year: "To those who destroyed his civilization, to the slave trader, to the lyncher, Afro-American poets only respond by peaceful words." As the West became mechanized and, by implication, spiritually sterile, black Americans, he felt, were writing the only worthwhile poetry in American letters, even though they romanticized Africa and its supposedly primitive cultures. At the same time, Senghor staked out a middle course over assimilation. In his view, Africans didn't need to accept the complete package of European civilization—they had the right to be selective. "Let us take from it what is best, what is seminal, and allow us to give you back the rest."[14]

Retracing these philosophical discussions of poetry and self-image from almost a century ago can feel like floating up in a hot-air balloon—and the air gets thin. And yet there were genuine, indeed *urgent*, concerns behind late-night typing of manuscripts and debates in the Montmartre cafés. Senghor didn't always have his head in the clouds, and he had his bread-and-butter teaching career to think about. On a trip to Dakar, he was offered the job of inspector of education in French West Africa, but he turned it down, knowing he'd never be able to change policy the way he liked and effect real change. Ideas won out, and he returned to Paris to teach and take courses at the Sorbonne.

The Second World War nearly ended him. Called up as a private in the French army, he was among the troops who tried in vain in 1940 to hold a bridge at a small town near Vichy. As soon as his unit was captured, the Nazis yanked the black soldiers out of the lines and put them up against a wall to be shot. Rifles were raised. Senghor and the other soldiers yelled out, "*Vive la France! Vive l'Afrique noir!*" The firing squad took aim. And then, as if the moment had been scripted out of a Jean Renoir film, a French officer convinced the Nazis to stop. Such an action would surely dishonor the German army. Senghor would live. The gruesome moment of literally staring down the barrel of a gun gave him a new motivation to live and accomplish his artistic goals. Despite the poor food and miserable conditions in the different prisoner-of-war camps he stayed in for months, Senghor worked on his poetry and made new friends in soldiers from the French African diaspora; the prisoners even managed to entertain themselves on occasion with a crude version of a kora.

By 1944, he had refined an idea he had back before the war, a strikingly original proposal of collaboration between colonizer and colonized: Africa had things to teach France in terms of both the human heart and the artistic mind. "It is not a question of sending France to an African school; it is not even a question of assimilating African elements of which French writers and painters have begun to be aware." Instead, he thought Africa could help France "to uncover her original and authentic face that lies beneath the ugliness which modern evolution has superimposed."[15] Here is a precursor of appreciation for multicultural diversity, about fifty years before it found expression in schools in Europe and North America.

Ever the Francophile, he saw acceptance of some Western values and modernism as essential to African survival. In 1946, he posed a question: "In what way can we understand France's civilizing mission? We think that no nation is more suited than she to play the role of awakening drowsy civilizations and of fertilizing civilizations, which, even if young, are not primitive." Senghor was already thinking of a life in politics, so it would be easy to make a cynical conclusion that this was a convenient posture. It was anything but, because the fashionable left already rejected European methods. Senghor's stand was quite unique when he later suggested that Africans had to "forget old suffering to render justice to Europe and admit its necessity."[16]

Another apostle of *Négritude* and a distinguished member of the French Senate, Alioune Diop, founded the quarterly magazine *Présence Africaine* in 1947. Diop and a circle of about ten young, passionate students "wanted to create an African cultural renaissance in Paris" and believed, as the Beninois journalist Paulin Joachim put it, "our vocation was essentially to insert African culture into the civilization of the white man. It was to affirm our presence, our African presence, because the colonizers had always negated our culture, as if there could be a people without culture."[17] Diop saw a key target audience for his quarterly in the youth of Africa who lacked "intellectual food" and he also hoped to persuade African elites into reconnecting with other social classes and bridging Africa with the Western world.[18]

The first issue featured the work of French intellectuals such as André Gide, Jean-Paul Sartre, and Georges Balandier. It also included the work of Senghor, Bernard Dadié of Côte d'Ivoire, and American literary lights such as Gwendolyn Brooks and novelist Richard Wright. In the years that followed, *Présence Africaine* published some of the greatest writers in African literature. In 1948, as France tried to forget the nightmare of the Nazi occupation, losing itself in a fresh wave of jazz, literature, and art, Senghor put out an *Anthology of the New Black and Malagasy Poetry in the French Language*. It was a collection of poets from the Antilles, Madagascar, and French colonial Africa, and it made quite a splash—more so because Senghor persuaded Jean-Paul Sartre to write its introduction, titled "Black Orpheus."

More than half a century later, it still reads as an ambiguous critique, and you're left unsure if it's the work of an ally. Sartre begins on a downright accusatory note to a presumably white French audience: "When you removed the gag that was keeping these black mouths shut, what were you hoping for? That they would sing your praises? Did you think that when they raised themselves up again, you would read adoration in the eyes of these heads that our fathers had forced to bend down to the very ground?" Strong stuff. But as he delves into *Négritude*, he undermines it, declaring it "an anti-racism racism." This charge, more than any other, punctuated the discussions of the concept over the next few decades. Sartre rhapsodized that *Négritude* was "in essence, poetry" but only a few lines earlier wrote that it was "a sad myth full of hope, born of Evil and pregnant with future Good, living like a woman who is born to die and who feels her own death even in the richest moments of her life . . .

it also remains the existential attitude chosen by free men and lived *absolutely*, to the fullest [emphasis in the original]."[19]

Senghor himself later acknowledged that *Négritude* was a myth, but it had been a useful one that allowed for constant reinterpretations, and he was no dogmatist. He kept writing poetry as his political career threatened to eclipse his literary one. First, he worked for the colonial administration and then was elected as a deputy of the National Assembly. Senghor had already decided in the 1930s that for France and West Africa, "our destiny is one and the same." Eventually, he would become the first president of independent Senegal. His old university friend Georges Pompidou would become France's prime minister and later president.

Senghor, however, always preferred to think of himself as more poet than statesman. It's just as well, given that his political career received far fewer rave reviews than his poetry, especially from Senegalese who lived through his tenure. Amid regular accusations of his being a "neocolonialist," he steered his country into the dismal shoals of economic stagnation. When protests rocked the University of Dakar campus in 1968, just as they erupted around the world, many students were tossed into military camps, and Senghor even "suggested that the head of Senegal's army, General Jean-Alfred Diallo, take power if he wished."[20] Yet he was the first and one of the very few postindependence leaders in Africa to ever voluntarily give up power, retiring in 1984, but not before he paved the way for his handchosen successor. That same year, at the age of seventy-four, he was inducted as the first African member of the Académie Française.

The reader was warned at the beginning that we wouldn't dive deep into the political careers of African thinkers who became leaders. But Senghor requires this brief note of context because he capitalized greatly on his image as an intellectual and a literary giant. As scholar Florian Bobin writes, "Although Senegal did not experience the same political crises as its neighbors, the mythification of 'poet-president' Senghor has blurred our understanding of his political action. Under the single-party rule of the Senegalese Progressive Union (UPS), authorities resorted to brutal methods; intimidating, arresting, imprisoning, torturing, and killing dissidents. Recalling he was both a poet and a president is a matter of fact but associating both, while refusing to recognize the authoritarianism he displayed, is historical nonsense."[21]

Nevertheless, Senghor remains a chief architect of one of the most controversial yet influential African ideas. *Négritude* would always have its critics, both black and white. Communists particularly loathed it because it defied their pigeonholing of black peoples into their own elaborate ideology and the greater class struggle. As the years rolled on, others rejected *Négritude* as a catchall that mistakenly elevated emotion above reason. Wole Soyinka once dismissed *Négritude* as an "inherently invalid doctrine" and Senghor as a romanticist expat: "The duiker will not paint 'duiker' on his beautiful back to proclaim his duikeritude; you'll know him by his elegant leap. The less self-conscious the African is, and the more innately his individual qualities appear in his writing, the more seriously he will be taken as an artist of exciting dignity."[22]

His criticism was often repeated in the years to follow in the pithier, "A tiger does not proclaim his tigritude." Yet even Soyinka qualified his views on *Négritude* with the advance of decades and suggested that "for me, Senghor remains the first—albeit unannounced—African winner of the Nobel Prize for Literature."[23]

In the end, *Négritude* served a purpose, at least as a bridge. It helped solidify the budding unity between Caribbean intellectuals and their African counterparts. If its loose collection of vague, lyrical notions and metaphysical posturing annoyed some Africans, *Négritude* was at least something of their own now to reject, and they could build a new substantial edifice, whether it was in literature, criticism, or philosophy. As Tyler Stovall put it, *Négritude* "proclaimed that peoples of African descent contributed significantly to the civilization of the world, and in praising the culture of a people so often deemed inferior and degraded, it struck a powerful blow for racial equality and self-respect."[24]

In the 1930s, Paris had the jazz and the art, but if you wanted to see the future of the intellectual landscape for much of Africa and the Caribbean, you really had to go to London. The future leaders and activists of an independent Ghana, Kenya, and other countries were often studying, working, and rushing through Britain's capital to take part in rallies or editorial meetings of radical publications. Eric Williams, when he wasn't tunneling through files and receipts over the Atlantic slave trade, was on the fringes of the radical activist movement but never a hard-core member. He would take the train in from Oxford to show up for a few meetings but mostly remained the bookish student.

Not that anyone was likely to recognize their potential anyway. Many of these student radicals were stone-cold broke. One of them studied anthropology at the London School of Economics, and he had to sneak out of his tiny flat near Victoria Station to avoid his landlady when the rent was due. Entering his forties, he sometimes peeled the stamps off letters to sell just for a bun to eat, and his clothes were so shabby that his friends dragged him off to shops to buy him new pieces of clothing. If he was lucky, the phonetics department at University College paid him ten shillings an hour for his expertise in the Kikuyu language. The world would know him as Jomo Kenyatta, and one day he would be the first president of an independent Kenya.

It would have been difficult to believe from meeting the man in 1930s London. His early schooling had been unimpressive. He'd had various jobs, from moving livestock to reading water meters, and had managed to escape serving like other Kikuyu for the British effort in World War I, taking few risks when he joined those working for independence. The Kikuyu Central Association sent him to London in 1929 to lobby officials at the Colonial Office, but its representative—then calling himself Johnstone Kenyatta—spent his expense money on clothes and living the high life with a couple of English prostitutes.

University studies, writing articles for British magazines and newspapers, and his activities in politics all gave Kenyatta an excuse not to go home through the next decade. He befriended Trinidad radical George Padmore, who by then—amazingly—had worked as a reporter in Germany before the Nazis forced him to leave. Padmore had a great influence on his political thinking. Then, during World War II, Kenyatta waited out the conflict as a farm laborer in Sussex. When he finally chose to return home in 1946, he abandoned his English wife, who was pregnant with his second child, knowing they would be political liabilities as he rejoined the fight with the KCA.

But back in the 1930s, he had already made a major contribution to African ideas. He wrote a book called *Facing Mount Kenya*.

On first blush, it can be a dry read; it's often interesting but far from a page-turner. And a modern reader can be forgiven for expecting they'll be in for a slog when they find passages such as this: "When crops are about four or five inches high, the weeding of the ground is started. During this time, people join a collective weeding."[25] But it also contains some fascinating gems: "The disobedient or careless son or daughter lives under the fear of [a dying parent's curse] every day. '*Orokanyararwo ne ciana ciaku otogwo onyarareete*' May your children treat you with disrespect as you have treated me."[26] Page by page, Kenyatta builds up a portrait of a people through its social groupings, its religious practices, and its initiation ceremonies.

But what makes *Facing Mount Kenya* such a remarkable and lasting achievement is that it's a major work both in ethnography and as a Pan-African manifesto. White observers certainly could have cataloged all the practices and beliefs of the Kikuyu, but here was a study by an insider. Kenyatta *was* Kikuyu. The frontispiece of the book had a photograph of him holding a spear while dressed in traditional garb (which he borrowed from a friend). He could write authoritatively about their practices of worship and medicine because he used to help his grandfather, a traditional healer. He made the case that whatever the failings of the Kikuyu's traditional system of government, individuals enjoyed rights under their own system and could live as they pleased. When Europeans came along, their first step in oppression was to confiscate the best lands.

Keep in mind, his words were published in 1938, when most Africans were treated as either savages or children. But by now, the momentum of the 1920s and early thirties had pushed open windows in Europe and America to allow in fresh thinking. And in a bitter irony, the political threat against Jews and other minorities meant their cultures were being reevaluated, so it only made sense to look again at African ones. Today, we've seen the same phenomenon with articles asking, "Who are the Yezidis?"—a people in Iraq called "devil worshippers" and who were persecuted by ISIS. But like the Yoruba and the Kikuyu, the Yezidi were always there (and in fact had suffered devastating persecution for at least 200 years under the Ottoman Empire while the West stayed mostly oblivious). Kristallnacht took place in November 1938; the Nazis showed the world once again that white Europeans could be devalued as easily as Africans.

Not that Kenyatta's work didn't meet with criticisms, as he certainly had his own spin on many things. His academic mentor at the London School of Economics was Professor Bronislaw Malinowski, a star at the time in the rising field of anthropology and a sincere advocate for indigenous people to have their own say about their cultures. But when he wrote the introduction for the book, he couldn't resist weighing in. For instance, Kenyatta championed the practice of female circumcision, claiming extravagantly that a Kikuyu female specialist uses a razor "with the dexterity of a Harley Street surgeon" while the unfortunate girl "hardly feels any pain." Malinowski declared he wasn't aware of any case when a performing London surgeon and a Kikuyu had been observed side by side and that the "principles of sepsis are certainly not prominent in the ritual surgery of any African tribe."[27]

Others went further. The anthropologist Louis Leakey, who knew the Kikuyu well enough to be fully fluent in their language and was a bitter critic of Kenyatta's hyperbole, once had a shouting match with him over the issue at an anthropology seminar in 1935.

The merits of the specific cultural practices, however, aren't what give Kenyatta's work its legacy. Here was an African defining his people—and *insisting* that an African version be the definition. He concluded his book by arguing that "by driving him off his ancestral lands, the Europeans have robbed [the African] of the material foundations of his culture and reduced him to a state of serfdom incompatible with human happiness. The African is conditioned, by the cultural and social institutions of centuries, to a freedom of which Europe has little conception, and it is not in his nature to accept serfdom forever. He realises that he must fight unceasingly for his own complete emancipation; for without this he is doomed to remain the prey of rival imperialisms, which in every successive year will drive their fangs more deeply into his vitality and strength."[28]

In recent years, it's been suggested that Kenyatta never wrote *Facing Mount Kenya*. The doubts are fueled in part by one of the founders of the Mau Mau, Bildad Kaggia, who claimed Kenyatta had never even read his own book; he ascribes its authorship to "a British lady."[29] It has to be remembered that while Kaggia was a regular ally of Kenyatta in the fight for independence, he was also a political rival. As for the "British lady" he referred to, this can only be Dinah Stock, the English woman Kenyatta lived with in London and the Sussex countryside. It's a fact that she did organize his various university essays for their inclusion in the book and corrected his English grammar and spelling.[30]

But to suggest Stock authored the book is a hard sell. While Kenyatta reportedly had difficulties with English when he first arrived in London, he was penning articles for the *Daily Worker* as early as 1929 and one for the *New Statesman* in 1936. He was already at the LSE when he met Dinah Stock for the first time at a rally in Trafalgar Square in May 1937. She edited the draft of *Facing Mount Kenya* in three weeks—hardly the time window needed to meticulously research a life's worth of experience of Kikuyu culture and then ghostwrite a whole book on it and infuse it with a spirit of nationalism.[31]

When the book was first released, it sold a pathetic 517 copies. But as time passed, it gained steam, perhaps because it was well received by experts and was published in Britain, a country where people were still expected to know and keep to their class but who couldn't help notice things were changing. Only a couple of years before, anti-Fascists and Oswald Mosley's Black Shirts were brawling in the infamous Battle of Cable Street in London's East End. And one year before Kenyatta's book was released, George Orwell's *The Road to Wigan Pier* came out, brutally dissecting working-class life in the Midlands and Yorkshire. Notice the phrasing in Kenyatta's lines quoted above: *a freedom of which Europe has little conception.*

Perhaps the most accurate and lasting verdict on the book is the one handed down by Jomo Kenyatta's biographer, Jeremy Murray-Brown. He called *Facing Mount Kenya* "a propaganda tour de force" and "a skillful blend of fact and polemic."[32]

One of Kenyatta's friends in the 1930s was the most famous black man in the world, singer and actor Paul Robeson.

Standing six foot three, handsome, and with a deep bass voice that spellbound audiences whether in dialogue or song, there seemed nothing he couldn't do. A remarkable athlete, a charismatic performer who had starred in Broadway revivals of *Show Boat* and Eugene O'Neill's play *Emperor Jones*, Robeson moved in 1933 to London, where he could enjoy theatrical and film opportunities without the oppressive constraints of the American racial divide. Respected widely in liberal and intellectual circles on both sides of the Atlantic, he was in a unique position to express his opinions on Africa and stir the public imagination in ways that academics couldn't. Not only is he still underappreciated as a civil rights advocate, he provides us with an interesting measure of the standing of African culture and ideas in the interwar period.

"I 'discovered' Africa in London," Robeson explained two decades later, and the continent "profoundly influenced my life."[33] Enrolling at London's School of Oriental and African Studies, he learned the intricacies of Yoruba and Asante Twi, and this brought him into the circle of impoverished but energetic student activists, such as Kenyatta and Ghana's future first president Kwame Nkrumah. He would become a patron of the West African Students' Union in Camden Square.[34] At the same time, his celebrity allowed him to socialize with established and prominent figures like H. G. Wells and Jawaharlal Nehru. He also claimed that thanks to his research and growing interest in socialism, he was paid a call by British intelligence.[35]

While many African American activists and radicals of his time still thought of the mother continent as backward, Robeson was able to talk to men like Kenyatta who felt they had nothing to apologize for over their cultures, and this made a deep impression on him. For an op-ed piece in *The Spectator* in 1934, he noted how even some black Americans were under the delusion that Africans were so primitive that they were "practically incapable of speech and merely used sign language!" But to Robeson, it was "astonishing" and "fascinating to find a flexibility and subtlety in a language like Swahili, sufficient to convey the teachings of Confucius, for example."[36]

That same year, he expressed a desire to visit Nigeria to discover pure African music and to further learn languages "so that as soon as I arrive, I can feel at home." He envisioned himself settling permanently in Africa one day. One incredulous reporter challenged him on whether he had in mind a village in the Congo, to which Robeson shot back, "Why not? They are my own people, and I would be on my native soil. Among white men, I am always lonely."[37]

Months later, he clarified his intent in an article for London's *Daily Herald*, one that declared boldly from its opening line, "Sometimes I think I am the only Negro living who would not prefer to be white." Yes, he was interested in living in Africa, but he wasn't about to abandon his career. "Where I live is not important. But I am going back to my people in the sense that for the rest of my life, I am going to think and feel as an African—not as a white man." And he offered a political analysis that is strikingly modern and familiar to our era. "Only those who have lived in a state of inequality will understand what I mean—workers, European Jews, women . . . those who have felt their status, their race, or their sex a bar to a complete share in all that the world has to offer."[38]

Yes, his student friends in London thought of themselves and their fellow Africans in an anticolonial context, and some, like George Padmore, framed it as a Marxist class struggle, but Robeson went further. He defined the African as a specific alienated group on an equal status with populations that were recognized at the time as oppressed minorities, such as Jews. His article was published not only in London but appeared across the Atlantic in the *Chicago Defender*.

It's worth dwelling for a moment on what a landmark this was. It was one thing for Jomo Kenyatta to demand respect for his people's traditional ways, and it was another thing for West Indian intellectuals to team up with African expats in Paris over literary magazines. But it would take years for their respective impacts to be felt beyond their circles. Paul Robeson was a worldwide American celebrity. Like Josephine Baker, he sold records and was a box office draw. And he was *choosing* to be African and stated it publicly. In 1936, he wrote another magazine article with the ironic title "Primitives," defending African intellectual achievement and civilization.

Reminding his readers of Pushkin's and Alexandre Dumas's African roots, he anticipated the tired comeback that these were exceptions, and even if the African "thinks as Confucius thought . . . where are his philosophers, his poets, his artists?" Robeson's reply was that "Africa has produced far more than Western people realize. More than one scientist has been struck by the similarity between certain works by long-dead West African artists and exquisite examples of Chinese, Mexican and Javanese art. . . . It is now recognized that African music has subtleties of rhythm far finer than anything achieved by a Western composer."[39]

Robeson never fulfilled his own promises of exploring interpretations of "pure" African music—he was always more comfortable with spirituals and folk songs. But he found other ways to express his African identity and support Africa politically. His efforts had mixed results and left him with some bittersweet memories.

In 1934, for instance, the Korda Brothers—makers of such film classics as *The Four Feathers* and *The Thief of Baghdad*—adapted the shlock imperialist adventure novel *Sanders of the River* by Edgar Wallace. They gave the major part of African chief Bosambo to Robeson, winning him over with the sales pitch that this film would be different than past portrayals of the continent. And it was true that spectacular B-roll footage was shot in central Africa: traditional rituals and dancing, wildlife, stunning scenery, the works. Most of the action for the plot, meanwhile, was filmed on a London set, albeit one that employed Africans living in the city. Robeson—who had long believed he was a descendant of Nigeria's Igbo people—managed to strike up friendly conversations with Nigerian extras, relying on a few Igbo words and phrases he claimed had been passed down to him through his family.[40] His friend Jomo Kenyatta played one of the warriors in the movie.

Before the cameras rolled, Robeson thought *Sanders* would enlighten moviegoers about the real Africa. He was appalled by the finished movie, and it's not difficult to see why. Over a fluttering Union Jack, the film opens with the bombastic claim that "tens of millions of natives under British rule, each tribe with its own chieftain, are governed and protected by a handful of white men whose everyday work is an unsung saga of courage and efficiency." The film offers a nauseating portrayal of Africans as superstitious children in need of a white savior. "I hate the picture," Robeson said years later.[41]

He had the chance, however, to subvert the standard colonial narrative when he was asked in 1936 to film a prologue and record the theme song to a documentary film about South Africa. This was *My Song Goes Forth*, directed by Joseph Best and released in some locations as *Africa Looks Up*.

Best himself delivered most of the narration in the film, which by turns made condescending and even insulting judgments on the figures who passed in front of his lens. As Charles Musser wrote in *Film History*, the people—both black and white—"clearly have no idea that they are to be the objects of such unremitting evaluation. Best applied such an approach to every one of significantly lower status. In a native market place, he filmed a wide variety of people, who pose good-naturedly for his camera. At one point his commentary intones: 'An intelligent looking native is followed by an unintelligent looking white. One of the poor white class.' The white man poses for Best in a relaxed, friendly manner—unaware that the camera man would subsequently add a humiliating evaluation of his demeanor." An African couple is shown dressed up for a date, hardly aware that their time together would be contrasted with "traditional courting practices."[42]

Robeson's contribution was therefore a breath of fresh air. He revised the original script of the prologue to make a much bolder on-screen statement. "Every foot of Africa is now parceled out among the white races. Why has this happened? What has prompted them to go there? If you listen to men like Mussolini they will tell you it is to 'civilize'—a divine task, entrusted to the enlightened peoples to carry the torch of light and learning, and to benefit the African people. . . . Africa was opened up by the white man for the benefit of himself—to obtain the wealth it contained." For the first time, British audiences sat in theaters and heard a distinguished black man in a sharp suit candidly inform them "there is no difference whatever between the capacity of the African and of the Europeans."[43]

The film earned only tepid reviews. Best, try as he might, could not persuade distributors in South Africa to take the original cut. After re-editing the picture, he still couldn't get a release for it in the U.S. well into the 1940s, and it's unclear just how well the film did, if it did any business at all, in America. Nevertheless, it was seen and reviewed in the place where it could perhaps be most effective: the seat of the British Empire. We should still think of it as a milestone, not least because motion pictures were still a young medium. *My Song Goes Forth* failed to give South Africans their dignity, but it did have Paul Robeson. The man who chose to think of himself as African now spoke *for* Africans, and, more important, he was recognized as an intermediary for their cultures. Between his articles and his efforts in cinema, Robeson, in modern parlance, took African ideas into the mainstream.

For decades, Robeson spoke out and lobbied mainly through the auspices of the Council on African Affairs, which was formed in 1937 (he was later its chairman). With the force of his celebrity and his natural eloquence, he was a sharp critic of colonialism and the right-wing elements in the postwar world which tried to keep a grip on Africa. J. Edgar Hoover, just as he'd targeted Marcus Garvey and would years later persecute Martin Luther King Jr., had his agents spy on him. It's beyond the scope of this book to dwell on the impressive civil rights activism and personal struggle of Robeson, but it's worth mentioning his second appearance before the House Committee on Un-American Activities in 1956. The testimony of such writers as Arthur Miller and Lillian Hellman usually get the attention in retelling the dark days of HUAC, but no one ever defied the committee as Robeson did, literally telling it, "Go to hell."

Through the 1950s and sixties, the relentless harassment by authorities, including the State Department spreading disinformation about him and at one point denying him a passport, took a heavy toll on his career. Then on his mental state and inevitably on his physical health. Before his tragic breakdown and death, however, he was a staunch advocate of African liberation. In 1954, Oliver Tambo invited him to send a statement to the annual conference of the African National Congress. Robeson wrote that he was "deeply proud that you are my brothers and sisters and nephews and nieces—that I sprang from your forebears. We come from a mighty, courageous people, creators of great civilizations in the past, creators of new ways of life in our own time and in the future. We shall win our freedom together. Our folks will have their place in the ranks of those shaping human destiny."[44]

13

Tanks versus Spears

It was the war in Africa that changed the world. Tens of thousands of people once poured into the streets of different capitals for its cause, but many people have never even heard of this conflict. And so few celebrate its victory.

When the spark lit in early December 1934, the *New York Times* ran a tiny item on page 11 of its edition, an Associated Press story about an oasis in the middle of nowhere, which it incorrectly stated was in Italian Somaliland. The truth was that Fascist troops had moved in and interfered with a joint British–Ethiopian border commission. During the tense standoff, the British soldiers left. The Ethiopians were on their own and were hopelessly outmatched. In a skirmish days later, they suffered heavy casualties. The confrontation was billed in the press as a border dispute, but the Italians—according to their own maps—were more than *sixty miles* within Ethiopian territory. Worse, Italy's dictator Benito Mussolini had been planning to start this fight as early as 1932.[1]

Mussolini had always been a thug. In World War I, the British paid him to lead gangsters in Milan who would beat up antiwar protesters. Then he turned his career as a journalist and publisher into a platform to gain power. Fake news didn't start in our modern era; it really began in more sophisticated forms about 100 years ago when "Il Duce"—the Leader—and his

cronies adjusted the facts to their liking. "With astonishing success, the *Fascisti* have not only cut off true contemporary record
of their deeds but have invented a whole history of their past
which is usurping the suppressed truth," observed the journalist William Bolitho in 1925. "In another five years, every scrap of
material evidence of the real history of Fascism will have disappeared as thoroughly as the dossier of Mussolini from the Swiss
Police Bureau."[2]

But Mussolini couldn't erase Italy's humiliating defeat at
Adwa. With an adolescent's conception of military valor, he
wanted it avenged. Invasion of Ethiopia could serve a practical
purpose, too. Only a few years after he came to power, Mussolini claimed in public that Italy's colonies—Eritrea, Libya, its
own parcel of Somaliland—couldn't satisfy the country's needs.
The truth was that Italy stayed poor because of incompetence.
The Fascist approach to economics was a set of industrial guilds
and corporate boards, each one too bungling and bureaucratic to
lift the country out of its doldrums. The south stayed undevel-
oped, with areas where malaria was endemic.

On the morning of May 24, 1934, Mussolini rode through the
Piazza Venezia in a carefully staged show of power. "The Italian infantry is now so developed that it can contend against any
infantry in the world," he boasted. "Better to live a day as a lion
than a century as a sheep. Italy wishes peace but is ready for any
eventuality. Are you all ready?"

And the crowd shouted back, "*Yes! Yes!*"[3]

We can never be sure how much pro-war feeling there was
in the country, as attendance at the Duce's speeches and public
events was always mandatory.

Planes, tanks, armored cars, and huge quantities of ammunition were shipped over to Italian African territory, and we have
evidence of his predatory ambitions from his own words: "The
more rapid our military action, the less will be the danger of
diplomatic complications. No one in Europe will raise any difficulties for us if the conduct of military operations rapidly creates
an accomplished fact."[4]

Mussolini clearly expected the rest of Europe to let Italy
have "its place in the sun," but this was the 1930s, not the era of

Belgium's King Leopold, and Ethiopia's Emperor Haile Selassie took his grievance to the League of Nations. This should have settled the matter. The League's own Covenant stated an "all for one, one for all" doctrine of collective security and defense of its members. Britain's delegate, Anthony Eden—handsome, intellectual, a fashion icon of the day, and fluent in multiple languages—sincerely believed in it. Unfortunately, his own Tory government did not. It included men who grew up in the "glorious" years of the Raj and the Battle of Rorke's Drift, and after the slaughter of the Great War, they were happy to sit on the sidelines and watch someone else's colonial adventure. They also dreaded the prospect of getting ensnared in another mechanized, trench-laced horror.

They certainly wouldn't start it over a country *in Africa*. Ethiopia, complained critics, was a backward nation that still had slavery (ignoring the fact that Haile Selassie had taken several steps to eradicate slavery in the country). The other great superpower of the time was France, but like Britain, it was more concerned with keeping Mussolini happy and in an alliance against Hitler. Some of the efforts to prevent war were scuttled by French Prime Minister Pierre Laval, an odious, cynical toady for the dictators who later helped lead the Vichy regime (and who would be ignominiously shot by a firing squad in 1945 after his hidden cyanide capsule failed to work).

So, an independent African nation exposed the underlying conceit behind the great idea promoted by the League of Nations. Collective security was a veil, one the dictators would pull down and rip into shreds.

The League dithered for months, dragging the dispute all the way into the summer of 1935, and Mussolini, though frustrated by his government having to file counterpetitions, motions, and be accountable, had more time for his arms buildup as statesmen kept pondering and debating in Geneva. Then a strange thing happened, and everyone, Mussolini most of all, was unprepared for how the narrative of righteous conquest got away from him.

Ordinary people—in London and Paris, New York and Mexico City, Chicago and Madrid—expressed solidarity with Ethiopia. On August 3, about 20,000 African Americans and sympathetic whites turned out for two marches to a rally in Harlem. There were more demonstrations by African Americans across the U.S. In Toulouse, protesters attacked a group of Italian sailors who were on their way home to join the fight. In Accra and Cape Town, thousands of black residents tried to sign up as soldiers for Ethiopia. Muslim Arabs in Morocco even organized their own force to cross the Sahara and work their way along the Nile to fight on the side of Haile Selassie.

"The Ethiopia Crisis," as it was dubbed until war broke out, now dominated the headlines. For a while, Mussolini became more bellicose and let it be known that he was willing to attack Malta if he didn't get his way. The British government temporarily rediscovered its spine and sent ships into the Mediterranean, putting some overseas bases on alert. We might easily have had World War II about four years early. But at the center of the fight was Ethiopia, a land where barefoot warriors were often armed only with spears, buffalo-hide shields, and rifles from the last century. They needed modern arms. They needed modern medical supplies and more doctors. Most of all, they needed their allies to stop hand-wringing and start helping.

The world, especially residents of African American neighborhoods in the U.S., watched with growing apprehension. "Haile Selassie was the first black emperor I ever saw in a newsreel," recalled James Baldwin, who witnessed the drama unfold as a ten-year-old child in a movie theater. "He was pleading vainly with the West to prevent the rape of his country. And the extraordinary complex of tensions thus set up in the breast, between hatred of whites and contempt for blacks, is very hard to describe."[5]

Everything, it seemed, now had an angle related to the crisis—it even spilled over to the sports pages. Boxers Joe Louis and Primo Carnera become political pawns when they met in the ring at Yankee Stadium. Carnera naturally stood for Italy, while Louis was cast in the role of champion for Ethiopia. "They put a heavy weight on my twenty-year-old shoulders," Louis complained later. "Now, not only did I have to beat the man, but I had to beat him for a cause."[6] He did beat him, and Harlem erupted in ecstatic celebration. Months later, a Broadway play funded through the New Deal's Federal Theater Project—a "living newspaper" about Ethiopia—was shut down by the U.S. government because real politicians were portrayed onstage.

Celebrities weighed in throughout the struggle, but there was no consensus. Josephine Baker—then involved with an Italian stonemason pretending to be a count and who became her manager—stunned everyone by siding with the Fascists. "I am ready to travel around the world to convince my brothers that Mussolini is their friend. If need be, I will recruit a Negro army to help Italy."[7] For a short while, she became a pariah among African Americans. Radio pioneer Guglielmo Marconi claimed he was working on a microwave weapon to bring down British planes, but no weapon ever materialized. George Bernard Shaw told a reporter, "Mussolini means blood. Don't forget if it is white versus black, we shall have to come in with the Italians."[8]

On the other side, Trotsky argued that if Mussolini won, it would discourage colonial peoples in Africa and elsewhere. Mohandas Gandhi wanted to organize a Red Cross unit for Ethiopia but admitted he had trouble raising interest among Indians. In London, Marcus Garvey wrote in his bully pulpit of a newspaper, *The Black Man*, that Italy's dictator was "a tyrant, a bully, an irresponsible upstart," while Emperor Haile Selassie was a "sober, courteous and courageous gentleman."[9] He warned that there were millions of black people willing to fight for the cause. It was true that there *were* scores of black volunteers ready and willing to go fight, both in the U.S. and in British and French colonies. But their governments took fierce steps to keep them from participating, and the State Department deliberately denied passports to African Americans.

The League of Nations imposed an arms embargo, but this did little against Italy, which could easily get around the rules and had already shipped most of what it needed, while Ethiopia couldn't possibly catch up. The League imposed economic sanctions, but despite pressure from Anthony Eden, these didn't include oil. Meanwhile, the British government lost its nerve for any confrontation with Mussolini, and the dictator knew it—an Italian spy worked as a messenger in the British embassy in Rome. Worse, MI6 *knew who he was*. But Britain's ambassador

Volunteers in Harlem sign up in the hopes of going to fight for Ethiopia. *Courtesy Critical Past.*

to Italy refused to accept the warning and less than two years later even invited the man and his wife to the coronation of King George VI.

Finally, Mussolini's soldiers crossed the Mareb River into Ethiopia on October 3, 1935. The small, two-seater tanks made by Fiat had "Adwa" written on their sides, and the Fascist planes made a point of bombing Adwa and other small towns to drive home the message of vengeance—they then issued a denial, even though Mussolini's own sons, who were pilots, bragged about their mission.

In London, Kwame Nkrumah heard a newsboy shouting and noticed the headlines. "At that moment, it was almost as if the whole of London had suddenly declared war on me personally. For the next few minutes I could do nothing but glare at each impassive face wondering if those people could possibly realize the wickedness of colonialism, and praying that the day might come when I could play my part in bringing about the downfall of such a system."[10] In South Africa, Nelson Mandela was a teenager. "I was seventeen when Mussolini attacked Ethiopia, an invasion that spurred not only my hatred of that despot but of fascism in general."[11]

Protests went on, massive and multiple ones, and in New York City, there were ugly fights between African Americans and Italians in the streets and in school yards. London was another arena where left and right collided. In Soho Square, Oswald Mosley and his British Black Shirts handed out pamphlets, declaring that "finance, oil, the Jews, and the Reds want war." Police had to break up fights between his men and demonstrators. Nearby, you found African and Caribbean expatriates and students working hard for the activist group, International African Friends of Ethiopia. Kwame Nkrumah was a member, as was Jomo Kenyatta.

So were West Indies writers and activists such as C. L. R. James and George Padmore. Marcus Garvey's ex-wife, Amy Ashwood Garvey—an accomplished music producer and lyricist as well as a talented speaker in her own right—founded the Florence Mills Social Club, where the radicals liked to meet, plan, and relax. In a brief article for *The New Leader*, the paper for the Independent Labour Party, C. L. R. James wrote, "Let us fight against not only Italian imperialism, but the other robbers and oppressors, French and British imperialism."[12] By the time he started drafting *The Black Jacobins*, his classic on Toussaint Louverture and the Haitian Revolution, he "had reached the conclusion that the centre of the black revolution was Africa, not the Caribbean."[13]

Jomo Kenyatta became so immersed in the cause that he grew a beard in imitation of Haile Selassie and took to wearing a fez and cloak. In the flat he shared with Dinah Stock in London's Camden Town, he painted the furniture in the traditional colors of Ethiopia. Stock remembered Kenyatta "half jestingly, half seriously, quizzing a distinguished aircraft designer—who happened to be a Communist—on the most effective way of sabotaging an airplane on the ground with a spear."[14]

In America, the emperor's one-time physician turned activist and fund-raiser Malaku Bayen also took innovative steps to enlist African Americans. He knew that for the residents of

Harlem and the struggling communities in major cities across the United States, Ethiopia was a matter of racial pride. Long before Martin Luther King, before Angela Davis and *Roots*, Malaku Bayen preached the message, "Think black, act black and be black."[15] A strong believer in Pan-Africanism, he even broke off his engagement to the daughter of Ethiopia's foreign affairs minister just so that he could marry an African American woman.

Protests stirred the heart and raised awareness, but ultimately, the Ethiopians were left to face the enemy alone. Haile Selassie, knowing his forces were outmatched, pulled back his armies and allowed the Fascists to push deep into the country—dangerously overextending their supply lines. The Italians had planes and tanks, but the Ethiopians at least had geography on their side. In the Danakil, for instance, the two-seater tanks made by Fiat, built out of cheap tin, might as well have been ovens when the temperature rose to 120 degrees. In several ways, the war was fought as if it were happening in the previous century. Blacksmiths were called up for military service because the Italian army relied so much on horses. Mussolini's commanders repeatedly used a three-column attack formation. And while their artillery hammered away with brutal effect, the struggle for ground often came down to two armies clashing in bloody hand-to-hand combat.

To everyone's surprise, the Ethiopians managed to hold their own for several weeks, hurting the Italians badly with serious losses and slowing their momentum to a crawl. It's astonishing that they won as many engagements as they did. But culture was part of their undoing. Thanks to the dictates of feudal custom, the generals in charge were high-ranking nobles, each one a ras, and *none* of them had any experience with modern warfare. Only one had ever even been under fire: Ras Mulugeta Yeggazu, a hero of the Battle of Adwa, and he was now old, cantankerous, and alcoholic. Besides sometimes undermining his fellow commanders, he mistreated prisoners and let his soldiers loot peasant villages.

Haile Selassie had urged his people not to fight in the open, to dye their brilliant white shammas brown to better camouflage them in the countryside. They didn't listen. To duck behind hills, to sneak up on the enemy went against a long warrior tradition. Ethiopian battles almost never continued past sundown, and the Italians were taken aback when the Ethiopians had the advantage, only to suddenly break off and retreat. Only one resourceful commander, the emperor's own cousin, Ras Imru, took the advice of guerrilla warfare to heart and made impressive raids on the enemy all the way into Eritrean territory.

Meanwhile, Britain's foreign secretary at the time was Samuel Hoare, a man who once served as the MI6 handler for Mussolini when he was smashing the skulls of peace activists. Hoare was another old-school Tory who saw the Ethiopians as savages and had no problem with Italy gobbling up the country. That December, he met with France's Pierre Laval, who kept negotiating with Mussolini in secret. Laval and Hoare cooked up a scheme of their own to finally abandon Ethiopia, and during the talks, Laval frequently called up the Duce to get his opinion. The deal came to be known as the Hoare-Laval Pact. To avoid more war, Italy would receive about *half* of Ethiopia as well as the means to capture the rest. The consolation prize for the loser would be Assab, a port to the sea—but Ethiopia wouldn't be allowed to build a railway to it.

Haile Selassie, of course, rejected the plan. But the scandal over the shameful deal and betrayal of an ally nearly took down the British government, and Samuel Hoare was forced to quit. Anthony Eden was made foreign secretary, but behind his back, officials at the Foreign Office kept towing the same old agenda.

And so the war went on. Mussolini gave direct orders to increase bombings and the use of poison gas. In several cases, their bombs deliberately hit and obliterated Red Cross hospitals. The poison gas was devastating, killing scores of warriors while leaving others with severe, excruciating burns and often permanent damage to their lungs. Marcel Junod, a Swiss doctor with the Red Cross, remembered coming over a hill after one Italian raid and seeing the burn victims moaning, "*Abiet . . . Abiet. . . .* Have pity."[16] Cattle thrashed in helpless panic, dying in agony. When stories of these clear violations of the Geneva Convention went public, Rome offered more denials and did its best to stonewall investigations. They also engaged in public smears of a Polish Red Cross doctor they had taken prisoner and tortured.

Journalist George Steer reported on the sadistic bombing of the unfortified town of Harar, warning that if such a tactic could be used with impunity on African civilians, then eventually it would be employed on Europeans. Only months later, he investigated the bombing of Guernica, prompting international outrage and inspiring Picasso's famous mural. But it was Harar that taught the Fascists what they could get away with.

One by one, the armies under the great rases fell, their generals and officers either killed or captured. Haile Selassie, who had manned an antiaircraft gun at his headquarters in Dessie, went into the field himself to command one final push back. But he ignored his own advice and led a conventional assault. After the hopeless final battle, the Ethiopians were forced into a long retreat, bombed and gassed repeatedly as they straggled south. In the middle of it, the emperor broke away with a small unit of soldiers to visit the incredible complex of Lalibela, with its recessed churches hewn out of volcanic rock. He prayed for a miracle. He prayed for two straight days, without food or drink. The miracle never happened.

After Haile Selassie reached his capital, he was faced with a horrible choice. Stay and be taken prisoner, to be inevitably executed after creative humiliations by the Fascists? Or flee into exile? He chose exile. General Rodolfo Graziani, a man who reveled in cruelty, wanted to bomb the emperor's train to Djibouti, but Mussolini knew this would be the breaking point of the world's conscience. He shrewdly allowed his prey to escape.

When Haile Selassie arrived in London, he was cheered by crowds of British well-wishers. Marcus Garvey and his small delegation showed up at Waterloo station, eager to meet his hero, but the emperor failed to notice them. This was traumatic to Garvey, who took it as a personal slight, and his entire perspective changed. In his newspaper, he dropped his gushing praise of the emperor and launched increasingly bitter attacks, condemning him for running away. "It is a pity that a man of the limited intellectual caliber and weak political character like Haile Selassie became Emperor of Abyssinia at so crucial a time in the political history of the world."[17] His new stand was so unpopular that followers began to abandon his movement in droves, and other black radicals shunned him.

There were other shifts in attitude. Only days after the emperor's arrival, the British government dropped its sanctions against Italy.

The emperor settled in a mansion in Bath called Fairfield House, and to this day, stories persist that he fled Ethiopia with immense wealth—a fantasy pushed by Italian propaganda. His situation was quite the opposite. He, his wife and children, and his small entourage lived austerely on modest funds. They were in such dire straits that at one point the emperor put a collection of family silver up for public auction. Another time, the director of the local power company visited Fairfield House, intent on making Haile Selassie pay his overdue bill. Led into the cold main sitting room of the house, he found the emperor in a chair with a blanket over his knees. The director decided to drop the matter on the spot.[18]

The civil war in Spain soon took over the front pages of the world's newspapers. Many African Americans in the U.S. still wanted to fight Fascism but having learned their lesson from the State Department's obstruction, they went to France first before joining the Spanish Republican brigades. As one black volunteer put it in a short story, "I wanted to go to Ethiopia and fight Mussolini. . . . This ain't Ethiopia, but it'll do."[19] Haile Selassie, however, was not willing to let the League of Nations forget his nation's plight. In June 1936, he became the first head of state to address the assembly.

As he came to the podium, Italian reporters blew whistles and shouted insults from the gallery, and they had to be ejected by security guards. Then, speaking in Amharic, he scolded the men and women who had failed his country. "You, Great Powers, who have promised the guarantee of collective security to small states over whom hangs the threat that they may one day suffer the fate of Ethiopia, I ask: What measures do they intend to take? Representatives of the world, I have come to Geneva to discharge in your midst the most painful of duties for the head of a state. What answer am I to take back to my people?" As he left the podium, he told them, "It is us today. It will be you tomorrow."

His address is considered one of the greatest political speeches in history. But at the time, it had little effect. The League, blithely ignoring how it had calcified into a talk shop of political irrelevance, tabled its motions and did nothing to stop the horrors of Spain either. Nor would its members stop what happened to Czechoslovakia. And in Ethiopia, things only got worse.

From the very first day Fascist troops entered Addis Ababa and took control of other major towns, they systematically rounded up and slaughtered suspected resistance fighters, priests, and traditional healers. Intelligence reports sent on to the British Foreign Office tell of Fascist soldiers marching into consular missions to physically abuse staff and throw their weight around. Women, both black and white, were raped. *Times* of London reporter George Steer was deported, as were other "enemies" of the new Italian African Empire. Ethiopians woke up to find themselves living under a system of apartheid. They could no longer enter certain restaurants or sit where they pleased in a movie theater. Socially mixing, let alone romance between the two races, was now strictly forbidden.

The Ethiopian resistance fought back. For many years, it was thought that two young Eritreans, Moges Asgedom and Abriha Deboch, acted alone in the most famous strike against the occupation; in fact, they were part of a coordinated effort by resistance leaders.[20] On February 19, 1937, outside what used to be the emperor's small palace, the Italian viceroy, General Graziani, distributed alms to a crowd of old, sick, and disabled Ethiopians in a shameless public relations move (Graziani even complained about how long it was taking). Then Moges and Abriha threw grenades from a ground-floor window. When the first one went off, Graziani—the "hero" of the new Italian Empire—turned tail and ran. But a second grenade slashed his back with shrapnel.

The soldiers on guard didn't know where the explosions came from, so they panicked and fired into the crowd. Moges and Abriha escaped and joined a guerrilla unit but were eventually hunted down and executed in the field. Back in the capital as Graziani was taken to surgery, the Italian officer left in charge gave the Black Shirts three days of *carta blanca*—three days to destroy, kill, and do what they pleased to the Ethiopians. At 6:00 that evening, a massacre began. The Italian reporter Ciro Poggiali recorded in his diary, "Soon the streets around the *tukuls* [huts] are strewn with bodies."[21] A Hungarian doctor named Ladislas Shaska, writing under the pseudonym Ladislas Sava, was another witness. "Whole streets were burned down, and if any of the occupants of the houses ran out from the flames, they were machine-gunned or stabbed with cries of '*Duce! Duce! Duce!*'"[22]

From the second floor of his family house, which overlooked the capital's Menelik Square, a young boy named Imru Zelleke saw Italian soldiers and civilians beating and killing Ethiopians. What shook him to the core "was the extreme and indiscriminate violence inflicted on peaceful people."[23] Ethiopians to this day mark the date of this massacre, which in their calendar is *Yekatit 12*, and meticulous historical research puts a conservative estimate of at least 20,000 people murdered.[24] Even after the "official" three-day orgy of violence, the killing didn't end. It merely went on under the official guise of execution. There was slaughter in towns all through the occupied region as well as massacres of thousands more at the Debre Libanos monastery.

Young Imru Zelleke, his mother, and two sisters were taken to the Danane concentration camp, some twenty-five miles south of Mogadishu, where they would spend close to two years. Several such camps were established in Somalia and Eritrea, and for each one, conditions were appalling: horrible food, rampant diseases such as malaria and typhus, cynical neglect. Of about 6,500 prisoners at Danane, only half would survive. Incredibly, photos of the camp were used in postcards, captioned in German and Italian.

Ethiopians kept dying. And yet the concept of Ethiopia was stubbornly resilient. When a Russian-made documentary film about the war was shown at the Isis Theatre in Shanghai, a mob of Italian sailors stormed in. They tossed smoke bombs, beat the men in the projection booth, and stole the movie. All they accomplished, however, was provoking more headlines around the world.

Fascism also needed to constantly reassure itself. That meant adorning Addis Ababa, just as in Rome, with portraits of Mussolini. It meant stealing works of art, such as the equestrian statue of Menelik from its spot in front of St. George's Cathedral. It meant carting off the massive stones of the Aksum Obelisk and shipping them to Rome, where they were fitted together as a trophy and stood for decades. A brisk trade in pornographic postcards exhibiting nude Ethiopian, Eritrean, and Somali women thrived. There were also more respectable shots of "exotic" Africana, reminiscent of the human zoo depictions of the Somalis around the turn of the twentieth century. Maaza Mengiste, author of the celebrated novel about the war, *The Shadow King*, noticed the patterns of "natives in front of huts . . . natives staring back" and tweeted in 2019, "Africans are the foreign currency that validates the white man's life; he gains meaning through them while they remain stereotypes; he shines as adventurer, holder of greater knowledge."[25]

The adventurer, however, was losing his grip. Mussolini had to replace Graziani, paranoid and deranged after his attack, with the aristocratic Duke of Aosta as viceroy. Though Aosta charmed British guests over polo matches, he still promised to kill women and children if the guerrillas didn't surrender. His threats had little effect. Desertions by Italian soldiers became a problem, and there were incidents of panic and cowardice when the *arbegnoch*, the "Patriots" of Ethiopia, attacked train stations and outposts.

Among the Patriots were some courageous and flamboyant characters worthy of legend. There was the boy general Jagama Kello, who started fighting at fifteen, and by the time of the Liberation, he commanded about 3,500 men. It wasn't unusual for smart, tough-as-nails Ethiopian women to lead guerrilla units, and one of them was Lekelash Bayan, whom her soldiers dubbed *Belaw*, which meant "Strike him!" These were the words she used when she encouraged her soldiers to fire on the enemy: "*Strike him! Strike him!*" Once, cut off from her unit, she hid in a tree for five days, and when a couple of enemy soldiers passed by, she dropped down and ambushed them.[26]

The "boy general" Jagama Kello, center, with two other Ethiopian Patriots.

So, as much as the war is presented with a fixed date of "conquest," the reality is that Italian forces occupied only about half the country, for which they held a tenuous hold at best.

In 1938, Franklin Roosevelt, having won his second term, knew he could be more daring now in his foreign policy. He had a plan for world peace, but its success hinged entirely on British cooperation. The plan had a breathtaking scope. It advocated principles of international conduct, arms reduction, and, in times of war, respect for what he called humanitarian conditions. But Britain's prime minister by then was Neville Chamberlain, a petty, narrow-minded man who had Foreign Secretary Anthony Eden's phone tapped. Without ever consulting Eden, Chamberlain sent off a reply to Washington that turned Roosevelt down. And he included a bombshell: he was ready to recognize the Italian conquest of Ethiopia.

The Americans were furious. Through the back-and-forth, it became clear that Chamberlain was also setting up separate talks with Germany that would also shut out Washington. Roosevelt shelved his grand plan. Eden and one of the president's clos-est advisers, Sumner Welles, agreed that no other opportunity ever came after 1938 that could have prevented the approaching inferno of World War II. But Eden had done his best through the years to rein in the worst of Tory impulses, and he would get his chance to redeem himself.

An African emperor had warned other nations, "It will be you tomorrow." Now he was proved right. France soon collapsed under the Nazi juggernaut. Mussolini, anxious to be on the win-ning side, decided to throw in with Germany. "I only need a few thousand dead," he told his generals, "so that I can sit at the peace conference as a man who has fought."[27] The Underground in France got advance word of his decision from of all people, Josephine Baker.

Famously frivolous, ditzy Josephine turned out to be a bril-liant spy, above suspicion thanks to her old stand on Ethiopia. As a welcome guest at embassy parties for the Axis powers, she could pick up bits of intel, and she also hid members of the French Resistance at her private chateau and helped them get passports. She even scribbled down notes in invisible ink on her music sheets. And for all this courageous work, she helped change the course of the war and was later given France's Legion of Honor.

The news of Italy joining the war was a cause for celebra-tion among many in London. Churchill's government was now free to attack Italy's colonies. Meanwhile, the head of the Black Shirts in East Africa was fuming over his own lack of resources. There were soldiers who didn't have water bottles, native troops reduced to rags. There was a lack of sandals, a lack of ammuni-tion, a lack of everything except Ethiopians who wanted to kill them. He warned his superiors that if there was an emergency, his men wouldn't be able to hold out against an attack. And as soon as the Royal Air Force dropped leaflets announcing that the emperor was on his way, Italian desertions rose higher.

When the Liberation came, it happened with remarkable speed. On almost all sides, conventional British forces swept in like bulldozers. Their numbers included South Africans,

Indians, colonial Kenyans, Nigerians, Sudanese, and soldiers from the Caribbean. In the south, as the British swept up from Kenya and captured Mogadishu, the Italians fled so rapidly that the Allies struggled to keep up with those running away.

Meanwhile, the Patriot forces—who had sometimes been fighting themselves almost as much as the Italians—were convinced to give up their petty feuds and coordinate with a British commando initiative called Mission 101 under an old Ethiopian expert, Colonel Daniel Sandford. At the same time, a brilliant, often insubordinate madman of a tactician, Major Orde Wingate, led what he called "Gideon Force." It was an elite unit that went on commando raids, stinging the Fascist forces where it hurt and convincing them that larger armies were on their way. The incredible bluff worked. Military historians love to dissect the assaults and initiatives of Sandford and Wingate, but these British commanders were successful largely because the Ethiopians themselves, over five years of guerrilla war and resistance, had worn the Italians down to a nub.

As the Allies captured Italian soldiers, they often confiscated photos that the men kept as souvenirs. They were disturbing, horrific shots of smiling troops and civilians posing in front of hanged Ethiopians or captured guerrillas tortured and killed. More were found in the Italian archives when Addis Ababa was liberated.

Haile Selassie returned to his capital on May 5, the very day the Italians captured it five years before. "Do not reward evil for evil," he told his people. "Do not commit any act of cruelty like those of which the enemy committed against us up until this present time. Do not allow the enemy any occasion to foul the good name of Ethiopia. We shall take his weapons from the enemy and make him return by the way that he came."

Before the guns fell silent, there was talk of war crime trials. Winston Churchill said he didn't care whether Mussolini was shot or locked away until the end of the war. As Italy's defenses crumbled, the top Fascists in Rome kicked their dictator out and put in charge General Pietro Badoglio, one of the brutal commanders who had bombed and gassed Ethiopians in 1935. But Roosevelt and Churchill—eager to take Italy out of the conflict—were willing to negotiate with him. The Foreign Office came up with a rationale that barred Ethiopia from even having a seat on the War Crimes Commission.

Badoglio never faced justice over his crimes in Ethiopia. Rodolfo Graziani *was* convicted as a war criminal but not for anything he did in Africa. His official transgression was staying loyal to Mussolini and collaborating with the Nazis in the final phase of the war. A military tribunal sentenced him to nineteen years, but he was let out after only a few months. Mussolini's end, of course, was famously gruesome, ending up shot, his corpse mutilated and then hung upside down from a hook at a gas station in Milan. On hooks beside his body were the corpses of his mistress and some associates.

In 1941, Ethiopia became the *first* occupied nation to be liberated by the Allies. But with the British House of Commons bombed by the Luftwaffe only days before and things still dire in Europe, this accomplishment was all but eclipsed. Mere days after Italy's surrender, the East Africa Command and the War Office decided to help themselves to everything from railway construction goods to a brick factory, all resources and materials Ethiopia could have used to rebuild itself. Worse, the British chose not to leave entirely, occupying the Ogaden for seven years.

The British Foreign Office liked to cast the 1935 war and the Liberation as two separate conflicts. So do most history books. But these struggles should be viewed as a single continuous one given the ongoing insurgency during the Italian occupation. What then is the legacy of this war? How did the ideas that emerged from it change Africa and the rest of the world? As it turns out, its impact, both positive and negative, has been immense.

The standard line when the war is thought of at all is to point out how Ethiopia's struggle highlighted the impotence of the League of Nations. But this says little about Ethiopia and more about the League. Japan's invasion of Manchuria in 1931 and the Spanish Civil War offer the same lesson. Far more important, Ethiopia signaled to Hitler that he could get away with his own plans for capturing much of Europe. This is not an inference or speculation; it's fact. In 1938, Mussolini himself told Hitler that if the League had imposed an oil embargo, he would have had to give up on Ethiopia within a week. "That would have been an incalculable disaster for me."[28] To sit idly by and allow the devaluing of one people grants a license for the devaluing of anyone. Haile Selassie's bitter warning in Geneva went unheeded.

Disillusioned by the British throwing their weight around after the war, Haile Selassie recognized it was time for the Lion of Judah and the Albion Lion to go their separate ways. Franklin Roosevelt, ailing but still determined to be an architect of the postwar future, expressed a great interest in meeting the emperor. So, in 1945, the two titans came face to face aboard the *USS Quincy* in the Suez Canal. They spoke in French. There was little tangible that came out of the session, and yet it marked a seismic shift in international relations. This was when the United States began to factor Africa seriously into its foreign policy, seeing it as one of the vital theaters for its long Cold War with the Soviet Union.

We also need to examine the idea of *nationhood* itself in the Horn of Africa. Before the Italians ever came along, Eritrea had spent much of its existence passing through the hands of different kingdoms, including Aksum, as well as the medieval political entity known as the Medri Bahri and the Ottoman Empire. Its various rulers had clashed now and then with Ethiopia, and its people had no say whatsoever in the treaty in which Ethiopia's emperor Menelik recognized the boundaries of the Italian colony. But to this very day, Eritreans and Ethiopians share many elements of culture. Haile Selassie decided that if he couldn't hold Italian war criminals to account, his consolation prize would be Eritrea. It was his insurance that his kingdom would never be landlocked and helpless again, and he lobbied for this through the United Nations.

Many Eritreans welcomed the idea of uniting with Ethiopia. Others opposed it. In the early postwar period, Eritrea developed some of the basic infrastructure of democratic government with an elected assembly. But as Ethiopia gradually took over, it shut this down and closed the one independent newspaper. By this time, Imru Zelleke was a smart, young official for the imperial government, and Ras Kassa, a member of the emperor's inner circle, told him not to bother working on Ethiopia's constitutional revisions, which were expected by the UN as a prerequisite before union with Eritrea. "Don't waste your time on this affair; in any case, whatever changes are made will never be implemented."[29] When Haile Selassie annexed Eritrea outright in 1962, there was already a small guerrilla army, the Eritrean Liberation Front, carrying out raids and lighting the fuse for one of the longest, bloodiest wars in African history.

Yet the emperor's reputation on the international stage grew immensely in the postwar years. There was, until the prison martyrdom of Nelson Mandela, simply no one else who seemed so much to embody for the West the African conscience. It would be years before the story was more widely told of how he had asked the Royal Air Force to put down a rebellion in Ethiopia's Tigray region in 1943, planes dropping warning leaflets and then bombs on Mekelle and Corbetta.[30] After the Tigray People's Liberation Front attacked the Northern Defense Forces of the Ethiopian government in Tigray in late 2020 (before its main conventional army was humiliatingly crushed in less than a month), its supporters often referred to this infamous raid in social media debates.

Haile Selassie was an autocrat—those who knew him don't dispute this—and we'll come back to his final years later. But on a philosophical level, at least, he had always believed in African unity and individual autonomy for Africans. The Europeans, after all, had talked big about friendship but had let him down time and again. The Americans, taking over from the British as global policemen, were interested in his country first and foremost as a place to park their jet fighters as they kept an eye on the Middle East. No doubt his bitter experiences with diplomacy and the war inspired him to help found what became the African Union, still based today in Addis Ababa.

When the emperor came to speak at the UN in 1963, he had a new warning for the world. "That until the philosophy which holds one race superior and another inferior is finally and permanently discredited and abandoned . . . the dream of lasting peace and world citizenship and the rule of international morality will remain but a fleeting illusion, to be pursued but never attained." These words are famous, partly because Bob Marley placed them in another classic reggae anthem.

Meanwhile, the activists, writers, and scholars who took up the cause of Ethiopia's fight against Fascism—men such as Jomo Kenyatta, Kwame Nkrumah, Eric Williams, C. L. R. James, and George Padmore—would shape pan-African thought for the next twenty years. Even Marcus Garvey owes part of his cultural immortality to the war. In 1938, he spoke to supporters in Sydney, Nova Scotia, where he again criticized the emperor and discussed the Fascist invasion, promising his audience, "We are going to emancipate ourselves from mental slavery because whilst others might free the body, none but ourselves can free the mind." Bob Marley shortened this line and incorporated it into another classic tune, "Redemption Song."

Other impacts of the war have a darker legacy. George Steer returned to East Africa for the Liberation not as a reporter but as a captain in charge of propaganda services. He developed innovative strategies and methods for what is now called "psy-ops"—ones that would be used later in the wars in Vietnam, Iraq, and Afghanistan. One of his tactics was to play Italian music through loudspeakers to Fascist troops, reminding them of home; another was to enlist deserters to persuade their former comrades to give up the fight. Steer was always an advocate of the underdog and the oppressed, so you have to wonder what he would make of the adaptations of his methods, with sound trucks blasting heavy metal music during modern military sieges.

Anthony Eden was haunted by the 1930s failures of the democracies. He became prime minister of Great Britain in 1955, and when the Suez Crisis broke, he equated Gamal Nasser with his Fascist enemies of the past. Nasser, it was true, had national-ized the canal and knew how to whip supportive crowds into a nationalist fervor. Eden, however, chose to respond by conspir-ing with France and Israel in a cynical ploy to invent a provo-cation; he then sent British troops to attack Egypt. But under political and financial pressure from the U.S., he was forced to announce a cease-fire and later resigned. "I am still unrepentant about Suez," he remarked years later. "People never look at what would have happened if we had done nothing. There is a parallel with the thirties. If you allow people to break agreements with impunity, the appetite grows to feed on such things."[31]

Then there are the areas where the war should have had a lasting impact . . . yet never did. It should have spawned its own inspirational legend like the Spanish Civil War. Langston Hughes wrote poems about it. George Schuyler, one of the lights of the Harlem Renaissance, wrote a pulp novel about it in serial form for readers of the *Pittsburgh Courier*. The war had its own music, with a Calypso tune, "The Gold in Africa," by Neville Mercano. There were heroic exploits in black newspapers about John Robinson, the "Brown Condor," who led Ethiopia's tiny air force. If more African Americans had been allowed to go fight, it's quite probable that their contribution would be remembered today in the same manner that black members of the Lincoln Brigade are finally getting their due. The U.S. State Department made sure they couldn't.

And a new generation of black radicals grew up in America and Africa, idolizing Nkrumah and Kenyatta—and later Mandela—with some perhaps never learning about the conflict that helped form their political outlooks and characters. Fortunately, there's been renewed interest in the war. A bust of John Robinson along with a reading garden named after him are now parts of the American embassy in Addis Ababa. And the Aksum Obelisk, a treasure stolen by the Fascists during the occupation, was returned to Ethiopia in 2005 at Italy's own expense of $8 million. The reassembled obelisk was unveiled in 2008.

We might consider this "progress" in attitudes toward history. But it's an uneven process and always has been. When Italy invaded Greece and Yugoslavia, it was a Fascist invasion. When Italy invaded Libya and Ethiopia, these were supposedly *colonial* ventures. Why the difference in terminology? (Especially one that implies a foregone conclusion.) This allowed certain Fascists to portray the war in Ethiopia as if it were a grand adventure, as if they were red-coated British soldiers boldly fighting Zulus hand to hand instead of dropping poison gas and bombs or tossing chained Ethiopian prisoners out of planes high over mountains—a practice the soldiers called "Taken up to Rome."

One of these apologists was the famous journalist and author Indro Montanelli, who led a battalion of Eritrean soldiers before he got a job in the Fascist Press and Propaganda Office. In his memoir, *The Twentieth Eritrean Battalion*, he confided how he thought of the war as a "long and marvelous holiday, a reward given to us by 'Big Daddy' for thirteen years of work at our school desks."[32] In 1969, on the Italian TV show *The Hour of Truth*, he smugly recalled how at twenty-four, he bought an Eritrean girl, Desta, from her father. "I think I chose well. She was a beautiful girl of twelve years. Excuse me, but in Africa, it was another thing."[33]

In the audience was Elvira Banotti, the Italian Eritrean journalist and feminist, who was not going to let this slide. She bluntly accused him of colonialism and rape.

"Madam, there was no violence," claimed Montanelli. "Girls get married at twelve in Ethiopia."

Banotti wouldn't let up, prompting him to admit that if had he done such acts in Europe with a twelve-year-old, yes, he would have been guilty of rape. "Exactly," shot back Banotti. "So what difference is there physically or psychologically?"[34]

It's worth noting that before returning to Italy, Montanelli handed off his "wife"—whom he also sometimes referred to as a "small animal"—to another Italian officer who became infamous for war atrocities. He retold his child-bride story for the rest of his life but adjusted the details to make himself more sympathetic. He died in 2001. Such was his reputation in journalism that a statue of him was erected in a park in Milan that also bears his name. In more recent years, however, it's become a target for repeated vandalism; in 2019, it was splattered with pink paint and in 2020 doused again with red paint and the words "racist" and "rapist" scrawled on its side. Yet Milan's mayor refused to bow to pressure to have the statue removed.[35]

Nor was Montanelli ever alone in trying to rewrite the past. In 2012, Rodolfo Graziani's hometown of Affile, east of Rome, opened an ugly block of a memorial to its native son, the

"Butcher of Fezzan." There was international protest and wide-spread liberal condemnation, and in 2017, the town's mayor and two of its councilors went to jail for commissioning it. In 2019, the Duce's own granddaughter and a member of the European Parliament, Alessandra Mussolini, threatened on social media to sue anyone "offending" the memory of her grandfather. Given the sheer volumes of evidence, she would lose in any court, but it would make for an interesting spectacle.

Lost in the noise is consideration of what Africa endured, and the problem is that our understanding of the scourge of Fascism comes with a hierarchy of victims. There are Holocaust museums and memorials in the U.S., Canada, Poland, France, Germany, Austria, even Japan. Posts on Facebook and Twitter remind us to never forget—as we shouldn't—the millions of Jews murdered. As if in afterthought, some attention is spared for the Communists, Catholics, mentally retarded, reporters, homosexuals, and Jehovah's Witnesses who also went to their deaths. Even if one recalls these other victims, the attention is focused on *Europe*. The Libyans, Algerians, Somalis, Ethiopians, and Eritreans who fell under Fascist boot heels are neglected. While a monument to those killed in the Graziani massacre stands in Addis Ababa, there is no museum dedicated yet to the war itself in Ethiopia, let alone one in another country.

The warning in recent times has been over Western nations allowing themselves to slide into autocratic rule, abandoning their democracies. The warning might have more resonance if it talked about how Fascism was first defeated in Africa.

14

Success Stories

The postwar conduct of the Allies also enabled a perverse and self-serving revisionism on Fascist Italy. The Americans and British found it useful not to dwell on past crimes, but this meant Italy wasn't subjected to the same efforts of "de-Nazification" that Germany went through. Instead of their territory being liberated, people in Italian Somaliland woke up to find the colonial powers had merely switched places. The Italians had used a system of slavery and harsh conscription. So did the British. When they took over, they kept the old practices of forced labor and "collective punishment," the seizing of assets and holding an entire clan responsible for the crimes of one person. One activist wrote an open letter to British Prime Minister Clement Attlee, complaining how "the workers are brutally flogged in public for routine offences" and that protesters armed with pitiful sticks and stones were shot.[1]

Britain proposed that the different parts of Somali territory be united under its control. But this notion met with resistance from various quarters, including Haile Selassie's Ethiopian government, which hungered to absorb Somali territories into its domain. So in 1948, a Four Power Commission was set up (the U.S., the Soviets, France, and Britain) to investigate and decide what to do. Only days after its delegation arrived in the country, there was a massive riot in Mogadishu on January 11. The evidence suggests that right-wing Italian elements wanted to cause trouble—they were the only ones with firearms. But the sheer numbers of native demonstrators meant fifty-one Italians were killed to fourteen Somalis. In Italy, memorial services were held in churches for the Italian "martyrs," while newspapers ran inflammatory and often racist reports on the episode.[2]

As the Four Power Commission did its job, it became clear that some of its representatives listened more to Italian lobbying than to the voices that spoke for the colony's inhabitants, such as the Somali Youth League. America's representative and ambassador-at-large, Philip Jessup, declared that because the Somalis were largely "tribal" and pastoral, "We can hardly expect these people to be in a position to determine for themselves what means might best assure their achievement of self-government and independence and the fulfilment of their national aspirations."[3] In the end, London held on to British Somaliland, while in 1950, the UN gave Italy back its former colony under a trusteeship intended to last ten years. This was like rewarding a beaten Nazi Germany with the Netherlands.

The Italian administration in Mogadishu—packed with pro-Fascist elements and even familiar names of the worst war criminals in the region—soon chose to wind back the clock in terms of courts, the use of torture on political suspects, and the bullying of the civilian population. The administration also liked to play on clan and ethnic divisions to undermine Somali unity. The UN Trusteeship Council noted how "in the first contact between administration officials and any members of the Somali Youth League, in courts or in any other proceedings, the first question that would be asked of the member of the Somali Youth League would be: 'To what tribe do you belong?'"[4]

But the administration was living on borrowed time, managing a territory where most of the populace would not cooperate. By 1953, it made overtures to reach a compromise agreement with the League so it could fulfill its mandate. In the first legislative assembly elections of 1956, the writing was on the wall for the administration, as the League captured the most seats, forty-three.[5] Four years later, British Somaliland and Italian Somaliland joined to become the independent nation of Somalia, which doesn't get nearly enough attention in the West for its relatively successful parliamentary democracy through the 1960s—a time when much of Africa slid into despotism and chaos.

Professor Abdi Ismail Samatar points out that despite the young nation's "trailblazing democratic record, little has been written about it. Somalis have been tormented for over forty years by a dictatorship, warlords, tribalist fiefdoms . . . pseudo-religious tyrants, and corrupt, incompetent transitional and federal regimes. Neither the large Somali diaspora nor the young generation in the country know much about this vital history, and both groups are surprised when they hear about a Somalia that led the continent in democratic practice and the high quality of its leadership."[6]

Somalia's first president, Aden Abdulle Osman, rose from the hard life of an orphan doing odd jobs and working on plantations in the southern Janale district. While serving in an administrative position for the Italian colonial regime in 1939, he had an ugly encounter with Fascist racism reminiscent of the ordeal for Rosa Parks. Like so much else under the regime, buses were segregated. And during a journey when the driver ignored the bell for the bus to stop, Osman politely challenged him. The driver began shouting abuse, even getting off the bus and following Osman as he trudged away for the long walk to his destination. "If you call me an SOB," Osman told him, "then you are one, but go ahead and hit me." A mob of white men then poured out of a restaurant and dragged Osman and another Somali to a cell, releasing him only when they found out he worked as an officer for the colonial administration. Despite pressure over months, he refused to apologize for standing up for himself.[7]

He climbed the ranks of the Somali Youth League to become a respected statesman, acting on his deep convictions and faith in his new country's institutions. What's particularly interesting is that while other anticolonial activists looked to Marxism as a cure-all, leading them toward autocratic methods, Osman took a different path. For Professor Samatar, who interviewed him at length and had access to his diaries, this position was rooted in the lessons of culture, and Osman would have had them in mind in developing his views. "There is a part of Somali tradition prior to colonialism in which by and large there was no centralized authority in terms of government. There were no prisons, for instance, across the country. So how did they deal with questions of crime? Well, the community got together and reprimanded the person, and . . . put sanctions on that person. Or ostracized him out of that community or things of that nature. And there was no class structure, in the sense that everybody had access to the range of farms and land, and basically it was what Karl Marx might have called primitive communism of a sort."[8]

There were collaborations among people but no authority over one another. "And so it gave him a sense of confidence in himself and his people, and that he could separate democracy as sort of an independent regime from the dominance of imperial powers who claimed to be democratic."[9] As the president for the infant republic's first government in 1960, Osman had the responsibility of nominating the prime minister, settling on Abdirashid Ali Sharmarkee, who in turn managed to secure a healthy parliamentary mandate. Sharmarkee in turn picked a "team of rivals" for his cabinet, sharing power with men from the opposition parties to reduce the risk of friction and conflict in parliament as the nation took its first steps in governing itself.

He also made a tour of the country to understand its problems better and was "overwhelmed" by the extent of the poverty in the north, what would soon become former British Somaliland, where there was little infrastructure but its inhabitants were terribly impoverished.[10] After the cabinet was decided, Osman gave a speech, telling Somalis that "it is my modest opinion that only you, citizens, can strengthen democracy; in fact democracy does not mean anarchy but the power invested in the people in accordance with order and based on the laws. . . . All of us must respect and the laws that we have made for ourselves and love one another and resolve our controversies in a peaceful and fraternal order." The U.S. embassy in Mogadishu called the speech "remarkable."[11]

The road ahead had its potholes, as some of Sharmarkee's cabinet ministers from opposition parties stoked old ethnic resentments to oppose the government's new constitution, pitting northerners against southerners. Northerners, however, had grounds for complaint. With unification, the city of Hargeisa was reduced to a provincial backwater, and it didn't help that foreign officials who were holdovers from the colonial regime had packed up and headed south, taking their spending money and families with them.[12] And yet the constitution referendum passed, with results that were more nuanced than a simple "north–south" divide on first blush (for instance, a slim majority of the central parts of a couple of northern regions said yes).[13]

The government would weather considerable storms in its short life, such as a bill to reduce the cabinet size and petty, political squawking over the salaries of members of parliament. Dealing with an attempted coup in December of 1961 was no mere pothole but a threat to blow up the entire bridge, not only between north and south but the path leading to strengthening the democracy.

It happened in Hargeisa, with a group of "Sandhurst-trained lieutenants" from the north who chose to arrest their superior officers from the south and then claim falsely that the commander of the national forces, General Daud Hirsi, backed them and had assumed power after rioting in Mogadishu. But the leaders of the coup weren't acting out of any great regional patriotism—they simply didn't like how others had been promoted over them. And for all the legitimate complaints that northerners could make, they didn't pour into the streets of Hargeisa or anywhere else in massive crowds to rally to the cause. Worse for the coup leaders, General Hirsi—a national hero and loyalist—went on Radio Mogadishu to deny any involvement. In fact, the regional police commissioner, a northerner himself, wouldn't help them, and it was northern soldiers who put down the coup within hours, killing one of the officers.[14]

So far, this will sound like familiar territory to the cynics who pass judgment on African history. What's more interesting is what followed. When northern MPs pushed for clemency, Osman told them it was beyond his constitutional powers. The government went to great lengths to ensure the coup leaders received a fair trial, meeting a request to bring in foreign lawyers for the proceedings and even picking up part of the cost of their fees. While the guilt of those on trial was overwhelmingly clear, the British judge threw out the case on a technicality. Osman and other senior officials were flabbergasted, even more so when the judge ruled out any appeal. But they wouldn't push the issue. As Abdi Samatar writes, "This was the first time in Africa's post-independence history that a government released coup makers without any retribution. In fact, most of the coup plotters were rehabilitated a year later when border hostilities broke out between Ethiopia and Somalia."[15]

The lesson here is not the mere unicorn spotting of democracy in a turbulent Africa—it's that leaders of profound moral character stuck to a system of rules they had set up for themselves, not falling back on opportunistic excuses to get around it for the result they wanted. They reasserted their faith in it through their conduct. That's worth celebrating whatever the geography. Consider that in that same year of 1961, a military junta in Turkey that *had* succeeded with a coup hanged the nation's former prime minister. Europe was reeling from the construction of the Berlin Wall. Kennedy sent thousands of military advisers to Vietnam and authorized the use of napalm. In other words, some fifteen years after the last "just" war, World War II, the world didn't blink twice over rhetoric for democracy being substituted with expediency.

Yet Somalia was managing to live up to its early democratic promise. In 1964, Abdirazak Hussen became prime minister. A man whose childhood was spent partly as a camel herder, Hussen later experienced the cruelties of British colonial rule in the early postwar period just as Osman had encountered the Italian variety. Like the older president, Hussen was incorruptible, with a fierce diligence to his work. While in power, his cabinet ministers had to disclose their assets and declare that they didn't hold any properties or stock holdings. Hussen himself lived in the same house, paying the same rent as he had during his tenure as an MP. And "as if to set a benchmark, he visited random ministries at the start of the workday and closed to the gates to those, including the minister, who came late to work."[16]

It would lead us too far off our journey to retell the story of "what went wrong" in terms of Somalia's democracy, but the simplest explanation perhaps is that the fledgling system didn't have more time for its roots to thicken. There were still notorious instances of corruption, nepotism, and bribery; Abdirashid Sharmarkee wasn't above doling out cash and plum positions to win support.[17] Yet in 1967, Aden Osman became the first democratically elected president in modern African history to be defeated in an election, graciously accepting the will of the people and relinquishing his power. He was replaced by Sharmarkee. The rot, however, was setting in despite the best efforts of officials who cared.

In October 1969, Sharmarkee was murdered by his own bodyguard during a tour of Lake Anod, though the assassination wasn't viewed at the time as political but driven by revenge.[18] Only eleven days later and the day after Sharmarkee's funeral, General Siad Barre led a military coup. Osman and Hussen were among those locked up for three and a half years without trial, and it says something about these two incredible men in how they each reacted when Barre tried to intimidate the prisoners upon their release. Osman told the general that if "the regime was looking for excuses to deprive them of their rights," its soldiers might as well take the men back to prison. Pulled aside from the others, Hussen told Barre point blank he wouldn't be a spy.[19] Barre's ruthless dictatorship would last more than twenty years. Osman spent most of them in quiet seclusion on a farm in Janale, while Hussen fled his job as Somalia's UN ambassador in 1977 to seek political asylum in the United States.

When I spoke to Professor Abdi Samatar in late 2020, I asked him what he would say to those who might suggest he exaggerates the importance of Somalia's first democrats; after all, Osman and Hussen still had to contend with the type of political shenanigans and corruption that would plague other parts of Africa. The professor had a brilliant counterargument: should the United States give up on more hundreds of years of history because of the corruption of the Trump administration? "So do we romanticize American democracy and ignore all the garbage that's sailing underneath that?"

And he argued that it's worth examining how we measure the implementation of democracy—the fight against colonialism was part of it. Besides the struggle against Italy, there was "the resistance against the British . . . the longest liberation war in Africa [that] started in 1899 and ended in 1921, almost 21 years. The place where the British first and foremost used war planes in the colonies was in northern Somalia. That resistance was part of the democratic project—I'm saying 'democratic' in the modern version if you like of elected officials and what not. But the democratic spirit of the Somali people has been there to put the strongest resistance to British colonialism anywhere in the world at that point in time. . . . So what you see from 1960 to 1969 is the tip of the iceberg."

In 1960 when Somalia became independent, almost 5,000 kilometers away, democracy also advanced in the British Protectorate of Bechuanaland, where its prominent leaders pushed London into creating a multiracial legislature; true, London insisted on packing the chamber with about a third of its own choices, but it was a significant step, and only six years later, Bechuanaland became the independent nation of Botswana.

But spare a thought for a moment for the hand dealt to this country. Being overrun by greedy imperialists could be horrible, but Bechuanaland suffered the indignity of being the country that was merely in the white man's way. In 1853, a chief went to Cape Town to ask the British to help protect his land from the Boers. Not interested, said the British. In fact, they bothered to pay attention only after the Germans parked themselves in South West Africa. As for Bechuanaland, a high commissioner declared bluntly in 1885, "We have no interest in the country . . . except as a road to the interior; we might therefore confine ourselves for the present to preventing that part of the protectorate being occupied by either filibusters or foreign powers doing as little in the way of administration or settlement as possible."[20]

Ten years later, three powerful chiefs for the Tswana states of Bechuanaland, anxious to keep their vulnerable territory away from Cecil Rhodes and his rapacious British South Africa Company, traveled all the way to London to firmly toss their lot in with the British government. It was decided that "The chiefs will rule their own people much as at present," while Colonial Secretary Joseph Chamberlain promised, "We will take the land that we want for the railway and no more."[21] They did, and the suits in Whitehall fulfilled Chamberlain's promise, satisfied overall with their policy of benign neglect.

When Botswana celebrated its freedom, it was with a midnight ceremony literally in the middle of a sandstorm blowing off the Kalahari Desert. A traditional healer among the spectators at Independence Stadium promised the storm was an "omen of new life for our country." Meanwhile, Boy Scouts pitching in for the ceremonies raced around, trying to retrieve the windblown foam-rubber cushions put out for guests. The fireworks went ahead that night while a bonfire was lit at the top of Kgale Hill.[22]

The nation was already expected to fail, the odds against it, and critics could rattle off plenty of reasons. For one, this nation about the size of Texas was landlocked and prone to regular drought—400,000 head of cattle were lost in the summer of 1966 alone.[23] If you stood in Botswana, you had apartheid-era South Africa on one side, along with its stooge satellite, South West Africa (later Namibia), and on the other side, you had newly independent and struggling Zambia next door to white-ruled Rhodesia (later Zimbabwe). Your links to the outside world, even your food in times of drought except for meat, depended on the railway that ran from Cape Town to Salisbury—today's Harare. A reminder of its vulnerability came mere weeks after the independence ceremony when a management switch failed on the line, holding up food supplies; Rhodesian Railways, taking over the line from South Africa, blamed the screwup on "teething troubles and staff shortages."[24]

And your neighbors wouldn't leave you alone. The worst offender by far was Pretoria, its brutal reaction to the Soweto uprising in 1976 driving thousands of South Africans to Botswana's refugee camps. Pretoria also accused Botswana of allowing freedom fighters of the African National Congress to use the country as a staging ground for attacks. Just as the Nixon White House was willing to destabilize Cambodia to fight the North Vietnamese, so the apartheid regime thought nothing of sending its commandos into Botswana to reap bloody vengeance. In May 1985, they planted a house bomb that murdered the son of a prominent trade union official living in exile. In June, they brazenly drove into Gaborone after midnight, firing mortars and machine guns at spots throughout the capital for half an hour, killing at least sixteen people. Those whom white-ruled South Africa murdered as "terrorists" included a six-year-old child and an innocent Dutch national.[25]

And yet Botswana not only met the challenges of being hobbled by its enemies, it exceeded everyone's expectations. Much of the credit for that goes to a single individual. While the "great man" theory has long been shelved by academics, there is something to be said for figures of lion-size integrity stepping forward right when they're needed. For Botswana, it was the man newspapers called "handsome" and "heavy-set"—Seretse Khama.

In 1966, at the age of forty-five, he became president. The man who would have been king. He'd relinquished his title as chief years before and endured a five-year exile because he dared stay true to his English wife, Ruth Williams, an office typist whom he'd met at a dance in London. Choosing her had gone against the wishes of his uncle, the regent of the dominant Bangwato people, and the British exploited the issue, arguing his marriage was somehow "endangering the security" of the Bangwato, who never wanted another chief but Seretse.[26] But two lovers defying an empire and a jealous political rival was a tale that resonated with the British public, and Seretse's situation inspired a public protest campaign that included top intellectuals and actors, including Alec Guinness.[27] In 1956, Seretse Khama finally returned home with his wife—and without his title thanks to a deal struck with Whitehall. The love story behind his marriage inspired the recent film *A United Kingdom*.

Even without the title, Khama was still a political force to be reckoned with. "When he first went on political campaigning," recalled scholar Willie Henderson, "humble villagers were astonished by his readiness to shake hands and by his willingness to exchange a joke, share a story or dispute a point. It is hard for us to grasp hold of this astonishment today. We are used to the idea of politicians working a crowd, but kings did not behave in this way in the Bechuanaland Protectorate."[28] Khama also became known for his wit. He once remarked how being a capitalist among socialist African leaders, he was the only one to fly to a conference on a hired plane.[29]

And he had a clear vision of the protectorate's problems. Better still, he understood what was needed. Schools were integrated, and their improvement made a priority. A firm but flexible neutral posture was the most sensible course of action over neighbors, but he denounced apartheid and reached out to Zambia over economic collaborations. Only a year before he assumed the presidency, he visited Fordham University to collect an honorary degree and told the audience how he recognized the harsh reality of politics. "It is not my ambition to sit on the fence between East and West and to place Bechuanaland at the disposal of the highest bidder. . . . [But] If I cannot meet the needs of my people, they will turn to my political opponents, who already operate with funds from Communist countries." In that same speech, he famously remarked, "We stand virtually alone in our belief that a nonracial society can work now, but there are those among our neighbors who will be only too delighted to see our experiment fail."[30]

Strong character for leadership, however, did not imply that he thought of himself as irreplaceable. Quite the contrary. Like Somalia's Osman and Hussen, the goal was to establish a democratic tradition. Khama impressed this upon a U.S. diplomat who paid a call on him, pointing out that his vice president, Ketumile Masire, could immediately take over if ever needed.[31] Khama's biographer Susan Williams notes how Masire informed her in personal correspondence that the new leaders of Botswana "were determined to learn from the failures of other African countries. As far as they were concerned, ideology was a luxury, and they had to be pragmatic—what mattered was not something on the political Left or the Right, but what was good for Botswana."[32]

Well, what *was* good for Botswana? As it turned out, something it already had. Its tradition of tribal assembly, the *kgotla*—like other African antecedents we discussed in chapter 6—was largely democratic in spirit (it has to be noted, however, that the *kgotla* was for men only, though women occasionally served as regents).[33] The system appreciated merit, and the rules of the *kgotla*, in fact, "were interpreted to remove bad rulers and allow talented candidates to become chief."[34] As Professor Zibani Maundeni later told *The Economist*, "Before any big decision, [Tswana leaders] consulted the general population. There was a strong culture of hearing the views of ordinary people."[35]

In the postwar period, a process had gathered momentum of formalizing *kgotlas* into advisory councils that reviewed and vetted legislation.[36] While the *kgotla* system was adapted into constitutional modern governance, a few years after independence, the Khama administration wisely put the power over land allocation into the hands of committees, ensuring that no chief could ever abuse the setup and build his own little fiefdom. And like Somalia's early democracy project, Botswana put its faith in a parliament with multiple political parties, encouraging an open and free press along with a society that enjoys the races living together in tolerance.

And of course, the diamonds helped.

Okay, but other African nations have diamonds. Angola has diamonds. South Africa has diamonds. Sierra Leone tragically became infamous for a few years because of its blood diamonds. Yet when De Beers made its big find in Ngwato territory about a year after independence, Botswana's leaders knew how to proceed responsibly. While the nation was still a protectorate, they had actively discouraged mining operations, knowing what ills could follow with greater European development; before news of the major discovery went public, Seretse Khama pushed for legislation that meant all of Botswana would benefit from diamond wealth, not simply one tribe or region.[37]

What also made a huge difference was the government's commitment not to squander what they gained. Profits were sunk into infrastructure, water access, health care, and other needs. As economist George Ayittey (whom we'll meet later) points out, the government didn't try to replace or compete with the private sector in terms of industries—it used its windfalls and kept a tight rein on its purse during the good years, relying on its saved capital as a "cushion to ride out the lean years."[38] This method was especially critical in the early 1980s when the diamond market hit a temporary slump.[39]

Just as important was how the Khama government delicately threaded the needle in terms of foreign relations. The critics and naysayers expected that Botswana would soon become another "Bantustan" for South Africa, one of the black homelands under apartheid that made a farce of the very concept of autonomy. It didn't happen. And that's because Khama masterfully promoted his new nation to the world as a state that deserved to be respected as such. He secured big loans from the World Bank, the U.S., and other countries for major mining development. He shunned South African and Rhodesian racism yet wouldn't harbor guerillas fighting their regimes, only legitimate refugees, earning valuable credibility on the international stage. After Ian Smith had the border closed for a while between Rhodesia and Zambia, Khama outflanked him. Botswana seized the opportunity to work with Zambia on building the Nata-Kazungula Road in the 1970s, enlisting the help of other African states and creating a new lifeline for development.[40]

Despite its prosperity, the small nation couldn't prevent the thuggish apartheid regime of South Africa invading its soil and throwing its weight around. But by that 1985 attack when raiders murdered sixteen people in Gaborone, sympathy was resoundingly on Botswana's side, with even Ronald Reagan's administration recalling the U.S. ambassador to South Africa in protest. Apartheid had only five years left. Seretse Khama didn't live long enough to see its end, dying of cancer in 1980, but he clearly understood such a toxic system of relentless oppression was unsustainable, and so he played the long game.

Botswana has had its troubles, and its halo lost some of its glow in the decades that followed. It was tragically ravaged by AIDS but implemented one of the most progressive treatment programs on the continent. In the late 1980s and nineties, it endured scandals over corruption, mismanagement, and incompetence, particularly in its banking and housing sectors. While these are troubling, we should ask ourselves, does that make it another *African* state—or just a *nation* state? The 2008 financial crisis is now more than a decade behind us, and as you might recall, prisons in the U.S. did not fill up with the Wall Street executives who ruined countless lives and sent monetary shock waves around the world. After America knocked the world economy off its axis, no one accused it of being irredeemably corrupt or politically unstable. And so Botswana goes on as well. Despite having its own share of political scandals, its democracy appears reasonably intact.

People have unfortunately missed the real stunning achievement of Seretse Khama and Botswana. Building a nation with integrity and good governance wasn't the main feat to be commended in a strife-torn Africa. Peoples all over the world *expect* as a bare minimum that their governments won't be corrupt and look after them—they're entitled to. But Seretse Khama and his ministers achieved these things while wedged between the last two behemoths of white supremacy. And the country that white men first ignored and then tried to slowly crush and starve is still around, in no small part due to how it chose to enter the modern world on its own terms.

Part III

DEPTHS

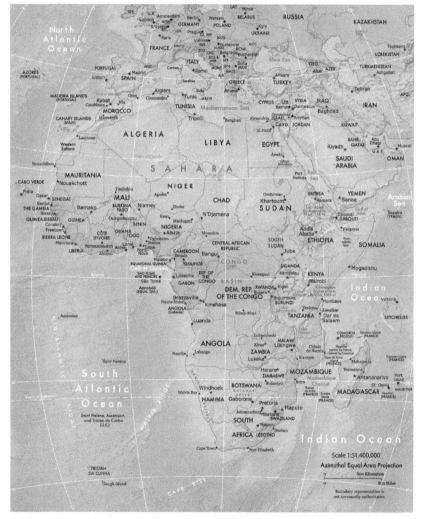

Modern Africa as we know it today, but the map still demonstrates something about how we view and interact with the continent. Many old colonial labels have been replaced with African names, some reflecting the glories of old empires. But it's a map of nation-states with fixed borders, even though multiple cultures and peoples may fall under one domain or be scattered across the artificial lines. *Courtesy Getty Images.*

15

The Worth of Words, the Value in Pictures

The 1940s and the postwar era would be an exciting time and a key transitional phase for the dissemination of African ideas. It wasn't just that independence movements in African countries like Somalia and Botswana began to make themselves felt as never before; African thinkers and scholars were hungry for knowledge, eager to spread the message of what they learned. Fatima Massaquoi was one of those exceptional individuals, and while she never developed any new, groundbreaking theories or school of thought that was picked up by innovators, her example and life's work ensured that others gained opportunities, and in this respect, she made an enormous difference.

Her life's journey came with certain advantages. For one thing, she was literally born a princess around 1904 in southern Sierra Leone to Momolu Massaquoi, king of the Gallinas people of Liberia, while her grandmother was also a queen of the Vai. Life, of course, for African royalty was completely different than their European counterparts, and Massaquoi's autobiography is an ethnographic treasure trove of details on Vai life and social customs in Sierra Leone and Liberia at the time she grew up.

When she was a child, one of Momolu's wives and her stepmothers once imposed a punishment that involved the little girl standing on a box with her hands raised and bound; today, we wouldn't simply call this abuse, it would qualify as outright torture. Fatima fell off the box, and the rope disfigured her hands and injured the bones. Though self-conscious for the rest of her life over the scars, she still forgave her stepmother and became a skilled violinist.

For her father, Momolu, a full education was essential, and he studied in Boston, New York, and Nashville in the late 1800s and later at Oxford, impressing on his children the virtues of learning. He was especially hard on Fatima. In 1928, when she managed to get ranked tenth in her class, her father's reply was a perfunctory compliment followed by this admonition: . . . "But before you leave that class, you must be the *first. First* was always my place in every class I have ever entered and every post I have ever occupied [emphasis in the original]." His paternal love was genuine, but he still warned her that "thousands are looking upon you."[1]

It was true, however, that he was remarkably accomplished. Momolu Massaquoi held several key posts in the Liberian government and is considered by some to be the first indigenous African diplomat in modern Europe, serving as Liberia's consul general in Hamburg. Young Fatima accompanied her parents to Germany. Scholar Raymond Smyke, a friend to her in her later years, put it well when he wrote that in Hamburg, Momolu Massaquoi "became a magnet, attracting the young men and women from all over Africa, studying in England and elsewhere. The consulate became an unofficial clearing house of ideas, thoughts and aspirations for Africa. . . . Fatima recalled W. E. B. Du Bois, sitting on the sofa, relaxed, cigar in hand, sharing his thoughts on Pan-Africanism and the future of the race with visitors."[2] Marcus Garvey, by then exiled forever from America and soon to settle into his new life in London, was another visitor. Fatima had to recite a poem at a dinner reception given in his honor at a hotel in 1928.

Momolu Massaquoi should also get credit for being one of the first activists to lobby for the return of African artifacts. German filmmaker Hans Schomburgk apparently smuggled a stone sculpture of an alligator away from Liberia's Gola territory (he claimed he bought it for £1), and Momolu's steady letter-writing campaign in 1924 to German newspapers prompted a court to order the sculpture's return. It's still unclear, however, whether the sculpture ever made its way back to its proper place.

Fatima was naturally a witness to the political chaos going on in 1920s Germany, at one point getting caught in a riot in 1925 that prompted her and her little brother to flee into a dairy store. In the 1930s, she developed a correspondence with the Latvian American philosopher and peace activist Jacob Loewenberg, who had a strong influence on her. She "found that many of his teachings have come true," and though she first argued with his notion that "nobody could acquire wealth without hurting and tramping on the rights and privileges of others in some way," she came around to seeing his point.[3] She socialized with and sometimes acted as interpreter for young Africans who were active Communists. Momolu, however, worried: "Be careful—I don't want you to become involved and implicated with German political life."[4]

Having a daughter who might become indiscreet over the country's endless political talks, lectures, and rallies would have been a terrible embarrassment in his position, though we shouldn't discount a father's natural protectiveness. But she had a good head on her shoulders, and she clearly found Nazism repellent while not understanding how it could appeal to so many people. While she enjoyed a small circle of German friends that included those sympathetic to Hitler, the Nazis were busy trying to get back the African colonies they lost as spoils to the victors of the Great War; Germans bought up land in what is now Namibia, while the Hitler Youth circumvented a legal ban on their party there and held their activities under the name of the "Pathfinders."[5]

At first, she was interested in studying medicine but finally decided on becoming a teacher. With life becoming increasingly difficult and outright dangerous for black people in Germany, it was decided in 1937 that she ought to pursue her studies in the United States. She had little to say in her autobiography on what life for her was like in the first years of the Nazi regime, but we can get insights from her nephew Hans Massaquoi, who wrote the best-selling memoir of his childhood there, *Destined to Witness*. Hans drew a vivid portrait of his Aunt Fatima, calling her a genius, fluent in multiple languages and skilled in math, chemistry, and biology. To Hans, she loved "being the center of attention," and in an era when black American women straightened their hair to mimic white hairstyles, she "wore an Afro so huge it would have aroused the envy of a Fiji Islander" while sporting a "bright yellow leopard-skin coat." Hans overheard Fatima complain to his mother "about the frequent insults she and [her German boyfriend] drew from indignant Nazis whenever they were seen in public together."[6]

Coming to America, her very presence in town could be news, at least in the black press. "Princess Fatima Massaquoi Guest at Elaborate Reception," ran the headline for a story in the *Indianapolis Recorder* in August 1937. But the African royal chose to take sociology at Lane College in Jackson, Mississippi—in the heart of the Jim Crow South. When she arrived at her college, some of the girls dressed up in blackface and were about to beat tin can drums. Confronted with a young black woman dressed in an elegant ensemble, the hazers quickly backed down.

To bring money in, Massaquoi often gave lectures about her home to churches and schools, selling masks, native cloths, ivory, and other artifacts that her father mailed to her; he had supported himself with talks and selling items when he took his own education in the U.S. She also needed to adapt from the European way of learning to the American one, and her view gives us insight into how she would later be regarded as a great educator. "I still maintain that a thing may be false in one sense and can be true in another," she wrote in her autobiography, "and unless a true or false statement leaves out all other possibilities, it is unfair. Most teachers do not have questions or statements that can truly be answered with 'true' or 'false.' Also, the matter of answering a question with one word is unjust to students. While that one word may be accurate or has been used by a special class, there are often numerous words that can describe a topic or serve as a keyword. I have felt keenly all along that teachers who give objective tests do not wish to be bothered with reading and grading too many written papers."[7]

After graduating from Lane, she moved on to Fisk University in Nashville, where she studied sociology and anthropology and taught Vai to try to cover her expenses. By 1944, Fisk could brag about having dozens of enrolled students hailing from different parts of the Caribbean and Africa. And the university's president, Thomas Jones, made all the right noises about African scholarship, telling the *Pittsburgh Courier*, "The time has come when we Americans must realize the value of African culture as an important part of our liberal arts education in the same way as we study the cultures of Europe."[8] How he and his faculty sought that value was another story.

Encouraged by her professors, Massaquoi first drafted an autobiography as her thesis, but she didn't want the material becoming public. After coercion from her thesis adviser, Mark Watkins, she handed it in, though she subsequently earned her MA with another thesis on nationalist movements in West Africa. To make a long, convoluted story short, Watkins and others dragged their feet on developing her manuscript as a book to be published by the school, telling her it needed editing because her composition wasn't good enough. They fed her other excuses to hold on to her work, doling out occasional small stipends. This also screwed up Massaquoi's plans to attend graduate school in Boston, and it seems the faculty wanted to sponge off her ethnological knowledge and language expertise in Vai as much as they could before letting her go.

Massaquoi finally confronted Watkins in 1944, demanding the return of her manuscript, and now the university's line was that it owned it outright, having paid for it with a few of the pittances they had given to string her along. Worse, Watkins had begun using her material for classroom study and even publishing some of it under his own name. As well, according to Massaquoi, when she tried to retrieve the manuscript from Watkins's safe, he assaulted her.[9] With little recourse left, she first appealed to the Board of Trustees then finally sued the university.

Her lawsuit against Fisk takes us back to the sad, familiar ground of questions over authenticity. Here was an African woman who had to claim her voice, as white American men felt perfectly entitled to steal her work and pass it off as their own. But Massaquoi won her battle, with a judgment that gave her "all property rights to the manuscript and any financial returns from its publication."[10] It's mildly astonishing that her victory— a black African woman winning in a *southern* court *in 1945*—isn't celebrated more as a civil rights landmark. It certainly made the

African American press at the time, with even the sub-headline "Seeks to Preserve African Culture."[11]

"I never wrote my story for Dr. Watkins or Dr. Jones to take away," Massaquoi told the *Baltimore Afro-American* newspaper. "My autobiography is my soul and my heritage, and I couldn't go home to Liberia and look my family in the face after selling my culture and heritage for a mess of pottage [stew]."[12] Ironically, her revised version of it was never published within her lifetime but salvaged from a microfilm copy and edited decades later.

After her studies in Boston, Massaquoi returned to Liberia in 1946 to help found what would become the University of Liberia in Monrovia, and "she taught in almost every department."[13] By 1960, she was dean of its College of Liberal and Fine Arts. Two years later, she founded the university's program of African Studies. But the woman who once cut a flamboyant figure with her Afro and leopard-skin coat in Hamburg was still a rebel. Long before it was acceptable and fashionable for Liberians to wear their own native clothing in Monrovia, Fatima Massaquoi routinely went off to teach in traditional outfits; as a result, when she went to meetings at the Executive Mansion (the official residence of the president), she was often stopped by security.[14] She campaigned successfully against the rule that forced students to wear academic gowns on campus; she also lobbied students to keep their own indigenous names instead of taking foreign ones.[15]

"The most highly educated indigenous woman of her generation," as Smyke called her, "she was special to the increasing number of students who came from the hinterland and from the tribes of Liberia . . . the symbol of what the majority in the country could aspire to."[16]

In 1945—the final year for Fatima Massaquoi's studies in Boston—a Belgian Franciscan missionary to the Congo, Placide Tempels, brought out a book titled *Bantu Philosophy*. It offered his own interpretation of what he called "Bantu ontology." The term *Bantu* itself is a misleading one that's lost much of its old currency—and for good reason. It was once used to refer to hundreds of different peoples speaking close to 700 languages across southern Africa.

But as it turns out, Tempels's focus was on the thinking of a single people, the Baluba of the Congo. In boiling down their metaphysics, he argued, "The key principle of Bantu philosophy is that of vital force. The activating and final aim of all Bantu effort is only the intensification of vital force. To protect or to increase vital force, that is the motive and the profound meaning in all their practices. It is the ideal which animates the life of the '*muntu,*' the only thing for which he is ready to suffer and to sacrifice himself."[17]

The Baluba people, argued Tempels, built their philosophy on a foundation of internal and external evidence. "Songs, fables, mythological traditions and ceremonies of initiation assure instruction in Bantu thought. However, they draw other arguments from their own experience. Since their ancestors proceeded from God himself, should not they have a longer knowledge than they themselves? Besides, their ancestors lived by this philosophy, preserved and handed down life through their recourse to these natural forces, and saved the Bantu people from destruction. Consequently, their wisdom seems sound and sufficient."[18]

But reading Tempels's book, you also come across jarring arguments such as this: "We do not claim, of course, that the Bantu are capable of formulating a philosophical treatise, complete with an adequate vocabulary. It is our job to proceed to such systematic development. It is we who will be able to tell them, in precise terms, what their inmost concept of being is."[19]

Nevertheless, *Bantu Philosophy* was well received when it first came out. A striking exception was, ironically, the Catholic Church; one bishop tried to convince the Vatican to condemn the book as heresy. Alioune Diop, the founder of *Présence Africaine*, wrote an introduction for the French edition in which he considered Tempels's book "the most influential work he had ever read."[20]

With time and evolving politics, however, the work has come in for harsher verdicts, particularly from African thinkers. About twenty years after the book appeared, Ugandan poet and critic Okot p'Bitek wrote, "Can serious African scholars concerned with a correct appraisal and analysis of African beliefs and philosophies afford this kind of cheap generalization? Would they not prefer a cool, sober, methodical, and comparative approach, based on a detailed study of a number of African traditional societies?" Tempels, he reminded his reader, claimed that "by living with the Baluba for a long time, without knowing how, he attained the ability to think like the Bantu and to look upon life as they did."[21] To Okot p'Bitek, this was anecdotal personal experience and intuition passing itself off as scholarship.

Still later, philosopher Paulin Hountondji of Benin was happy to strip Tempels of his honorary membership in the pantheon of African thought: "The best European Africanists remain Europeans, even (and above all) if they invent a Bantu 'philosophy,' whereas the African philosophers who think in terms of Plato or Marx and confidently take over the theoretical heritage of Western philosophy, assimilating and transcending it, are producing authentic African work."[22]

Far more interesting perhaps than Tempels's conclusions about the Baluba is the way things have since been reversed: African thinkers now get to decide how to catalog European observers and see if they'll allow their conclusions or even their relevance to such discussions. But if anything, there is a spirit of consistent generosity to the African mind. Cameroon philosopher Pius Mosima is well aware how condescending Tempels got in his work but points out that the Belgian still became the student of the Africans and made "a significant break from classical anthropology."[23]

He notes that for Tempels, Africans were "incapable of articulating the way they perceive and understand the world," a Eurocentric assumption that implies "that indigenous African peoples predominantly articulate their beliefs and values through rites, rituals, and masquerades, rather than using discursive verbal statements such as proverbs and myths." And those who hold this view—as everything in our discussions of written script, the traditions of griots and griottes, the legacy of African antecedents—show us they are thunderously *wrong*. Still, Mosima believes *Bantu Philosophy* has "served as a basis and reference point for all future attempts at formulating and constructing an indigenous African philosophical system."[24]

And Mosima goes further. He maintains, "We need both the born Africans and the Africans by choice in our move towards a new African philosophy," and contends that "the majority of

African thinkers do not find it in any way aberrant to consider Tempels as the father of contemporary African philosophy."[25]

Others have disagreed. "The main contribution of Tempels is more in terms of sympathy and change of attitude than perhaps in the actual contents and theory of his book." This line comes from *African Religions and Philosophy* by John Mbiti, a professor and Anglican priest, and his own study was published fourteen years after Tempels's work came into print and about a decade after *Bantu Philosophy* first saw English translation.

Mbiti was born in Mulango, Kenya, in 1931, the son of two farmers. Because he was raised Christian, he naturally took on a borrowed Western scorn for indigenous faith. Around the same time in the 1950s that he earned his PhD in theology at Cambridge, he was ordained by the Church of England as well. He began looking into traditional African religions for a purely practical reason—he didn't know anything about them, but he'd managed to land a job teaching the subject at the University of Makerere in Kampala, Uganda.[26] By the time he wrote *African Religions and Philosophy*, he would claim these traditional faiths deserved the same respect as Christianity, Judaism, Buddhism, and Islam.

His work is a significant and even profound examination of the subject. Mbiti argued, for instance, that for many traditional African societies, such as the Kikuyu, "time is a two-dimensional phenomenon, with a long *past*, a *present* and virtually *no future* [emphasis in the original]."[27] Since events haven't yet taken place, they can't very well exist, and therefore this future time doesn't exist either. When it comes to conceptions of God, evil, and justice, there are societies "in which people do not feel they can offend against God," and for several peoples, such as the Zande of the Congo, the Ankole of Uganda, and the Swazi of modern Eswatini and the province of Mpumalanga in South Africa, "God has no influence on people's moral values."[28]

Instead, people in these cultures are concerned with offending intermediaries such as spirits and what Mbiti refers to as the "living-dead," ancestors such as kings and patriarchs. Mbiti's 1969 first edition also contained some fascinating ethnographic details, such as how the Wolof people of Senegal, Mauritania, and The Gambia mixed Islam with traditional beliefs, such as a fear of witchcraft and a cult of spirit possession.[29]

While academics mostly welcomed Mbiti's book as an innovative study, some also criticized him for assessing African religions from a Christian perspective. A professor in Nigeria, while commending Mbiti's diligent research, thought he "overplayed his hand" in places by claiming Christianity was indigenous to Africa.[30] The anthropologist Aylward Shorter wrote in *African Affairs* that Mbiti's book contained little actual philosophy per se and that one "disturbing element is Professor Mbiti's profound pessimism about the value of African traditional religions" and for his "conviction that African and other non-Christian religions are a preparatory and 'even essential ground' in the search for the Ultimate, conducted more surely and explicitly by Christianity."[31]

Not surprisingly, Okot p'Bitek wasn't impressed either. He included Mbiti in a list of African nationalists, such as Kenyatta, Senghor, and Ghana's Joseph Danquah, who "protest vigorously against any Western scholar who describes African cultures and religions in disparaging terms." And so they "dress up African deities in Hellenic robes and parade them before the Western world."[32]

Mbiti, however, ignored his critics and doubled down on one of his boldest assertions. "The God described in the Bible," he wrote years later, "is none other than the God who is already known in the framework of our traditional African religiosity. The missionaries who introduced the Gospel to Africa in the past 200 years did not bring God to our continent. Instead, God brought *them* [emphasis in the original]. They proclaimed the name of Jesus Christ. But they used the names of the God who was and is already known by African peoples—such as Mungu, Mulungu, Katonda, Ngai, Oludumare, Asis, Ruwa, Ruhanga, Jok, Modimo, Unkulunkulu and thousands more."[33] Here, incidentally, is a progression in thinking and a new perspective that eluded Edward Wilmot Blyden over indigenous religions.

The *New York Times* once asked him about the growing influence of Africa on Christianity. "The days are over when we will be carbon copies of European Christians," said Mbiti. "Europe and America westernized Christianity. The Orthodox easternized it. Now it's our turn to Africanize it."

Let's not grumble too much here that Christianity was already "Africanized," first thanks to Augustine, plus the Ethiopians and Nubians; we know Mbiti was talking about the specific context of sub-Saharan Africa and the "import" of the faith from westerners. And what he suggested was remarkable. For 2,000 years, the religion had imposed itself on other cultures, and their believers had to conform to its rules. For the last few times that somebody didn't like that arrangement, there was a split in empire, a Reformation, and an English king who needed a divorce. Mbiti, however, declared that Africans could be agents of change for their faith, and they would obviously be conscious of the process of cultural modification.

Mbiti went on to write other books though none as groundbreaking and provocative as his landmark work, and in recent years, scholars have taken issue with his analysis of African concepts of time.[34] But with his death at age eighty-seven in 2019, the tributes poured in, including from Justin Welby, the Archbishop of Canterbury, who called him a key father of African theology. Despite the limitations of his analysis, Mbiti elevated the discussion of African religion in the same way that Jomo Kenyatta changed the conversation over cultural and social practices of a native people.

When World War II ended, folks wanted to dance again. In Paris, they wanted to eat well and listen to jazz as they once did. Black Americans and African students took up residence again in the Latin Quarter and near the Café de Flore. Meanwhile, Londoners still had to pick their way through rubble and put up with rationing. In the summer of 1948, the *Empire Windrush* brought more than 800 West Indian migrant workers to the port of Tilbury in Essex, the first wave of a new immigrant class that would reshape and reinvigorate Britain. Independence movements were getting louder and more aggressive in different parts of Africa, and to many English and French, Belgians and Italians, all reading their newspapers and trying to forget the recent nightmare of bombs and death camps, why shouldn't these Africans have their own liberation?

If the 1930s and forties were key decades for transition, then the 1950s deserve to be remembered as one of the most inspiring decades for the progression and spread of African ideas and culture in modern history. *Négritude* was at the height of its intellectual currency in France. Cheikh Anta Diop was teaching in Paris and would soon rock the field of Egyptology; Frantz Fanon would change how people think about the anticolonialism struggle. We'll consider them both in following chapters. Chinua Achebe's classic novel *Things Fall Apart* would be published in 1958. If you knew where to look, African culture could be found practically everywhere. If you went into a theater in 1951 to watch the movie adaptation of *Cry the Beloved Country*, you heard part of the slow, beautifully haunting "Mbube," the Zulu song by South African musician Solomon Linda (though it was first recorded in 1939). You know this song—everyone does. Because it's been covered multiple times by Western artists in its faster, excruciatingly insipid pop version, "The Lion Sleeps Tonight."

And there was an explosion in new, exciting art. Only this time, African motifs and visions weren't filtered by a Picasso or a Matisse. Africans themselves created the works and received their proper due. Some were studying in London at traditional schools, some were in Paris, some were producing their work in their home countries. And the titan who stood above them all was Nigerian painter and sculptor Ben Enwonwu. According to his biographer Sylvester Ogbechie of the University of California, he was "one of the very few Nigerian artists who actually had a full-time professional career as an artist."[35] Most of the others had to balance their creative output with day jobs (and here, we're talking about artists in the modern sense rather than the staple indigenous crafts of, say, traditional sculpture or textiles). Enwonwu didn't just prosper. He was extraordinarily successful, and no one else came close to his height of fame and celebration. He was profiled regularly in newspapers and magazines, landing major commissions and even having Queen Elizabeth II sit for one of his sculptures.

He was born into a prominent family in 1917 in Nigeria's river city of Onitsha. His father was a traditional sculptor and his mother a cloth merchant. By the time he was in his late teens, his skills and incredible potential as an artist were recognized. At just twenty years old, his work was shown in a London gallery, and within a handful of years, he was earning competition prize money and awards as well as a scholarship to study in England. The honors would keep on coming.

By then, he had already spent a couple of years as an art teacher in Benin City. This was a place that inspired, provoked, frustrated him, and shaped his views. For Enwonwu, the Oba of Benin could be blamed for the community's decline in traditional arts as much as the British keeping their tight grip on Nigeria. Akenzua II, he complained, was "not interested in Benin art, nor does he help the present carvers of Benin," but Akenzua wasn't in a position really to sponsor the top creatives in ivory and bronze; the British had restored the outward trappings of monarchy (if not its real power) back in 1914 to foil Germany's ambitions for Nigeria.[36]

So here is more fallout from that destructive looting of the Benin Bronzes—that rupture in the continuity of governance had echoed on, inspiring Enwonwu's harsh criticism. At the same time, we can see how what was always essential in the culture had been rescued and was finding new expression. It didn't have to be stuck in a museum like a pinned butterfly under glass. As Ogbechie writes, the artist "derived a huge store of images and themes from his immersion in Benin culture, and these resurfaced in various forms throughout his career."[37]

In 1946, Julian Huxley—then running UNESCO—invited Ben Enwonwu to represent Africa at an international exhibition of modern art at the Musée D'Art Moderne in Paris. *Négritude* was one of the influences on him, and in his paintings of female nudes, Senghor and Césaire's concept comes sensually to life. According to his son, Oliver, the artist was "instrumental in creating a visual representation of the philosophy. If you look closely at that work on this *Négritude* theme, you can see how he shows the beauty of the black skin, the beauty of the African woman. He depicts this carefully in the work and it's all about being black and proud."[38]

In 1956, the landmark Conference of Negro-African Writers and Artists was held during a warm September at the Sorbonne's Amphitheatre Descartes. A pantheon of African and Caribbean thinkers was in attendance: Aimé Césaire and Léopold Sédar

Senghor were there, as well as Frantz Fanon. And Ben Enwonwu was a guest speaker, there to talk about the current problems of the African artist. His speech was later published in—where else—*Présence Africaine*. If it isn't already, this speech should be required reading in African Culture Studies and given to students at Fine Arts schools.

The problems for the African artist, as he saw them, fell under various categories: political, cultural, educational, social, even emotional. Enwonwu didn't keep his easel in a bubble. He was aware of politics and insisted his fellow artists do the same, that each one was "bound by the nature of traditional artistic style of his country, to express, even unconsciously, the political aspirations of his time; and for these expressions to be true, they must be an embodiment of the struggle for self-preservation."[39]

There were still traditional craftsmen and artists in villages, he noted, whose work was vital and relevant. At the same time, younger artists educated in Western techniques faced a difficult burden because "the preservation and continuity of the characteristic quality of African art depends largely on how modern African artists can borrow the techniques of the West without copying European art." No doubt, this remains an important question for those painting a canvas or sculpting a bronze in Cape Town or Abidjan, but it's not just a matter of aesthetics. "It would not have been necessary for the African artist of today to prove to the world that he can create objects of great beauty had the political problems that he has had to face not affected him so deeply, and his art as well."[40]

In a tangential way, he noted how African art revitalized Western traditions, and he must have had in mind Picasso and other European borrowers. The problem is that Western ideas and education couldn't return the favor; it could never keep alive "the native genius of the African peoples." He then made this shrewd observation. "And while Europe can be proud to possess some of the very best sculptures from Africa among museums and private collectors, Africa can only be given the poorest examples of English art particularly, and the second-rate of other works of art from Europe."[41] To Enwonwu, the African

Dancing Figure by Ben Enwonwu. *Courtesy of the U.S. National Archives.*

artist "faces the humiliation of having to listen to lectures on African Art in foreign art galleries and museums. He visits foreign museums in order to see a collection of the art of his own country, and very often he is shown round the museum by European curators."[42]

This grabs our attention immediately because it's of course true not only for African artists but for anyone of African descent who has wandered around Western institutions. Here was Ben Enwonwu, basically making the case if not a closing argument for the repatriation of African artifacts and treasures. When I asked Enwonwu's biographer Sylvester Ogbechie about this, he agreed with me and explained that the artist became invested in the idea because of his former art instructor and mentor, the Englishman Kenneth Murray. "Murray created the Nigerian museum system and fought the colonial government very hard to keep important examples of Nigerian art in Nigeria rather than being exported. Murray was doing this in the 1950s and the 1960s. . . . And I'm sure [Enwonwu] would have realized the impact of what he was doing."[43] Unfortunately, says Ogbechie, Murray was virtually alone in making such an argument in colonial Nigeria at that time.

And in 1956, no one—at least not on television or in the major newspapers—would have dared insist on *returning* such items to their original nations. It just didn't seem to occur to anyone back then, especially as much of Africa was still under colonial rule. Enwonwu didn't suggest it either. Even the Elgin Marbles, or the Parthenon Marbles as they're increasingly being referenced, didn't have a prominent international campaign for their return until the 1980s. Enwonwu eloquently expressed the sentiment that many Africans feel on seeing pieces of their heritage on display, far from home, and he deserves credit for being one of the first to write about the emotional impact of stolen artifacts.

On a royal tour in Africa, Queen Elizabeth II visited his studio in Lagos and commissioned him to make a sculpture of her. Sittings were done at both Buckingham Palace and his rented studio in Maida Vale, London, which allowed him to make a clay model, later cast in plaster and then in bronze by others.[44] It was a singular honor for Enwonwu, being the first African artist ever to create an official royal portrait, and he gave the first public showing at an annual art exhibition in London in 1957. While the *Times* art critic praised his contributions to the exhibition, the *Daily Mail*'s Pierre Jeannerat grumbled over "a distinct Africanization of the features" in the bronze queen. It was true that Enwonwu had given Elizabeth fuller lips in the portrait. It was also true that the queen herself liked the final sculpture.[45] So much for the grumblers, at least those in Britain.

"Ben Enwonwu is a slightly chubby but very energetic man," wrote an unnamed special correspondent for *The Guardian* in 1957. "At his house in the rich area of Lagos, he would often put a stack of long playing records on his gramophone, forget about a meal, try to finish off a painting or two, pick up a chisel when he felt like it, carve away for a while and then complain that he had stomach ache. He runs an American car and brought it over to England with him; here, he says, it is not necessary to have such a big car so he is thinking of changing to 'something more conservative like a Jaguar.'"[46]

In Africa, Enwonwu's success and stardom summoned pride, but it also sparked criticism over his laurels coming from the institutions of colonizers, especially given that Nigeria still waited for its independence. He defied stereotypes and easy classifications. "European artists like Picasso, Braque and Vlaminck were influenced by African art," he said in an interview for the BBC in 1958. "Everybody sees that and is not opposed to it, but when they see African artists who are influenced by their European training and technique, they expect that African to stick to his traditional forms, even if he bends down to copying them." He refused to do so. He pointed out that he knew the Italian sculptor Alberto Giacometti while in England. "I knew he was influenced by African sculptures. But I would not be influenced by Giacometti because he was influenced by my ancestors."[47]

His art has naturally proved to be his best testimonial, and its versatility is astonishing. His painting of his friend, American hairstylist Christine Davis, is faintly Impressionistic. His landscapes and his paintings of African dancers in traditional masks offer explosions of lush, vivid color. His sculpture *Anyanwu* ("Sun"), for the United Nations, is a symbolist work that depicts a thin woman in the garb of Benin royalty. *The Drummer*, mounted on the Nigerian Telecommunications headquarters in Lagos, can faintly remind you of Henry Moore. And his stunning masterpiece *Tutu* has been called a national icon of Nigeria.

Tutu is one of three portrait studies he made of Princess Adetutu Ademiluyi, the granddaughter of a former Ife king of the

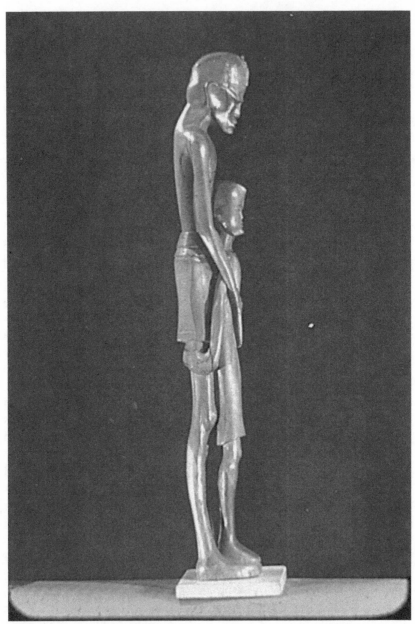

Father and Son by Ben Enwonwu. *Courtesy of the U.S. National Archives.*

Yoruba people. Enwonwu painted it in 1974 when the wounds of the horrific Nigerian Civil War, involving its breakaway province of Biafra, were still raw for the country's citizens. The Igbo people were a majority in Biafra, and Enwonwu was Igbo himself. But a painting of a Yoruba princess was considered a moving gesture of national reconciliation, and Nigerians hung prints of *Tutu* on their walls across the country.[48] The original went missing in 1975 and wasn't seen for decades until it was located in a London flat in 2017, an event that novelist Ben Okri called "the most significant discovery in contemporary African art in over fifty years."[49]

Enwonwu died in 1994 at the age of seventy-seven, and his art now sells for staggering prices. The recovered *Tutu* sold for a record $1.6 million in 2018. The next year, *Christine* sold for more than seven times its estimated price of $1.4 million at Sotheby's. By any measure—artistic accomplishment, fame, the skyrocketing valuations of his works—he is a success. And with luck, his expressions in print and in interviews of African Ideas will hopefully earn as much recognition one day as his sculptures and paintings.

Enwonwu's meteoric rise could never be matched, but other artists broke through. Gerard Sekoto, born in 1913 in Botshabelo, a Lutheran mission station in South Africa's Transvaal, achieved early success in his twenties and thirties. In 1940, the Johannesburg Art Gallery bought his composition *Yellow Houses — Sophiatown*, and for decades it remained the gallery's sole addition painted by a black South African artist. By its very inclusion, it rejected and subverted the conceit of white supremacy. But Sekoto still had to disguise himself as a cleaner just to sneak into the gallery and catch a glimpse of his work hanging there.

His early paintings are known for their social realism and scenes of dazzling color. He painted miners heading for their shift. He painted a lonely mother cradling a child in the impoverished squalor of District 6 in Cape Town. His politically blunt *Song of the Pick* shows a line of black laborers with pickaxes in front of a nonchalant white foreman; the workers, in perfect synch with their axes raised high over their heads, look almost poised to rebel and attack. *Sixpence a Door*, his famous depiction of Zulu dancers, was included in a touring exhibition of South

African art, and when it was shown at the Tate Gallery in London in 1948, the Queen Mother remarked that the painting that she liked the most was "the one by the native artist."[50]

Encouraged by his friend and fellow artist Ernest Mancoba, Sekoto moved to Paris because he understood it was the Mecca of the art world "and that there was also freedom of thought there."[51] Travel back then was still mostly by ship, and so he made a stopover in London, where Ben Enwonwu put him up for a few days; the two had some influence on each other's work during these postwar years.[52] Before he had left for Europe, Sekoto had asked himself first, "Am I going there to become a Frenchman?" The answer was no. "All I needed was to throw myself into the artistic fountain of Paris which attracts so many nationalities throughout the world, and to see what my feelings as an individual South African could gain."[53]

Life, however, is hardly ever so accommodating. He didn't speak French and wound up living in a cheap hotel in Saint-Germain-des-Pré, broke and playing the piano in jazz bars to survive. He also began to drink too much.

His first solo exhibition in Paris in 1949 was a flop in terms of sales. Worse, it sparked a physical fight with the gallery owner, Raymond de Cardonne, who called the cops on him. Feeling regret, de Cardonne learned to his horror that Sekoto hadn't been taken to jail but to a psychiatric hospital instead. He brought the artist charcoals and sketch paper, and Sekoto produced a set of pensive and somber portraits of his fellow patients.[54] Around this time, *Time* magazine featured him in its arts section of an August issue. Sekoto kept drawing and painting both contemporary scenes of life around him in Paris and scenes from memory of South African culture, and though sales and success came gradually, it did eventually arrive. Over the next decades, his work was exhibited in Sweden and Denmark, Italy, and the United States.[55]

"I had to come to Europe where I could be together with other artists and where there was no color bar," he recalled later. He didn't consider himself a political exile in France. "I came on my own to stay here and had never dreamed of gold, except of spiritual gold, at all costs."[56]

Unfortunately, even as his art took on new significance for a South Africa in its last years of apartheid, Sekoto was financially struggling and drinking heavily again. He lost his romantic partner of many decades, was evicted from her apartment, and then the authorities callously dumped him in a care home for seniors in the suburb of Corbeil, where "he felt restricted by the rules and regulations."[57] In 1983, he was injured badly after getting hit by a bus in Paris, limping through the final years of his life. Yet awards still came in, exhibitions were still organized. When a major retrospective exhibition on his work was held at the Johannesburg Art Gallery, Sekoto told a reporter, "I am very pleased about the exhibition, but I have no plans to come back home. This is where I live now."[58]

Relatively content at another retirement home for artists in the Parisian suburb of Nogent-sur-Marne, he died in 1993.[59] His reputation has grown even more after death, with retrospectives in the land he spent decades away from in exile and his paintings featured on South African stamps.

Critics are divided over any connection Sekoto had with *Négritude*. On the one hand, he certainly would have known its ideas through friends in the African diaspora community in Paris and perhaps from working with the magazine *Présence Africaine*; he urged his fellow creatives to go "now and then to Africa to draw their inspiration from spiritual sources, which have not been influenced by Western culture."[60] In 1966, he visited Senegal, where Léopold Sédar Senghor, by then the country's president, treated him as a hero. But one art historian has dismissed the notion of influence, contending that, for Sekoto, coming from the brutal environment of South Africa, "Sartre's philosophical platitudes about black culture and universalism could not have been more foreign or more fanciful."[61]

The critics and historians quibble, too, over when he did his best work: his years in South Africa versus his long exile in France. What is not in doubt is how he continues to resonate with modern audiences, his work distilling images of South African character and demonstrating, like Ben Enwonwu, that what makes African art does not need to stay contained only to Africa. That might come across initially as a facile point, but it's

Mother and Child by Gerard Sekoto. *Courtesy of the U.S. National Archives.*

an essential one. Until Enwownu, Sekoto, and others in the 1940s and fifties, visual African art was frozen—at least for the West and perhaps the rest of the world—as an anonymous, faceless, communal product. Sekoto quite literally took on the "starving artist" lifestyle in Paris (Mancoba had warned him about Van Gogh), but he stayed true to his culture and his vision. His name never became attached to any expat movement or Parisian school. The name "Sekoto" is synonymous with *South African* art.

In 1953, Richard Wright, the novelist who wrote the best sellers *Black Boy* and *Native Son*, forty-five years old and with his best literary work behind him, decided to visit Africa. It did not go well.

In the Gold Coast, only a handful of years before its independence, he expected to have a long talk with the man of the hour, Kwame Nkrumah, but Nkrumah gave him little attention. Used to living comfortably in France, Wright was unprepared for the rough conditions of an Accra hotel room with cockroaches and mold. Africans didn't know his name. They didn't treat this stranger sporting a pith helmet and wearing Western clothes as a celebrity at all. He was miserable. But he brought a lot of his own despair on himself, enraging locals by snapping photos of a traditional funeral ceremony. While he was no longer really a Communist, Wright's worldview was still shaped by Marxist historical theory, and he carried around an invisible footlocker of ingrained prejudices and pruderies.

He was offended by common nudity. He was offended that ordinary Africans didn't open up and explain their cultural practices. As one biographer put it, "He would ask questions—rather hostile questions that were the product of his Western assumptions—and the African, unable to find the words to explain an entirely different reality, would finally become impatient with the trap Wright seemed to be setting. Wright, irritated, would record the dialogue as yet another example of the African's 'chronic distrust.'"[62]

He thought tribal chiefs were "preposterous," strolling under "foolishly gaudy" umbrellas and with "outlandish regalia." In his notes, he complained, "Their claims about their ability to appease the dead is a fraud, their many wives are a seductive farce . . . their justice is barbaric, their interpretations of life are contrary to common sense." If he had his way, traditional religion would be harshly stamped out. When he noticed men holding hands in the streets [still a common practice in parts of Africa and the Middle East] or men dancing with each other, he felt "a sense of uneasiness . . . deeper than I could control."[63] He eventually cut his trip short.

The book that evolved out of his trip, Black Power, was published in 1954, and it hasn't aged well. Like a New Jersey college student on vacation in Sarajevo or Bangkok, Wright was shocked to realize that the strange land he was visiting constantly reminded him of his own American character. "I'm of African descent and I'm in the midst of Africans, yet I cannot tell what they are thinking and feeling."[64] His book includes a shrill appeal to Nkrumah to enact Fascist-style conscription as a way to "atomize the fetish-ridden past, abolish the mystical and nonsensical family relations that freeze the African in his static degradation."[65] Wright didn't know it, but when excerpts of Black Power were published in certain magazines, these were propaganda devices of the CIA's bogus organization, the Congress for Cultural Freedom.[66]

Two years later, Wright attended the Conference of Negro-African Writers and Artists at the Sorbonne, the same conference where Ben Enwonwu was a speaker. And Wright told his audience, "Today, a knowing black, brown, or yellow man can say: 'Thank you, Mr. White Man, for freeing me from the rot of my irrational traditions and customs, though you are still the victims of your own irrational customs and traditions!'"[67] In his view, Western plundering—despite its ugly motives—was in the end a boon to colonized peoples. "The partial overcoming of the forces of oppressive religions in Europe resulted, in a round-about manner, in a partial overcoming of tradition and religion of Asia and Africa." In our modern age, Henry Louis Gates has diagnosed Wright's "colonial condescension" as an attitude hardly more advanced than Edward Wilmot Blyden's views of traditional Africa at the turn of the twentieth century.[68]

Why should it matter what a fading black American novelist thought of Africa? Well, consider Wright's rambling address in which he detours into political territory. He talked of a Western-educated elite in Africa and Asia, "an elite more Western than the West." His fuzzy logic worked like this: to keep rational, civilized values in Africa and help it develop, the Western powers should leave the Africans to themselves, otherwise they would naturally resent even the most benign collaborations and oversight. Given how the colonial powers had brutalized Africa, they had no right to shake their heads or cluck their tongues over African affairs after they left. "The West must trust that part of itself that it has thrust into Asia and Africa. Nehru, Nkrumah, Nasser, Sukarno, and the Western educated chiefs of these newly created national states must be given *carte blanche* right to modernize their lands without overlordship of the West, and we must understand the methods they will feel compelled to use."[69]

Which, for the most part, is exactly what happened. It wasn't that Wright was particularly prescient. No one knew quite what to expect after African countries became independent, but the widespread expectation in the West—indeed the hope—was that the fledgling nations would replicate the democratic institutions of their former colonial overseers. Wright saw Marxist economic practices as a rejection of colonialism, which to many radical Africans was personified by big capitalism. Without even knowing the kind of African antecedents discussed in chapter 5, he was prepared to reject most of the continent's culture, even to stomp a Fascist boot down on it if necessary. Whether this view found sympathetic ears at the Sorbonne, history would sadly prove there were those in Africa who bought this rationale.

James Baldwin was in the audience that evening, covering the conference for a feature in *Encounter* magazine. When Wright argued that "what was good for Europe was good for all mankind," Baldwin dismissed this as "a tactless way of phrasing a debatable idea." He picked up on Wright's veiled endorsement of dictatorial methods, plus Wright's naive expectation that leaders like Egypt's Gamal Nasser and Indonesia's Sukarno would later voluntarily give up power. Wright, Baldwin noted, "did not say what would happen then, but I supposed it would be the second coming."[70]

In twenty years, the world had gone from Paul Robeson—a black American who wrote, "I want to be African"—to the open disdain of African cultures by Richard Wright. James Baldwin decided to see Africa for himself in 1962 and to write an article for *The New Yorker* magazine, but he admitted to a friend that he was worried about "being looked down upon as an American and afraid that something American in him might look down on Africans."[71] He, at least, brought more self-awareness to his travels than Wright did, and he visited Senegal and Sierra Leone and made short stops in Monrovia, Abidjan, and Accra. But while he kept notes on what he saw, "the things that really attracted him . . . he was unable to pursue in any depth."[72]

Given the cross-pollinating relationship of Africa and black America, it's a shame that two of the most gifted black American novelists of the twentieth century couldn't become fresh interpreters of African culture and aspirations. Neither was ever comfortable *in* or *with* Africa in the ways that Paul Robeson was or, as we'll see later, Malcolm X was. It is especially unfortunate in the case of Baldwin, the grandmaster of the personal essay.

Here, for instance, is what he had to say in *Notes of a Native Son* about the black American encountering the African student in Paris, and his descriptions ring true for both the students trying to get by in the 1930s and the ones who arrived in the postwar era. "In Paris, the African Negro's status, conspicuous and subtly inconvenient, is that of a colonial." The African expatriate in Paris understood that "his country must be given—or it must seize—its freedom." The colonial students, Baldwin noticed, all live together in the Latin Quarter in "ageless, sinister-looking hotels; they are all forced continually to choose between cigarettes and cheese at lunch."

He mused that while a black American might catch himself feeling homesick, he still "begins to conjecture how much he has gained and lost during his long sojourn in the American republic. The African before him has endured privation, injustice, medieval cruelty; but the African has not yet endured the utter alienation of himself from his people and his past . . . he has not, all his life long, ached for acceptance in a culture which pronounced straight hair and white skin the only acceptable beauty."[73]

Imagine what he might have come up with if he had more time among locals in the different countries of his tour.

16

The Shadow of Mau Mau and the Echoes of Algiers

The story of Britain's role in the Scramble for Africa has been told many times, including the "White Mischief" days of drugs, drinking, and hedonism in Kenya less than 100 years ago. But it's impossible to discuss the Mau Mau without a quick diversion into colonial history because Kenya didn't merely experience colonialism—it had a system of apartheid practically as brutalizing as the version in South Africa. And yet the situation had complexities all its own.

The British had first pushed their way in as a desperate bid to keep it out of the hands of their imperial rivals, funding a ludicrously expensive railway from Mombasa to Lake Victoria. In the raids that helped secure British control, the indigenous peoples who historically dominated the region, such as the Kikuyu and Nandi, put up the strongest fight, while the Maasai and Luo became British allies.[1] By the 1940s, one in eight Kikuyu had been reduced to being mere tenants—"squatters" as they were known—on farms owned by Europeans, and in 1925, Kenya's court system made it so that Africans could be evicted at the whim of a landlord.[2] Ironically, while the Mau Mau Uprising came to be associated most of all with the Kikuyu, other tribes had ended up with far less territory. The big losers were the Maasai, the Nandi, and the Kipsigis. African populations kept growing—as did their cattle herds—but

305

all were penned in on reserves, without further room for their animals to graze.[3]

While the tribes already had complex cooperative and competitive relationships of their own, the situation ensured their continued rivalry while the British kept the lion's share of the best land for cultivation over the next fifty years. David Anderson summed it up well when he wrote that after 1902 and the railway enterprise, "White political and economic domination, the alienation of African lands, and the oppression of Africans as a poorly paid and exploited laboring class had all followed in short order."[4] There were only four Africans in the colony's legislature, and none of them got to their positions through a ballot box—they had been carefully chosen by the government.[5]

Contrary to newspaper portrayals at the time of white settlers toiling away, carving out a nation, it was the Africans who did the hard labor, with the crueler farm bosses willing to flog workers with a hippo-hide whip. Africans coming and going from a native reserve were forced to carry a *kipande*, a pass with their name, tribe, fingerprints, and employment record. It was worn around the neck in a small, metal container that tinkled with the wearer's step; Kikuyus loathed it and called it *mbugi*, the goat's bell. A native Kenyan was at the mercy of his white boss, for if the employer didn't sign his *kipande*, it was illegal for anyone else to hire him. When working as a servant in the house, he or she often had to endure a derogatory nickname like "Stupid" assigned by the settler and his family members, who also referred to Africans as "monkeys."[6]

Against this backdrop of colonial entitlement and repression evolved a radical movement, one determined to exact vengeance and achieve liberation: Mau Mau.

But resistance had been tried before in Kenya. The government had left the education of Africans mostly up to Anglican, Presbyterian, and Methodist missions, and much of the anticolonial activism in the 1920s evolved out of these Christian African communities, which produced young professionals who worked in Nairobi. Many of them were Kikuyu. Radical leader Harry Thuku came up through their ranks, accusing the colonial regime of stealing Kikuyu land and declaring that missionaries were "preaching the word of the devil." His arrest in 1922 was inevitable. But when close to 8,000 Africans showed up at the police station to protest, nervous officers fired into the crowd, killing at least twenty-one people and perhaps as many as fifty-six.[7]

While the Mau Mau were poorly armed, they slipped out of the forest shadows and inspired dread with their attacks on white settler farms and on their fellow Africans whom they deemed to be collaborators. They mutilated settlers' cattle and nailed their beloved pets to walls with threatening notes to inspire terror. They were also capable of appalling atrocities, most of which in the end were committed more against their fellow Africans than against white settlers.

Those inducted into the Mau Mau took a loyalty oath, and its ceremony and wording would later fascinate the Western press, perhaps because it involved cutting the initiate and mixing his blood with that of a slaughtered goat, along with other rituals. In some published versions, the ritual included the promise that if you didn't follow specific rules, "may you die of this oath" or words to that effect. The anthropologist Louis Leakey (a harsh critic of Mau Mau) argued the oath was once a simple swearing-in and developed into a more elaborate ceremony based on traditional male initiation ceremonies.[8] Still, for the journalists reporting on the crisis, references to blood rituals and Kikuyu magic worked well with lurid photos and film showing how the Mau Mau preferred weapons of the *simi*, a sword, or a *panga*, a machete.

One of the Mau Mau's founders, Fred Kubai, explained decades later, "We knew our people were ignorant, and they were ruled by the traditional customs. And well, they held that the oath could kill, and we tried to exploit the ignorance of our people."[9] As the struggle intensified, oaths became more complicated. Creating Mau Mau turned the Western conception of the "primitive" African against itself. Out in the forest, however, the guerrillas organized themselves into disciplined military units, with leaders often sporting bits of British army uniforms, such as a beret or an overcoat.[10]

And yet Mau Mau had no real underlying philosophy, no doctrine that could be argued over or nitpicked. It was a nightmare of African vengeance given form, both as a rebellion and as an idea that slowly constructed its own legend. The leaders didn't even give the movement its name—that came from elsewhere. The word "Mau Mau" has no meaning in Kikuyu. One of the more plausible origin theories is that a Kenyan police officer heard a Maasai suspect mispronounce the Kikuyu word for oath, *muma*.

On October 20, 1952, the Kenyan government declared a state of emergency, and the police rounded up more than 180 suspects that they identified as Mau Mau leaders (Kenyatta among them). They were so confident in their presumption that white officers cheered each time one of them was led into the station. While some of those arrested were genuinely involved, the authorities didn't really understand their enemy, thinking the movement was centered in Nairobi. In truth, Mau Mau built its strength in the countryside, and rebel leaders liked to use the Kenya African Union as their political cover. In some cases, they met for the KAU in Nairobi, then held *another* meeting for the Mau Mau Central Committee later the same night. There was a fair number of moderates who regularly communicated with the Mau Mau, and some took oaths, recognizing it had similar goals.

White authorities and settlers were all convinced the KAU's front man and leader, Jomo Kenyatta, was the sinister brain behind Mau Mau. So did most Kikuyu. But when a documentary team asked one of its founders, Bildad Kaggia, point-blank how much Kenyatta knew about the organization of Mau Mau, he smiled and replied, "I think he knew nothing."[11] At a mass rally in Kiambu back in August 1952, established activists like Harry Thuku and others had denounced the movement. The town was Jomo Kenyatta's political turf, and he declared Mau Mau "has spoiled our country, and we do not want it."[12]

The press, both in Kenya and abroad, ate up this bit of theater and ran big headlines over it, but the militants, crouching in their hideouts, were not impressed. Kenyatta was summoned before a secret meeting where he met the true organizers of Mau Mau for the first time—and was told in no uncertain terms to back off. The leaders were already selecting chiefs and headmen they deemed too close to the government for assassination.[13] Kenyatta could be added to their list.

In November, the colony's governor, Sir Evelyn Baring, gave in to pressure from London to hold a trial of Mau Mau leaders. Kenyatta was arrested, and when the police and government picked up five other KAU executives, they hardly realized they had captured two of the *genuine* ringleaders, Bildad Kaggia and Fred Kubai. The settlers weren't placated—most would have preferred the men be taken off to detention or, better still, shot. Evelyn Baring had no qualms about brazenly approaching a judge and arranging a rigged conviction. His first choice turned him down. Baring's second choice insisted on £20,000 to help set him up in a new life back in Britain.[14]

The authorities then moved the trial to the middle of nowhere, a remote spot called Kapenguria without water, phone, or rail service. For the trial itself, the government relentlessly focused their prosecution efforts on Kenyatta, and the very first witness was one of his neighbors, a man named Rawson Macharia, who later turned out to have been bribed for his perjured testimony. The police also made a habit of harassing and arresting defense witnesses. Even Kenyatta's old nemesis from his university days back in London, Louis Leakey, was recruited to be a court interpreter. At one point, one of the defense lawyers caught him blatantly changing the response of a witness from a *no* to a *yes*.[15]

The cross-examination of Kenyatta gives us a brief glimpse of how African Ideas can also be feared as weapons. The prosecution asked him repeatedly about *Facing Mount Kenya* and whether the book reflected his current opinions. Kenyatta, however, knew how to verbally fence. "The book cannot necessarily be my guide during my whole life."[16] The prosecutor even debated with Kenyatta whether his denunciations of Mau Mau were sincere or sufficient, as if weakness of effort were itself evidence of collusion. Kenyatta was indignant. "You people have audacity to ask me silly questions. I have done my best, and if all other people had done as I have done, Mau Mau would not be as it is now. You made it what it is, not Kenyatta."[17] His protests never helped because the fix was in, and he and his fellow defendants were sentenced to seven years of hard labor, to be followed by "indefinite restriction."

As the trial had carried on, in late January 1953, the members of a typical settler family, the Rucks—a doctor, his wife, and their six-year-old son—were gruesomely hacked to death. The rebels had tricked their way onto the Ruck farm with the help of a trusted Kikuyu servant. The next day, a mob of about 2,000 settlers descended on Government House in Nairobi, demanding to be let in, and when refused, they stubbed out their cigarettes on the faces and arms of black police officers. They came close to breaking the doors down.

Meanwhile, out in the Nyandarua forest, there were Mau Mau camps with 400 people, sometimes 1,000 for base camps, with elaborate bamboo shelters, tidy common areas, and well-organized kitchens that could hide smoke from British reconnaissance planes and bombers.[18] And in March 1953, the guerrillas scored their most impressive victory, swooping down with eighty soldiers on the poorly defended police station in Naivasha, letting out its prisoners and helping themselves to more weapons—the whole raid took only about twenty minutes.[19] But the guerillas were always doomed to fail. They were clever at making their own weapons, and rifles might be stolen from farms, but the Royal Air Force pounded them with bombs and strafed them with machine gun fire.

The British wanted to choke off any support from the African population, and so the authorities rounded up thousands of Kikuyu on suspicion and detained them in concentration camps. Men lost years of their lives to the barbed-wire misery of what two leading historians of Mau Mau, David Anderson and Caroline Elkins, both call a gulag. Anderson found that during the state of emergency, 1,090 Kikuyus were hanged, a number which far exceeded the executions that France chose for Algeria's terrorist revolutionaries. It surpassed the numbers in other British colonial posts after World War II.[20] Women and children were not spared either, deported to reserves which were gulags in all but name, their food supplies tightly restricted to keep them out of rebel hands. The result was widespread famine.

In taking such extreme measures, the regime hoped to break the spirit and support for Mau Mau, but sympathy for the insurgents was never cut and dried, even within Kikuyu ranks. In 1954, the Kikuyu Home Guard numbered 25,600 men—5,000 more than the Mau Mau likely had as they kept on fighting in the Aberdares. A Kikuyu man in the Home Guard gained trading licenses, tax exemptions, and the valuable compensation of having the right to vote. These were powerful inducements, but they didn't automatically buy loyalty. Home Guard recruits sometimes didn't even volunteer but were dragged into units through "press gang techniques," and once in, their association with the government regime meant they could hardly leave; at the same time, there were cases where members collaborated with the Mau Mau and provided supplies.[21] And yet, Home Guard units were also responsible for some of the most brutal attacks on the insurgents and horrific assaults during interrogations.

It is not overstating it to say that British methods for questioning a rebel were on the level of Nazi horrors; some white settlers themselves referred to the police's Special Branch unit as "Kenya's SS." Beatings were the least of it. Men's testicles could be crushed with pliers, while the women were stabbed in the vagina with knives or beer bottles.[22] One white settler interviewed by historian Caroline Elkins and who stayed anonymous explained how Special Branch had a "way of slowly electrocuting a Kuke—they'd rough up one for days. Once I went personally to drop off one gang member who needed special treatment. I stayed for a few hours to help the boys out, softening him up. Things got a little out of hand. By the time I cut his balls off, he had no ears, and his eyeball, the right one, I think, was hanging out of its socket. Too bad, he died before we got much out of him."[23]

The Mau Mau, however, were capable of equal atrocities. One of their most heinous was a massacre in Lari, in which they targeted the families of chiefs and headmen they labeled collaborators. Having lured the Home Guard patrol away, gangs of disguised rebels set upon homesteads, tying ropes around huts to stop the occupants from pushing out their doors and escaping. Then the Mau Mau set their homes ablaze. As ordinary Kikuyu struggled to flee—most of them women and children—their attackers cut them to pieces with simis, pangas, and axes. There are accounts of body parts of one chief carried off like trophies. His youngest wife survived being "horrendously slashed across the chest and head. As she fell to the ground with blood streaming down her face, the young woman saw both her children killed, one a toddler, the other a baby."[24] The government was quick to exploit Lari for propaganda, but surviving film footage of small children in plaster casts, scarred for life, one burned across his face, offers its own indictment of cruelty.[25]

Bombing and isolation wore down the Mau Mau—the guerrillas could not advance, not when the white regime locked up virtually the entire Kikuyu population. As years passed, the authorities released some detainees but also forced others into hopeless positions of collaborating to win their release. The most "incorrigible" of Mau Mau suspects and troublemakers were put in the Hola detention camp near the Tara River. The authorities bulldozed Kenyatta's house and tried to erase his name in the African consciousness. But the gulag colony could not go on forever, and in 1959, land reforms were introduced, crop restrictions lifted, and a handful of Africans elected to the colony's legislative council.

That same year, when a group of Hola detainees refused to work, guards clubbed eleven men to death and seriously wounded dozens of others. The Kenyan authorities tried to cover it up, but with an election coming in Britain, the news got out, and the opposition had useful ammunition against the Tory government of Harold Macmillan.

One of the Hola scandal's most adroit critics in the House of Commons was, of all people, Tory Member of Parliament Enoch Powell, who argued that it didn't matter whether the eleven dead were "lowest of the low," as some had argued, and that "We cannot say, 'We will have African standards in Africa, Asian standards in Asia and perhaps British standards here at home.'. . . We must be consistent with ourselves everywhere."[26] Almost ten years later, Powell gave his shocking "Rivers of Blood" speech, which attacked increased immigration of nonwhites into Britain. Hola was never going to be enough to kick

Macmillan out of Downing Street, but it served as another spur for Britain to get out of Kenya.

When the state of emergency was lifted in 1960 and the decolonization process for Kenya switched into high gear, African politicians called for Kenyatta to be released. He was let out in 1961, and he soon accepted leadership of the relatively new Kenya African National Union. To placate whites determined to stay on, he talked about mutual forgiveness. This struck the right note as independence loomed, and it helped him secure the premiership, but Kenyatta was well aware that his internment and association with Mau Mau gave him political capital among Africans. On his visit to Kenya in 1964, Malcolm X wrote in his travel diary how he listened to a speech in which the prime minister took "complete responsibility for organizing the Mau Mau."[27]

The leopard changed his spots yet again as he secured power. To be fair, he now had the difficult task of uniting bitter loyalists and disillusioned freedom fighters. When former detainees and Mau Mau veterans banded together, presuming their sacrifices should be rewarded with land, Kenyatta turned them down and told them to go buy it like everyone else. With Jomo at the helm, the all-too-recent nightmare of detention, beatings, and mass slaughter were intrusions on the grand vision of a new, independent state. They were the family secrets not talked about, and they wouldn't be examined out in the open for some time.

Why should we care more than half a century later about the Mau Mau Uprising? And how does an extremist group—whether terrorists or freedom fighters—merit entry into our parade of African Ideas? We *should* care because Mau Mau has experienced an intellectual evolution of its own. We still wrangle with the question of how far a people are allowed to retaliate against an occupying force, and we have no lack of recent case studies. There are those who refuse to acknowledge the Boycott, Divest, and Sanctions movement as a legitimate protest against Israel and who maintain soldiers have every right to fire on Palestinian teenagers hurling rocks. What are the limits? Are there any? In Hong Kong in 2019, some pro-democracy demonstrators indulged in vandalism of shops as they played a dangerous game of confrontation with the police and Beijing's proxies. How far do we let things go?

Mau Mau burst onto the world consciousness a little over five years after an era when death and destruction could be rationalized as the "last just war." It erupted as the West was getting comfortable with the approach of nonviolent resistance introduced by Mahatma Gandhi. But Mau Mau didn't equivocate. It told the colonialist if you don't like what we do, especially what we're doing to you, get the hell out—get out *now*. As an idea, Mau Mau first lived in minds abroad as the very worst of the African heart, the dark flip side of Josephine Baker's erotic gyrations and the masks that found their way onto a Picasso canvas.

But for all the fear that Mau Mau inspired in settlers, only thirty-two whites were ever murdered, with twenty-six Asians slain. Mau Mau wrath fell heaviest on their fellow Africans, with more than 1,800 of them slaughtered, 3,000 African police murdered, and an unknown number of civilians wounded. Mau Mau history is still riddled with controversy over disputed figures. Historian Caroline Elkins's statistics have been hotly debated—one estimate puts the number of Africans held in detention camps at around 80,000, while Elkins claimed it was about 1.5 million.[28]

The uprising earned a fair amount of attention from the American media against a backdrop of increasing civil rights activity in the United States. In 1954, you heard on the news how the U.S. Supreme Court handed down its decision in *Brown v. Board of Education.* Then the northern states were shocked by Emmett Till's murder by lynching in Mississippi in August 1955. Then Rosa Parks refused to give up her seat on a bus in Montgomery, Alabama, that December. Black American activists had already adopted tactics of direct action and nonviolence resistance in the early fifties, but the newspapers and television informed everyone how Africans did *not* use quiet, polite methods. They used machetes. They were supposedly vicious and vengeful and unpredictable.

Besides striking fear into the heart of the British colonial mind, Mau Mau unnerved Americans with that unspoken nightmare of white consciousness: the angry black man.

Always ready to spot Communists under the bed, editorial writers raised the alarm of a "Red Africa," and reportage sometimes approached the hysterical. One story in a right-wing American magazine made the outlandish claim that Jawaharlal Nehru ran a corps of agents in Kenya who were provoking the natives and that the British government was even aware of this but feared Nehru would take India out of the Commonwealth.[29]

Nothing better personifies the white American view of Mau Mau than a long feature that appeared in *Life* magazine in February 1953. It was written by Robert Ruark, a popular columnist and writer who decided to travel to Kenya, adopt Hemingway's machismo, and spend his days roaming the veldts, killing large, exotic animals. Ruark painted a vivid picture of white settlers leaving their guns on the dining table, carrying a shotgun to market, and even having a pistol ready in a soap dish for baths. "There often is no way to be sure that a servant is *not* a member of the secret terrorist society. The news may come some dark night when he opens the door to his fellow Mau Mau, who will chop you into small bits with *simis* and *pangas* [emphasis in the original]."[30]

The white settler, he claimed, "does not want to leave the land he has painfully cleared and fenced and watered and planted." After a few secondhand anecdotes of terrifying encounters, he described sleeping over at an acquaintance's farm. "Nobody feels like a cowboy. There are too many bandaged arms and scarred faces about. There are too many pianos hacked to matchwood, too many fired drapes, too much smashed crockery and too many violent reports on the local news program in the evening radio schedule. Too many neighbors are dead, their heads chopped to bleeding shreds." For Ruark, the Mau Mau were "the few" preying on "many innocents," and its leadership had "cunningly exploited the grievances of many simple, misguided people."[31]

One could read this article and believe terrified whites lived their lives completely on the defensive. The truth was that in the first year of the state of the emergency, a substantial number of settlers hunted Kikuyu as they would a lion or elephant, and they didn't bother to ask their victims' politics before randomly murdering them. Only a few months after Ruark's article ran in *Life*, it devoted a photo spread to a popular spokesman for the settlers, Michael Blundell, and his family, again portraying them as digging in and making a stand. One of Blundell's bodyguards bragged to a British newspaper that he had killed thirty-three Mau Mau.[32]

A couple of magazine articles couldn't shape American perceptions, but Ruark didn't stop with *Life*. He wrote a well-reviewed novel, *Something of Value*, declaring in his foreword, "In order to understand Mau Mau it is first necessary to understand Africa" and "To understand Africa, you must understand a basic impulsive savagery that is greater than anything we 'civilized' people have encountered in two centuries."[33] One modern historian of the era has dismissed the author as "deplorably ignorant of Kenyan affairs."[34] Ruark was paid handsomely for the film rights by MGM, which naturally cast two obvious Americans, Rock Hudson and Sidney Poitier, as the leads. Both novel and film depict Kenyan farm life the way a romance novelist would pen a sequel to *Gone with the Wind*, offering "good" massahs and "bad" ones. Ruark himself had grown up in North Carolina.

Even before his novel hit the big screen, Americans could go to the theaters in 1955 and see a documentary called *Mau Mau*. Produced by Joe Rock, a has-been of the silent era, it was "filmed in flaming color," and filmgoers were told, "*See!* The secret killer society massacres that horrified the world!" Narrated by Chet Huntley before he rose to fame coanchoring NBC News, his gravitas couldn't make up for the poor production values, which didn't go unnoticed. The *New York Times* called its editing "piecemeal, and chronologically the scenes often are baffling. Although some ugly, fitting glimpses of the aftermaths of Mau Mau raids speak for themselves, the picture sandwiches in a handful of phony sniping scenes and two flagrantly staged marauding sequences."[35]

Presumably, its billing as a documentary helped it make an end run around censors to show topless black women wrestled to the ground. Yet the *Times* was impressed with the film's commentary, taking on faith that the narration got its facts correct even though the producers were willing to fabricate whole sequences. Jomo Kenyatta is referred to as the "ringleader" of the Mau Mau, who "has rejected the white man's established order and way of life and his superiority over the black races."[36]

We could dwell on the film's other shortcomings, but what's interesting here is how it's another sign that Mau Mau's legend created a bogeyman for white Americans.

Black Americans were naturally supportive in general of the Kenyan people, but their perspective was more complex. The NAACP first viewed "with alarm the terrorist methods of the Mau Mau in Kenya," then changed its tune. Hardly bothering to freshen up its language, it decided to "condemn the terrorist methods used against the Mau Mau and others who fight to abolish colonialism and racism."[37] In a bold stand, the *Pittsburgh Courier* considered the Mau Mau attacks "a normal and understandable reaction to white aggression."[38] The Pulitzer Prize–winning African American journalist Malcolm Johnson indulged in Ruark-style luridness for the *Chicago Defender* and the *Atlanta Daily World*, traveling to "primitive settlements where native tribesmen still buy their wives and sell their daughters in exchange for cattle" so he could investigate the "secret native terrorist society sworn to drive out the whites or kill them to achieve black supremacy." To Johnson, the Mau Mau oath "expresses fanatical hatred of all whites and of the Christian religion."[39]

Black activists and liberals wanted to highlight the cruel excesses of the British military and the apartheid regime in Kenya, but they always felt compelled to pay lip service to the obvious, that their indignation did not mean an endorsement of Mau Mau. When he wrote to President Eisenhower, A. Philip Randolph criticized the bombing of the Kikuyu but added that "the leaders of the African natives must be prevailed upon to see that violence and bloodshed cannot constitute a solution of their social, economic, and political problems."[40]

It would take a mind with a broader, more radical vision to abandon any tone of apology and claim Mau Mau as a force for revolution.

Five days before Christmas 1964 in Harlem, a church choir performed a song about Oginga Odinga, Kenya's vice president. Then Malcolm X gave a speech, predicting the Mau Mau would "go down as the greatest African patriots and freedom fighters that the continent ever knew."[41] The *New York Times* was on hand and plucked his more incendiary statements, such as "We need a Mau Mau" and "If the language is a shotgun, get a shotgun. But don't waste time talking the wrong language."

Malcolm X was appearing with civil rights activist Fannie Lou Hamer, who had endured being shot at, arrested, regularly harassed, and abused down in Mississippi, and his call to action was in the context of publicizing her experiences and her efforts to cofound a political alternative for representation in Congress, the Freedom Democratic Party. The *Times* didn't bother to mention her.[42] The FBI, however, dutifully transcribed the article and added it to its files.[43]

While making the common mistake of presuming Kenyatta genuinely led the movement, Malcolm suggested that activists could "best learn how to get real freedom by studying how Kenyatta brought it to his people in Kenya." He also floated the idea of an American Mau Mau as a tactical alternative. "When I was in Africa, I noticed some of the Africans got their freedom faster than others. Some areas of the African continent became independent faster than other areas. I noticed that in the areas where independence had been gotten, someone got angry."[44]

About two weeks later, while speaking to civil rights workers from Mississippi, he brought up Kenyatta and reminded his audience, "Five years ago, they said he was a leader of the Mau Mau. And they tried to make him appear to be a monster. As long as he didn't have his own independence, he was a monster. . . . He had a negative image five years ago because he wouldn't compromise. He was bringing freedom to his people by any means necessary. Now that his people have gotten their freedom, he's respected."[45]

Only an obtuse listener could interpret these remarks as promoting terrorism, nor was Malcolm X seriously interested in unleashing bands of guerrillas with machetes onto southern farms. Skillfully provocative, he believed in what seemed to him to be a commonsense position: self-defense for blacks not only in America but around the world. The debate will go on over just how radical Malcolm X stayed after his break with the Nation of Islam, but what is implied in his comment is that extremism, or at least what is depicted as an extremist view by others, can have a politically legitimate end goal, and it's one that doesn't merely seek a revolutionary purge but looks for scenarios in which black people achieve equality and may still have to occasionally deal with white power structures.

There is something else remarkable in his stand. When black American activists rejected Mau Mau violence, they were by implication also setting themselves apart from the iconic African "savage," asserting the standard line that the civilized black American had put unfathomable oaths and the age of spears behind him. Now here was Malcolm X telling anyone who listened properly that there was no difference in the struggle between the Kenyan and the African American. So why should the African American be ashamed of the Kenyan's methods?

He made this point only days later when speaking to the Militant Labor Forum at Palm Gardens in New York City after a reporter asked him to confirm the *Times* story. He thought "a person has a lot of nerve to ask me that in a society . . . where in 1964 three civil rights workers can be murdered in cold blood and—not the Mississippi government—but the federal government can't do anything about it. I say we need a Mau Mau when a Negro educator can be murdered in Georgia, and they know who murdered him, and the government can do nothing about it. I say we need a Mau Mau, and I'll be the first to join it. A lot of people that you don't think go for it will line right up behind me."[46]

He was an astute observer of African current affairs, following closely events in Angola and the Congo. (In a speech in Harlem, he once called the assassinated Congo leader Patrice Lumumba "the greatest black man who ever walked the African continent."[47]) African history always informed his outlook. When Brian Glanville interviewed him for the *New Statesman* in 1964, he asked, "Why Muslims?," to which Malcolm replied, "Our people are from Nigeria and Ghana. They tell us we're from West Africa, and I think historically that's sound doctrine." But when Africans were taken as slaves, they "had to be cut off from Islam." Glanville, who wrote mostly about soccer, couldn't resist inserting into his article a condescending rebuttal. "One can quarrel with his analysis here; white American motives for weaning their Negroes from Islam—if they did—were probably less devious and more evangelic."[48]

In late November 1964, Malcolm once again showed his depth of knowledge on New York radio when he commented, "The basic cause of most of the trouble in the Congo right now is the intervention of outsiders—the fighting that is going on over the mineral wealth of the Congo and over the strategic position that the Congo represents on the African continent. And in order to justify it, they are doing it at the expense of the Congolese by trying to make it appear that the people are savages. And I think . . . if there are savages in the Congo then there are worse savages in Mississippi, Alabama, and New York City, and probably some in Washington, D.C., too."[49] This serves as accurate for the depiction of the Congo's exploitation in the late 1990s through to the mid-2000s as it was in 1964; the Western media, especially broadcast networks, for instance, routinely referred to war in the region as a "tribal conflict" without even referencing coltan, the precious mining ore used for electronics, which was a key factor.

On a visit to Nigeria, his fame preceded him, and he knew how to appeal to his audience at a meeting over South African apartheid held at the University of Ibadan. When a fellow speaker criticized the visiting American's remarks, the crowd turned so belligerent that Malcolm stepped in to quiet folks down. "Perhaps I should take charge of the meeting."[50] Yes, he was a black man among a black people, but he was in a foreign country. Beyond what it says about the man's remarkable confidence, there's how his words and experiences resonated with listeners in a Nigeria only four years free from colonialism.

And in expressing his admiration for Kenyatta and the Mau Mau, Malcolm X gave an African leader and a movement validation that's had far-reaching influence; it's resulted in a creative and intellectual feedback loop. Mickie Mwanzia Koster, a professor at the University of Texas, traced Malcolm X as an inspiration for hip-hop artists in Kenya: "Malcolm's legacy is still unfolding because the seeds and connections created in the 1960s are still in motion. . . . Politically conscious Hip Hop artists in particular are using their political and social messages to educate and remind the masses of the struggles of Malcolm X and their Mau Mau forefathers."[51] Koster pointed out that a "massive image" of him was painted on a wall in the Dandora slum in Nairobi, and when she interviewed hip-hop artist Kamau Ngigi, he told her, "Malcolm X advocated for a true revolution. His ideologies are still completely relevant because we were given a fake independence. We as black people are still begging."[52] From Kenya to Harlem and back to Kenya again.

In 2013, in part because of the publicity over Caroline Elkins's research, the British government agreed to pay £20 million (about U.S. $30 million) in an out-of-court settlement as compensation to Mau Mau veterans. It also put its "sincere regret" for its colonial abuses into funding a memorial, which was unveiled two years later in Nairobi's Uhuru Park. Thousands gathered to inspect its statue, one that depicts a woman with a traditional kiondo basket handing food to a dreadlocked Mau Mau fighter. Many veterans and their relatives who showed up for the ceremony sported red T-shirts with the wording *shujaa wa Mau Mau*—"heroes of Mau Mau." The BBC reported that they "crowded around the monument as soon as it was unveiled to take pictures. There was a look of satisfaction on their faces. For many, it is a symbol of closure."[53]

And yet . . . A settlement and a statue are hardly the last words on Mau Mau, nor should they be. The times were more complex, as Bethwell Ogot has insisted, and he should know—he lived through them.

Ogot, who is of the Luo people, worked as a student teacher in Kagumo, which was "constantly under threat" from militant Mau Mau leaders from Nyeri, even though soldiers were stationed nearby. "The African members of staff had to literally obey two governments in order to survive," he recalled in his autobiography. "It was particularly difficult for me as a non-Kikuyu to survive in this environment of violence, hatred, fear and intolerance." At one point, he was expected to take part in all-night patrols, ones for which he was given only a "slasher" to defend himself and which would have been "suicide." He refused and then was directed to take a Kikuyu cleansing oath—he argued this would hardly work, not being a Kikuyu.[54]

To Ogot, the Mau Mau Uprising was a civil war, one that in the telling should properly incorporate the stories of the other peoples of the nation. In a perceptive review in 2005 of both Caroline Elkins's book and David Anderson's *Histories of the Hanged*, Ogot suggested that "many writers on Kenyan history, especially the history of decolonization, view everything from central Kenya. Otherwise, they would know that colonial rule in Kenya had always been brutal, and dirty methods were always used to crush any rebellion."[55] He cited two fascinating examples that deserve greater attention and are worth comparing to the troubled chronicle of the Mau Mau.

One is the resistance of the Nandi people, who fought their own brave war against colonial invasion around the turn of the twentieth century. Britain's Colonel Richard Meinertzhagen—who enjoyed killing Africans with a psychopath's pleasure—tricked the Nandi's leader, Koitalel, into meeting with him, and when Koitalel extended his hand, Meinertzhagen shot him at point-blank range. The Nandi were forced onto a gulag reserve of their own. If they left, they could be killed on sight. A land commission in 1934 determined that aside from the Maasai, the Nandi lost more land than any other native people in the colony.

But only a handful of years before the world learned the words "Mau Mau," two radicals, Elijah Masinde and Lukas Pketch, were leading *Dini ya Msambwa*, a revolt that called for all Europeans to be driven out of Kenya "and an African king anointed." Like Mau Mau, the movement mixed politics with African spirituality, and the followers were mainly from the Babukusu people and the nomadic, pastoralist Pokot. Again literally outgunned, these rebels took to hiding in caves. Pketch, who had a certain evangelical charisma, didn't rely on violence to win adherents, and, in fact, he strongly objected to using it to gain followers. He was among the fifty rebels killed in April

1950 in the Kolloa massacre. As for Masinde, he was sent to a mental hospital.[56]

Pokot men—and eventually women—were rounded up, their livestock confiscated, and they were packed off to concentration camps (which were soon badly overcrowded). Most were condemned to forced labor, and there were frequent cases of torture. Even after Pokot were released from the camps, they were sent to the remote area of Lomech, in what at the time was Uganda, where they again often faced torture, starvation, and disease. The colonial powers were still arresting and exiling suspected Pokot rebels right up to the year of Kenya's independence. Where, Ogot asked reasonably in more than one article, are their celebrations? Mau Mau, he's argued, has been used in Kenya as the final yardstick, but "Kenya had many voices in the anti-colonial movement who would not qualify to be on the official list of Mau Mau war heroes."[57] What about them?

Today, there is the memorial to Mau Mau in Nairobi, but if the protests against statues in 2020 have taught us anything, it's that the stone effigies of heroes may be dragged down and shattered at some future appointment for condemnation. And we already know that as noble as the overall struggle was against colonialism in Kenya, the Mau Mau Uprising was rich in haunting ambiguities, of forced collaboration and ruthless executions of those judged traitors, of massacres of the innocent who only hoped to eke out a living. How will people 100 years from now—or even a few decades—interpret the struggle? Ogot's many voices who don't qualify are owed their turn. One day, maybe they'll be heard. And if another generation can figure out those dilemmas of conscience that once plagued Kenya, maybe we'll finally banish the ghosts in places such as Vichy.

As with the Italian-Ethiopian War, the war in Algeria was a meteor slamming into an ocean, sending out tides and waves that we still experience today. It created two fascinating legacies, one in the work of a psychiatrist from Martinique and the other in an astonishing collaboration between Italian filmmakers and the revolutionaries themselves. But until the past twenty years or so, the French government wouldn't "even admit that there had been a war in Algeria; officially it was a peace-keeping operation in a French province."[58]

Even a whole nation can live in a state of denial, but Frantz Fanon preferred to diagnose the victim of abuse, the nation's colony across the Mediterranean. What he prescribed was a radical therapy that excited the left across the developing world.

Fanon grew up in a middle-class home but as a teenager fled Martinique when it was taken over by the more rabidly racist and collaborating forces of the Vichy regime. He joined the Free French, took part in the Battle of Alsace, and after getting wounded in the chest from a mortar round during enemy fire at Colmar, was awarded the Croix de Guerre. Like many African and Caribbean soldiers, he was appalled by the shabby treatment and lack of respect from the French citizens he had helped liberate. Still, France was the beacon of education for black francophones, and he chose to study medicine and psychiatry in Lyon.

He was still a psychiatric resident in 1952 when he finished his first major work, *Black Skin, White Masks*. But he nearly ruined his chances for publication when the book was being considered by *Éditions du Seuil*. Impressed with the manuscript, senior editor Francis Jeanson asked to meet the firebrand author at his office. When Jeanson started to compliment the book, Fanon—thinking he was being patronized—interrupted him and chose to be provocative, saying the equivalent of "Not bad for a n——!" Jeanson was so offended, he was ready to kick Fanon out of his office. His reaction apparently gained Fanon's trust, and it was Jeanson who suggested the ultimate title for the book.[59]

Black Skin, White Masks is a searing indictment of aspects of racism and colonialism, built on a foundation of psychological and cultural insight. From adjustments in language that black colonials need to make to how men and women of different races relate to each other, there's much to debate and discuss. In his famous essay "Shooting an Elephant," George Orwell had touched on the same theme. "I perceived in this moment that when the white man turns tyrant it is his own freedom that he destroys. He becomes a sort of hollow, posing dummy, the conventionalized figure of a sahib. For it is the condition of his rule that he shall spend his life in trying to impress the 'natives,' and so in every crisis he has got to do what the 'natives' expect of him. He wears a mask, and his face grows to fit it."[60] But Fanon, of course, looked at things from the perspective of those in the indigenous population; he recognized the masks that *they* wore. For the first time, someone examined the impacts of colonialism with an educated, psychoanalytical approach sympathetic to the oppressed.

His other great work, *The Wretched of the Earth*, is informed by his experiences in Algeria as the war for independence ripped the country apart.

Both sides in the conflict used torture. Declassified records paint a revolting portrait of the French army relying on beatings, electroshock, near drownings, rape, and sodomizing victims with bottles and sticks. Committing torture itself exacted a psychological toll, and as a psychiatrist at Blida-Joinville Psychiatric Hospital outside Algiers, Fanon treated individuals for a variety of conditions. On one occasion, a policeman who was haunted by the screams of the tortured ran into one of his own victims on the hospital grounds; the torturer suffered a panic attack, while the victim was so traumatized, he made a suicide attempt. Later in Tunis, at the L'hôpital Charles-Nicolle, Fanon gradually converted the hospital's modest neuropsychiatric unit into Africa's first psychiatric day clinic. During his tenure there, he again saw a steady parade of mental casualties from the war, from electroshock victims who were terrified to turn on a radio to women in refugee camps who suffered postpartum depression.

Fanon's sympathies for oppressed Algerians, plus his psychiatric work, soon led to his involvement with the Front de Libération Nationale, and he wasn't alone at the Blida hospital in aiding liberation efforts. Yet, despite his treating army officers and policemen who tortured, he didn't betray doctor–patient confidentiality except in one specific and arguably justified case—he learned from a female patient of an elaborate plot, one relying on petty criminals to assassinate French Prime Minister Guy Mollet on his visit to Algiers and to blame the murder on the FLN. Thanks to Fanon, the scheme was thwarted after "some old Free French networks from the 1940s in Algeria were reactivated."[61]

Fanon eventually tired of the double life of the colonial doctor who for appearances' sake tolerated the regime while serving revolution on the side. After he handed in a defiant resignation letter, he was summarily expelled from Algeria in 1957. After a brief time in Paris, he moved to Tunis, where he continued to write and work on behalf of the FLN and occasionally travel to represent the cause. Now an exile but still identifying with his adopted nation, he told a conference in Accra in 1958, "Every African must feel directly engaged and ready to answer the call of any and all territories and report in person," and that an "Algerian cannot be a true Algerian if he does not feel in his core the indescribable tragedy that is unfolding in the two Rhodesias or in Angola."[62] His sharpened and expanded attacks on colonialism would culminate in *The Wretched of the Earth*.

Like *Black Skin, White Masks*, it's a book that volleys between dense analysis and a compelling tide of righteous anger. "Europe is literally the creation of the Third World," he writes in the first essay. "The riches which are choking it are those plundered from the underdeveloped peoples."[63] He didn't pause to back up this accusation, but we know he wasn't wrong, given how the West has been enriched by coltan from the Congo, blood diamonds from Sierra Leone, the oil of Nigeria, and the gold of South Africa. He pointed out how a colonial power will try to sell the native on "individualism" and promote its own version of national history to justify its rule. And he reminded his reader about African antecedents—how self-reflection and the settling of disputes at public meetings were traditional practices.

But on the matter of culture, Fanon knew the glories of the Songhay Empire couldn't fill the bellies of their descendants, though with his psychiatrist's detachment, he praised the benefit of pride in the African past. And for him, *Négritude* had its limits of usefulness because the problems black Americans faced may not be at their essence the same as those faced by their African counterparts, and colonialism's insistence that there was no indigenous culture "inevitably leads to a glorification of cultural phenomena that becomes continental instead of national, and singularly racialized."[64] The problem is that many of these penetrating insights were matched by reckless conjecture.

"Before independence," Fanon argued, "the colonized painter was insensitive to the national landscape" and "specialized in still life." But once a country won its independence, the artist, in trying to reconnect with his own fellow citizens, gets trapped in portraying a "national reality which is flat, untroubled, motionless, reminiscent of death rather than life."[65] As the reader knows from chapter 14, this simply wasn't true and certainly doesn't speak at all to the nuances of experience and study of such masters as Ben Enwonwu or Gerard Sekoto. Such sweeping generalizations without justifying examples are one of the fundamental and unfortunate defects of Fanon's classic.

Probably the most famous arguments from *The Wretched of the Earth* deal with Fanon's rationale for justifying violence against colonial oppression. He argued that colonialism is violence—and it can be defeated only with violence. "At the individual level, violence is a cleansing force. It rids the colonized of their inferiority complex, of their passive and despairing attitude. It emboldens them and restores their self-confidence." Aware of what they've achieved through violence, he argued, the masses aren't so quick to fall under the sway of a "living god" or self-proclaimed "liberator."[66]

The idea of nonviolence, to Fanon, was a convenient ploy of the colonialist bourgeoisie to arrive at a compromise. And it worked in favor of the more moderate nationalists looking to gain power. Note the language here: "If events go one step further, the leader of the nationalist party distances himself from the violence. He loudly claims he has nothing to do with these Mau Mau, with these terrorists, these butchers. In the best of cases, he barricades himself in a no-man's-land between the terrorists and the colonists and offers his services as 'mediator'; which means that since the colonist cannot negotiate with the Mau Mau, he himself is prepared to begin negotiations."[67]

It's fascinating that while Fanon is most associated with the idea that violence is justified in terms of anticolonial struggle, "he proved to have a personal horror of violence," as Simone de Beauvoir noticed when she and Sartre enjoyed long talks with him during a visit in Rome. For the cause, he could rationalize it. On a visceral level, he was repulsed. "He thought, however, that his personal dislike of violence was a failing that reflected his position as 'an intellectual.'"[68] With what we know of the man and his psychiatric treatment of soldiers on both sides of the war, we might presume that, in truth, this shows his basic humanity.

For *The Wretched of the Earth*, Fanon revised and recycled material from essays published earlier, doing little research for the book, and he was gravely ill in Tunis when he rushed to get it into print. He wouldn't live to see the response to his work. Flying to the U.S. in the hope that he might fare better under the care of American doctors, he died in a hospital in Bethesda, Maryland, early in the morning of December 6, 1961. When the news of his passing reached Paris, police officers went around to bookstores and impounded copies of his final offering.

It would take a few years for *Wretched* to have its full impact, and the criticisms of the more staunchly conservative and centrist Western press were predictable. In its review of the Grove Press English translation, *Time* magazine called it the *Communist Manifesto* or *Mein Kampf* of the anticolonial revolution and declared, "This is not so much a book as a rock thrown through the windows of the West."[69] The sociologist commentator Lewis Coser relied on invective in *Dissent*, calling Fanon a "marginal man" who was "scarred and humiliated" with a "profoundly repellant" vision.[70]

But *The Wretched of the Earth* became a hit with a very different audience. In the mid-1960s, as Sly Stone and Jimi Hendrix blasted from stereos, university students of color and a few sympathetic, left-wing whites burrowed into Fanon's angry primer of radicalism, treating it as a "sacred text."[71] Black American activist Stokely Carmichael—who went on the Freedom Rides and stood in Alabama with others against the rawest, ugliest white supremacy—was sick and tired of polite tactics. He now began talking about killing instead of dying for meaningful change, and he often invoked Fanon in his speeches. "As a colonized people, we should look at some of the effects colonialism has on us. The major effect that colonialism has on any victim is that he, the victim, hates himself. Frantz Fanon points this out quite clearly in *The Wretched of the Earth*." Carmichael thought Fanon was a figure who provided "a lot of our ideological strength."[72] Bobby Seale recalled how "with my copy of Frantz Fanon's book, *The Wretched of the Earth*, in my hand, I found out where Huey [P. Newton] lived" to try to persuade him to start a new organization: the Black Panthers.[73]

Fanon's books traveled well, but any polemic, like war reporting or a muckraking exposé, usually has a shelf life pegged to the temperature of the times. The era of protest inevitably fizzled out, and Che Guevara became less of a role model and more of a dorm room poster. As with any "classic" of political literature, new readers will find in *Wretched* what is useful for their own struggle. But we should consider how prescient and relevant Fanon is for the country to which he was so devoted, a nation in Africa.

In an interview, his biographer David Macey noted that Fanon may well be considered "an embarrassment" for modern-day Algeria "in that his vision of the post-independent period departs significantly from that of the FLN. The FLN's proclamation of 1954, which was in effect a declaration of war, predicates the emergence of an independent Algeria upon an Arabic-Islamic identity (which is not to say 'Islamist' in the current sense of that term)." But Fanon looked forward "to an Algeria in which women would play a major role, and in which there is a place for the European minority (and, at least by implication, for Berber and Jewish minorities who would not necessarily define themselves as Arabi-Islamic). His nationalism is not, that is, based upon ethnicity, but rather upon a will-to-be-Algerian."[74]

As Algerians change how they think of themselves, no doubt they'll also change their minds about the man who exerted his will to be counted among them.

Algeria won its independence in 1962. And the Battle of Algiers inspired *The Battle of Algiers*, a film written by Franco Solinas and directed by Gillo Pontecorvo.

By any measure, it's an incredible work of art, telling the story of the Algerian guerrillas taking their fight in and out of the capital's casbah, only to be met with brutal tactics by the colonial authorities and French paratroopers. The film opens, in fact, with a suspect in his underwear, clearly traumatized from an "enhanced interrogation" only moments before. For many years, when you watched the film in theaters or older video releases, it came with a disclaimer that not one foot of archival or news footage was used—this was done because its powerful documentary style is so convincing, with unsettling re-creations of bomb attacks and mass protest scenes, that you'd swear that they must have relied on *some* real-life footage. They didn't.

With its dispassionate reserve, you can watch *The Battle of Algiers* as a thriller, but why it's worth viewing again and again is because it's a film of ideas. Modern methods of terrorism— indeed, the whole pointless "war on terrorism"—started in Algiers in the 1950s, and the movie re-creates these origins. We see nervous revolutionaries walk up and shoot colonial police officers. The early terrorists don't harm women or children—it's the *pied noirs* who with vigilante ruthlessness choose to bomb the casbah and start the nightmare spiral of escalation. And this depiction is factually correct. We see a young woman plant a bomb in a café and the horrifying result.

The film explores the whole controversy of searching women in traditional Muslim clothing. The icy cool French commander, Colonel Mathieu—whom the viewer can't help but admire because he sees the struggle with no illusions—remarks casually during a briefing, "ID checks are ludicrous. If anyone's papers are in order, it's the terrorist's." Later, when reporters bombard him with questions, he asks them for news from Paris. He's told that Sartre wrote another critical article. Pausing a moment, he wonders a little morosely, "Why are the Sartres always born on the other side?"

The film doesn't demonize the French, nor does it romanticize the revolutionaries, which is remarkable, as the Algerians working with the Italian producers originally envisioned a story slanted to their side. But when asked if any pressure was given, screenwriter Franco Solinas replied, "None whatever. Let's say that they might have preferred a more traditionally heroic film."[75] The stylistic feat is even more astonishing when you realize that the two main Algerian characters are played by *senior members of the FLN who were in the struggle*. Its star, Saadi Yacef, became one of Algeria's senators after the war for independence.

The Battle of Algiers was nominated for three Academy Awards, won a slew of other awards—and was banned for five years in France. As film writer Peter Matthews pointed out, the tactical methods of the FLN "are so explicit" that the movie amounted to a training manual for groups such as the Black Panthers, the early Palestine Liberation Organization, and the Irish Republican Army.[76] But there were lessons, too, for occupiers if they bothered to pay attention.

In 2003, it became increasingly clear that George W. Bush's invasion of Iraq was a quagmire, one built on a fiction about weapons of mass destruction and attacking an autocratic regime that, while brutal, had absolutely nothing to do with 9/11. While Guantanamo was filling up with detainees, the Pentagon's Directorate for Special Operations and Low-Intensity Conflict held a private screening of *The Battle of Algiers*. An official drafted up this invitation to the screening in a flyer: "How to win a battle against terrorism and lose the war of ideas. Children shoot soldiers at point-blank range. Women plant bombs in cafes. Soon the entire Arab population builds to a mad fervor. Sound familiar? The French have a plan. It succeeds tactically but fails strategically. To understand why, come to a rare showing of this film."[77]

Did those at the Pentagon sitting through those final minutes of *Battle*—with its swirls of smoke, ululating women, protesters overwhelming helmeted soldiers—learn anything? Given the long debacle of the Iraq War, followed by the rise and fall of ISIS, it doesn't appear so. If cinematic art couldn't make an impression, neither, it seemed, could history. In a fresh preface for the 2006 reprint of his classic work on Algeria, *A Savage War of Peace*, Alistair Horne mentioned how the staff for U.S. Defense Secretary Donald Rumsfeld asked him to send a copy of his book to their boss, "underscoring the evils of torture—and not least, the propaganda value even the least substantiated rumors of it can arouse. I received a flea in the ear—courteous, but a flea nevertheless—for my trouble."[78]

Stubborn attitudes at the Pentagon don't diminish the relevance of these two works or of the conflict that inspired them. It is almost reflexive for pundits and commentators today to revisit the *recent* current events that sparked the creation of ISIS or Al-Shabaab, focusing on these groups' sadism, extremist jihadism, and criminal operations. And if Fanon were alive today, he would certainly have an opinion on the psychological approach that seeks to "deprogram" and "de-radicalize" young militants (rather than simply tossing suspects in prison).

But to dismiss young extremists as merely looking to belong and getting steered down a dark path ignores what may be legitimate political grievances. At the heart of their groups in the developing world is a rage against a perceived authority—often the Western capitalist or his proxies who seem indistinguishable from the old colonial powers. Now imagine if today's tactic of de-radicalization was attempted on youth in 1950s Algeria or Kenya. Of course, the scenario is slightly ridiculous because they were colonial regimes, and such an approach would have been hopelessly misguided in its condescension. But they also would have failed because while the Mau Mau and FLN regularly drew condemnations for their methods from some, it was difficult to argue with the legitimacy of their goal: independence and self-autonomy for their peoples.

But if we ignore the actual political beliefs of today's militants, presuming they are only "misguided" or psychologically unbalanced, we are infantilizing an enemy at our peril. Let there be no mistake: no argument is being made here to legitimize an ideology and certainly not violence. What matters is the political and economic contexts that led to situations and crises that are eerily and sometimes depressingly familiar to us. And suppose we turn the scenario on its head and consider more benign causes? It's worth remembering that even young climate change activists today such as Greta Thunberg have been dismissed as "naive" or as pawns of more sinister forces.

17

The Sphinx and the Minotaur

Let's go back yet again to the Sorbonne's Amphitheatre Descartes, to that Conference of Negro-African Writers and Artists in 1956. Before Richard Wright gave his strange address praising the indirect benefits of colonialism, there was another speaker, one who annoyed James Baldwin because he ran over his time by twenty minutes. This was a doctoral candidate from Senegal named Cheikh Anta Diop, and Baldwin wrote that the question of whether the ancient Egyptians were black "has never greatly exercised my mind, nor did M. Diop succeed in doing so—at least not in the direction he intended." He conceded that Diop was a hit at the conference, and his claims "of the deliberate dishonesty of all Egyptian scholars may be quite well founded for all I know, but I cannot say that he convinced me."[1]

As it happens, Diop has been dividing writers and scholars ever since, and he may be one of the most contentious figures to appear in this book. To include him is controversial, but so would be ignoring him. He got several things wrong. But then so did Galen, and you won't find a comprehensive history of Western medicine without a section on Galen.

Diop started a conversation that was badly needed, and it's one that's still going on. As Nigerian historian Toyin Falola put it, some of the issues Diop raised "have become part of contemporary ideological backgrounds, even cultural warfare." His work and the debates it sparked "show how scholarship and politics can meet and clash and how defining identity for Africa and searching for ideas to uplift it remain open to controversy."[2] What Diop set out to do goes to the heart of why this book exists at all, and for that alone, we need to pay attention to him. While we can't resolve the questions still bitterly fought in some quarters, we can give his ideas hard scrutiny and perhaps a reassessment.

Cheikh Anta Diop was born in 1923 in the village Thieytou in the Diourbel region of Senegal. He pursued studies in both philosophy and sciences, gaining admission to the Sorbonne in 1946. When he presented his doctoral thesis, the professors informed him "that if he wanted to complete his dissertation, he would have to choose another topic."[3] His efforts weren't wasted, however, as he published them in his book, *Nations nègres et culture* (*Black Nations and Culture*) in 1954. Ten of its chapters would later be incorporated into the English translation of his work *The African Origin of Civilization*, published twenty years later in the U.S. He invested considerable time in politics over Senegal's independence and writing about his ideas for his country's development and later spent years teaching physics and directing a radiocarbon laboratory he founded in Dakar. But it's his relentless pursuit of Egyptian history that's our main interest here.

He began his efforts, as he explained to one interviewer, "via linguistics and history. But it was soon apparent that I would have to master various other fields, such as ethnology, anthropology and so on. Consequently, I was led to tackle biochemistry, physics, mathematics, philosophy, etc."[4]

Today, it may seem natural to accept that the ancient Egyptians had African roots, but if you recall from chapters 8 and 12, there were some in the West who could talk themselves into thinking Ethiopians were white. Race, in case we really need a reminder, is a concept without any foundation in hard science. The idea gained traction during the Enlightenment with various thinkers who busied themselves with measuring skull sizes and creating ridiculous categories for nose widths and skin pigmentation. The issue grew into an obsession for certain naturalists in the nineteenth century.

And then some intellectuals in Europe and America realized they had a problem. There was no getting around the fact that Egypt was in Africa, but if Egypt created the first civilization, how did this square with celebrating the glories of Greece and Rome and the later achievements of white Europe? Especially when there were inconvenient lines in Herodotus that claimed the Egyptians were "black skinned and wooly haired."[5]

By the mid-1800s, as the bitter debate over slavery in the U.S. intensified, American writers in particular pushed the notion that the ancient Egyptians must have been white. American physician Samuel George Morton of Philadelphia was an advocate of the theory that God created the races separately, and so he twitched his calipers over various skulls from ancient Egypt, and, like a crackpot with an old-fashioned divining rod, he concluded that "Negroes were numerous in Egypt, but their social position in ancient times was the same that it now is, that of servants and slaves."[6]

In 1851, a certain John Campbell, who fancied himself an intellectual, also from Philadelphia, published a book titled *Negro-mania: Being an Examination of the Falsely Assumed Equality of the Various Races of Men*. In his mind, the fact that white men had long oppressed black people testified to obvious Caucasian superiority. "The idea that the Negro race ever civilized Egypt is now exploded among learned men," wrote Campbell, "but we have among us persons who spurn at history [sic]," and he devoted a whole chapter to trying to poke holes in the accuracy of statements by Herodotus and Diodorus Siculus—two writers, incidentally, whom Diop would use 100 years later to help make his case and whom new critics would pounce on in turn.[7]

Complicating matters further, in 1902, the distinguished American Egyptologist James Breasted published a remarkable article about his examination of a slab of black granite with inscriptions kept at the British Museum. The ancient author of the text was unknown, but Breasted insisted that the work itself came from the priesthood for the god Ptah at Memphis, and he titled his paper *The First Philosopher*. The translation includes the lines, "Ptah the Great is the heart and tongue of the gods. . . . Everything that he wills. The gods fashioned the sight of the eyes, the hearing of the ears." Breasted argued that here was worship that evolved into abstract thinking: "The most remarkable feature of all this is the characterization of the god as the mind in everything, whether gods, men or beasts, and reminds one of Thales's statement, that 'all is full of gods.'"

He went further. The unknown Egyptian author's "conception of function of mind and idea in a philosophical system is so clear and so high that it is *even modern* in its superiority over those strange objective 'ideas' of Plato [emphasis in the original]." To Breasted, it was "now clear that valuable philosophical beginnings . . . existed in Egypt a thousand years before the first Greek philosophers was born. The objection to the origin of Greek philosophy in Egypt on the ground that no such material is to be found there, now falls away."[8]

But wait—the sad irony is that Breasted was quite happy to give credit to Egyptians but *not* to black Africans. In his 1926 work *Conquest of Civilization*, he asserted that the peoples who settled in North Africa and the Near East, going right back to prehistoric times, "have all been members of the white race." As for the "teeming black world of Africa," it had been "separated from the white race by the broad stretch of the Sahara Desert." Mostly cut off, "they remained uninfluenced by civilization from the north, nor did they contribute appreciably to this civilization."[9]

It's easy to see then why Diop faced an uphill battle to gain acceptance for his theories. In 1960, his critics could still trot out twenty-year-old books by anthropologist Carleton Coon, now discredited but still influential back then.[10] To give you a measure of Coon's thinking, his magnum opus in 1962 was called *The Origin of Races*, advancing the idea that five different races evolved into *Homo sapiens* at different times. Though he was forced to concede from Louis Leakey's excavations in Tanzania that, yes, humans originated in Africa, Coon insisted that "he soon dispersed, in a very primitive form, throughout the warm regions of the Old World. . . . If Africa was the cradle of mankind, it was only an indifferent kindergarten. Europe and Asia were our principal schools."[11] It's fair to say that segregationists *loved* Coon's work.[12]

No wonder then that in making his case, Diop sounds like he's issuing a call to arms. "The African historian who evades the problem of Egypt is neither modest nor objective, nor unruffled; he is ignorant, cowardly and neurotic."[13] It would be analogous to a researcher on Europe ignoring Greece and Rome. "Instead of presenting itself to history as an insolvent debtor, [the] black world is the very initiator of the 'western' civilization flaunted before our eyes today."[14]

Diop would not be the first to reclaim the Egyptians as black or insist on a Greek debt to Egyptian civilization. In 1887, Edward Wilmot Blyden remarked that "a superficial criticism, guided by local and temporary prejudices, has attempted to deny the intimate relations of the Negro with the great historic races of Egypt and Ethiopia. But no one who has travelled in North-Eastern Africa, or among the ruins on the banks of the Nile, will for a moment doubt that there was the connection, not of accident or of adventitious circumstances, but of consanguinity between the races of inner Africa of the present day, and the ancient Egyptians and Ethiopians."[15]

In 1954, a Guyanese American professor teaching in North Carolina and Arkansas, George G. M. James, went further and published a book titled *Stolen Legacy*, arguing, "For centuries, the world has been misled about the original source of the arts and sciences."[16] But James made several sloppy errors in his classics detective work (one of which we'll discuss later), and mainstream critics were not kind. He did, however, have his supporters, among them one of the great lights of African Studies, William Leo Hansberry (uncle of famous playwright Lorraine Hansberry). Hansberry conceded that "all the relevant facts and evidence may not absolutely sustain" James's more controversial propositions, but he found that the book held a "novel and more or less revolutionary thesis."[17]

Both Blyden and James relied on the same toolkit, the Greek and Roman classics, and demanded that their readers open their eyes to what was in front of them at the sites of ruins. Diop wasn't aware of *Stolen Legacy* when he began his research in the 1950s, but he would praise the book decades later.[18] What made his own arguments fresh and persuasive in the postwar era was that he combined Classical scholarship with an attempt at scientific scrutiny and a dissection of the prevailing Egyptology.

There is too much ground to cover to evaluate all of Diop's evidence. At his most brilliant, he skewered the more foolish claims of "white Egyptian" advocates and offered a panoramic alternative history of how Egypt was first perceived by the Greeks and how its culture was distorted over time. He tunnels through Herodotus and Strabo, digs into the notes of Jean Francoise Champollion (the genius who deciphered the hieroglyphics), and he quotes a minor eighteenth-century aristocrat, Constantin de Volney, who traveled through Egypt and decided that the race of its inhabitants, once black, had "lost the intensity of its original color" through mixing with other cultures.[19] In fact, the frontispiece to The African Origin of Civilization is an illustration made during Napoleon's expedition to Egypt by the artist and scholar Vivant Denon, who would become the first director of the Louvre. It shows in profile the Great Sphinx at Giza, with obvious black features. "This profile is neither Greek nor Semitic," declared Diop in a caption. "It is Bantu."

Now, if you're skeptical (or cynical), you might presume the artist indulged in racist caricature, which wouldn't be unusual for Europeans in the eighteenth century. But why would he in this case? Napoleon's band of scientists and ethnographers had no such agenda for their remarkable discoveries. The illustration is well known, but Denon's firsthand account of seeing the Sphinx isn't, and it's worth quoting: "Though its proportions are colossal, the outline is pure and graceful; the expression of the head is mild, gracious and tranquil; the character is African; but the mouth, the lips of which are thick, has a softness and delicacy of execution truly admirable; it seems real life and flesh. Art must have been at a high pitch when this monument was executed."[20]

The current thinking of experts is that the Great Sphinx of Giza was completed during the reign of the pharaoh Khafra during the Fourth Dynasty, about 2500 BCE. Whether the Sphinx was supposed to depict Khafra is another matter, but, as Diop might ask, if the ancient Egyptians weren't black or at least dark-skinned, why would they give such a magnificent monument black features?

Egypt's Great Sphinx, as illustrated by Vivant Denon.

But his evidence is not always persuasive, sometimes highly questionable, and often open to interpretation, which is why his work remains controversial, at least in the West. For instance, the ancient residents of Egypt called their country *Kemet*, which means "the black land," referring to the dark soil of the country. Diop insisted that the word referred to the black race, and any other definition was a "gratuitous distortion."[21] But the Egyptians also regularly referred to the desert regions as *Deshret*, "the red lands."[22] There is also a simple commonsense refutation to his argument, and it's useful here to think back to our discussion in chapter 9 about colonial Europeans imposing tribal names. As Marq de Villiers and Sheila Hirtle pointed out, such labels meant nothing to Africans, who had "no need to be instructed who they are. They were *The People*. It didn't matter what others called them."[23] In the same vein, why would ancient

Egyptians—ancient Africans of a specific region—define themselves with a term that contrasts them to others?

Diop devoted much attention to the color shades of sculpted figures, pointing out the reddish tint used for Egyptians and black used for Nubian statues, which provoked its own thread of controversy. His detractors could say rightly there were other colors in the Egyptian palette, and indeed we see blue, green, yellow, and red used for certain gods. But consider the example of Mentuhotep, clearly shown in some depictions (though not all) with black skin. Mentuhotep was a southern king who reunited Egypt after the First Intermediate Period, so experts believe he was likely of Nubian descent. Diop placed much of his faith as well in Herodotus and other Classical writers like the geographer Strabo for both his argument that the ancient Egyptians were black and his claim that the Egyptians gave much of their culture to the Greeks. The problem is that we know Herodotus, Strabo, and others aren't always reliable.

To be fair, the Classical scholars who indict these sources get to have it both ways: by casting doubt on, say, the Greek "Father of History," they can paradoxically keep Greece as the wellspring of "Western civilization." This doesn't, however, resolve certain problems. For instance, Diop believes Strabo when he wrote that the Egyptians settled Colchis, a tiny state in what is now Georgia on the Black Sea. So far, there's no archaeological or other tangible evidence that this ever happened. He also places undue significance on parts of the Bible as if they can be trusted, at least partially, as sources for historical evidence instead of as religious mythology.

And yet . . . Diop brought scientific ingenuity to the debate. He came up with a clever test for melanin in samples taken from mummies found during the excavations by Auguste Mariette in 1851 at Saqqara in Egypt. Looking at the samples under a microscope, he concluded that the ancient Egyptians "were unquestionably among the black races." He invited other scholars to examine his samples and data for themselves.[24] One of the most famous episodes of his career was when he presented his radical ideas in 1974 to a small symposium in Cairo on "the Peopling of Ancient Egypt and the Deciphering of the Meroitic

Script." It must have been one hell of a lively conference, as the clashes between Diop and his critics ring loud and clear through the understated academic prose that summarized the sessions.

"Professor Diop was not in favor of setting up commissions to verify patent facts which, at the present time, simply needed formal recognition: in his view, all the information currently available, even that which derived from the superficial studies made in the nineteenth century, supported the theory that in the most ancient times the Egyptians were black-skinned and that they remained so until Egypt ultimately lost its independence." And later, "During the discussion, nothing was conceded by either side."[25]

This version gives the impression that Diop could be intransigent. But much time seems to have been spent (or wasted) at the symposium on quibbling over nostril widths and hair textures of supposed blackness, with standards that Diop considered arbitrary and must have found exasperating. At the same time, he cited details of outward appearance when they were useful to him, advancing at the time an idea that there were two black races, one with smooth hair and another with "crinkly hair."

And in an interview a decade later, he still underscored the importance of appearances even as he criticized how ethnographers changed the definition of what "black" was when information proved inconvenient: "If we speak only of genotype, I can find a black who, at the level of his chromosomes, is closer to a Swede than [white South African politician] Peter Botha is. But what counts in reality is the phenotype. It is the physical appearance which counts. This black, even if on the level of his cells he is closer to a Swede than Peter Botha, when he is in South Africa he will still live in Soweto. Throughout history, it has been the phenotype which has been at issue, we mustn't lose sight of this fact . . . which makes us say that Europe is peopled by white people, Africa is peopled by black people, and Asia is peopled by yellow people. It is these relationships which have played a role in history."[26]

The abandonment of the notion that Egyptians were white had already begun years before Diop struggled to get his thesis accepted. French scholar Emile Massoulard brought out his book *Prehistory and Proto-History of Egypt* in 1949, likely the very first "to recognize, or at least to articulate in print, that the civilization of dynastic Egypt was largely an indigenous development, with its most fundamental roots in the culture of the Predynastic period." Unfortunately, scholars were still pushing the theory of a "dynastic race—a 'master race' of invaders from the east, thought to be responsible for imposing civilization on the 'primitive' and unsophisticated indigenous Egyptians" right into the early 1970s.[27]

Diop's ideas were so radical for the time that when he wrote the opening chapter for the second volume of UNESCO's *General History of Africa*, the editors felt it necessary to warn readers that experts didn't share his conclusions, while he got his own shot in with this line: "It will be understood how difficult it is to write such a chapter in a work of this kind, where euphemism and compromise are the rule."[28]

Through Diop, we can trace another path of the cultural momentum of African ideas. He invoked Tempels's *Bantu Philosophy* to suggest Egyptians and other African peoples held similar beliefs in the origins of the cosmos and ignored the important criticism by John Mbiti and Okot p'Bitek about the sweeping generalizations drawn from the Luba to other African religious beliefs. In his early writings, when discussing cultural alienation among black peoples, Diop quoted lines from Aimé Césaire and Léopold Sédar Senghor.

But by the time he came to write his last book, *Civilization or Barbarism*, he wanted to thoroughly debunk any remaining pseudoscientific characterizations of blacks as "emotional" and "sensual" beings rather than fully rounded individuals capable of rational thought and discovery, and he saw how *Négritude* exponents could help perpetuate such clichés. The movement's writers "did not at the time [between the world wars] have the scientific means to refute or to question these types of errors. Scientific truth had been white for such a long time that . . . all these affirmations made under the scientific banner had to be accepted as such by our submissive peoples. Therefore, the *Négritude* movement accepted this so-called inferiority and boldly assumed it in full view of the world."[29]

Diop would not—and spent a lifetime refuting it.

Having looked for answers with radiocarbon technology, he no doubt would have been the first to enthusiastically embrace the latest techniques we have today for DNA testing. But they wouldn't have given him all the answers he expected. A study published in 2017 examined 166 samples from 151 mummies excavated at Abusir-el-Meleq, which dated from the New Kingdom to the Roman era, from 1388 BCE to 426 CE. "The ancient DNA data revealed a high level of affinity between the ancient inhabitants of Abusir el-Meleq and modern populations from the Near East and the Levant." It also "found an influx of sub-Saharan African ancestry after the Roman Period," for which there might have been a variety of historical causes.[30]

Does that settle the issue? Far from it. The town became something of a trade hub during Ptolemaic rule all the way to the Roman period, so we shouldn't be too surprised, for instance, to find the impact of Greek, Latin, Hebrew, Canaanite, and other populations in samples dated later. And the study itself cautions that all the genetic data was "obtained from a single site in Middle Egypt and may not be representative for all of ancient Egypt. It is possible that populations in the south of Egypt were more closely related to those of Nubia and had a higher sub-Saharan genetic component, in which case the argument for an influx of sub-Saharan ancestries after the Roman Period might only be partially valid and have to be nuanced."[31] Various other studies done on modern Egyptians have produced different results, with some finding connections to Middle Eastern populations and others highlighting North African ties. Diop, however, always conceded that racial mixing was a factor in the ancient Egyptian population.

As things stand, modern scholarship rejects the concept of race as a biological construct and recognizes the immense difficulty of assigning skin tone to ancient human remains. Ancient Egyptians certainly were descendant from indigenous North African peoples, and as such, they likely had a range of skin tones, not unlike modern peoples of the Nile Valley, with southerners tending to have darker skin tones than northerners.

If you recall, we discussed in chapter 1 the probable migrations of African ancestors, including pastoralists in the Sahara, and the ancient peoples of what is now Sudan and Ethiopia who headed north and settled in the Upper Nile basin. We also discussed the cultural exchanges with Mesopotamia and the Middle East and how the Nubians conquered Egypt and set up their own short-lived dynasty.

We should always remember that this was an *African* empire, even if it absorbed influences from the Near East. As mentioned before, many experts are now revising their views, suggesting the Nubians may have been responsible for certain aspects of Egyptian culture yet deserve closer study to see how they were distinct. Hopefully by now, the reader knows that there's enough glory in the ancient and medieval civilizations of Africa—north, east, west, and south—to go around.

If Cheikh Anta Diop had only championed the cause of black Egyptians, his reputation as an innovative historian, even with the ongoing arguments over his controversial evidence, would probably be secure. But he had a wider vision than race, and with a physicist's mind, he sought a grand unifying theory. He dived into studying cultural practices and linguistics, seeing similarities in royalty practices of ancient Egyptians and peoples of sub-Saharan Africa, between ancient Egyptian words and his own native tongue of Wolof. The experts have been debating his conclusions ever since. He believed that "Egyptian civilization originated from the heart of Africa, going from south to north, and that the Nubian kingdom predated and gave birth to that of Upper Egypt."[32] But today's archaeologists will tell you that the evidence for complex societies is much older in Egypt than in Nubia. That being said, the first unification of Egypt in the Early Dynastic Period is thought to be the result of a king of southern polities defeating a coalition of polities in the north.

Diop cited as proof artifacts found at Qustul near Abu Simbel in Sudan, but most experts today don't find these conclusive either. Still, he anticipated the growing interest in the Nubians and a shift in thinking about their significance.

All these conjectures had a higher purpose than merely convincing colleagues at symposiums or gaining citations in journals. "The historic consciousness of African peoples has dimmed, and we have become progressively an amnesic people, cut off from our history," said Diop in 1985. "We must restore the historical awareness of the African peoples and Afro-Americans, and this restoration will come through a knowledge of Egyptian history which is the first manifestation of culture in Africa. The first African experience was that of Egypt. That is why, if we are to return to the source culturally, it must be at the foundation of our humanities. We must teach it systematically and show all that our people contributed to other peoples of the world before passing the torch."[33]

Honors, if not clear vindication, came late in his life. In 1985, he visited Atlanta, Georgia, where the mayor at the time, Andrew Young, declared April 4 "Cheikh Anta Diop Day." Feted by his hosts, Diop was given an honorary degree from Morehouse College and had the chance to meet with Coretta Scott King. According to one writer, "Because of Diop's political position in Senegal, he had been isolated in many circles in Dakar. Hence, Diop's trip to Atlanta was one of the few times in his life, if not the only, that he was ever 'treated like a VIP.'"[34]

What then is his legacy? He was a pioneer. He scooped up the ancient Egyptians and put them back into an African context, rescuing them forever from that stodgy island of academia where they were useful as precursors to the Greeks but with little relevance to the lands beyond the Nile Basin. Others may have tried to advance an enlightened perspective on Egypt, but Diop captured attention. At the same time, we can't overlook his errors, and while science has given weight to some of his claims, this is not the same thing as validating his selections for evidence. Diop himself expressed disappointment that his work and ideas were never given the "proper feedback," with rigorous testing and exhaustive discussion.[35] Despite the grumbles in the mainstream that turned into an irritable silence, he set himself the task of wrestling the study of ancient Egypt out of the hands of complacent European scholarship, and in this respect, he succeeded. From a thesis rejection in Paris and casual dismissal decades ago at a small conference in Cairo, he's now accepted as part of the curriculum at many universities.

Today, you'll still find *The African Origin of Civilization* in bookshops. The digital artist Adé Olufeko created a unique portrait of Diop in 2014, with the scholar's black-and-white image seeming to burst from the canvas with shards of vivid yellow and green. The painting was unveiled at the Sixteenth African Business Conference of Harvard Business School, where Olufeko was also a panel speaker.[36] And in Senegal, there's an even greater tribute to him. In 1987, the University of Dakar was renamed Cheikh Anta Diop University.

About a year after Cheikh Anta Diop died, Martin Bernal published the first book in his three-volume study *Black Athena: The Afroasiatic Roots of Classical Civilization*—with a fourth volume written years later to respond to his critics. Born in Britain and educated at Cambridge, Bernal moved to the U.S. and joined the faculty of Cornell. Like Diop, he began in a different field, as a scholar of Chinese. Not surprisingly, many of his critics took issue with his translations of ancient Egyptian. Unlike Diop, he had no burning passion at first to rebalance the historical scales. Instead, he was suffering a midlife crisis in the 1970s, disillusioned by the Vietnam War, and interested in his own roots, he began to study the language of the ancient Jews, which led him to Greek, which led him to researching the ancient Egyptians—and he concluded that the ancient Egyptians had invaded and spread across Greece and other parts of the Mediterranean.

He would devote thick volumes to trying to prove that locales such as Crete and Boeotia were once ancient colonies of this earlier civilization. A quick example: he reminds us that bulls were of "great cultic significance" in Upper Egypt during reigns of pharaohs taking the name of Mentuhotep. Crete had its own bull cult and is famously associated with the legend of the minotaur. To Bernal, it was "plausible to suppose that the Cretan developments directly or indirectly reflected the rise of the Egyptian Middle Kingdom."[37] Because Egypt imported silver from Greek mines and Egyptian objects have been found in Crete, he inferred "this could be the result of . . . Egyptian power" during the Eleventh Dynasty. But there is a very simple, alternative explanation: trade. Even Bernal conceded that "the connection still appears tenuous on archaeological grounds alone."[38]

Yet *Black Athena* "disturbed the peace" in the West far more than *Black Nations and Culture* did when it was released. Of course, Diop faced obstacles for a breakthrough that Bernal never had. He was far away in Senegal, and he wrote originally in French in the sunny, bland, postwar 1950s. It took time for his efforts to make an impact. An English translation of *African Origins of Civilization* wouldn't be published until 1974 when the last angry flashes of student radicalism were sputtering out. By then, Black Panther Huey Newton had fled to Cuba, and the Vietnam War was winding down. University faculties were more receptive to new ways of thinking, but step away from the campus, and Africa was still low on the priorities for the U.S. and Europe, preoccupied then with bombings by the Irish Republican Army and Basque separatists and with the Middle East oil crisis and Watergate.

Skip forward to 1987 when *Black Athena* hit bookstores, and the West was on the brink of another seismic shift in cultural attitudes. Ronald Reagan and Margaret Thatcher were both in office. That same year, philosopher Allan Bloom brought out his best seller *The Closing of the American Mind*. With a curmudgeonly flair, Bloom attacked a malaise of moral relativism and grumbled how university students didn't read anymore, and if they did, they weren't reading the so-called Great Books that encapsulate Western thought. This was one of the first shots in the culture wars, and against this backdrop and the rise of the political correctness movement (which started on college campuses), here was Bernal, telling people that the Greeks didn't really build their culture as we thought and that much of it came from the Egyptians.

Black Athena inspired arguments on radio shows, news coverage on TV, magazine articles, and as with the works of physicist Stephen Hawking, it was a book that regular people talked about more than they read. When his second volume came out in 1991, one reviewer quoted Bernal's introduction: "I have based my case in this whole project on the principle of competitive plausibility rather than certainty." Then the reviewer added this caustic rebuke, "Undergraduate term papers are failed every day for indulging in 'competitive plausibility'" and suggested Bernal's work deserved no less academic rigor.[39]

The *New York Times* enlisted Egyptologist John Baines to review Bernal's second volume, and he found the methodology in it wanting. Bernal, he wrote, "rightly says that Egypt's influence on the ancient Middle East and the Aegean has been underestimated. But this does not mean or require that Egypt conquered Anatolia and the Aegean. Besides, his argument for that conquest is problematic. He uses legends from a late period to establish the reality of great events of an earlier period, and then seeks to support that reality with minute pieces of contemporary evidence . . . the word he uses for Asia probably refers to Syria-Palestine and not Anatolia; the archeological destructions he cites cannot be closely dated; and the legend reported by Herodotus is, after all, a legend. Thus, the conjunction he constructs for these materials could be pure coincidence."[40]

Egyptologist Peter Lacovara points out that Bernal "posited that the relationship between Classical Greece and Egypt was much the same as between Japan and China, with Japan's wholesale adoption of much of Chinese culture. . . . The basic problem was in Bernal's erroneous model, which was an easy target. The fact is that pharaonic Egypt did have a tremendous impact on the development of the Classical world, but it was more nuanced, transmitted and modified over the millennia through the civilizations of the ancient Middle East and the Mediterranean."[41]

Without Diop, it's hard to imagine that Bernal would have had much impact, and yet our pioneer from Senegal gets little attention in *Black Athena* and only a few citations. For all his discussion of what he labels "Ancient" versus the "Aryan" models, Bernal wasn't interested in the question of race for the ancient Egyptians. "Research on the question usually reveals far more about the predisposition of the researcher than about the question itself," and then, as if cornered, he at last chose a side: he believed the Egyptians were fundamentally African and that many of the most powerful dynasties "were made up of pharaohs whom one can usefully call black."[42]

In fact, Bernal comes across today as cringingly naive on the issue of race. "An even more powerful inhibitory factor to the restoration of the Egyptian aspect to the Ancient Model has been that . . . these black scholars have been outside academia." He was genuinely surprised that George James's *Stolen Legacy*, though popular, was "not considered as scholarship by academics and not even stocked by libraries."[43] It was eight years before a white scholar born in Hampstead, England, and who immigrated to the States learned about a history book written by a black autodidact—and published in the last years of Jim Crow.

He finished the introduction to his first volume with this challenge: "The political purpose of *Black Athena* is, of course, to lessen European cultural arrogance." This line, which has its own hint of smugness, suggests a debate on the author's terms. But he didn't get the fight he wanted. Instead, race and African identity, the two elements he largely ignored in *Black Athena*, became the dominant themes of bitter feuds that lasted years. And these hold a valuable cautionary lesson for our pursuit of African Ideas.

Classics scholar Mary Lefkowitz became one of the fiercest critics of Bernal's work and similar approaches, first reviewing it for *The New Republic* magazine and then publishing *Not Out of Africa: How Afrocentrism Became an Excuse to Teach Myth as History*. Unlike Bernal, her command of ancient Greek is unassailable, and she used it to powerful effect in criticizing his analysis. She also went after the more dubious claims of other past scholars, such as George James, who had suggested in *Stolen Legacy* that Aristotle—with the help of Alexander the Great—plundered valuable Egyptian texts from the Library of Alexandria. The problem, as Lefkowitz pointed out, is that a) Alexandria wasn't even a bustling city until after Aristotle died in 322 BCE, b) the library wasn't running until around 297 BCE with one of Aristotle's own students taking charge, and c) most of the books in it were Greek.[44] Bernal didn't make mistakes along such lines, but he was lumped in with the others.

Lefkowitz, however, could occasionally summon our modern goddess, Hyperbole: "Any attempt to question the authenticity of ancient Greek civilization is of direct concern even to people who ordinarily have little interest in the remote past. Since the founding of this country, ancient Greece has been intimately connected with the ideals of American democracy."[45] This is laying it on thick. It implies that to ask innocently about Greek civilization threatens the very foundation of America. Besides, both idylls are myths. In the age of Pericles, only Athenians who met a strict definition of citizenship could vote, which left out slaves, women, and other categories. As for the American Revolution, that was started by wealthy landowners who relied on their extended family networks and who already controlled the provincial assemblies. Besides, why should a concept of "democracy" inhibit pursuit of historical truth anyway?

Bernal took his revenge by reviewing *her* book, plus the collection of critical essays on *Black Athena* that she edited, for the *London Review of Books* (it would be interesting to learn how the paper's editor navigated the ethics of this). And back and forth it went. Lefkowitz also clashed in print with one of the major exponents of Afrocentricity, Molefi Asante, and with Egyptologist Ann Macy Roth of Howard University. If Lefkowitz could take Bernal to task over his Greek, Roth could take Lefkowitz to school over her understanding of ancient Egyptian culture, pouring cold water on her arguments over hieroglyphics and religious rituals.[46]

The tragedy is that the debate seemed to not only polarize attitudes but also calcify them. It's certainly valid to question historical revisionism. But it's equally valid to challenge such stubborn resistance to new interpretations. Diop and Bernal were not tossing out the Greek sources and certainly not the Greeks; on the contrary, they picked their argument with scholars of the nineteenth century who pushed an "Aryan" narrative for Greek civilization that even the Greeks never believed. One had to ask—and still ask—why Africa should still be marginalized even if flaws or mistakes are found in Diop and Bernal's research? The ancient Greeks tell us a debt was owed. The sums may be added up wrong, but that doesn't cancel the debt.

In the end, one of the most perceptive criticisms belonged to John Baines, who, in his *New York Times* review of *Black Athena* and Diop's *Civilization or Barbarism*, observed that while both authors promoted Africa, "they remain Eurocentric in their approach and method. Neither work attempts to show that the values or achievements of African societies are independent of the West or superior to it. Rather, they are concerned with establishing that African achievements were anterior to those of classical and later Western civilization and that these achievements were subsequently diffused to much of the world." Baines also highlighted the fact that great civilizations were perfectly capable of developing "independently, without any outside influence," and rattled off such examples as Great Zimbabwe and Aksum.[47]

In the late 1980s, *Black Athena* was considered highly provocative. More than thirty years on, it's substantially less so, certainly less than Diop's work. The reason is a simple and an ironic one. There's very little "African-ness" in Bernal's work, even though it's supposed to be an argument that certain Africans gave Greeks their culture. Unlike Diop, Bernal was squarely in the camp that Mesopotamia got civilization rolling, "with the possible exception of writing." And his end goal was always a reinterpretation of *Greek* culture, not the African one, the Egyptians.[48]

As we've seen, Diop already claimed this ground and more, and he saw ancient Egypt as having significant links to other societies and kingdoms nearby and beyond the Sahara. Bernal's vision was at root a very conservative one. He may have called his Athena black, but she was hardly African. His series of books are ultimately a backhanded way of validating Classical civilization. Diop thought of ancient Egypt as the source, and his goal was to elevate African civilization and secure it a place side by side as an equal to Greek, Roman, Persian, and other cultures. For any mistakes he may have made, one can build on the road he cleared and head in different directions: to Nubian influence in Assyria or to interactions with Punt or perhaps farther west and south. Bernal's journey only takes us into a frustrating maze back to the minotaur, to the "glory" that was Greece.

Year after year, more scholarship is done that explores how much ancient Egypt gave to the world, including its impact on the rest of Africa. Scholar Jock Agai recognizes similarities in cultural practices between ancient Egyptians and the Yoruba people of Nigeria, such as burial rituals.[49] Zambian professor Chisanga Siame has taken a philological approach that "tries to link pharaonic names to traditional African rulers, hinting at possible historical continuities."[50] These are interesting, even fascinating theories worth exploring, though we can't leap to conclusions yet about their veracity. Just as the archaeologists keep digging, so those who work the texts and gather research in the field will keep building their cases. "Diffusion and population movements did exist in the past, but they must be carefully demonstrated," warns the *Oxford Encyclopedia of Ancient Egypt.*[51]

But why, one may ask, must we cling to cultural diffusion? This doesn't take issue with the ideas mentioned above, but our obsession with finding a single "first" grandeur. It's a model that's been used before to validate a culture—worse, to validate a mere interpretation of it. It's what blinded Frobenius at Ife, and a century later, his fanciful Greeks from Atlantis have been supplanted by far more credible but unconfirmed pharaohs. The digging goes on, research goes on . . . But whether a decisive link is found should not alter the appreciation that's grown over time for the multiple civilizations across the continent. The point made by Baines should be well taken, that civilizations can also develop on their own.

So as we race back occasionally to the pyramids, we must keep a cautious eye out for another legendary feature of the desert: the mirage.

As Kenya's independence began to look inevitable in the post-war period, one of its brilliant trade unionists and top activists was thinking ahead to the country's future after the Union Jack was pulled down.

Tom Mboya was a man who believed in the practice of an old advertisement, "Growl now, smile later." It is remarkable how much he accomplished when he was only in his twenties. As a sanitary inspector of milk, he ran into the typical racism of the time and got involved in union politics, one of the few legal avenues available to fight the colonial regime and push for reforms, and he traveled abroad and got the word out about the British atrocities during the Mau Mau Uprising, helping to win international support. But he knew that some fights were with logistics and empty pockets. As with earlier generations, there were brilliant young Africans, including his fellow Kenyans, who couldn't pursue the scholarships they'd been offered because they couldn't afford the trips abroad and other expenses.

As it was, there were damn few of them. In the postwar era when much of the world could still be marked in red for the British Empire, there were only about 400 colonial students at U.K. educational facilities, and only about 100 of them held scholarships; in 1946, there were 600 scholarship students, but only 100 of them were Africans.[52] That same year, the head of the Welfare Department of the Colonial Office, a man who had worked as an official for Rhodesia, wrote sympathetically, "It is almost impossible to find any lodgings for Africans in the center of London, and they are having to live in remoter suburbs and incur additional expenses in fares and waste time travelling. Owing to color prejudice, the African student has been, and still is being, denied free access to lodgings which may be available to other classes of students."[53]

Most African students in Europe and America struggled financially and emotionally to get by. While pursuing his studies in the U.S., Nnamdi Azikiwe wound up broke, unemployed, and depressed in Pittsburgh, where he decided to end his life by lying down on a railway track and letting a tram run over him; a Good Samaritan yanked him out of danger, talked him out of suicide, and later gave him five dollars and helped set him up with a job as a dishwasher.[54]

Tom Mboya had first studied at a Catholic school in Kenya where the annual fee exceeded his father's monthly income as a plantation overseer, and he later lived with a tutor in a mud hut. He would be one of the lucky ones. As his union activities and activism earned him an international profile, he was invited to study at Ruskin College at Oxford in 1955, though he still had to jump through hoops to obtain an exit visa. London was also not above enlisting American authorities to intimidate and expel

Kenyan activists studying in the U.S. Writer Mugo Gatheru was pulled off the street, questioned for hours, and had to fight deportation; he was later refused permanent residence.[55]

At first, a member of the American Committee on Africa (chaired at the time by Martin Luther King Jr.) shelled out personally for fifty-three Kenyans to fly over to the U.S., but this obviously wasn't a long-term solution. Then in 1959, Mboya went across America on a speaking and organizational tour and had the opportunity to drum up more scholarships.[56] He soon discovered another hurdle: the U.S. government demanded that every student arrive with $300 in hand. Kenyan families "worked furiously" to raise money, and a charter airplane ferried eighty-one students over to the States that year, among them, Mboya's future wife.

The operation mushroomed—so successful, in fact, that other countries resented Kenyan students getting virtually all the placements, and they pushed hard to have their own students included. Mboya had been the only African director of the African American Students Association, but after a couple of years, he was joined by Tanzania's Julius Nyerere, Zambia's Kenneth Kaunda, and Joshua Nkomo, who would be Robert Mugabe's arch-rival for decades in Zimbabwe. By January 1963, the initiative had placed 1,011 students—with 132 of them women—in the U.S. and 100 at universities in Canada.[57]

For a young man or woman from Kenya or Tanzania to be educated abroad in those early years was *an event*. Families scraped up the funds, took out debts, or sold off valuable pieces of land. For the second charter flight, thousands showed up at the airport, even with the takeoff at four in the morning, just to see their pride-and-joys depart. Mboya recalled that "spontaneous singing and dancing, and the excited chatter of old and young, made a happy bedlam of the otherwise austere airport building."[58]

Instead of support for the airlifts, both the British colonial administration and American foundations turned up their noses disapprovingly, probably because "our airlift was a challenge to them, to the institutions which had paid lip service to the African struggle but had done until then virtually nothing to help."[59]

Mboya and his allies basically responded with, Okay, let's see you do better. Other initiatives by the Americans and British would follow while the original carried on. In 1960, Mboya flew again to the United States, only to run into a State Department that offered him no financial help and Richard Nixon, who made sympathetic noises but ultimately did nothing (Nixon, a vulgar racist in private like Ronald Reagan, was cunning enough to disguise his sentiments when needed). But Mboya did get a meeting with an influential young senator, John Kennedy, at his home in Hyannis Port, Massachusetts, managing to talk his way into securing $100,000 for four charter planes, plus some funds for the students' expenses.

Such obstacles—especially the financial resistance—make it difficult to believe (okay, many of us won't *want* to believe) allegations that Mboya could have been a paid CIA asset or that his airlift project served the agency's agenda "to groom future pro-American leaders of newly independent English-speaking states in Africa."[60] Being possibly used and knowing you've been used can be two different things. After all, through the 1950s to the late sixties, the CIA managed to fund *Encounter*, a high-brow literary and political magazine in Britain, right under the nose of its own founder and editor Stephen Spender, and we already discussed Richard Wright being duped in chapter 15. Who then is to say that Mboya wasn't smarter than the spies, so arrogantly presumptuous of an American university system that could guarantee future geopolitical loyalty? If he did take their money, perhaps he understood it could be funneled into a greater purpose.

His efforts have been rightly celebrated because the educational initiative he helped start changed the world in very tangible ways. Barack Obama's father wasn't among those airlift passengers, but he was a recipient of the scholarship program Mboya set up, and perhaps if Obama Sr. hadn't attended university in Hawaii . . . well, you know the rest. One of the airlift recipients was Wangari Maathai, whom we'll meet later. Another was noted geneticist Reuben Olembo, a future architect of the UN Environment Programme.

The merits to the African airlifts may appear obvious in hindsight, and scrutiny over President Obama's background led to articles and profiles of the initiative more than fifty years later. What often gets left out is how Mboya faced criticism from both the British, who didn't like the Americans educating their colonials, and some Americans, who nitpicked at the airlift initiative. In an article for *Harper's* magazine in 1961 headlined, "Africans Beat on Our College Doors," Albert Sims, an education administrator for the State Department who moved on to the Peace Corps, rattled off a bunch of criticisms and argued that "neither we nor the Africans can afford the random mating of our people and institutions in the style of the 'crash' program for East African students."[61] The word choice, you might say, is telling.

Mboya thought all these through and in his political memoir, *Freedom and After*, offered his defense. "The ideal for East Africa is to educate many more at home; but even so, it would still be desirable for a good number to go overseas for further education. The experience broadens their minds and helps them to be able to interpret the thinking of foreign nations to their own people when they return. Such students are also needed as ambassadors-at-large, to bring closer to other peoples the ideas and problems of our countries."[62] Clearly thinking of the example of Nkrumah and Kenyatta in London in the 1930s, Mboya pointed out that it was from studying abroad that several future African leaders had made their first friendships.

The airlift program always worked on the assumption that these bright young Africans would eventually *go home* to help build their countries as they became independent states and take over as its rising stars. But why couldn't they get their education in their native lands? Simple. There were pitifully few places, if any, for them to obtain the kind of quality education they so badly wanted, and even as the colonial powers knew their sun was setting, they made little effort to help. Uganda's Makerere University had started as a technical school, and it didn't even offer certificate courses until 1937; it became a university only in 1949. There was no question of education abroad creating a "brain drain" because from a cultural perspective, most of these students relied on family support networks—they not only felt obligated to come home, they *wanted* to return.

Mboya clearly had in mind more than a Pan-African vision but an international one, his initiative reaping a crop of students who would learn to "interpret the thinking of foreign nations" while serving as ambassadors-at-large. He fully expected Kenya and its neighbors to take their spots with the economic power-houses of the late twentieth century.

Sadly, in 1969, Tom Mboya walked out of a pharmacy on what is now Moi Avenue in the busiest district of Nairobi, and a political assassin shot him dead. A statue of him was erected on the same street, while nearby Victoria Street was renamed in his honor.

It's worth pausing to consider Tom Mboya over his thoughts on another issue. In the spring of 1969, he spoke in Harlem about African independence, and as he finished, he answered questions about the idea of a new "back to Africa" movement. It's difficult to tell if there was ever any growing popularity for this, but certainly, as mentioned before, there was a new kind of "Africa chic" in the late sixties and much of the seventies threading its way through pop culture, fashion, and radical politics at the time (and just as today, when Africa is used this way, many Africans are exasperated by the superficiality). Mboya didn't think much of a proposed exodus, and he was surprised when a few radicals interrupted him, one of them throwing eggs. "His aim was as bad as his manners."[63]

In a long opinion piece for the *New York Times*, he pointed out that, yes, the black struggle in the U.S. and the independence movements in Africa were related, but radicals who looked to African political thinkers like Frantz Fanon to superimpose the colonial struggle onto the U.S. situation were confused. "African nationalism is, by its very nature, integrationist, in that its primary objective is to mold numerous tribes into a single political entity." This is interesting for several reasons. As a Luo of Kenya, Mboya knew how tribalism got in the way of fighting the common colonial enemy, and he also backed Jomo Kenyatta as the natural choice to lead his country when it became independent. To him, the Americans were already far down the path of having created something distinct, and, in fact, they might come back to Africa to collaborate politically and culturally with native peoples, but the two were now on separate paths.

Sure, black Americans could move to Africa if they wanted, he wrote in his *Times* piece, but they were kidding themselves if they thought they could "throw off their American culture and become African." There were some who thought they could simply do it with a shaggy beard or an affectation of clothing. "An African walks barefoot or wears sandals made of cheap tires not because it is his culture but because he lives in poverty."[64] He was aware of what he called "a great debate" over African culture at the time, and his views are startlingly relevant to our own era. "I do not share the view of those who demand Black Studies and then insist that white students be barred from them. Such an attitude reflects a contradiction, and conflicts with our search for recognition and equality. Freedom for both Africans and black Americans is not an act of withdrawal, but a major step in asserting the rights of black people and their place as equals among nations and peoples of the world."[65]

18

Because Biko

A lawyer for Steve Biko's family summed up his fate with a stark eloquence: "He died a miserable and lonely death on a mat on a stone floor in a prison cell."[1]

It happened like this. He was arrested with his friend and fellow activist, Peter Jones, at a roadblock late one night in mid-August 1977, accused of driving from the community of King William's Town to the city of Cape Town, where he supposedly intended to distribute pamphlets to incite a riot. Leaving his hometown was a crime—he was a "banned" person, restricted in his travel. Meeting more than one person at a time (aside from family members) was a crime. Speaking out was a crime. Distributing pamphlets was a crime. So now they had their excuse, and they hauled him away, keeping him under Section 6 of South Africa's Terrorism Act in a cold cell at the Walmer Police Station in Port Elizabeth, naked and in manacles for days.

And one day, probably September 6, they beat him to a pulp so horribly in Interrogation Room 619 that he bled into his spinal fluid. By September 11, he was in a coma, and the authorities had to do a better cover-up. So they tossed their suspect into the back of a Land Rover—naked and shackled to its floor—and drove *750 miles* to a prison hospital in Pretoria. He was pronounced dead the next day. Stephen Bantu Biko was only thirty years old.

The excuses that emerged were pathetically far from convincing. The public was first told he was on a hunger strike and that he starved to death. For the inquest later, police testified that he had a wild expression on his face and threw a chair during an interrogation. When it came out that he had suffered brain injuries, the government stooge of a doctor who first saw him in his cell expressed shock that Biko had died in custody. "It was quite obvious that we had missed something."[2]

Worse was how the apartheid regime inevitably reacted when the outraged black majority—and the world—vented its anger and dismay over the murder and cover-up. When more than 1,200 students at the University of Fort Hare (450 miles south of Johannesburg) held a memorial service for Biko in a sports field, a small army of police and attack dogs descended on them and tossed people in jail for ten days. At a National Party conference, South Africa's Justice Minister James Kruger earned laughs from his white audience when he remarked that Biko had the "democratic right to die" and that his death "leaves me cold."[3] He was still offering grotesque bon mots weeks later, telling reporters, "A man can damage his brain in many ways. I can tell you that under press harassment, I've also felt like banging my head against the wall, but now reading the Biko autopsy, I realize it may be fatal."[4]

South Africa was already an international pariah, but Biko's murder inspired a fresh wave of revulsion. Lest we forget, in 1977 there was not one but *two* white supremacist governments still functioning in Africa, one in Pretoria and the other in Rhodesia. And the more "enlightened" nations were shocked that the South African regime would exercise its savagery on a prominent activist—a strange reaction given that it never hesitated to show its true face when challenged. The world had let the Sharpeville massacre happen in 1960, and it expressed its impotent shock again when police slaughtered children in the Soweto uprising in 1976.

Though apartheid was in its last gasping years, you would never know it from the institutionalized permanence of it. Even when faced with sanctions, it found its way around them, buying weapons from Israel. Headline performers like Frank Sinatra and Elton John quietly flew over and performed at the country's luxury resort, Sun City. Ronald Reagan shamelessly vetoed antiapartheid legislation passed by both houses of Congress in 1986 and argued disingenuously that sanctions would only hurt the country's blacks. A little more than a decade earlier, he had referred to African delegates to the UN as "monkeys" in a private phone call with Richard Nixon.[5] As you strolled through Trafalgar Square in London in the mid-eighties you often saw a group of antiapartheid protesters chanting and dancing on the steps of St. Martin-in-the-Fields, which is as close as they were allowed to get to the target of their outrage, South Africa House. Nelson Mandela was not a white-haired, smiling grandfather; he was a young man in black-and-white posters and placards that called for his release. Since no one outside Robben Island had seen him in years, his features were frozen in time in that black-and-white photo.

Biko understood what could happen to him. Interviewed by an American businessman, he recalled how the authorities had killed a friend days before one of his own recent arrests. "You are either alive and proud or you are dead, and when you are dead, you can't care anyway. And your method of death can itself be a politicizing thing." But his tactical thinking went deeper than mere acceptance of the inevitable. As is common in despotic regimes, the torturer, the brute muscle, has instructions to go only so far. Biko counted on this. In a previous interrogation, he had told police officers, "Listen, if you guys want to do this your way, you have got to handcuff me and bind my feet together, so that I can't respond. If you allow me to respond, I'm certainly going to respond. And I'm afraid you may have to kill me in the process even if it's not your intention."[6] If he put up a fight in his last hours, it wasn't out of a last impulse of defiant machismo but knowing he could make his death politically useful.

At first, commemorations were small. South Africa's great artist in exile, Gerard Sekoto, painted an homage to him in 1978, depicting his mother with downcast, mourning eyes. In 1980, Peter Gabriel created the haunting requiem for him which incorporated in its lyrics the Xhosa phrase, *Yehla Moja*—"Come

Spirit"—and which featured an excerpt of the antiapartheid song "Senzeni Na?" ("What Have We Done?"). In fact, Gabriel used a recording of the song as sung at Biko's funeral at the Victoria Stadium in King William's Town.[7] South African censors promptly banned it (and somewhat comically let it slip past them when it was used as background music for an aired episode of the cop show *Miami Vice*).[8]

And still Biko grew as an icon. A decade after he was beaten to death in his cell, he was brought back to life in the film *Cry Freedom*. Directed by Richard Attenborough, it suffered from a poor script that chose to see Biko, played by Denzel Washington, mainly through the eyes of the liberal reporter Donald Woods, portrayed by Kevin Kline. Half the movie didn't even focus on Biko at all but followed Woods and his family's desperate escape from South Africa after the murder. Even while South African censors dithered—and then surprisingly allowed it to be shown—pirate videotapes were already being smuggled into the country. Still, the subject matter was too much for ten British Tories, including former prime minister Edward Heath, who all declined to attend the film's London premiere.[9]

It's been said many times that Steve Biko achieved a fame in death that he never had in life. While true, this does him a disservice; had he lived, his notoriety would have been assured through recognition of his eloquence and his charisma. If his murder has eclipsed his ideas, it's mainly because the man himself isn't around to champion them, to refresh them and take them in new directions. We can only guess how his views might have changed in a postapartheid South Africa, but we can be certain from his powerful intelligence that they *would* have evolved. And they're worth reconsidering.

Unfortunately, the circumstances of his death will always compete for significance, and, as we'll see, these circumstances still test a much-cherished doctrine that secured the peaceful transition of South Africa from the hated apartheid era to its new dawn as a democratic nation.

Steve Biko's thinking came out of a gradual disillusionment in the way student political groups were fighting apartheid while he was a young medical student at the University of Natal in the 1960s. The National Union of South African Students was dominated and funded at the time by mostly white liberals, who seemed to be big on talk but short on making the same sacrifices or commitment as their black counterparts. Things came to a head in 1967 for a NUSAS conference at Rhodes University in Grahamstown, when the whites and Indians had places to stay in the dormitories but no one gave any thought to the black delegates.

The primary opposition to apartheid had been a multiracial integrated approach. The implication was, take away the brutal segregationist machinery, and everything will be fine. But the hypocrisy of the white students for NUSAS amply demonstrated to Biko that, no, all will *not* be fine and that apartheid was simply the ugliest manifestation of deeper problems in South African race relations. He and others formed their own group in 1968, the South African Students' Organization, known as SASO, and as he became more immersed in recruiting, fund-raising, traveling to conferences, he developed what came to be called "Black Consciousness."

At its root, Biko saw Black Consciousness as restoring the self-esteem of black citizens, an essential step before they could achieve their freedom from apartheid. Black people had to know they were worthy of their own emancipation. Biko liked to use the old catchphrase "Black is beautiful" and made it clear that *black* was also inclusive. The Black Consciousness Movement was happy to ignore the traditional tribal categories and open the door to Indians as well as those the regime defined as "colored." Apartheid had always liked to pit one racial segment of the nonwhite majority against the other with different economic privileges and levels of acceptance. The Black Consciousness Movement plowed through this distraction. Biko probably never heard of Malaku Bayen, Ethiopia's activist who in the 1930s insisted African Americans "Think black, act black and be black," but each was dealing with an apartheid, and so the same philosophical approach had to be summoned.

Biko also had some scathing criticism for white liberalism, noting how "even those whites who see much wrong with the system make it their business to control the response of the blacks to the provocation."[10] They conveniently "vacillate between two worlds," making the right complaints while still enjoying their "exclusive pool of white privileges," but they needed to understand that black people didn't need a go-between.[11] No surprise, both the apartheid regime and the liberal press (including at first his future friend, journalist Donald Woods) cast the Black Consciousness Movement as extremist, pushing a form of black racism. But Biko wasn't rejecting white allies—he merely insisted they defer to black leadership in efforts for emancipation.

Reading the phrases above, there's another frisson of recognition for our own era, with its bitter debates over cultural representation and what's now being called the "politics of respectability," that is, just how those in the group try to police themselves and their marginalized members. Who gets to be an ally? What are the best tactics to use? However they're decided, the essence of Biko's approach still holds: black people speaking for themselves and setting their own agenda. Black Lives Matter would explore this ideological terrain generations later.

By 1972, Biko had neglected his medical studies so much that he was kicked out of the University of Natal. He was interested in taking law, but this would also fall by the wayside as he committed his time to the struggle. The government did not make it easy. In March 1973, he was served with the banning order that penned him up in King William's Town and made it illegal for him to be quoted in the media.

Though he was a vital leader for Black Consciousness, the movement kept going, and organizers found ways around the restrictions. Black Consciousness birthed the Black People's Convention, and in 1974, some in SASO and the BPC wanted to hold mass rallies to celebrate the independence of Mozambique. Biko opposed the idea, knowing the official response would be more bans and arrests, and, sure enough, the regime landed hard on activists across the country and put nine of the SASO/BPC leaders on trial. Biko volunteered to speak on behalf of the accused, and though nothing could save the men in the dock from being shipped off to Robben Island, he used his testimony over four days in May 1976 as a "platform for spreading the cause of Black Consciousness." His biographer Xolela Mangcu has highlighted how Biko had to avoid handing the judge the noose to hang him with while conveying an articulate, reasonable defense of the movement's ideas.[12]

While the men on trial faced charges over their words, he talked about "police charging against people in places like Sharpeville without arms, and I am talking about the indirect violence that you get through starvation in townships."[13] Such acts indicated "more terrorism than what these guys have been saying." When the prosecution asked him, "What do you think of Africans who work for the Security Police?," his answer was blunt: "They are traitors." He said this in a room "ringed" by armed white and black officers.[14]

The great historian of the Xhosa, Noël Mostert, had the chance to meet Biko once and considered him the "first original late twentieth-century voice to emerge from African protest," and that he "personified, through his lack of anti-white sentiment, his gentleness and articulate rationality, so many of the characteristic attributes of the missionary-educated African elite which had assumed African leadership after the last of the frontier wars exactly a century before; yet he embodied as well a complete rupture with that tradition."[15] This is highly perceptive: Mostert is suggesting that Biko inherited the mantle of such figures as Harry Thuku and John Chilembwe but carved out a path of his own. Xolela Mangcu went further and traced Biko's intellectual lineage all the way back to the views and resistance efforts of prominent Xhosa chiefs of the seventeenth century.[16]

Steve Biko had his own opinions on history. In correcting the abysmal self-image the black man had of himself, Biko recognized how white authorities didn't just graft their version of the past on to the colonial mind-set; they also distorted the native individual's understanding of his own roots, depicting his history as a parade of tribal conflicts. Instead of deliberate migrations, the African was supposedly always fleeing another despotic chief. Of course, the black child absorbing such textbook libels naturally identified with the most successful model presented to him: white civilization. Fanon had made a similar point.

Biko used the term *African culture* in a slightly ambiguous way, one that could be taken as both generic but also specific to Xhosa or South African contexts. Nevertheless, we can find echoes in his work of several themes regarding African antecedents that we discussed earlier. "One of the most fundamental aspects of our culture is the importance we attach to Man," he wrote in a paper delivered at a conference. "Ours is a Man-centered society. Westerners have in many occasions been surprised at the capacity we have for talking to each other—not for the sake of arriving at a particular conclusion, but merely to enjoy the communication for its own sake."[17]

Biko went on to describe a gregarious, mutually supportive culture, and while his portrait might be a little too rosy, it has truth in it. He mentioned how a stranger knocking on a door in the West will be typically met with a challenge. And he's right; the standard "Can I help you?" really translates to "What are you doing here? Why are you in *my* space?" To Biko, the African is not suspicious by nature. "This attitude to see people not as themselves but as agents for some particular function either to one's disadvantage or advantage is foreign to us."[18] Having to live together isn't a "mishap" that requires people to fiercely compete, it's an "act of God" that's intended to inspire a collective solving of life's problems. Nor was poverty thought about as it is in the West. If it happened, it was due to some natural disaster, and it wasn't taboo or offensive to call on neighbors to help you out.

His short analysis of cultural concepts wasn't the first of its kind, and he quoted Zambia's president Kenneth Kaunda twice to help make his case (one wonders, however, what he would have made of Kaunda's later career and stubborn clinging to power). But Biko articulated these concepts well—so well that a comparison to humanism is unavoidable. Biko's line about "the importance we attach to Man" and how "Ours is a Man-centered society" is right up there with the maxim we learn in school from Protagoras: "Man is the measure of all things."

But there are differences between these belief systems, too. If you're European or from North America, think back to how you were first taught humanism, probably in secondary school.

You were likely given examples of *a* man, *a* great scientist-artist like Leonardo da Vinci, *a* thinker like Erasmus or Voltaire. Individual accomplishments radiating out, affecting the Renaissance and Enlightenment civilizations. Great institutions like say, the formation of the American system of government, we were told, sprung out of the debates of keen minds and strong individual personalities.

Without straying too far down other roads, consider how the Enlightenment philosophers thought of what's known as the "Social Contract." Having no recourse to anthropology, most of those keen minds fell back on speculation about early human beings and assumed they were competitive savages. And then their debate turned to just when and how humans developed society and government and how values were—and should be— imposed by a chosen power. That Africans developed their own society in a more organic way—as cultural practice and tradition and with accountability for their leaders that wasn't necessarily written down—was beyond their comprehension and imagination. Both are philosophical ideals, but we might even go so far as to say that African humanism is far more *humane*.

In the 1980s, South Africa's president P. W. Botha allowed concessions such as interracial marriage while authorizing some of the bloodiest crackdowns on resistance, including bombing countries that were antiapartheid allies, such as Zambia and Zimbabwe. Steve Biko was dead. The African National Congress surged in popularity as the true believers of Black Consciousness who weren't in prison or in exile lost precious momentum through factional squabbles. Xolela Mangcu, a student at the time involved in the politics, admits that the movement's decline was in part "self-inflicted."[19]

After the jubilation over Nelson Mandela's release in 1990 and the wave of worldwide support for his rise to the presidency of his nation, the question became how to suture old wounds in a free South Africa. Instead of a Nuremberg trial approach borrowed from Europe, the Mandela government treated apartheid as a crime against humanity but set up an investigative and legal body with a uniquely African approach, one that remains controversial to this day. It was the Truth and Reconciliation Commission. The thinking behind it was already enshrined in the country's interim constitution: "There is a need for understanding but not for vengeance, a need for reparation but not for retaliation, a need for *ubuntu* but not for victimization."[20]

You'll recall we discussed *ubuntu* back in chapter 9. According to academic Michael Onyebuchi Eze, one of its core principles is the power of forgiveness: "I forgive you because every human being is an irreplaceable subject in our discursive formation. Within this formation, forgiveness does not weaken me, it empowers me."[21] Here was an African Idea made tangible in an indigenous form of justice. Chaired by Archbishop Desmond Tutu, the commission offered amnesty to those who stepped forward and offered the truth about apartheid's systematic terror and political crimes. It accepted more than 20,000 victim statements—and, interestingly, rejected more than 5,000 amnesty applications, granting only about 849.

While its televised hearings in 1996 captured much of the world's imagination, many were dissatisfied with the process. The BBC suggested their criticism "stems from a basic misunderstanding about its mandate. It was never meant to punish people, just to expose their role in crimes committed under apartheid."[22] But this was off the mark. Black South Africans could follow the good intentions just fine. Some merely didn't see the approach as useful. Others feared retribution from the old diehards who once did the dirty work for the much-hated security forces.[23] There were other problems, too. One of the most infamous former colonels in charge of the police's counterterrorism unit frustrated investigators by withholding details; he was already in prison, serving more than 200 years and two life sentences for six murders plus a host of other crimes.[24]

The international media coverage sometimes brought a certain level of critical cynicism to the proceedings: "Witnesses, handpicked for the spotlight, were encouraged to weep," reported Reuters, "and often a woman sat next to them patting them on the back and offering tissues." Some critics were willing to admit the hearings "brought peace to some victims . . . which divisive, lengthy and costly trials might not."[25] Yet by the time the TRC shut its doors in 1998, there were still 477 cases of missing individuals and probably thousands of others that went unreported to the commission by their families. "What has changed?" asked one of its own commissioners in 2007. "For the average, ordinary citizen, very little." This was Yasmin Sooka, the prominent international human rights lawyer. "Reparations have been miniscule and from a very small group of people. In terms of real, meaningful redistribution, what's actually happened? Almost nothing."[26]

Nothing better illustrated the limits of Truth and Reconciliation than the case of Steve Biko. The five policemen implicated in his death were brought one by one before the commission to testify, and most of them verbally ducked and weaved when they were challenged. In making their amnesty applications, one admitted to lying at the inquest into Biko's death even about when a doctor was brought in, blaming this on orders from his superiors (who were conveniently dead). Two admitted that their suspect was beaten with a hose pipe, but still they wouldn't come clean over the whole story.

George Bizos, the lawyer for the Biko family, cornered retired colonel Harold Snyman over the implausible details in his testimony. "In your version, the police acted in self-defense, all four of them against an attack by Biko."

"He bumped his head," replied Snyman.

Bizos wasn't buying it. He gave the audience of some 2,000 people "a long look over the top of his glasses" and said, "If that story is true, it's his fault and not the fault of anyone else. You and your colleagues are blameless."

Snyman answered, "As I said, there had been an assault."[27]

The five were all refused amnesty, but the commission's decision didn't matter. Twenty years had passed, which put their crimes outside the statute of limitations.

While the TRC was given critical postmortems when the job was done—looking at who didn't give a full confession and who still wanted a more punitive form of justice—the media scrutiny didn't bring the discussion back to the values the commission had espoused: *ubuntu*. Yes, there was plenty of debate over forgiveness. But *ubuntu* encapsulates much more, the strengthening of community through the forgiveness and reconciliation. No one seemed to notice that the TRC's quest for answers and its theater of catharsis also represented a clash of cultures.

The table had been flipped when Mandela took over, and those who once clubbed and bullied and murdered for apartheid now had to negotiate with an indigenous power structure, one with a value system they didn't understand. Indeed, it was one they had never wanted or tried to understand. The commission also brought several Africans accused of political crimes before its hearings, including a defiant, unrepentant Winnie Mandela, who was implicated in gruesome kidnappings and murders by her bodyguards. She laughed out loud when one of her accusers testified.[28] To the TRC, "it became evident at times that she regarded [its inquiries] as a personal vendetta being waged against her by the Commission. This might also explain her contemptuous attitude towards certain witnesses and her reprimands to those who asked her questions that she did not like."[29]

In seeking justice through the ideal of *ubuntu*, Desmond Tutu and others didn't factor in what Steve Biko had long tried to tell everyone: that there had been a break in the continuity of African cultural concepts. The "inferiority complex" of black South Africans wouldn't be cured overnight, and it made some young activists highly susceptible to a once-heroic figure like Winnie Mandela turned demagogue. Even her role in the murders didn't bring her down. She walked out of the TRC hearings a free woman. Instead, she went to prison later for five years for corruption and fraud.

But Truth and Reconciliation in South Africa has inspired others to adopt the *ubuntu* model. Chile used such a commission to investigate the thousands of murders and human rights abuses under dictator Augusto Pinochet. Canada's Truth and Reconciliation Commission faced the disgraceful abuse of Aboriginal children in what was known as the Indian residential school system. Germany held two commissions over the human rights abuses that took place in Communist East Germany.

An African form of justice, whatever its debatable flaws, has gained validation around the world.

In 1967, the year that Steve Biko's comrades were getting fed up at a NUSAS conference in Grahamstown, one of Africa's rising intellectual stars essentially made his debut.

At just thirty-four years old, Ali Mazrui published three different books, including his important study *Towards a Pax Africana: A Study of Ideology and Ambition*. Heavily influenced by Kwame Nkrumah's Pan-Africanism, Mazrui articulated a vision of political nonalignment as a larger search for dignity and for Africa to "matter in the world." Herbert Spiro, the political scientist and future ambassador to Cameroon, gave it his highest praise and gushed that Mazrui did for Africa what "Professor Louis Hartz did for America in *The Liberal Tradition in America*."[30] Over a career of almost fifty years in which he taught in Uganda, Nigeria, and the U.S., Mazrui churned out a dizzyingly prolific number of books. He was given honors by universities and even the British House of Lords, and he was always a stimulating and often hotly controversial figure in African Ideas.

When his landmark documentary series, *The Africans: A Triple Heritage*, sparked trouble for the PBS network in 1986, he was interviewed by the entertainment journalist Arthur Unger for the *Christian Science Monitor*. By then, Mazrui was in his fifties, a bear of a man with salt-and-pepper hair and a mustache. Unger, thinking he was cute, opened his feature with the quip that his interview subject didn't arrive in a daishiki but an Ivy League suit. The journalist said he disagreed with many of the professor's opinions but found his ideas challenging. "Dr. Mazrui smiled. 'Good,' he said, with just the hint of a sigh. 'Many people disagree with me. My life is one long debate.'"[31]

Mazrui was born in Mombasa into one of the most prominent families of Kenya in 1933, the son of a leading Muslim judge. Earning his MA at Columbia and his PhD from Oxford, he taught at the University of Makerere in Kampala, which in the 1960s and early seventies had to be one of the most interesting and stimulating institutions for study on the continent. John Mbiti was on staff. Ngũgĩ wa Thiong'o came for the very first African Writers Conference in 1962. Novelist and travel writer Paul Theroux taught English there in 1965. Ugandan novelist Okello Oculi was studying political science at the same time.

A staggering roster of prime ministers, presidents, film stars, authors, and athletes are among its alumni.

Mazrui had a prestigious teaching post, and he was on a roll. He wrote op-ed pieces for the *Times* of London. But he also attracted the wrong kind of attention—including from Uganda's genocidal dictator Idi Amin, who put out an invitation through intermediaries that he could have a job with the administration. Mazrui decided it was time to move along. "I was, in a sense, running away from Idi Amin," he told the *New York Times* years later. "For a while, I was in good standing in Uganda. But I declined his invitation to be his Kissinger, a special adviser. I might have done some good. Or, possibly, I wouldn't have been alive to talk to you here today."[32]

In a way, Mazrui was trying to build for political history and culture what John Mbiti attempted to do with religion and spiritual traditions, looking for common denominators and postulating a grand unifying theory. Both men represented a new academic class, one that wouldn't tolerate African culture being demeaned, and they certainly weren't going to omit the legacy of colonialism.

Whether he was conscious of it or wanted to acknowledge it at all, Mazrui's theories owed much to that brain trust in London in the 1930s that protested the Italian-Ethiopian War, that collective of friends and associates—Jomo Kenyatta, George Padmore, C. L. R. James—who shaped the perspectives of his main early influence, Kwame Nkrumah. Later, Mazrui would claim in his TV documentary series that "something of the flame of Africa refuses to be extinguished deep in the black American soul." With scenes of evangelical Christian worshippers dancing and wailing up a storm, he opined, "In no area of life is Africa's primeval power more alive than in black Americans' styles of worship."[33] Mazrui seemed to have little time for *Négritude*, but the suggestion that there's a unique psychological and spiritual heritage for the African peoples and the diaspora echoes one of its core premises.

One of his most provocative ideas was expressed in a BBC Reith Lecture in 1979. Mazrui envisioned a Pax Africana. To keep the peace in Africa, self-government was implied, and "the logical conclusion of the whole process of decolonization lay in Africa's ambition to be its own policeman."[34] If that was the case, then Africa should also contribute to world security, even though it was the most politically marginalized continent. He then argued that Africa, specifically economic powerhouses like Nigeria, should develop nuclear capability. This was his logic: "When little white children misbehave in some Western societies the mother may sometimes say, 'Behave yourself—or a big black man will come and take you away.' Today we are dealing not with little white children, but with white grown-ups in northern chanceries who need to be threatened with the danger of big black men wielding nuclear devices. I realize this will sound outrageous to many people. Imagine Emperor [Jean-Bédel] Bokassa playing Napoleon with a nuclear bomb—or Idi Amin doing a war dance with an atomic device! How can I even contemplate putting nuclear weapons into the hands of such tin pot dictators?" His answer was that such dictators would have such power anyway "unless we declare these weapons illegitimate for *everybody* [emphasis in the original]." Mad rulers don't come only from Africa, but maybe the dread of them could frighten "northern war-mongers" back to sanity.[35]

This idea naturally reaped a backlash of criticism. But Mazrui made an interesting point that goes beyond nuclear proliferation. Why shouldn't the Africans, or black people anywhere, have the means to defend themselves? In the 1960s, when the Black Panthers took advantage of open-carry gun laws—which was their right—the reaction of the FBI and Ronald Reagan's government in California was to vilify and persecute them. "Big black men" with guns indeed scared white authorities. And in our own era, while shootings and police beatings of black people have continued to outrage America, white protesters carrying assault rifles were allowed to storm the Michigan State Capitol to protest COVID-19 measures.[36]

But Mazrui didn't leave the issue with just this reasonable defense. He made a case for nuclear deescalation that relies on the fear of black men with guns, an argument many find deeply offensive. He conceded that Idi Amin "could indeed kill a lot of people" but doubted he could destroy the whole world—hardly a compelling argument and more of a callous rationale. Mazrui's words on the cold page tempt you to hope he's making an ironic, Swiftian "Modest Proposal," but he clung to his premise over the years with genuine sincerity.

No less divisive was his "Triple Heritage" theory, which was the ultimate expression of his conceptual thinking on Africa. He began advancing this theory in articles and would later expand on it in his TV series and its companion book. The essence of it was that Africa was shaped by three major influences: its own indigenous cultures and spiritual belief systems, the spread of Islam across the continent, and Western colonialism. Mazrui naturally had other corollaries to this view, arguing that the continent suffered from fragmentation and that, while gigantic in size, it was the most politically marginal, but it was his three-plank architecture that became his staple.

It's a reductive view, and it prompted scathing criticism. Scholar Hailu Habtu wrote that one of Mazrui's articles promoting his vision made for "interesting reading. That is perhaps the only kind thing one can say about it." Hailu zeroed in on a serious flaw in the thesis, that its "hidden premise is the existence of an African cultural vacuum, or near-vacuum, destined to be filled by 'universalistic' civilizations such as Greco-Roman (Christian, European, Western, etc.) or Judaeo-Arabic (Semitic, Hebraic, Arabic, etc.)," and he considered it not only incorrect, it was "to say the least, offensive." While yes, Mazrui had factored in some indigenous cultures, it wasn't clear whether they had equal weight to the imported ones in his grand theory or if he was merely paying them lip service. Hailu made his criticism in 1984, and interestingly, he pointed out, "The line of inquiry most African and Africanist scholars are reluctant to pursue is the African contribution to Judaic, Greco-Roman, Arab, Indian, Western, and other civilizations."[37]

At the other end of the spectrum was the attitude in a long article for *Encounter* magazine written in 1980 by Peter Bauer of the London School of Economics. Bauer was an unapologetic libertarian later honored by the right-wing Cato Institute. Oddly, though, he devoted less space to attacking Mazrui over economics than to his interpretations of history. "In historical times," Bauer declared loftily without identifying a specific era, "the achievement of black Africa . . . has been negligible compared to that of Asia and Europe."[38] He then rattled off many of the stock replies to the horrors of slavery and the virtues of colonialism that we've already discussed, plus he included a disturbing apologist rationale over the massacres in Soweto and Sharpeville, South Africa.

But his few economic criticisms did land some hits: "Professor Mazrui proposes extensive replacement of Western imports and foreign personnel, technology and capital by local resources. Where are these to come from and who will pay?" A little later, he pounced on Mazrui's argument for "official restrictions of commercial contacts with the West, thereby depriving people of what they want and can afford."[39] Mazrui never did offer adequate defenses to such criticisms, nor did they seem to hurt his academic standing. Ensconced for many years at the University of Michigan and later at Binghamton University, he enjoyed accolades and prestigious scholarly appointments to everywhere from Nairobi to Singapore.

His series *The Africans: A Triple Heritage* was an ambitious coproduction of a PBS affiliate and the BBC, along with the usual funding partners for the American public network, including the National Endowment for the Humanities. At a cost of $3.5 million—a lot of money in 1986 for a TV documentary series—it was naturally a product of its time. The nine episodes had beautiful cinematography, enough that the viewer didn't lose interest in the cerebral musings of its host, and it was the kind of show that followed in the footsteps of *Civilisation* by Kenneth Clark and *The Ascent of Man* by Jacob Bronowski. The famous Brits who hosted these programs gave their on-screen delivery as if they were still in lecture halls. Yes, Mazrui could sometimes be pompous in his episodes, but to his credit, he talked to his viewer more like an urbane uncle stopping in to share what he'd seen on his travels. The *New York Times* noted that when his series was shown first in the U.K., it received "generally respectful reviews."[40]

Enter Lynne Cheney. Yes, *that* Lynne Cheney, right-wing conservative and wife of the career politician Dick Cheney, who would rise to become vice president under George W. Bush. At the time, she was chair of the National Endowment for the Humanities, and she didn't like what she saw in Mazrui's series. She dashed off a letter of complaint to the Washington PBS station, the lead partner for the network, objecting to the apparent effort in the series "to blame every technological, moral, and economic failure of Africa on the West."[41] Essentially, the same indignant reaction as Peter Bauer once had to Mazrui's work. She insisted the NEH's credit be taken off the program, and as an appeasement, the producers added two words to the title credit, *A Commentary* (as if this wasn't already obvious). There was one other concession: Mazrui had called Karl Marx "the last of the great Jewish prophets," and this line was cut from the American broadcast of the episode.[42] Meanwhile, the storm in a teacup spilled onto the pages of the major newspapers' second sections for a day or so.

No one, of course, squawked this much when Alistair Cooke made personal observations in his TV series on America. No one complained very loudly when James Burke expressed opinions about science in his brilliant show, *Connections*, especially about the threat of nuclear war. But now an African was offering his views in the same medium and in the same tradition. Mazrui laughed off the criticisms, and he could afford to since PBS clearly stood behind its host and its program; not one network affiliate dropped the show. As for Lynne Cheney, she found a new way to be an unwelcome irritant when years later she complained publicly about explicit pop song lyrics. Her efforts there proved as equally short lived and irrelevant.

To watch Mazrui's series today, however, can be a frustrating experience, as it hasn't aged well. With the authority of his academic status and the novelty of being the first African to explain the continent for a sprawling TV series, he made sweeping generalizations that don't hold up under the simplest scrutiny. In the first episode, he talked about great explorers like Columbus. "One of the gaps in African experience has been the relative absence in this interest in what lies beyond the horizon." To him, there were "no Nelsons coming from Africa, there are no adventurers seeking new lands to conquer."[43] Oh, really?

Hailu Habtu's criticisms over an article could equally apply to the show: "Mazrui's verdicts, sometimes as equivocal as they are facile, stretch the imagination almost to breaking point."[44]

He would court controversy for the rest of his long career until his death in 2014. When Henry Louis Gates hosted a TV series on Africa for PBS in 1999, Mazrui dashed off a peevish critique that fooled no one with its jealous resentment. Wole Soyinka wrote an article in response, bluntly suggesting that "Mazrui should have kept quiet."[45] He didn't. Mazrui might well have been one of the first to publicly compare Israel's policies against Palestinians with the apartheid regime of South Africa, an opinion that has gained substantial currency today even among left-wing Jewish critics. Back in the late 1980s, however, the comparison was incendiary enough that one of his publishers refused to print his book *Cultural Forces in World Politics*.

After Iran's Ayatollah Khomeini openly called for the assassination of Salman Rushdie because of his novel *The Satanic Verses*, Mazrui wrote an opinion piece for the *Toronto Star* in 1992 that called Rushdie a cultural traitor and suggested he was the architect of his own troubles. While he claimed his "sympathies were strong with Rushdie on the issue of censorship," he rattled off examples of American and Israeli treatment of traitors, implying a double standard on the part of the West.[46] This sidestepped the core issue: how was it right that a nation could use terrorism—in this case against one individual rather than, say, a passenger jet full of hostages—because its regime didn't like what that person wrote?

What *is* surprising, in retrospect, is that Mazrui didn't suffer professionally from advocating this opinion, which implied Tehran was right to order the assassination of a writer. Mazrui kept teaching in America, the self-proclaimed land of freedom of speech, and he kept publishing books with American publishers. While no thinker with a substantial body of work should be reduced to a single opinion, fans of his books and his TV series will need to reconcile this view—and the academic privilege he enjoyed in the West—with the rest of his contributions. In the end, it smacks of the kind of hypocrisy he often attributed to the West.

Nevertheless, he moved the dialogue of African ideas forward. A case can be made that he accomplished this most of all as a "popularizer" of Africa in the same way that Kenneth Clark popularized great art in his *Civilisation* series and Carl Sagan enlightened millions over science in *Cosmos*. By spreading his personal vision, always heavily tinted by his Muslim Kenyan outlook, he made himself a lightning rod for debate. Now with everything getting a second life on YouTube, his attempt has proved more durable than his actual ideas. Who today in academia, let alone the forums of politics and culture, wants seriously to cling to Mazrui's Triple Heritage? Today, we know more than we used to about Africa's past. There is more interest today in the Africa that existed prior to colonization. And, as some have argued, the continent has always been far more diverse and complex than his problematic vision.

But his attempt to identify key influences and unifying forces was a noble attempt. Mazrui was from the generation that saw traditional colonialism wither and die, and he was an important observer and critic of the transitional phase in governance despite his more radical assertions. Those who followed would take even bolder, more aggressively realist approaches.

19

Trees and Oil, Cheetahs and Hippos

In the beginning, independent Africa showed astonishing promise. For instance, when Ghana first raised its flag in place of the Union Jack, its gross domestic product was double that of South Korea, and its per capita income rivaled that of Spain.[1] And we've already discussed the encouraging example of Botswana. Yet things soon turned horribly wrong. From the heartbreaking wars in Angola and Mozambique to brutish despots like Mobutu Sese Seko, it was clear by the 1970s that most of the continent couldn't save itself, at least not for a prolonged period of time. No one has been more critical of the postindependence record than the generation of Africans who came to maturity in those initial years. Having lived through them, they know better than anyone the failings of the different regimes.

The colonial powers that ruled these countries had set an example of kleptocracy instead of good governance. Just as no mugger ever steals your wallet then dusts you off and points you to the subway, so the Europeans hadn't thought ahead to their victims' lives after they boarded their jets and flew away. And native residents who worked with the British, French, Portuguese, or Belgians as high-ranking civil servants were collaborators in all but name, and so they never gave a damn about the indigenous people either. Technocrats hired to stay on because of their expertise weren't about to change character, but they were in positions to keep feathering their own nests.

At the same time, the anticolonialism leaders who swept into office as heroes could tell you all about the Marxist dialectic but nothing about how to finance the construction of a bridge or how to promote investment in small business. Nor did they hesitate to treat themselves to new lives of luxury as rewards for their long struggles. They weren't interested in allowing voices of dissent, whether they came from a reporter's typewriter or from across the aisle in a parliament. On top of all the incompetence and venality developed a culture of dependence on foreign aid that became as addictive and spiraling as heroin to a street addict.

These are not my conclusions. They represent in part or full the views of some of the great minds to come out of Africa and make their reputations in the 1980s and nineties. These big brains were responsible for a tectonic shift in Africa's political discussions, one started with the debate that still goes on over the fairness of the colonial aftermath. One prevailing rationale went: Now that the Europeans have gone, turn yourself around, shake yourself off, go be productive, and have freedom of the press. Create transparent government and economic sustainability. It's been five minutes, what's taking you so long? The standard counter to this, not without some justification, was, Wait a minute, look what a mess we've inherited. But the new thinkers argued, Why shouldn't African peoples have economic prosperity, good governance, and all the other virtues right away? Especially when so many of the administrations, such as those of Nigeria or Zambia, were rapidly squandering capital and goodwill. The sins of past colonial masters were no excuse for the African regimes' corruption and incompetence. Nor was this new generation blind to the repackaged colonialism of predatory corporate enterprises.

Nigeria's Ken Saro-Wiwa recognized the threat. He worked in academia and as a federal administrator for the oil port of Bonny, but it's as a brilliant writer that he really made his name. His 1985 novel about the Nigerian Civil War written in idiomatic and pidgin English, *Sozaboy*, is now considered a classic. He wrote poems, radio and stage plays, and children's books, and he created Nigeria's hugely popular sitcom *Basi and Company*. But as the nineties began, he was preoccupied with the rights and autonomy of his native people, the Ogoni, and how Royal Dutch Shell ran roughshod over their coastal lands, destroying their crops with acid rain and slaughtering wildlife as "uncontrolled oil spills dotted the landscape with puddles of ooze the size of football fields. Virtually all fish and wildlife . . . vanished."[2]

What Shell and Chevron were doing in the region, he wrote, amounted to genocide. For the Ogoni, "the land is a god and is worshipped as such"; a traditional belief is that human souls can transfer into animals, including aquatic ones, and if something destructive happens to them, it can harm the people who have a duty to look after them.[3] His younger brother, Owens, a doctor, saw for himself how the environmental damage was affecting their people and joined his effort.

Saro-Wiwa kept a large reserve of outrage for Yakubu Gowon, Nigeria's military leader for nine years who ran the country during its bloody civil war in the 1960s before he was kicked out by his own army officers in 1975. Gowon had ignored Nigeria's constitution for a blatant grab of all offshore oil. But Saro-Wiwa also blasted in print the leaders who followed him. "The new men . . . created seven new states, most of them in the ethnic majority areas of the Hausa-Fulani, Igbo and Yoruba, increasing thereby the share of oil revenues by these groups while exacerbating ethnic tension. They went further to revise the revenue allocation formula agreed before independence, so to give the ethnic majorities a still greater share of oil revenue. The areas from which oil was being extracted were now forced to accept twenty per cent instead of fifty percent of the proceeds of mining rents and royalties."[4]

Since the Nigerian government of the 1990s was mired in corruption and happy to collude and protect the oil companies, Saro-Wiwa's crusade ran smack into the regime, which tossed him in prison for months. Undeterred despite repeated arrests, he kept at it, organizing marches, demanding oil revenues for the Ogoni, enduring harassment by the military and security

service, even deportation from Ogoniland. Shell was later implicated in cases of army torture and the killing of protesters—it
"provided the Nigerian army with vehicles, patrol boats and
ammunition, and to have helped plan raids and terror campaigns against villages."[5]

Then Saro-Wiwa and eight other Ogoni leaders were arrested
in 1994 on trumped-up charges related to the killings of four
Ogoni chiefs by a mob. Human rights groups launched complaints, including the PEN American Center, which noted in
an open letter signed by illustrious members such as Chinua
Achebe and Ben Okri that at the courthouse, the authorities let
in an observer from Shell but kept BBC News out. There were
unconfirmed reports that "when defense lawyers objected to
the military's heavy-handed screening policy, military personnel assaulted them."[6] The fix was in for the defendants from the
beginning, and many witnesses for the prosecution later admitted they were bribed.

At one point, Owens Wiwa went to seek help at the British embassy and ended up dealing with an official fresh from
London on his very first foreign posting. No sooner did Owens
finish going over the issues involved in Ogoniland and Shell's
conduct than the young man informed him bluntly, "Owens,
Shell is Britain's biggest investment in Nigeria. In fact, it's 90
percent of the British investment in Nigeria. I'm in this office
because of Shell. In a way, Shell is paying my salary. We don't
tell Shell what to do. Shell tells us."[7]

Years before, Ken Saro-Wiwa had written a short story about
a young merchant seaman who turned to armed robbery, bitter
over "the open looting of the national treasury" and his homeland's rampant corruption. In a letter to a girlfriend he hasn't
seen in ten years, his hero imagines facing a firing squad with
his accomplices in a stadium where the poor come to take in
the spectacle. "So now, dear girl, I'm done. My heart is light as
the daylight which seeps stealthily into our dark cell. I hear the
prison guard jangle his keys, put them into our keyhole. Soon
he'll turn it and call us out. Our time is up."[8]

But Ken Saro-Wiwa wouldn't die as a cynical bandit, the
object of derision by an unsympathetic crowd. Only days before

the execution verdict was handed down for him and the others, he was nominated for a Nobel Peace Prize. Thousands of Nigeria's troops and riot police were mobilized in case public outrage turned violent.[9] The condemned men were to die not by a firing squad but on the gallows. On November 10, 1995, Saro-Wiwa was selected as the first to be hanged, and he made a stirring speech in a courtyard before being taken away. "I have always been a man of good ideas, and whether I be killed, my ideas will live forever and Ogoni, for which I am dying, will one day be emancipated from the shackles of oppression."[10] In a grotesque turn of events, the gallows wouldn't work. He was brought back later, but again the mechanism failed, and as journalist J. Timothy Hunt put it, the hanging "was attempted several times and was cruel beyond imagination."[11]

In the wake of the executions, the Clinton White House recalled its ambassador from Nigeria and imposed travel restrictions on the regime in protest. Owens Wiwa, along with his wife and child, were forced to go on the run and escape into exile, managing in the end to move to Canada and live there for years. More recently, he has served as director of a nonprofit health initiative back in Nigeria. Meanwhile, there have been novels, songs, sculptures, and films inspired by Ken Saro-Wiwa's life and activist martyrdom.

There was some justice—of a kind—exacted from Shell in 2009 over its involvement in the human rights abuses of the Ogoni and the executions. The oil giant paid out $15.5 million to settle a legal action brought mainly by relatives of the hanged leaders, one of the largest payouts of its time. Stephen Kretzmann, director of Oil Change International, told *The Guardian* that Shell "knew the case was overwhelming against them, so they bought their way out of a trial."[12]

Ken Saro-Wiwa, as he said himself, was a man of good ideas. He appreciated the big picture of how an indigenous people and their way of life, their very home and natural world, were all threatened by a relentless conglomerate, one that was willing to help murder him for the sake of business as usual. As has happened so often before, what was done in one part of Africa demonstrated a pattern of corporate abuse and neglect that could be easily repeated elsewhere.

It took until the 1960s for human beings to seriously begin taking care of their planet, but environmentalism is often still thought of as a goal for aesthetics or preserving wildlife, not saving *us*. It would be nice to save the whales. It would be nice not to let trash clog the rivers. It's only in the last twenty years that we in the West have begun to "usefully panic," horrified at last that we are ingesting microplastics from garbage dumped in oceans, that our car exhausts are literally killing us. We are waking up to realize that while recycling has been fobbed off on us as a neighborly duty, corporations still lobby with big bucks so they can obliterate forests or, like Shell, lay waste to fragile ecosystems with their oil spills. Ken Saro-Wiwa's work and his sacrifice offers a poignant reminder that our passive concern is not enough; environmental abusers must be confronted and fought, especially when they are indulged by our governments.

His last words were widely reported as "Lord take my soul, but the struggle continues."[13]

Another one of the bright new minds that would fight for African environmentalism was Wangari Maathai. As mentioned earlier, she was one of the fortunate beneficiaries of the Mboya scholarship airlift, earning degrees in biology at colleges in Atchison, Kansas, and in Pittsburgh. She came home to be Kenya's first female PhD and Nairobi University's first female professor. In 1977, she founded the Green Belt Movement, an organization that tackled the massive problems caused by deforestation. If you're a Kenyan farmer in a remote area, the lack of wood fuel can have serious consequences. With fewer trees, you have less fuel and therefore cook *less*, which means you'll likely fall back on less healthy food.[14] The effects can be that simple and devastating.

Her initiative began with farmers relying on seedlings from government nurseries but evolved into what Maathai called with justifiable pride a revolution for Kenyan women. They developed their own innovations, such as making seedbeds out of broken pots and granaries to keep seeds safe from domestic animals.[15] The movement would end up planting tens of millions of trees and training thousands of women in professions such as forestry, agriculture, and beekeeping. This alone would have assured her a legacy, but Maathai set her sights higher. She went into politics . . . Which by that time, was no easy task in Kenya. The nation had rapidly transformed into a one-party oligarchy after Jomo Kenyatta's vice president and handpicked successor, Daniel arap Moi, came to power in 1978. "Everyone should sing like a parrot after me," said the new president, and under his regime, bribery and corruption chewed away at the country's judicial system like gangrene while academics and activists were left to rot without due process in underground cells, "some of them partly filled with water."[16] Nor had ethnic rivalries dissipated as Kenya marked more than fifteen years of independence. This was the troubled, shabby stage on which Maathai wanted to assume a role and speak her lines from the heart.

The winding narrative of Maathai's clashes with Moi is a long one. From her perspective, the president and his cronies didn't like her because she was Kikuyu, well educated, and had gone through a very public, acrimonious divorce, making no apologies for wanting her freedom in a society that still clung to traditional views of women's roles. But when it came down to it, rationales hardly matter to an autocrat. Moi didn't like this woman building a broad-based pro-democracy movement. At first, his regime used legal shell games to keep her out of positions of influence and parliament. Then it tried to clamp down on the Green Belt Movement's activities.

A major flash point was the government's shameless attempt to build a skyscraper in Uhuru (Freedom) Park in Nairobi—one that, among other things, would house the headquarters of Moi's KANU party and its mouthpiece, the *Kenya Times*, partly owned by the shadowy British tabloid magnate Robert Maxwell. As Maathai wrote in her memoir, Uhuru Park is as much a recreational oasis for Nairobi residents as Hyde Park is for people in London or Central Park is for New Yorkers: "It was a bitter irony that the park, named to celebrate our independence, was subjected like so many of Kenya's public goods to land-grabbers in the government."[17] When her lobbying efforts to fight the construction of the Times Tower fell on deaf ears, she wrote to the British high commissioner and to the UN. Members of parliament who backed Moi devoted forty-five minutes in the chamber to a torrent of personal abuse aimed at her and her followers, dismissing them as a "bunch of divorcees" and a "clique of women."[18]

Moi himself engaged in personal attacks, even in his address for Republic Day in 1989 marking Kenya's independence. "According to African traditions, women must respect their men," he declared as his audience laughed (like obedient parrots). "I ask you women. Can't you discipline one of your own?" For a while, it looked like the crusade over the Times Tower would be a lost cause. Construction was still set to go ahead, and with petty vindictiveness, the regime evicted the Green Belt Movement out of its offices—the government owned the building. But Maathai's relentless criticism and lobbying drew the attention of international media, and investors pulled out.

The battle of wills went on for more than a decade. In January 1992, when Maathai and others warned that Moi might use a staged coup as an excuse to prevent democratic elections, police burst through her barricaded home and arrested her. Her time in a cold cell aggravated her arthritis so badly that she needed to be carried into court on a stretcher. Nevertheless, she made bail and next month started a hunger strike with other activists in Uhuru Park, demanding the release of political prisoners. This time, riot police came and clubbed her and others unconscious.[19] The charges against her were eventually dropped, but the protests continued. During the elections of 1997, Maathai fought against cynical efforts to exploit ethnic resentments. When the government wanted to give away big chunks of Kakura Forest to its political cronies, she fought that, too.

A few years later, the government tried again to privatize precious land, and again, she was willing to get arrested more than once to raise attention. But by then, Maathai was such an internationally recognized figure that she couldn't be so easily packed off to a cell or rudely dismissed. In the end, she simply, stubbornly outlasted Moi, who was closing in on eighty years old and who finally chose to retire in 2002. The reins of power were handed over to Jomo's son, Uhuru Kenyatta, who's had a controversial tenure of his own. But that same year, Maathai was elected to parliament and served for a couple of years as assistant environment minister. Then in 2004, she became the first African woman to win the Nobel Peace Prize. In its announcement, the Norwegian Nobel Committee said, "She represents an example and a source of inspiration for everyone in Africa fighting for sustainable development, democracy, and peace."[20]

Not that life was guaranteed to be smooth after a Nobel medal was around her neck. Only a day before she was supposed to pick up her prize, she had to do damage control over comments she allegedly made about AIDS. Nairobi's *East African Standard* reported that at a workshop in Nyeri that August, she had compared the disease to a biological weapon and said, "Do not be naïve. AIDS is not a curse from God to Africans or the black people. It is a tool to control them from some evil-minded scientist."[21]

Maathai issued a statement, later published on the Green Belt Movement's website, writing that she was "shocked" over what she was "purported to have said." And no, she insisted, she did not "say nor believe that the virus was developed by white people or white powers in order to destroy the African people. Such views are wicked and destructive."[22] The day after the prize announcement, the *East African Standard* decided to run another inflammatory quote she allegedly made linking the disease to white scientists.

Life after her Nobel Prize was one of mostly anticlimax. She failed to win seats in two elections. She wrote books. At sixty-eight years old, she still took part in protests and got teargassed for her trouble. She died while undergoing cancer treatment in 2011.

In 2015, Kenyan writer and political analyst Nanjala Nyabola marked the four years that had passed since Maathai's death, noting there was only a handful of tepid tributes. "If an alien landed in Kenya this week, they'd think Moi was a hero and Maathai a mere footnote in national history. Her legacy is a victim of both the casual misogyny and the political schizophrenia that characterizes Kenya's public sphere. In Kenya, we want women to be strong and opinionated, but not too strong and not too opinionated—not like Maathai."[23]

Africa's heroes and martyrs, just like African Ideas, have a habit, though, of being rediscovered, and Wangari Maathai accomplished too much for her to be marginalized for long. Of course, environmentalism has been around for more than 100 years—in fact, it got its *start* in Kenya, a fact that Maathai herself acknowledged in one of her books.[24] Chief Josiah Njonjo and an eccentric English botanist, Richard St. Barbe Baker, pioneered in 1922 what was called *Watu wa Miti*, "People of the Trees." A movement that pushed the virtues of forestation and conservation. Today, it's known as the International Tree Foundation.

Like Ken Saro-Wiwa, Wangari Maathai linked environmentalism to the urgent problems of trying to carve out a livelihood and live in rural Africa. She made it about cooking fuel and female education. She demonstrated how the potential loss of a public park stripped away the veil on political greed and an open contempt for ordinary citizens. In her Nobel acceptance speech, Maathai said, "Initially, the work was difficult because historically our people have been persuaded to believe that because they are poor, they lack not only capital, but also knowledge and skills to address their challenges. Instead, they are conditioned to believe that solutions to their problems must come from 'outside.' Further, women did not realize that meeting their needs depended on their environment being healthy and well managed. They were also unaware that a degraded environment leads to a scramble for scarce resources and may culminate in poverty and even conflict. They were also unaware of the injustices of international economic arrangements."[25]

It's not a question of whether Maathai identified all these connections first. What matters is that she addressed them through a focused, practical effort that placed economic, political, and personal power into the hands of thousands of women. And in Kenya, for now at least, the trees are many, and they are still green and tall.

While Ken Saro-Wiwa and Wangari Maathai put their energies into fighting the powerful and corrupt in their home countries, someone else took on the whole collection of African leaders turning into despots. He thundered away that they had betrayed their peoples' trust and that it was high time for Africans to give up the blame game over colonialism and do the proper *work*. This was George Ayittey, and he's still at it, speaking his mind and defying the image of the tweedy, quiet economist who digs into a folder of stats. Ayittey has those, to be sure, but he also points an accusing finger at deeds. An associate scholar with the Foreign Policy Research Institute, he founded and helms the Free Africa Foundation. He served as an adviser to Barack Obama's administration and was once ranked among *Foreign Policy* magazine's "Top 100 Public Intellectuals."

Born in Ghana, he attended Adisadel College, one of the boarding schools for Africans set up during the colonial era. His friend and contemporary, retired Ghana diplomat Patrick Hayford, says such schools were the rough equivalents of Britain's Eton and Harrow, producing "almost the entire elite of colonial Africa" (Hayford himself attended Adisadel's rival institution, Mfantsipim School).[26] Ayittey studied at university in the late sixties and seventies, during some of the most tumultuous years on the African continent. Mobutu Sese Seko tightened his grip on Zaire (later the Democratic Republic of Congo) and made it into a police state. Meanwhile, Idi Amin evicted thousands of South Asians from Uganda and turned the Nile into a river of blood with the corpses of journalists, lawyers, religious leaders, and ordinary victims of different ethnic groups, such as the Ancholi and Lango peoples.

As the 1980s began, Ayittey's own native Ghana was steered by a military junta and riddled with corruption; the country's police, for example, drove around in expensive BMWs, claiming they needed these flashy cars to apprehend criminals.[27] Ayittey, however, was half a world away getting his master's in London, Ontario, and his PhD in economics at the University of Manitoba in Winnipeg, a Canadian city famous for its bone-chilling temperatures in winter (this author, by the way, was across town, attending high school).

When I asked Ayittey whom he considered influences on his work, he replied that no particular person—African or westerner—had shaped his outlook. "I have always felt 'alone' intellectually." And yet he shares an iconoclastic streak with several of the innovators we've discussed so far. Like Cheikh Anta Diop, he ran into trouble with his doctoral thesis. He wrote that Africa faced an impending crisis due to ongoing misguided leadership, corruption, senseless civil wars, military vandalism, and tyranny. "My thesis committee hit the roof and ordered me to expunge all references to internal factors from my thesis. I refused, and for nine months I battled them." In the end, however, he gave in because a job was waiting for him at Wayne State College in Nebraska.[28]

He managed to get his provocative opinion pieces published in the *Wall Street Journal* in the mid-eighties Long before pop stars and pundits advocated for Third World debt to be forgiven, Ayittey argued the opposite. He believed many countries had misused or squandered their loans, and forgiving such debts simply rewarded irresponsible, incompetent behavior. Instead, creditors should insist on reforms.[29] For his article titled "A Double Standard in Black and White," he conceded that "apartheid is an abomination" but reminded his readers that many African dictators advocating for majority rule in South Africa had declared themselves "presidents for life." Ayittey noted how the UN didn't condemn the tyranny in black regimes lest it be viewed as interfering in domestic affairs. "South Africa is not a sovereign nation, it might be argued—its government is illegitimate and unrepresentative of its people. But what African government *is* legitimate and representative?"[30]

By his own account, this article put him on the map. He received invitations to write for other newspapers, congressmen asked him to testify, think tanks requested he write books. The Hoover Institution was eager to get him as a National Fellow, and later he joined the Heritage Foundation as a Bradley Resident Scholar. But his strong views also made him a target. "In Africa, they [the authorities] banned my books, trailed my movements, raided my hotel room in Nairobi."[31] One especially bizarre episode happened in Dakar, Senegal, in 1994.

He was making a quick purchase at the airport when the cashier offered change in West Africa CFA francs. Ayittey refused, knowing they were virtually worthless and insisted that he get dollars back. "Soon, some kind of altercation took place," recalled Ayittey, "and they went and brought the police inspector. The police inspector saw me and said, 'I know this guy, he's a troublemaker.'" Ayittey tried to explain his position and for his trouble wound up in detention for hours. "I was trying to tell them that the money was worthless. And to them that was an insult."[32]

Granted one phone call, he reached out to a cousin who worked at the United Nations, and the cousin rushed down to the airport, bringing along one of Ayittey's books with his picture on the back cover. "And he told them, 'You know who you have put in the cell?' And I think that sort of worked them up a bit."[33] It took another hour and a missed flight, but he eventually walked free.

"What made his writings so powerful was that he always had his data, his irrefutable facts," recalls Patrick Hayford. Hayford, now retired, served as a distinguished diplomat for Ghana, including as high commissioner to South Africa, acting high commissioner to the U.K., and director for African affairs in the office of UN Secretary-General Kofi Annan. Ayittey "was brutally frank and frankly brutal in setting out in stark terms the corruption, the malfeasance, the incompetence, the stupidity, the cruelty of Africa's leadership as well as of the elites. He regularly named names. He quoted specific incidents, he highlighted gross human rights abuses. At that time, nobody else had the courage to do this. That is why he was attacked so viciously."[34]

In reviewing Ayittey's *Africa in Chaos* for the *New York Times Book Review* in 1998, Jeremy Harding called the economist "a writer who takes no prisoners—especially when it comes to Africa's postcolonial leaders—and his description of a continent in chaos at the end of the millennium has one or two poignant echoes of Fanon's Africa in the twilight of the colonial period. There's a distinct echo, above all, in Ayittey's call for radical change the length and breadth of the continent. But his 'common-sense' revolution could not be farther from Fanon's. Not only is it hostile to the old Marxist paradigms; it is based on a profound suspicion of history."[35]

In his 2004 book *Africa Unchained: The Blueprint for Africa's Future*, Ayittey concluded, "Africa is a mess—economically, politically and socially." He ripped into figures such as Liberia's Charles Taylor, writing, "The leadership in Africa is a despicable disgrace to black people. I won't back down from these 'harsh words' because I am angry—very angry—and I am not alone in feeling this way."[36] And in his 2011 book *Defeating Dictators*, he directed some of his wrath at America and Europe, pointing out how "Tunisian pro-democracy demonstrators got no help from the West—zilch." The biggest impediment to democracy in Africa, he argued, has been the West's national security agenda. "Democratization efforts are often abandoned when they clash with these interests. The argument here is not that the West should abandon its interests—all countries pursue their own national interests—but that it should be honest about the fact that promoting democracy is not its primary goal."[37]

Now at an age when most scholars would enjoy retirement and an "emeritus" attached to their names, he's still ready to jump on a plane for keynote speaking engagements halfway around the world. He's also a feisty, even combative personality on Twitter who has both his fans and his detractors, quite willing to debate Africa's economics and its history over social media. "What kind of stupid question is this?" he once replied to a rather vulgar attack that accused him of playing up to a white establishment.[38] On an April morning in 2020, he commented in a retweet, "The character of many South African politicians stinks. Quack revolutionaries, crocodile liberators, vampire elites, briefcase bandits. Where is my cutlass?"[39]

He has, however, modified his old view over forgiving African debt, arguing that it wasn't the powerless African peoples who accrued staggering sums but their corrupt and incompetent leaders. His position remains a nuanced one. "In the past, African governments borrowed recklessly and spent the money on economically unproductive investments and projects. So if you wipe the slate clean, if you don't put a set of provisions on it, it will give them the incentive to borrow and waste the money again." He also insists that debt relief should go only to the countries that "at least have some democratic accountability."[40]

He is perhaps best known today for developing his unique categories of "hippos" and "cheetahs." The hippos are the corrupt, greedy leaders and complacent bureaucrats who have betrayed the continent. The cheetahs are the young entrepreneurs who have the potential to save it, individuals who value a free market economy and who might be able to attract foreign investment. Only a handful of years ago, Ayittey had talked about trying to develop a fund to supply promising cheetahs with mezzo capital—roughly between $10,000 up to $200,000, "but they are not well organized into a formidable force that I would have liked," and the initiative has fallen behind. He would "hate to go to Western donors and ask them for it because that would be counter-productive and counter to everything I stand for. Nor will I go to African governments and ask them for money after me being so critical of their governments."[41]

While another leg of his cheetah generation concept is to build a network of those with potential, this initiative has also stalled for the time being—mainly because many successful businesses in Africa thrive on their connections to corrupt governments. "So if I was to sort of promote the idea of a cheetah generation, which is clean, it will be difficult for me to go to such businesses with bad reputations." Such setbacks seem to only reinforce his condemnations of the overall state of Africa.

Jeremy Harding noted that "without the active presence of the United States and France in central Africa during the 1960s, we might never have heard of Mobutu Sese Seko. Ayittey has surely not forgotten that in the dark days of the Cold War, many of Africa's dictators were puppets—and that the strings were pulled chiefly in Washington, Paris and Moscow."[42] Whether Ayittey remembers them or not, he has never been patient with those who shift the blame or trace the continent's problems back to the colonial era, which he has called "disingenuous."

Yet those who praise his books can misunderstand his outlook as easily as his critics. After lauding Ayittey's "brave and reflective" *Africa in Chaos*, Geoffrey Wheatcroft—a veteran of the right-wing papers in Britain who once reported on South Africa—opined in the *Wall Street Journal*, "My own view is that Europe played a mean trick on Africa, going beyond imperial malice or greed, through the extremely short duration of formal empire. Africa would be better off if Europeans had either never colonized it in the first place or stayed there much longer, until political and economic institutions had taken root in reality rather than theory."[43]

Such a rehash of White Man's Burden couldn't be further from what Ayittey has recommended as a cure for the continent's ills, which has urgent relevance to our examination of African Ideas. He has long been a champion of the continent's own homegrown mechanisms of government, the kind discussed in chapter 4, and its native practices of market economy. He wrote an entire book on the subject, *Indigenous African Institutions*. Not everyone agrees. I put his ideas to Abdi Ismail Samatar, whom you'll remember from chapter 15. He respects Ayittey as a scholar but parts company with him over a wholesale revival of such practices. "Colonialism has changed the world whether we like it or not," and instead, he argues, we should look to what principles can be teased out of the old traditions.

"What are the principles that guided such cultures and societies for problem solving? . . . How can we revisit them in a modern area in a world that's different from what it used to be?" These are the takeaways for Samatar "rather than bringing the whole thing forward lock, stock, and barrel."[44]

And with our seemingly inexorable drift away from traditional ways of life into the Amazon drone deliveries and Netflix binges of our disposable global culture, you might be skeptical of a return to the governing models of village elders.

"No, no, no, you are arguing just like an African," Ayittey told me during a phone call. "Listen, we still have kings in Africa. We still have chiefs in Africa. We still have village markets in Africa. We still have our traditional systems in Africa." When countries implode through political turmoil or civil war, such as Somalia, the Congo, or Ethiopia, "the only things that are left are two things: their religions and their traditional systems, the elders and the chiefs, they are still there. Now take a look at the U.S. The U.S. Constitution is more than 200 years old. I have never, ever heard anybody . . . an American, say that, 'Look, we can't go back to that ancient constitution because it is too old.'" In the traditional model, a chief is held to the principle of accountability. "It's nothing new to Africa. If a chief is corrupt, we remove him from power. We are still doing it."[45]

To Ayittey, there were three reasons for the early regimes in postcolonial Africa abandoning their own indigenous institutions. First, they believed the colonial mythology that such institutions were backward and primitive, so they couldn't rely on them to engineer a socialist state. Second, many African leaders associated free markets and democracy with the capitalism of the West. "Since colonialism was evil and exploitative, they believed that capitalism, too, was evil and exploitative. So they rejected capitalism and chose the antithesis of capitalism, which was socialism."[46] Third, many leaders during the struggle for independence got support from communist and socialist countries such as Cuba, so it was natural for them to adopt their economic systems.

Our conversation took place when for the first time in close to 100 years, Americans could openly, seriously discuss socialism without being branded as dangerous radicals and tossed into jails. But many young leftists and liberals fail to make a distinction between "pure" socialism, with the government owning the means of production, and the kind of democratic social welfare net (for example, national health care) that's developed in much of Europe. Similarly, a whole generation of Africans in different countries are growing up fully aware of regime corruption but perhaps not realizing how Marxism was once treated as a panacea that plunged their nations into economic ruin.

Part of the problem comes from a misinterpretation of the idea of the African collective. For instance, in 1984, Nigerian poet and philosophy professor Ifeanyi Menkiti wrote that a crucial distinction "exists between the African view of man and the view of man found in Western thought: in the African view it is the community which defines the person as person, not some isolated static quality of rationality, will, or memory." Because "personhood is something at which individuals could fail," wrote Menkiti, African societies "emphasized the rituals of incorporation and the overarching necessity of learning the social rules by which the community lives" so that the individual can attain "social self-hood."[47]

Let's focus on the last statement about learning social rules. Well, what is so different here than what we find in myriad examples of accepted rituals in Western culture? From today's early games taught in kindergarten to admission interviews for university, from marriage dowries in the Middle Ages to behavior of audiences at the theater in Boswell's and Johnson's time, Western behavior has always had its rituals, too. It's only in our modern era that we've come to see society as growing less formal and having less structure. But community defined human beings in the West for centuries as much as it did in African cultures, so Menkiti is one of many who saw through the mirage of exceptionalism.

It's worth noting that in his essay, he drew on Placide Tempels's old conceptions and John Mbiti's ideas, as well as traditional Nigerian Igbo thought. In other words, Menkiti seems to have looked at the problem, as so many others have before, through a very narrow spectrum. You could argue that so did Steve Biko, but his approach, which indicates an "African humanism," doesn't imply an oppressive, stifling communal rule. The narrower view is perhaps how so many made the leap from a sense of African community to Marx.

In contrast, Ayittey dug through the history texts. His *Indigenous African Institutions* offers a survey on an almost exhaustive range of cultures across the continent. And he argues that in traditional Africa, the means of production has always been privately owned. When you visited a village and asked who the land belongs to, you were told, "The land belongs to us." But this casual answer referenced a specific definition. It meant the villager's extended family or clan, "which were immediately misinterpreted by Europeans," as the land belonged to "every Tom, Dick and Harry in the village. The extended family is the basic social and economic unit in Africa." The extended family was, in fact, a *private* entity. Such ideologies as communism were never indigenous to the continent. "There were free village markets in Africa, there was free enterprise in Africa, there was free trade in Africa. These are ancient institutions that are as valid today as they were back then. And this is what we have to go back to and build upon."[48]

We can quibble over the potential effectiveness and the minutiae of how Ayittey's recommended policies would work, but at least his ideas are meticulously derived *from* and tailored *to* the continent, unlike so many of the "solutions" imposed on Africa before. This alone makes listening to Ayittey worthwhile and should earn him a place in the pantheon of African innovators. The modern world doesn't keep many slots for prophets, but it will listen now and then to the economist. Few ever become famous or household names like John Maynard Keynes, Milton Friedman, and Robert Reich. Being an economist is a little like being a novelist, always in danger of losing that most valuable of currencies, relevance. As with his colleagues, time will decide if George Ayittey is right.

But in time, he may come to be valued as one of the world's great economic historians. No one else has given such a detailed, devastating critique of the political dynamics of African nations and their economic fallout. True, his books like *Defeating Dictators* and *Africa Unchained: The Blueprint for Development* were not intended to be read as histories but as serious explorations of what was happening in Africa at the time they were written. They were critical studies, urgent warnings. Nevertheless, one or two may become classics.

We still read Adam Smith's *The Wealth of Nations*, and we read it not only as theory but as economic history. John Kenneth Galbraith's *The Great Crash of 1929* was written in 1954 as history, and it's reprinted again and again with each major stock market peril. So, it should not surprise anyone if a couple of George Ayittey's books, such as *Africa Betrayed* and other works, are eagerly thumbed through by students and analysts of future generations.

20

Exiles and Expats

In 2016, a young, vivacious Ethiopian woman named Selam Kebede landed a great job researching tech start-ups in the developing world. Travel was a given—in fact, she needed to visit more than twenty countries for work. But Selam soon discovered that having a passport wasn't enough to go jaunting around Africa. She needed visas, and getting them involved not only exasperating paperwork but processing fees from the various nations—some as high as U.S.$70. When they were all tallied up, they might cripple her budget.

The embassy of one nation on her itinerary demanded that she get verification from Ethiopia's Foreign Ministry that she wasn't a criminal. Then the people she would be working with abroad would have to send her a formal invitation, one verified by *their* Foreign Ministry that they were entitled to do this and that they agreed to assume legal liability for her. Even after the various hoops she had to jump through, the visa would still take about three weeks to process. At another embassy, "the guy at the desk went ahead and kind of proposed. He said he is looking for a wife and I might just be her. He had to take my number for 'work purposes' while saving it on his phone and told me to come back on Monday to know how long it would take to get the visa."[1]

Why, she asked in a *Medium* article that year, was it so difficult for Africans to travel in Africa? "What are we afraid of, or more like, why are we afraid of ourselves?" Given how Americans and Europeans had "messed the whole continent up," she found it ironic that Americans and Europeans "could simply walk in to almost all of the African countries" while she and her fellow citizens who lived in Addis Ababa—the capital that served as headquarters for the African Union—had the least access to the continent.[2]

But Selam persevered. She learned that part of the logistical nightmare is that where you apply can decide the result. She'd naturally begun by submitting her applications to embassies in Addis Ababa. "Some countries are almost impossible," she explained to me in an interview in 2020. "I couldn't go to Angola—it would have taken at least six months to even try and get the visa, which I wouldn't have even been guaranteed to get. Same with Botswana and the DRC [Democratic Republic of Congo]."[3] She says she went to the Foreign Ministry of Ethiopia in the hopes of securing a letter of support, but it was beyond the officials' comprehension that an African needed to travel frequently for business. Immigration bureaucracy, both in Africa and in the West, believes the most secure way of controlling traffic is to let the African visit—and then ensure the African goes directly home.

Only Selam had to journey to multiple destinations. "They couldn't even process that, and their system doesn't allow for that as well." So after getting the visas she *could* secure at home, she basically winged it, hopscotching along, visiting Nigeria and getting her visa to Ghana from there; from Ghana, getting into Mali; and so on.

Just as troubling is the fact that many Africans cannot even *leave* the continent. One of the things most white British, Americans, Germans, French, and so on take utterly for granted is their ability to travel to almost anywhere they please. They can decide on the spur of the moment to see Paris. They can study in Brussels or Munich. This is denied to much of the world's population. One of Europe's leading intellectuals of African descent, Asfa-Wossen Asserate, drives home this lesson in his book *African Exodus*: "Whenever there is talk of 'illegal' or 'irregular' migrants, one thing should always be borne in mind: for

Africans there is virtually no possibility of emigrating to Europe by legal means. The freedom of movement that most Europeans take for granted simply does not exist for Africans. The majority of those who live in the Southern Hemisphere are prevented from moving around the world freely."[4]

The European Union has its Schengen area, in which more than two dozen countries work as a single jurisdiction, allowing its nationals to move about freely and live and work where they please under normal circumstances. As Asfa-Wossen points out, to get a visa for the Schengen, the average African "must state their reason for wishing to travel and prove that they will not pose a financial or other risk to their host country. In addition, they are required to present bank statements, a business license or proof of income, a return ticket and valid health insurance documentation. It takes an outlay of several thousand euros to amass all the documents that are needed to get a visa. The requirements for issuing a visa to citizens of West African states like The Gambia are even more strict. European consulates there often demand that an applicant present letters of invitation from each host country he or she intends to visit, or declarations of surety for potential financial expenses."[5]

The data prove his point. Immigration from outside the EU is still the responsibility of its individual member states. For years, Germany took in more applicants for asylum than any other country in the EU.[6] But times have changed, and when DW News pored over visa applications between 2014 and 2017, it discovered that African nationals topped the list of those Germany rejected—twice as many as applications from Asia and with only one in five applications given a thumbs-up.[7] Despite the German Foreign Ministry claiming otherwise, the numbers strongly suggest that applicants were being penalized for the political situations in their home countries. Twenty-eight percent of applicants from Ghana were rejected, while a whopping 44 percent of applicants from Cameroon were rejected; South Africa, seen whether rightly or wrongly by the West as one of the more stable nations on the continent, had only 6 percent of their applicants rejected.

It's not just a bias at visa centers—it starts right at the policy level. Germany wanted to add Maghreb states to the list of "safe countries," which would mean refugees from those nations would be almost instantly rejected if they tried to seek asylum. The strategy would shamelessly ignore the persecution of LGBTQ people that goes on in Morocco, Tunisia, and Algeria as well as turn a blind eye to those tortured and persecuted for being political dissidents.[8]

Things are not better in Britain, as revealed in a report published by the All-Party Parliamentary Group on Africa in 2019. Its researchers crunched the numbers of Home Office quarterly statistics and found that while 12 percent of all visa applications for visits were refused between 2016 and 2018, the refusal rate for Africans was 27 percent, more than double the norm. According to the report, "some case studies demonstrated questionable and sometimes offensive reasons for refusals." A celebrated choreographer and two dancers from the Democratic Republic of Congo were set for a performance that drew on their personal experiences of the country's civil war. The entry clearance officers turned them down because they "could not understand why dancers from the UK could not fill these roles."[9]

The U.K. visa system appears rigged in ways that might be hauntingly familiar to African Americans dealing with voter suppression in the United States. An applicant can be sent off again and again to provide more paperwork. Kenyan author Nanjala Nyabola considers the system "inhumane and degrading."[10] Assumptions are made about an applicant's financial status, and even when the applicant has a credible U.K. sponsor that will foot the whole bill, the person is forced to jump through hoops and can still be turned down over minor discrepancies. Government ministers and African Union commissioners aren't immune from the humiliating process either, one that demands they provide highly personal information. "Despite many years of independent evidence showing alarmingly high levels of errors and inconsistency in decision making, there is no right of appeal or redress for applicants."[11]

Even past success is no guarantee of seeing Europe again. After studying electrical engineering in Ethiopia, Selam Kebede earned a scholarship to get her master's degree in Helsinki and lived in Finland for five years before deciding to return home. Eight months later, she was invited to a conference back in Finland—only the embassy denied her a visa. "It was the funniest thing ever!" says Selam. "It was so confusing, I don't understand. That's when I created havoc."[12]

Because she had many contacts in Finland plus knew the conference organizer in Ethiopia, she could draw on a wide network for her lobbying efforts. As a result, "now I'm even awarded [the status of] a Finnish special envoy for Ethiopia, so I'm like an ambassador," she laughs. "I work a lot with the Finnish embassy to try to strengthen the Finnish-Ethiopian relationship, especially for Ethiopian students who went to Finland and want to come back, or for Finnish students who want to come to Ethiopia. I really am very active to try to help out whenever I can, so they gave me this honorary title, which is great. . . . I love the country, I go there, we do a lot of work—even now, I try to bring a lot of Finnish investors to come to Africa and help my school in Finland to support more international students."

And her stories of visa troubles don't even stop there. While still working on her master's in Helsinki, she was once the team lead on a project that was supposed to take her to Pace University in New York. The U.S. embassy kept denying her visa because it claimed she didn't have sufficient ties to Finland to believe that she would return there after visiting America. Embassy officials pointed out that she wasn't married and didn't have children—the kind of rebuke that would prompt an American woman to launch a discrimination lawsuit if this were done in a job interview in Seattle or Boston. Her university was adamant that she was essential to the trip to New York. "They made me go four times. It was such a drama. The university in New York was writing, our university, the dean . . . everyone's writing them."

She says at her first try, the official at the embassy didn't spend two minutes and denied her on the spot. On her second attempt, another official expected her to go all the way home to Ethiopia to apply to the U.S. embassy there and told her, "You know why we do this is because unfortunately, we look at data, and in the past a lot of people from your country went to the U.S. and never came back." This failed to impress Selam. "And I'm like, 'How is that my problem?' First of all, this makes no sense. That should not be a reason how you measure another person's opportunity. . . . You can't really decide for me based on what other people have done. Why are you penalizing me? And the fact that they don't get that treatment when they come here [to Africa], it's just what bothers me the most."

In the end, the official dealing with her fourth visa application chose to "take a risk."

And these are the experiences of only one individual and a highly accomplished one at that. Selam Kebede was awarded a Mandela Washington Fellowship at Dartmouth College in 2016. Now living in Nairobi, she's a director at a venture capital firm working with tech start-ups. But in November 2019, she wanted to travel to Indonesia for a diving holiday and still ran into trouble, though she can laugh about it now. She believes the authorities probably first assumed she was an American, as they might have seen more black American women, but when they saw her Ethiopian passport, they demanded, "What are you doing here? 'I'm here to dive.' What? By *yourself?* Where did you get the money from? So obviously, you're a drug mule or something. No, this story doesn't add up, so let's interrupt you for a bit. This happens a lot."

Even Canada—the country that's enjoyed so many laurels from the world over its liberal values and tolerance—has a terrible record for how it treats African migrants. The country's national network, the CBC, discovered that Africans are least likely to obtain visas than visitors from any other continent.[13] For at least two years running, Ottawa refused dozens of visas to African applicants hoping to attend an artificial intelligence conference in Vancouver. What makes these policies doubly foolish is that they also hurt the sectors in the host country because organizers—tired of seeing their delegates rejected and anticipating the worst—opt to move their conferences to more receptive locales. Or not hold them at all.

Europeans first came to Africa for its gold and other goods. Then it decided it wanted Africa's people *as* goods and loaded them with the grim efficiency of stacking cordwood into the holds of ships. Time passed, and after various pieties that veiled a reconsideration of balance sheets, Europe and America decided that slavery wasn't very profitable, morally or economically, yet less than twenty years after the U.S. Civil War, the Great Powers of Europe could rationalize forced labor. In their Scramble for Africa, they were hungry for palm oil, ivory, rubber, and, most important, land. African people could either get out of the way, preferably by dying from a machine gun—or pick up a basket or pickax. Time passed, and while nations across Africa celebrate their independence each year, the West still wants to raid its stores.

As for the people? To the West, they're still inconvenient.

It wasn't always like this. In July 1964, Malcolm X spoke at a Cairo summit of the Organization for African Unity, the forerunner to the African Union. His speech was a call for solidarity with blacks in America facing abuses of their civil rights, and he made these remarkable observations. "Recently," he said, "three Kenyan students mistaken for black Americans were brutally beaten by the New York police. Shortly afterwards, two Ugandan diplomats were also beaten by the same police, who had mistaken them for African Americans. If Africans are treated like that when they are just visiting America, imagine the multiple sufferings that your brothers and sisters who live on this earth endure. Our problem is your problem.

"No matter how much independence Africans gain on the mother continent, if you do not wear the traditional dress of the country you come from all the time when you visit America, you could be mistaken for one of us and suffer the same mutilations that we go through on a daily basis. Your problems will never be fully solved until ours are solved. You will never be fully respected until we, too, are respected. You will never be recognized as free human beings until we, too, are recognized and treated as free human beings."[14]

He then pleaded with his audience for African states to lobby the UN so it would investigate American police brutality and systemic racism. Not much came of this notion, and if he was serious about this tactic, then he vastly overestimated the clout of the newly independent countries. But what's fascinating here is that Malcolm X anticipated that Africans would someday be *back* in the wider world again more than ever before. He saw the future—that Europe would still frequently echo America's contempt for any black face that dared show itself in distant capitals. While it is true that he was speaking of Africans visiting the U.S., he was naturally aware of the racism that Africans encountered in Britain, France, and elsewhere. The crisis of thousands of African refugees seeking asylum in Europe—with thousands being turned away—would have caused him profound concern.

In 1968, when Asfa-Wossen Asserate first came to Germany as a student, he didn't need a visa. This was way back before the euro, back when each country had its own brightly colored, idiosyncratic notes: British pounds, French francs, German deutsche marks. He was nineteen years old, and when he stepped off the plane, he didn't have any European currency. "Do you know what I had? Ethiopian dollars. I went into Frankfurt airport. There was a bank there, I took out my Ethiopian *birr*, put it on the counter and got DM 1.65 for one Ethiopian *birr*. The only currency that was convertible in Africa! Why? It was backed by gold. The first and last time that Ethiopian currency has been exchangeable—ever since then, forget it. What is it today? One euro amounts to forty-five *birr*. How are we going to explain this to another generation?"[15]

Without knowing it at the time, he would make Germany his home for decades, and he would be one of the lucky ones.

In 1973, reports of famine emerged in Ethiopia's Wollo province. Elderly and isolated, Emperor Haile Selassie had clung to power but had grown to rely on a circle of petty courtiers. While blame would fall on his shoulders for the famine, retired ambassador Imru Zelleke—who knew the man, who recognizes his faults and virtues—believes that court officials kept much of the truth about the famine from the emperor. The next year on the heels of public outrage, the Marxist Derg came to power, hijacking the student revolution that sought reforms over the country's crushing economic problems and social disparities. It summarily executed more than sixty politicians and government figures, including Asfa-Wossen's father, Prince Asserate Kassa, who was the last president of Ethiopia's Imperial Crown Council. The young student couldn't go home now even if he wanted to. When his passport expired, he couldn't obtain a new one.

It was just as well that he didn't go back. Having killed dozens of members of the government, it was no great leap for the Derg to murder the emperor, and there's strong evidence that its leader, Mengistu Haile Mariam, committed the act himself, suffocating the weak and elderly Haile Selassie with a pillow. The regime embarked on a campaign of slaughter, rape, torture, and destruction from 1977 to 1978 that made them the Khmer Rouge of Africa. There's even a museum for the Derg's "Red Terror" in Addis Ababa, where during my visit I saw plastic boxes loaded with skulls and bones.

To this day, it's unclear how many thousands the Derg murdered, perhaps as many as 500,000 people.[16] First, they went after the idealistic students who sparked the initial revolution as well as the old royals; then it was Eritrean nationalists and Oromo separatists, and, in the end, their targets could be practically anyone. Then they began cannibalizing their own, killing the brain trust behind their literacy and land reform programs. A bloody civil war ended them, but they were replaced by the controversial Ethiopian People's Revolutionary Democratic Front.

Asfa-Wossen Asserate was luckily absent for all of this. In fact, in 1974, he was such a rarity in Frankfurt am Main as a political refugee that it took no more than a week for his asylum claim to be accepted. After seven years, he would obtain his German citizenship. While still in university, he founded the first human rights group for his native land—the Council for Civil Liberties in Ethiopia—pushing for the release of all political prisoners. (He stopped operating it years later after the renowned academic Mesfin Woldemariam started the Ethiopian Human Rights Council—the move was so the two organizations wouldn't have to compete.) Once out of school, he worked as a freelance journalist and press officer and over time carved out a reputation in Germany as a distinguished political analyst, writer, and consultant advising midsized German companies on their investments in Africa.

By 1991, he was big enough for *The Spectator* to notice, and it sent Ian Buruma around to profile him, interviewing him at The Traveller's Club in London, where he was a member. Buruma wrote that it was tempting to see Asfa-Wossen as a comic opera figure, "a bit like those White Russians in Paris in the 1930s, dreaming of restoring the Tsar, even as they were reduced by unfortunate circumstances to guarding the doors of fashionable restaurants, selling, as it were, their aristocratic allure."[17]

This comparison was not meant to be cutting—quite the opposite. Buruma took Asfa-Wossen's ambitions seriously, including his goal to start a new political party in Ethiopia, which by then had at last kicked out the Derg. And you can still see what Buruma meant. Always impeccably dressed in a tailored suit, Asfa-Wossen Asserate is from an older generation that learned to speak their minds in proper, complete sentences—not a barnacle nonsense word of "like" ever clinging to his perfectly rounded Oxbridge tones. The political ambitions, however, had to be quickly shelved as Ethiopia traded one repression for another, adopting a system of ethnic federalism that ensured the country's different cultural groups would be at each other's throats for the next thirty years. The victor of these petty ethnic political feuds was the Tigray People's Liberation Front, and its legacy of corruption, oppression, and torture over twenty-seven years is still fresh for many Ethiopians and why there was substantial support in the country for Prime Minister Abiy Ahmed's crackdown on the TPLF's rebellion in 2020.

Discussing the war on a DW News talk show that year, Asfa-Wossen Asserate declared, "For me, the root of all evil is the Ethiopian constitution." The country remains unique in having set up in the 1990s an ethnic federation. "Ethiopia became the most racist country in the world. We're the only place in Africa where in our identity cards, you have the word *race* written on it." All the politics in the country had been based on ethnicity. "The parties were ethnic, our borders were ethnic. And you know, we have seen in the world where you have ethnic borders, ethnic cleansing is not very far away."[18] He was right, for the year was stained with the blood of multiple massacres.

Asfa-Wossen Asserate. *Author's private collection.*

Insight is a rare gift for a writer. Good style, sensing the market, these are useful skills, but *understanding*—that's talent. In his 2003 best seller *Manieren* ("Manners"), he examined the basis for European civilization. He wrote a widely praised biography of his great-uncle, Haile Selassie, *King of Kings.* And then he turned his attention to the problems of Africa. His success has not blunted his compassion. Here is how he punctures the miserly distinction people draw between refugees fleeing terrorism and war and those who are branded "economic refugees," a dirty label these days for immigration officials. "Anyone who fears for his life because he doesn't have enough to eat finds himself in just as desperate a situation as a person who is being persecuted for his faith or his political convictions. Food and water shortages, a lack of work, an inadequate educational system and a non-existent health service: can a person escaping such a situation be said to be fleeing voluntarily?"[19]

But many of Europe's leaders have stopped caring. They have made their continent into a high-tech fortress with sea patrols, drones, cameras, and biometric data, and as if that's not enough, they are determined to keep Africans from even leaving home. As Asfa-Wossen points out, dictators in northern Africa, such as Tunisia's Zine el-Abidine Ben Ali and Libya's Muammar

Gaddafi, performed Europe's dirty work for years. Internment camps held those who tried to flee their nations while they were richly rewarded with the lifting of sanctions and arms embargoes and the disbursement of billions of euros to be used for "refugee control."[20] The Arab Spring upset this cozy arrangement with both leaders kicked out of power, but Europe keeps finding ways to prevent Africans from reaching its shores.

In 2018, a leaked document revealed that the EU thought of building "migrant processing centers in north Africa in an attempt to deter people from making life-threatening journeys to Europe across the Mediterranean."[21] But it hardly needed to—as has always worked before, it just went ahead with paying autocratic states in Africa to keep their people at home. In 2019, Eritrea received €20 million from the EU for construction of a road, a project that was supposed to improve the country's infrastructure—the regime relied on its familiar supply of military conscripts to get the job done. To the EU, this was no problem, even after alarm bells were raised by the media; it sent Eritrea another €95 million.[22]

What is especially disturbing about all this, aside from turning Africa into a virtual prison, is that it revives the toxic rationale of "See, they do it to themselves. . . . They sold themselves into slavery." But as with the slave trade and colonialism, Europe has incentivized African nations to hurt their own citizens and hold them back.

In such conditions, it's little wonder then that middle-class and wealthier Africans can't even use legal means to travel. Asfa-Wossen recalls an incident involving one of his clients, a publisher in the Ivory Coast with a net worth he guesses at $15 million. The publisher wanted to visit Germany to buy a Heidelberg press but was told by embassy officials in Abidjan, "Forget it, you're only going there so that you will be able to hand in your asylum details and you want to stay."

It was a ridiculous notion. What would the man do in Germany when he was one of the richest men in his own country? But this is why people hire consultants. Asfa-Wossen Asserate called up the Foreign Ministry to have a word with the head of the African department. "And I said to him, 'I'll give you exactly two hours to come back to me, because the next telephone call is going to *Der Spiegel*. They would love this."[23] Here, after all, was Berlin trying to compete for African business with Beijing, and yet it wouldn't allow potential buyers of German manufacturing into the country. Asfa-Wossen says the official promised that in half an hour, the publisher's visa would be waiting for him at the embassy in Abidjan.

We have to keep in mind that the publisher had the wealth and position to afford a skilled advocate. Others aren't so lucky and can't even advocate for themselves as effectively as Selam Kebede does. And we're left with the question of why this phenomenon is happening at all. Is it merely another knock-on effect of colonialism? Or is it perhaps an expression of contempt and dread that the developed world has adopted toward postindependent Africa, plagued by coups, terrorism, and instability?

"Well, I think it's a little bit of both of what you said," replies Asfa-Wossen Asserate, and as we examine the problem together, it's clear there is no easy binary answer. To him, the Europeans never really left, and he can correctly point to the financial grip and military presence that France has over francophone Africa. Realpolitik, he insists, has for ages been "the basis of all African policies of all European countries. And what does it mean for us Africans? What does *realpolitik* mean? It means only you can be the greatest culprit that has ever existed in this world. As long as you are in power, we democrats will come crawling on our knees to worship you—God save you if you are no longer in power."

He was quick to remind me of what he calls the Roosevelt factor. The famous story goes that in the 1930s, while Nicaragua was occupied by U.S. Marines, Franklin Roosevelt was asked about Anastasio Somoza, the petty despot who rose to power and who was already demonstrating his indifference to human suffering in his country. Roosevelt purportedly said, "Somoza may be a son of a bitch, but he's *our* son of a bitch." So, Africa is no different than other continents: it's never lacked for SOBs who can be rented or bought outright.

"Now this is the one side," says Asfa-Wossen. "But on the other hand, one also has the right to ask all the other African countries, 'Well you had sixty years now where you could really be independent. What have you done for your people?'" He brought up the issue of massacres. The slaughter in Rwanda is still fresh in memory. "And this is my question: Where has Africa gone to? Where has African humanity gone to? Are we really better off without the colonialists or as leaders of our people, aren't we far, far more inhumane than they were?"

I suggested that this was perhaps dangerous logic. It was clear he wasn't justifying colonialism, but colonial apologists certainly enjoy making such comparisons. He countered that given how people are suffering, "we have to ask the question: What is the reason why Africans are leaving their families, their homes, their own people—is it really only for money? No. It is because the majority of them cannot live a normal life in their own country, because the rulers are of a different religion or they have a different ethnic group or they don't allow you to believe in your political visions."[24]

In reviewing his book, the *Financial Times* sniffed that "Much of the criticism is fair, if hardly groundbreaking," and *Foreign Affairs* conceded, "Even if one does not agree with his normative argument, Asserate is clearly right that in the long run, the only way to moderate illegal migrant flows from Africa is to improve the welfare of Africans at home."[25] I wondered why the reactions were so politely tepid, and I think I've hit on the answer.

Wangari Maathai's books still offer a satisfying "hero's journey" in an African figure overcoming persecution and addressing a problem herself. And some of those who applaud George Ayittey's blistering attacks on African dictators will try to absolve themselves of collective responsibility for Western plundering. Both Maathai and Ayittey make it abundantly clear in their writings that they hold the West accountable, but as we saw with Ayittey's work, this can get overlooked. What is different in Asfa-Wossen Asserate's case is that his arguments can't be easily compartmentalized. He's no bleeding-heart liberal insisting on debt forgiveness, nor does he expect Africa to solve its problems all on its own.

Like any set of useful reforms, his suggestions for improving Africa have depth and require careful consideration. Among them, he wants to see Europe end its unfair trade practices and its dumping of cheap agribusiness goods on developing nations, a practice that turns African farmers into paupers. Europe should stop prowling Africa's coastlines, draining its valuable fishing stocks. He naturally backs the encouragement of good governance, and he favors the idea of an international "audit office" that would check on how development aid is being used and who it's really going to—or not going to. After having the pendulum swing back to "Africa, heal thyself" (or simply, "Africa, go away"), it is indeed a novelty to see a view that incorporates the continent into a globally connected, cooperative economic order.

We can only hope that the rest of the world wakes up and finally recognizes the value of Africa's people, treating them as equals rather than as puzzles or problems to be solved while their goods are carted away. The dissemination of African Ideas doesn't rely completely on the free movement of Africans, but it is strengthened by the opportunity for them to move as they please, gathering and sharing experiences, the same way Europeans and others do. This isn't realpolitik. This isn't sophisticated policy. It's common sense, informed by the natural human compassion that's supposed to be inherent in us all. It is Biko's "importance we attach to Man." All we need to do is start by opening the door. We don't need to menacingly ask, "Can I help you?" We can ask the question with sincere interest . . . and hold the door open.

21

Concluding Remarks

In a fine introduction to an edition of *From Dawn to Decadence*, Peter Conrad noted that its author, Jacques Barzun, disapproved of the method of historians like Arnold Toynbee and Oswald Spengler, who "both looked at events teleologically, determined to find 'a system and a purpose' in the muddled course of human affairs."[1] This, as we know, isn't an unknown impulse among African thinkers. Ibn Khaldun decided that history had cycles and expected decadence, which to him as to Barzun meant decline. Ali Mazrui had his less-than-convincing Triple Heritage. But why does there need to be a system and a purpose at all? Why should historians treat Africa the way that physicists try to shoehorn quantum mechanics into a unifying theory of everything? I find myself siding with Barzun on this one.

We have a different problem with interpretations. History is an educational narrative, but it's also frequently a sales job we pitch ourselves. I mentioned Bronowski and Mazlish's *The Western Intellectual Tradition* back in my introduction. The authors saw the 500 years they covered from Leonardo da Vinci to Hegel as a growing expression of two fundamental ideas: the development of the human personality and the right to dissent. These are fine notions, and there's a lot to be said for them. But it was easy in 1960—with the last world war over and consigned to memory—to think of these expressions of Western civilization culminating before our eyes. It's now routine to dissect its underlying fallacy in university lecture halls, that progress was always inevitable.

An uglier expression of such pride can be found in the work of Bruce Gilley, a professor of political science at Portland State University. In 2019, only weeks after The 1619 Project filled an August issue of the *New York Times Magazine* and inspired scores of African Americans, Gilley had an article posted on the website of the right-wing National Association of Scholars titled "Was It Good Fortune to Be Enslaved by the British Empire?" He argued with no evidence that "the life chances of those enslaved under the British empire improved markedly compared to what they would have been in Africa even as freemen, and certainly compared to other slave colonies in the Americas. Within a flourishing capitalist system, the value put on slaves meant that slave owners had every interest in keeping them healthy."[2]

This, aside from being deeply offensive, borders on grotesque over its distortion of the facts given what we know of the countless beatings, whippings, mutilations, murders, and rapes of African slaves in the British Empire. Only two years before, Gilley had caught the attention of newspapers when his article titled "The Case for Colonialism" was published in *Third World Quarterly*, which later retracted it. The article found a new home at a conservative journal. Gilley openly called for "some areas to be recolonized. Western countries should be encouraged to hold power in specific governance areas (public finances, say, or criminal justice) in order to jump-start enduring reforms in weak states."[3]

In his slavery article, he mischaracterized the destruction and looting by British soldiers of Benin City. In his case for colonialism, he argued there was widespread support for it among indigenous populations. The success of his approach relies on the ignorance of the impressionable. Now, I did not set out to write my chapters on antislavery and colonial resistance with Gilley in mind (I don't think I'd even heard of him when I first drafted the chapters), but nothing brings into relief more the urgent need for accurate renditions on these topics than such perversions of history.

Less overtly racist but no less destructive is *The Right Side of History* by Ben Shapiro, who earns his bread and butter as a right-wing polemicist. "Jerusalem and Athens built science. The twin ideals of Judeo-Christian values and Greek natural law reasoning built human rights. They built prosperity, peace, and artistic beauty. Jerusalem and Athens built America, ended slavery, defeated the Nazis and the Communists, lifted billions from poverty, and gave billions spiritual purpose."[4]

And he goes on like this. *The Right Side of History* is a thin tome (because Shapiro's readers shouldn't be taxed to read too much). It's a lazily written book for lazy people. Shapiro likes to cherry-pick quotes, especially from social sciences and psychologists, while leaving his more sweeping generalizations without any proof. "The United States has freed billions of people." Really? When? How? The statement is ridiculous on its face because of the obvious legacy of slavery and the betrayal of Reconstruction. But even if you wanted to be generous and try to include America's victories in the first and second World Wars over "freeing billions," it didn't act alone but each time as part of a multinational allied force, and in both cases, the United States showed up conspicuously late in the day to do the right thing.

Of course, there is little to no historical context provided for many of Shapiro's declarations. It serves his purpose to talk about democracy as a gift from the Greeks and to trot out Plato's ideas, but Plato had nothing to do with the reality of Athens as a city-state or its government. It's *this* reality that is the true inheritance of Western culture, not just Plato's philosophical musings. It's a democratic model influenced by Pericles, who lived and died before Plato was even born. Shapiro mentions the Donatists in passing, but they're useful only in making a point about Augustine—no mention either that he was African. In fact, Africa doesn't merit a single reference in his index.

What stands out most of all in the book is its breathtaking conceit. For Shapiro, the ideals and values of the Enlightenment "arose in the Judeo-Christian West alone."[5] This is another shamelessly ignorant position. We can argue, if you like, about how far Ethiopia's Zera Yacob got with his philosophy, but the fact that he communicated his ideas at all to his student Walda

Heywat demonstrates that, no, sorry, neither the gardens of Europe nor the soil of America were magically prepared by God (Hebrew or Christian) for the cultivation of liberal ideas. I don't fault Shapiro for not knowing a great Ethiopian thinker, I condemn him for not bothering to look for one—or any other example that contradicts his assertion. Again, lazy. And arrogant. For propagandists like Shapiro, civilization can never be a potluck dinner where different cultures bring what dishes they have to the feast. It must be a competition with a clear winner. It's a pernicious, even dangerous attitude, and, if nothing else, I hope *The Gifts of Africa* has whittled a stake for slaying the vampire of Western exceptionalism.

Those who want to bang on about democracy in ancient Greece forget that even in the time of Pericles, there was no pure democracy. Athens was run by males who had citizenship, and *they* were the ones who got to vote. We talk about democracy as a product of the West in sloppy, imprecise terms when what we're really discussing is an emphasis on *good governance*, one that is accountable to its citizens. And African cultures have clearly had this.

If we go back to the examples of Africans developing a smallpox vaccine and sophisticated techniques for caesarean section, it's obvious that a scientific methodology developed, yet we can't see the gradual steps for it in Africa as often as we do with Western medicine. Nevertheless, the evidence of methods clearly implies a process. Bronowski and Mazlish argued, "The rational analysis of society as a construction to serve and satisfy human needs also begins at the Renaissance." Well, maybe for Europe it does, but as we've seen, much of Africa had already developed cultures in which people were in harmony with their environment and with each other. If West Africa doesn't offer a parade of iconoclastic philosophers and rebels, perhaps it's because the enlightened mechanisms in its societies had no need of them.

This is not the same as judging their cultures unsophisticated. Quite the contrary. You'll recall the Xhosa legal scholars who could take on all comers in debate. Nor do I want to suggest these African cultures were utopias. But they had a place for the skilled artist. There was a place for the talented sculptor and the musician, the architect and the griot, just as the Italian Renaissance had places for Botticelli and da Vinci. The Xhosa jurist who kept the equivalent of a law library in his head probably mulled over heavy philosophical questions all the time, and in working them out, he fulfilled a recognized social function. Why would he want to play the rebel and bring the whole structure of society down? He was part of that structure, as was the most ordinary, humble tender of cattle.

We prize individuality, freedom, and rebellion in the West because we are accustomed to these values, which on a grand timescale are relatively recent additions. But we also appreciate them because they are part of the sales pitch of history that we've written for ourselves, the "epic journey towards the actualization of the individual": Thomas More being obstinate with Henry VIII, the French revolutionaries at the barricades (of course, bursting into catchy Broadway show tunes), rich, white landowners in Virginia and Massachusetts who owned slaves and heroically stood up over taxes to an enemy a whole ocean away. Yet in parts of a larger, greener continent, there was already relative social harmony and communal productivity.

You might search this alternate harmonious reality for an inertia, a lack of innovation, which is a criticism usually tossed at the heavy bureaucratization of Chinese dynasties, but on the whole, I suspect you'll fail. Remember the amazing wonders of a Benin City with public street lighting, Africa's medical innovations and its wealth of manufacturing, the dazzling production of refined, beautiful art. Its cultures were thriving and *progressing* until they were cruelly interrupted. Some have survived, at least partially. The point is that they were never static.

Nor, as we've seen with the revolt against Susenyos and the example of Walatta Petros, was Africa ever without its own conflicts for self-determination and values, its own renegade individualists. Let's not forget Bilali, the slave revolt leader in Sierra Leone who fought for decades. We are so used to measuring by European progress and by dating Africa from either the Atlantic Slave Trade or the colonial Scramble that only a few academics

and historians seem to have evaluated these cultures in terms
that don't compare or contrast them with the West.

Now, if we must identify themes in the narrative of African
ideas, then we can start with the most recognizable one: the
human being's relationship with his own group. Before you sigh and
expect me to rehash *ubuntu* again in terms of the Zulu, Shona,
etc., let me assure you I have another direction in mind. I think
we can find the concern of a human being's place within his
group—the "I am because we are"—in many of the thinkers
profiled. What is Augustine's debate with the Donatists if not a
struggle over group loyalties? And it's no coincidence that Ibn
Khaldun, collecting information from tribes of Amazighs, is the
"father of sociology." Olaudah Equiano suffered the traumatic
memory of being torn from Igbo society, kidnapped and forced
into a strange, new culture in which he was forced to adapt, one
that used him but would never fully accept him. It's no wonder
then that Equiano later sympathized with vulnerable groups
such as the working poor and Irish radicals. The "I am because
we are" is a value, but it's not a solved equation. Africans such
as Augustine, Ibn Khaldun, Equiano, and others have been
expanding on it through the centuries.

Another theme (if it can be called that, for maybe it's more of
a working premise) is the *cooperative nature of African disciplines.*
In Western culture since at least the Middle Ages, science and
faith have been at odds with each other—and still are. Protestants had the Spanish physician Michael Servetus burned at the
stake. The Roman Catholic Inquisition put Galileo on trial and
forced him to recant his scientific findings. Western history is
full of lurid examples of scientists being persecuted, and yet
we hardly learn of similar cases in ancient and medieval Africa.
True, a lack of written sources skews our perception, but we do
retain some historical records. And for all the authoritarianism
of ancient Egypt and Nubia, we have the paradox that mathematics, physics, medicine, and astronomy all flourished under
the pharaohs.

It's also interesting that the scientific advancements and
philosophical development that were fostered in Timbuktu and
at the University of Qarawiyyin didn't spark a crisis in African

Islamic thought, not in the way that heliocentrism threatened institutional Christianity. Africans have always shown a receptiveness to and enthusiasm for scientific innovation and practice. In the summer of 1866, epidemics of cholera, smallpox, and typhus broke out in Ethiopia. Emperor Tewodros had the good sense to consult the Europeans at his royal court over how they handled such crises, and he moved his capital to higher ground and practiced what today we call "social distancing" while quarantining the sick.[6] The West has often compartmentalized its disciplines. Africans have long recognized that science and history, faith and responsible governance, can inform each other.

Still another theme is the deeply ingrained sense of *justice* in African cultures tempered with *compassion*. For example, customary law in Somali culture is unique in its development, and it doesn't even borrow any foreign words for its legal vocabulary. It wasn't punitive but compensatory; for grievous bodily assault, the convicted assailant had to give his victim fifty camels.[7]

That same spirit of fairness can be found in the cousin of jurisprudence, diplomacy. Remember that the kings of Kongo and Dahomey first tried appeals to reason and a sense of humanity over the deep incursions into their lands from the Atlantic slave trade. Centuries later, after the horrors of civilian bombings, poison gas, massacres, and concentration camps, Ethiopia's Haile Selassie told his people in his very first speech after the liberation on May 5, 1941, "Do not reward evil for evil. Do not commit any act of cruelty like those of which the enemy committed against us up until this present time." The Truth and Reconciliation hearings of South Africa aspired to restore balance. Justice for Africans is about order as it is on other continents, but it's not about order for only a government or system of regulation—it's for the *people's harmony*. Which arguably makes it the worthiest justice of all.

It's been put to me that an argument can be made that these are exceptions to a more general phenomenon of bad rule, with numerous examples of Europeans summarily executed. But I would say that, by and large, we tend to measure European and North American governments and systems of justice on the basis of their philosophical ideals as much as their case studies—in other words, their original intent and the best case scenario of them in practice. We celebrate America's Declaration of Independence and France's Declaration of the Rights of Man. We respect Britain and the United States for court systems in which you're judged by a jury of your peers, and it's only recently over the long time line of centuries that their systems have been rigorously challenged over class and racial inequities. Why then do we not give the same benefit of the doubt to African governance and justice? Naturally, we must look at justice in practice as much as justice conceived, but it's interesting that our go-to position for Africa is often its excesses, its corruption, and brutality before the loftier aims of its legal architecture.

The great convulsions of the slave trade and European colonialism imposed three other themes on Africa—Africans certainly didn't create them or set them into motion, but they have been forced to respond to these negative burdens ever since. One is the *psychological impact of these cataclysms*, the collective trauma from these events. As we've seen, those who first examined and dissected the scars and wounds of the African psyche, who first wrote sympathetically and movingly about their effects, were not Africans at all but sons of the Caribbean: Edward Wilmot Blyden, Marcus Garvey, Frantz Fanon. Nevertheless, African thinkers, as well as African American ones, would follow in their footsteps, and they would agree either partially or fully with their analyses and build on their insights.

The second negative theme that grew out of these cataclysms is what I call the *demand for authenticity of experience*. We see it again and again with the questioning of whether Zera Yacob wrote his "Inquiry," the veracity of Olaudah Equiano's narrative, the doubts over the epics of the griots and the oral history of the elders, and the whitewashing of the ancient Egyptians. The people of Africa are entitled to ask, Why is it that every time we make something, you in the West doubt whether we did the job? Even the critical nitpicking over the creations of Ben Enwonwu is essentially a nasty shot on whether the artist was "African enough" or "too African" to be counted among the world's greatest sculptors and painters. The debate over the return of African artifacts and treasures also falls under this category. It is not enough that your culture made these. We have them now. Prove to us you are authentically civilized (according to our measure) and can be trusted with the responsibility of holding on to your own inheritance.

The third negative theme is the *weighing of worth of culture*. Every immigrant, whether expatriate or refugee, is forced to confront the value of one's own culture to him- or herself. When you live in a different country, you quickly discover what you're willing to keep or discard of the identity you brought with you, forcing you to adapt, while at the same time circumstances, experience, and duration will refine the process, sometimes without you even knowing it. It is always a compromise, and there's at least the consolation that you can play an active role in this personal evolution. How worthwhile is your culture to you? But the African has been forced to confront this problem in a very urgent sense in his *own* country.

Throughout time, dominant powers have sought to exterminate not only targeted populations but also their identities. A recent example of this is China's repression of Uyghurs. There is also the persecution of the Rohingya in Myanmar and the Yezidi in Iraq. But never has it been on such an appalling, massive scale as on the African continent, where invaders came and demanded, "Why should this matter, even to you? Get rid of it. It's barbaric, primitive." Or, in so many words, "This is pointless and retards your modernizing."

Blyden took up these issues, and so did economist Gebrehiwot Baykedagn in his own way. Kenyatta's *Facing Mount Kenya* was a fierce response to this demand. Fanon, of course, would offer the most detailed and penetrating critique of his time for weighing the worth of culture in *The Wretched of the Earth*. Diop's work on Egypt was another response. But the theme has persisted. Such was the devastation of these two cataclysms, the slave trade and European colonialism, that Africans have debated it long after the most conspicuous outward trappings of colonialism were gone. But the Europeans never really left. They just switched the game and became "corporate investors." Observers such as Asfa-Wossen Asserate have identified this phenomenon in their works.

So, while we might find themes, there are no *fixed* conclusions to be drawn here because the process of discovery continues. Acquired knowledge has a cultural momentum, and new interpretations will develop as they always do. By considering the negative themes, we are not defaulting to a Eurocentric mode; we're not defining Africans as constantly "reacting to" the issues and traumas imposed by the West. This would be no more accurate for Africans than believing that China still fixates on the Boxer Rebellion. But hopefully, after our long journey together, the reader now appreciates that one of the most silly, patronizing notions is that the African joined the wider world during the independence period. Africans may be assessing their place in the new globalized reality, but so are Europeans and South Americans. So are we all. We should view the responses to these cataclysms as reflections of a wider historical context and recognize that Africans have *always* been active participants in world history and not just victims of events.

In fact, those who study Africa may focus on these two cataclysms and fail to discover another positive theme, which has been apparent throughout our entire tour of African ideas. It is why I find Ali Mazrui's contention that there was no "interest in what lies beyond the horizon" such a criminally ignorant thing to say. In chapter after chapter, we have seen Africans personally and culturally invested in "what's beyond." The ancient Egyptians and Ibn Battuta went to find it, Augustine tried to reconcile it—home with Rome—and Mansa Musa brought "the beyond" right to his own doorstep and his center of learning. But because of the eclipsing power of the slave trade and colonialism, we often ignore the theme before us, the truth that *Africans are "citizens of the world."* They have always had interest not only in their immediate surroundings but in the rest of the globe.

So the irony, the tragedy, is that many Western nations seem hell-bent on keeping Africans at home and preventing even *legal* migration for study, tourism, and putting down roots abroad.

I don't intend for this list of themes I've given here to be a definitive and exhaustive one, and they are useful only up to a point, just as Barzun's themes were for interpreting Western history. Of the ones I've listed, most of the attention that the

West has ever paid to Africa has overwhelmingly dwelled on the two cataclysms, the ones manufactured for the continent. Even with these, the West never quite escapes its own self-absorption. What did *we* do to the African, and can *we* trust what Africans say about themselves? (This second question is more veiled than it used to be, but the challenge is still there.) Sometimes, there is the odd speculation about what would become of Africa had the European powers never colonized it or practiced chattel slavery. I think a better thought experiment is, what would become of Europe had the Africans taken it over?

This is not an original idea for fiction. The writer Bertène Juminer of French Guiana explored it in his short novel *Bozambo's Revenge*. Steven Barnes dreamed up an alternate history of Africa colonizing the New World and using white Europeans as slaves for his novels *Lion's Blood* and *Zulu Heart*. Black British author Malorie Blackman imagined a scenario of Africans colonizing Europe for her young adult novel series *Noughts and Crosses*.

And it remains an intriguing premise to explore from the factual side over how civilization might have developed. You may say, "But we do know, don't we? What about Moorish Spain?" What Muslims called *Al-Andalus*. And it's an interesting case. There, "literacy was far more widespread than in any other country of the West. Almost every branch of study was pursued, from poetry to medicine and philosophy."[8] While instructive, however, Muslim Spain reflects only the conduct of Amazigh and Arabic cultures. I propose two other scenarios worth considering . . .

Let's return to 1324 CE, 724 in the year of the Hijra, and check on the great sultan Musa I on his epic pilgrimage to Mecca. He reaches Cairo, and people have never seen the like. *Come see, come see!* The chant weaves its way through the dusty alleys and roads of the city in the late morning, spreading the word: The fabulous king is making a stop! Here? *Here?* The date sellers and fruit marketers leave their stalls with their sons and daughters. The rich merchants stop fanning themselves in the arcades. Oxcarts block roads and spark petty arguments, which are soon forgotten because now the Legend has been made flesh.

But imagine if during Musa's stop in Cairo, word of his pilgrimage has already reached Rome or Florence and one of these city-states decides to make the biggest bank heist in history.

Landing at Alexandria, Italian soldiers and mercenaries rush across the open country to strike. Only they're not used to the punishing heat, they don't know this land, and the Mali cavalry and skilled warriors with their *tamba*, their javelins, make short work of these foolish knights under the sun. Musa leaves a pitiful, cowering handful of them alive so that a message can be sent back to Europe: *You saw the shine of our wealth from across the sea. You should know: It is the light reflecting off our spears. We will be coming.*

The Italian prince who launched the attack has no idea of the historical forces he's set in motion. After Musa fulfills his religious obligations for the Hajj, he's free to pursue a new agenda along his return leg home. And that is to gather and recruit those who will help him avenge the assault on his procession. His people know nothing of ships or maritime navigation. But taking a page from his enemies, he can *buy* such expertise. Corsairs who plunder the waters around Greece and Rhodes, Cyprus and the Turkish coast, hear of his offers and sign up to join the expedition.

Two years pass from the failed attack in Cairo. And then Italians in Ostia wake up one morning in disbelief as an armada sails into their harbor. The locals know nothing of the Malinke, skilled in saber and spear, easily beating the city's halfhearted army. The Mali army sweeps up and down the peninsula, wrestling away control of Pisa, Genoa, Milan, Florence, Naples. The first mosque in Italy is completed in Florence in 1332, its minaret built almost a century before Brunelleschi's dome on the Cattedrale di Santa Maria del Fiore. Italians can worship as they please in every city-state, but those who don't convert to Islam are subject to the *jizyah*, the tax on nonbelievers. Many, of course, are happy to convert to escape this financial burden, just as many subject peoples did under the Ottoman Empire. And still others, particularly merchants' sons and nobles, make the arduous journey down to the universities of Qarawiyyin in Fez and in Sankoré in Timbuktu.

Is it so preposterous? In this book, I've cited several examples in which European and African forces were on relatively level playing fields in terms of weaponry and military technology, ones where the Africans came out on top. Certainly, the examples of the Moorish conquest of Spain and the Portuguese helping the Ethiopians against invasion tell us it's more than plausible. Edward Gibbon could certainly picture it. He famously imagined in his *Decline and Fall of the Roman Empire* an entirely different outcome for the Battle of Tours in 732 CE, noting "the Rhine is not more impassable than the Nile or Euphrates, and the Arabian fleet might have sailed without a naval combat into the mouth of the Thames. Perhaps the interpretation of the Koran would now be taught in the schools of Oxford, and her pulpits might demonstrate to a circumcised people the sanctity and truth of the revelation of Mahomet."

By Gibbon's time, racist attitudes toward black people had become entrenched, and so his scenario entertains Arabs, not Africans, and is fixed along religious lines. But Europe could have been Africanized without Islamization.

Think back to chapter 5, when we discussed how Ethiopia's emperor Yeshaq suggested a double marriage to forge strong ties with Aragon. It didn't work out. But suppose Yeshaq had found a receptive monarch elsewhere. The first European diplomats to Ethiopia came from France.[9] Instead of Charles VII pinning his hopes of political survival on a teenage Joan of Arc, suppose he bets his fortune on Orthodox Africans finding their way across the Mediterranean?

As the alliance grows stronger over time between Ethiopia and France (or Aragon or even Portugal), there never is a civil war for Susenyos in the 1600s because there's no need for one. The Orthodox Church enjoys a mild resurgence in Western Europe, and it also attracts a young philosopher, Zera Yacob, to settle in the Dutch Republic, where his astonishing notions about individual liberty and doubt over God's existence find a greater audience beyond manuscripts in Ge'ez to readers of Latin. He writes a persuasive case against slavery, inspiring an abolitionist movement just as Portugal and Britain are set to embark on one of the worst genocides of human history—but it's halted before it can progress.

Okay, all these speculations are just that, speculations—fanciful and perhaps mildly entertaining. The point is that even when we consider alternatives in African history, by habit, we hardly ever consider the plausibility of their cultures shaping *our* world, just as Europe shaped Africa. And yet they already have. Yes, they often did it far less dramatically, but the impacts and the contributions are there if only we would recognize them. It perhaps requires a different mind-set or, more precisely, a return to an earlier, more classical mind-set. But one with an adjustment . . .

The culture wars have been going on for some time now, not only in the West but in Africa.

In 2017, at the University of Cape Town, militants blacklisted, vandalized, and burned various artworks during protests—not just work by white artists, but black artists as well. They included two collages that celebrated the life and work of antiapartheid activist Molly Blackburn. As Ivor Powell wrote later for the *SA Art Times*, "some seventy-four works of art from the university's collection—by some of the country's most acclaimed artists—have been taken down or covered up 'on the grounds of their vulnerability to potential damage' or because 'some members of the campus community have identified certain works of art as offensive to them—for cultural, religious or political reasons.'"[10] One of those removed was a portrait of Nelson Mandela.

Ideas matter. The spread or suppression of them can have tangible consequences. It has been less than a century since black South Africans were not even recognized as full citizens of their own homeland nor allowed to fully express themselves, and now ideas by accomplished painters, sculptors, and writers have been under attack.

The knee-jerk response of the media in the wider world might consider this an "African" problem in the same way it treats other issues on the continent with patronizing dismissal. But what happened on the UCT campus demonstrates that South Africa is plugged into the global intellectual network like everywhere else. In Cape Town, we may see art burned, but on

American campuses, there has been violence over controversial speakers invited to lecture. Censorship, whether official or by a small group of extremists, is no more innately African than it is French or American.

If only a select, vetted few can write or teach African history, if only a select, vetted few can create art about Africa, it is only a short step to allowing a select few to *read* African history or view its art. I don't think that's a world that any of us want to live in. It's certainly not the world that Kenya's Tom Mboya hoped for, which is part of why he wrote his opinion piece for the *New York Times*.

While the final draft of this book was being prepared in 2020, the Black Lives Matter movement gathered further momentum and swept the world. That summer, statues of slave traders in Britain and Confederate generals in America were pulled down, and some took issue with how far protesters were willing to go to sweep the board clean. In London, for instance, there was consternation over the statue of Winston Churchill in Parliament Square getting vandalized—Churchill, the cigar-chomping British bulldog who stared down the threat of Nazi invasion (but who indeed was also a notorious racist). Textbooks were pulled, to be reconsidered and revised. The 1619 Project was still being debated on social media. Add to this, a healthy debate went on over appointing more people of color and of African descent as faculty members for African Studies programs.

Yet for watching Africa itself, the obvious has escaped hard scrutiny. Only a year later, few in the West questioned why in the age of Black Lives Matter, most of the correspondents in Africa for major news brands are *white*: Declan Walsh, the chief Africa correspondent for the *New York Times*; Max Bearak, the East Africa bureau chief for the *Washington Post*, its West Africa bureau chief in Nairobi, Danielle Paquette; Jason Burke for *The Guardian*; Sarah Carter, the bureau chief in Johannesburg for CBS News; Alexandra Zavis, the bureau chief in Johannesburg for Reuters; Tom Gardner, who writes from Addis Ababa for *The Economist*; and the list goes on.

While these individuals might all be passably competent at their jobs, that has never been the point. And there is no contradiction with the argument made a moment ago. I am certainly not advocating that only a select few be allowed to report on Africa any more than it's a good idea to have only a vetted few teach African history. But just as African Studies faculties need to do better on diversity, so do bureaus for Western news outlets. Background and frame of reference naturally affect perceptions, and this is especially important when many of Africa's conflicts are rooted in the past. How well does a correspondent know a nation's history or the intricacies of the many cultures involved? And not just for a single country but the whole region?

Moreover, in the age of Black Lives Matter, Western news outlets still make a regular habit of running to nongovernmental organizations, think tanks, and human rights organizations, such as Human Rights Watch or Amnesty International, for juicy quotes and to "interpret" Africa. It is simpler (and lazier) for a white reporter to go to a white conflict analyst in, say, London or New York—because inevitably such experts tend to be conflict analysts rather than historians—to explain why a civil war has broken out in this or that part of the continent. Don't worry about finding proper sources, Amnesty will always pick up the phone. For Western correspondents, their go-to white expert can be someone they're comfortable with and who usually has had media training or interview experience; the expert knows exactly what you want, a complex situation reduced to a convenient sound bite.

As Ethiopia's Tigray situation dominated the headlines in late 2020 and much of 2021, Deutsche Welle chose for one story not to speak to any Africans *at all*, only three white experts: a conflict analyst, an academic, and a journalist and author.[11] In tweeting about the controversy, Gerry Simpson, an associate director at Human Rights Watch, sometimes didn't bother to even use photos of Ethiopia but ones from the Gulf War, Iraq War, and Somalia. Ethiopians spotted these errors and were understandably annoyed.[12] Perhaps Simpson thought no one would give a damn in Bangor, Maine, or Cardiff. When caught in one instance, he apologized on Twitter for "mistakenly using the wrong photo."[13] But he used a wrong photo on at least three different occasions.

Amnesty International chose to investigate an alleged massacre in Aksum in late November 2020 by phoning survivors long distance more than a month after it happened, with seemingly little attention paid to verifying who its staff were talking to or whether the witness accounts were factual.[14] Amnesty also reported hundreds of ethnic Amhara being stabbed and hacked to death in Mai Kadra that same November, blaming the Tigray People's Liberation Front (the death toll would later be revised by researchers at the University of Gondar to more than 1,500). Mere weeks later, Amnesty changed its tune and suggested to the Associated Press that Amhara could have also targeted Tigrayans.[15] On both occasions, Western media didn't bother to question the organization's methodology. Nor did most of the big news operations bother to follow up and speak to survivors in Mai Kadra itself, who told photojournalist Jemal Countess in March 2021 how there were signs the massacre was planned well in advance by the TPLF.[16] When pushed over slanted coverage, some reporters reflexively blamed the Ethiopian government for restricting access to the region (which can often be a matter of course for governments with war zones), and it doesn't explain how Countess could find what they didn't. Nor does it account for their heavy reliance on the *same* white experts and the *same* organizations over and over again to explain Africa.

The truth is that Human Rights Watch and Amnesty are concerned primarily with persuading North Americans and Europeans to donate and to back their crusades. They are private organizations. Deferred to as moral arbiters of the world, there is no accountability to Africans over what they say or write about the continent and how much they may get wrong.

In 2020, a report by a human resources consultancy found that Amnesty International UK had an office culture of overt racism in which senior officials regularly questioned the capability of black staff and used the *n*-word, with "colleagues labelled over-sensitive if they complained."[17] The report wasn't released to the public. According to *The Guardian*, the international board of Amnesty e-mailed its staff that same year over Black Lives Matter and admitted that "racism was encoded into the 'very organizational model' of the human rights body, which had been shaped by the 'colonial power dynamics and borders' that were 'fresh' at the time of its founding in 1961."[18] This is who's judging Africa and whom reporters regularly consult. And the ugly reality is that Western journalists still often prefer to talk to such intermediaries instead of Africans themselves.

This should bother us. A lot. Not only for our news today but our history tomorrow. Today's headlined war is tomorrow's textbook chapter, and the definitive narrative of events often hinges on the accuracy of accounts presented at the time of their unfolding. It would help tremendously if journalism schools across the United States and Europe imposed mandatory courses in world history, with ones focused on specific regions. How can you cover, say, the treatment of minorities in Turkey if you know next to nothing about the Ottoman Empire or Atatürk? How can you truly understand Somalia without looking back at its interval of postwar democracy? For much of Africa, the past is still alive and affecting the present. Google and a last-minute trip to Waterstones or Barnes & Noble won't cut it. You need to have the critical judgment to evaluate whether your source's version of history is well founded instead of the predictable cop-out of, "Well, I quoted accurately what was said."

But in our current culture wars, attention over the past has largely and stubbornly remained on representation in a limited scope, on simply evicting the "dead white males" from their home turfs in North American and European universities, museums, and libraries. We can and should go deeper. Against the backdrop of all the controversy over statues and classic Western texts in 2020, Glenn Loury, economics professor at Brown University, and Columbia's John McWhorter (both black Americans), had one of their free-flowing discussions on the online video talk program *The Glenn Show*. Loury made a crucial argument: the new faculty of color at a university might complain that "all the portraits on the wall of the venerable dining room . . . are old white males. 'I don't see any gay people, I don't see any women.' This is what they say, okay? So you have, by crediting this kind of talk, bought into the assumption that the student will be disserved if in a moment of distress they don't have a faculty person of color to be able to confide in.

"You dare not say to them, 'Look, we are human beings here. This is a humanistic enterprise that we're engaged in. We will be communing with Socrates—he's been dead for thousands of years. We're going to be learning languages that you have never heard before, because in those literary traditions are great insights of the human spirit that are rendered in a way that will transform your life if you acquaint yourself with them. You don't see anybody who looks like you? Are you kidding me? Everybody here is a human being."[19]

Shadi Hamid, a Senior Fellow at the Brookings Institute and a contributor to *The Atlantic*, passed along this clip and wrote his own Twitter thread on it, remarking that "the idea that the Western canon isn't part of my heritage because I'm brown is absurd and patronizing. If you're American and you live in the West, then the Western canon is yours. If they [Western thinkers] were smart and had something useful to say, I could care less about their skin color."[20]

Why Loury's and Hamid's points feel like such a breath of fresh air is because for years, knowledge has been weaponized, and we've been led to believe that the Western canon and alternative banks of thought and culture are in opposition to each other. You can't help but roll your eyes when you come across—and this is genuine—someone claiming online that Newtonian physics is "based on a Eurocentric world view not founded in reality."[21] All right, you say, now things have *really* gone too far. And yet it can't be denied that many of those who taught the Western canon in the past failed to convey Shadi Hamid's point, that these works by the great masters are for *everyone*, not just the sons and daughters of Europe and North America.

So now let's flip it. Can white European and American students and ordinary readers dig into the works of Frantz Fanon and Steve Biko? Can they appreciate them? Of course they can. It's true that Fanon and Biko had in mind black readers first, African and Caribbean readers above all. They were writing to help liberate their respective peoples. Well, Thomas Paine no doubt pictured individuals like himself when he penned *Rights of Man*. The writer consciously or subconsciously directs his or her thoughts toward a reflection. So the answer to the seeming exclusivity of the Western canon is not to throw out all the "dead, white males." We merely need to add another wing to the pantheon, one where we'll discover new faces. Some of the major thinkers profiled in the last few chapters, Wangari Maathai, George Ayittey, and Asfa-Wossen Asserate, didn't write their works and outline their thinking only for Africans—these are ideas for the whole world.

This is what I mean by a return to a classical mind-set but with an adjustment. It is the engagement in Loury's humanistic enterprise, the recognition of the African canon and placing it alongside the traditional Western one. If we have Herodotus, we have room for Ibn Khaldun. If we dwell on the military genius of Napoleon, why not spend time as well on the tactics of Shaka Zulu? The Western canon and the Gifts of Africa are not in competition with each other. It is simply high time that Africa's history and its contributions were woven into the great narrative we tell ourselves. What an amazing era of enlightenment we'll have when that time finally comes.

Acknowledgments

It started a handful of years ago with one of those sparkling, rambling phone conversations with Asfa-Wossen Asserate, which I always hope one day will be less rare because he's a delight to converse with (but hey, the man is busy and has his own books to write). Aware of my monumental hubris, I timidly broached the concept of this book. What did he think? Should I do it? And he encouraged me—wonderfully so. Being a dope, it didn't occur to me until later that he should be *in* the book, and so I e-mailed him in 2018, and two and a half hours later, I got a reply: "Dear Jeff, 'NIHIL OBSTAT!' Will get in touch soon."

And yes, thanks, I did have to look up what *Nihil Obstat* means. I belong to that generation that took typing class in Grade 9 and that learned geography from books and not cell phones but was mercifully spared from Latin. The point is that there are far wiser, more educated souls than yours truly, and so yes, I shamelessly begged for their help. I thank my good fortune that they took pity on me and rescued me from some embarrassing errors. But the reader should understand that any mistakes of either fact or interpretation in this tome are my responsibility alone.

I should thank first my long-suffering test readers, chief among them Thomas A. Hale, now retired after serving as professor of African, French, and comparative literature at

Pennsylvania State University. I also owe a huge debt to the following for reading certain sections of the book: Nourredine Bessaldi; Bereket Kelile; Nicholas Rankin; Peter Lacovara, director of the Ancient Egyptian Archaeology and Heritage Fund; Sylvester Ogbechie of the University of California, Santa Barbara; Dan Hicks of the University of Oxford and the Pitt Rivers Museum; Verena Krebs of Ruhr University; and Alemayehu Geda of Addis Ababa University.

Then there are the interview subjects who patiently endured my long-distance interrogations and occasional follow-ups: Asfa-Wossen Asserate, George Ayittey, Sylvester Ogbechie, Thomas A. Hale, Al Haji Papa Bunka Susso, Patrick Hayford, Selam Kebede, and Abdi Ismail Samatar. I am extremely grateful to the following who granted me permission to quote, cite, and rely on their works: Thomas A. Hale, Marq de Villiers, Konrad Tuchscherer of St. John's University in New York, Derrick M. Nault of the University of Tokyo, Sarah Cunningham-Scharf, Verena Krebs of Ruhr University, Maaza Mengiste, Peter Lacovara, Louis Takács, Jeremy Murray-Brown, Yirga Gelaw Woldeyes of Curtin University in Perth, Wendy Belcher of Princeton University, J. Clark Reith of the University of Western Ontario, and Ken Menkhaus of Davidson College, North Carolina. My great thanks to Nadia Naqib, senior commissioning editor at the American University in Cairo Press, for graciously allowing me to quote from chapters of *Ancient Nubia*, and to Abdi Ismail Samatar and to Indiana University Press for allowing me to quote from Professor Samatar's *Africa's First Democrats*. And thanks as well to Åsa Rönngren and George Hoyningen-Huene Estate Archives for permission to use the stunning portrait of Josephine Baker.

There are so many others who helped, made brilliant suggestions, offered tips, and nudged me in cool new directions. Elshadaie Getenet kept finding a treasure trove of fascinating bits of Ethiopian history, which he shares on Twitter, and thanks to him, I discovered Gebrehiwot Baykedagn. Other heroes include Ambo Mekasa, Socrates Mbamalu, Hind Makki, Antonella Piazza, Dawit Yehualashet, Seifesilassie Gebremeskel, and Deocliciano Okssipin. A sincere thanks as well to staff at the U.K.

National Archives and at the Toronto Reference Library, which has a surprisingly impressive collection on African Studies.

At Prometheus Books, acquisitions editor Jake Bonar was the first to see the merit in this book, and so I have him to thank for it making it into print.

Notes

Introduction

1. "German Discovers Atlantis in Africa," *New York Times*, January 29, 1911.

2. Leo Frobenius, *The Voice of Africa* (London: Hutchinson & Co., 1913), 98.

3. Suzanne Marchand, "Leo Frobenius and the Revolt against the West," *Journal of Contemporary History* 32, no. 2 (April 1997).

4. Michael Glover, "Kingdom of Ife: Sculptures from West Africa, British Museum, London," *The Independent*, March 4, 2010.

5. Leo Frobenius, "Early African Culture as an Indication of Present Negro Potentialities," *Annals of the American Academy of Political and Social Science* 140 (November 1928).

6. W. E. B. Du Bois, *The World and Africa* (Oxford: Oxford University Press, 2007), xxxiii.

7. Wole Soyinka, Nobel Lecture, December 8, 1986, Nobelprize.org.

8. Jacqueline Trescott, "Myriad Voices from an Unsung Continent," *Washington Post*, December 15, 1999.

9. Boris Johnson, "If Blair's So Good at Running the Congo, Let Him Stay There," *The Telegraph*, January 10, 2002.

10. Boris Johnson, "Cancel the Guilt Trip," *The Spectator*, February 2, 2002.

11. Jacques Barzun, *From Dawn to Decadence* (London: Folio Society), 3.

12. Rudolph Windsor, *From Babylon to Timbuktu* (1969; repr., Atlanta, GA: Windsor Golden Series, 1988), 137.

13. Michael Palin, *Sahara* (London: Weidenfeld & Nicolson, 2002), 95.

14. Chinua Achebe, "Spelling Our Proper Name," in *Black Writers Redefine the Struggle: A Tribute to James Baldwin* (Amherst: University of Massachusetts Press, 1989), 9.

15. Tim Jeal, *Stanley: The Impossible Life of Africa's Greatest Explorer* (New Haven, CT: Yale University Press, 2007), 15.

16. Edward Wilmot Blyden, *Christianity, Islam and the Negro Race* (1887; repr., Baltimore, MD: Black Classic Press, 1994), 131.

Chapter 1

1. Toby Wilkinson, *The Rise and Fall of Ancient Egypt* (New York: Random House, 2010), 48.

2. G. Mokhtar, ed., *UNESCO General History of Africa*, vol. 2, *Ancient Civilizations of Africa* (London: James Currey, 1990), 91.

3. Wilkinson, *Ancient Egypt*, 366–69.

4. Anthony Leahy, "The Libyan Period in Egypt: An Essay in Interpretation," *Libyan Studies* 16 (1985): 62.

5. Pierre Briant, *From Cyrus to Alexander: A History of the Persian Empire* (University Park, PA: Eisenbrauns, 2002), 54.

6. Mokhtar, *UNESCO General History of Africa*, 165.

7. 3.25, Herodotus, *The Landmark Herodotus*, ed. Robert Strassler (New York: Anchor Books, 2007), 218.

8. Bertrand Russell, *History of Western Philosophy* (1905; repr., New York: Simon & Schuster, 1945), 3–7.

9. Abouelhadid Sherif, "The Sacred Geometry of Music and Harmony," in *Petrie Museum of Egyptian Archaeology: Characters and Collections* (London: UCL Press, 2015), 62.

10. Wu Mingren, "Nilometers: Ancient Egypt's Ingenious Invention Used until Modern Times," Ancient Origins.net, March 21, 2020.

11. Andrew Lawler, "Writing Gets a Rewrite," *Science*, n.s., 292, no. 5526 (June 29, 2001).

12. Konrad Tuchscherer, "Recording, Communicating and Making Visible: A History of Writing and Systems of Graphic Symbolism in Africa," in *Inscribing Meaning: Writing and Graphic Systems in African Art* (Washington, DC: Smithsonian Institution, 2007), 37–53.

13. Toby Wilkinson, *Writings from Ancient Egypt* (London: Penguin, 2016), xiv.

14. Mokhtar, *UNESCO General History of Africa*, 107.

15. Wilkinson, *Writings*, 286–87.

16. Gay Robins and Charles Shute, *The Rhind Mathematical Papyrus: An Ancient Egyptian Text* (London: British Museum Publications, 1987), 42, 46.

17. Rosalie David, *Handbook to Life in Ancient Egypt*, rev. ed. (Oxford: Oxford University Press, 2007), 261.

18. Marshall Clagett, *Ancient Egyptian Science: A Source Book, Volume Three: Ancient Egyptian Mathematics* (Philadelphia: American Philosophical Society, 1999), 51.

19. Jacques Jouanna, *Greek Medicine from Hippocrates to Galen*, trans. Neil Allies (Leiden: Brill, 2012), 4.

20. Jouanna, *Greek Medicine*, 5–6.

21. Homer, *The Odyssey*, trans. Robert Fagles (New York: Penguin, 1996), 131.

22. Diogenes Laertius, *Lives of the Eminent Philosophers*, trans. Pamela Mensch (New York: Oxford University Press, 2018), 136.

23. 2.8.4, Herodotus, *The Landmark Herodotus*, 152.

24. Jouanna, *Greek Medicine*, 10.

25. Basil Davidson, "The Ancient World and Africa: Whose Roots?" *Race and Class* 29, no. 2 (1987).

26. Joyce Tyldesley, *Hatchepsut: The Female Pharaoh* (London: Penguin, 1996), 145.

27. Warren Dawson, "Pygmies and Dwarfs in Ancient Egypt," *Journal of Egyptian Archaeology* 24, no. 2 (December 1938).

28. "Baboon Mummy Tests Reveal Ethiopia and Eritrea as Ancient Land of Punt," *Archaeology News Network*, April 23, 2010; Own Jarus, "Baboon Mummy Analysis Reveals Eritrea and Ethiopia as Location of Land of Punt," *The Independent*, April 26, 2010.

29. Thomas Schneider, "The West beyond the West: The Mysterious 'Wernes' of the Egyptian Underworld and the Chad Palaeolakes," *Journal of Ancient Egyptian Interconnections* 2, no. 4 (2010).

30. Schneider, "The West beyond the West."

31. Thomas Schneider, "Egypt and the Chad: Some Additional Remarks," *Journal of Ancient Egyptian Interconnections* 3, no. 4 (2011).

32. Peter Lacovara, "The Land of Nubia," in *Ancient Nubia: African Kingdoms on the Nile*, ed. Marjorie Fisher (Cairo: The American University in Cairo Press, 2012), 6.

33. Holland Cotter, "America's Big Museums on the Hot Seat," *New York Times*, March 18, 2020.

34. Stuart Tyson Smith, *Wretched Kush: Ethnic Identities and Boundaries in Egypt's Nubian Empire* (London: Routledge, 2003), 99–135, 197, 20.

35. Lacovara, "The Art and Architecture of Kushite Nubia," in Fisher, *Ancient Nubia*, 108.

36. Susan Doll, "Texts and Writing in Ancient Nubia," in Fisher, *Ancient Nubia*, 160.

37. Lisa Heidorn, "The Horses of Kush," *Journal of Near Eastern Studies* 56, no. 2 (April 1997).

38. Heidorn, "The Horses of Kush."

39. Marjorie Fisher, "The History of Nubia," in *Ancient Nubia*, 10.

40. Terence Spencer, "The Race to Save Abu Simbel Is Won," *Life* 61, no. 23 (December 2, 1966).

41. Doll, "Texts and Writing in Ancient Nubia," 163, 166.

42. Joyce Haynes and Mimi Santini-Ritt, "Women in Ancient Nubia," in Fisher, *Ancient Nubia*, 172–73.

43. Haynes and Santini-Ritt, "Women in Ancient Nubia," 174.

44. Ibid., 184.

45. Peter Lacovara and Yvonne Marowitz, "The Treasure of a Nubian Queen," in Fisher, *Ancient Nubia*, 55.

46. Peter Schwartzstein, "Changing Egypt Offers Hope to Long-Marginalized Nubians," *National Geographic*, February 1, 2014.

47. Kahled Mahmoud, "Dashing Nubians' Hopes of Returning Home," Carnegie Endowment for International Peace, August 13, 2018.

48. Schwartzstein, "Changing Egypt."

49. Salma Islam, "Egypt's Indigenous Nubians Continue Their Long Wait to Return to Ancestral Lands," *GlobalPost*, July 24, 2017.

50. Mahmoud, "Dashing Nubians' Hopes of Returning Home."

51. Mahmoud, "Dashing Nubians' Hopes of Returning Home."

52. Ahmed Megahid, "First Nubian Language Dictionary Published by Volunteers," *The Arab Weekly*, January 19, 2020; "Dreaming of Returning Home, Egypt's Nubians Revive Language," France24.com, April 23, 2020.

53. "Dreaming," France24.com, April 23, 2020.

Chapter 2

1. Robin Lane Fox, *The Classical World* (New York: Basic Books, 2006), 304.

2. Robert Graves, *The Golden Ass* (New York: Farrar, Straus and Giroux, 1951), 3.

3. Graves, "Introduction," in *The Golden Ass*, ix.

4. Emmanuel Plantade and Nedjime Plantade, "Lybca Psyche: Apuleius' Narrative and Berber Folktales," in *Apuleius and Africa*, ed. Benjamin Todd Lee, Ellen Finkelpearl, and Luca Gervarini (London: Routledge, 2014), 180.

5. Augustine, *Confessions* (London: Penguin, 1961), 46.

6. D. A. Masolo, "African Philosophers in the Greco-Roman Era," in *A Companion to African Philosophy*, ed. Kwasi Wiredu (Oxford: Blackwell, 2004).

7. Masolo, "African Philosophers in the Greco-Roman Era."

8. Maurice Frost, "A Note on the Berber Background in the Life of Augustine," *Journal of Theological Studies* 43, no. 171/172 (July/October 1942).

9. Miles Hollingsworth, *Augustine of Hippo: An Intellectual Biography* (Oxford: Oxford University Press, 2013), 52.

10. Norman F. Cantor, *Civilization of the Middle Ages* (New York: HarperCollins, 1994), 51–52.

11. Michael Brett and Elizabeth Fentress, *The Berbers* (Cambridge, MA: Blackwell, 1996), 55.

12. Peter Brown, "Christianity and Local Culture in Late Roman Africa," *Journal of Roman Studies* 58, pts. 1–2 (1968).

13. Kevin Shillington, *History of Africa*, 3rd ed. (London: Palgrave Macmillan, 2012), 75.

14. Henry Chadwick, "Introduction," in Augustine, *Confessions*, xi–xii.

15. Augustine, *Confessions*, 126.

16. Stephen Greenblatt, "How St. Augustine Invented Sex," *The New Yorker*, June 19, 2017.

17. Greenblatt, "How St. Augustine Invented Sex."

18. Bertrand Russell, *History of Western Philosophy* (1905; repr., New York: Simon & Schuster, 1945), 341.

Chapter 3

1. Stuart Munro-Hay, *Aksum: An African Civilization of Late Antiquity* (Edinburgh: Edinburgh University Press, 1991), 180.

2. Yuri Kobishchanov, *Axum*, trans. Lorraine Kapitanoff (University Park: Pennsylvania State University Press, 1979), 37, 39.

3. Yuri Kobishchanov, "On the Problem of Sea Voyages of Ancient Africans in the Indian Ocean," *Journal of African History* 6, no. 2 (1965).

4. Kobishchanov, *Aksum*, 91–95.

5. Pekka Masonen and Humphrey Fisher, "Not Quite Venus from the Waves: The Almoravid Conquest of Ghana in the Modern Historiography of Western Africa," *History in Africa* 23 (1996).

6. Masonen and Fisher, "Not Quite Venus from the Waves," 201.

7. Ibid., 205.

8. Osire Glacier, "Fatima al-Fihri," in *Dictionary of African Biography* (Oxford: Oxford University Press, 2012), 357.

9. Mohammad Enan, *Ibn Khaldun: His Life and Work* (Lahore: Ashraf Press, 1962), 4.

10. Allen Fromhertz, *Ibn Khaldun: Life and Times* (Edinburgh: Edinburgh University Press, 2011), 84.

11. Jack Weatherford, *Genghis Khan and the Making of the Modern World* (New York: Broadway Books, 2004), 252–53.

12. Ibn Khaldun, *The Muqaddimah: An Introduction to History*, trans. Franz Rosenthal (1969; repr., Princeton, NJ: Princeton University Press, 2005), 11.

13. Fromhertz, *Ibn Khaldun*, 116–17.

14. Robert Irwin, *Ibn Khaldun: An Intellectual Biography* (Princeton, NJ: Princeton University Press, 2018), 47–48.

15. Ibid., 55.

16. Ibid.,144–52.

17. Fromhertz, *Ibn Khaldun*, 129–30.

18. Arnold Toynbee, *A Study of History*, 6 vols. (London: Oxford University Press, 1948), 3:322, 10:136.

Chapter 4

1. Basil Davidson, *The African Past* (Boston: Little, Brown, 1964), 76.

2. Michael Gomez, *African Dominion: A New History of Empire in Early and Medieval West Africa* (Princeton, NJ: Princeton University Press, 2018), 108.

3. N. Levtzion, "The Thirteenth- and Fourteenth-Century Kings of Mali," *Journal of African History* 4, no. 3 (1963): 341–53; Francoise-Xavier Fauvelle, *The Golden Rhinoceros* (Princeton, NJ: Princeton University Press, 2018), 165.

4. Joan Baxter, "Africa's 'Greatest Explorer,'" BBC News, December 13, 2000.

5. Marq de Villiers and Sheila Hirtle, *Timbuktu: The Sahara's Fabled City of Gold* (Toronto: McClelland & Stewart, 2007), 73.

6. Gomez, *African Dominion*, 113.

7. De Villiers and Hirtle, *Timbuktu*, 75–76; Gomez, *African Dominion*, 119.

8. Ibid., 80.

9. Ibid., 87.

10. Ibn Battuta, *Travels in Asia and Africa*, trans. H. A. R. Gibb (London: Routledge & Sons, 1953), 326.

11. Battuta, *Travels in Asia and Africa*, 329–30.

12. Fauvelle, *The Golden Rhinoceros*, 192.

13. Pekka Masonen, "Leo Africanus: The Man with Many Names," *Al-Andalus Magreb* 8–9 (2001).

14. Ibid.

15. Ibid.

16. Natalie Zemon Davis, "'Leo Africanus' Presents Africa to Europeans," in *Revealing the African Presence in Europe*, ed. Joaneath Spicer (Baltimore, MD: Walters Art Museum, 2012), 65.

17. Basil Davidson, *The African Slave Trade* (Boston: Little, Brown, 1980), 26.

18. Joshua Hammer, *The Bad-Ass Librarians of Timbuktu* (New York: Simon & Schuster, 2016), 16.

19. Josef Meri, *Medieval Islamic Civilization: An Encyclopedia* (London: Routledge, 2005), 765; Gomez, *African Dominion*, 255.

20. As quoted by A. Adu Boahen, *Topics in West African History* (London: Longman, 1986), 38.

21. Toby Green, *A Fistful of Shells* (London: Allen Lane, 2019), 64.

22. Lee Cassanelli, *The Shaping of Somali Society: Reconstructing the History of a Pastoral People, 1600–1900* (Philadelphia: University of Pennsylvania Press, 1982); see chapters 1 and 2 on the societal background and on the Ajuran in history and tradition.

23. Ibn Battuta, *Travels in Asia and Africa*, 110.

24. Ibid.

25. Vasco Da Gama, *A Journal of the First Voyage of Vasco da Gama, 1497–1499*, trans. E. G. Ravenstein (London: Hakluyt Society, 1898), 88.

26. Samuel Wilson, *The Emperor's Giraffe and Other Stories of Cultures in Contact* (Boulder, CO: Westview Press, 1999), 124; Peter Greste, "Could a Rusty Coin Rewrite Chinese-African History?," BBC News, October 18, 2010.

27. Debbie Challis, "From China to Sudan," in *Petrie Museum of Egyptian Archaeology: Characters and Collections* (London: UCL Press, 2015), 92.

28. Charles Parker and Jerry Bentley, eds., *Between the Middle Ages and Modernity: Individual and Community in the Early Modern World* (Lanham, MD: Rowman & Littlefield, 2007), 160.

29. Wilson, *The Emperor's Giraffe and Other Stories of Cultures in Contact*, 121.

30. Ibid., 124.

31. Jerome Osorio and James Gibbs, trans., *The History of the Portuguese during the Reign of Emmanuel*, 2 vols. (London: Millar, 1752), 1:286.

32. Cassanelli, *The Shaping of Somali Society*, 93. But Cassanelli is quoting Enrico Cerulli's *Somalia*, 3 vols. (Rome: Instituto Poligrafico dello Stato, 1957–1964), 2:248. It's useful to recall here the mention of colonial agendas in the historiography and how we are stuck sometimes with highly biased material. Cerulli, for instance, was supposed to have faced war crimes for his record when Italian Fascists occupied Ethiopia, and it's only through the appalling lack of due diligence by Allied authorities in pursuing his true record—as well as certain political expediencies of the postwar era—that he didn't find himself in a dock or standing on a gallows. This creates a problem. But even if the reader finds Cerulli's work suspect, I believe we can trust the scholarship of Cassanelli, who makes clear in his book that he weighed oral narratives and colonial sources very carefully.

Chapter 5

1. Stuart Munro-Hay, *Aksum: An African Civilization of Late Antiquity* (Edinburgh: Edinburgh University Press, 1991), 180.

2. Richard Greenfield, *Ethiopia: A New Political History* (London: Pall Mall Press, 1965), 28.

3. Richard Pankhurst, *The Ethiopians: A History* (Oxford: Blackwell, 2001), 39–40.

4. David Northrup, *Africa's Discovery of Europe* (New York: Oxford University Press, 2009), 4.

5. Verena Krebs, *Medieval Ethiopian Kingship, Craft, and Diplomacy with Latin Europe* (Cham: Palgrave Macmillan, 2021), 20, 23, 39. I am extremely grateful to Dr. Krebs for allowing me to rely heavily on her research for this section.

6. Krebs, *Medieval Ethiopian Kingship*, 63. Different sources have identified Alfonso's relative, with Peter Garretson identifying her as his sister and David Northrup suggesting it was her daughter; I'm inclined to go with Krebs's more recent research and detailed account of the lady in question.

7. Ibid., 187 (p. 32 regarding the use of Arabic).

8. Ibid., 64.

9. Ibid., 65.

10. Ibid., 87, 117n.

11. Marco Bonechi, "Four Sistine Ethiopians? The 1481 Ethiopian Embassy and the Frescoes of the Sistine Chapel in the Vatican," *Aethiopica*, no. 14 (2011).

12. Pankhurst, *The Ethiopians*, 77–78.

13. Krebs, *Medieval Ethiopian Kingship*, 27.

14. Roger Crowley, *Conquerors: How the Portuguese Forged the First Global Empire* (New York: Random House, 2015), 8.

15. Pankhurst, *The Ethiopians*, 62.

16. Sylvia Pankhurst, *Ethiopia: A Cultural History* (Woodford Green: Lalibela House, 1955), 302.

17. Pankhurst, *The Ethiopians*, 105, 107.

18. Pankhurst, *Ethiopia*, 355.

19. C. F. Beckingham and G. W. B. Huntingford, *Some Records of Ethiopia, 1593–1646* (New York: Routledge, 2016), 76–77.

20. There are different renditions of this speech given by Hiob Ludolf, James Bruce, and modern scholars. Instead of merely quoting one of them, I've chosen to amalgamate and adapt the speech into our current vernacular.

21. Greenfield, *Ethiopia*, 60.

22. Pankhurst, *The Ethiopians*, 108.

23. Yirga Gelaw Woldeyes, "Colonial Rewriting of African History: Misinterpretations and Distortions in Belcher and Kleiner's Life and Struggles of Walatta Petros," *Journal of Afroasiatic Languages, History and Culture* 9, no. 2 (2020).

24. Woldeyes, "Colonial Rewriting of African History."

25. Pankhurst, *Ethiopia*, 360.

26. Claude Sumner, "The Significance of Zera Yacob's Philosophy," *Ultimate Reality and Meaning* 22, issue 3 (September 1999).

27. Claude Sumner, *Ethiopian Philosophy*, vol. 2 (Addis Ababa: Commercial Printing Press, 1976), 250.

28. Sumner, *Ethiopian Philosophy*, 233–35.

29. Sumner, "The Significance of Zera Yacob's Philosophy."

30. Sumner, *Ethiopian Philosophy*, 237–38.

31. Sumner, *Ethiopian Philosophy*, 238.

32. Dag Herbjørnsrud, "The African Enlightenment," Aeon, December 13, 2017.

33. Claude Sumner, *Classical Ethiopian Philosophy* (Addis Ababa: Commercial Printing Press, 1985), 227.

34. Frederick Douglass, "The Abilities and Possibilities of Our Race," as quoted in William R. Scott, *The Sons of Sheba's Race* (Bloomington: Indiana University Press, 1993), 19. Scott devotes an entire chapter to the Ethiopian tradition, which chronicles extensively how it played a role in early African American life.

35. Wendy Belcher, "From Sheba They Come: Medieval Ethiopian Myth, U.S. Newspapers and a Modern American Narrative," *Callaloo* 33, no. 1 (Winter 2010).

Chapter 6

1. Yash Tandon, "Recolonization of Subject Peoples," *Alternatives* 19, no. 2 (Spring 1994).

2. Basil Davidson, *The Slave Trade* (Boston: Little, Brown, 1980), 31.

3. Harold Courlander and Ousmane Sako, *The Heart of the Ngoni: Heroes of the African Kingdom of Segu* (New York: Crown Publishers, 1982), 5.

4. Ibid.

5. A. Adu Boahen, *Topics in West African History* (London: Longman, 1986), 78–79.

6. Ibid., 82.

7. Robert Edgerton, *The Fall of the Asante Empire* (New York: Free Press, 1995), 25.

8. Enid Schildkrout, ed., *The Golden Stool: Studies of the Asante Center and Periphery* (New York: Anthropological Papers of the American Museum of Natural History, 1987), 86.

9. Noel Mostert, *Frontiers* (New York: Knopf, 1992), 199–201.

10. William Holden, *The Past and Future of the Kaffir Races* (Port Natal: Richards, Glanville and Co., 1866), 178–79.

11. Boahen, *Topics in West African History*, 98.

12. Marq de Villiers and Sheila Hirtle, *Into Africa* (Toronto: Key Porter Books, 1997), 189.

13. Ibid., 225.

14. Ibid.

15. Elliott Skinner, "The Mossi and Traditional Sudanese History," *Journal of Negro History* 43, no. 2 (April 1958): 125.

16. Ibid., 125–26.

17. Ibid., 127.

18. Ibid., 127, 129.

19. "Qui est le Mogho Naaba, au centre des négociations au Burkina Faso?," SlateAfrique.com, September 23, 2015.

20. Uri Friedman, "What's Actually in the Magna Carta?," TheAtlantic.com, June 15, 2015.

21. Basil Davidson, *Let Freedom Come* (Boston: Little, Brown, 1978), 63–65.

22. A. G. Hopkins, *An Economic History of West Africa* (New York: Routledge, 1973), 48.

23. Davidson, *Let Freedom Come*, 66.

24. George Ayittey, *Indigenous African Institutions*, 2nd ed. (Ardsley, NY: Transnational Publishers, 2006), 352.

25. E. A. Ritter, *Shaka Zulu* (1955; repr., London: Penguin, 1978), 395–96.

26. I. M. Lewis, *Understanding Somalia and Somaliland* (New York: Columbia University Press, 2008), 22.

27. Stephen Coss, *The Fever of 1721: The Epidemic That Revolutionized Medicine and American Politics* (New York: Simon & Schuster, 2017), 75.

28. D. D. O. Oyebola, "Yoruba Traditional Bonesetters: The Practice of Orthopaedics in a Primitive Setting in Nigeria," *Journal of Trauma* 20, no. 4 (April 1980).

29. Oyebola, "Yoruba Traditional Bonesetters."

30. Harry Johnston, *The Uganda Protectorate* (London: Hutchinson, 1902), 750.

31. John Roscoe, *Twenty-Five Years in East Africa* (Cambridge: Cambridge University Press, 1921), 147.

32. P. Amaury Talbot, *In the Shadow of the Bush* (London: Heinemann, 1912), 278–79.

33. Hana de Goeij, "A Breakthrough in C-Section History: Beatrice of Bourbon's Survival in 1337," *New York Times*, November 24, 2016.

34. J. N. P. Davies, "The Development of 'Scientific' Medicine in the African Kingdom of Bunyoro-Kitara," *Medical History* 3, no. 1 (January 1959).

35. Edgerton, *The Fall of the Asante Empire*, 38.

36. Fred Pearce, "African Queen," *New Scientist*, issue 2203 (September 11, 1993).

37. Mawuna Koutonin, "Story of Cities #5: Benin City, the Mighty Medieval City Now Lost without a Trace," *The Guardian*, March 18, 2016.

38. Howard Zinn, *A People's History of the United States* (1980; repr., New York: HarperCollins, 2003), 26.

39. De Villiers and Hirtle, *Into Africa*, 226.

40. Ron Eglash, *African Fractals: Modern Computing and Indigenous Design* (New Brunswick, NJ: Rutgers University Press, 2002), 20.

41. Kate Torgovnik May, "Architecture Infused with Fractals: How TED Speaker Ron Eglash Inspired Architect Xavier Vilalta," blog.ted .com, October 25, 2013.

42. Ibid.

43. Nick Compton, "This Stylish African Architecture Will Blow You Away," Wired.co.uk, August 29, 2017.

44. Ibid.

45. Neo Maditla, "How Architect Mariam Kamara Is Masterminding a Sustainable Future for Niger," CNN Style, March 16, 2020.

46. Christopher Hitchens, *The Quotable Hitchens*, ed. Windsor Mann (New York: Da Capo Press, 2011), 58.

47. De Villiers and Hirtle, *Into Africa*, 226.

48. Philip Igbafe, "The Fall of Benin: A Reassessment," *Journal of African History* 11, no. 3 (1970).

49. Ibid.

50. For the Foreign Office's concern about not enough troops, see Igbafe, "The Fall of Benin," 395–96; on the confirmation of arrangements, see also Dan Hicks, *The Brutish Museum* (London: Pluto Press, 2020), 90.

51. Alan Boisragon, *The Benin Massacre* (London: Methuen, 1897), 59.

52. Igbafe, "The Fall of Benin," 396–97.

53. Hicks, *The Brutish Museum*, 125.

54. Felix Roth, "A Diary of a Surgeon with the Benin Punitive Expedition," *Journal of the Manchester Geographical Society* 14 (1898); Reginald Bacon, *Benin: The City of Blood* (London: Edward Arnold, 1897), 87.

55. Percy Talbot, *The Peoples of Southern Nigeria*, vol. 3 (Oxford: Oxford University Press, 1926), 862.

56. Bacon, *Benin: The City of Blood*, 13.

57. Ibid., 89–90.

58. Hicks, *The Brutish Museum*, 142.

59. Bacon, *Benin*, 91–92.
60. Jeanette Greenfield, *The Return of Cultural Treasures*, 3rd ed. (Cambridge: Cambridge University Press, 2007), 124.
61. Greenfield, *The Return of Cultural Treasures*, 12.
62. Richard Gott, "The Looting of Benin," *The Independent*, February 22, 1997.

Chapter 7

1. Basil Davidson, *The Slave Trade* (Boston: Little, Brown, 1980), 40–41.
2. Robert Edgerton, *The Fall of the Asante Empire* (New York: Free Press, 1995), 25.
3. Martin Delany, *Official Report of the Niger Valley Exploring Party* (New York, 1861), 309.
4. Gomes de Azurara, *The Chronicle of the Discovery and Conquest of Guinea*, vol. 1, trans. Charles Beazley (London: Hakluyt Society, 1899), 84.
5. Linda M. Heywood, *Njinga of Angola: Africa's Warrior Queen* (Cambridge, MA: Harvard University Press, 2017), 27.
6. Cécile Fromont, *The Art of Conversion: Christian Visual Culture in the Kingdom of Kongo* (Chapel Hill: University of North Carolina Press, 2014), 9–10.
7. Martin Meredith, *The Fortunes of Africa* (New York: Public Affairs, 2014), 103–4.
8. Basil Davidson, *A History of West Africa* (New York: Anchor Books, 1966), 297.
9. John Thornton, "Legitimacy and Political Power: Queen Njinga, 1624–1663," *Journal of African History* 32, no. 1 (1991).
10. Donald Burness, "Nzinga Mbandi and Angolan Independence," *Luso-Brazilian Review* 14, no. 2 (Winter 1977).
11. Heywood, *Njinga of Angola*, 51.
12. Ibid., 107.
13. Thornton, "Legitimacy and Political Power."
14. Marquis de Sade, *Philosophy in the Boudoir*, trans. Joachium Neugroschel (New York: Penguin, 2006), 68.
15. Georg Hegel, *Lectures on the Philosophy of History*, trans. Ruben Alvarado (Aalten: Wordbridge Publishing, 2011), 90, 91.

16. Fernando Martinho, "The Poetry of Agostinho Neto," *World Literature Today* 53, no. 1 (Winter 1979); Burness, "Nzinga Mbandi and Angolan Independence."

17. Kwame Arhin, "The Role of Nana Yaa Asantewaa in the 1900 Asante War of Resistance," *Le Griot* 8 (2000).

18. Francis Fuller, *A Vanished Dynasty: Ashanti* (London: John Murray, 1921), 188.

19. Edgerton, *The Fall of the Asante Empire*, 191–92.

20. Ibid., 226, 235.

21. Myles Osborne and Susan Kingsley Kent, *Africans and Britons in the Age of Empires, 1660–1980* (London: Routledge, 2015), 116.

22. T. C. McCaskie, "The Life and Afterlife of Yaa Asantewaa," *Africa: Journal of the International African Institute* 77, no. 2 (2007).

23. Arhin, "The Role of Nana Yaa Asantewaa."

24. McCaskie, "The Life and Afterlife of Yaa Asantewaa," 163–74.

25. Mike Dash, "Dahomey's Women Warriors," Smithsonian.com, September 23, 2011.

26. Dash, "Dahomey's Women Warriors."

27. Fleur Macdonald, "The Legend of Benin's Fearless Female Warriors," BBC.com/Travel, August 27, 2018.

28. Stanley Alpern, "On the Origins of the Amazons of Dahomey," *History in Africa* 25 (1998). Alpern discusses the difficulties with pinning down who founded their corps in detail.

29. Ibid.

30. Stanley Alpern, *Amazons of Black Sparta: The Women Warriors of Dahomey* (New York: New York University Press, 1998), 193.

Chapter 8

1. Mary-Antoinette Smith, *Essays on the Slavery and Commerce of the Human Species*, ed. Thomas Clarkson and Ottobah Cugoano (London: Broadview Editions, 2010), 22; David Olusoga, *Black and British* (London: Macmillan, 2016), 85; Olusoga discusses at length the issue of contradictory estimates for the black population and their living conditions.

2. Hugh Thomas, *The Slave Trade* (New York: Simon & Schuster, 1997), 489.

3. Olaudah Equiano, *An African's Life, 1745–1797: The Life and Times of Olaudah Equiano* (London: Continuum, 2000), 152.

4. Ibid., 152.

5. Olusoga, *Black and British*, 158–86; Olusoga offers one of the best detailed retellings of the Sierra Leone settlement debacle.

6. Ibid., 186.

7. Adam Hochschild, *Bury the Chains* (2005; repr., New York: Mariner Books, 2006), 133.

8. John Bugg, "The Other Interesting Narrative: Olaudah Equiano's Public Book Tour," *PMLA* 121, no. 5 (October 2006).

9. John Bugg, "The Sons of Belial: Olaudah Equiano in 1794," *Times Literary Supplement*, August 1, 2008.

10. Stephen Manning, "Professor Questions Accuracy of Famed Slave Narrative," The Ledger.com, September 23, 2005.

11. Robin Blackburn, "The True Story of Equiano," *The Nation*, November 2, 2005; Teresa Wiltz, "For Slave's Biographer, Truth Contains a Bit of Fiction," *Washington Post*, September 10, 2005; Manning, "Professor Questions Accuracy of Famed Slave Narrative."

12. Wiltz, "For Slave's Biographer, Truth Contains a Bit of Fiction."

13. Vincent Carretta, *Equiano the African: Biography of a Self-Made Man* (2005; repr., New York: Penguin, 2007), 147.

14. Bugg, "The Other Interesting Narrative."

15. Ibid.

16. Carretta, *Equiano the African*; Bugg, "Deciphering the Equiano Archives," *PMLA* 122, no. 2 (March 2007).

17. David Dabydeen, "Poetic License," *The Guardian*, December 3, 2005.

18. Paul Lovejoy, "Autobiography and Memory: Gustavus Vassa, alias Olaudah Equiano, the African," *Slavery and Abolition* 27, no. 3 (December 2006).

19. Southern Poverty Law Center, *Teaching Hard History: American Slavery* (Montgomery, AL: Southern Poverty Law Center, 2018), 9.

20. Annabelle Timsit and Annalisa Merelli, "For 10 Years, Students in Texas Have Used a History Textbook That Says Not All Slaves Were Unhappy," *Quartz*, May 11, 2018.

21. Hochschild, *Bury the Chains*, 372.

22. In what is an otherwise brilliant and insightful study of the postcolonial period, *The State of Africa*, Martin Meredith relies on Kapuściński and credits him with "compiling a vivid picture of life at the old imperial palaces" under Haile Selassie, only noting that "critics claimed it was a little too imaginative." In fact, critics like John Ryle of the Rift Valley Institute and his recent biographer, Artur Domosławski, have exposed Kapuściński as an outright liar on numerous occasions,

which begs the question as to why he is still relied on for historical information related to Africa.

23. Peter Englund, "Fact and Fiction," *Financial Times*, August 24, 2012.

24. Eric Williams, *Inward Hunger: The Education of a Prime Minister* (London: Andre Deutsch, 1969), 49–50.

25. Ibid., 182.

26. Ibid., 209.

27. Ibid., 211.

28. Sally-Anne Huxtable, "Wealth, Power and the Global Country House," in *Interim Report on the Connections between Colonialism and Properties Now in the Care of the National Trust, Including Links with Historic Slavery* (Swindon: National Trust, 2020), 8.

29. Greg Grandin, "Capitalism and Slavery," The Nation, May 1, 2015.

30. Richard Huzzey, "1900–2007: The Legacies of Slavery and Anti-Slavery," BBC Local Oxford, November 27, 2014.

31. Sylviane Diouf, ed., *Fighting the Slave Trade: West African Strategies* (Oxford: James Currey, 2003), 145.

32. Diouf, *Fighting the Slave Trade*, 145.

33. Edward Wilmot Blyden, "Report on the Expedition to Falaba, January to March 1872," *Proceedings of the Royal Geographical Society of London* 17, no. 2 (1872–1873): 117.

34. Ibid., 120.

35. Ibid., 118.

Chapter 9

1. Apollos Nwauwa, "Far Ahead of His Time: James Africanus Horton's Initiatives for a West African University and His Frustrations, 1862–1871," *Cahiers d'Études Africaines* 39, no. 153 (1999).

2. Ibid.

3. Craufurd Goodwin, "Economic Analysis and Development in British West Africa," *Economic Development and Cultural Change* 15, no. 4 (July 1967).

4. James Africanus Horton, *Political Economy of British Western Africa; with the Requirements of the Several Colonies and Settlements* (London: W. J. Johnson, 1865), 8; James Africanus Horton, *West African Countries and Peoples, British and Native: A Vindication of the African Race* (London: W. J. Johnson, 1868), 21.

5. Goodwin, "Economic Analysis."

6. Horton, *West African Countries and Peoples, British and Native*, 108.

7. Horton, *West African Countries*, 58.

8. Ibid., 82–83.

9. Horton, *Letters on the Political Condition of the Gold Coast since the Exchange of Territory between the English and Dutch Governments* (London: W. J. Johnson, 1870), 138.

10. Goodwin, "Economic Analysis."

11. Horton, *West African Countries*, 247.

12. James Ciment, *Another America: The Story of Liberia and the Former Slaves Who Ruled It* (New York: Hill and Wang, 2013), 8–10.

13. Ibid., 29–30.

14. Ibid., 55.

15. Charles Thomas, *Adventures and Observations on the West Coast of Africa and Its Islands* (New York: Derby & Jackson, 1860), 156.

16. Hollis Lynch makes this point in his introduction to Edward Wilmot Blyden, *Selected Letters of Edward Wilmot Blyden* (Millwood, NY: KTO Press, 1978), 15–16.

17. James Fairhead, Tim Geysbeek, Svend E. Holsoe, and Melissa Leach, eds., *African-American Exploration in West Africa: Four Nineteenth Century Diaries* (Bloomington: Indiana University Press, 2003), 26.

18. Edward Wilmot Blyden, *The Aims and Methods of a Liberal Education for Africans: Inaugural Address* (1882; repr., New York: George Young, 1920), 13.

19. Edward Wilmot Blyden, *Christianity, Islam and the Negro Race* (London: W. B. Whittingham, 1887), 146.

20. Ibid., 14.

21. Ibid., 15–16.

22. Ibid., 26–27.

23. Hollis Lynch, *Edward Wilmot Blyden: Pan-Negro Patriot, 1832–1912* (Oxford: Oxford University Press, 1967), 74–77.

24. Blyden, *Selected Letters of Edward Wilmot Blyden*, 14.

25. Ibid., 183.

26. "The Berlin Conference," *New York Times*, January 30, 1885.

27. Lynch, in Blyden, *Selected Letters of Edward Wilmot Blyden*, 80.

28. George Washington Williams, *An Open Letter to His Serene Majesty Leopold II*, 1890, reprinted on BlackPast.org.

29. Derrick M. Nault, *Africa and the Shaping of International Human Rights* (Oxford: Oxford University Press, 2021), 19.

30. Roger Casement, *Congo Report*, submitted to U.K. Parliament, February 1904, 60.

31. Casely Hayford, "Introduction," in *West Africa before Europe and Other Addresses* (London: C. M. Phillips, 1905), i.

32. Douglas Wheeler, "Nineteenth Century African Protest in Angola: Prince Nicolas of Kongo (1830? – 1860), *African Historical Studies*, 1, no. 1 (1968).

33. Colin Grant, *Negro with a Hat* (Oxford: Oxford University Press, 2008), 40.

34. Ibid., 169.

35. Richard Greenfield, *Ethiopia: A New Political History* (London: Pall Mall Press, 1965), 109.

36. Raymond Jonas, *The Battle of Adwa* (Cambridge, MA: Belknap Press, 2011), 215.

37. Ibid., 269.

38. Ibid., 112.

39. *New Times and Ethiopia News*, July 18, 1936.

40. Sylvia Jacobs, *The African Nexus: Black American Perspectives on the European Partitioning of Africa, 1880–1920* (Westport, CT: Greenwood Press, 1981), 196.

41. Bahru Zewde, *Pioneers of Change in Ethiopia* (Oxford: James Currey, 2002), 49–52.

42. Ibid., 51.

43. Ibid., 52.

44. Greenfield, *Ethiopia*, 155.

45. Paul Henze, *Layers of Time* (New York: Palgrave, 2000), 211–12.

46. Tenkir Bonger, "Introduction" in Gebrehiwot Baykedagn and Tenkir Bonger, *The State and Economy in Early 20th Century Ethiopia* (London: Karnak House, 1995), 18.

47. Baykedagn and Bonger, *The State and Economy in Early 20th Century Ethiopia*, 53–54.

48. Ibid., 163.

49. Ibid., 115.

50. Ibid., 110–11.

51. Bonger, "Introduction," 34–35; Baykedagn and Bonger, *The State and Economy*, 106.

52. Ibid., 71.

53. Matteo Salvadore, "A Modern African Intellectual: Gabre-Heywat Baykadan's Quest for Ethiopia's Sovereign Modernity," *Africa: Rivista Trimestrale di Studi e Documentazione dell'Istituto Italiano per l'Africa e l'Oriente* 62, no. 4 (2007).

Chapter 10

1. Konrad Tuchscherer, "Recording, Communicating and Making Visible: A History of Writing and Systems of Graphic Symbolism in Africa," in *Inscribing Meaning: Writing and Graphic Systems in African Art* (Washington, DC: Smithsonian Institution, 2007), 37–53. I am grateful to Professor Tuchscherer for allowing me to rely heavily on this chapter for explaining written scripts.

2. Konrad Tuchscherer, "The Lost Script of the Bagam," *African Affairs* 98, no. 390 (January 1999).

3. James Africanus Horton, *Political Economy of British Western Africa; with the Requirements of the Several Colonies and Settlements* (London: W. J. Johnson, 1865), 12.

4. Dianne Oyler, "Re-Inventing Oral Tradition: The Modern Epic of Souleymane Kanté," *Research in African Literatures* 33, no. 1 (Spring 2002).

5. Oyler, "Re-Inventing Oral Tradition."

6. Tuchscherer, "Recording, Communicating and Making Visible."

7. Oyler, "Re-Inventing Oral Tradition."

8. Rohit Inani, "Language Is a 'War Zone': A Conversation with Ngũgĩ wa Thiong'o," *The Nation*, March 9, 2018.

9. "Language at the Centre of Decolonisation," University of Witwatersrand, Johannesburg site, March 3, 2017.

10. Socrates Mbamalu, "How Can African Languages Be Protected?," This Is Africa website, March 22, 2017.

11. Ibid.

12. Oluwamuyiwa Aikomo, "Trevor Noah Slams South African Xenophobic Attacks, Receive Praises from Nigerians," Nollywoodalive .com, September 3, 2019.

13. Christian Grade, "The Historical Development of the Written Discourses on Ubuntu," *South African Journal of Philosophy* 30 (October 2013).

14. Michael Onyebuchi Eze, *Intellectual History in Contemporary South Africa* (New York: Palgrave Macmillan, 2010), 191.

15. Thomas A. Hale, *Griots and Griottes* (Bloomington: Indiana University Press, 1998), 186.

16. Ibid.

17. Interview with the author, February 13, 2020.

18. Hale, *Griots and Griottes*, 10. Hale offers a more specific breakdown of the label in different languages across western Africa. I am indebted to Professor Hale for allowing me to rely heavily on his work for this section.

19. The governor-general was Jules Brévié, as quoted by Hale in *Griots and Griottes*, 222.

20. Ibn Battuta, *Travels in Asia and Africa*, trans. H. A. R. Gibb (London: Routledge & Sons, 1953), 328.

21. Lucy Durán, "Ballaké Sissoko, Malian Kora Player Has His Kora Destroyed by USA Customs," February 5, 2020, Facebook, Ballake Sissoko fan page.

22. Interview with the author, February 13, 2020.

23. Joe Penney, "How US Customs Officers Damaged a Revered West African Artist's Custom-Built Kora," Quartz Africa website, February 6, 2020.

24. Thomas A. Hale, "De Sotuma-Sere à New York City, L'Itinéraire de Jali Papa Bunka Susso, Griot Gambien," *Africultures*, no. 61 (October–December 2004).

25. Interview with the author, February 13, 2020.

26. Hale, *Griots and Griottes*, 23.

27. Interview with the author, October 9, 2019.

28. Ibid.

29. Hale, *Griots and Griottes*, 80.

30. Geoffrey Haydon and Dennis Marks, eds., "Introduction," in *Repercussions: A Celebration of African-American Music* (London: Century Publishing, 1985), 9.

31. Arnold Lubasch, "'Roots' Plagiarism Suit Is Settled," *New York Times*, December 15, 1978.

32. Philip Nobile, "Alex Haley's Hoax," *Village Voice*, February 23, 1993.

33. Adam Henig, *Alex Haley's Roots: An Author's Odyssey* (CreateSpace, 2014), 47–48. Henig relies on reportage by Phil Stanford and his article "Roots and Grafts on the Haley Story," *Washington Star*, April 8, 1979.

34. Henig, *Alex Haley's Roots*, 46.

35. Philip Nobile, "The Prize That Taints the Pulitzer's Ethics and Honor," History News Network, April 20, 2018, https://historynews network.org/article/168815.

36. Alex Haley, *Roots: The Saga of an American Family* (New York: Doubleday, 1976), x.

37. Mark Ottaway, "Tangled Roots," *Sunday Times*, April 10, 1977.

38. Nobile, "Alex Haley's Hoax."

39. Ibid.

40. Donna Britt, "Rooting Up Haley's Legacy," *Washington Post*, March 2, 1993.

41. Clarence Page, "Alex Haley's Facts Can Be Doubted, but Not His Truths," *Chicago Tribune*, March 10, 1993.

42. Nobile, "The Prize That Taints the Pulitzer's Ethics and Honor."

43. Alex Haley, "My Furthest-Back Person—'The African,'" *New York Times Magazine*, July 16, 1972.

44. Donald Wright, "Uprooting Kunta Kinte: On the Perils of Relying on Encyclopedic Informants," *History in Africa* 8 (1981).

45. Hale, *Griots and Griottes*, 253.

46. Ibid., 254–55.

47. Ibid., 255.

48. Interview with the author, October 9, 2019.

49. E. A. Ritter, *Shaka Zulu* (1955; repr., London: Penguin, 1978), 7.

50. "Shaka," Wikipedia page entry.

51. Ritter, *Shaka Zulu*, 237.

52. Hale, *Griots and Griottes*, 256.

53. Ngũgĩ wa Thiong'o, "The Myth of Tribe in African Politics," *Transition*, no. 101 Looking Ahead (2009), Indiana University Press on behalf of the Hutchins Center for African and African American Research at Harvard University, p. 17.

54. Martin Meredith, *The State of Africa: A History of the Continent since Independence* (London: Simon & Schuster, 2011), 155.

55. Marq de Villiers and Sheila Hirtle, *Into Africa* (Toronto: Key Porter Books, 1997), 104.

56. Gérard Prunier, *The Rwanda Crisis: History of a Genocide* (New York: Columbia University Press, 1997), 26.

57. Prunier, *The Rwanda Crisis*, 47–54.

58. Jamal Mahjoub, *A Line in the River* (London: Bloomsbury Publishing, 2018), 91.

59. Louis Takács, "Issa Somali [1914]," *Let Me Get There: Visualizing Immigrants, Transnational Migrants & U.S. Citizens Abroad, 1914–1925* website. Takács cites and shows key documents, including the Chicago manifest and newspaper articles covering the Somalis. I am indebted for his kind permission in letting me rely on his research.

60. "Freaks in Paris Togas," *Washington Post*, March 24, 1914.

61. Takács, e-mail to the author, September 23, 2019.

62. Takács, "Issa Somali [1914]."

63. Barnum & Bailey advertisement, *New York Sun*, March 22, 1914.

64. "The Assembly Ground of the Nations," *Muncie Sunday Star*, July 26, 1914.

65. Takács, "Issa Somali [1914]."

Chapter 11

1. Basil Davidson, *Let Freedom Come* (Boston: Little, Brown, 1978), 155.

2. Roger Tangri, "Some New Aspects of the Nyasaland Native Rising of 1915," *African Historical Studies* 4, no. 2 (1971): 305.

3. George Shepperson and Thomas Price, *Independent African: John Chilembwe and the Origins, Setting and Significance of the Nyasaland Native Rising of 1915* (Edinburgh: Edinburgh University Press, 1987), 174.

4. John McCracken, *A History of Malawi, 1859–1966* (Rochester, NY: James Currey, 2013), 148.

5. Robert Rotberg, *The Rise of Nationalism in Central Africa* (Cambridge, MA: Harvard University Press, 1965), 82–83.

6. E. V. Debs, "Statement to the Court," September 18, 1918, https://www.marxists.org/archive/debs/works/1918/court.htm.

7. Tangri, "Some New Aspects of the Nyasaland Native Rising of 1915," 311.

8. Rotberg, *The Rise of Nationalism in Central Africa*, 84.

9. McCracken, *A History of Malawi, 1859–1966*, 141.

10. McCracken, *A History of Malawi, 1859–1966*, 127.

11. Michael Crowder, "The First World War and Its Consequences in Africa," UNESCO, 1985, https://en.unesco.org/courier/news-views-online/first-world-war-and-its-consequences-africa.

12. Safaa Kasroui, "Moroccan Soldiers Fought in All Major Battles of WWI," *Morocco World News*, November 12, 2018.

13. Davidson, *Let Freedom Come*, 171.

14. *Lagos Weekly Record*, June 12, 1919, as quoted in James Coleman, *Nigeria: Background to Nationalism* (Berkeley: University of California Press, 1971), 184.

15. Edmund Hogan, *Cross and Scalpel: Jean-Marie Coquard among the Egba of Yorubaland* (Ibadan: HEBN, 2012), 451–63.

16. *Nigerian Pioneer*, September 7, 1917, as quoted in Coleman, *Nigeria*, 453.

17. Cheryl Johnson, "Grass Roots Organizing: Women in Anticolonial Activity in Southwestern Nigeria," *African Studies Review* 25, no. 2/3 (June–September 1982): 137–57.

18. Judith Van Allen, "Sitting on a Man: Colonialism and the Lost Political Institutions of Igbo Women," *Canadian Journal of African Studies* 6, no. 2 (1972): 170.

19. Marc Matera, Misty Bastian, and Susan Kingsley Kent, *The Women's War of 1929* (New York: Palgrave Macmillan, 2012), 2–3; C. L. R.

James, *A History of Pan-African Revolt* (Oakland, CA: PM Press, 2012), 72.

20. A. E. Afigbo, "Review of *Igbo Village Affairs*, 2nd ed., by M. M. Green," *Journal of the Historical Society of Nigeria* 4, no. 1 (December 1967): 187; Margery Perham, *Native Administration in Nigeria* (Oxford: Oxford University Press, 1962), 212, 246.

21. Gelett Burgess, "The Wild Men of Paris," *Architectural Record*, May 1910, 401.

22. Burgess, "The Wild Men of Paris," 407–40.

23. Alfred Barr, ed., *Picasso: Forty Years of His Art* (New York: Museum of Modern Art, 1939), 60, 62.

24. Andrew Meldrum, "Stealing Beauty," *The Guardian*, March 15, 2006.

25. André Salmon, "Negro Art," *The Burlington Magazine for Connoisseurs* 36, no. 205 (April 1920): 166.

26. Salmon, "Negro Art," 166.

27. Rachel Gould, "In Montreal, Picasso Comes 'Face-to-Face' with the African Art That Inspired Him," Culture Trip, July 17, 2018, https://theculturetrip.com/north-america/canada/articles/in-montreal-picasso-comes-face-to-face-with-the-african-art-that-inspired-him.

28. Adeline Adams, "Of Gains Tossed Aside," *American Magazine of Art* 17, no. 9 (September 1926): 488–90.

29. Melville Herskovits, "Negro Art: African and American," *Social Forces* 5, no. 2 (December 1926): 294.

30. Aldon Morris, *The Scholar Denied: W. E. B. Du Bois and the Birth of Modern Sociology* (Berkeley: University of California Press, 2017), 210–11. At the annual meeting of the African Studies Association in Atlanta in 2018, its president, Jean Allman, gave a lecture titled, "#Herskovits Must Fall? A Meditation on Whiteness, African Studies, and the Unfinished Business of 1968." While Allman "chronicled . . . how the field became dominated by white men," scholar Marius Kothor noted in an essay that the audience was predominantly white, and "the resounding applause made it clear to me that the majority of the people in attendance were convinced that the issues Allman had discussed were outside of that room—somewhere out there in the big bad racist world." See Marius Kothor, "Race and the Politics of Knowledge Production in African Studies," Black Perspectives, April 8, 2019, https://www.aaihs.org/race-and-the-politics-of-knowledge-production-in-african-studies.

31. Janet Flanner, *Paris Was Yesterday, 1925–1939* (1972; repr., New York: Mariner Books, 1988), xx–xxi.

32. Lynn Haney, *Naked at the Feast* (London: Robson Books, 1981).

Chapter 12

1. Tyler Stovall, *Paris Noir: African Americans in the City of Light* (New York: Houghton Mifflin, 1996), 104.

2. Janet Vaillant, *Black, French and African: A Life of Léopold Sédar Senghor* (Cambridge, MA: Harvard University Press, 1990), 79.

3. Vaillant, *Black, French and African*, 91.

4. Eslanda Robeson, "Black Paris," *Challenge: A Literary Quarterly* 1, no. 4 (1936): 12–13.

5. Maurice Delafosse, *The Negroes of Africa*, trans. F. Fligelman (1931; repr., Washington, DC: Associated Publishers, 1968), 249–50.

6. Oswald Spengler, *The Decline of the West* (1918; repr., Oxford: Oxford University Press, 1991), 254.

7. Edward Wilmot Blyden, *West Africa before Europe and Other Addresses* (London: C. M. Phillips, 1905), 140.

8. *La Revue du Monde Noir*, Autumn 1931 (1st issue).

9. Paulette Nardal, "The Awakening of Race Consciousness," *La Revue du Monde Noir*, April 1932.

10. Alain Locke, *The New Negro* (1925; repr., New York: Touchstone, 1999), 14.

11. Nnamdi Azikiwe, *My Odyssey* (New York: Praeger, 1970), 143–44.

12. Kora Véron and Thomas A. Hale, *Les Ecrits d'Aimé Césaire: Bio-bibliographie commentée (1913–2008)*, 2 vols. (Paris: Honoré Champion, 2013), 1:21.

13. Thomas A. Hale, explanation in private e-mail sent to the author, March 25, 2020; the translation of Senghor's "Emotion" phrase comes from the *Stanford Encyclopedia of Philosophy*.

14. Jacques-Louis Hymans, *Léopold Sédar Senghor: An Intellectual Biography* (Edinburgh: Edinburgh University Press, 1971), 90.

15. Hymans, *Léopold Sédar Senghor*, 102.

16. Hymans, *Léopold Sédar Senghor*, 84–85.

17. Paulin Joachim as quoted in Jules-Rosette Bennetta, *Black Paris: The African Writers' Landscape* (Urbana: University of Illinois Press, 1998), 35.

18. Bennetta, *Black Paris*, 36.

19. Jean-Paul Sartre, "Black Orpheus," trans. John MacCombie, *The Massachusetts Review* 6, no. 1 (Autumn 1964–Winter 1965): 13–52. MacCombie's was the first American translation and publication, and it was pointed out in the issue that only one previous English translation had been available in an obscure and out-of-print French African magazine in 1951.

20. Florian Bobin, "Poetic Injustice: The Senghor Myth and Senegal's Independence," *Review of African Political Economy*, June 12, 2020.

21. Bobin, "Poetic Injustice."

22. Obiajuru Maduakor, "Soyinka as a Literary Critic," *Research in African Literature* 17, no. 1, Special Issue on Criticism and Poetry (Spring 1986), 3–4.

23. Wole Soyinka, *The Burden of Memory, the Muse of Forgiveness* (Oxford: Oxford University Press, 1999), 144.

24. Stovall, *Paris Noir*, 112.

25. Jomo Kenyatta, *Facing Mount Kenya* (London: Heinemann Educational Books, 1979), 59.

26. Kenyatta, *Facing Mount Kenya*, 114.

27. Bronislaw Malinowski, "Introduction," in Kenyatta, *Facing Mount Kenya*, xi.

28. Kenyatta, *Facing Mount Kenya*, 318.

29. Bildad Kaggia, W. de Leeuw, and Mwaganu Kaggia, *The Struggle for Freedom and Justice: The Life and Times of the Freedom Fighter and Politician Bildad M. Kaggia* (Nairobi: Transafrica Press, 2012), 114.

30. Jeremy Murray-Brown, *Kenyatta* (New York: Dutton, 1972), 231.

31. W. Maloba, *Kenyatta and Britain: An Account of Political Transformation, 1929–1963* (London: Palgrave Macmillan, 2018), 64.

32. Murray-Brown, *Kenyatta*, 222.

33. John Clarke, "Paul Robeson: The Artist as Activist and Social Thinker," *Présence Africaine*, no. 107 (1978): 231.

34. Susan Williams, *Colour Bar* (London: Penguin, 2016), 11.

35. Gerald Horne, *Paul Robeson: The Artist as Revolutionary* (London: Pluto Press, 2016), 6–7.

36. Paul Robeson, "The Culture of the Negro," *The Spectator*, June 15, 1934, 916.

37. Martin Duberman, *Paul Robeson* (New York: Knopf, 1989), 176.

38. Paul Robeson, *Daily Herald*, January 26, 1935.

39. Paul Robeson, "Primitives," *The New Statesman and Nation*, August 8, 1936, 191–92.

40. Sterling Stuckey, "'I Want to Be African': Paul Robeson and the Ends of Nationalist Theory and Practice, 1914–1945," *The Massachusetts Review* 17, no. 1 (Spring 1976): 100.

41. Duberman, *Paul Robeson*, 182.

42. Charles Musser, "Presenting: 'A True Idea of the African of Today': Two Documentary Forays by Paul and Eslanda Robeson, *Film History* 18, no. 4 (2006): 424.

43. Musser, "Presenting," 427.

44. Duberman, *Paul Robeson*, 341.

Chapter 13

1. The evidence for this is in documents and in the memoir of Mussolini's first commander of the invasion, General Emilio de Bono, *Anno XIIII*. The basis for many of the additional facts in this chapter can be found in Jeff Pearce, *Prevail: The Inspiring Story of Ethiopia's Victory over Mussolini's Invasion, 1935–1941* (New York: Skyhorse Publishing, 2014), which tells the whole story of the war in far greater detail.

2. Stand-alone quote for George Seldes, *Sawdust Caesar* (New York: Harper & Brothers, 1935).

3. David Darrah, *Hail Caesar!* (New York: Hale, Cushman & Flint, 1936), 275.

4. George W. Baer, *The Coming of the Italian-Ethiopian War* (Cambridge, MA: Harvard University Press, 1967), 60.

5. James Baldwin, *Nobody Knows My Name* (New York: Dell Press, 1963), 73.

6. Richard Bak, *Joe Louis: The Great Black Hope* (New York: Da Capo Press, 1998), 90.

7. Lynn Haney, *Naked at the Feast* (London: Robson Books, 1981), 196.

8. Geoffrey Harmsworth, *Abyssinia Marches On* (London: Hutchinson & Co., 1941), 26–27.

9. *The Black Man*, July 1935.

10. Kwame Nkrumah, *Ghana: The Autobiography of Kwame Nkrumah* (London: Thames Nelson & Sons, 1957), 27.

11. Nelson Mandela, *Long Walk to Freedom* (Boston: Little, Brown, 1994), 292.

12. C. L. R. James, "Is This Worth a War? The League's Scheme to Rob Abyssinia of Its Independence," *New Leader*, October 4, 1935.

13. Alan Mackenzie, "Radical Pan-Africanism in the 1930s: A Discussion with C.L.R. James," *Radical History Review* 1980 (Fall 1980): 68–75.

14. Jeremy Murray-Brown, *Kenyatta* (New York: Dutton, 1972), 362n.

15. William R. Scott, "Malaku E. Bayen: Ethiopian Emissary to Black America, 1936–1941," *Ethiopian Observer* 15 (1972): 132–38.

16. Marcel Junod, *Warrior without Weapons*, trans. Edward Fitzgerald (London: Jonathan Cape, 1951), 61.

17. *The Black Man*, March–April 1937.

18. Interview with Keith Bowers, author of *Imperial Exile*, December 6, 2017.

19. Danny Duncan Collum, ed., *African Americans in the Spanish Civil War: "This Ain't Ethiopia, but It'll Do"* (New York: Macmillan, 1992), 5.

20. The best source on the intricacies is the brilliantly researched book by Ian Campbell, *The Plot to Kill Graziani: The Attempted Assassination of Mussolini's Viceroy* (Addis Ababa: Addis Ababa University Press, 2010).

21. Poggiali, *Diario AOI*, as quoted and translated by Christopher Duggan, *Fascist Voices* (London: The Bodley Head, 2012), 289.

22. Ladislas Sava, *New Times and Ethiopian News*, December 14, 1940.

23. Imru Zelleke, *A Journey*, self-published memoir, 2016, 29.

24. For a detailed breakdown of numbers and identification of nobles, intellectuals, and other victims, see the appendices in Ian Campbell, *The Addis Ababa Massacre* (London: Hurst, 2017).

25. Twitter, @MaazaMengiste, 3:38 p.m., 3:41 p.m., December 4, 2019.

26. Tsehai Berhane-Selassie, "Women Guerrilla Fighters," *North East Africa Studies* 1, no. 3 (1979–1980): 73–83.

27. Christopher Hibbert, *Mussolini: The Rise and Fall of Il Duce* (New York: St. Martin's Griffin, 2008), 124.

28. Anthony Eden, *Facing the Dictators: The Eden Memoirs* (London: Cassell, 1962), 297.

29. Imru Zelleke, *A Journey*, 112.

30. Patrick Gilkes, *The Dying Lion* (Los Angeles: Tsehai Publishers, 2007), 180; David Killingray, "'A Swift Agent of Government': Air Power in British Colonial Africa, 1916–1939," *Journal of African History* 25, no. 4 (1984): 443.

31. Alden Whitman, "Anthony Eden Is Dead at 79," *New York Times*, January 15, 1977, 6.

32. As quoted by Angelo Del Boca, *The Ethiopian War, 1935–1941* (Chicago: University of Chicago Press, 1969), 65.

33. "The Story of the Statue of Indro Montanelli Defaced in Milan," *Il Post*, March 10, 2019.

34. "The Story of the Statue of Indro Montanelli Defaced in Milan"; Lorenzo Tondo, "Milan Mayor Refuses to Remove Defaced Statue of Italian Journalist," *The Guardian*, June 14, 2020.

35. Tondo, "Milan Mayor Refuses to Remove Defaced Statue of Italian Journalist."

Chapter 14

1. Sylvia Pankhurst, *Ex-Italian Somaliland* (London: Watts & Co., 1951), 163.

2. Pankhurst, *Ex-Italian Somaliland*, 222–23; Abdi Ismail Samatar, *Africa's First Democrats* (Bloomington: Indiana University Press, 2016), 43–44.

3. Pankhurst, *Ex-Italian Somaliland*, 304.

4. UN Trusteeship Council, *Official Records*, 11th session, 415th meeting, June 9, 1952, https://digitallibrary.un.org/record/1627097?ln=en, 18.

5. Samatar, *Africa's First Democrats*, 59. I am greatly indebted to Professor Samatar for allowing me to rely heavily on his works for this chapter.

6. Samatar, *Africa's First Democrats*, 185.

7. Ibid., 22–24.

8. Interview with the author, December 23, 2020.

9. Ibid.

10. Samatar, *Africa's First Democrats*, 95, 96–97.

11. Ibid., 96, 246n.

12. I. M. Lewis, *A Modern History of Somalia* (Boulder, CO: Westview Press, 1988), 172.

13. Lewis, *A Modern History of Somalia*, 100.

14. Ibid., 173–74; Samatar, *Africa's First Democrats*, 110–14.

15. Samatar, *Africa's First Democrats*, 115.

16. Ibid., 147, 156, 192.

17. Ibid., 175.

18. Ken Menkhaus, "Calm between the Storms? Patterns of Political Violence in Somalia, 1950–1980," *Journal of Eastern African Studies*, August 22, 2014, 9.

19. Samatar, *Africa's First Democrats*, 207.

20. Daron Acemoglu, Simon Johnson, and James Robinson, "An African Success Story: Botswana," Massachusetts Institute of Technology, Department of Economics Working Papers 01-37, July 2001, 13.

21. "Mr. Chamberlain and Bechuanaland," *Irish Times*, November 16, 1895; Daron Acemoglu and James Robinson, *Why Nations Fail* (New York: Crown Publishing, 2012), 405.

22. "Bechuanaland Now Nation of Botswana," *New York Times*, September 30, 1966, 1.

23. Richard Stevens, "The New Republic of Botswana," *Africa Report*, October 1, 1966, 17.

24. UPI, *Washington Post*, "Botswana Rail Troubles Arise," October 22, 1966, A14.

25. UPI, *Los Angeles Times*, "S. Africa Raid in Botswana Kills 13; U.S. Recalls Envoy," June 16, 1985, 1; UN Chronicle, "'Unprovoked and Unwarranted Attack' on Botswana Condemned by Security Council," June 1985, 22.

26. "From Exile to President," *New York Times*, October 1, 1966, p. 10.

27. Willie Henderson, "Seretse Khama: A Personal Appreciation," *African Affairs* 89, no. 354 (January 1990): 30.

28. Henderson, "Seretse Khama," 38.

29. Ibid., 47.

30. Seretse Khama, "A Policy of Prudence" (address at Fordham University, October 1965), *Africa Report*, October 1, 1966, 19.

31. Susan Williams, *Colour Bar* (London: Penguin, 2016), 321.

32. Ibid., 322.

33. J. Clark Leith, *Why Botswana Prospered* (Montreal: McGill-Queen's University Press, 2005), 36.

34. Acemoglu and Robinson, *Why Nations Fail*, 407, 411.

35. "Africa's Prize Democracy; Botswana," *The Economist*, November 6, 2004, 50.

36. Leith, *Why Botswana Prospered*, 26.

37. Acemoglu and Robinson, *Why Nations Fail*, 412.

38. George Ayittey, *Indigenous African Institutions*, 2nd ed. (Ardsley, NY: Transnational Publishers, 2006), 515.

39. J. Clark Leith, "Botswana: A Case Study of Economic Policy, Prudence and Growth," World Bank Working Paper, August 31, 1999, 4.

40. Willie Henderson, "Independent Botswana: A Reappraisal of Foreign Policy Options," *African Affairs* 73, no. 290 (January 1974): 47.

Chapter 15

1. Raymond Smyke, "Fatima Massaquoi Fahnbulleh: Pioneer Woman Educator, 1912–1978," 1990 article reprinted in *Liberian Studies Journal* 31 (2006): 46.

2. Smyke, "Fatima Massaquoi Fahnbulleh," 53n11.

3. Fatima Massaquoi, *The Autobiography of an African Princess* (New York: Palgrave Macmillan, 2013), 158.

4. Massaquoi, *The Autobiography of an African Princess*, 159.

5. Nick Rankin, *Telegram from Guernia* (London: Faber and Faber, 2003), 154. For a more in-depth study of the German efforts, see George Steer, *Judgment on German Africa* (London: Hodder and Stoughton, 1939).

6. Hans Massaquoi, *Destined to Witness* (New York: HarperCollins, 1999), 61.

7. Massaquoi, *The Autobiography of an African Princess*, 224–25.

8. "Nearly Fifty Alien Students at Fisk U," *Pittsburgh Courier*, March 4, 1944.

9. Massaquoi, *The Autobiography of an African Princess*, 247n6.

10. "Autobiography Judged Hers," *Baltimore Afro-American*, February 10, 1945.

11. "Autobiography Judged Hers."

12. "Autobiography Judged Hers."

13. Smyke, "Fatima Massaquoi Fahnbulleh," 49.

14. Vivian Seton, speaking about *The Autobiography of an African Princess* for a Library of Congress video, YouTube, October 2, 2014, https://www.youtube.com/watch?v=ZzpGrSJZ5sw.

15. Ayodeji Olukoju, *Culture and Customs of Liberia* (Westport, CT: Greenwood Press, 2006), 105.

16. Smyke, "Fatima Massaquoi Fahnbulleh," 44.

17. Placide Tempels, *Bantu Philosophy*, facsimile of English ed. (Paris: Présence Africaine, 1959, by Centre Aequatoria), 76.

18. Tempels, *Bantu Philosophy*, 36.

19. Tempels, *Bantu Philosophy*, 17.

20. Pius Mosima, *Philosophic Sagacity and Intercultural Philosophy* (Leiden: African Studies Centre, 2016), 46.

21. Okot p'Bitek, "Fr. Tempels' Bantu Philosophy," *Transition*, no. 13 (March–April 1964): 15.

22. Paulin Hountondji, *African Philosophy: Myth and Reality*, 2nd ed. (Bloomington: Indiana University Press, 1996), 53–54.

23. Mosima, *Philosophic Sagacity and Intercultural Philosophy*, 45.

24. Mosima, *Philosophic Sagacity and Intercultural Philosophy*, 46, 45.

25. Mosima, *Philosophic Sagacity and Intercultural Philosophy*, 13.

26. Richard Sandomir, "John Mbiti, 87, Dies; Punctured Myths about African Religions," *New York Times*, October 24, 2019.

27. John Mbiti, *African Religions and Philosophy* (London: Heinemann, 1969), 17.

28. Mbiti, *African Religions and Philosophy*, 207.

29. Mbiti, *African Religions and Philosophy*, 244–45.

30. G. O. M. Tasie, Review, *Journal of Modern African Studies* 12, no. 2 (June 1974): 327.

31. Aylward Shorter, Review, *African Affairs* 69, no. 277 (October 1970): 392.

32. Okot p'Bitek, *Decolonizing African Religions*, reprint of *African Religion in Western Scholarship* (New York: Diasporic Africa Press, 2011), 19.

33. John Mbiti, "The Encounter of Christian Faith and African Religion," *Christian Century*, August 27–September 3, 1980, 817–20, version reproduced at Religion Online.

34. Kibuijo M. Kalumba, "A New Analysis of Mbiti's 'The Concept of Time,'" *Philosophia Africana* 8, no. 1 (2005): 11–19.

35. Interview with the author, May 21, 2020.

36. Sylvester Ogbechie, *Ben Enwonwu: The Making of an African Modernist* (Rochester, NY: University of Rochester Press, 2008), 62.

37. Ogbechie, *Ben Enwonwu*, 62.

38. "After Nigerian Painting Fetches $1.8M, Artist's Son Says: 'I Hope It's Coming Back to Lagos,'" story transcript, *As It Happens*, CBC Radio, October 17, 2019.

39. Ben Enwonwu, "Problems of the African Artist Today," speech reprinted in *Présence Africaine*, June–November 1956, 174.

40. Enwonwu, "Problems of the African Artist Today," 175.

41. Ibid., 176.

42. Ibid., 178.

43. Interview with the author, May 21, 2020.

44. "Statue to Commemorate Royal Visit to Nigeria," *Manchester Guardian*, June 11, 1957, 5.

45. Ogbechie, *Ben Enwonwu*, 138–39.

46. "Statue to Commemorate Royal Visit to Nigeria."

47. Naima Mohamud, "Ben Enwonwu: The Nigerian Painter behind 'Africa's Mona Lisa,'" BBC News, October 17, 2019, https://www.bbc.com/news/world-africa-50071212.

48. Ciku Kimeria, "A Recently Found Ben Enwonwu Painting Has Sold at Seven Times Its Valuation of $1.4 Million," Quartz Africa, October 16, 2019, https://qz.com/africa/1729512/nigerian-artist-ben -enwonwu-painting-sold-by-sothebys-at-1-4m.

49. "Decades after It Went Missing, Nigerian Masterpiece Is Found in London Apartment," story transcript, As It Happens, CBC Radio, February 7, 2018.

50. Barbara Lindop, Sekoto: The Art of Gerard Sekoto (London: Pavilion Books, 1995), 15.

51. Gerard Sekoto, "Autobiography," Présence Africaine, no. 69, 190.

52. Interview with the author, May 21, 2020. Ogbechie says Enwonwu told him directly how he had let Sekoto stay with him for a short while and how they influenced each other.

53. Sekoto, "Autobiography," 190.

54. Lindop, Sekoto, 19.

55. Chloë Reid, "The Artist: Sekoto's Life," Gerard Sekoto Foundation, https://www.gerardsekotofoundation.com/artist-overview.htm.

56. "Leading Black South African Painter Staying in Paris despite Acclaim at Home," Reuters, November 23, 1989.

57. Reid, "The Artist."

58. "Leading Black South African Painter Staying in Paris despite Acclaim at Home."

59. Lindop, Sekoto, 26, 29.

60. Christine Eyene, "Sekoto and Négritude: The Ante-room of French Culture," Third Text 24, no. 4 (July 5, 2010): 430.

61. Richard Powell, Black Art: A Cultural History (New York: Thames & Hudson, 2002), 114.

62. Hazel Rowley, "Richard Wright's Africa," The Antioch Review 58, no. 4 (Autumn 2000): 417–18.

63. Rowley, "Richard Wright's Africa," 414.

64. Richard Wright, Black Power: Three Books from Exile (New York: HarperCollins, 2008), 172.

65. Ibid., 417.

66. Susan Williams, White Malice (New York: PublicAffairs, 2021), 61–63.

67. Richard Wright, "Tradition and Industrialization: The Plight of the Tragic Elite in Africa," Présence Africaine, nos. 8–10 (June–November 1956): 355.

68. Henry Louis Gates, Tradition and the Black Atlantic: Critical Theory in the African Diaspora (Philadelphia: Basic Civitas, 2010), 12.

69. Wright, "Tradition and Industrialization," 358.

70. James Baldwin, *Nobody Knows My Name* (New York: Dell Press, 1963), 48.

71. David Leeming, *James Baldwin: A Biography* (New York: Knopf, 1995), 207.

72. Leeming, *James Baldwin*, 210.

73. James Baldwin, *Notes of a Native Son* (1955; repr., Boston: Beacon Press, 2012), 123.

Chapter 16

1. M. P. K. Sorrenson, *Origins of European Settlement in Kenya* (Oxford: Oxford University Press, 1968), 272.

2. David Anderson, *Histories of the Hanged* (London: Weidenfeld & Nicolson, 2005), 25.

3. Sorrenson, *Origins of European Settlement in Kenya*, 275–77.

4. Anderson, *Histories of the Hanged*, 3.

5. Ibid., 9.

6. Robert Edgerton, *Mau Mau: An African Crucible* (London: I. B. Tauris, 1990), 20.

7. Don Barnett and Karari Njama, *Mau Mau from Within* (New York: Monthly Review Press, 1970), 36–37; Anderson, *Histories of the Hanged*, 17.

8. Louis Leakey, *Defeating Mau Mau* (1954; repr., London: Routledge, 2004), 42–49.

9. *End of Empire—Kenya*, Granada Television, United Kingdom, 1985.

10. Marshall Clough, *Mau Mau Memoirs: History, Memory and Politics* (London: Lynn Rienner Publishers, 1998), 131.

11. Interview with Bildad Kaggia, *End of Empire—Kenya*.

12. Jeremy Murray-Brown, *Kenyatta* (New York: Dutton, 1973), 290–93.

13. Murray-Brown, *Kenyatta*, 290–93.

14. Interview with Bildad Kaggia, *End of Empire—Kenya*.

15. Bildad Kaggia, *Roots of Freedom: 1921–1963* (Nairobi: East African Publishing House, 1975), 130.

16. Murray-Brown, *Kenyatta*, 312.

17. Ibid., 316.

18. Clough, *Mau Mau Memoirs*, 136.

19. M. P. K. Sorrenson, *Land Reform in the Kikuyu Country* (Oxford: Oxford University Press, 1967), 98.

20. Anderson, *Histories of the Hanged*, 7.

21. Daniel Branch, *Defeating Mau Mau, Creating Kenya* (New York: Cambridge University Press, 2009), 75–77.

22. Edgerton, *Mau Mau*, 159.

23. Caroline Elkins, *Imperial Reckoning* (New York: Henry Holt, 2005), 86–87.

24. Anderson, *Histories of the Hanged*, 125–27.

25. *End of Empire—Kenya*.

26. U.K. Hansard, July 27, 1959.

27. Manning Marable, *Malcolm X: A Life of Reinvention* (New York: Viking, 2011), 372.

28. Elkins, *Imperial Reckoning*, xiv.

29. A. S. Cleary, "The Myth of Mau Mau in Its International Context," *African Affairs* 89, no. 355 (April 1990): 227–45.

30. Robert Ruark, "Your Guns Go with You," *Life*, February 16, 1953.

31. Ruark, "Your Guns Go with You."

32. Edgerton, *Mau Mau*, 151.

33. Robert Ruark, "Foreword," in *Something of Value* (1955; repr., Cutchogue, NY: Buccaneer Books, 2009).

34. Clough, *Mau Mau Memoirs*, 38.

35. "Documentary 'Mau Mau!' at Embassy," *New York Times*, July 14, 1955.

36. *Mau Mau*, Rock-Price Productions, 1955.

37. Gerald Horne, *Mau Mau in Harlem? The U.S. and the Liberation of Kenya* (New York: Palgrave Macmillan, 2009), 115; James Meriwether, "African Americans and the Mau Mau Rebellion: Militancy, Violence, and the Struggle for Freedom," *Journal of American Ethnic History* 17, no. 4 (Summer 1998): 63–86.

38. Cleary, "The Myth of Mau Mau in Its International Context," 227–45.

39. Meriwether, "African Americans and the Mau Mau Rebellion," 63–86.

40. Meriwether, "African Americans and the Mau Mau Rebellion," 63–86.

41. Malcom X's speech to rally at the Williams Institutional CME Church in Harlem, December 20, 1964; this is sometimes described as taking place in recent sources at the Audubon Ballroom, but there is no reason to believe the *New York Times* sent its reporter to the wrong venue and presumably reported the location properly.

42. "Malcolm Favors a Mau Mau in U.S.: At Harlem Rally, He Urges Negroes to 'Even Score'" *New York Times*, December 21, 1964, 20.

43. FBI memo dated December 21, 1964, now publicly released and available at https://vault.fbi.gov.

44. Malcom X's speech to rally at the Williams Institutional CME Church in Harlem, December 20, 1964.

45. Question-and-answer session after Malcolm X's speech to civil rights workers from Mississippi, January 1, 1965.

46. Malcom X's speech to Militant Labor Forum at Palm Gardens, New York, January 7, 1965.

47. Malcolm X's speech to Organization of Afro-American Unity, Audubon Ballroom, Harlem, New York, June 28, 1964.

48. Brian Glanville, "Malcolm X," *New Statesman*, June 12, 1964, 901.

49. Malcolm X on WMCA Radio, New York, November 28, 1964.

50. Abram Martin, "Apartheid and Malcolm X," *The New Leader*, June 22, 1964, 9.

51. Mickie Mwanzia Koster, "Malcolm X, the Mau Mau, and Kenya's New Revolutionaries: A Legacy of Transnationalism," *Journal of African American History* 100, no. 2 (Spring 2015): 250–71.

52. Koster, "Malcolm X, the Mau Mau, and Kenya's New Revolutionaries," 250–71.

53. "Kenya Mau Mau Memorial Funded by UK Unveiled," BBC News, September 15, 2015, https://www.bbc.com/news/world-africa-34231890.

54. Bethwell Ogot, *My Footprints in the Sands of Time* (Victoria, BC: Trafford Publishing, 2003), 57–58.

55. Bethwell Ogot, Review, *Journal of African History* 46, no. 3 (2005): 495.

56. B. E. Kipkorir, "The Kolloa Affray, Kenya 1950," *Transafrican Journal of History* 2, no. 2 (1972): 114–29.

57. Bethwell Ogot, "Mau Mau & Nationhood: The Untold Story," in *Mau Mau and Nationhood*, ed. E. S. Odihambo and John Lonsdale (Oxford: James Currey, 2003), 34.

58. Peter Lennon, "A Call to Arms," *The Guardian*, January 13, 2001.

59. Alice Cherki, *Frantz Fanon: A Portrait*, trans. Nadia Benabid (Ithaca, NY: Cornell University Press, 2006), 24.

60. George Orwell, "Shooting an Elephant," *New Writing*, 1936.

61. David Macey, *Frantz Fanon: A Biography* (London: Verso, 2012), 272.

62. Cherki, *Frantz Fanon*, 141.

63. Frantz Fanon, *The Wretched of the Earth*, trans. Richard Philcox (New York: Grove Press, 2004), 58.

64. Ibid., 154.

65. Ibid., 161.

66. Ibid., 51–52.

67. Ibid., 24.

68. Macey, *Frantz Fanon*, 457.

69. Review of "Prisoner of Hate," *Time*, April 30, 1965.

70. Lewis Coser, "The Myth of Peasant Revolt," *Dissent*, May–June 1966, 298–303.

71. Philip Toynbee, "The Student Revolution: A Case for the Defense," *Globe and Mail*, June 25, 1968, 7.

72. Stokely Carmichael, *Stokely Speaks* (1971; repr., Chicago: Chicago Review Press, 2007), 136, 146.

73. Stephen Shames and Bobby Seale, *Power to the People: The World of the Black Panthers* (New York: Abrams Books, 2016), 22.

74. Simon Dawes, "Interview with David Macey on Fanon, Foucault and Race," *Theory, Culture & Society*, January 5, 2011.

75. Interview with Franco Solinas by PierNico Solinas (no relation) in booklet for Criterion release, 2004.

76. Peter Matthews, "The Battle of Algiers: Bombs and Boomerangs," booklet for Criterion release, 2004.

77. Michael Kaufman, "Film Studies," *New York Times*, September 7, 2003.

78. Alistair Horne, "2006 Preface," in *A Savage War of Peace* (New York: New York Review Books, 2006).

Chapter 17

1. James Baldwin, *Nobody Knows My Name* (New York: Dell Press, 1963), 43.

2. Toyin Falola, *Nationalism and African Intellectuals* (Rochester, NY: University of Rochester Press, 2004), 45–46.

3. Lafayette Gaston, "Past Afrocentricity: Reassessing Cheikh Anta Diop's Place in the Afrocentric Frame," special issue, *The Liberator* 8, no. 23 (2009).

4. Carlos Moore, "Conversations with Cheikh Anta Diop," *Présence Africaine*, n.s., no. 149/150 (1989): 376.

5. 2.104, Herodotus, *The Landmark Herodotus*, ed. Robert Strassler (New York: Anchor Books, 2007), 161.

6. Samuel George Morton, *Crania Aegyptica: Observations on Egyptian Ethnography* (Philadelphia: John Pennington, 1844), 65.

7. John Campbell, *Negro-mania: Being an Examination of the Falsely Assumed Equality of the Various Races of Men* (Philadelphia: Campbell and Power, 1851), 10.

8. James Breasted, "The First Philosopher," *The Monist* 12, no. 3 (April 1902): 321–36.

9. James Breasted, *The Conquest of Civilization* (New York: Harper and Brothers, 1926), 43–45.

10. Cheikh Anta Diop, *The African Origin of Civilization*, trans. Mercer Cook (Chicago: Lawrence Hill, 1974), 238.

11. Carleton Coon, *The Origin of the Races* (New York: Knopf, 1962), 656.

12. John Jackson Jr., "'In Ways Unacademical': The Reception of Carleton S. Coon's *The Origin of Races*," *Journal of the History of Biology* 34 (2001): 247–85.

13. Diop, *The African Origin of Civilization*, xiv.

14. Diop, *The African Origin of Civilization*, xiv.

15. Edward Wilmot Blyden, *Christianity, Islam and the Negro Race* (1887; repr., Baltimore, MD: Black Classic Press, 1994), 176n2.

16. George G. M. James, *Stolen Legacy* (New York: Philosophical Library, 1954), 10.

17. William Leo Hansberry, "Book Review: Stolen Legacy," *Journal of Negro Education* 24, no. 2 (Spring 1954):127–29.

18. Moore, "Conversations with Cheikh Anta Diop," 375–76.

19. Diop, *The African Origin of Civilization*, 27–28; see also Cheikh Anta Diop and Yaa-Lengi Ngemi, *Civilization or Barbarism* (Chicago: Lawrence Hill, 1991), 1.

20. Vivant Denon, *Travels in Upper and Lower Egypt during the Campaigns of General Bonaparte in That Country*, trans. Arthur Aiken (New York: Heard and Forman, 1803), 140.

21. Diop, *The African Origin of Civilization*, 7.

22. Toby Wilkinson, *The Rise and Fall of Ancient Egypt* (New York: Random House, 2010), 2.

23. Marc de Villiers and Sheila Hirtle, *Into Africa* (Toronto: Key Porter Books, 1997), 104.

24. G. Mokhtar, ed., *UNESCO General History of Africa*, vol. 2, *Ancient Civilizations of Africa* (London: James Currey, 1990), 20, 37.

25. Mokhtar, *UNESCO General History of Africa*, 20, 52, 53.

26. Charles Finch, "Conversations with Cheikh Anta Diop," *Présence Africaine*, n.s., no. 149/150 (1989): 367.

27. Toby Wilkinson, *Early Dynastic Egypt* (London: Routledge, 1999), 14.

28. Mokhtar, *UNESCO General History of Africa*, 31.

29. Diop and Ngemi, *Civilization or Barbarism*, 217.

30. Verena Schuenemann, Alexander Peltzer, Beatrix Welte, W. Paul van Pelt, Martyna Molak, Chuan-Chao Wang, Anja Furtwängler, Christian Urban, Ella Reiter, Kay Nieselt, Barbara Teßmann, Michael Francken, Katerina Harvati, Wolfgang Haak, Stephan Schiffels, and Johannes Krause, "Ancient Egyptian Mummy Genomes Suggest an Increase of Sub-Saharan African Ancestry in Post-Roman Periods," *Nature Communications* 8 (2017), article no. 15694.

31. Schuenemann et al., "Ancient Egyptian Mummy Genomes Suggest an Increase of Sub-Saharan African Ancestry in Post-Roman Periods."

32. Diop and Ngemi, *Civilization or Barbarism*, 5.

33. Finch, "Conversations with Cheikh Anta Diop," 368.

34. Gaston, "Past Afrocentricity."

35. Finch, "Conversations with Cheikh Anta Diop," 372.

36. Chika Ezeanya-Esiobu, "Adé Olufeko and the Resurrection of Cheikh Anta Diop," *Pambazuka News*, November 24, 2016.

37. Martin Bernal, *Black Athena: The Afroasiatic Roots of Classical Civilization*, 4 vols. (New Brunswick, NJ: Rutgers University Press, 1987–1994), 2:22, 1:18.

38. Bernal, *Black Athena*, 2:22.

39. Robert Pounder, "Black Athena 2: History without Rules," *American Historical Review* 97, no. 2 (April 1992): 461–64.

40. John Baines, "Was Civilization Made in Africa?," *New York Times*, August 11, 1991, 12.

41. Peter Lacovara, "Not Out of Africa, Not: Ancient Egypt, Nubia and the Roots of Western Civilization," draft article shared with the author, September 8, 2020.

42. Bernal, *Black Athena*, 241–42.

43. Bernal, *Black Athena*, 401.

44. Mary Lefkowitz, *Not Out of Africa* (New York: Basic Books, 1996), 137.

45. Lefkowitz, *Not Out of Africa*, 6.

46. Ann Macy Roth, "Africa—Review of Books," *American Historical Review* 102, issue 2 (April 1997): 493–95; Ann Macy Roth, "To the Editor," *American Historical Review* 102, issue 4 (October 1997): 1306–7.

47. John Baines, "Was Civilization Made in Africa?," *New York Times*, August 11, 1991, 12.

48. Bernal, *Black Athena*, 12, 14.

49. Jock Agai, "An Investigation into the Ancient Egyptian Cultural Influences on the Yorubas of Nigeria," *HTS Teologiese Studies/Theological Studies* 69, no. 1 (2013): 01–09.

50. Chisanga Siame, "Katunkumene and Ancient Egypt in Africa," *Journal of Black Studies* 44, no. 3 (April 2013): 252–72.

51. Donald Redford, ed., *The Oxford Encyclopedia of Ancient Egypt* (Oxford: Oxford University Press, 2001), 27.

52. J. L. Keith, "African Students in Great Britain," *African Affairs* 45, no. 179 (April 1946): 65.

53. Keith, "African Students in Great Britain," 65.

54. Nnamdi Azikiwe, *My Odyssey* (New York: Praeger, 1970), 101–2.

55. Tom Schachtman, *Airlift to America* (New York: St. Martin's Press, 2009), 43–44.

56. Ibid., 46, 48.

57. Tom Mboya, *Freedom and After* (1963; repr., Nairobi: East African Educational Publishers, 2008), 138.

58. Ibid., 141.

59. Ibid., 143.

60. Susan Williams, *White Malice* (New York: PublicAffairs, 2021), 79–80, 205–6.

61. Albert Sims, "Africans Beat on Our College Doors," *Harper's*, April 1, 1961, 58.

62. Mboya, *Freedom and After*, 150–51.

63. Tom Mboya, "The American Negro Cannot Look to Africa for an Escape," *New York Times*, July 13, 1969.

64. Ibid.

65. Ibid.

Chapter 18

1. Steve Biko and Millard Arnold, "The Inquest into the Death of Stephen Bantu Biko," in *Black Consciousness in South Africa*, ed. Louis Pollak (New York: Vintage Books, 1979), 343.

2. Reuters, "Something Missed, Biko Inquest Told," *Globe and Mail*, November 23, 1977, 11.

3. "1,210 Mourners Held in S. Africa Swoop," UPI, reprinted in *Toronto Star*, September 16, 1977, A10.

4. "Ugly Humor," editorial, *Toronto Sunday Star*, November 13, 1977, A8.

5. Lauren Gambino, "Ronald Reagan Called African UN Delegates 'Monkeys', Recordings Reveal," The Guardian, July 21, 2019, www.theguardian.com/us-news/2019/jul/31/ronald-reagan-racist-recordings-nixon.

6. "Biko on Death," The New Republic, January 7, 1978, https://newrepublic.com/article/122784/biko-death.

7. Durrell Bowman, *Experiencing Peter Gabriel: A Listener's Companion* (Lanham, MD: Rowman & Littlefield, 2016), 91–92.

8. Reuters, "Miami Vice Viewers Hear Banned Song," *Globe and Mail*, July 22, 1986, A10.

9. Reuters, "Banned Film Being Sold Underground," *Globe and Mail*, August 3, 1988, A8; Deborah Telford for Reuters, "British Conservatives Shun Anti-Apartheid Premiere," *Globe and Mail*, November 25, 1987, C7.

10. Steve Biko, "Black Consciousness and the Quest for a True Humanity," in *Black Theology: The South African Voice*, ed. Basil Moore (London: Hurst & Co., 1973), 38.

11. Steve Biko, "Black Souls in White Skins?," in *I Write What I Like* (New York: Harper & Row, 1978), 21.

12. Xolela Mangcu, *Biko: A Life* (London: I. B. Tauris, 2014), 192–97.

13. Millard Arnold, ed., *The Testimony of Steve Biko* (London: Maurice Temple Smith Publishers, 1979), 139.

14. Steve Biko, preamble to "The Righteousness of Our Strength," in *I Write What I Like*, 121.

15. Noël Mostert, *Frontiers: The Epic of South Africa's Creation and the Tragedy of the Xhosa People* (New York: Knopf, 1992), 1278.

16. Mangcu, *Biko* (see the chapter "Steve Biko in the Intellectual History of the Eastern Cape: The African Elite and European Modernity").

17. Steve Biko, "Some African Cultural Concepts," in *I Write What I Like*, 41.

18. Biko, "Some African Cultural Concepts," 42.

19. Mangcu, *Biko*, 295.

20. Constitution of the Republic of South Africa, Act 200 of 1993: Epilogue after Section 251, as quoted in Christian Gade, "The Historical Development of the Written Discourses on Ubuntu," *South African Journal of Philosophy* 30, issue 3 (2011): 311.

21. Michael Onyebuchi Eze, *Intellectual History in Contemporary South Africa* (New York: Palgrave Macmillan, 2010), 191.

22. "South Africans Reconciled?," BBC News, October 30, 1998, http://news.bbc.co.uk/2/hi/special_report/1998/10/98/truth_and_reconciliation/142673.stm.

23. Donna Bryson for the Associated Press, "Truth Commission Regarded with Suspicion in South Africa," *Globe and Mail*, April 8, 1996.

24. Suzanne Daley, "Apartheid-Era Assassin Accused of Whitewashing His Past," *Globe and Mail*, July 20, 1999.

25. Richard Meares for Reuters, "An 'Evil Compromise' to Save a Nation," *Globe and Mail*, September 28, 1997, F1.

26. Stephanie Nolen, "What's Bred in the Bones," *Globe and Mail*, October 20, 2007, p. F1.

27. Kate Dunn, "The Elusive Truth about the Death of a Hero," *Toronto Star*, September 28, 1997, F7.

28. Associated Press, "Winnie Mandela Faces Accusers," *Globe and Mail*, November 25, 1997, A14; Hein Marais, "Winnie Mandela Cool at Probe," *Globe and Mail*, November 28, 1997.

29. *Truth and Reconciliation Commission of South Africa Report*, vol. 2, 581.

30. Parviz Morewedge, ed., *The Scholar between Thought and Experience* (Binghamton, NY: Institute of Global Cultural Studies, 2001), 105.

31. Arthur Unger, "Mazrui: 'My Life Is One Long Debate," *Christian Science Monitor*, October 6, 1986.

32. Herbert Mitgang, "Looking at Africa through an African's Eyes," *New York Times*, October 5, 1986, 27.

33. Ali Mazrui, *The Africans: A Triple Heritage*, episode 9: "Global Africa," BBC-PBS-WETA production.

34. Ali Mazrui, "Lecture 6: In Search of Pax Africana," *Reith Lectures 1979: The African Condition*, BBC Radio 4, December 12, 1979.

35. Mazrui, "Lecture 6."

36. Tess Owen, "People with Guns (and No Masks) Swarmed the Michigan State Capitol to Protest the Coronavirus Lockdown," *Vice*, April 30, 2020; "Coronavirus: Armed Protesters Enter Michigan Statehouse," BBC News, May 1, 2020.

37. Hailu Habtu, "The Fallacy of the 'Triple Heritage' Thesis: A Critique," *Issue: A Journal of Opinion* 13 (1984): 26.

38. Peter Bauer, "Ali Mazrui, a Prophet out of Africa," *Encounter*, June 1980, 70.

39. Bauer, "Ali Mazrui, a Prophet out of Africa," 78.

40. Mitgang, "Looking at Africa through an African's Eyes," 27.

41. Mitgang, "Looking at Africa through an African's Eyes," 27.

42. Mitgang, "Looking at Africa through an African's Eyes," 27.

43. Ali Mazrui, *The Africans: A Triple Heritage,* episode 1: "The Nature of a Continent," BBC-PBS-WETA production.

44. Habtu, "The Fallacy of the 'Triple Heritage' Thesis," 27.

45. Wole Soyinka, "Ali Mazrui and Skip Gates' Africa Series," *The Black Scholar* 30, no. 1 (Spring 2000): 7.

46. Ali Mazrui, "Salman Rushdie: The Last Hostage?," *Toronto Star,* January 7, 1992, A13.

Chapter 19

1. Asfa-Wossen Asserate, *African Exodus* (London: Haus, 2018), 57.

2. Entry for Ken Saro-Wiwa as recipient of 1995 Goldman Environmental Prize.

3. Ken Saro-Wiwa, *Genocide in Nigeria,* 12–13.

4. Saro-Wiwa, *Genocide in Nigeria,* 85.

5. Ed Pilkington, "Shell Pays Out $15.5 Million over Saro-Wiwa Killing," *The Guardian,* June 9, 2009.

6. Robert Stone et al., "The Case of Ken Saro-Wiwa," *New York Review of Books,* April 20, 1995.

7. J. Timothy Hunt, *The Politics of Bones* (Toronto: McClelland & Stewart, 2005), 230.

8. Ken Saro-Wiwa, "Africa Kills Her Sun," in *Adaku and Other Stories* (Epsom: Saros International Publishers, 1989), 162.

9. Frank Aibogun, "Nigerian Activist's Last Words: 'The Struggle Continues,'" AP News, November 12, 1995.

10. Ken Wiwa, *In the Shadow of a Saint* (Toronto: Knopf Canada, 2000), 172.

11. Hunt, *The Politics of Bones,* 230n.

12. Pilkington, "Shell Pays Out $15.5 Million over Saro-Wiwa Killing."

13. Frank Aibogun, "Nigerian Activist's Last Words."

14. Wangari Maathai, *The Green Belt Movement* (New York: Lantern Books, 2003), 19–20.

15. Maathai, *The Green Belt Movement,* 28.

16. "Moi, Kenyan Strongman Who Presided over Rampant Graft, Dies," Reuters.com, February 4, 2020, www.reuters.com/news/picture/moi-kenyan-strongman-who-presided-over-r-idUSKBN1ZY0LW.

17. Wangari Maathai, *Unbowed* (New York: Anchor Books, 2007), 185.

18. Maathai, *Unbowed*, pp. 190–91.

19. Geoffrey Lean, "How They Cut Down the Tree Woman of Kenya," *The Observer*, March 8, 1992.

20. "The Nobel Peace Prize for 2004," NobelPrize.org, www.nobelprize.org/prizes/peace/2004/summary.

21. Walter Gibbs, "Nobel Peace Laureate Seeks to Explain Remarks about AIDS," *New York Times*, December 10, 2004.

22. Wangari Maathai, "The Challenge of AIDS in Africa," Greenbeltmovement.org, December 12, 2004, www.greenbeltmovement.org/wangari-maathai/key-speeches-and-articles/challenge-of-AIDS.

23. Nanjala Nyabola, "Wangari Maathai Was Not a Good Woman: Kenya Needs More of Them." *African Arguments*, October 6, 2015.

24. Maathai, *The Green Belt Movement*, 7–8.

25. Wangari Maathai, Nobel Lecture, Oslo, December 10, 2004.

26. E-mail to the author, June 24, 2020.

27. George Ayittey, *Africa Unchained: The Blueprint for Africa's Future* (New York: Palgrave Macmillan, 2005), 402, 404.

28. E-mail to the author, May 2, 2020.

29. E-mail to the author, May 2, 2020.

30. George Ayittey, "A Double Standard in Black and White," *Wall Street Journal*, July 22, 1985.

31. George Ayittey, e-mail to the author, May 2, 2020.

32. Sarah Cunningham-Scharf and Jeff Pearce, "Hungry, Hungry Hippos," *Corporate Risk Canada* 4, no. 2 (Summer 2015).

33. Cunningham-Scharf and Pearce, "Hungry, Hungry Hippos."

34. E-mail to the author, June 24, 2020.

35. Jeremy Harding, "Scapegoating History," *New York Times Book Review*, March 8, 1998, 7.

36. Ayittey, *Africa Unchained*, 183–84.

37. George Ayittey, *Defeating Dictators* (New York: St. Martin's Press, 2011), 217, 219.

38. George Ayittey, @ayittey, Twitter, April 28, 2020, 12:59 a.m.

39. George Ayittey, @ayittey, Twitter, April 9, 2020, 9:33 a.m.

40. Cunningham-Scharf and Pearce, "Hungry, Hungry Hippos."

41. Interview with the author, December 16, 2018.

42. Harding, "Scapegoating History."

43. Geoffrey Wheatcroft, "Things Still Fall Apart," *Wall Street Journal*, February 26, 1998, A15.

44. Interview with the author, December 23, 2020.

45. Interview with the author, December 16, 2018.

46. Interview with the author, December 16, 2018.

47. Ifeanyi Menkiti, "Person and Community in African Traditional Thought," in *African Philosophy: An Introduction*, ed. R. Wright (Lanham, MD: University Press of America, 1984).

48. Interview with the author, December 16, 2018.

Chapter 20

1. Selam Kebede, "Africa in the Eyes of an Ethiopian, Part 1: Traveling Africa while Ethiopian," Medium, April 7, 2016, https://medium.com/akoma-media/africa-in-the-eyes-of-an-ethiopian-a532e22f868a.

2. Kebede, "Africa in the Eyes of an Ethiopian, Part 1."

3. Interview with the author, August 26, 2020.

4. Asfa-Wossen Asserate, *African Exodus* (London: Haus, 2018), 150.

5. Asserate, *African Exodus*, 150.

6. Jennifer Rankin and Jon Henley, "EU to Consider Plans for Migrant Processing Centres in Africa," The Guardian, June 19, 2018, www.theguardian.com/world/2018/jun/19/eu-migrant-processing-centres-north-africa-refugees.

7. Gianna-Carina Grün and Daniel Pelz, "Why Few Visas Are Issued for Africans Wanting to Come to Germany," DW.com, June 7, 2018, www.dw.com/en/why-few-visas-are-issued-for-africans-wanting-to-come-to-germany/a-44097212.

8. Keith Walker and Timothy Jones, "Germany's List of 'Safe Countries of Origin' and What It Means," DW.com, February 15, 2019, www.dw.com/en/germanys-list-of-safe-countries-of-origin-and-what-it-means/a-46262904; Jefferson Chase, "German Bundesrat Says Maghreb States Not Safe for Refugees," DW.com, March 10, 2017, www.dw.com/en/german-bundesrat-says-maghreb-states-not-safe-for-refugees/a-37882572.

9. *Visa Problems for African Visitors to the UK*, July 16, 2019, All-Party Parliamentary Group Report for Africa, 8, 25.

10. Helen Warrell and David Pilling, "Africans Twice as Likely to Be Refused UK Visa, Say MPs," FT.com, July 16, 2019, www.ft.com/content/00e1ad38-a7c3-11e9-984c-fac8325aaa04.

11. *Visa Problems for African Visitors to the UK*, 8, 27.

12. Interview with the author, August 26, 2020.

13. Idil Mussa, "African Visitors Least Likely to Obtain Canadian Visas," CBC.ca/news, November 26, 2019, www.cbc.ca/news/canada/ottawa/canada-s-temporary-visa-approval-rate-lowest-for-african-travellers-1.5369830.

14. Jeune Afrique, "George Floyd: Malcolm X's Visionary Speech in Africa," The Africa Report, June 2, 2020, www.theafricareport.com/29196/george-floyd-malcolm-xs-visionary-speech-in-africa.

15. Interview with the author, July 24, 2020.

16. "US Admits Helping Mengistu Escape," BBC News, December 22, 1999.

17. Ian Buruma, "Paternalist Prince," *The Spectator*, August 17, 1991.

18. Asfa-Wossen Asserate on *To the Point*, "Ethiopia's Abiy Ahmed: From Peace Laureate to Man of War?," DW.com, December 3, 2020, www.dw.com/en/ethiopias-abiy-ahmed-from-peace-laureate-to-man-of-war/av-55811355.

19. Asfa-Wossen Asserate, *African Exodus*, 18.

20. Asfa-Wossen Asserate, *African Exodus*, 142–43.

21. Rankin and Henley, "EU to Consider Plans for Migrant Processing Centres in Africa."

22. Matina Stevis-Gridneff, "How Forced Labor in Eritrea Is Linked to E.U.-Funded Projects," New York Times, January 8, 2020, www.nytimes.com/2020/01/08/world/europe/conscription-eritrea-eu.html; Matina Stevis-Gridneff, "Eritreans Sue E.U. over Use of Forced Labor Back Home," New York Times, May 14, 2020, www.nytimes.com/2020/05/13/world/europe/eritrea-eu-lawsuit-forced-labor.html.

23. Interview with the author, July 24, 2020.

24. Interview with the author, July 24, 2020.

25. David Pilling, "African Exodus by Asfa-Wossen Asserate: Thwarted Ambitions," FT.com, June 8, 2018, www.ft.com/content/42e9adce-4eec-11e8-9471-a083af05aea7; Nicolas van de Walle, "African Exodus: Migration and the Future of Europe," Foreign Affairs, March/April 2019, www.foreignaffairs.com/reviews/capsule-review/2019-02-12/african-exodus-migration-and-future-europe.

Chapter 21

1. Peter Conrad, "Introduction," in *From Dawn to Decadence*, by Jacques Barzun (London: Folio Society), xv.

2. Bruce Gilley, "Was It Good Fortune to Be Enslaved by the British Empire?," National Association of Scholars, nas.org., September 30, 2019, www.nas.org/blogs/article/was-it-good-fortune-of-being -enslaved-by-the-british-empire.

3. Bruce Gilley, "The Case for Colonialism," *Third World Quarterly*, 2017.

4. Ben Shapiro, *The Right Side of History* (New York: Broadside Books, 2019), xxiv–xxv.

5. Shapiro, *The Right Side of History*, 179.

6. Richard Pankhurst, *An Introduction to the Medical History of Ethiopia* (Trenton, NJ: Red Sea Press, 1991), 163.

7. George Ayittey, *Indigenous African Institutions*, 2nd ed. (Ardsley, NY: Transnational Publishers, 2006), 79–80.

8. C. W. Previté-Orton, *The Shorter Cambridge Medieval History*, vol. 1 (Cambridge: Cambridge University Press, 1971), 377.

9. Previté-Orton, *The Shorter Cambridge Medieval History*, 377.

10. Ivor Powell, "Behind UCT's Removed Art: The Writing on the Wall," SA Art Times, October 23, 2018.

11. The three experts interviewed were William Davison, a senior analyst for Crisis Group whom the Ethiopia government deported in 2020; academic Kjetil Tronvoll, who has written articles openly sympathetic to the Tigray People's Liberation Front; and journalist Michela Wrong, arguably the only credible expert and the author of a book on Eritrea, *I Didn't Do It for You*, and, more recently, *Do Not Disturb*, about Rwanda. "Once Enemies, Ethiopia and Eritrea Ally against Tigray," DW.com, November 29, 2020, www.dw.com/en/once -enemies-ethiopia-and-eritrea-ally-against-tigray/a-55763490.

12. @BDR_Photography, Twitter, November 23, 2020, 11:26 p.m.

13. @GerrySimpsonHRW, deleted tweet, https://twitter.com/ GerrySimpsonHRW/status/1331223600540639234.

14. The alleged Aksum massacre remains controversial. See Amnesty International, "The Massacre in Axum," February 26, 2021, www .amnesty.org/en/documents/afr25/3730/2021/en. I criticized Amnesty's claims in an article ("Ethiopia: Lies, Damn Lies, Axum and the West," Medium.com, March 4, 2021), pointing out that Amnesty claimed that hundreds of bodies were found in the streets on November 30, 2020 and that a major church celebration was canceled as people

hid in their homes, but there is TV footage taken that day of the church services going ahead as planned, with people casually relaxing on benches in the sunshine and walking around freely; the footage was uploaded on December 4, well before the accusations of the massacre were made. And yet we are expected to believe that folks in the town casually went out and attended an annual religious occasion only a day or two after Eritrean soldiers slaughtered scores of residents. Virtually the entire Western media chose that season to ignore this evidence, except for one Italian journalist. See Francesca Ronchin, "Axum: Il massacre denunciato dale ong," Panorama.it, March 25, 2021.

15. "Ethiopia: Investigation Reveals Evidence That Scores of Civilians Were Killed in Massacre in Tigray State," Amnesty.org, March 12, 2021, www.amnesty.org/en/latest/news/2020/11/ethiopia-investigation -reveals-evidence-that-scores-of-civilians-were-killed-in-massacre-in -tigray-state; Fay Abuelgasim, Nariman El-Mofty, and Ana Cara, "Shadowy Ethiopian Massacre Could Be Tip of the Iceberg," APNews .com, December 12, 2020, www.cbs17.com/news/shadowy-ethiopian -massacre-could-be-tip-of-the-iceberg.

16. https://www.gettyimages.co.uk/photos/jemal-countess-mai -kadra?family=editorial&phrase=jemal%20countess%20mai%20 kadra&sort=newest#license. See also Jeff Pearce, "Ethiopia: Mai Kadra, Metekel, and the Media Shame That Won't Be Forgotten," Medium .com, April 8, 2021.

17. Nazia Parveen, "Amnesty International Has Culture of White Privilege, Report Finds," The Guardian, April 20, 2021, www.theguard ian.com/world/2021/apr/20/amnesty-international-has-culture-of -white-privilege-report-finds.

18. Parveen, "Amnesty International Has Culture of White Privilege, Report Finds."

19. Glenn Loury on "The Dark Arts," The Glenn Show, July 23, 2020.

20. Shadi Hamid, @shadihamid, July 28, 2020, 4:50 p.m.

21. I could cite the source, but rather than subject the individual to even more ridicule than earned, the reader will simply have to trust that the quote is accurate.

Select Bibliography

Books

Achebe, Chinua. "Spelling Our Proper Name." On *Black Writers Redefine the Struggle: A Tribute to James Baldwin*. Amherst: University of Massachusetts Press, 1989.

Ajayi, J. F. Ade, ed. *UNESCO General History of Africa*. Vol. 6, *Africa in the Nineteenth Century until the 1880s*. London: James Currey, 1998.

Akyeampong, Emmanuel, and Henry Louis Gates Jr., eds. *Dictionary of African Biography*. Oxford: Oxford University Press, 2012.

Alpern, Stanley. *Amazons of Black Sparta: The Women Warriors of Dahomey*. New York: New York University Press, 1998.

Anderson, David. *Histories of the Hanged*. London: Weidenfeld & Nicolson, 2005.

Asfa-Wossen Asserate. *African Exodus*. London: Haus, 2018.

Augustine. *Confessions*. London: Penguin, 1961.

Ayittey, George. *Africa Unchained: The Blueprint for Africa's Future*. New York: Palgrave Macmillan, 2005.

———. *Indigenous African Institutions*. 2nd ed. Ardsley, NY: Transnational Publishers, 2006.

———. *Defeating Dictators*. New York: St. Martin's Press, 2011.

Azikiwe, Nnamdi. *My Odyssey*. New York: Praeger, 1970.

Bacon, Reginald. *Benin: The City of Blood*. London: Edward Arnold, 1897.

Baer, George W. *The Coming of the Italian-Ethiopian War*. Cambridge, MA: Harvard University Press, 1967.

———. *Pioneers of Change in Ethiopia*. Oxford: James Currey, 2002.

Baldwin, James. *Notes of a Native Son*. 1955. Reprint, Boston: Beacon Press, 2012.

———. *Nobody Knows My Name*. New York: Dell Press, 1963.

Barnett, Don, and Karari Njama. *Mau Mau from Within*. New York: Monthly Review Press, 1970.

Barzun, Jacques. *From Dawn to Decadence*. 2001. Reprint, London: Folio Society, 2015.

Baykedagn, Gebrehiwot, and Tenkir Bonger. *The State and Economy in Early 20th Century Ethiopia*. London: Karnak House, 1995.

Beckingham, C. F., and G. W. B. Huntingford. *Some Records of Ethiopia, 1593–1646*. New York: Routledge, 2016.

Bennetta, Jules-Rosette. *Black Paris: The African Writers' Landscape*. Champaign: University of Illinois Press, 1998.

Bernal, Martin. *Black Athena: The Afroasiatic Roots of Classical Civilization*. Vols. 1–4. New Brunswick, NJ: Rutgers University Press, 1987–1994.

Biko, Steve. *I Write What I Like*. Edited by Aelred Stubbs. New York: Harper & Row, 1978.

———. *Black Consciousness in South Africa*. Edited by Millard Arnold. New York: Vintage Books, 1979.

———. *The Testimony of Steve Biko*. Edited by Millard Arnold. London: Maurice Temple Smith Publishers, 1979.

Blyden, Edward Wilmot. *The Aims and Methods of a Liberal Education for Africans: Inaugural Address*. 1882. Reprint, York: George Young, 1920.

———. *Christianity, Islam and the Negro Race*. 1887. Reprint, Baltimore, MD: Black Classic Press, 1994.

———. *West Africa before Europe and Other Addresses*. London: C. M. Phillips, 1905.

———. *Selected Letters of Edward Wilmot Blyden*. Edited by Hollis Lynch. Millwood, NY: KTO Press, 1978.

Boahen, A. Adu. *Topics in West African History*. London: Longman, 1986.

Boisragon, Alan. *The Benin Massacre*. London: Methuen, 1897.

Branch, Daniel. *Defeating Mau Mau, Creating Kenya*. New York: Cambridge University Press, 2009.

Breasted, James. *The Conquest of Civilization*. New York: Harper and Brothers, 1926.

Brett, Michael, and Elizabeth Fentress. *The Berbers*. Cambridge, MA: Blackwell, 1996.

Briant, Pierre. *From Cyrus to Alexander: A History of the Persian Empire*. University Park, PA: Eisenbrauns, 2002.

Campbell, Ian. *The Addis Ababa Massacre*. London: Hurst, 2017.

———. *The Plot to Kill Graziani: The Attempted Assassination of Mussolini's Viceroy*. Addis Ababa: Addis Ababa University Press, 2010.

Cantor, Norman F. *Civilization of the Middle Ages*. New York: HarperCollins, 1994.

Carretta, Vincent. *Equiano the African: Biography of a Self-Made Man*. 2005. Reprint, New York: Penguin, 2007.

Cassanelli, Lee. *The Shaping of Somali Society: Reconstructing the History of a Pastoral People, 1600–1900*. Philadelphia: University of Pennsylvania Press, 1982.

Cerulli, Enrico. *Somalia*. 3 vols. Rome: Instituto Poligrafico dello Stato, 1957–1964.

Cherki, Alice. *Frantz Fanon: A Portrait*. Translated by Nadia Benabid. Ithaca, NY: Cornell University Press, 2006.

Ciment, James. *Another America: The Story of Liberia and the Former Slaves Who Ruled It*. New York: Hill and Wang, 2013.

Clagett, Marshall. *Ancient Egyptian Science: A Source Book, Volume 3: Ancient Egyptian Mathematics*. Philadelphia: American Philosophical Society, 1999.

Clarkson, Thomas, and Ottobah Cugoano. *Essays on the Slavery and Commerce of the Human Species*. Edited by Mary-Antoinette Smith. London: Broadview Editions, 2010.

Clough, Marshall. *Mau Mau Memoirs: History, Memory and Politics*. London: Lynn Rienner Publishers, 1998.

Coleman, James. *Nigeria: Background to Nationalism*. Berkeley: University of California Press, 1971.

Coon, Carleton. *The Origin of the Races*. New York: Knopf, 1962.

Coss, Stephen. *The Fever of 1721: The Epidemic That Revolutionized Medicine and American Politics*. New York: Simon & Schuster, 2017.

Courlander, Harold, and Ousmane Sako. *The Heart of the Ngoni: Heroes of the African Kingdom of Segu*. New York: Crown Publishers, 1982.

Crowley, Roger. *Conquerors: How the Portuguese Forged the First Global Empire*. New York: Random House, 2015.

Da Gama, Vasco. *A Journal of the First Voyage of Vasco da Gama, 1497–1499*. Translated by E. G. Ravenstein. London: Hakluyt Society, 1898.

David, Rosalie. *Handbook to Life in Ancient Egypt*. Rev. ed. Oxford: Oxford University Press, 2007.

Davidson, Basil. *The African Past*. Boston: Little, Brown, 1964.

———. *A History of West Africa*. New York: Anchor Books, 1966.

———. *Let Freedom Come*. Boston: Little, Brown, 1978.

———. *The African Slave Trade*. Boston: Little, Brown, 1980.

Darrah, David. *Hail Caesar!* New York: Hale, Cushman & Flint, 1936.

De Azurara, Gomes. *The Chronicle of the Discovery and Conquest of Guinea*. Vol. 1. Translated by Charles Beazley. London: Hakluyt Society, 1899.

De Bono, Emilio. *Anno XIIII: The Conquest of an Empire*. London: Cresset Press, 1937.

Delafosse, Maurice. *The Negroes of Africa*. Translated by F. Fligelman. 1931. Reprint, Washington, DC: Associated Publishers, 1968.

Delany, Martin. *Official Report of the Niger Valley Exploring Party*. New York, 1861.

Del Boca, Angelo. *The Ethiopian War, 1935–1941*. Chicago: University of Chicago Press, 1969.

Denon, Vivant. *Travels in Upper and Lower Egypt during the Campaigns of General Bonaparte in That Country*. Translated by Arthur Aiken. New York: Heard and Forman, 1803.

De Villiers, Marq, and Sheila Hirtle. *Into Africa*. Toronto: Key Porter Books, 1997.

———. *Timbuktu: The Sahara's Fabled City of Gold*. Toronto: McClelland & Stewart, 2007.

Diogenes Laertius. *Lives of the Eminent Philosophers*. Translated by Pamela Mensch. New York: Oxford University Press, 2018.

Diop, Cheikh Anta. *The African Origin of Civilization*. Translated by Mercer Cook. Chicago: Lawrence Hill, 1974.

———. *Civilization or Barbarism*. Translated by Yaa-Lengi Ngemi. Chicago: Lawrence Hill, 1991.

Diouf, Sylviane, ed. *Fighting the Slave Trade: West African Strategies*. Oxford: James Currey, 2003.

Duberman, Martin. *Paul Robeson*. New York: Knopf, 1989.

Du Bois, W. E. B. *The World and Africa*. 1979. Reprint, Oxford: Oxford University Press.

Edgerton, Robert. *Mau Mau: An African Crucible*. London: I. B. Tauris, 1990.

———. *The Fall of the Asante Empire*. New York: Free Press, 1995.

Eglash, Ron. *African Fractals: Modern Computing and Indigenous Design*. New Brunswick, NJ: Rutgers University Press, 2002.

Elkins, Caroline. *Imperial Reckoning*. New York: Henry Holt, 2005.

Enan, Mohammad. *Ibn Khaldun: His Life and Work*. Lahore: Ashraf Press, 1962.

Equiano, Olaudah. *An African's Life, 1745–1797: The Life and Times of Olaudah Equiano*. London: Continuum, 2000.

Eze, Michael Onyebuchi. *Intellectual History in Contemporary South Africa*. New York: Palgrave Macmillan, 2010.

Fairhead, James, Tim Geysbeek, Svend E. Holsoe, and Melissa Leach, eds. *African-American Exploration in West Africa: Four Nineteenth Century Diaries*. Bloomington: Indiana University Press, 2003.

Falola, Toyin. *Nationalism and African Intellectuals*. Rochester, NY: University of Rochester Press, 2004.

Fanon, Frantz. *The Wretched of the Earth*. Translated by Richard Philcox. New York: Grove Press, 2004.

Fauvelle, Francoise-Xavier. *The Golden Rhinoceros*. Princeton, NJ: Princeton University Press, 2018.

Fisher, Marjorie, ed. *Ancient Nubia: African Kingdoms on the Nile*. Cairo: The American University in Cairo Press, 2012.

Fox, Robin Lane. *The Classical World*. New York: Basic Books, 2006.

Frobenius, Leo. *The Voice of Africa*. London: Hutchinson & Co., 1913.

Fromhertz, Allen. *Ibn Khaldun: Life and Times*. Edinburgh: Edinburgh University Press, 2011.

Fromont, Cécile. *The Art of Conversion: Christian Visual Culture in the Kingdom of Kongo*. Chapel Hill: University of North Carolina Press, 2014.

Fuller, Francis. *A Vanished Dynasty: Ashanti*. London: John Murray, 1921.

Gates, Henry Louis. *Tradition and the Black Atlantic: Critical Theory in the African Diaspora*. Philadelphia: Basic Civitas, 2010.

Gomez, Michael. *African Dominion: A New History of Empire in Early and Medieval West Africa*. Princeton, NJ: Princeton University Press, 2018.

Grant, Colin. *Negro with a Hat*. Oxford: Oxford University Press, 2008.

Graves, Robert. *The Golden Ass*. New York: Farrar, Straus and Giroux, 1951.

Green, Toby. *A Fistful of Shells*. London: Allen Lane, 2019.

Greenfield, Jeanette. *The Return of Cultural Treasures*. 3rd ed. Cambridge: Cambridge University Press, 2007.

Greenfield, Richard. *Ethiopia: A New Political History*. London: Pall Mall Press, 1965.

Hale, Thomas. *Griots and Griottes*. Bloomington: Indiana University Press, 1998.

Haley, Alex. *Roots: The Saga of an American Family*. New York: Doubleday, 1976.

Hammer, Joshua. *The Bad-Ass Librarians of Timbuktu*. New York: Simon & Schuster, 2016.

Haney, Lynn. *Naked at the Feast*. London: Robson Books, 1981.

Harmsworth, Geoffrey. *Abyssinia Marches On*. London: Hutchinson & Co., 1941.

Hayford, Casely. *West Africa before Europe and Other Addresses*. London: C. M. Phillips, 1905.

Henig, Adam. *Alex Haley's Roots: An Author's Odyssey*. CreateSpace, 2014.

Henze, Paul. *Layers of Time*. New York: Palgrave, 2000.

Herodotus. *The Landmark Herodotus*. Edited by Robert Strassler. New York: Anchor Books, 2007.

Heywood, Linda M. *Njinga of Angola: Africa's Warrior Queen*. Cambridge, MA: Harvard University Press, 2017.

Hicks, Dan. *The Brutish Museum*. London: Pluto Press, 2020.

Hitchens, Christopher. *The Quotable Hitchens*. Edited by Windsor Mann. New York: Da Capo Press, 2011.

Hochschild, Adam. *Bury the Chains*. 2005. Reprint, New York: Mariner Books, 2006.

Holden, William. *The Past and Future of the Kaffir Races*. Port Natal: Richards, Glanville and Co., 1866.

Hollingsworth, Miles. *Augustine of Hippo: An Intellectual Biography*. Oxford: Oxford University Press, 2013.

Homer. *The Odyssey*. Translated by Robert Fagles. New York: Penguin, 1996.

Horne, Alistair. *A Savage War of Peace*. New York: New York Review of Books, 2006.

Horne, Gerald. *Mau Mau in Harlem? The U.S. and the Liberation of Kenya*. New York: Palgrave Macmillan, 2009.

———. *Paul Robeson: The Artist as Revolutionary*. London: Pluto Press, 2016.

Horton, James Africanus. *Political Economy of British Western Africa; with the Requirements of the Several Colonies and Settlements*. London: W. J. Johnson, 1865.

———. *West African Countries and Peoples, British and Native: A Vindication of the African Race*. London: W. J. Johnson, 1868.

———. *Letters on the Political Condition of the Gold Coast since the Exchange of Territory between the English and Dutch Governments*. London: W. J. Johnson, 1870.

Hountondji, Paulin. *African Philosophy: Myth and Reality*. 2nd ed. Bloomington: Indiana University Press, 1996.

Hunt, J. Timothy. *The Politics of Bones*. Toronto: McClelland & Stewart, 2005.

Hymans, Jacques-Louis. *Léopold Sédar Senghor: An Intellectual Biography*. Edinburgh: Edinburgh University Press, 1971.

Ibn Batuta. *Travels in Asia and Africa.* Translated by H. A. R. Gibb. London: Routledge & Sons, 1953.

Ibn Khaldun. *The Muqaddimah: An Introduction to History.* Translated by Franz Rosenthal. 1969. Reprint, Princeton, NJ: Princeton University Press, 2015.

Imru Zelleke. *A Journey.* Self-published memoir, 2016.

Irwin, Robert. *Ibn Khaldun: An Intellectual Biography.* Princeton, NJ: Princeton University Press, 2018.

Jacobs, Sylvia. *The African Nexus: Black American Perspectives on the European Partitioning of Africa, 1880–1920.* Westport, CT: Greenwood Press, 1981.

James, George G. M. *Stolen Legacy.* New York: Philosophical Library, 1954.

Jeal, Tim. *Stanley: The Impossible Life of Africa's Greatest Explorer.* New Haven, CT: Yale University Press, 2007.

Johnston, Harry. *The Uganda Protectorate.* London: Hutchinson, 1902.

Jonas, Raymond. *The Battle of Adwa.* Cambridge, MA: Belknap Press, 2011.

Jouanna, Jacques. *Greek Medicine from Hippocrates to Galen.* Translated by Neil Allies. Leiden: Brill, 2012.

Kagan, Donald. *Pericles of Athens and the Birth of Democracy.* New York: Free Press, 1991.

Kaggia, Bildad. *Roots of Freedom: 1921–1963.* Nairobi: East African Publishing House, 1975.

Kaggia, Bildad, and Mwaganu Kaggia. *The Struggle for Freedom and Justice: The Life and Times of the Freedom Fighter and Politician Bildad M. Kaggia.* Nairobi: Transafrica Press, 2012.

Kenyatta, Jomo. *Facing Mount Kenya.* London: Heinemann Educational Books, 1979.

Kobishchanov, Yuri. *Axum.* Translated by Lorraine Kapitanoff. University Park: Pennsylvania State University Press, 1979.

Krebs, Verena. *Medieval Ethiopian Kingship, Craft, and Diplomacy with Latin Europe.* Cham: Palgrave Macmillan, 2021.

Leeming, David. *James Baldwin: A Biography.* New York: Knopf, 1995.

Lefkowitz, Mary. *Not out of Africa.* New York: Basic Books, 1996.

Leith, J. Clark. *Why Botswana Prospered.* Montreal: McGill-Queen's University Press, 2005.

Lewis, I. M. *A Modern History of Somalia.* Boulder, CO: Westview Press, 1988.

———. *Understanding Somalia and Somaliland.* New York: Columbia University Press, 2008.

Lindop, Barbara. *Sekoto: The Art of Gerard Sekoto*. London: Pavilion Books, 1995.

Locke, Alain. *The New Negro*. 1925. Reprint, New York: Touchstone, 1999.

Lynch, Hollis. *Edward Wilmot Blyden: Pan-Negro Patriot, 1832–1912*. Oxford: Oxford University Press, 1967.

Maathai, Wangari. *The Green Belt Movement*. New York: Lantern Books, 2003.

———. *Unbowed*. New York: Anchor Books, 2007.

Macey, David. *Frantz Fanon: A Biography*. London: Verso, 2012.

Mahjoub, Jamal. *A Line in the River*. London: Bloomsbury Publishing, 2018.

Maloba, W. *Kenyatta and Britain: An Account of Political Transformation, 1929–1963*. London: Palgrave Macmillan, 2018.

Mangcu, Xolela. *Biko: A Life*. London: I. B. Tauris, 2014.

Marable, Manning. *Malcolm X: A Life of Reinvention*. New York: Viking, 2011.

Massaqoi, Fatima. *The Autobiography of an African Princess*. New York: Palgrave Macmillan, 2013.

Massaquoi, Hans. *Destined to Witness*. New York: HarperCollins, 1999.

Matera, Marc, Misty L. Bastian, and Susan Kingsley Kent. *The Women's War of 1929*. New York: Palgrave Macmillan, 2012.

Mazrui, Ali. *The Africans: A Triple Heritage*. Boston: Little, Brown, 1986.

Mbiti, John. *African Religions and Philosophy*. London: Heinemann, 1969.

Mboya, Tom. *Freedom and After*. 1963. Reprint, Nairobi: East African Educational Publishers, 2008.

McCracken, John. *A History of Malawi, 1859–1966*. Rochester, NY: James Currey, 2013.

Meredith, Martin. *The State of Africa: A History of the Continent*. London: Simon & Schuster, 2011.

———. *The Fortunes of Africa: A 5000-Year History of Wealth, Greed, and Endeavor*. New York: PublicAffairs, 2014.

Mokhtar, G., ed. *UNESCO General History of Africa*. Vol. 2, *Ancient Civilizations of Africa*. London: James Currey, 1990.

Morton, Samuel George. *Crania Aegyptica: Observations on Egyptian Ethnography*. Philadelphia: John Pennington, 1844.

Moses, Wilson. *The Golden Age of Black Nationalism, 1850–1925*. Hamden, CT: Archon Books, 1978.

Mosima, Pius. *Philosophic Sagacity and Intercultural Philosophy*. Leiden: African Studies Centre, 2016.

Mostert, Noel. *Frontiers: The Epic of South Africa's Creation and the Tragedy of the Xhosa People.* New York: Knopf, 1992.

Munro-Hay, Stuart. *Aksum: An African Civilization of Late Antiquity.* Edinburgh: Edinburgh University Press, 1991.

Murray-Brown, Jeremy. *Kenyatta.* New York: Dutton, 1972.

Nault, Derrick M. *Africa and the Shaping of International Human Rights.* Oxford: Oxford University Press, 2021.

Northrup, David. *Africa's Discovery of Europe.* New York: Oxford University Press, 2009.

Odihambo, E. S., and John Lonsdale, eds. *Mau Mau and Nationhood.* Oxford: James Currey, 2003.

Ogbechie, Sylvester. *Ben Enwonwu: The Making of an African Modernist.* Rochester, NY: University of Rochester Press, 2008.

Ogot, Bethwell. *My Footprints in the Sands of Time.* Victoria, BC: Trafford Publishing, 2003.

Ogot, B. A., ed. *UNESCO General History of Africa.* Vol. 5, *Africa from the Sixteenth to the Eighteenth Century.* London: James Currey, 1999.

Okot p'Bitek. *Decolonizing African Religions.* Reprint of *African Religion in Western Scholarship.* New York: Diasporic Africa Press, 2011.

Olukoju, Ayodeji. *Culture and Customs of Liberia.* Westport, CT: Greenwood Press, 2006.

Olusoga, David. *Black and British.* London: Macmillan, 2016.

Osborne, Myles, and Susan Kingsley Kent. *Africans and Britons in the Age of Empires, 1660–1980.* London: Routledge, 2015.

Pankhurst, Richard. *An Introduction to the Medical History of Ethiopia.* Trenton, NJ: Red Sea Press, 1991.

———. *The Ethiopians: A History.* Oxford: Blackwell, 2001.

Pankhurst, Sylvia. *Ex-Italian Somaliland.* London: Watts & Co., 1951.

———. *Ethiopia: A Cultural History.* Woodford Green: Lalibela House, 1955.

Pearce, Jeff. *Prevail: The Inspiring Story of Ethiopia's Victory over Mussolini's Invasion, 1935–1941.* New York: Skyhorse Publishing, 2014.

Perham, Margery. *Native Administration in Nigeria.* Oxford: Oxford University Press, 1962.

Powell, Richard. *Black Art: A Cultural History.* New York: Thames & Hudson, 2002.

Previté-Orton, C. W. *The Shorter Cambridge Medieval History.* Vol. 1. Cambridge: Cambridge University Press, 1971.

Prunier, Gérard. *The Rwanda Crisis: History of a Genocide.* New York: Columbia University Press, 1997.

Rankin, Nick. *Telegram from Guernia.* London: Faber and Faber, 2003.

Redford, Donald, ed. *The Oxford Encyclopedia of Ancient Egypt*. Oxford: Oxford University Press, 2001.

Ritter, E. A. *Shaka Zulu*. London: Penguin, 1978.

Robins, Gay, and Charles Shute. *The Rhind Mathematical Papyrus: An Ancient Egyptian Text*. London: British Museum Publications, 1987.

Roscoe, John. *Twenty-Five Years in East Africa*. Cambridge: Cambridge University Press, 1921.

Rotberg, Robert. *The Rise of Nationalism in Central Africa*. Cambridge, MA: Harvard University Press, 1965.

Russell, Bertrand. *History of Western Philosophy*. 1905. Reprint, New York: Simon & Schuster, 1961.

Samatar, Abdi Ismail. *Africa's First Democrats*. Bloomington: Indiana University Press, 2016.

Saro-Wiwa, Ken. *Adaku and Other Stories*. Epsom: Saros International Publishers, 1989.

Schachtman, Tom. *Airlift to America*. New York: St. Martin's Press, 2009.

Schildkrout, Enid, ed. *The Golden Stool: Studies of the Asante Center and Periphery*. New York: Anthropological Papers of the American Museum of Natural History, 1987.

Scott, William R. *The Sons of Sheba's Race*. Bloomington: Indiana University Press, 1993.

Shapiro, Ben. *The Right Side of History*. New York: Broadside Books, 2019.

Shepperson, George, and Thomas Price. *Independent African: John Chilembwe and the Origins, Setting and Significance of the Nyasaland Native Rising of 1915*. Edinburgh: Edinburgh University Press, 1987.

Shillington, Kevin. *History of Africa*. 3rd ed. London: Palgrave Macmillan, 2012.

Smith, Stuart Tyson. *Wretched Kush: Ethnic Identities and Boundaries in Egypt's Nubian Empire*. London: Routledge, 2003.

Sorrenson, M. P. K. *Land Reform in the Kikuyu Country*. Oxford: Oxford University Press, 1967.

———. *Origins of European Settlement in Kenya*. Oxford: Oxford University Press, 1968.

Soyinka, Wole. *The Burden of Memory, the Muse of Forgiveness*. Oxford: Oxford University Press, 1999.

Steer, George. *Caesar in Abyssinia*. London: Hodder and Stoughton, 1936.

———. *Judgment on German Africa*. London: Hodder and Stoughton, 1939.

———. *Sealed and Delivered*. London: Hodder and Stoughton, 1942.

Stevenson, Alice, ed. *Petrie Museum of Egyptian Archaeology: Characters and Collections*. London: UCL Press, 2015.

Stovall, Tyler. *Paris Noir: African Americans in the City of Light*. New York: Houghton Mifflin, 1996.

Sumner, Claude. *Ethiopian Philosophy*. Vol. 2. Addis Ababa: Commercial Printing Press, 1976.

———. *Classical Ethiopian Philosophy*. Addis Ababa: Commercial Printing Press, 1985.

Talbot, Percy. *In the Shadow of the Bush*. London: Heinemann, 1912.

———. *The Peoples of Southern Nigeria*. Vol. 3. Oxford: Oxford University Press, 1926.

Tempels, Placide. *Bantu Philosophy*. Facsimile of English edition, Paris: Présence Africaine, 1959, by Centre Aequatoria.

Thomas, Charles. *Adventures and Observations on the West Coast of Africa and Its Islands*. New York: Derby & Jackson, 1860.

Thomas, Hugh. *The Slave Trade*. New York: Simon & Schuster, 1997.

Toynbee, Arnold. *A Study of History*. 6 vols. Oxford: Oxford University Press, 1948.

Tyldesley, Joyce. *Hatchepsut: The Female Pharaoh*. London: Penguin, 1996.

Vaillant, Janet. *Black, French and African: A Life of Léopold Sédar Senghor*. Cambridge, MA: Harvard University Press, 1990.

Véron, Kora, and Thomas A. Hale. *Les Ecrits d'Aimé Césaire: Biobibliographie commentée (1913–2008)*. 2 vols. Paris: Honoré Champion, 2013.

Wheeler, Douglas and René Pélissier. *Angola*. London: Pall Mall Library of African Affairs, 1971.

Wilkinson, Toby. *Early Dynastic Egypt*. London: Routledge, 1999.

———. *The Rise and Fall of Ancient Egypt*. New York: Random House, 2010.

———. *Writings from Ancient Egypt*. London: Penguin, 2016.

Williams, Eric. *Capitalism and Slavery*. Richmond, VA: William Byrd Press, 1944.

———. *Inward Hunger: The Education of a Prime Minister*. London: Andre Deutsch, 1969.

Williams, Susan. *Colour Bar*. London: Penguin, 2016.

———. *White Malice*. New York: PublicAffairs, 2021.

Wilson, Samuel. *The Emperor's Giraffe and Other Stories of Cultures in Contact*. Boulder, CO: Westview Press, 1999.

Wiredu, Kwasi, ed. *A Companion to African Philosophy*. Oxford: Blackwell, 2004.

Wiwa, Ken. *In the Shadow of a Saint*. Toronto: Knopf Canada, 2000.

Wright, Richard. *Black Power: Three Books from Exile*. New York: HarperCollins, 2008.
Zinn, Howard. *A People's History of the United States*. 1980. Reprint, New York: HarperCollins, 2003.

Academic, Museum, and Government Publications

Acemoglu, Daron, Simon Johnson, and James Robinson. "An African Success Story: Botswana." Massachusetts Institute of Technology, Department of Economics Working Papers 01-37, July 2001.
Afigbo, A. E. "Review of *Igbo Village Affairs*, 2nd ed., by M. M Green." *Journal of the Historical Society of Nigeria* 4, no. 1 (December 1967): 186–90.
Agai, Jock. "An Investigation into the Ancient Egyptian Cultural Influences on the Yorubas of Nigeria." *HTS Teologiese Studies/Theological Studies* 69, no. 1 (2013).
Alpern, Stanley. "On the Origins of the Amazons of Dahomey." *History in Africa* 25 (1998).
Arhin, Kwame. "The Role of Nana Yaa Asantewaa in the 1900 Asante War of Resistance." *Le Griot* 8 (2000).
"Baboon Mummy Tests Reveal Ethiopia and Eritrea as Ancient Land of Punt." Archaeology News Network website, April 23, 2010.
Belcher, Wendy. "From Sheba They Come: Medieval Ethiopian Myth, U.S. Newspapers and a Modern American Narrative." *Callaloo* 33, no. 1 (Winter 2010).
Blyden, Edward Wilmot. "Report on the Expedition to Falaba, January to March 1872." *Proceedings of the Royal Geographical Society of London* 17, no. 2 (1872–1873).
Bobin, Florian. "Poetic Injustice: The Senghor Myth and Senegal's Independence." *Review of African Political Economy*, June 12, 2020.
Bonechi, Marco. "Four Sistine Ethiopians? The 1481 Ethiopian Embassy and the Frescoes of the Sistine Chapel in the Vatican." *Aethiopica*, no. 14 (2011).
Breasted, James. "The First Philosopher." *The Monist* 12, no. 3 (April 1902).
Brown, Peter. "Christianity and Local Culture in Late Roman Africa." *Journal of Roman Studies* 58, pts. 1–2 (1968).
Bugg, John. "The Other Interesting Narrative: Olaudah Equiano's Public Book Tour." *PMLA* 121, no. 5 (October 2006).

Burness, Donald. "Nzinga Mbandi and Angolan Independence." *Luso-Brazilian Review* 14, no. 2 (Winter 1977).

Carretta, Bugg. "Deciphering the Equiano Archives." *PMLA* 122, no. 2 (March 2007).

Casement, Roger. *Congo Report*. Submitted to U.K. Parliament (February 1904).

Challis, Debbie. "From China to Sudan." In *Petrie Museum of Egyptian Archaeology: Characters and Collections*, ed. Alice Stevenson. London: UCL Press, 2015.

Cleary, A. S. "The Myth of Mau Mau in Its International Context." *African Affairs* 89, no. 355 (April 1990).

Davidson, Basil. "The Ancient World and Africa: Whose Roots?" *Race and Class* 29, no. 2 (1987).

Davies, J. N. P. "The Development of 'Scientific' Medicine in the African Kingdom of Bunyoro-Kitara." *Medical History* 3, no. 1 (January 1959).

Davis, Natalie Zemon. "'Leo Africanus' Presents Africa to Europeans." In *Revealing the African Presence in Europe*. Baltimore, MD: Walters Art Museum, 2012.

Dawson, Warren. "Pygmies and Dwarfs in Ancient Egypt." *Journal of Egyptian Archaeology* 24, no. 2 (December 1938).

Eyene, Christine. "Sekoto and Négritude: The Ante-room of French Culture." *Third Text* 24, no. 4 (July 5, 2010).

Finch, Charles. "Conversations with Cheikh Anta Diop." *Présence Africaine*, n.s., no. 149/150 (1989).

Frobenius, Leo. "Early African Culture as an Indication of Present Negro Potentialities." *Annals of the American Academy of Political and Social Science* 140 (November 1928).

Frost, Maurice. "A Note on the Berber Background in the Life of Augustine." *Journal of Theological Studies* 43, no. 171/172 (July/October 1942).

Gade, Christian. "The Historical Development of the Written Discourses on Ubuntu." *South African Journal of Philosophy* 30, issue 3 (2011).

Gaston, Lafayette. "Past Afrocentricity: Reassessing Cheikh Anta Diop's Place in the Afrocentric Frame." *The Liberator* 8, no. 23 (2009).

Goodwin, Craufurd. "Economic Analysis and Development in British West Africa." *Economic Development and Cultural Change* 15, No. 4 (July 1967).

Grade, Christian. "The Historical Development of the Written Discourses on Ubuntu." *South African Journal of Philosophy* 30 (October 2013).

Hailu Habtu. "The Fallacy of the 'Triple Heritage' Thesis: A Critique." *A Journal of Opinion* 13 (1984).

Hale, Thomas A. "De Sotuma-Sere à New York City, L'Itinéraire de Jali Papa Bunka Susso, Griot Gambien." *Africultures*, no. 61 (October–December 2004).

Hansberry, William Leo. "Book Review: Stolen Legacy." *Journal of Negro Education* 24, no. 2 (Spring 1954).

Heidorn, Lisa. "The Horses of Kush." *Journal of Near Eastern Studies* 56, no. 2 (April 1997).

Henderson, Willie. "Independent Botswana: A Reappraisal of Foreign Policy Options." *African Affairs* 73, no. 290 (January 1974).

———. "Seretse Khama: A Personal Appreciation." *African Affairs* 89, no. 354 (January 1990).

Huxtable, Sally-Anne. "Wealth, Power and the Global Country House." In *Interim Report on the Connections between Colonialism and Properties Now in the Care of the National Trust, Including Links with Historic Slavery*, UK National Trust, September 2020.

Igbafe, Philip. "The Fall of Benin: A Reassessment." *Journal of African History* 11, no. 3 (1970).

Jackson, John, Jr. "'In Ways Unacademical': The Reception of Carleton S. Coon's *The Origin of Races*." *Journal of the History of Biology* 34 (2001).

Johnson, Cheryl. "Grass Roots Organizing: Women in Anticolonial Activity in Southwestern Nigeria." *African Studies Review* 25, no. 2/3 (June–September 1982).

Kalumba, Kibuijo M. "A New Analysis of Mbiti's 'The Concept of Time.'" *Philosophia Africana* 8, no. 1 (2005).

Keith, J. L. "African Students in Great Britain." *African Affairs* 45, no. 179 (April 1946).

Killingray, David. "'A Swift Agent of Government': Air Power in British Colonial Africa, 1916–1939." *Journal of African History* 25, no. 4 (1984).

Kipkorir, B. E. "The Kolloa Affray, Kenya 1950." *Transafrican Journal of History* 2, no. 2 (1972).

Kobishchanov, Yuri. "On the Problem of Sea Voyages of Ancient Africans in the Indian Ocean." *Journal of African History* 6, no. 2 (1965).

Koster, Mickie Mwanzia. "Malcolm X, the Mau Mau, and Kenya's New Revolutionaries: A Legacy of Transnationalism." *Journal of African American History* 100, no. 2 (Spring 2015).

Lacovara, Peter. "Not out of Africa, Not: Ancient Egypt, Nubia and the Roots of Western Civilization." Draft article shared with the author, September 8, 2020.

Leahy, Anthony. "The Libyan Period in Egypt: An Essay in Interpretation." *Libyan Studies* 16 (1985).

Leith, J. Clark. "Botswana: A Case Study of Economic Policy, Prudence and Growth." World Bank Working Paper, August 31, 1999.

Levtzion, N. "The Thirteenth- and Fourteenth-Century Kings of Mali." *Journal of African History* 4, no. 3 (1963).

Lovejoy, Paul. "Autobiography and Memory: Gustavus Vassa, alias Olaudah Equiano, the African." *Slavery and Abolition* 27, no. 3 (December 2006).

Maduakor, Obiajuru. "Soyinka as a Literary Critic." *Research in African Literature* 17, no. 1 (Spring 1986).

Mahmoud, Khaled. "Dashing Nubians' Hopes of Returning Home." Carnegie Endowment for International Peace, August 13, 2018.

Mahoney, Anne Louise, ed. *Documenting the Red Terror*. Ottawa: ERT-DRC, 2012.

Marchand, Suzanne. "Leo Frobenius and the Revolt against the West." *Journal of Contemporary History* 32, no. 2 (April 1997).

Martinho, Fernando. "The Poetry of Agostinho Neto." *World Literature Today* 53, no. 1 (Winter 1979).

Masonen, Pekka. "Leo Africanus: The Man with Many Names." *Al-Andalus Magreb* 8–9 (2001).

Masonen, Pekka, and Humphrey Fisher. "Not Quite Venus from the Waves: The Almoravid Conquest of Ghana in the Modern Historiography of Western Africa." *History in Africa* 23 (1996).

Mbiti, John. "The Encounter of Christian Faith and African Religion." *Christian Century*, August 27–September 3, 1980.

McCaskie, T. C. "The Life and Afterlife of Yaa Asantewaa." *Africa: Journal of the International African Institute* 77, no. 2 (1995).

Menkhaus, Ken. "Calm between the Storms? Patterns of Political Violence in Somalia, 1950–1980." *Journal of Eastern African Studies*, August 22, 2014.

Meriwether, James. "African Americans and the Mau Mau Rebellion: Militancy, Violence, and the Struggle for Freedom." *Journal of American Ethnic History* 17, no. 4 (Summer 1998).

Moore, Carlos. "Conversations with Cheikh Anta Diop." *Présence Africaine*, no. 149/150 (1989).

Musser, Charles. "Presenting: 'A True Idea of the African of Today': Two Documentary Forays by Paul and Eslanda Robeson." *Film History* 18, no. 4 (2006).

Nardal, Paulette. "The Awakening of Race Consciousness." *La Revue du Monde Noir*, April 1932.

Nwauwa, Apollos. "Far ahead of His Time: James Africanus Horton's Initiatives for a West African University and His Frustrations, 1862–1871." *Cahiers d'Études Africaines* 39, no. 153 (1999).

Ogot, Bethwell. Review. *Journal of African History* 46, no. 3 (2005).

Oyebola, D. D. O. "Yoruba Traditional Bonesetters: The Practice of Orthopaedics in a Primitive Setting in Nigeria." *Journal of Trauma* 20, no. 4 (April 1980).

Oyler, Dianne. "Re-Inventing Oral Tradition: The Modern Epic of Souleymane Kanté." *Research in African Literatures* 33, no. 1 (Spring 2002).

P'Bitek, Okot. "Fr. Tempels' Bantu Philosophy." *Transition*, no. 13 (March–April 1964).

Pounder, Robert. "Black Athena 2: History without Rules." *American Historical Review* 97, no. 2 (April 1992).

Roth, Felix. "A Diary of a Surgeon with the Benin Punitive Expedition." *Journal of the Manchester Geographical Society* 14 (1898).

Roth, Ann Macy. "Africa—Review of Books." *American Historical Review* 102, issue 2 (April 1997).

Rowley, Hazel. "Richard Wright's Africa." *The Antioch Review* 58, no. 4 (Autumn 2000).

Salvadore, Matteo. "A Modern African Intellectual: Gabre-Heywat Baykadan's Quest for Ethiopia's Sovereign Modernity." *Africa: Rivista Trimestrale di Studi e Documentazione dell'Istituto Italiano per l'Africa e l'Oriente* 62, no. 4 (2007).

———. "The Ethiopian Age of Exploration: Prester John's Discovery of Europe 1306–1458." *Journal of World History* 21, no. 4 (2011).

Schneider, Thomas. "Egypt and the Chad: Some Additional Remarks." *Journal of Ancient Egyptian Interconnections* 3, no. 4 (2011).

Schuenemann, Verena, Alexander Peltzer, Beatrix Welte, W. Paul van Pelt, Martyna Molak, Chuan-Chao Wang, Anja Furtwängler, Christian Urban, Ella Reiter, Kay Nieselt, Barbara Teßmann, Michael Francken, Katerina Harvati, Wolfgang Haak, Stephan Schiffels, and Johannes Krause. "Ancient Egyptian Mummy Genomes Suggest an Increase of Sub-Saharan African Ancestry in Post-Roman Periods." *Nature Communications* 8 (2017), article no. 15694.

Sherif, Abouelhadid. "The Sacred Geometry of Music and Harmony." In *Petrie Museum of Egyptian Archaeology: Characters and Collections*, ed. Alice Stevenson, 62–63. London: UCL Press, 2015.

Siame, Chisanga. "Katunkumene and Ancient Egypt in Africa." *Journal of Black Studies* 44, no. 3 (April 2013).

Skinner, Elliott. "The Mossi and Traditional Sudanese History." *Journal of Negro History* 43, no. 2 (April 1958).

Smyke, Raymond. "Fatima Massaquoi Fahnbulleh: Pioneer Woman Educator, 1912–1978." 1990 article reprinted in *Liberian Studies Journal* 31 (2006).

Southern Poverty Law Center. *Teaching Hard History: American Slavery*. Montgomery, AL: Southern Poverty Law Center, 2018.

Soyinka, Wole. "Ali Mazrui and Skip Gates' Africa Series." *The Black Scholar* 30, no. 1 (Spring 2000).

Stuckey, Sterling. "'I Want to Be African': Paul Robeson and the Ends of Nationalist Theory and Practice, 1914–1945." *Massachusetts Review* 17, no. 1 (Spring 1976).

Sumner, Claude. "The Significance of Zera Yacob's Philosophy." *Ultimate Reality and Meaning* 22, issue 3 (September 1999).

Tandon, Yash. "Recolonization of Subject Peoples." *Alternatives* 19, no. 2 (Spring 1994).

Tangri, Roger. "Some New Aspects of the Nyasaland Native Rising of 1915." *African Historical Studies* 4, no. 2 (1971).

Thornton, John. "Legitimacy and Political Power: Queen Njinga, 1624–1663." *Journal of African History* 32, no. 1 (1991).

Tsehai Berhane-Selassie. "Women Guerrilla Fighters." *North East Africa Studies* 1, no. 3 (1979–1980).

Tuchscherer, Konrad. "The Lost Script of the Bagam." *African Affairs* 98, no. 390 (January 1999).

———. "Recording, Communicating and Making Visible: A History of Writing and Systems of Graphic Symbolism in Africa." In *Inscribing Meaning: Writing and Graphic Systems in African Art*. Washington, DC: Smithsonian Institution, 2007.

Unger, Arthur. "Mazrui: 'My Life Is One Long Debate.'" *Christian Science Monitor*, October 6, 1986.

Van Allen, Judith. "Sitting on a Man: Colonialism and the Lost Political Institutions of Igbo Women." *Canadian Journal of African Studies* 6, no. 2 (1972).

Wright, Donald. "Uprooting Kunta Kinte: On the Perils of Relying on Encyclopedic Informants." *History in Africa* 8 (1981).

Wright, Richard. "Tradition and Industrialization: The Plight of the Tragic Elite in Africa." *Présence Africaine*, nos. 8–10 (June–November 1956).

Yirga Gelaw Woldeyes. "Colonial Rewriting of African History: Misinterpretations and Distortions in Belcher and Kleiner's Life and Struggles of Walatta Petros." *Journal of Afroasiatic Languages, History and Culture* 9, no. 2 (2020).

Articles in Newspapers, Magazines, and Online Media

Aikomo, Oluwamuyiwa. "Trevor Noah Slams South African Xenophobic Attacks, Receive Praises from Nigerians." Nollywoodalive.com, September 3, 2019.

Ayittey, George, "The Truth in Lending to Third World Governments." *Wall Street Journal*, October 11, 1984.

———. "A Double Standard in Black and White." *Wall Street Journal*, July 22, 1985.

Baines, John. "Was Civilization Made in Africa?" *New York Times*, August 11, 1991.

Bauer, Peter. "Ali Mazrui, A Prophet out of Africa." *Encounter*, June 1980.

Bernal, Martin, "Whose Greece?" *London Review of Books* 18, no. 24 (December 12, 1996).

Blackburn, Robin. "The True Story of Equiano." *The Nation*, November 2, 2005.

Britt, Donna. "Rooting Up Haley's Legacy." *Washington Post*, March 2, 1993.

Bugg, John. "The Sons of Belial: Olaudah Equiano in 1794." *Times Literary Supplement*, August 1, 2008.

Clarke, John. "Paul Robeson: The Artist as Activist and Social Thinker." *Présence Africaine*, no. 107, 1978.

Compton, Nick. "This Stylish African Architecture Will Blow You Away." Wired.co.uk, August 29, 2017.

Cunningham-Scharf, Sarah, and Jeff Pearce. "Hungry, Hungry Hippos." *Corporate Risk Canada* 4, no. 2 (Summer 2015).

Dabydeen, David. "Poetic License." *The Guardian*, December 3, 2005.

Dash, Mike. "Dahomey's Women Warriors." Smithsonian.com, September 23, 2011.

de Goeij, Hana. "A Breakthrough in C-Section History: Beatrice of Bourbon's Survival in 1337." *New York Times*, November 24, 2016.

"Dreaming of Returning Home, Egypt's Nubians Revive Language." France24.com, April 23.

Enwonwu, Ben. "Problems of the African Artist Today." Speech reprinted in *Présence Africaine*, June–November 1956.

Englund, Peter. "Fact and Fiction." *Financial Times*, August 24, 2012.

Friedman, Uri. "What's Actually in the Magna Carta?" TheAtlantic.com, June 15, 2015.

Gaston, Lafayette. "Past Afrocentricity: Reassessing Cheikh Anta Diop's Place in the Afrocentric Frame." *The Liberator* 8, no. 23 (2009).

Gibbs, Walter. "Nobel Peace Laureate Seeks to Explain Remarks about AIDS." *New York Times*, December 10, 2004.

Gilson, Dave. "'I Will Disappear into the Forest'": An Interview with Wangari Maathai." *Mother Jones*, January 5, 2005.

Glanville, Brian. "Malcolm X." *New Statesman*, June 12, 1964.

Glover, Michael. "Kingdom of Ife: Sculptures from West Africa, British Museum, London." *The Independent*, March 4, 2010.

Gott, Richard. "The Looting of Benin." *The Independent*, February 22, 1997.

Gould, Rachel. "In Montreal, Picasso Comes 'Face-to-Face' with the African Art That Inspired Him." *Culture Trip*, July 17, 2018.

Grandin, Greg. "Capitalism and Slavery." The Nation.com, May 1, 2015.

Greenblatt, Stephen. "How St. Augustine Invented Sex." *The New Yorker*, June 19, 2017.

Greste, Peter. "Could a Rusty Coin Rewrite Chinese-African History?" BBC News website, October 18, 2010.

Haley, Alex. "My Furthest-Back Person—'The African.'" *New York Times Magazine*, July 16, 1972.

Harding, Jeremy. "Scapegoating History." *New York Times*, March 8, 1998.

Herbjørnsrud, Dag. "The African Enlightenment." Aeon, December 13, 2017.

Huzzey, Richard. "1900–2007: The Legacies of Slavery and Anti-Slavery." BBC Local Oxford website, November 27, 2014.

Inani, Rohit. "Language Is a 'War Zone': A Conversation with Ngũgĩ wa Thiong'o." *The Nation*, March 9, 2018.

Johnson, Boris. "If Blair's So Good at Running the Congo, Let Him Stay There." *The Telegraph*, January 10, 2002.

Johnson, Boris. "Cancel the Guilt Trip." *The Spectator*, February 2, 2002.

Kasroui, Safaa. "Moroccan Soldiers Fought in All Major Battles of WWI." *Morocco World News*, November 12, 2018.

Kimeria, Ciku. "A Recently Found Ben Enwonwu Painting Has Sold at Seven Times Its Valuation of $1.4 Million." Quartz Africa, October 16, 2019, https://qz.com/africa/1729512/nigerian-artist-ben-enwonwu-painting-sold-by-sothebys-at-1-4m.

Koutonin, Mawuna. "Story of Cities #5: Benin City, the Mighty Medieval City Now Lost without a Trace." *The Guardian*, March 18, 2016.

Lawler, Andrew. "Writing Gets a Rewrite." *Science*, n.s., 292, no. 5526 (June 29, 2001).

Lennon, Peter. "A Call to Arms." *The Guardian*, January 13, 2001.

Lubasch, Arnold. "'Roots' Plagiarism Suit Is Settled." *New York Times*, December 15, 1978.

Macdonald, Fleur. "The Legend of Benin's Fearless Female Warriors." BBC.com/Travel, August 27, 2018.

Maditla, Neo. "How Architect Mariam Kamara Is Masterminding a Sustainable Future for Niger." CNN Style, March 16, 2020.

Manning, Stephen. "Professor Questions Accuracy of Famed Slave Narrative." Associated Press as published online for *The Ledger*, September 23, 2005.

May, Kate Torgovnik. "Architecture Infused with Fractals: How TED speaker Ron Eglash Inspired Architect Xavier Vilalta." TED Blog, October 25, 2013.

Mazrui, Ali. *The Africans: A Triple Heritage*. BBC-PBS-WETA production, 1986.

Mbamalu, Socrates. "How Can African Languages Be Protected?" This Is Africa, March 22, 2017.

Megahid, Ahmed. "First Nubian Language Dictionary Published by Volunteers." *Arab Weekly*, January 19, 2020.

Meldrum, Andrew. "Stealing Beauty." *The Guardian*, March 15, 2006.

Mitgang, Herbert. "Looking at Africa through an African's Eyes." *New York Times*, October 5, 1986.

Nobile, Philip. "The Prize That Taints the Pulitzer's Ethics and Honor." History News Network, April 20, 2018.

Nobile, Philip. "Alex Haley's Hoax." *Village Voice*, February 23, 1993.

Nyabola, Nanjala. "Wangari Maathai Was Not a Good Woman: Kenya Needs More of Them." *African Arguments*, October 6, 2015.

Ottaway, Mark. "Tangled Roots." *Sunday Times* (London), April 10, 1977.

Page, Clarence. "Alex Haley's Facts Can Be Doubted, but Not His Truths." *Chicago Tribune*, March 10, 1993.

Pearce, Fred. "African Queen." *New Scientist*, issue 2203, September 11, 1993.

Pearce, Jeff. "Ethiopia: Lies, Damn Lies, Axum and the West," Medium .com, March 4, 2021.

———. "Ethiopia: Mai Kadra, Metekel, and the Media Shame That Won't Be Forgotten," Medium.com, April 8, 2021.

Penney, Joe. "How US Customs Officers Damaged a Revered West African Artist's Custom-Built Kora." Quartz Africa, February 6, 2020.

Pilkington, Ed. "Shell Pays Out $15.5 Million over Saro-Wiwa killing." *The Guardian*, June 9, 2009.

Pilling, David. "African Exodus by Asfa-Wossen Asserate: Thwarted Ambitions." Financial Times website, June 8, 2018.

"Qui est le Mogho Naaba, au centre des négociations au Burkina Faso?" SlateAfrique.com, September 23, 2015.

Rankin, Jennifer, and Jon Henley. "EU to Consider Plans for Migrant Processing Centres in Africa." *The Guardian*, June 19, 2018.

Ronchin, Francesca. "Axum: Il massacre denunciato dale ong." Panorama.it, March 25, 2021.

Ruark, Robert. "Your Guns Go with You." *Life*, February 16, 1953.

Sartre, Jean-Paul. "Black Orpheus." Translated by John MacCombie. *The Massachusetts Review* 6, no. 1 (Autumn 1964–Winter 1965).

Schwartzstein, Peter. "Changing Egypt Offers Hope to Long-Marginalized Nubians." *National Geographic*, February 1, 2014.

Sekoto, Gerard. "Autobiography." *Présence Africaine*, no. 69.

Seton, Vivian. Speaking about *The Autobiography of an African Princess* for a Library of Congress video, YouTube, October 2, 2014.

Spencer, Terence. "The Race to Save Abu Simbel Is Won." *Life*, December 2, 1966.

Stone, Robert, et al. "The Case of Ken Saro-Wiwa." *New York Review of Books*, April 20, 1995.

Takács, Louis. "Let Me Get There: Visualizing Immigrants, Transnational Migrants and U.S. Citizens Abroad, 1914–1925."

Timsit, Annabelle, and Annalisa Merelli. "For 10 Years, Students in Texas Have Used a History Textbook That Says Not All Slaves Were Unhappy." Quartz website, May 11, 2018.

Trescott, Jacqueline. "Myriad Voices from an Unsung Continent." *Washington Post*, December 15, 1999.

Van de Walle, Nicolas. "Capsule Review." *Foreign Affairs*, March/April 2019.

Wiltz, Teresa. "For Slave's Biographer, Truth Contains a Bit of Fiction." *Washington Post*, September 10, 2005.

Wu Mingren. "Nilometers: Ancient Egypt's Ingenious Invention Used until Modern Times." Ancient-Origins.net., March 21, 2020, *End of Empire—Kenya*. Granada Television, United Kingdom, 1985.

Additional News Stories

Africa Report
Architectural Record
Baltimore Afro-American
Daily Herald
Dissent
Globe and Mail
Guardian
Harper's
Lagos Weekly Record
Los Angeles Times
Manchester Guardian
Muncie Sunday Star
New Leader

New Republic
New Statesman and Nation
New Times and Ethiopia News
New York Times
Observer
Pittsburgh Courier
Reuters
Spectator
Time
Times of London
Toronto Star
Washington Post

Interviews by Phone, Video Call, Documentary Film Shoot, and E-Mail

Asfa-Wossen Asserate, May 22, 2018; July 24, 2020
George Ayittey, December 16, 2018; May 2, 2020
Keith Bowers, December 6, 2017
Thomas Hale, October 9, 2019
Selam Kebede, August 24, 2020
Sylvester Ogbechie, May 21, 2020
Abdi Ismail Samatar, December 23, 2020
Papa Susso, February 13, 2020

Index

.